American Character and Culture in a Changing World

Recent Titles in
Contributions in American Studies
Series Editor: Robert H. Walker

A Divided People
Kenneth S. Lynn

The American Dream in the Great Depression
Charles R. Hearn

Several More Lives to Live: Thoreau's Political Reputation in America
Michael Meyer

The Indians and Their Captives
James Levernier and Hennig Cohen, editors and compilers

Concerned About the Planet: *The Reporter* Magazine and American Liberalism, 1949–
1968
Martin K. Doudna

New World Journeys: Contemporary Italian Writers and the Experience of America
Angela M. Jeannet and Louise K. Barnett, editors and translators

Family, Drama, and American Dreams
Tom Scanlan

Hemispheric Perspectives on the United States: Papers from the New World Conference
Joseph S. Tulchin, editor, with the assistance of María A. Leal

"Ezra Pound Speaking": Radio Speeches of World War II
Leonard W. Doob, editor

The Supreme Court: Myth and Reality
Arthur Selwyn Miller

Television Fraud: The History and Implications of the Quiz Show Scandals
Kent Anderson

Menace in the West: The Rise of French Anti-Americanism in Modern Times
David Strauss

Social Change and Fundamental Law: America's Evolving Constitution
Arthur Selwyn Miller

American Character and Culture in a Changing World

SOME TWENTIETH-CENTURY PERSPECTIVES

edited by John A. Hague

CONTRIBUTIONS IN AMERICAN STUDIES, NUMBER 42

GREENWOOD PRESS
WESTPORT, CONNECTICUT ● LONDON, ENGLAND

Library of Congress Cataloging in Publication Data

Main entry under title:

American character and culture in a changing world.

   (Contributions in American studies; no. 42
ISSN 0084–9227)
   Edition of 1964 published under title: American
character and culture.
   Bibliography: p.
   Includes index.
   1. United States—Civilization—20th century—
Addresses, essays, lectures. 2. National charac-
teristics, American—Addresses, essays, lectures.
I. Hague, John A. II. Hague, John A., ed.
American character and culture.
E169.1.H138 1979   973.9   78–67568
ISBN 0–313–20735–6

Library of Congress Catalog Card Number: 78-67568
ISBN: 0-313-20735-6
ISSN: 0084-9227

First published in 1979

Greenwood Press, Inc.
51 Riverside Avenue, Westport, Connecticut 06880

Printed in the United States of America

10 9 8 7 6 5 4 3 2 1

FOR JANET

Contents

Illustrations and Tables   ix

Preface   xi

PART ONE—American Character—Past and Present   1

The Romantic Heritage and American Character   3
    John A. Hague
Diagnosing the American Dream   17
    Marshall W. Fishwick
The American Quest for Affluence   27
    Gerald E. Critoph
America and the Post-Affluent Revolution   51
    John A. Hague

PART TWO—Literature and the Changing Culture   63

Patterns in Recent American Literature   65
    Robert H. Walker
Literature and Politics: The Case of Ezra Pound Reconsidered   81
    Robert A. Corrigan
A Morphology of the Modern Fable   99
    Bruce A. Lohof
How to Learn History from Sinclair Lewis and Other Uncommon Sources. 111
    Nelson Manfred Blake

PART THREE—History and the Changing Culture   125

Henry Adams's Historical Paradigm: A Reexamination of the Major Phase 127
    David W. Marcell
The Contending Americas   143
    Gerald E. Critoph
Technology in American Culture   157
    Morrell Heald
Public Opinion—A Democratic Dilemma   171
    Stow Persons

Was Nat Turner Right? Violence in American History   185
    Nelson Manfred Blake
Foreign Relations, American Style   197
    Morrell Heald

PART FOUR—Special Groups—Visions and Problems   207

American Women and the American Character   209
    David M. Potter
American Women and the American Character: A Feminist Perspective   227
    Alice Kessler-Harris
Some Issues in the Proper Study of Black America   243
    Benjamin D. Berry, Jr.
Bridging the Gap: The Challenge of Interfacing American Studies
and Afro-American Studies   253
    Peter W. Dowell and Delores P. Aldridge
Visions and Versions of Childhood   275
    Albert E. Stone
Henry James and Childhood: *The Turn of the Screw*   279
    Albert E. Stone
Autobiography and the Childhood of the American Artist: The Example
of Louis Sullivan   293
    Albert E. Stone

PART FIVE—Personality and Culture   323

Poor Richard: Nixon and the Problem of Innocence   325
    David W. Marcell
The Hero in the Context of Social Change   339
    Marshall W. Fishwick
Slavery and Personality: A Problem in the Study of Modal
Personality in Historical Populations   349
    Norman R. Yetman
Culture, Character, and Personality   367
    Murray Murphey

Bibliography   379

Index   387

Illustrations

Carson, Pirie, Scott & Co., Chicago. Detail of cast iron 303
over entrance.

Plate 16 from Louis Sullivan, *A System of Architectural* 304
Ornament According with a Philosophy of Man's Powers.

Tables

1. Linear Structure 101
2. Linear Structure in "To Trust in Andy" 101
3. Type of Problem by Percentage 107
4. Demographic Analysis 108

Preface

The first edition of *American Character and Culture* appeared in 1964 and represented, in the main, essays which had been published under the auspices of the Charles E. Merrill lecture series in American Studies at Stetson University. In 1964, I noted that "these articles furnish the reader with an overview of some of the striking new developments which have resulted from interdisciplinary studies in the past fifteen years. They also offer an impressive variety of fresh insights into the nature of American character and experience."

Nine of the ten essays which appeared in the first edition are reproduced here. The fifteen new essays included in this volume reflect both continuity and change. They remain focused on the broad themes of character and culture, and like the essays in the first volume, stress the role of ideas in twentieth-century society. Nevertheless, there are significant changes in the concerns and also in the methods of the contributors to this edition. Thus, Marshall Fishwick insisted in the first edition that "The Great Debate of our time rages between Traditionalists and Existentialists," but he begins his new essay by declaring "A new international style and outlook are surfacing in every part of the world." Fishwick, like several other authors in this volume, believes, moreover, that the new style transcends "political, class, language and racial barriers." If the authors recognize that it is no longer possible to study American culture in isolation from the rest of the world, they are also discovering that a profound approach to the study of any culture requires the crossing of disciplinary lines and the use of techniques which will have validity in any society or culture. Thus, in turning to autobiography, Albert Stone finds it necessary to make use of the work of historians and psychoanalysts as well as literary scholars, and he also finds it imperative to consider the methodological problems which are involved in "studying one creative person in depth."

There is also a change of tone in the new essays. In his afterword to "Patterns in Recent American Literature," Robert Walker says that the one generalization in the original article (written in 1967) which he would seriously qualify is "the one that found current literature, on balance, to be an affirmation of the human condition in the American setting.'' Walker finds that ''many kinds of popular literature are less abundant and sunny,'' and that there are few examples of writers whose works ''harbor sustained consideration of the age's large moral issues.'' In the foreword to the first edition, I wrote that ''there remains ground for cautious optimism on the part of those who seek to preserve and transmit the heritage of their civilization.'' While the contributors to the second edition have not lost hope, they have grown more cautious and even anxious about the future of their society.

Finally, essays in the second edition repeatedly call attention to ways in which our culture is rapidly and radically changing. But, even as they describe the changes, the authors simultaneously point to elements of stability or to factors which seem change resistant. Thus, Morrell Heald, while noting changes in American foreign policy, describes in a fascinating manner the ways in which isolationist and international voices continue their dialogue in contemporary America. My own essay, though finding some institutions undergoing radical change, argues that values relating to equality and personal achievement are surprisingly durable.

The essays in Part One discuss the ideas and forces which have shaped, and are reshaping, American character in the twentieth century. They remind us of the extent to which affluence, or at least the hope of achieving it, has given us a romantic and hopeful legacy, but they also point out parochial and transient elements of affluence which raise hard questions for American institutions and individuals.

In the second and third sections, the essays explore a variety of themes which relate literature and history to a changing culture. Robert Walker examines literary patterns which have emerged as writers have felt compelled to face the dark side of our existence. He sees current literary experiments reflecting both nostalgia for a simpler way of life and a transition toward an uncertain future affirmation. Robert Corrigan's case study involving Ezra Pound reminds us that our creative and political lives are intertwined, and Bruce Lohof demonstrates that popular fiction is likely to reflect widely held beliefs and shared traditions. Finally, Nelson Blake suggests that a careful use of literary materials can enhance the scholarship of historians and students of culture.

The efforts of historians to deal with change are too numerous to catalog, but a half-dozen essays in Part Three open a series of windows on twentieth-century America which will repay careful examination. No one, as David Marcell suggests, was more anxious to understand the changes pouring over the modern world than Henry Adams. To confront his ''paradigm'' is to question the meaning of education in the modern world. Gerald Critoph analyzes contending traditions which affect our perception of meaning, and Heald takes a careful look at the ambiguity which surrounds our use and worship of technology. In his essay on ''Public Opinion,'' Stow Persons acknowledges that polling appears ''to be in accord with the theory of direct democracy," but he also points out that direct democracy is open to several important criticisms, and that polling techniques create a dilemma rather than a panacea for those who participate in democratic institutions. Blake examines a theme which has surely reached "center stage" in our world, and relates violence to the broad spectrum of values which shape American character. Finally, Heald shows how our conduct of foreign affairs uniquely reflects our experiences, hopes, and values.

The fourth part, by focusing on some specific—and often neglected—groups, enables us to reexamine the relationship among culture, institutions, and personal values. David Potter's famous essay on "American Women and American Character" reminds us that many studies of national character have focused primarily on male roles and activities. Alice Kessler-Harris gives us a challenging, disturbing, but ultimately hopeful feminist perspective on the future of our society. The essays by Benjamin Berry, Peter Dowell and Delores Aldridge, and Albert Stone not only afford important insights into the experiences of blacks and children, but also tell us something about tools and approaches which we can use to make our study and teaching of American civilization more cosmopolitan and humane.

The study of national character, according to Potter, "is properly a branch of the study of group character and of personality."[1] It is appropriate, therefore, to conclude this volume with a series of essays dealing with personality and group character.

In the first essay of the final section, Marcell relates the personality of Richard Nixon to middle-class aspirations which derive from a tradition of innocence. Nixon, as Marcell reminds us, wanted to be an American hero. In the second essay of this section, Fishwick suggests that old-style heroes are no longer functional, and that today's heroes must set a new tempo and master a new style.

Norman Yetman's article provides us with a model for relating personality types to a social system. Using sociological and psychological concepts to examine the relationship between personality types and the social system of slavery, he reappraises Stanley Elkins's "Sambo" thesis and concludes by noting "The basic objective of research dealing with the issue of slavery and personality should be to determine not whether there was diversity of personality types among American slaves, but whether there was a systematic pattern of distribution of these personality types and the relation of these patterns to location within the slave social system."

In the final essay, Murray Murphey reminds us that "personality and culture are not identical" and that "The significant problem is how drives, habits, and social groupings are related." By focusing on such relationships rather than a simple interaction of culture and personality, we can begin the painstaking task of discovering "the interrelations of drives and habits in individuals and sets of individuals."

The study of American character is an ongoing inquiry. Those who pursue it rarely come to identical conclusions, but they do discover a common bond in the questions they ask. These questions cross disciplinary lines and frequently take those who pose them beyond the walls of the academy. That is surely one of the things that keeps volumes like this from being parochial. The questions which bear upon our character touch our humanity as well.

JOHN A. HAGUE
Stetson University
April 28, 1978

Note

1. David M. Potter, *People of Plenty* (Chicago: University of Chicago Press, 1954), p. 33.

PART ONE
American Character—
Past and Present

JOHN A. HAGUE

The Romantic Heritage and American Character

*John A. Hague is a graduate of the American Studies program
at Yale University. He is Professor of the Charles E. Merrill
Program of American Studies at Stetson University in
DeLand, Florida. His articles have been concerned with
recent intellectual history and studies of American character.
From 1971 to 1977 he was the Director of the National
American Studies Faculty.*

In 1858 Oliver Wendell Holmes celebrated Puritanism's demise by describing
the collapse of the deacon's wonderful shay. One hundred years later American
writers, responding to the tensions of the cold war and the machine age, were
noting the collapse of romantic attitudes and ideals which had held sway in the
nineteenth century. Arthur Winner, the protagonist in a novel by James Gould
Cozzens, discovered that his legal ethics and personal values could not easily
mesh. By contrast, his father had never known such a conflict. Seemingly
Americans were experiencing a loss of innocence. The collapse of romantic
idealism appeared real and complete.

We now know that Puritanism did not die in 1858. It had stepped out for a
change of clothes, but it was by no means stripped of its influence. Indeed
twentieth-century scholars have rediscovered both its influence and its value. In
the 1940s, for example, Ralph Barton Perry wrote a large opus which proclaimed
the impact of Puritanism and democracy on American life. Perry astutely noted
the ways in which these traditions reinforced each other as well as the ways in
which they clashed. He pointed out that America's debt to both traditions was
large.

Similarly, one wonders if romanticism is really dead. Certainly some of the
values and attitudes which it fostered are in jeopardy, but evidence of its
influence can be found almost everywhere in American culture today. It is my
purpose in this paper to define the nature and impact of romanticism on American
character. Such an analysis will, I believe, provide some insights about the

serviceability of the romantic heritage in the twentieth century. Specifically, it may indicate the general direction the romantic American's education ought to take.

I

In the nineteenth century a romantic tradition found fertile soil on a developing continent and succeeded in modifying the legacy of the preceding centuries. In order to understand American romanticism let us examine briefly two movements which did much to define its tone. Frontier evangelism, on the one hand, and transcendentalism, on the other, furnished the context out of which lasting romantic influences sprang. The evangelical religion of the frontier was a response to the insecurities and loneliness of the frontiersman's life. The evangelist preached a gospel of love, redemption and salvation. He called upon sinners to forsake their evil ways, to wash in the blood of the lamb and become "as white as snow." The impact of the resulting conversion experience transfigured the frontiersman's life. Beholding a vision of a future life in a golden city, he went back to his farm to live courageously "at" his future rather than "in" the present. His life, regardless of the physical circumstances which surrounded it, had acquired a new significance and a heroic dimension.

The transcendentalists were also intent on tapping the spiritual resources of the human condition. They too had conversion experiences, although they were less likely to refer to a single and total transformation than were the pioneering farmers. Nevertheless, they found within themselves, in those moments when they touched the oversoul, a sense of wholeness and strength which filled the present with a spark of eternity. Such experiences persuaded the transcendentalists that greatness was a state of being and that life was a journey in which the traveler constantly searched for the heroic virtues. Although the heroic virtues arose from the spiritual self-reliance of the individual, most transcendentalists expected men to translate these virtues into lives of useful service. Emerson could not completely conceal a tinge of exasperation when he thought of Thoreau captaining a huckleberry party.

A number of conditions aided and abetted the growth of a romantic outlook. Men were conquering a continent—in an unbelievably short span of time. In the process they had to be self-reliant and daring. Secondly, America was engaged, in the words of Walt Rostow, in its drive to maturity. Americans were applying a growing technology to all sectors of the economy, and many witnessed in their own lifetime the full impact of the industrial revolution. Third, it was a century of mass migration to the new world. Nearly sixty million Europeans left Europe in the nineteenth century, and approximately thirty-six million settled in the United States. The image of the melting pot is not altogether accurate, but we can recognize that the availability of sizable rewards created a pressure on the immigrant to strive for success that was virtually irresistible. Many people argued that it was the influx of new blood that gave America her strength and vitality.

II

David Riesman has noted many of these factors in describing the "inner direct-ed" American. The inner-directed style of conformity was presumably in its heyday during the late nineteenth and early twentieth centuries. Riesman cited the fact that the inner-directed individual was success oriented and therefore work oriented. Since his work had to do with problems related to industrializa-tion or the agricultural conquest of the continent, the inner-directed man typically found himself engaged in hard physical labor. He took vacations in order to work more effectively, and he strove to achieve an ever higher status in the communi-ty. His source of strength came from the values which the community instilled and subsequently rewarded.

In Riesman's view, the world of inner-directed activity separated work from play, adults from children, and social classes from each other in a clear cut fashion. As a result the inner-directed society had a sense of direction and purpose which reflected the clearly defined class lines and values it contained. Riesman argued further that the images of power coincided pretty closely with the actualities of power in the nineteenth century.

Riesman's concepts of tradition, inner and other directed modes of conformity, are models, just as the second law of thermodynamics is a model. The real question which we must ask about his models is how useful are they? Do they help us understand more clearly and precisely the reasons for the responses which we have made and are making? In this instance does the concept of inner direction provide a useful key to understanding the behavior of the "romantic" American of the late nineteenth century?

Its usefulness is decidedly limited. Carl Degler has already observed that a good deal of evidence points to the conclusion that Americans have always been other directed.[1] In addition, I believe that other factors explain more carefully and fully the behavioral responses which Riesman has noted. Many of Riesman's insights are remarkably fruitful, but the model itself is a trifle suspect.

Before I examine the "other" factors I think it is well to point out that Riesman's models were designed primarily to explain middle- and upper-middle-class behavior. With this I have no quarrel. A great many observers have insisted that America has consistently demonstrated a fondness for middle-class values, and Americans themselves have been quick to apply the label to their own position in society.

The fact remains, however, that the nineteenth-century middle class was a much smaller group, both absolutely and relatively, than its twentieth-century counterpart. As a result, when we talk about the inner-directed middle classes of a previous generation we are talking about a fairly restricted group that defined its status in rather explicit terms. Success meant a house in the right neighborhood, the requisite number of servants, the right kind of household furnishings, and membership in the respectable community organizations and churches. Under these circumstances one can readily appreciate what Carl Becker meant when he said, shortly after the turn of the century, that American individualism was marked by achievement rather than eccentricity, by conformity rather than revolt.[2]

When Riesman began to examine twentieth-century American society he discovered that individuals were often directed with reference to the groups in which they were participating. Thus the bohemians of Greenwich Village, far from being highly individualistic, were other directed with reference to each other. In other words, these individuals discovered a group whose approval they needed and coveted. The evidence seems to indicate a similar state of affairs with reference to the inner-directed middle classes of the earlier period. When Sinclair Lewis created George Babbitt in 1920, he portrayed a middle-class businessman who finally admitted to himself that he simply could not subsist without the approval of his peers. One can argue, of course, that Babbitt symbolizes neatly the emergent other-directed character structure, but his upbringing and community ties suggest strongly a middle-class inner-directed value profile.

One factor which explains a good deal about the responses of nineteenth-century Americans, as well as twentieth-century Americans, is their constant struggle to be upwardly mobile. To be mobile in a production-oriented society one must work long and hard at the process. For Americans just entering the ranks of the middle classes leisure was almost nonexistent. It is not hard to separate work and leisure when leisure is such a rare commodity to begin with. Some confined leisure to Saturday afternoons, and others, living in more isolated areas, combined leisure and religion once a year in a week-long revival.

In 1900 a majority of Americans still lived in rural areas or in small towns and villages. Frederick Lewis Allen has pointed out that middle-class Americans, prior to the first world war, did remarkably little traveling.[3] When one combines these facts with the observation that middle-class status was a minority status, one gains additional insight into the homogeneous character of this group. Parents separated the adult world from the child world because they felt confident about their ability to retain control of the socialization process in which their children were participating. A child who could handle father's inquiry about where he'd been by saying "Out," and then dispose of "What did you do?" by replying "Nothing," was part of a social structure father knew and understood.

Perhaps this gets to the heart of the matter. Cora DuBois argues that four value premises underlie American middle-class behavior. In brief, "(1) the universe is mechanistically conceived, (2) man is its master, (3) men are equal, and (4) men are perfectible."[4] One does not need to idealize the circumstances under which the middle class toiled. Their lives had a grubby side and a dull side, and they longed unmistakably for a better day. But they believed that life, in the general sense, was manageable; that those who understood what they wanted and made proper use of their talent would secure their just deserts. In short a manageable world was one in which men were capable of creating and maintaining the conditions under which people got what they deserved.

As a result of this attitude, the middle-class American maintained a strong personal orientation in most of his value judgments. Christopher Newman, the protagonist of Henry James's novel, *The American,* made a determined effort to get the aristocratic Bellegardes to disregard tradition and to evaluate his suit for their daughter on its own merits. Huck Finn made his decision to go to Hell on the basis of his personal loyalty to Jim. And few nineteenth-century Americans would have understood the novel that Melville completed at the century's close. In *Billy Budd* Melville produced a "romantic-tragic" book which juxtaposed the sympathetic individualism of the romanticist with the detached impersonalism of the tragedian. Appropriately the book was not published until 1924.

It is perfectly true that many American businessmen were beginning to think in corporate terms. Rockefeller's willingness to sacrifice individual buds for the sake of the larger, more perfect bloom is a case in point. By and large, however, the personal orientation prevailed. Despite all of the differences which separated the New Nationalism of Theodore Roosevelt and the New Freedom of Woodrow Wilson, both men took strong personal views of the economy. Wilson wanted to make it possible for individuals to compete with corporations, and Roosevelt wanted to hold corporations accountable to a personal ethic. The speeches of both were redolent with phrases which reflected a personalized ethic.

In 1912 the good ship *Titanic* left England on its maiden voyage to the United States. The ship was unsinkable. Thus it symbolized man's ultimate triumph over nature. Walter Lord has given us a dramatic account of the ship's last hours in the icebound North Atlantic. What is of significance for our purposes is the fact that the tragedy was made possible and then compounded because no one acted on the assumption that the ship could sink. The crew of a nearby vessel, seeing the distress flares of the *Titanic*, assumed that the passengers of the stricken vessel were having a celebration, because the *Titanic* could not be in trouble. Such an assumption was logical if one believed that he lived in a knowable and manageable world. Proceeding on such an assumption one expected nature to be harnessed. One expected the growth of knowledge to reduce the hazards of daily life and to make more certain the achievement of the good society. We recognize today that Karl Marx was one of the great optimists about human nature in the nineteenth century. But he was not alone. Emerson, Thoreau, Henry George, and many others had their own concept of the withering away of the state, and their hopes for a brave new world ran high.

Perhaps enough has been said to provide a significant summary of the late-nineteenth-century middle-class American and his attitudes. He strove for upward mobility and his life was work oriented. Because of the context in which he lived and worked, he separated adult activities from child activities and also work from leisure. His individualism was an individualism of conformity rather than one of eccentricity. His value orientation was personal rather than corporate, provincial rather than cosmopolitan; and the symbols which denoted success seemed clearly defined. Living in a manageable world, he was prepared to make an heroic effort to achieve his goals. His goals, of course, were for the most part those which society wanted him to want. His response to success or failure, joy or sorrow, happiness or despair was highly personal, and his behavior reflected warmth and compassion or coldness and indifference, depending on the individual circumstances which prevailed.

Since the world was supposed to be knowable and manageable, the American labeled the forces and events which threatened to disrupt his world as immoral. He regarded the outbreak of war in Europe in 1914 with disbelief and horror, and described it in terms of barbarism and backsliding. Even those Americans, like James and Dewey, who rebelled against the absolutes with which conservatives sought to defend the status quo, insisted upon man's ability to control his fate.

As a result, the American moralized and romanticized his choices. By these terms I mean first, that he tended to decide matters on a black and white basis, and, second, that he did not examine critically the probable consequences of his choices. From this conclusion I draw two inferences. First, the American, as of 1914, had little reason or wish to criticize the direction in which he believed his society was going. Second, he was in no sense introspective about his convictions or his role in society. If these inferences are accepted, the likelihood that his individualism was one of conformity is accentuated.

Such a complex of attitudes and values made the American inventive, shrewd, and practical on a short run basis, and helpless, naive, and unrealistic on a long range basis. I am contending that it was not simply the frontier that made the American inventive, shrewd, and practical. These traits resulted from the American's preoccupation with short range and manageable problems. Henry Ford's biography provides a case in point. Few industrialists have been more ingenious than he. Yet, the very qualities which brought him such magnificent success almost brought about the destruction of the company he founded. His failure to assess the developing trends within American industry made the formulas by which he built up the Ford Motor Company a millstone for his executives. Thus the American's shortsightedness has frequently petrified his inventiveness and practicality. As far back as 1830 de Tocqueville was noting the tendency of Americans to generalize readily on the basis of quick success and limited experience.

III

What are the principal changes which the twentieth century has brought about? First, it has seemingly crowned American efforts with very great success. At least in a material sense Americans have been able to achieve many of the things which nineteenth-century orators held out as the symbols of the good life. In a remarkably short period of time Americans have transformed their living conditions, their life expectancy, and their position as a world power. Second, the ranks of the middle class have been greatly enlarged. No longer is the middle class a minority group which can easily secure hired help. Third, Americans have become far more mobile, both physically and socially, than ever before. Only 5 percent of the American people occupied the same dwelling in 1960 that they inhabited in 1940. The average real income of the bottom four-fifths of American families doubled between 1940 and 1960. Fourth, the stream of immigrants has dried up to a mere trickle. As one might expect, the problems of the American city and the American school have accordingly changed. Fifth, the public school, particularly the public high school, has come of age as an institution. It now serves a greater percentage of the population, and finds itself subject to a wider variety of demands and standards. Sixth, the twentieth century is in the process of becoming an age of automation and cybernation. In consequence the traditional institutions of work and property no longer fulfill their historic roles. The evidence clearly seems to support the conclusion that an increasing number of people will have to define their work along radically different lines. It also suggests that the possession of property no longer supplies an individual with a meaningful stake in society. Rather it is the possession of an education which furnishes the individual that stake. Seventh, the twentieth century has witnessed the development of bureaucracy and the centralization of power. Put another way this is an era which has attained elements of a corporate society. Eighth, the mass media of communication have tied the American people together in a way that was never before possible. In an age which has made a wide variety of goods and services available to the American people, their instruments of communication have, paradoxically, tightened the bonds of conformity. Similarly, in an age which has produced more and better education for increasing numbers of people, the media, by virtue of the huckster's persistent effort to reach the lowest common denominator, have forced an almost continual oversimplification of ideas and issues. Ninth, the physical frontiers of American society have closed, as Frederick Jackson Turner said they would. While few would question that significant opportunities remain, many would assert that they are sometimes hard to find. Others insist that the growth rate of a mature society must slow down, and that Americans ought to adjust to the fact. David Potter, for example, has suggested that modern society does not need so many highly mobile individuals, and that it may be possible to strike a different balance between the demands of mobility and those of status.[5] Tenth, for many Americans the twentieth century has brought fragmentation and alienation. Finally, the twentieth century has become an era in which war has become total and in a sense permanent. Walter Lippmann has pointed out that modern man has learned that war is not rational and that he cannot make peace. Thus he must learn to live with frustration.

IV

Before appraising the impact of these developments on the romantic tradition, I want to say a word about intellectual developments which have shaped the twentieth-century mind all over the Western world. Intellectually the twentieth-century citizen is the heir of Darwin, Freud, and Einstein. There are many, many consequences of these three revolutions of which we are still only vaguely aware, but it seems clear that they have extended our intellectual horizons, and that they have complicated forever the forces we must understand in order to discipline our lives intelligently. We cannot help being aware of the fact that we live in a particular culture, operate on fallible assumptions, and act with limited vision. The knower knows that he cannot dissociate what he knows from the concepts he used to discover the knowledge, and that the concepts were in turn shaped by a culture which he inherited. Rheinhold Neibuhr suggests an awareness of such facts when he argues that it is man's nature to seek an ultimate meaning and his fate to see every meaning which he achieves threatened.[6] Under such circumstances man is enjoined to accept his relativity which is to say his finiteness and his mortality.

The list of changes cited above is not intended to be exhaustive. It may, however, give us a basis upon which to make a comparison between the late nineteenth-century middle-class American and his mid-twentieth-century counterpart. Many twentieth-century Americans are probably less work oriented than their predecessors. They are apparently just as bound by conformity, although they travel more, read more, and have a wider range of choice when it comes to purchasing goods and services. The choice is wider both because of what is being produced and because of what people have to spend. Simultaneously the middle classes have become greatly enlarged. In the process the symbols which denote success have lost their clarity, and individuals have begun to work harder at the business of securing acceptance of the credentials they have already earned. De Tocqueville warned that in a democratic society the bonds of affection would be extended but relaxed. The twentieth-century American has witnessed the extension of said bonds, and he has also seen them become increasingly superficial. The existential search for identity has become more difficult, and so the American has frequently sought identity through a conformity marked by its totality and its compulsiveness.

David Riesman has correctly pointed out that the totality of the conformity has made it difficult for the individual to separate his work and leisure, and it has also made it difficult for him to find constructive channels of escape. In Riesman's terminology it is difficult for the other-directed citizen to turn off his radar set.

The roots of alienation in the modern world spread out over a wide territory. I believe that one important sector into which the roots reach is the romantic tradition itself. The romantic's search for truth and meaning frequently led him to rebel against form and tradition. His quest also caused him to turn in upon himself and to begin an existential journey in pursuit of an inner and spiritual truth. In the nineteenth century romantics like Emerson and Thoreau were supported by a community with which they had personal ties. Later on a writer like Mark Twain discovered that the supporting community was disappearing and that he was left more and more to depend solely upon his own endeavors. As the support of the community faded, the burden of the existential journey grew increasingly heavy. In the twentieth century the romantic found little support in form, tradition, or community, and his rebellion often took on a pathetic or ridiculous character.

I would hazard a guess that the value orientation of the twentieth-century American remains personal, although, as the preceding analysis suggests, he finds himself subject to a great many corporate structures and pressures. There is an interesting contrast between the personally oriented statements of most college and university catalogues and the impersonal operation of their bureaucracies. The American's value orientation has, however, shed a good deal of its provinciality, and has undoubtedly become somewhat more tolerant of other points of view.

The American's world is both manageable and unmanageable. It is manageable in the sense that he achieves on a day-by-day basis many of the immediate objectives which he pursues. His life span is increasing, and he secures transportation, education, and recreation for himself and the members of his household. Yet he is not immune to accidents; he is not impervious to boredom, and he is most decidedly not immune to the big bomb. He is not at all sure that he can translate his more or less successful management of daily life into successful management of the world scene. Furthermore, he finds that few choices are clear-cut. He has to live with ambiguity and frustration. He is a man with a headache that won't go away.

Caught in such a predicament, some Americans have begun to wonder if they have been pursuing the right goals. The circumstances which have surrounded them with indecision and boredom have forced them to become introspective—to undertake the existential journey. Others rebel and follow prophets like Barry Goldwater and Norman Vincent Peale who assure them that life is not complicated, and that the goals are clear after all. Such men evoke an image of an earlier, simpler America, and exert an emotional appeal based on a romantic dream world which they themselves inhabit.

That we have been a goal-seeking people is clear. Whether the goals themselves remain clear is another question. The search for goals, or purpose, or identity betrays a basic anxiety on the part of the American people. We have reached so many of the goals we have pursued that we are a little puzzled about where we should go next. After World War II Americans confronted a crisis in Europe and in the developing nations. We responded quickly, and the period which gave birth to the Marshall Plan, the North Atlantic Alliance, and the Point Four Program will surely rank as one of the most creative in the history of our foreign affairs. Since that time, however, our policies appear to have grown more rigid, and we have displayed increasing uncertainty in our efforts to cope with conditions around the globe. When the Russians launched the first Sputnik, Americans began an all-out effort to match the Russian space age scientific achievements. In summer of 1964 this effort appears to have been remarkably successful, and simultaneously we seem to be somewhat at a loss in planning our next moves. Walt Rostow has already noted that Americans may be becoming somewhat bored with the miracle of high mass consumption. His observation simply underscores the fact that people who build their lives on the attainment of finite goals are likely to have a sense of emptiness when they reach their objective. How many novelists never overcame a first success? What would have happened to William Faulkner if Yoknapatawpha County had integrated in 1938, or in 1929? Like the bear that went over the mountain, we now know that there is not a Garden of Eden on the other side. There is just another mountain. Moreover, the mountains are getting harder to climb.

V

Can the romantic heritage serve us in some fashion in such a time? Serve us it must, since it is part of our very beings. But it must adapt to the changed context of the twentieth century. I believe that three major adaptations are required. First romanticism must be disciplined by a sense of tragedy. There is a meaningful link between nineteenth-century romanticism and twentieth-century existential-ism, and, on the surface at least, there is no incompatibility between romanticism and tragedy.

Lincoln managed the combination in the nineteenth century. Scott Buchanan, in a discussion published by The Center for the Study of Democratic Institutions, argues that "power politics is tragic in its life course."[7] The beginning of political wisdom, he continues, lies in an understanding of *Oedipus Rex*. The high point of the play comes when Oedipus discovers that he himself is the criminal for whom he has been searching. "Everything he had done had a double meaning which now began to be disclosed. And finally the tragic fact came out that he was the criminal. He thereupon destroyed his sight and said, 'I see.' "[8] The world, concludes Buchanan, needs the wisdom of Oedipus.

If you don't know that there is going to be a calamity, you are a silly, pathetic person. If you do know there is going to be a calamity and you just accept it, you are silly again. The only way to make it mean something is to be heroic about it. But the heroism is not the heroism of the Nazis—what they called realistic heroism, where you act heroic as a big gesture. You don't do that; you just discover things, and it makes life noble and grand while it is happening.[9]

Buchanan is asserting that the heroic vision can be combined with the tragic vision.

George Santayana said much the same thing in his only novel, *The Last Puritan*. Oliver Alden finally comes to recognize that his friends will never thank or repay him for the gifts he bestows. Neither will he forsake his duty, even when it requires that he lay down his life. The romantic tragedean understands and accepts the necessity of commitment to imperfect causes. He recognizes the necessity of striving for perfection at the same time that he accepts the fact that he cannot reach it. He knows, but is never complacent about, the fact that men do not always get what they deserve. He has something of the quality which Christopher Newman, in James's *The American*, shows when he refuses to exact an ''eye for an eye'' from the Bellegardes. He has something of the quality which George Webber displays in *You Can't Go Home Again* when he refuses to accept the notion that something or even anything is impossible. Yet he knows that only a little *is* possible.

The second adaptation involves the capacity to appraise realistically the world in which man lives. The American must examine critically the events and movements which surround him, and he must acquire as much and as precise information as he can about social structures and the way people interact with them.

The third adaptation involves the perspective of the romantic. He must acquire a sense of history which he has rarely had. For he must learn to set the short view against the long view, and he cannot do this until he comes to terms with his own past. Jack Burden, in *All the King's Men,* finally accepts the burden of his past because he discovers that one cannot hope for the future until he accepts the past. In short one must both understand and *accept* the past in order to assess what is possible in the present and in the future.

The romantic who attempts these adaptations will discover that he needs self-discipline and self-knowledge. He will need to measure carefully his capacities and his limitations, and all his choices ought to reflect a continuous and agonizing self-appraisal.

Heightened self-knowledge and the adaptations discussed above require a high price. Personal struggle and suffering are involved. The crucial question is whether a significant number of Americans are able and willing to pay the price. Put another way, the question asks whether Americans can recognize the tasks which this age presents and accept them while accepting also the limitations under which they must act.

We must define the tasks carefully, because the very complexity of our times makes it terribly easy to be caught fighting the wrong battles at the wrong time and in the wrong place. Look at the furor over the question of prayer in the public schools. A dialogue concerning the relation which ought to exist between church and state is valuable and constructive, but those who delude themselves into thinking that an opening prayer makes a secular institution a religious one or that it does something significant by way of protecting historic values are really blind. Instead of strengthening the school in areas where moral problems are involved, such as control or elimination of houseparties and fraternity initiations, or regulation of automobiles by students, or curbing an athletic program that has become parasitic, these people prefer to fight it out on an oversimplified issue which they can understand and which they hope somehow to control. Then when they do win, which is not very often, they persuade themselves that the devil has been licked. Ironically their success strengthens the very forces they wish to curb.

The real tasks our age presents are numerous and complex. For example, how can we make bureaucracies both efficient and responsible? At the same time how can we enable them to deal more effectively with individual differences? The problem is extraordinarily difficult but not impossible. Some of the most creative thinking going on in educational circles today lends fresh hope to the possibility of making educational institutions more efficient and simultaneously capable of dealing with a wider range of individual differences.

There are many other tasks, but all involve the same attitudes and complexities. Each asks the question of whether we are capable of extending and conserving a heritage which involves self-affirmation and self-denial. If we can determine what it is that must be affirmed, we may discover what we must deny in order to make the affirmation. Self-denial has been a consistent theme in our literature and in our experience. Often we hear that the trouble with contemporary Americans is that they are fat; that they have not had to deny themselves anything of consequence. There is an important element of truth in the charge. Is it possible, however, that our failure stems from the fact that we have not related what must be denied to what must be affirmed?

The contemporary age also seems to have marked a central task rather plainly for this generation of Americans. Historically the American people have fought to secure for widening groups of people the circumstances and conditions essential for the achievement of freedom and dignity. One can argue that conditions have often pushed us into the fight. Conditions are pushing us again. The price of preserving the heritage is that of making it applicable in areas we never knew existed. We are today in the position of the nineteenth-century men of wealth whose spending was marked by "conspicuous consumption." They learned, with difficulty, that they could not keep their wealth and ignore the "have-nots" in their own society. Today Americans find themselves in the middle of a much more vast revolution involving diverse cultures and millions upon millions of people.

The mid-twentieth century American may have some advantages, however. His growing self-awareness may make it possible for him to accept the fact that his efforts will be misunderstood; that he will not get proper credit for what he undertakes. His sense of history may keep him from being easily discouraged and may even allow him to perform his tasks cheerfully. His sense of tragedy will acknowledge the problems on the other side of the mountain. Thus equipped he may discover the applicability to his immediate circumstances of what Paul

Tillich has called "the eternal now." That is to say he may discover that in feeding hungry Congolese he is taking a step made necessary by an acceptance of his own past, and made significant for its own sake by the fact that it offers a link with the future.

The problem for the American who has lived at the future rather than in the present is to learn to see life whole; to accept the past which represents his limitations; to enjoy the present for its own sake; and to accept the future with hope, even a future which ends in death. The American heritage, extending back to the days of Puritanism, can be of real service here. Americans in the past have understood that they lived under a judgment which commanded perfection and in circumstances which denied the possibility of achieving it. Born to this agony, the Americans can bear it by accepting the tasks which come out of history and by leading the way toward a future for which they can accept some small, but significant, measure of responsibility.

The miracle of America has been a miracle of rebirth. The miracle has never taken place without pain and suffering, misunderstanding and anguish. But it occurs. We have denied the Negro his rights, but our guilt would not down. We wanted isolation, but we could not make it stick. We dreamed of a nation of farmers, but we surrendered the dream. Put this way the task of those who educate is to initiate a process of self-criticism, to force people to reexamine assumptions, and to look at alien viewpoints. If the educator can help people to discover their limitations, feel sorry about them, and define for themselves responsibilities which are worthy of them, he will have done what he can to help Americans conserve the values that make them what they are.

Curiously enough, the age belongs to the educator in a way. Precisely because this is an age of introspection and analysis, it falls to the intellectual and educator to make the process of maturation significant. If the teacher is content to win smiles and to reinforce complacency, he will kill what Sherwood Anderson called the young thing that keeps us alive. The young thing is, perhaps, man's urge to seek the truth. When men try to possess it, to reduce it to dogma, they kill it. If they do not kill it, however, Americans will have an answer to Nikita Khrushchev's boast that he will bury them. The answer goes something like this. "Our civilization will change, even in ways that we do not foresee. Yours will, too. Your notion of utopia is surely doomed to suffer the fate of all utopias. But you do not understand the source of our strength. The source of our strength is our commitment to seek the truth and to dignify human existence. The source of our strength explains the miracle of our rebirth. For the truth to which we testify is indeed the truth that sets men free. We know that this truth is not our exclusive possession. No one can freeze it, or make it his personal property, but men can witness to the truth and thereby pass on their inheritance to future generations. The thing that gives us strength, the thing to which *we* dedicate *ourselves*; the thing which we affirm and for which we can indeed deny ourselves; that thing *is* eternal."

Notes

1. Carl N. Degler, "The Sociologist as Historian: Riesman's, *The Lonely Crowd,*" *American Quarterly* 15, no. 4 (Winter 1963): 483 – 97.

2. Carl L. Becker, "Kansas," reprinted in *Everyman His Own Historian* (New York: F. S. Crofts & Co.. 1905), p. 9.

3. Frederick Lewis Allen, *The Big Change* (New York: Harper & Brothers, 1952), pp. 7 – 8.

4. Cora DuBois, "The Dominant Profile of American Culture," *American Anthropologist* 57, no. 6, pt. 1 (December 1955): 1233.

5. David M. Potter, *People of Plenty* (Chicago: University of Chicago Press, 1954), p. 109.

6. William Hordern, *A Layman's Guide to Protestant Theology* (New York: Macmillan Company, 1955), p. 152.

7. Center for the Study of Democratic Institutions, "Tragedy and the New Politics" (Santa Barbara: The Fund for the Republic, 1960), p. 21.

8. Ibid.

9. Ibid., p. 22.

MARSHALL W. FISHWICK

Diagnosing the American Dream

Marshall Fishwick did his graduate work at the University of Wisconsin and Yale and has taught at Washington and Lee, the University of Minnesota, Delaware, Lincoln, and Temple universities. He is now a professor in the Department of Performing Arts and Communications at Virginia Polytechnic Institute and State University. He has made American Studies a part of the world community and has taught in Denmark, Germany, Poland, India, England, and Italy. His most recent book is entitled Popular Culture in the New Journalism.

I

The play's the thing: it holds the mirror up to man. What, in our time and place, does it show?

Sounds, syntax, and logic jumbled beyond recognition. In Samuel Beckett's plays, men might sit on nothing identifiable, which exists in a gray space. The whole world crawls from left to right along an invisible track. One character resembles the square root of 2. Twenty-eight people yearn for the day when their combined total ages will be exactly 1,000 years. The Butcher in Arnold Weinstein's *The Red Eye of Love* busies himself building a skyscraper out of used meat. Can *this* be "the land of the free, and the home of the brave"? What has happened to the American Dream?

The Theatre of the Absurd reveals not the rational world of our eighteenth-century forefathers but a world that has gone mad. "Man attempts to make sense out of his senseless position," the brilliant young playwright Edward Albee says, "in a world that makes no sense. The social structures man has erected to 'illusion' himself have collapsed." Albee's attack on America in *The American Dream* is one of the telling documents of our generation. Our diagnosis may well begin here.[1]

In the play his whole theme is understated. Instead of shouts and curses we confront the trite speech and clichés of everyday life, turned into a formula for ritual communication. Accurately and meticulously he reveals the neurosis inside our everyday assumptions. Suddenly we realize that individuality and creativity are squelched by the conformist way of life—killed (so far as the play itself is concerned) in the person of a foster-son murdered for disobedience. The old Emersonian phrases seem to mock us from the wings. Self-reliance merely leads to group revenge.

The Zoo Story, another Albee play, presents us with ironic suicide staged as imitation murder. Jerry, who seems unable to find any sense of community, suffers from "a great weariness." Neither Bohemian nor Beat, he simply cannot respond to the phony world around. In fact, he cannot even communicate with his landlady's dog. In reaching out for a more meaningful life, he is only moving towards his own death.

If American Studies as an intellectual enterprise in the 1960s is to be vital and effective, it must move beyond the time-honored clichés about American optimism and confront rampant pessimism. Students of our culture must move from behind the façade of a chrome-covered culture and confront the main issues where they really exist.

The Great Debate of our time rages between Traditionalists and Existentialists. The former insist on keeping the inherited house tidy; the latter on discarding it and building anew. That we face unprecedented crises, no one denies. But what should our response be? Should we guard the fort, or abandon it for the frontier? Considering our predicament, what should our attitude and policy be? Anguished apprehension has brought us, in fear and trembling, to accept the paradoxicality or absurdity of the universe. Obsessed with the spectre of annihilation itself, we "rediscover" poets like Rilke; novelists like Melville; philosophers like Kierkegaard, whose comment on old-style system builders sums up our modern dilemma in a sentence: "Most systematizers stand in the same relation to their systems as the man who builds a great castle and lives in the adjoining barn."

Existentialism, which claims Kierkegaard as a fountainhead, has rapidly become a major force in the twentieth century. Some claim its origins are rooted in the ancient Greeks; others that it springs from François Villon, and after him Rabelais and Montaigne; still others see it as a reaction against the rationalism which dominated western thought from Descartes through Hegel. Whatever Existentialism's origins, it has spilled out of the philosophic mold, into literature, drama, theology, politics, history, and mass media—not so much a system as a protest *against* systematizing. Particularly in the physical sciences, "laws" and "certainties" of the Newtonian world have been superseded. "To what appeared to be the simplest question," J. Robert Oppenheimer writes in *Science and the Common Understanding,* "we now tend to give either no answer or an answer which will at first sight sound like a strange catechism."

This "strange catechism" attempts to analyze the great emptiness of modern life; with nothingness that lies curled at the heart of being like a worm. Jean Paul Sartre holds that there are two kinds of being: *l'être en soi* (being in itself) and *l'être pour soi* (being for itself). The first is characterized by infinite density—a rock, for instance—the second by mutability and desire. Man—project plus facticity—is in the second category. Existence is action and involvement. Haunted by the gnawing passion to thwart meaninglessness, man gravitates towards ruts, pigeonholes, and fantasies. "Stop!" Existenialists cry. "Only when you struggle are you human. The uncommitted life isn't worth living."

The real enemy is inauthentic existence.[2] Its hallmarks are abstractions, circumlocutions, and pomposity. Meaning emerges only in the struggle between creativity and inquisition. "A creative period in art," Albert Camus wrote, "can be defined as an order of style applied to the disorder of an age." And again, in a poignant description of modern man's plight: "I have always felt that I lived on the high seas, menaced, at the heart of a royal happiness."

No matter what existentialism's cultural origins or terminology, its diagnosis has striking relevance in contemporary America. Wrapped in an ethnocentric cocoon, we find ourselves acting as if today's values were permanent fixtures. We are serious about trivialities (electric toothbrushes, sports cars, hair-dos), trivial about reality (life, encounter, death). We insist on convenient categorical pegs on which to hang every conception; despise uncertainty and disorder; and impose both certainty and order where none exists. So it is at home, in the market place, in the university. Instead of real education we offer adjustment, pressing pliant human beings into patterns, filling curricula with supermarket knowledge conveniently packaged and labeled. Pat answers masquerade as truth. Some intellectuals have almost reverted to the eighteenth century's excessive adulation for reason. Fighting flux with formalism, they are reconciled to superficiality in every phase of life.

We accord ultimate meaning to the useful, but refuse to ask: useful for *what?* Increasingly we find ourselves being transformed into things—cogs in the universal system of organized production and consumption. We are lonely in crowds, trapped in organizations, entranced by status symbols, stripped of privacy in a naked society.

Hence W. H. Auden's caustic invitation:

Come to our well run desert
Where anguish comes by cable
And the deadly sins can be bought in tins
With instructions on the label.

He joins the long procession of those who warn against size, titilation, and triviality. A century ago Walt Whitman asserted that a mouse is miracle enough to stagger sextillions of infidels. Paul Elmer More had strong opinions about sterile abstractions:

The absolute, the abstract, and the infinite—absolute unity, abstract being, and infinite actuality—are the most impertinent and pernicious words in the vocabulary of philosophy. Their devastation effect is in exact proportion to their lack of meaning, as a vacuum is the most deadly power in nature. These conceptions are the sterile eggs of reason never fecundated by sense; the scholar who brooks them may addle them and his own brain, but will hatch nothing.[3]

In more and more areas of American life the ability or even advisability of promulgating air-tight theories and infallible propositions is being questioned. Better honest doubt than dishonest certainty. Thus Robert A. Dahl comments on the contemporary concept of power:

We are not likely to produce—certainly not for some considerable time to come—anything like a consistent, coherent 'theory. . . .' We are much more likely to produce a variety of theories of limited scope, each of which employs some definition that is useful in the context of the particular piece of research or theory but different in important respects from the definitions of other studies.[4]

This viewpoint has been expressed time and again by "Realists" in the field of political theory—Reinhold Niebuhr, Walter Lippmann, Hans Morgenthau, George Kennan, and Kenneth Thompson. Learn to resist the great American impatience, they tell us; live with ambiguities which make quick generalizations untenable. Look behind the verbiage for *real* issues and positions. Make possibilities the function of actuality; but never consider actuality the only possibility.

In a more bizarre and less articulate way, America's rebels and beats have made the same point. Lacking the positive philosophy of their predecessors, those proto-existentialists in the Jazz Age Bohemia, they have nevertheless denounced sham and false rhetoric. Oscar Handlin acknowledges this in *The Americans: A New History of the People of the United States.* Norman Mailer, the beats, the hipsters, and the *sick* comedians knew what they were against, Dr. Handlin comments, but they were unable to say what they were for. The mass media deluged their generation with an array of images—confused, distorted, disordered. "Violence smothered the sentimental platitudes; they believed none of it or all of it, with equal coolness." Some pushed on to a *reductio ad absurdum*. "My name is John Filler and I represent the latest rage in American Freaklore, the hip-beat author who doesn't write," an account in the July 1963 *Esquire* began. "I don't write because it is the tradition of my school to stop, once enough insight is gained to graduate from student to mastery. You only put on paper what you hope somebody will buy. This school is sort of a fraternity, but none of us pledged it."

The historical revolution now under way, J. H. Hexter predicts, will not consist in the creation of ambitious general theories, but in piece-meal advances. Historian after historian will reexamine "the place and time with which he is mainly concerned, and [will seek] to contrive, for telling about what went on in that bounded time and place, a vocabulary of conceptions better suited to bring out its character."[5] On today's intellectual scene the force of an idea does not depend on its grandiosity.

Yet in the workaday world, discrepancies and gaps between practice and outmoded theory are ignored. Historians, David Potter notes, constantly work with separate items of data, so that relationships are a chief part of their work. "Yet," Potter continues, "the literature of their method and the procedures of their training give so little attention to the systematic analysis of such relationships that a majority of those trained in history have never confronted the general question of the nature of causation or of motivation or of group identity." Many are not even aware that they *haven't* confronted these questions; many who train them are not aware of it either. To this observation John William Ward adds another. Historians seldom face the embarrassment of those in American Studies, confronting the demand to define their field. "Protected by tradition against such rude and unsettling questions, left free to do what their inclinations, conscious or otherwise, call them to, historians remain content to teach their courses and write their books, hardly bothered that their generic title refers not at all to their function but to the institutional fiction which gathers them under a single umbrella."[6]

Not only history, but all formal education runs the danger of divorcing itself from reality. Teachers abstract and generalize by inclination and habit. Students memorize phrases and formulae without learning how and when to apply them. What starts as erudition can quickly degenerate into irrelevance. Hamlet's old lament takes on new significance: "Words, words, words." Yet even the reign of words is coming to an end, along with man's bondage to the earth. Today science is able to do things that cannot be made fully intelligible in words, but only in formulae. Thus (as Mary McCarthy points out) we may be abolishing speech as vital communication between men; "and this implies that the life of action, the matching of great words with great deeds, is finished."[7]

Such basic doubts deserve primary consideration. The same generation that produced existentialism also produced American Studies.[8] Today the pressing task for those engaged in it seems not to be so much *defending* a position or culture as in defining it. *Despite* the numerical growth of American Studies departments and courses many academicians are still skeptical. In a world long marked by Cartesian fixed points, fluidity and relativism are threatening. Colleagues who are friendly over coffee can become formidable in committees and departments. It is one thing to say, with Howard Mumford Jones, that the departmental system splits us into little groups conducting internecine wars; and quite another thing to do much about it.[9]

II

In so diffuse and decentralized an activity as American Studies, it is also hard to know just what has been, or is being, done. "What might be said in general terms?" Professor Riesman asked recently. "Has American Studies grown faster in state or private universities; in newer or in older ones; in universities or in colleges? How about denominational institutions? Since Robert Walker's book came out[10] there must have been great changes. Have you any sense of these trajectories? Is it still a matter of missionaries and their devoted disciples?'' No one has attempted to give Professor Riesman a definite or authoritative answer.

Meanwhile, C. Vann Woodward's "Age of Reinterpretation" rushes on. Western imperialism is collapsing. New nations spring up. Power is polarized between two nuclear giants.[11] Questions of protocol and precedent are dwarfed by the titanic struggle for survival. A query once posited by an eighteenth-century immigrant farmer named de Croevecoeur orbits, like a satellite, around the world: "What then *is* an American?" He is *homo sapiens* struggling in a broadbacked and boisterous culture featuring Paul Bunyan's strength and Yukon Ike's verve; Casey Jones' daring and Salvation Sal's devotion; John Henry's rhythm and Huck Finn's charm. He lives in a big, foolish, generous land, wide as the Mississippi or prairies nature hesitated to enclose; white as Cape Cod sand, black as West Virginia coal; flat as Salt Lake basin, too steep for Rocky Mountain goats.

The land is full of turbulent cities, with fingers of power reaching out into space; plantations, warmed by the glow of golden memories; river land, with earth richer than the treasures of Solomon. It abounds with poor boy sandwiches, atomic reactors, foot-long hot dogs, Charles Addams gothic, Hopi Indians, imitation castles, block slums, freedom marches, glass domes, beatniks, little magazines, big sells, wetbacks, greenbacks, comebacks. Fastened on it are fascinating names to set a poet musing—Dry Bones, Nantucket, Go-to-Hell Gulch, Lost Mule Flat, Machopongo, Bubbleup, Wounded Knee, Roanoke, Purgatory Creek, Lake June in Winter, Okaloacoochee Slough, and Boot Hill. Here is a group of vaguely united states searching for an epic.

In 1864 the transcendentalist George P. Marsh called this Republic "the first example of the struggle between civilized man and barbarous uncultivated nature."[12] Generally the culture hero is the savage, the theater a wilderness, and the drama one of slow progress against nature. But in America the full energies of advanced European civilization were "brought to bear at once on a desert continent." The whole process of civilization was enormously accelerated; the cultural opportunity and diversity multiplied beyond calculation.

The one valid tag for such a landscape is *pluralism*. With two powerful weapons—dynamism and the will to experiment—the continent was conquered. In the national motto and destiny, the *unum* was counterbalanced by *pluribus*. Whatever else American Studies is or is not, it must be inextricably bound up with the nation's dramatic growth and her emergence as a world power. In a positive sense, it is allied to contemporary movements within the scholarly community to regain concepts of meaning which served humanistic scholarship through the Renaissance, but which were sometimes lost in overspecialization later on. Negatively, it articulates a protest against rigid categories of knowledge, and the tendency to treat everything American as a mere extension of European culture. Both tendencies appear in essays by such pioneers in the field as Tremaine McDowell, Stanley Williams, Ralph Gabriel, Henry Nash Smith, and

Robert Spiller. In 1948 Professor McDowell formulated his First Law of American Studies: It would present the complex design of American life, thus revealing the fundamental diversity of human experience within which the student should eventually find a fundamental unity.[13]

Ten years later the question of just *how* to present this complex design remained unanswered. Some who had manned the front line sounded a bit fatigued when they made their 1958 battle report in *Studies in American Culture; Dominant Ideas and Images*. No ready-made method for American Studies was in sight, concluded Professor Henry Nash Smith. "We shall have to develop one for ourselves, and I am afraid that at present we shall have to be content with a very modest program," he continued. "The best thing we can do, in my opinion, is to conceive of American Studies as a collaboration among men working from within existing academic disciplines but attempting to widen the boundaries imposed by conventional methods of inquiry."[14]

Appearing five years later, Walter Johnson's brochure on *American Studies Abroad* took a position which was, like Smith's, basically conservative. In fact, he seemed more anxious to retrench than to go forward in the far-flung outposts American Studies has set up since World War II, thanks to the Fulbright program and other international grants:

It is hoped that the newly established American Studies Foundation [in Japan] will avoid overemphasis on the United States as an area study and instead will stimulate the more solid and productive growth of American subjects through the interested academic disciplines.[15]

Exporting American Studies is one of the most difficult, and still most promising, aspects of the whole current picture. Wherever the enterprise smacks of cultural imperialism, it will be challenged or rejected. Wherever it seeks to present an accurate picture of a complex and powerful culture in transition, it will be welcomed and appreciated. As Edward R. Murrow, former head of the United States Information Agency, pointed out, we must be willing to include "warts and all" in the picture we present. Even the well developed academic disciplines (American literature, history, and government) are not too well known abroad, and run the risk of being labeled "propaganda." Courses bearing the label "American Studies" will be more suspect still.

As early as 1953, Dr. Francis A. Young (Executive Secretary of the Conference Board of Associated Research Councils) pointed out that there were too few qualified candidates to meet the needs of the Fulbright-Hays program; in 1962 the chairman of the British Association of American Studies warned that visiting mediocrities would do more harm than good, reinforcing rather than eliminating prejudices against the United States, its universities, and its American Studies curricula.[16] By putting our house in order at home—developing mature and able scholars of American culture—we shall automatically improve our offerings overseas.

III

Meanwhile, the struggle between generalists (who would examine the macrocosm) and specialists (obsessed with the intricacy of the microcosm) continues. The former are impatient to achieve the grand synthesis. The latter insist that we must know much more about the elements we are trying to synthesize. Instead of deploring this disagreement, we should encourage it. Whether or not they concede it, each group is dependent on the other for growth and survival. The fate of interdisciplinary scholarship depends on an increase, not a diminution of questions—provided they are relevant to the issues of our time.

Let me mention six recent books which do precisely that. Despite certain weaknesses and flaws (which reviewers quickly pounced on), they point towards new ways of dealing with complex problems—perhaps even towards a new methodology for American Studies. As yet the shore is only dimly seen: but the voyage is under way.

The first title is Thomas C. Cochran's *Railroad Leaders, 1845 – 1890: The Business Mind in Action* (1953). Professor Cochran's primary aim is "to establish some norms of thought and attitude for American railroad presidents" between 1845 and 1890; to arrive at a "profile of presidential attitudes" on such matters as competition, social problems, expansion, and innovation. By analyzing the letter-files of sixty-one railroad presidents, he arrives at a picture far different from that of most historians, economists, and political scientists. He has given new insight into a complex and pivotal nineteenth-century institution—the railroad.

In *The American Adam: Innocence, Tragedy, and Tradition in the Nineteenth Century* (1953), R. W. B. Lewis sets out to discover a masked pattern in American literature, and by implication in American culture. On the surface our literature shows the authentic American as a "figure of heroic innocence and vast potentialities, poised at the start of a new history." Underneath, Dr. Lewis asserts, is a very different American. The images and metaphors used in literature express masked anxieties and value premises. As we know these, a much more accurate picture of the nineteenth-century American emerges.

Daniel J. Boorstin's *The Americans: The Colonial Experience* (1958) shows how American history can be reinterpreted in the light of recent interdepartmental surveys. Dr. Boorstin does not hold with the time-honored notion that America was a "second chance" for Europe; that our culture is merely an extension of the old world's. Like Turner, Parrington and Beard before him (who may be the real Founding Fathers of American Studies) Boorstin finds new categories: an American frame of mind, the ideal of the undifferentiated man, culture without a capital, the fusion of law and politics, poetry without poets, backwoods farming, and a nation of minute men. A later Boorstin book called *The Image: What Happened to the American Dream?* (1961) is more provocative, but less successful. *The Image* must be counted a failure, but a significant one.

David M. Potter's *People of Plenty* (1954) attempts to discover how economic abundance has affected American life. Can one establish a valid concept of national character by pooling the work of historians and behavioral scientists, Potter asks in his introduction; his book provides an affirmative answer. He conceives of abundance not in terms of a storehouse of fixed assets, but as something residing in a series of physical potentialities, which have never been inventoried at the same value for any two cultures. He goes on to show how some aspects of child rearing in the United States are as distinctively American (when compared with other countries) as any Yankee traits that have ever been attributed to the American people; and he opens the door to a whole series of investigations of contemporary life.

One of the most impressive recent books—*America and the World Revolution* (1962)—has the virtues of an outsider looking in. The English author Arnold Toynbee sees us in a perspective which natives could never hope to attain. In this study he shows how the historian can bring personal observation, moral concern, and comparative criteria into a single focus. For generations, Toynbee maintains, America symbolized the revolutionary concern of the many in a world controlled by the few. Knowing that the disease of liberty is highly contagious, Americans deliberately spread it throughout the world. By a twist of fate, we now find ourselves leading the anti-revolutionary forces. We have abandoned the world majority and joined the world minority. In our time, technology is within sight of being able to produce enough material benefits to provide for the whole human race. The millions who stand on the starvation line know this and intend to do something about it. What will the American response be?

More optimistic, and no less original, is *A New History of the People of the United States* (1963), by Oscar Handlin. His story centers on vast and lasting nervousness before a vast and lasting empty space. Handlin's theme is inner conflict and loneliness; American history echoes the ancient Greek sin of *hubris*. The rage to tame the wilderness outside and inside us has long been an obsession. We have sought security, at different times, in land, slaves, stocks, or SAC airplanes. Who are we, anyway? Does anybody know? In asking, we continue to chase Melville's white whale. That mythic beast symbolizes our uncertainty: corruption and innocence, purpose without point, invasion without destination.

Whether or not one agrees with the analysis and conclusions of Cochran, Lewis, Boorstin, Potter, Toynbee, and Handlin, he realizes that each is attempting diligently to diagnose the American dream. Instead of repeating the old platitudes, they are making fresh starts, running new tests. They seek to probe, not to pontificate.

Those who profess and practice American Studies might do well to study and emulate them. We must be equipped to perceive our uniquely American heritage, and prepared to supersede it. In a fast-changing world, the need for the kind of Americans Emerson envisioned a century ago remains: "Men and women of original perception and original action, who can open their eyes wider than to a nationality—to the considerations of benefit to the human race . . . men of

elastic, men of moral mind, who can live in the moment and talk and take a step forward.''

Notes

1. Published in 1961, the play was extensively reviewed and discussed. See, for example, *Catholic World,* August 1961; *Christian Century,* March 1, 1961; *Horizon,* July 1961; *Nation,* February 11, 1961; *New Yorker,* February 4, 1961; *Saturday Review,* February 11, 1961; and *Theatre Arts,* March 1961. For a discussion of Albee's position in current drama, see Walter Kerr, *The Theater in Spite of Itself* (New York: S & S, 1963).

2. A fine introduction to the subject is Paul Tillich's *Theology of Culture* (New York: Oxford University Press, 1959). See also Simone de Beauvoir, *The Ethics of Ambiguity* (New York: Philosophical Library, 1948); Jean Paul Sartre, *Existential Psychoanalysis* (1962 ed., Gateway Editions Ltd.); Jethro Bithell, *Modern German Literature, 1880–1950,* 3d. rev. ed. (London: Methuen, 1959); Hugh Kenner, *Samuel Beckett, a Critical Study* (New York: Grove Press, 1961); Thomas Hanna, *The Lyrical Existentialists* (New York: Atheneum, 1962); Walter Ong, *The Barbarian Within* (New York: Macmillan, 1962); and Gabriel Marcel, *The Existential Background of Human Dignity* (Cambridge: Harvard University Press, 1963).

3. Paul Elmer More, *Pages from an Oxford Diary* (New York: 1951 ed., Kennikat), p. 28.

4. Robert A. Dahl, "The Concept of Power," *Behavioral Science* 3 (July 1957): 201–15.

5. J. H. Hexter, *Reappraisals in History* (New York: Harper Torch-books, 1961), p. vii. Professor Hexter's devastating attack on "Tunnel History" and factor analysis make this one of the pivotal books in the field. The Social Science Research Council has been much concerned with these matters. See, for example, their Bulletin 54, *Theory and Practice in Historical Study* (1946), Bulletin 64, *The Social Sciences in Historical Study* (1954), and *Generalizations in the Writing of History* (Chicago, 1963).

6. John William Ward, "Generalizations upon Generalizations," in *American Quarterly* 15, no. 3 (Fall 1963): 465. In this article Dr. Ward includes the quotation from Dr. Potter which appears above; it is from an essay included in *Generalization in the Writing of History* (Chicago, 1963).

7. Mary McCarthy, reviewing Hannah Arendt's *The Human Condition* in the *New Yorker,* October 18, 1958.

8. In *American Studies in the United States* (Baton Rouge: L.S.U. Press, 1958) Robert Walker reports that the movement dates largely in the years since World War II. More recent summaries may be found in the *American Quarterly.*

9. Howard Mumford Jones, *Education and World Tragedy* (Cambridge, Mass.: Harvard University Press, 1947). Pointing out that the departmental system is the creation of the past seventy or eighty years Professor Jones notes that it is "regarded by most professors as something absolute and inescapable."

10. See Walker, *American Studies.*

11. C. Vann Woodward, *The Age of Reinterpretation* (Washington: Service Center for Teachers of History, 1960), Pamphlet No. 35.

12. George P. Marsh, *Man and Nature; or Physical Geography as Modified by Human Action* (New York: Scribner's, 1864). Quoted by Arthur A. Ekirch, Jr., *Man and Nature in America* (New York: Columbia University Press, 1963), p. 71.

13. Tremaine McDowell, *American Studies* (Minneapolis: University of Minnesota Press, 1948), p. 51.

14. Henry Nash Smith, "Can 'American Studies' Develop a Method?" in Joseph J. Kwiat and Mary C. Turpie, eds., *Studies in American Culture; Dominant Ideas and Images* (Minneapolis: University of Minnesota Press, 1960), p. 14.

15. Walter Johnson, *American Studies Abroad, Progress and Difficulties in Selected Countries* (Washington, 1963).

16. "The Fulbright Program," *News Report* (National Academy of Sciences – National Research Council), March – April 1953, p. 22; and Johnson, *American Studies Abroad,* p. 57.

GERALD E. CRITOPH

The American Quest for Affluence

*Gerald E. Critoph is Professor of American Studies
at Stetson University, DeLand, Florida. He received
his doctorate in the American Civilization Program at the
University of Pennsylvania and taught at Colgate and
Michigan State before coming to Stetson. He has recently
written a musical play,* Reluctant Rebel, *dealing with the
American Revolution.*

There is a poignantly persistent belief held by many Americans that most of the Europeans who came to America in the colonial period were motivated by the urge to establish a society in which each person would be free to worship as he pleased. However, a careful study of the settlers of North America reveals that the great majority of immigrants, right from the beginning, crossed the ocean to improve their economic positions in life. The subsequent struggle to conquer the wilderness and spread across the continent has been marked by a continuous drive to raise the material standard of living for more and more Americans.[1] This quest for affluence is still characteristic of the nation, having been intensified tremendously since World War II.

In 1776, Thomas Jefferson wrote, with the approval of many of his countrymen, "We hold these truths to be self-evident, that all men are created equal, that they are endowed by their Creator with certain unalienable rights, that among these are life, liberty and the pursuit of happiness." While these lofty ideals have been variously interpreted, sometimes rather narrowly, they have continued to be considered by most Americans to be fundamental to the American Way of Life. What is significant to this essay is that, at all stages of U.S. history, these ideals have been widely identified by Americans with the accumulation and possession of material goods through some socially acceptable occupation.

In the two centuries of debate over what Jefferson meant by "all men are created equal," the most consistent agreement has been that it expressed an ideal: the equality of opportunity that all Americans *ought* to have. It has emphasized that all Americans should have equal opportunities in gaining access to and in earning a share of the goods and services that society produces in any one period.

In interpreting the "right to life," Americans generally have not meant just sustaining life with the requisite food and shelter. They have usually defined this kind of minimum as mere existence. Instead, they have assumed that the right to life included living at a standard deemed decent according to the means available at any particular time.

Jefferson took for granted that the "right to liberty" was based on the possession of property. Like many other Enlightenment writers, he agreed with John Locke that each person had a right to own property. He maintained that a person was not really independent of the influence of others unless he owned enough property to support himself and his family. According to this point of view, the more property a person held, the more liberty he had.

In the "pursuit of happiness," eighteenth-century Americans tended to believe that possessions held the key. The rapidly expanding industrial developments of the nineteenth and twentieth centuries convinced their beneficiaries that they were right. Americans have joked about it, saying that "Money isn't everything, it can't buy happiness, but it certainly can finance the search for it." Their behavior much more eloquently declares that happiness is usually determined by the goods and services they have had at their disposal.

These attitudes could be documented by quoting Americans from all levels of society throughout American history. However, since this essay concentrates on the period since World War II, statements from the two presidents who held office just before that time suggest some prevailing attitudes. On March 4, 1929, Herbert Hoover reflected the national enthusiasm with the unprecedented economic achievement of the 1920s when he said in his inaugural address: "In a large view we have reached a higher degree of comfort and security than ever existed before in the world. . . . I have no fears for the future of our country. It is bright with hope."[2] Less than eight months later, the New York stock market crashed and the United States began a decade of the worst depression in its history.

The depression and the world war that followed it were important factors in increasing the material desires of most Americans. They became convinced that a solid base in property ownership was essential to their personal security. President Franklin D. Roosevelt expressed the hopes of millions of Americans in a press conference on December 28, 1943, by saying: " . . . when victory comes, . . . it seems pretty clear that we must plan for, and help bring about, an expanded economy which will result in more security, in more employment, in more recreation, in more education, in more health, in better housing for all our citizens, so that the conditions of 1932 and the beginning of 1933 won't come back again."[3]

Americans believed that the end of the war would bring about a sudden burst of civilian goods onto the market. Members of the armed forces were anxious to get out of uniform and into civilian clothes, get behind the wheels of their own new cars, and, like their civilian countrymen, buy some of the fabulous products that the forecasters were promising. Americans were hungry for the goods and services that depression and war had denied them. They were sure that the improved technology of the war industries would be put to work making more terrific things than ever before.

Their war experiences had persuaded millions of Americans that an enlarged portion of those goods would be within their reach. Factory workers had more than doubled their average weekly incomes between 1939 and 1945. Because of wartime shortages of civilian goods, much of their increases went into various forms of savings. Servicemen had also saved a part of their pay. By the time hostilities had ceased, Americans had accumulated around $140 billion in savings, $129 billion of which were in easily convertible forms.[4]

In June 1945, Congress passed what came to be known as the G.I. Bill. Its provisions had profound effects on the American quest for affluence, as well as contributing to the successful attempt to avoid a traditional postwar depression. The bill provided a subsistence income of $20 a week for a maximum of fifty-two weeks for veterans looking for a job or waiting to go back to school. The Veterans Administration (VA) guaranteed mortgages for veterans who wanted to own their own homes. This turned out to be a boon to the construction industry as well as the veterans. Also, VA backing of small business loans reduced the risk that veterans had to run in starting in business for themselves. The G.I. Bill gave a boost to the economy while it made the veterans' personal reconversion to peacetime a smoother one.

Probably the greatest investment that Americans made through this law was in the veterans who went back to school and college. By July 1951, the U.S. government had spent $14.5 billion educating 7.8 million veterans. Over 2 million attended college. The United States has been reaping the benefits of this expansion of knowledge ever since, not only in the original group who received more education, but in the subsequent raising of educational sights for millions of families.[5]

Even though the immediate postwar years were full of strikes and shortages of raw materials, the volume of goods and services increased at an amazing pace. Americans could indulge in some of the richer tastes they had developed with the enlarged incomes they continued to enjoy. In 1950, a U.N. survey revealed just how much richer Americans were than anyone else. The United Nations estimated the per capita annual income in real purchasing power in the United States at $1,453. The three closest countries were Canada, New Zealand, and Switzerland, all of which fell into the $800–$900 per capita range.[6]

Because food is a basic human need, a nation's eating patterns provide a good measure of its affluence. By the middle of the 1950s, it had become apparent that American eating habits were changing rather drastically. *Life* magazine recognized this in a special issue on food dated January 3, 1955. Its cover showed a loaded supermarket shopping cart with the subheading declaring: "Mass Luxury: A $73 Billion Market Basket." The issue's introduction asserted: "Americans who are as well fed as any people in the world are also prize specimens of what good feeding does to a people. Each generation is taller, bigger and healthier than the preceding one—and each has a longer life expectancy.''[7]

The issue emphasized that the national diet was more substantial and more varied. For one thing, Americans were eating more meat than ever before. According to the American Meat Institute, 1954 was a record meat-eating year—156 pounds per person were consumed.[8] More kinds of vegetables were served in American homes, and in greater quantities. It was also becoming apparent that some Americans were eating too much, causing Adlai Stevenson to note that the United States was the world's only nation where overeating was a major problem.

Food was being produced more and more by giant food factories like Seabrook Farms of New Jersey with 50,000 acres growing 100 million pounds a year. It was sold increasingly in the 18,000 supermarkets across the country, constituting 5 percent of the 360,000 grocery stores, but accounting for nearly 50 percent of the total food sales. The giantism of the producers and retailers of the middle 1950s greatly impressed Americans at the time, but it was just the beginning.[9]

The American achievement of a large degree of affluence in the 1950s was also indicated by the astounding pile of agricultural surpluses that was building up. By the end of 1959, the U.S. government reported that it owned surplus farm products worth over $9 billion.[10] The mounds of food just sitting in warehouses gave the illusion of a well-fed nation. Most Americans *were* well fed, but there were still substantial groups of citizens who went to bed hungry each night. Affluence in the 1950s was not for all Americans.

A prime example of the American quest for affluence has been the automobile. It started out as a plaything for the rich at the beginning of the twentieth century, but, within fifteen years, it was considered a necessity by many in the middle classes. By 1940, despite the depression, there were about 32 million cars, buses, and trucks in use in the United States. In 1950, there were approximately 49 million on the road, even though no civilian cars were built during four of the years between 1940 and 1950.[11]

The extent of the automobile industry in 1950 was revealed by an article in *Life* magazine for January 1, 1951, describing the General Motors Corporation. It declared:

General Motors Corporation . . . is the biggest, most successful and most profitable manufacturing enterprise in the history of man. . . . In 1950 GM had not only its most profitable year but the most profitable year of any corporation any time—the net income reaching about $900 million. In that year GM made almost half of all the 6,650,000 automobiles built in the U.S., as well as 647,000 trucks, 2,200 buses, over 2,000 diesel locomotives and millions of other products like electric refrigerators, jet engines, and oil burners. It employed 516,000 wage or salary earners, virtually enough to support a city the size of Cleveland, indirectly employed about 200,000 more in the privately owned sales agencies for its products and by spending about half its gross income of $7 billion on materials and services gave employment to possibly 250,000 more. Its tax bill ($800 million) is bigger than all the federal income taxes paid collectively by 14 of the states.[12]

During the 1950s, Americans bought an annual average of 6 to 7 million cars, making at least one of their postwar dreams come true.[13]

While automobiles constituted a significant item in the American consumer's budget, other products also demonstrated the affluence that Americans were achieving. In 1949, U.S. manufacturers produced 543 million pairs of nylons, sufficient to furnish every woman over fourteen in the country with at least 9 pairs. In 1950, the *Scientific Monthly* stated that, after allowing for price rises, Americans spent 96 percent more for books than in 1940, 140 percent more for toys and sporting equipment, 129 percent more for flowers and seeds, 219 percent more for photograph developing and printing, and 263 percent more for phonographs, records, musical instruments, radios, and television sets. *Life* magazine for January 5, 1953, cited a survey of the appliance industry for 1952. It said that a million electric ranges were sold, plus 720,000 water heaters, 3,400,000 refrigerators, 1,200,000 food freezers, and 500,000 automatic dryers.[14]

As the decade progressed, affluence became possible for more and more Americans. Millions acquired a second car, usually used or compact. Two million families owned a second home in 1959, with 75,000 more being planned. About 70,000 families built swimming pools in 1959 at an average cost of $4,000. In 1950, there had been 3,600 residential pools in the United States. By 1959, there were 250,000.[15] These statistics merely suggest the volume of extras that the rest of the world considered luxuries, but which many Americans were beginning to think of as necessities in their efforts to maintain their desired social status.

Life magazine celebrated the end of the decade in a special issue entitled "The Good Life," dated December 28, 1959. One article stated that Americans were paying $40 billion a year for their leisure activities. An estimated 30 million people put up $2.6 billion for fishing expenses in 1959, while the related activity of boat building and maintenance drew a gross income of over $2 billion. Movie houses recorded 2.2 billion admissions and receipts of over $1.2 billion. When other forms of show business were included, a total of $4 billion was spent on entertainment. Bowling became a $1 billion business in 1959, and the National Golf Association said that golfers paid out $750,000 for their favorite sport.[16]

The rising interest in sports shown by Americans in the 1950s reflected their expanding affluence in both time and money spent. In *Trends in the Sporting Goods Market* (1965), Richard Snyder described the increased expenditures for sporting goods in the two decades following World War II. He noted that total consumer purchases of sporting goods exceeded $1 billion for the first time in 1947. This constituted 0.93 percent of the total paid for all consumer goods by Americans. This ratio held fast until 1952, when the $1.372 billion spent for sporting goods was 0.95 percent of the total. The percentage continued to climb, hitting 1 percent in 1956 at $1.693 billion and reaching 1.06 percent in 1959 when spending for sporting goods went beyond $2 billion for the first time.[17]

Attendance at spectator sports events also blossomed after World War II. An example of this was baseball, by far the most heavily attended professional sport in the prewar period. After the war, the two major baseball leagues increased their paid admissions, reaching around 20 million in 1947, where it stayed for the next two seasons. In 1949, the National Association, governing body for baseball's minor leagues, announced that the total paid attendance for the 59 leagues was almost 42 million. This was the fourth consecutive year that they had posted record audiences.[18] These marks might have been exceeded if the newly developing use of television for broadcasting sports events had not begun to compete seriously as a way for spectators to view their teams.

Television's effect on spectator sports was mixed in 1950. There was an immediate decline of 8 million admissions in baseball's minor leagues and a drop of 3 million among the major league clubs. On the other hand, the National Football League announced that 1950 was the best attendance year in its history, and the numbers attending college football games were greater than ever before.[19]

The reduction in attendance at major league baseball games continued until the 1953 season when the total hit a low for the decade at 14.383 million. A reversal, beginning in 1954 with a total of 15.935 million, seems to have been in response to the Braves' shift from Boston to Milwaukee in 1953 (the first such change in fifty years), the Browns' move from St. Louis to Baltimore, where they became the Orioles in 1954, and the Athletics' transfer from Philadelphia to Kansas City in 1955. Moves in 1958 took the Dodgers from Brooklyn to Los Angeles and the Giants from New York to San Francisco. By the end of the decade, major league baseball was being played in fifteen metropolitan areas instead of the ten represented at its start. The shifts responded to changes taking place in the population and the economy, and enabled more baseball fans to see major league action firsthand. By 1959, total attendance was more than 19 million, close to the 20 million totals achieved in the late 1940s before television entered the competition. These developments contributed to the sharply declining attendance at minor league contests, revising drastically the patterns of baseball viewing in the 1950s.[20]

Television may have forced adjustments in the structure of professional baseball, but it had a salutory effect on a number of others. It introduced a variety of sports into millions of homes. Sports like football, basketball, hockey, wrestling, boxing, and track captured the interest of many Americans who saw these contests played at a professional level for the first time on television.

Football, both college and professional, seems to have profited from this exposure. Except for 1954 and 1957, both recession years, attendance at college games increased steadily. Total paid admissions at National Football League games rose each year of the decade, going above 3 million in 1958. Interest in professional football had grown to such an extent that a group of promoters organized the American Football League in 1959 to start in the fall of 1960.[21]

Two other sports attracted increased investment of time and money—thoroughbred horse racing and harness racing. In 1952, about 27.5 million attended the nation's running tracks, 12 percent more than in 1951, and bet a total of over $1.921 billion, an increase of 19.8 percent. Harness racing fans totaled 7.9 million and wagered $362.8 million, both records. Both forms of racing attracted more fans to their tracks each year throughout the decade and betting totals were greater each year. By 1959, thoroughbred horse racing in the twenty-four states which allowed parimutuel betting on horse racing attracted a total of over 30.4 million fans who bet $2.391 billion on their favorites. Harness racing in that year drew more than 14.1 million fans who wagered $793.8 million.[22]

It was suggested earlier that the postwar outpouring of goods and services was generated by a conjunction of expanded taste and buying power among consumers and an increased productive capacity in U.S. industries. Another factor which cannot be overlooked in the American quest for affluence is advertising. In *People of Plenty* (1954), David Potter wrote:

If we seek an institution that was brought into being by abundance, without previous existence in any form, and, moreover, an institution which is peculiarly identified with American abundance rather than abundance throughout Western civilization, we will find it, I believe, in modern American advertising.[23]

While advertising might have been brought into existence by abundance, it has been an important element in exploiting that abundance by persuading American consumers to buy all they can of the products of that abundance.

The importance given to advertising in the 1950s can be seen by the amount of money spent by U.S. businesses on it. In 1947, they invested $5 billion on advertising of all sorts. By 1951, this had risen to more than $6.5 billion and to over $9 billion in 1955. In 1957, business paid $10.4 billion, more than double the bill of the previous decade.[24]

According to *Printers' Ink*, there were 374 U.S. companies that spent at least $1 million on advertising in 1956. Of the fifteen categories most heavily advertised that year, the greatest investments were made by companies manufacturing soaps, drugs, and cosmetics, for which the total bill reached $390 million. Advertising for food and soft drinks totaled $371 million, and, for automobiles, $239 million. The other categories of goods and services were, in order of their advertising expenditures: home equipment, $191.8 million; alcoholic beverages, $135.3 million; tobacco, $110.7 million; petroleum products, $79.4 million; industrial machinery, $63.2 million; clothing, $31 million; travel, $29.1 million; industrial chemicals, $27.6 million; rubber goods, $27.1 million; insurance, $19.3 million; magazines and books, $18.9 million; and paper and plastic products, $18.3 million.[25]

Ernest Havemann commented, in *Life* magazine for April 28, 1958: "The expansion of advertising seems to be due chiefly to the revolution in marketing and purchasing habits since the war. The supermarket, super-drugstore and discount house have practically eliminated the influence of the oldtime floor salesman; customers now have to be sold before they get into the store."[26] Advertising in the 1950s was playing a significant role in showing consumers the way in their quest for affluence.

It is quite apparent that, despite recessions in 1954 and 1957, the country's production expanded at a vigorous pace. More Americans partook of the available abundance than in any other previous era, and they seemed anxious to continue their participation in the good life. As the nation entered the 1960s, another recession threatened to reduce the opportunities to consume as joyously as before. However, the economy was righted and Americans experienced a decade of material growth greater than the one that had preceded it.

The 1960s were not marred by recession until the very end, but they were plagued by an undeclared war in Southeast Asia and violent unrest in the cities and on the college campuses. Even so, the great majority of Americans, both silent and noisy, continued the feverish quest for more and more affluence. Their efforts resulted in a more technologically sophisticated society in which even larger percentages of Americans were able to enjoy the good life. In an evaluation of the decade, the *New York Times* for January 11, 1970, reported that the gross national product (GNP) had increased from around $504 billion in 1960 to over $932 billion in 1969. While some of this reflected a rise in prices, there was a substantial expansion of the volume of goods and services. By the end of 1969, the United States, whose residents comprised 6 percent of the world's population, was consuming 35 percent of the world's annual production of raw materials. Income per capita in the United States still outpaced the rest of the world at $3,803 in 1969. In the two countries closest to that mark, Sweden and Canada, per capita incomes were less than $2,900 a year.[27]

One ramification of this amazing expansion was the great number of families rising above the poverty level designated by the U.S. government in 1959 at $3,000 a year for a nonfarm family of four. In that year, out of a population of 179,245,000, over 39,500,000 persons were living on an income below that line. In 1969, with a population of 204,342,000, the number of persons below the poverty line of $3,800 was recorded at about 24,100,000. During the same period, the rolls of the employed grew by 12 million workers, from 65.6 million in 1959 to 77.9 million in 1969.[28]

A more luxurious diet was indicative of the expanding participation by more and more Americans in the pleasures of affluence. The rise in meat consumption was especially striking, from the average 156 pounds per person previously noted for 1954 to an average of 181.5 pounds per person in 1968, up 4 pounds from 1967. The only other nations which exceeded this amount were Argentina, Uruguay, Australia, and New Zealand.[29]

Americans were overeating even more prodigiously than they had in the 1950s. *Life* magazine asserted in its issue for August 21, 1970:

The U.S. produces the greatest agricultural bounty the world has ever known. Yet some 10 million Americans go to bed hungry each night, while tens of millions more suffer from a more subtle form of malnutrition: they eat too much of the wrong kinds of food.

Today, only half of all U.S. families eat a good diet. Most of us overeat. And our eating habits are steadily deteriorating. Today we consume 83% more potato chips, 79% more soft drinks and 31% more alcohol than we did 15 years ago. At the same time, we are eating fewer fruits and vegetables (which provide vitamins and minerals) and drinking less milk (our major source of calcium).[30]

U.S. farms were producing at a rate sufficient to provide every person in the country with an interesting and nutritious diet. However, much of that production appeared on the market in the form of junk foods high in calories and low in real nourishment.

The proliferation of household gadgets intended to make life more comfortable and pleasant went on at a rapid pace in the 1960s. By the end of the decade, there were more than two hundred different kinds of electrical appliances available for home use. The ordinary family owned more than twenty of these, some possessing as many as fifty. They had heaters, refrigerators, radios, TV sets, clocks, lights, vacuum cleaners, stoves, air conditioners, hair dryers, shavers, washing machines, and power tools, to name only a few. These appliances were consuming about 30 percent of the electricity generated nationally, which totaled 1.6 trillion kilowatt hours in 1970. Despite the rise in the cost of electricity, largely from the increased price of oil at the end of the decade, few Americans were considering a cutback in their dependence upon electric gadgets.[31]

Another illustration of the growing affluence in the 1960s was the increase in the sales of new automobiles over the previous decade from a 6 to 7 million annual average in the 1950s to a 9 million annual average in the late 1960s. The Motor Vehicle Manufacturers Association found in a 1971 survey that 4 out of 5 American households owned cars. One-car households constituted 50.2 percent of the national total, while 25 percent owned two, and 4.8 percent owned three or more cars. More than 111 million persons were licensed drivers, and over 90 million cars and trucks were registered in 1971.[32]

The annual increase in new cars on the road was accompanied by trends responding to what William A. McWhirter called in *Life* magazine for April 11, 1969, "an unparalleled public craving for larger, lustier and more lavish automobiles," spawning "a 'Power and Glory' market." However, he noted a countertrend toward imported compacts, which "took just over 10% of the total market," a feat that had not been achieved since 1959. Despite the minority who were moving toward more economical cars, most Americans considered that the proper measure of one's social status was the obvious extravagance symbolized by a powerful, well-equipped automobile.[33]

Life magazine depicted some aspects of the national affluence achieved by the decade's end in two special issues: "The '60s, Decade of Tumult and Change" (December 26, 1969) and "Into the '70s" (January 9, 1970). An article in the former issue began: "In our affluence we constructed a culture based on congestion." The three accompanying photographs illustrated the point. One showed an end-to-end lineup of jet airliners waiting to take off from LaGuardia in New York. In another, all sorts of boats crowd pier after pier in a harbor, prompting the comment that "In harbors like California's Redondo Beach, man's last great open frontier, the sea, began to take on the look of a supermarket parking lot. Encouraged in part by a technology that has learned how to stamp out fiber-glass yachts like so many costly cookies, 50 million Americans were afloat by the end of the decade." The third was of the Ford Foundation Building in New York, a twelve-story gallery of offices looking inward across a roofed courtyard. According to *Life*, this was an exception to the pattern evolving in the 1960s: "Manacled by the economic need to cram ever more people onto the limited real estate of Manhattan island, most architects were forced to design what amounted to towering filing cabinets." [34]

More photographs of congestion appeared in "Into the '70s": a line of persons waiting to enter a Los Angeles museum, cars crowding a San Francisco street with people thronging the sidewalks, a packed Manhattan subway, a crowd waiting for luggage at an airport, long lines in a San Francisco bank, a man squirming out of his car in a squeezed parking spot among rows and rows of cars in the Washington airport, an overflowing new baby nursery in a Chicago hospital, and tombstones jammed in row on row in a New York cemetery. With affluence came congestion. With congestion the hectic pace of activity accelerated. [35]

All of this made it seem even more necessary to escape. The number of families who could cool off from the heat of the race in their own private swimming pools soared from 250,000 in 1959 to nearly 650,000 in 1969. Families owning second homes went from around 2 million in 1959 to almost 3 million in 1969, with some 100,000 starting to build them. Millions hit the road in a variety of ways. Some took to their bicycles, the sales of which reached more than 7 million by 1970. A great many traveled by car and stayed in the rapidly proliferating motels across the country. Mainland Americans traveling as tourists to Hawaii totaled 1.5 million in 1970, compared with 243,000 in 1959. Others traveled in what have come to be known as recreational vehicles. This was reflected in the sales figures for 1968: 115,200 travel trailers, 79,500 truck-bed campers, and 13,200 motor homes. By 1970, there were 2.5 million recreational vehicles transporting American families away from their humdrum routines to vacation places around the country. While most of them were just moderately comfortable, some were elegantly furnished and cost up to $20,000. [36]

Camping had become a big business. The U.S. Department of Commerce estimated that Americans paid over $2 billion in 1970 for camping equipment, excluding vehicles. It concluded that at least one out of five Americans spent some time each year camping out in one form or another.[37] It was back to Nature, but the trip was taken in style and affluence.

Many Americans were indulging in another kind of trip—journeys into the fantasyland of sex. Legal attitudes had been changing toward the depiction of sex in writing, films, and still photography. The courts struggled with definitions of obscenity and pornography in a number of cases. The result was an opening up of the market to lawful exploitation. In *Morals '68*, a Cowles publication, UPI correspondent Harry Ferguson wrote: "The U.S. Post Office Department thinks the traffic in pornography may run as high as $500 million a year." *Life* magazine for August 28, 1970, carried an article called "Pornography Goes Public," by John Neary, who called it "a $1 billion-a-year low-overhead business where the profit margins run up to 10,000%."[38]

Professional sports continued to attract more and more fans, with TV coverage playing a significant role in enabling tens of millions to watch their favorite teams. While TV viewing cut down on minor league baseball and small college football attendance, it encouraged expansion of major league sports franchises to cities which had had minor league teams or none at all. This was true in baseball, football, basketball, and hockey. As a result, Americans could increasingly indulge their sports-viewing tastes all year in all parts of the country. More and more of their leisure time and more of their disposable income was being spent to see professional athletes compete in an increasing variety of events.

At the same time, they were spending more money on their own participation in athletic activities. In *The Sporting Goods Market at the Threshold of the Seventies* (1969), Richard Snyder described this steady rise. Taking the $1.872 billion which Americans spent for sporting goods in 1958 as a base index of 100, he found that the index of spending was 119.9 for the 1960 total of $2.244 billion. There was a substantial increase each year, and, in 1969, the total, at an index number of 217.7, reached more than $4 billion for the first time.[39]

Various kinds of racing also attracted millions of American viewers. By the middle of the decade, harness racing was bringing in more than 20 million paid admissions annually to its tracks, while thoroughbred horse racing had surpassed an annual average total of 40 million admissions. By the end of the decade, auto racing was recording an annual attendance of over 40 million fans at its tracks. Betting on the horses totaled $2.481 billion at the legal parimutuel windows in 1960. By the middle of the decade, that total had doubled and continued to increase each year until it exceeded $5 billion in 1969.[40]

Americans wagered more money illegally each year on a broad variety of sports. Steve Cady, writing a wrap-up article for sports in the 1960s in the *New York Times* for December 28, 1969, declared: "It was a profitable decade for the bookie, a dangerous one for the compulsive gambler." Some experts, he said, estimated that the total bet illegally on sports each year averaged around $50 billion.[41] It was a clear reflection of opulent affluence, assuming that most of the money wagered was considered surplus by the bettors.

The affluence went beyond just comfort in the 1960s. In its issue entitled "Into the '70s,'' *Life* magazine listed some random statistics that demonstrated the proliferation of goods and services over the ten years. For instance, pantyhose, introduced in the late 1960s, went from 200 million pairs sold in 1968 to 624 million pairs in 1969. There were 500 women enrolled in judo classes in 1960, compared with 20,000 in 1969. At an average of $3 a jump, 5,000 persons went skydiving in 1960, while 30,000 participated in 1969. Retail sales of wigs totaled $35 million in 1960, and rose to $500 million in 1969. (*Life* magazine for October 16, 1970, noted a fad in wigs for little girls, some under ten years of age. J. C. Penney was concentrating on the ten to sixteen age group with wigs in fifteen different colors, costing from $7 to $19 each.) Sales of sunglasses went from $14.5 million in 1960 to $39 million in 1969. Guitar sales rose from $35 million in 1960 to $130 million in 1969. Undoubtedly, this was accelerated by the rock and roll craze which featured guitars. As part of this, the Beatles invaded the United States from England and in two successive years filled New York's Shea Stadium with over 100,000 bodies wriggling to their music.[42]

One way to pay for all this was to charge it. Credit card billings totaled $8 billion in 1960. They soared to $17.5 billion in 1969.[43] Enjoy now and pay later had become a way of life for a large number of Americans.

Americans entered the 1970s with puzzled ambivalence concerning the future of their affluence. Despite promises from political leaders to pull out of the Southeast Asian war, the fighting continued to drag on, costing lives and billions of dollars. Despite cocky statements of establishing a businesslike conduct of the nation's economy, ominous indicators of difficulty such as persistent inflation and rising unemployment refused to be resolved.

Public concern for the future was reported by *Life* magazine for August 15, 1969, in an article headlined "The New Math of Inflation." It summed up the results of a Harris opinion poll conducted for *Life*:

For a decade it's been called "the affluent society," but suddenly the U.S. public is beginning to think all those dazzling statistics and ever-rising curves are a giant con game. Between inflation, which today is at an annual rate of 7.2%, and the relentless increase in federal, state and local taxes, we are all running to stand still. In fact, many have begun to fall behind, and the average citizen is furious about it. . . .

There is real political dynamite in this widespread anger, for it is a middle-class revolution in the making, a fact acknowledged by Congress in its current debate on tax reform. What emerges most starkly from the poll, in Harris' words, is "a portrait of a silent, unblack, unurban, unaffluent America in seething revolt." Moreover, the heart of that potential revolt is also the heart of "Nixon country": skilled wage-earners and the property-owning middle-income groups—white, respectable, suburban and small-town. They are convinced that big business and the rich are getting away with murder in exploiting tax loopholes and subsidies. Many people are equally convinced that the poor are boondoggling on relief payments. In both cases they feel the middle class is bearing the brunt of others' greed or laziness. . . . Sixty percent of all families feel that between inflation and taxes they are worse off this year than last, and over a ten-year period, . . . they are very close to being right. Adding their frustration to the discontent of the blacks and the young, Harris concludes, ''Today it is hard to find any part of this country which is not deeply disturbed about some major aspect of our national life.''[44]

As part of the poll, the interviewers asked the persons in the sample what they wanted money for. They established what items the respondents already had, then asked if they wanted what they did not possess. For example, 17 percent had a comfortable retirement assured them; 70 percent did not have it but wanted it. Among other things, 34 percent had a color TV, 46 percent did not but wanted it; 45 percent had steak and roast beef whenever they wanted it, 37 percent did not but wanted it; 34 percent had entertainment out at least once a week, 28 percent did not but wanted it; 66 percent owned a house, 26 percent did not but wanted one; 63 percent had a vacation at least once a year, 24 percent did not but wanted one; 77 percent had at least one automobile, 16 percent did not but wanted one.[45] While this catalog of possessions and desires was published to demonstrate discontent in the United States, it also illustrated an extremely high level of achievement for a large proportion of Americans.

An end-of-the-decade opinion poll run by Harris for *Life* magazine, published January 9, 1970, suggested greater satisfaction with life in the United States than the poll taken in the summer of 1969. The analysis of the poll by Bayard Hooper, headlined ''The Real Change Has Just Begun,'' refuted Harris's earlier statement which characterized many Americans as ''deeply disturbed'' and ''in seething revolt.'' Hooper declared:

For the most part, Americans seem quite contented with their working lives. With the average work week at 39.5 hours, only managers and executives complain of working too hard, while 64% even of those with an eighth-grade education find their work ''important and significant.'' . . . Given a chance between making more money and getting more time off, only 45% opt for the money, and when asked to choose between 10% more income in an interesting job or 50% more income in a boring job, 75% of all people choose the interesting job. In short, Americans do not appear to be as compulsively dissatisfied and materialistic as they are always accused of being.[46]

While the two polls did not examine exactly the same things, a comparison of them seems to indicate some significant disagreement as to what the future of American affluence would be, as well as what kind of affluence Americans desired. However, the polls did stress that Americans expected to continue to live in the midst of an abundance that would exceed what had gone before.

The first half of the 1970s proved to confound economists and other social scientists more than any previous period. The economists, especially, had difficulty agreeing on explanations for the confusing developments. In particular, the combination of an increasingly high rate of inflation and an equally high rate of unemployment forced economists of all persuasions to revise their basic theories of how economies operate.

After a decade of steady economic growth, whether measured in current or constant dollars, the GNP in 1958 dollars was about the same in 1970 as it had been in 1969. An inflation rate wavering between 7 and 8 percent had wiped out any real growth in the production of goods and services, even though the total value in current dollars almost reached the magic figure of $1 trillion. Simultaneously, the unemployment rate climbed sharply, going from just under 4 percent of the labor force in January 1970 to about 6.1 percent in December. Economic growth picked up some in 1971, almost 3 percent more than 1970, while the unemployment rate hovered just under 6 percent for most of the year. Economic activity revived vigorously in 1972, with expansion in 1958 dollars at 6.2 percent and the unemployment rate dropping gradually to almost 5 percent. The year 1973 was another good year, with the real GNP expanding by 5.9 percent and the unemployment rate dropping to a low of 4.6 percent in October before rising once more. In the process, over 9 million jobs had been added to the labor force in the first four years of the decade, totaling 85.6 million by the end of 1973. However, fuel oil shortages in 1973 combined with other economic factors to force a reversal to take place in 1974. Inflation rose sharply to a painful 14.4 percent in the last quarter of the year, while the unemployment rate soared to an equally painful 7.1 percent in December, the highest it had been in more than thirteen years. This combination resulted in a decline of 2.2 percent in the real GNP for the year, even though the cost in 1974 dollars of total goods and services rose to about $1.39 trillion. In the last quarter of the year, the reduction of real GNP was going at an annual rate of 9.1 percent, the sharpest drop in thirty years.[47]

Some indication of the impact that the economic difficulties of the 1970s were to have on the American quest for affluence came in a survey released in May 1975 by the Union Bank of Switzerland comparing GNP figures on a per capita basis for the nations of the world. As might be expected from the skyrocketing oil prices in the previous two years, three oil-producing nations recorded the highest per capita GNPs. Kuwait, at $11,000, was the highest, with Qatar and the United Arab Emirates next in order. Then came Switzerland with $7,270, Sweden with $6,840, Denmark with $6,800, the United States with $6,595, Canada with $6,340, and West Germany with $6,215. The United States was no longer the most affluent nation in the world.[48]

Americans continued to eat more in the 1970s, despite sharply rising food prices. They consumed an average of 182.6 pounds per person in 1969. Their consumption increased to a record high of 191.4 pounds per person in 1971. It dropped slightly to 189 pounds per person in 1972 and rapidly to 178 in 1973, reflecting price rises and consumer boycotts. However, it rose again to 187.5 pounds per person in 1974. Evidently, Americans could not give up the joys of eating meat just because it cost more. According to U.S. Public Health surveys published at the end of 1973, 25 to 45 percent of all American adults were more than 20 percent overweight.[49]

They also fed their pets well. Philip H. Dougherty, in his "Advertising" column in the *New York Times* for February 20, 1975, said that Americans spent $1.4 billion just for dog food in 1974. They spent over $2 billion to feed all kinds of pets.[50]

The acquisition of appliances and gadgets continued to play an important role in the American quest for affluence. While sales for electrical products declined as the recession worsened in 1974, Americans were still buying in large volume. In the *New York Times* for January 23, 1975, the Electronics Industries Association reported that sales of television, radio, and phonograph goods totaled over 62.7 million units in 1974. Even though this was an 11.8 percent drop from the 71.1 million units sold in the record year of 1973, it certainly was a substantial addition to the luxury items owned by Americans. The extent of TV ownership was indicated in an article by Georgia Dullea in the *New York Times* for December 20, 1974. She stated that 95.5 percent of the country's 68 million occupied housing units contained television sets. She also noted that 40 percent of them were color sets.[51]

In a *New York Times* News Service story published in the Daytona Beach *Sunday News-Journal* for May 13, 1973, reporter Wayne King described the life-style of an Italian-American who grew up in the same South Philadelphia neighborhood as the singer Mario Lanza. He was the son of a working-class family, but in 1973 he had a position with the Philadelphia Housing Authority with an annual income of just under $20,000. He owned a four-story brownstone house in downtown Philadelphia, where he lived with his wife and two children. His life story was right out of the "Gospel of Success" followed by generations of millions of Americans.[52]

His electrically operated possessions constitute a significant element of this fairly typical upper-middle-income family. On what King identified as a basic list, the family had "an electric blender, coffee maker, freezer, frying pan, two irons, eight radios, a refrigerator, two black and white television sets, two toasters, and three vacuum cleaners." In addition, they owned "two small record players and a stereo set, two electric toothbrushes, two electric clocks, two tape recorders, an electric sewing machine, an electric 'water pick,' and the odd items like an old electric train and a woodburning set." While he had a hand-powered lawnmower, the husband did own "two electric saws, a sander and a drill." He also owned an electric typewriter on which he did some of the work he brought home from his office. As added luxury, he had an electric hair dryer and his son used an electric hot comb.[53]

"On the other hand," King noted, "they do not have air conditioners... and they have passed up items like sunlamps, electric knives, can openers, waffle irons, food waste disposers, hotplates and buffet ranges, rotisseries, slide and movie projectors, popcorn poppers, electric garage doors, outdoor lawn lights, electric razors, humidifiers and what not."[54]

All of these appliances have added tremendously to the nation's consumption of energy. King made some striking comparisons:

Ten years ago, 19 percent of the families living in homes wired for electricity had room air conditioners. Today the figure is 47 percent. The number of families with electric blankets has doubled to more than 50 percent. Nearly half the nation's families have electric can openers compared to 11 percent 10 years ago . . . . Today, 99.9 percent of families in wired homes have electric irons, radios, refrigerators and black and white television sets; 97 percent have clothes washers and vacuum cleaners. Moreover, the number of wired homes has grown from 53.7 million in 1962 to 67.3 million today— more Americans using more power at an increasing rate.[55]

The oil crises of the 1970s caused sharp rate boosts for electricity in late 1973 and 1974, but cutbacks in use were quite moderate.

Automobile buying continued to increase to the record annual total of 11.4 million passenger cars in 1973. As a combined effect and cause of the increasing economic strains, Americans cut their purchases of cars to 8.8 million in 1974, a 23 percent drop. Sales of automobiles were even lower in the first half of 1975 than they had been in the first half of 1974, forcing industry-wide layoffs that had started building up in the last quarter of 1974. Harvard economist Wassily Leonief demonstrated in a study reported in the *New York Times* for December 8, 1974, that the layoffs and reduced production volume in the automobile industry caused cutbacks in related industries that altogether brought about 40 percent of the increased rate of unemployment taking place in 1974. Obviously, the stability of the automobile industry was of prime importance in maintaining the stability of the nation's economy and providing the means to continue the American quest for affluence.[56]

By the middle of the 1970s, Americans were showing evidence of some changes in automotive patterns. While there were approximately 105 million cars registered in the United States, a report of the Federal Highway Administration published in the *New York Times* for December 31, 1974, stated that travel on U.S. streets and highways had declined 3 percent in 1974 from 1973. A Gallup poll reported in the *New York Times* for February 16, 1975, that there was a 5 percent reduction in the number of Americans using cars to get to work in 1974 from 1973. It revealed that 79 percent of those going to work in 1973 went in private autos, while in 1974, the percentage dropped to 74. There was also an increasing interest in more economical vehicles, evidenced by the buyers' attraction to imported cars. In February 1974, 16.7 percent of the cars sold in the United States were imported, while in February 1975, foreign-made cars constituted 21.3 percent of the market. In addition, U.S. companies increased the sale of their compacts and planned for further expansion of their small-car production.[57]

One ramification of the oil crisis was an upsurge in the sales of motorcycles. An Associated Press story of July 30, 1974, stated that the Motorcycle Industry Council reported that sales of motorcycles had jumped 50 percent in the first quarter of 1974 to a total of over 700,000 new bikes. The U.S. Department of Transportation had estimated that 4.2 million motorcycles were on the road at the end of 1973.[58]

Some of this increased interest in motorcycles can be attributed to Americans' attempts to get back to nature or, at least, into the outdoors. As the 1970s began, Americans had more time and money to spend on leisure activities, a circumstance celebrated by *Life* magazine in a special issue called "The Endless Weekend," published on September 3, 1971. The editors introduced the issue by saying: "This entire issue of LIFE is about one of the happier products of our hardworking civilization: the leisure to escape. These days we are escaping at a rapidly accelerating rate and heading for the outdoors, summer and winter, as if the year were one long weekend." They pointed out that more than 400,000 recreational vehicles were produced in the previous twelve months. *Life* editors said that over 100,000 "dune-buggy fanciers" were crowding the sands of the various shores, "with 3 million recreational vehicles on the road, and an estimated 45 million people taking camping trips this year," so that "the nation's best-known national parks and seashore areas have become crowded summer resorts."[59]

During the winter, "The Endless Weekend," marked by ice skating, skiing, and sledding, was enhanced for many by the development of the snowmobile. As described in *Life* magazine for February 26, 1971, the snowmobile was a "minitank on rubber treads and skis," which could "be seen and heard leaping and churning just about anywhere there is snow, winning thousands of new fans—and at least as many enemies." Just a few years before, the snowmobile was a novelty with fewer than a thousand operating. However, in 1971, as *Life* magazine put it, "A million snowmobiles noisily cruise the land." While some of them were used for productive transportation, "the real boom [was] among just plain folks whose idea of a good time is to zoom around, at speeds up to 60 mph, on the breast of the new-fallen snow, wherever they find it." By the end of 1972, the number of registered snowmobiles had increased to 1.25 million.[60]

Another craze developing in the beginning of the 1970s was that for "minibikes." They were designed to be ridden by children and were driven by a small gas engine. At the bottom of the craze was a seeming wish of boys and a few girls, six to ten years of age, to emulate their elders. As *Life* magazine put it in its issue for January 22, 1971:

To them, a minibike in motion is pure joy—just the right size to satisfy the nascent craving for power-driven wheels of one's own, and just noisy enough (in the chain-saw, or earsplitting, range) to let everyone know that young Easy Rider is around. Minibikes, which cost from $89 to more than $300, can go practically anywhere at speeds of from 12 to 40 mph—plenty fast enough to kill an inexperienced rider. At least two such deaths have been recorded. Perhaps as many as 1.5 million bikes are now blasting around parking lots, sidewalks, back roads and front lawns of unhappy neighbors all over suburban America. For Police, this sort of back-alley activity is hard to monitor. The problem increases with the bike population, which was zero a few years ago and is now increasing by 250,000 each year.[61]

Participatory sports were getting great play in other areas. According to a study published in the *New York Times* for December 31, 1972, "The leisure-time market now accounts for a total expenditure of $100 billion." Americans were pouring $1 billion of that into skiing. About 45.5 million were taking to the waterways, with an estimated 9 million boats crowding the rivers and lakes. The study noted that "There are now 10.4 million regular golfers and 2.35 million who play 15 or fewer rounds a year." William D. Smith, writing in the "Advertising" column of the *New York Times* for August 29, 1975, stated "There are 15 million golfers in the United States with about 4 million classed as heavy players, or people who play five rounds a month during the season."[62]

The survey identified tennis as a $420 million business. In its August 11, 1972, issue, *Life* magazine headlined an article on the sport by asking the question, "Tennis, Everyone?" According to *Life*, "Some 11.5 million ordinary Americans, nearly twice as many as a decade ago and 500,000 more than last year, are enthusiastically thonking fuzzy balls at one another." It stated that there were over 100,000 tennis courts in the United States, with 5,000 new ones being added each year. Smith noted that in 1975 "There are 19 million tennis players with about 5 million classified as serious players, or, people who play once a week during the outdoor season."[63]

Spectator sports broke attendance records in the 1970s, even though more events were seen on television. *New York Times* sportswriter Joseph Durso reported that "A record total of 135 million persons paid last year (1973) to watch baseball, football, basketball, hockey and racing." UPI reporter Frank W. Slusser estimated that about 29.8 million fans paid to attend major league baseball games in 1975. Sports enthusiasts spent $1.265 billion in 1974 for all sports contests held in the United States.[64]

Dog racing tracks were pulling in capacity crowds largely because of their low admission charges (around 50 cents) and because they appeared to be hard to fix. According to a *New York Times* story from Hollywood, Florida, published February 12, 1975, "greyhound racing has become the seventh largest spectator sport in the country with more than 15 million customers last year. It was that lack of human element that gave gamblers confidence to bet $1-billion last year on the dogs, although the only major urban areas with tracks are Miami and Boston."[65]

Betting on other sports attracted billions of dollars a year from Americans wishing to add quickly to their means to affluence. Steve Cady, writing a series of stories on sports betting for the *New York Times* during the week of January 19, 1975, stated that about $7 billion was wagered during 1974 on horse racing, dog races, and jai alai through parimutuel betting systems in the thirty-one states which allow it. He added that the New York City Off-Track Betting Corporation processed about $800 million in legal horse racing bets. However, the largest share of the money which Americans bet on sports was illegal, still estimated to be over $50 billion annually.[66]

Movies became more actively patronized in the 1970s than in the 1960s. According to Jack Valenti, president of the Motion Picture Association of America, in an interview in the middle of January 1975, Americans spent $1.9 billion at movie box offices. This was the first time that the 1946 record of $1.7 billion had been exceeded. The 1974 figure was 25 percent better than the one for 1973 and about 21 percent above the 1972 gross. There were about 1.01 billion paid admissions in 1974, 17 percent more than in 1973 and 8 percent better than 1972.[67]

Another kind of recreation expanded rapidly in the 1970s—the theme park. Pioneered by Disneyland in California in 1955, theme parks were built in response to a desire to recapture some element of the past or to pretend to visit some exotic place. Over forty-five of a comparable size were built during the past two decades. *Amusement Business*, an entertainment trade paper, estimated that one out of four Americans would visit a theme park in 1976.[68] That would put attendance at over 50 million.

Going to a theme park was usually part of a vacation. While vacation travel was somewhat curtailed in the second half of 1973 and 1974 because of gasoline shortages, many millions still managed to go on some sort of a trip anyway. Travel abroad dropped off substantially, but there were reports that hotels in the Catskills were having their best year in 1974 and Florida experienced an upsurge in its tourist trade during the final week of that year. Disney World in central Florida broke all its attendance records for that time. Previously concerned motel operators were speculating that many Americans were having a last fling before the economic crunch got any worse. It seemed that Americans were very reluctant to give up having some sort of escape experience.[69]

Despite signs of continuing economic difficulty in 1975, Americans were still "hitting the road." Reporting on 1975 Memorial Day travel, the Associated Press declared: "From the East Coast to the West, Americans appear to be returning to their old getaway habits during the first major good-weather holiday since the gasoline crisis abated." Later reports carried out predictions that the 1975 summer vacation period would be a "bonanza season."[70]

As the decade of the 1970s passed the midpoint, they increased their spending on recreation. *U.S. News & World Report* commented in its issue for April 25, 1977: "For all their complaints about inflation and the lingering impact of recession, most Americans are still splurging on 'the good life.'" The magazine detailed some of the spending:

In January alone, people's outlays for amusement and recreational services climbed 19 percent above a year earlier. Spending at hotels, motels and tourist courts jumped by 12 percent.

Vacations are becoming longer, more elaborate and costlier, with a record number in prospect this year. Foreign travel is more popular than ever. Requests for passports have been running 15 percent above a year earlier.

Leisure-time activities are creating an unprecedented boom in sales of related equipment. Spending by boaters totaled 5.3 billion dollars in 1976; by golfers, 4 billion, and by skiers, 2.3 billion—all record highs. Sales of mini motor homes jumped by 90 per cent last year. And people bought 250,000 snowmobiles, 700,000 campers, 700,000 boats, 470,000 outboard motors and 700,000 recreational vehicles.

Spending for travel, lodging, meals and spectator amusements in the past year was estimated at 69 billion dollars—another all-time high. . . .

In total, leisure is accounting for a large and growing portion of the U.S. economy. Spending for such things last year amounted to nearly 146 billion dollars. This is not only a record for spending on the good life, but far exceeds annual outlays for all home building—or for national defense.[71]

An example of increased tourist travel is the Hawaii experience. *Newsweek* reported in its January 2, 1978, issue that 3.2 million tourists journeyed to the islands in 1977, as compared with 1.8 million in 1972. They spent $1.4 billion while they were there.[72]

While spending fabulous sums on a wide variety of recreational activities, Americans paid out lavish amounts on goods to enhance their lives. In a partial list, it might be noted that by the middle of the 1970s, their annual expenditures averaged: $29 to $30 billion for women's and children's clothes; $5 billion for cosmetics, toiletries, and fragrances; $1.6 billion for pantyhose and stockings; $6.6 billion for toys; $3 billion for books; $13.27 billion for radios, TVs, records, and musical instruments; $25 billion for alcoholic beverages; $1 billion for chewing gum; $4 billion for electric houseware appliances; and $118.5 billion for health care.[73]

As the nation passed the mid-decade point, the economy began to improve and the sales of America's favorite item, the automobile, rose in response. The 8.6 million purchased in 1975 was a drop of almost 200,000 from 1974. An upsurge in 1976 resulted in a total of new car sales of 10 million. Sales in 1977 were even greater—11.2 million.[74]

Automobile affluence was exemplified even more impressively by the *U.S. News & World Report* comment in its April 25, 1977, issue: "With more people and cars on the highway, one third of all U.S. households now own two or more autos." It also noted the increase of citizen-band radios in automobiles. There were 799,000 licenses in 1973 and 7.7 million in 1976.[75]

As practically everything tends toward big corporate production, advertising has become even more important in generating sales. This is illustrated by a more than tripling of the amount spent on it by business since 1960. The total advertising bill for the 1970s rose at a rate of over $1.6 billion a year in the first half of the decade to $28.2 billion in 1975. The total jumped sharply to $37.9 billion in 1977.[76]

Then, increasing affluence on the individual and corporate levels adds to the temptations of crime against property. With the exception of 1972, when it had a momentary decline, the nation's crime rate has risen each year in the 1970s. This has been especially expensive to business. The U.S. Department of Commerce estimated in 1972 that crime was costing business $16 billion a year. One set of responses by Americans was to get more protection than that provided by law enforcement agencies. This has spawned a variety of security systems—human, mechanical, and electronic. As Reginald Stuart said in an article describing this development in the *New York Times* for March 30, 1975, "Although very little data exist discussing the extent to which Americans have plunged into the private security business, estimates are that $10-billion to $15-billion a year is spent on guards, electronic detection devices, alarm systems, armored car services and a variety of other gadgets, devices and services for protection." Selwyn Raab reported in the *New York Times* for January 12, 1978, that the security guard business in the United States grossed $12 billion in 1977 and employed a million people as full and part time guards, "double the number of police officers in the country."[77]

This essay is too short to do more than suggest some of the great variety of goods and services that make up the affluence of U.S. culture. It would appear that Americans have generally been succeeding in their quest for the things that enhance life. Of course, the good life is still not enjoyed by all. However, there are forces at work that might make this goal come true, too.

At the same time, all is not good in this quest. One of the obvious drawbacks to the national accumulation of goods is the turnover or garbage problem. Where do we put all of the things produced, once they are worn out, out of fashion, or rendered useless? The rubbish heaps of communities all over the nation are mounting to terrifying proportions.

Another physical problem is the pollution that results from the manufacture of the products—the fouling of the air and water that used to be free and pure. This pollution is not only found coming from the smoke that pours out of stacks and the sewage that spews out of drainage pipes, but in the oil spillage that occurs much too often off our coastlines. A corollary to this kind of pollution comes in the difficulty of breaking down chemically the detergents and containers used by consumers or some of the pesticides used by farmers.

While the physical degenerative effects on our culture are bad enough, it seems that there is an even greater danger from the nation's drive to greater and greater affluence. That is the tendency to expect that these trappings of great wealth are unalienable rights for the tiny minority of the world's population that the affluent Americans constitute. The American nation has developed a tremendous potential for succeeding in the pursuit of happiness, at least as it is manifested in material goods and services. The question that Americans might ask themselves is "How much is it worth in effort, time, and money to gain all of these worldly goods, if there are still hundreds of millions of human beings who go to bed hungry each night?" Or, to put it another way, "On what basis can you justify 6 percent of the world's population enjoying over a third of the world's goods?" What price do we expect other human beings to pay so that we might enjoy the great measure of freedom we have in the way we work and in the way we consume?

Notes

1. Henry Bamford Parks, *The American Experience* (New York: Vintage Books, 1959), pp. 5–7. This is the theme of David M. Potter, *People of Plenty* (Chicago: University of Chicago Press, 1958).

2. Herbert Hoover, "Inaugural Address," *The Presidents Speak,* ed. by Davis Newton Lott (New York: Holt, Rinehart & Winston, 1969), pp. 223, 229.

3. Franklin D. Roosevelt, *The Public Papers and Addresses of ...,* compiled by Samuel I. Rosenman (New York: Harper & Brothers, 1950), 12: 573–74.

4. David A. Shannon, *Twentieth Century America,* 2nd ed. (Chicago: Rand McNally & Co., 1969), p. 477; Eric F. Goldman, *The Crucial Decade—And After, America, 1945–1960* (New York: Vintage Books, 1961), pp. 12–13; Oscar T. Barck, Jr., and Nelson Manfred Blake, *Since 1900,* 4th ed. (New York: Macmillan Co., 1965), p. 648.

5. Barck and Blake, p. 764.

6. Potter, pp. 81–83.

7. *Life,* January 3, 1955, cover, p. 2.

8. Ibid., p. 75.

9. Ibid., pp. 41, 38.

10. Shannon, pp. 582–84.

11. James J. Flink, *The Car Culture* (Cambridge, Mass.: MIT Press, 1976), p. 160; *Life,* January 5, 1953, p. 48.

12. *Life,* January 1, 1951, p. 56.

13. Shannon, p. 569; *New York Times,* April 25, 1960, pp. 43, 46.

14. *Life,* January 5, 1953, pp. 48, 92; "The American Explosion," *Scientific Monthly,* September 1952, p. 189.

15. *Life,* August 3, 1959, p. 50; December 28, 1959, p. 73.

16. *Life,* December 28, 1959, pp. 69–75.

17. Richard Snyder, "Trends in the Sporting Goods Market," in *Sport in the Socio-Cultural Process,* ed. by M. Marie Hart (Dubuque, Iowa: William C. Brown Co., 1972), p. 433.

18. Jim Becker, "Sports," *The Americana Annual,* 1950 (New York: American Corporation, 1950), p. 638.

19. Peter Brandwein, "Sports," *The Americana Annual, 1951* (New York: Americana Corporation, 1951), pp. 635, 638.

20. Brandwein, "Sports," *The Americana Annual, 1952* (New York: Americana Corporation, 1952), p. 669; *1953,* p. 661; *1954,* p. 675; *1955,* p. 694; George McNickle, "Sports, Games, and Shows," *The Americana Annual,* 1959 (New York: Americana Corporation, 1959), p. 715; *1960,* p. 721.

21. Ibid.

22. Brandwein, *1953,* p. 661; McNickle, *1960,* pp. 727, 728.

23. Potter, p. 167.

24. Ibid., p. 169; Ernest Havemann, "Turbulent Times for Advertising Business," *Life,* April 28, 1958, p. 150; Bureau of Census, *Statistical Abstract of the United States, 1975* (Washington, D.C.: U.S. Government Printing Office, 1975), p. 790.

25. Havemann, p. 153.

26. Ibid., p. 150.

27. *New York Times,* January 11, 1970, Section 12, p. 8.

28. *Statistical Abstract, 1975,* p. 399; *Monthly Labor Review,* May 1960, p. 492; *Monthly Labor Review,* February 1970, p. 42.

29. *New York Times*, January 12, 1969, Section 3, p. 11.

30. *Life*, August 21, 1970, p. 45.

31. *Life*, December 11, 1970, pp. 26F, 30, 31.

32. Sylvia Porter, "Your Money's Worth," Daytona Beach *Evening News*, p. 5; *New York Times*, March 14, 1971, Section 3, p. 28; *Times*, September 19, 1971, p. 59; *Times*, November 5, 1972, Section 12, p. 3; *Statistical Abstract, 1975*, p. 406.

33. William A. McWhirter, "Pray for Iacocca's Baby," *Life*, April 11, 1969, p. 70.

34. *Life*, December 26, 1969, pp. 82–83.

35. *Life*, January 9, 1970, pp. 8–15.

36. *Life*, January 9, 1970, p. 78; July 10, 1970, p. 66; July 30, 1971, p. 28; November 26, 1971, p. 58; *New York Times*, October 21, 1973, Section 11, p. 22; *Life*, August 14, 1970, pp. 21, 26–27.

37. *Life*, September 3, 1971, p. 49.

38. Harry Ferguson, "Filth Merchants and Censors," *Morals '68*, ed. by Jane Quinn (New York: Cowles Education Corp., 1968), p. 50; John Neary, "Pornography Goes Public," *Life*, August 28, 1971, p. 19.

39. Richard Snyder, "The Sporting Goods Market at the Threshold of the Seventies," in *Sport in the Socio-cultural Process*, p. 441.

40. Ernest A. Kehr, "Sports," *The Americana Annual, 1965* (New York: Americana Corporation, 1965), pp. 656, 658; *Life*, August 7, 1970, p. 2A; George McNickle, "Sports, Games, and Shows," *The Americana Annual, 1961* (New York: Americana Corporation, 1961), p. 717; Steve Cady, "A Decade for All Seasons," *New York Times*, December 28, 1969, Section 5, p. 2.

41. Cady, p. 2.

42. *Life*, January 9, 1970, pp. 78, 81; October 16, 1970, p. 34; December 26, 1969, p. 41.

43. *Life*, January 9, 1970, p. 78.

44. *Life*, August 15, 1969, p. 20.

45. Ibid., p. 22.

46. *Life*, January 9, 1970, p. 102.

47. A. H. Raskin, "The Labor Scene," *New York Times*, August 27, 1976, p. D1; Edwin L. Dale, Jr., *New York Times*, July 18, 1975, p. 1; July 21, 1976, p. 39; July 22, 1976, p. 1; Daytona Beach *Morning Journal*, May 21, 1975, p. 5B; *Newsweek*, March 31, 1975, p. 55.

48. *Newsweek*, March 19, 1975, p. 80.

49. Economic Research Service, *Food Consumption Prices Expenditures* (Washington, D.C.: U.S. Government Printing Office, 1975), 1975 Supplement to Agricultural Report No. 138, p. 26; CBS News, December 31, 1977; *House and Garden*, May 1976, p. 32.

50. Philip H. Dougherty, "Advertising," *New York Times*, February 20, 1975, p. 52; *New York Times*, January 27, 1974, Section 3, p. 3.

51. *New York Times*, January 23, 1975, p. 49; December 20, 1974, p. 44.

52. Daytona Beach *Sunday News-Journal*, May 13, 1973, Section E, p. 10.

53. Ibid.

54. Ibid.

55. Ibid.

56. *New York Times*, February 5, 1975, p. 47; December 8, 1974, Section 3, p. 1.

57. *New York Times*, December 28, 1974, p. 31; December 31, 1974, p. 36; February 16, 1975, p. 54; March 30, 1975, p. 1.

58. DeLand *Sun-News*, July 30, 1974, p. 4.

59. *Life*, September 3, 1971, pp. 8, 10, 52.

60. *Life*, February 26, 1971, p. 21; *New York Times*, December 31, 1972, Section 5, p. 14.

61. *Life*, January 22, 1971, pp. 58–59.

62. *New York Times*, December 31, 1972, Section 5, p. 14; William D. Smith, "Advertising," *New York Times*, August 29, 1975, p. 41.

63. *Life,* August 11, 1972, pp. 34, 36; Smith, p. 41.

64. *New York Times,* July 22, 1974, p. 38; Sarasota *Herald-Tribune,* April 18, 1976, Section F, p. 1; Bureau of Census, *Statistical Abstract of the United States,* 1976 (Washington, D.C., U.S. Government Printing Office, 1976), p. 218.

65. *New York Times,* February 12, 1975, p. 31.

66. *New York Times,* January 19, 1975, Section 5, p. 1.

67. *New York Times,* January 26, 1975, Section 5, p. 1.

68. *New York Times,* May 30, 1976, p. 20.

69. *New York Times,* March 10, 1975, pp. 1, 50.

70. DeLand *Sun-News,* June 2, 1975, p. 3; Daytona Beach *Sunday News Journal,* June 1, 1975, p. 1A.

71. *U.S. News & World Report,* April 25, 1977, pp. 26–27.

72. *Newsweek,* January 2, 1978, p. 30.

73. *New York Times,* November 25, 1974, p. 47; January 12, 1975, Section 3, p. 2; August 17, 1973, p. 47; December 24, 1976, Section 4, p. 3; March 14, 1976, Section 3, p. 15; December 4, 1977, Section 3, p. 1; December 18, 1977, Section 3, p. 1; *Statistical Abstract,* 1976, pp. 72, 218.

74. *New York Times,* January 6, 1977, p. 39; January 6, 1978, p. D1.

75. *U.S. News & World Report,* April 25, 1977, p. 26.

76. *Statistical Abstract,* 1976, p. 817; *New York Times,* January 8, 1978, Section 12, p. 59.

77. DeLand *Sun-News,* March 31, 1975, p. 2; Daytona Beach *Morning Journal,* February 11, 1972, p. 7; *New York Times,* February 22, 1974, p. 69; January 12, 1978, p. 31.

JOHN A. HAGUE

America and the Post-Affluent Revolution*

In 1969 Kenneth Keniston wrote an essay for the *New York Times* entitled "You Have to Grow Up in Scarsdale to Know How Bad Things Really Are." Mr. Keniston suggested that Americans were witnessing the end of one revolution and the birth of another, and he explained much of the turmoil in American life and values by arguing that we were struggling through a period between revolutions.[1]

The first revolution was the liberal democratic revolution. It was launched in the seventeenth and eighteenth centuries, and it sought to free individuals from the status-bound society of the Middle Ages. The goals of this revolution had to do with individual freedom and mobility. They held out the promise that if individuals could be educated and given the right to participate in their own governance, they could hope to achieve the conditions under which they and their successors could live in ever-increasing dignity and comfort. These goals, therefore, laid great stress upon equal opportunity, personal mobility, education, and self-government.

Keniston argued that by the decade of the 1960s American democracy had brought the goals of the first revolution within the grasp of most citizens. Moreover, the nation's capacity to bring the goals within the reach of *all* Americans had generated the conviction that failure to finish the tasks of the first revolution constituted grounds not simply for protest but for anger and outrage.

At the same time, however, a large number of Americans, particularly middle-class youth, had reached the conclusion that their affluent parents were unable to translate their material success into satisfying lives. Neither had they translated their affluence into a political force capable of ending the Vietnam War nor achieving full equality among all Americans. Not surprisingly, youth's response was an assertion that the costs of upward mobility were not worth the effort; that the search for human dignity and meaning had to be made in new ways and on fresh ground. In short, Keniston argued that a post-affluent society consciousness was forming, and that its torchbearers were searching for values which would be relevant and significant in a world where affluence could be taken for granted

* Portions of this essay originally appeared in the *Encyclopedia Americana* © 1976.

without being a prime objective. At the same time, however, the leaders of the new revolution demanded, as the price of even minimal participation in the establishment, the total fulfillment of the goals set by the earlier, liberal democratic revolution.

The consequences were varied, ironic, and ambiguous. Those who protested inequality and the war were more often than not demanding that American society fulfill its traditional promises. Those who sought new meaning and freedom at rock festivals and/or in drug cultures were often proclaiming the cancer of the old order and searching for a way of life entirely removed from its parameters. And, in many cases, the same individuals were alternatively fighting for traditional goals and protesting the futility of all efforts to reform the existing society.

Small wonder, then, that one begins to find significant characterological changes beginning to make themselves felt within American society. Nor is it surprising that these characterological changes express some of the tensions and ambiguities which stem from our efforts, simultaneously, to fulfill traditional goals while reaching for new ones.

One of the scholars who first recognized the fact that characterological changes were beginning to reflect these altered circumstances was Robert Lifton. In his essay "Protean Man," Lifton pointed out that many of the factors which produced cultural stability, and therefore fixed personality patterns, have disappeared. In Lifton's view there has been a worldwide sense of "historical dislocation, the break in the sense of connection which men have long felt with the vital and nourishing symbols of their cultural tradition," and, simultaneously, there has been a "flooding of imagery produced by the extraordinary flow of post-modern cultural influences over mass communications networks."[2] The result, Lifton thinks, is a protean man who seeks meaning and fulfillment in constantly changing roles which involve a "neverceasing quest for imagery of rebirth."[3] In short, all over the world people, cut off from traditional sources of security and meaning, are searching for activities that provide personal and social satisfaction.

American culture seems especially vulnerable to the conditions which Lifton describes. The application of sophisticated technology has changed the setting in which most Americans live. Heightened mobility, brought about by the affluence of the post-World War II era, has created a society of people who do not expect to live in one place, follow in their parents' occupational footsteps, or even complete their wage-earning years in a single occupation. The very forces which impel Americans in the direction of self-reliance cut them off from traditional sources of family and community support, and expose them to constantly changing peer group expectations.

Erik Erikson points out that role confusion sets in during adolescence, and that many Americans never transcend the confusion or the immaturity of their teenage experiences.[4] Given the fact that American culture is literally wired for sound, the emerging adolescent inevitably finds him- or herself exposed to an over-whelming variety of messages and models to imitate. Lifton apparently believes that to cope with this situation one must avoid fixed personality patterns and acquire the ability to adapt to constantly changing situations and groups.

Erikson, on the other hand, finds that failure to achieve a clear sense of identity tends to impede the ability to establish intimate relations with other adults and ultimately produces patterns of stagnation rather than growth.[5]

Whether one sides with Lifton or Erikson, however, one needs to recognize that the situation is complicated by the changing goals which we are pursuing. To the extent that Americans find meaning by seeking traditional forms of recognition and success, they are likely to be competing for promotions and salary increments, and attempting to fulfill the goals of the liberal democratic revolution. To the extent that they find meaning in cooperative, service-oriented activities, they are likely to be caught up in some phase of the post-affluent revolution. What is at stake in this conflict is the vision of what a just and humane society requires.

It is also helpful to remember that America has been a profoundly hopeful society. Ours has been a *romantic* democratic faith—one which has held out the promise that *everyone* can have a rewarding, satisfying life. Indeed the demand for satisfying, fulfilling experiences seems to have intensified with every generation. At the same time, however, role confusion—both with respect to peer group pressures and life goals—has increased. The result, in David Riesman's view, is that we often know what we like but not what we want and are therefore vulnerable to the appeals of advertisers and politicians who compete for our dollars and our votes.[6] Small wonder, then, that individuals are caught up in activities that seemingly push them in conflicting directions.

The remainder of this essay will consider the consequences which Americans experience as a result of simultaneously pursuing the goals of the liberal democratic revolution while searching for goals that are relevant to a world in which the hope of affluence no longer exerts as compelling an influence as it traditionally has done.

First, it seems clear that there *is* a sense in which the 1960s brought Americans in view of what they had always regarded as the promised land; that is, a land in which all people could utilize their talents to achieve comfortable living conditions and a fairly governed society; a land in which, as Eric Goldman argued, every individual's "rendezvous with destiny was a rendezvous with a better tomorrow." In 1960, 31.5 percent of all American families had an income of less than $4,000. By 1972, only 21.6 percent of American families had incomes of less than $6,000. In 1960 the percentage of American families with incomes over $7,000 was approximately 44; by 1972 the percentage of families with incomes in excess of $10,000 was approximately 56.[7] While this prosperity was clearly uneven (women were not getting equal pay for equal jobs, and black family income was only 62 percent of white family income), there were some grounds for believing that the inequalities might finally yield to the impact of sustained prosperity. In 1960 black family income had been only 56 percent of white family income. Moreover, in 1960 58.7 percent of Americans who were at least twenty-five years of age had *not* finished high school, whereas by 1973 this figure had declined to approximately 20 percent.[8]

The figures reveal both the fulfillment of traditional goals and *very* significant failures. Whereas 80 percent of all Americans over twenty-five had finished high school in 1973, only 40 percent of blacks over twenty-five had done so. Yet this was double the number of blacks over twenty-five that had finished in 1960.[9] If 31 percent of blacks, as compared with 10 percent of whites, were below the poverty line in 1970, it was still true that blacks doubled their purchasing power in the 1960s. The data suggest that large numbers of Americans crossed the poverty line in the 1960s and that large numbers also crossed the comfort line. The data also suggest that it is much harder for the bottom quintile of the population to become mobile than it is for the next-to-bottom quintile. Since minority groups account for a disproportionately large number of the bottom quintile, the prosperity of the 1960s made a small dent in existing inequalities, but did not remove them.

Inevitably, periods of prolonged prosperity create rising expectations. As Gerald Critoph points out in "The American Quest for Affluence," the 1960s enlarged and diversified the American appetite for consumption. The *average* American family now owns more than twenty electrical appliances, and a fourth of American families own two cars.[10] As family income increased in the 1950s and 1960s, Americans consistently spent more money on houses, cars, recreation and medical care, the very items which low-income families can least afford. Thus, for those left behind, the gap in living standards may very well have sharply increased.

The context of the 1960s was, nevertheless, as Keniston suggested, one which assumed the affluence of America. The hope of the Great Society was, after all, the hope that prosperity, fairness, and humane treatment were not finally incompatible. What changed? First America engaged in a long, fruitless war which did not achieve its publicly proclaimed objectives. "Peace with honor" was neither peaceful nor honorable and left Americans face to face with the realization that their great power was extremely fragile. Simultaneously, the emerging unity of oil-producing nations underscored American dependence on a world it could not control. Third, the combination of mounting inflation with rapidly rising unemployment created a new kind of recession—one which defied conventional analysis and treatment.

The recession-depression of the 1970s has underscored some of the basic problems of contemporary American society. After the United States recovered from the Great Depression, it entered an unparalleled era of high mass consumption. Basic to this era was the growth of a complex and sophisticated technology—one which made it possible for fewer persons working shorter hours to produce more goods. But, as the late Walter Reuther put it when being shown through an automated plant, the machines don't buy cars. Consequently, the problem of creating enough jobs to enable people to consume enough goods to keep the system functioning has become increasingly acute. An indication of the difficulty in which the advanced industrial nations find themselves may be found in the fact that they are competing bitterly for the dubious prize of arming the very nations capable of becoming the tinderbox for World War III.

From the standpoint of the individual a recession threatens job security. Inflation, on the other hand, makes many of the services he deems essential more and more costly. Traditionally, the individual—in collaboration with society—has sought to guard against economic disaster through a variety of insurance programs. Society provides unemployment compensation and social security; the individual insures his car, property, health, and life. Historically all of the insurance schemes were based on the assumption that widely spread risks would reduce costs and keep disasters within manageable proportions. Theoretically, insurance plans which were all inclusive provided the lowest premiums and returned the maximum benefits. Yet something has gone wrong. Automobile insurance, for example, has become virtually compulsory, but its costs have risen inexorably. Accidents have multiplied and awards have skyrocketed, and the end result not only dramatically increases the cost of insurance but actually makes some people uninsurable. In many cases, moreover, the loss of a car effectively removes a person from a significant sector of the job market.

A similar situation has developed in the medical profession. Here, also, there have been dramatic breakthroughs in medical technology in recent decades. At the time of the American Revolution life expectancy at birth was 35 years. In 1900, 125 years later, the figure had increased only to 45 years. By 1972 life expectancy at birth had reached 67.4 years for males and 75.2 years for females.[11] As Americans we are committed first and foremost to the concepts of equal opportunity and equal treatment. Precisely because we know how to deal with a greater variety of medical problems, we are also committed to the proposition that the knowledge shall be used professionally and equitably. Now manifestly this is an ideal which we have met very imperfectly. The distribution of health care services is one of the major problems in modern America. What the layman perceives is that doctors, as a group, are wealthy, and that, as a group, they seem to give preferential treatment to wealthy clients. The layman's revenge comes in the form of exorbitant judgments in malpractice suits. Moreover, his judgment of what constitutes malpractice is based not only on his belief that the doctor should give the patient attentive care, but also on his conviction that the doctor must use the best knowledge that is available. Since the growth of knowledge is steadily accelerating, the doctor who attempts to keep pace with it can only do so by sharply curtailing the number of patients he treats. Since it is easier to assign blame for something the doctor *did* do rather than for something he *didn't* do, the doctor also finds it safer to restrict his practice. Thus the clear possibility emerges that the advance of knowledge can create a situation in which that advance results in less equity rather than more equity.

In order to understand the implications of what has been said about the automobile and medical practice one must recognize that the liberal democratic revolution of the seventeenth and eighteenth centuries was based on a belief that the world was rational and orderly. Rational persons, therefore, could manage the world and indeed perfect it. If there is a single common thread in the arguments of American reformers throughout history, it is the belief that it is possible to create the kind of open society in which virtually everyone gets rewards which are commensurate with his or her abilities and efforts. While accidents and misfortunes are inevitable, it is society's responsibility to reduce these to a minimum and to compensate the victims who suffer through no fault of their own. If the technology which can save life and make it more comfortable cannot be used equitably, and if the automobile, upon which we depend for employment and personal freedom, becomes a vehicle we cannot afford to drive, then the world will have become for many Americans fundamentally irrational and unmanageable.

Predictably, American responses to such conditions are ambiguous. On the one hand, they respond by seeking additional job security. College youth, skeptical about the values of their elders, nevertheless seek courses and programs which will guarantee their employment. Studs Terkel's 1972 study of work reveals a strong tendency among all kinds of workers to avoid behavior which produces friction or ill will, and an equally strong tendency to accept whatever indignity a job requires for the sake of keeping it and for the hope of promotion.[12] Americans also respond by developing programs like "no fault insurance" which are attempts to create new forms of rationality.

On the other hand they also respond by various forms of withdrawal from society. Many, for example, are not having children. Whether this choice reflects an idealistic concern for the world population explosion or a fear about raising children in contemporary society, it amounts, in some sense, to a lack of confidence in the future. The figures are dramatic. In 1960, when the total population was 180 million, there were 20.3 million American children under five. In 1973, when the population had reached 210 million, there were only 16.7 million children under five. Other kinds of withdrawal take such diverse forms as the exclusive residential suburb and the various communal groups which exist both in the city and in the country. They are diverse, of course, because there is little resemblance between the life-style of suburbia and that of most communal societies. Nevertheless, both types manifest withdrawal symptoms. The suburb, as Richard Sennett has reminded us, is an attempt to wall out the disorders of the modern world, and to create a sheltered and protected area which limits personal growth. The communal group more often represents an outright rejection of prevailing cultural values and/or life-styles, but it also constitutes an effort to establish an island where reason and light may prevail against the darkness of the outside world.

When Keniston wrote his article in 1969, he was uncertain about the direction and substance of the post-affluent revolution. In retrospect his analysis appears, in some aspects at least, to have been overly simplistic. His confidence in the economy's capacity to fulfill the goals of the liberal democratic revolution did not take into account environmental problems or the difficulties which the "stagflation" of the 1970s produced; and he undoubtedly underestimated the continuing attraction of very traditional goals for large numbers of Americans.[14]

Nevertheless, the 1970s have been difficult years for traditional institutions. The family, the school, and the church, in addition to economic and political organizations, have found themselves threatened by changes which they do not fully understand or control. What participants in these institutions do understand is that many traditional practices and roles have lost their effectiveness. And, indeed, many sense that in the changing performances of our institutions we will find clues to the shape and posture of the future.

It is not possible in an essay of this size to examine in depth the performances of American families, schools, and churches. Indeed we do well to remind ourselves that family, school, and religious practices differ both among ethnic and regional groupings. Nevertheless, we can discern forces which, in varying degrees, impinge upon these institutions and hence upon all our lives. According to a 1975 report which Kenneth Keniston released in his role as head of the Carnegie Council on Children, a majority of school-age children, for the first time in American history, have mothers who work outside the home. Thirty years ago this was true for only 10 percent of the school-age children. If one combines this fact with a 700 percent increase in the divorce rate during the past fifty years, one recognizes that the socialization process is being taken over by schools, peers, and the "flickering blue parent," television.[15] Family loyalties remain very strong, but family styles are becoming more varied and peer group relationships more extended at earlier ages. What seems to be true—especially in middle-class families—is that significant numbers of children feel no special compulsion to replicate the family pattern of their parents.

The Carnegie Quarterly, commenting on *All Our Children,* notes that the revolutionary change within the family which has occurred during the past several centuries is that families which "were largely self-sufficient agricultural units, . . . [now] consume as a unit, but do not produce as a unit."[16] The result in economic terms is that children, who were formerly economic assets, have now become enormous liabilities. The Carnegie Council on Children estimates, conservatively, that "The total costs of housing, feeding, clothing, and educating one child through high school can total more than $35,000 for a family earning roughly $10,000 a year."[17] Consequently wives who choose to have children must choose to enter the labor market. But the pressures are also psychological. The Council declares:

American parents today are worried and uncertain about how to bring up children. They feel unclear about the proper balance between permissiveness and firmness. They fear they are neglecting their children, yet sometimes resent the demands their children make. Americans wonder whether they are doing a good job as parents, yet are unable to define what a good job is. In droves, they seek expert advice. And many parents wonder whether they ought to have children at all. [18]

A second case in point is the church. Historically the institutional church has conceived of its mission in priestly and prophetic roles. As priest the church must minister to the needs of those people within its reach. It must provide rest to the weary, comfort to the suffering, aid to the needy, nurture to the faithful, and forgiveness to the contrite in heart. Above all it must witness to its belief in God's redemptive grace. As prophet the church must put the community under judgment. It serves the community by questioning the morality of its acts; by constantly reminding it of its failures and shortcomings. Because the church sees itself as God's instrument in history, it must—to fulfill its calling—exercise a transforming effect upon the lives of its members and the community which surrounds it.

The church has always found it difficult to be both priest and prophet. Even when the church was the focal point of community life, it tended to be more successful in one role than in the other. As it lost its centrality, it tended to separate its priestly and prophetic functions with the result that it carried out its priestly tasks primarily for its own members, and it often ignored or minimized its prophetic role. In recent years inflation has further eroded the capacity of the church to fulfill its self-appointed tasks. Even though most denominations have raised more funds in the 1960s and 1970s to support missionaries, they have in the same period been forced to reduce the number of people actually serving in the mission field. In this situation people are likely to perceive a growing gap between what the church claims as its duty and what the church actually achieves.

Nevertheless, the very fact that Americans in the mid-1960s found themselves within sight of the promised land of affluence intensified their belief in the possibility of perfecting the social order. Indeed, those churches in the 1960s which spoke out for desegregation and integration experienced a modest rejuvenation. Thus a time emerged in which people were ready to take the *claims* of the church seriously. It is therefore not especially surprising to read credos of college students and find expressed in them a prevailing belief in many traditional Christian doctrines. It is also not surprising to discover that these same students, on the whole, do not see the institutional church as a crucial vehicle for implementing these beliefs.

Even educational institutions have lost some of their credibility. Serious questions have been raised about the capacity of schools to furnish equal opportunity to all Americans. Traditionally Americans have supported educational institutions because they believed these institutions trained people for responsible social roles and because they also furnished youth with opportunities to develop and use their natural abilities. Two factors explain the erosion of confidence. One is the arrival of mass education. Far larger and more diverse groups seek educational opportunities, and schools and colleges have found it increasingly difficult to accommodate the needs of their clienteles and maintain credible standards. The second factor is the increasing cost of education. As costs continue to rise, taxpayers and legislators search more intensely for ways of trimming educational budgets. Ironically, the more they trim, the greater the likelihood becomes of creating a situation in which schools and colleges *cannot* fill their traditional objectives and hence are *not* worth what they cost.

The foregoing analysis suggests some conclusions about both of Keniston's revolutions. First, the liberal democratic revolution *is* incomplete, and, as Keniston declared, a great deal of pressure exists to finish it. Second, recessions widen the gaps between the professed goals and the actual achievements, and therefore intensify the desires of Americans to achieve affluence and security—measured in rather traditional ways. If affluence cannot be taken for granted, people will struggle harder to achieve it. Thirdly, many Americans are skeptical about the manageability of their world and indeed of their own personal lives. They doubt the capacity of traditional institutions to meet new situations, and they are not confident about their own abilities to establish effective alternatives. Thus they are open to new strategies which hold out the possibility of reestablishing meaning in their lives. In this sense, they are on the edge of what Keniston called "the post-affluent" revolution.

The struggle to reestablish meaning has taken several forms. Women, for example, are not seeking merely to compete in traditional terms, but to transform the meaning of work by introducing cooperative attitudes and values. Youth are searching for socially significant occupations and many insist that material rewards are of secondary importance. Simultaneously many Americans are reestablishing a sense of place and community loyalty, and are forgoing the rewards of mobility.

But meaning cannot be restored by ignoring the demands of the earlier revolution. Those demands require, minimally, the establishment of equal opportunity and equal treatment and the creation of conditions in which the available opportunities are worth equalizing. If one assumes that fewer people working shorter hours can produce more goods, and if one also assumes that American society depends upon maintaining a very low rate of unemployment, then it becomes apparent that work and the satisfactions which it produces must be redefined. There simply are not enough jobs of the traditional variety to go around. In the next decade, therefore, Americans will have to employ more people in the arts, in sports, and a wide variety of leisure activities. They will have to employ more people in the delivery of health care services, and they will need to use a far greater number of people in teaching situations—whether in traditional schools or alternative educational programs.

Such developments give meaning to the post-affluent revolution. In the past it has been possible to invite wider participation in the affluent society by enlarging the pie to be divided rather than by redividing the pie. The top fifth of American families, measured by income, received approximately 60 percent of all family income in 1947. In 1970 they still received about 56 percent of the income. Some redistribution occurred in the postwar era, but it was modest. The economy will not function, however, unless nearly all Americans can participate in it. In order to preserve their affluence Americans will, in the 1980s, have to accept the most significant redistribution of income in their history.

That redistribution will be accompanied by three significant developments. First, there will be a wider variety of jobs available. For example, there may be fewer million-dollar athletes, but many more participatory recreational programs. Second, the expansion of service occupations and service-related jobs will make it possible to accommodate individual differences far more effectively than in the past. For example, the size of school classes will be significantly reduced when the teaching force is greatly enlarged. When this happens, the school will be an effective vehicle for improving the quality of American life and also for fulfilling the traditional goals of a democratic, upwardly mobile society. Finally, by redirecting their efforts toward meeting the pluralistic needs of a mass society American institutions can recover their effectiveness and their creditability. As they change, they will also find it possible to conserve traditional values and some of their traditional roles.

For these things to happen a new "message" must be given to those who govern and spend our dollars. Defense industries, thriving on deficit budgets, threaten to bankrupt us without even providing enough different kinds of jobs to alleviate the problem of unemployment. A redistribution of income which will create new definitions of work and meaningful new jobs requires, in terms of public spending, what William James called a "moral equivalent of war." We must, in short, send a "message" which "demands" that spending be related to the goals we most earnestly seek—the goals which give meaning to satisfaction to the lives of *all* Americans.

Notes

1. Kenneth Keniston, "You Have to Grow up in Scarsdale to Know How Bad Things Really Are," *New York Times Magazine,* April 27, 1969, pp. 27–29.

2. Robert J. Lifton, "Protean Man," *Partisan Review* 35 (Winter 1968): 27.

3. Lifton, p. 27.

4. Erik H. Erikson, *Childhood and Society,* 2nd ed. (New York: W. W. Norton and Company, Inc., 1963), p. 307.

5. Erikson, pp. 263–66.

6. David Riesman, *The Lonely Crowd,* rev. ed. (New Haven, Conn.: Yale University Press, 1961), Chap. 4, pp. 83–108.

7. *Statistical Abstract of the United States* (Washington, D.C.: U.S. Government Printing Office, 1975), Section 13, pp. 390, 391, 397.

8. *Statistical Abstract of the United States,* Section 4, p. 118.

9. *Statistical Abstract of the United States,* Section 4, p. 119.

10. Gerald E. Critoph, "The American Quest for Affluence," in *American Character and Culture in a Changing World,* John A. Hague, ed. (Westport, Conn.: Greenwood Press, 1979), p. 35.

11. *Statistical Abstract of the United States,* Section 2, p. 59.

12. Studs Terkel, *Working: People Talk About What They Do All Day and How They Feel About What They Do* (New York: Random House, 1972).

13. *Statistical Abstract of the United States,* Section 1, pp. 6–7.

14. See, for example, Conal Furay, *The Grass Roots Mind in America* (New York, London: New Viewpoints, a Division of Franklin Watts, 1977). Also Robert Coles recently published an essay entitled "The 'Ordinary American' and Us" (Bloomington, Ind.: Poynter Essay, the Poynter Center, Indiana University, December, 1977), in which he stated:

He (the ordinary American) does not need to be romanticized: the heroic "common man," good at heart, but corrupted by an evil or immoral society. He has his selfish, greedy, demanding, insular, narrow, even hateful moments, as do all of us, including the moralists, the chiding preachers among us—of which my ilk has become an especially prominent sectarian version. But he works hard for others as well as himself; he prays hard at church; he gives to charities—despite his economic worries, his social vulnerabilities; and not least, he does indeed love his country, and wants to respond to its higher principles, as enunciated by the occasional statesman who comes our way, and puts them into practice here and there through laws or programs.

15. See Kenneth Keniston and the Carnegie Council on Children, *All Our Children: The American Family Under Pressure* (New York: Harcourt Brace Jovanovich, 1976).

16. *Carnegie Quarterly* 25, no. 4 (New York: Carnegie Corporation of New York, Fall 1977), p. 2.

17. Ibid.

18. Ibid., p. 1.

PART TWO
Literature and the Changing Culture

ROBERT H. WALKER

Patterns in Recent American Literature *

Robert H. Walker's compilation American Studies in the United States *(1958) is a landmark referred to more than once in this collection. He has taught and administered in this field at several universities since 1953, at George Washington University since 1959. Senior Editor of* American Studies International *since 1970, Walker has written and edited a number of books, the latest of which is* The Reform Spirit in America *(1976, 1977).*

What is new about recent American literature? The surest way to answer this question intelligently is to begin by discovering what is old about it. Most of this essay is devoted to arranging fiction and verse of the past twenty years so as to comment on the degree to which it has continued to reveal established and important patterns. Has it become a democratic literature, by and for the people? Has it painstakingly reproduced its distinctive environment, natural and social? Has it formed an important and responsible part of the American social process, calling attention to problem areas and pointing toward needed change? Has this literature engaged life in a constructive manner, optimistically focusing on the "smiling aspects"? Has it displayed the American conscience, the concern for rightness as well as expediency, the need to base all arguments on a fundamental moral law?

It has been convenient for me to mix verse with fiction in this discussion but to omit dramatic literature. Recent drama, I think, would only strengthen the generalizations. I am aware of the vulnerability of many of my judgments, but I have been happy to see in many of my colleagues here an equal willingness to risk infallibility in order to explore contemporary areas of interest. Writing in the mid-sixties, one must apologize for lacking the necessary perspective to judge most of these works confidently, and for taking advantage of this flaw by deliberately mixing popular with serious literature.

---

* This essay is taken from public lectures delivered during the 1965 Summer Program in American Studies at Stetson University to an audience of high school teachers and general public. The text was edited in 1967 and again in 1978.

It is becoming increasingly difficult, as a matter of fact, to draw a line between the literature of the critics and the literature of the people. Do the novels of John P. Marquand or Louis Auchincloss, for example, demand a place in the literary histories as well as on the book-of-the-month lists? Was Raymond Chandler "just" a writer of profitable detective tales, or ought an anthology of accomplished American prose to include a sample of his work? That it is even remotely possible to consider questions like these demonstrates how drastically the demography of literature has been altered. Not four generations ago, Emily Dickinson wrote for her audience of two, Henry James for a relative few, and Ned Buntline for the multitudes. The gap between pulp and polite fiction was enormous. Now college professors, along with other people in bus stations and drugstores, pick up paperbound copies of John Barth, John Cheever, John O'Hara, and John Updike.

One consequence of the apparent narrowing of the gap between serious and popular fiction has been the impressive popular acceptance of the writers most elaborately praised by the critics. William Faulkner and Ernest Hemingway, undisputed favorites of the professors, were also dear to the public at large, increasingly so toward the end of their careers. *Life* magazine, one recalls, devoted its enormous circulation to the original printing of *The Old Man and the Sea*.[1] *A Moveable Feast* sold thousands of copies in its first week, and even single letters from the pen of Faulkner earned headlines as they were brought to light after his death.[2] The novel which created the greatest furor among the nation's top critics during the 1950s, *By Love Possessed,* became not only a best seller, but also—oh Everest of Everests—a *Reader's Digest* condensed book. Katherine Anne Porter delivered her long-awaited novel, *Ship of Fools,* not just to classrooms in the American novel but also to the coffee tables of hundreds of thousands of homes.[3]

These phenomena are part of the predictable consequences experienced by any nation in which an industrial revolution has been accomplished by a rise of the middle class and a consequent elevation of public education. The bull market for culture, following the close of World War II, was partly responsible for a soaring publications record which in little more than a decade saw American book production increase from one-half billion to one billion. As government subsidies for texts have extended beyond the original crop of G.I.'s and into the wars on poverty and cultural deprivation, the rate of growth has anything but slackened. Statistics, especially from publishers, are often unreliable and never conclusive. Much of the culture explosion may indeed be phony, as many fault-finders have insisted; surely the vast bulk of what is printed and bound has little to do with "belles-lettres." And yet the culture boom has some substantial qualitative as well as quantitative aspects. Now, for example, the writer need not come from a small wealthy and educated class. If he has talent, he can acquire the necessary training and education as part of his birthright, virtually. The availability of libraries and classrooms, bookstores and critical journals has never been greater. Nor need he the luck of a patron or the sinecure of a political job. Rather, with the broadening marketplace for good literature, the writer can perform at the very top of his abilities. If he is any good, and if he breaks the initial print barrier, he can expect a return on his talent which will enable him to live, self-supported as a writer, not as a customs house clerk or as a freak-in-residence at a castle or campus. A true democratization of culture, if there is such a thing, is a long way off; but writers today come noticeably from "the people," rather than from a particular class or stratum; and if they succeed, it will be with the many as well as the few.

The democratization of culture, because it has been shared by so many nations to a greater or lesser degree, is probably the least distinctive aspect of American literature. The most distinctive aspect continues to be the manner in which this literature reflects, with astounding literalness, the environment out of which it is produced. Considering the strength and persistence of this characteristic, there are remarkably few literary historians who have made much of it. Yet from Samuel Sewall's literary enslavement to the factual details of his natural and social environment to the latest political novel of Gore Vidal, the literature produced by this culture has been almost hopelessly involved with factual detail. What made *Moby Dick* a representative American novel? In part, the answer to this question rests with the chapter on cetology and the explicit insistence of Melville that even a metaphorical romance must be colored by the facts of whales and whaling.[4] What made *Leaves of Grass* the supreme poem of the United States?[5] The answer to this question cannot ignore Walt Whitman's catalogs of rivers, crops, states, and tribes—the map of his beloved subject. Theodore Dreiser, they say, was incapable of putting a fictional character on a street corner or streetcar unless he had previously checked his city directory and tram schedule. In recognition of this tendency, we have come to recognize the documentary fiction of John Dos Passos as contributing to a literary tendency more extreme in his work than elsewhere but well established nonetheless: namely, the mixture of the facts of environment—past and present—with the products of the creative imagination.

Nor has this tendency disappeared in the last generation. Beginning with an unusually literal rendering of World War II, the writer returned to the tradition of business and political novels in which accurate and authentic reporting supplied a necessary background for the action. Marketers of this literature, recognizing that American readers demand verisimilitude as an anchor to the imagination, make use of the dust jackets to persuade the potential reader that he will not only be skillfully and gracefully entertained but also reliably informed. Thus, a best-selling business novel, *Executive Suite*, gave prominent note on its cover to the fact that its author, Cameron Hawley, had in fact been vice-president of a large corporation not dissimilar in nature from the one whose top-management power struggle was the subject of the book.[6] (Might not a French publisher, say, try to hide the fact that his novelist had been a businessman?) The publishers of Gore Vidal's political novels make no secret either of his kinship to political celebrities or of his own abortive career as office seeker. Allan Drury's years as a political reporter in Washington provided him the material to compose a study of the senatorial mores sufficiently authentic to be included on the reading lists of political science courses, albeit *Advise and Consent* may never be required in a literature class.[7] Even in the area of historical romance, Pulitzer Prizewinning Robert Lewis Taylor saw fit to buttress his fictitious *Travels of Jamie McPhee-ters* with a bibliography of manuscript and printed sources which he had consult-ed for the sake of credibility.[8] Although one might interestingly debate the effect of fidelity to literal details on the quality of American writing, he would still be forced to concede that as a force in literature it waxes rather than wanes. The attitudes which pervade this literal-mindedness produce the answers to the remaining questions; at this stage one can note that the American writer and his readers regard the real, contemporary world as an interesting and worthy subject for literature. This attitude is no small thing in itself.

Social protest as an aspect of American literature is at least as old as *Two Years Before the Mast, Uncle Tom's Cabin,* and "Essay on Civil Disobedi-ence."[9] It reached one climax in the muckraking days of the late nineteenth and early twentieth centuries when the politico-economic preoccupations of the journalists spilled over into the novels of David Graham Phillips and Upton Sinclair, the verse of William Vaughn Moody and Eugene Field. It reached another in the bitter reactions to the Great Depression, the communism of the Federal Theatre, and the proletarianism of *The Grapes of Wrath.*[10] The years since World War II may not have seen a novel which produced such direct political action as Upton Sinclair's *The Jungle* nor a poem which struck so tender a social membrane as Edwin Markham's "The Man with the Hoe," but neither has it witnessed the abandonment of literature's social relevance.[11]

The focus of today's literary attention is divided unequally between the problems of urban life and of international relations. The first of these questions is by far the larger for the writer; the city is, to an amazing extent, the American novel, short story, and verse. From E. A. Robinson's "Tilbury Town" through William Carlos Williams's *Paterson* was recorded the shift from village to metropolis in life as well as in literature.[12] The opening lines of Stephen Crane's *Maggie* which so shocked his contemporaries now seem almost quaint.[13] All aspects of urban life have come under literary scrutiny. As guides to the various ethnic ghettos, one may choose between Edwin O'Connor and the Boston Irish, Nelson Algren and the Chicago Poles, Gerald Green and the Brooklyn Jews. Philip Roth showed what happened when Jewish culture went suburban (*Good-bye Columbus*), and John McPartland looked with more than sociological perception at the impact of life in "homogeneous" housing developments (*No Down Payment*).[14] Not all of these writers are reformers, by any means, but they use literature as a means of spotlighting conditions which need improvement.

The mark of the muckrake seems more in evidence when one turns to the plight of the urban Negro. The essays of James Baldwin and the speeches of Martin Luther King are probably more important than any fictionalization of similar material. Nevertheless, it is hard to read today *The Invisible Man* of Ralph Ellison and be surprised at the summer violence of Watts, Detroit, and points in between.[15] Richard Wright's *Native Son* served long and well as a twentieth-century counterpart to Harriet Beecher Stowe's incendiary work.[16] The nearest postwar equivalent is probably Claude Brown's impressionistic Harlem autobiography, *Manchild in the Promised Land*.[17] At least a U.S. Senate committee investigating urban crime sought and received the testimony of Brown in 1967.

The other major focal point of international involvement, war and peace, has been covered not so elaborately but equally spectacularly. Fletcher Knebel and Charles W. Bailey chilled readers with the dire possibilities of superpower in the hands of the military (*Seven Days in May*), while Eugene Burdick and Harvey Wheeler were dramatizing global tragedy as a consequence of compound electronic malfunction *(Fail Safe)*.[18] Legions of science fiction writers have made their futuristic points by opening their narratives after the holocaust. The muckraking novel concerning the role of the United States in Vietnam was written by the Briton Graham Greene before the American military was directly involved (*The Quiet American*),[19] but Eugene Burdick and Charles Lederer, two Americans, pointed out some reasons for the less-than-total success of American diplomatic programs in Southeast Asia. This book, *The Ugly American*, apparently caused serious repercussions in Washington and led to a much more exhaustive training program in the language and culture of foreign areas for American personnel about to serve their nation abroad.[20] One hears, also, that *Fail Safe* caused a reexamination of the safeguards against accidental initiation of nuclear warfare. These cause-and-effect relationships are all but impossible to prove. (We still say that *The Jungle* may have contributed to the passage of the Pure Food and Drug Act.)[21] Still, it seems a safe guess that the international muckrake has not been wielded without tangible results.

American literature is still involved with its environment and a conspicuous fraction of it is engaged with dramatizing social problems. But does the writer still believe that American endings are happy endings, or has he despaired of a shiny Roman culture slowly burying itself under films of carbon monoxide, sewers of stubborn detergent bubbles, and slowly rusting carcasses of Hupmobiles and Edsels? This is the hardest question to answer for several reasons. Hyperbole and overstatement have always been part of the literary arsenal, and it is sometimes impossible to distinguish pure despair from a tirade intended to produce action. Furthermore, much of the antisocial excrescence that passes for literature is chronologically analogous to a boy's first night out on the town; that is, there seems to be a lot of violence and obscenity which exists mainly to prove that Victorians and Puritans are not so powerful as they once were. There are these and other reasonable explanations for the appearance of a significant group of nay-sayers among the writers of the 1950s and 1960s, but it would be a great mistake to attempt to explain them away.

They are here. Nathanael West's *Day of the Locusts* has spread across the land.[22] Katherine Anne Porter, the sweetest and most charming of our living literary lionesses, has produced in her only full-length novel an absolutely acid comment on the degrees of venery and culpability which are all that distinguish one voyager from another on the *Ship of Fools* we call life.[23] Paul Bowles, one of our most talented artisans in the craft of writing, has explored existentialism only to find a congeries of brutal examples of the meaninglessness of meaning. Is war sick and insane? Yes, answered Joseph Heller in *Catch-22*, but hardly less so than the human dilemma at large.[24] In James Purdy, there is only a contrasting of the malevolence of ignorance with the malevolence of superficial cultivation. In William Burroughs, when he leaves off his purely clinical discussions of narcotics, there is left the frightening symbol of addiction representing the passive, possessed position occupied by most of us. Bernard Malamud, who has seen the human situation with sympathy, perception, and patience, has—in the end—held up his characters as microbes in a stoppered test tube. To John Cheever, and the many who have gone his way, the civilization we accept is but a veneer over the basic and enduring framework of our lusts and violence. When the moon is full over Westchester County, cracks in the veneer show through.

The dark side of our continent has been weirdly illuminated by this group of talented "black humorists" and black tragedians. Are there more of them now than in the days of Hearn and Bierce? Yes. Are they the Cassandras of our declining age? If so, there is nothing to do but continue to disbelieve them. Is there any historical explanation for their presence? Perhaps. Perhaps they are the consequences of our age of conformity, our great middle, our mass culture, our other-directedness. What must frustrate the writer, who is by definition an abstainer at least and frequently a dissenter, is the absence of reasonable alternatives to the central position. When labor unions sponsor golf tournaments, when giant corporations assume large responsibilities in the job corps, and when the president of the United States labels himself a "progressive conservative," where does one find a loyal opposition? On the Vietnam War, the answer is easy and obvious. But when Senator Goldwater tried to establish a distinguishable conservatism, he found that even party loyalty held only a small percentage of the voters to his program. To disagree fundamentally with the majority in postwar America has been to place oneself automatically on the lunatic fringe. As reasonable dissent has become more difficult, the writer has exploded his frustrations into tales of violence, perversion, addiction, and insanity.

To suggest that overconformity to the great middle may have provoked the normally neurotic dissenter into a psychotic rejection of his culture is not, of course, to explain away the Porters and Purdys. It is rather to admit that in addition to writing good fiction, they were telling us something about our civilization to which we ought to pay heed.

However disturbing are the products of the alienated imagination, they are far from occupying the majority literary position. Though more closely contested in

1967 than in 1897, an election between the sunny Howells and the sour Bierce school of American writing would still go to William-the-Dean. For to most of our good poets—William Meredith, Richard Eberhart, James Dickey, as well as to most of the writers of fiction, contemporary life is still something to be engaged in delightedly. A Richard Bissell can still perform with the exuberance of a young Mark Twain. A Gerald Green can make a bitter Brooklyn doctor heroic enough to convert a flatulant adman to Thoreau and the hard-yet-beautiful truths of nature and man. In fact, if one were to attempt a giant plot summary of the great mass of popular and some serious fiction, he would conclude that American life, to the writer, is well worth living and stands in very little need of change.

For a representative protagonist to succeed he must be wary of two principal dangers: the overly possessive demands of his family and the hypnotic fascinations of career itself. The wife of a corporation vice-president may suppress the message which would have made her husband president because she fears that her son would never again see dad in the little league grandstands once he assumed higher office. The wife of a public relations man argues the virtues of the suburbs and expensive schools just when her husband is trying to prove to himself that principles do have meaning in a compliant world of lobbies and expense accounts. Contrary to some sociological studies, the heroes tire not of the routines and scrambles. The danger to them is that they will, seduced not by money or power alone but by the fascinating intricacies of professional life, sleep on an office couch and make vice-president by twenty-nine. If the protagonist gives in to the unreasonable demands of his family or yields to the sire-call of career, he will be forever immature or warped. If he harks to conscience and self-trust, however, he can have a reasonable and gratifying success as a member of a family, a profession, and a community. Furthermore, he will recognize in himself a degree of meaningful individuality and independence which allows him to call himself his own man. The creators of this collective master plot will not have made much memorable fiction, but they have already recorded a majority viewpoint more clearly hopeful than the minority of their grim contemporaries.

One of the three basic tenets of the American democratic faith, wrote Ralph H. Gabriel, is a belief in a fundamental moral law from which all temporal directions must be taken.[25] Mr. Gabriel's conclusions were based as much on literary evidence as on any other kind, and it is true that the nineteenth-century writers support him well. Emerson, Whitman, Hawthorne, Melville, Longfellow, Howells, James, Robinson—all were men for whom literature and morality were inseparable. It is worth asking whether this preoccupation has persisted into the twentieth century. The answer is not simple; for, as this century opened, the stage was beginning to be dominated by a group of novelists and short story writers who were attempting to demonstrate that moral law was but an outworn fiction in a universe governed by indifferent natural law. These "naturalists"—Crane, London, Dreiser, Norris—failed to rid themselves completely of moral values and preoccupations, but they expended considerable effort toward so doing. In a somewhat parallel manner, the writers who came of age in the 1930s were so occupied with the crashing social and economic problems created by the depression that they dealt with collective morality, if any, or with those impersonal laws discovered by Karl Marx.

Between naturalism and the depression came World War I and the 1920s, a period which introduced more writers of substance than any in our history. Those who were still writing importantly in the 1950s stood for a sufficiently impressive involvement of literature with morality to make Ralph Gabriel's generalization still appropriate. To make the strongest case would be to begin with T. S. Eliot, whose flight from the wasteland to the cathedral formed the principal fact of his personal as well as his literary life. Without moral values, wrote Eliot in a number of ways and on a number of levels, life is without meaning or interest. Publicly, he recommended the large religious metaphors of druidism, the Crusades, Hinduism, and the Resurrection. Privately, he affirmed a conversion to the Anglican Catholic Church. No less committed to a religious frame of reference was William Faulkner. *Light in August* and *The Fable,* written at rather distant points in his career, attested his lasting interest in the meaning of Christ's life on earth.[26] More important to his canon was the broad Old Testament metaphor in which he has endowed the planter families—Sutphen, Compson, Sartoris—with the patriarchal sins of possession—unholy possession of a land and a people. Wreaking the vengeance of the Lord came a blight known as Snopes to burn the barns and lead the daughters astray. The only hope for either planter or dirt farmer lay in the far side of retribution and repentence.

If Eliot and Faulkner represented the enduring literary explorations of moral questions which began in the second and third decades of the century, Ernest Hemingway stood for a long time as their opposite number. His terse, uneditorialized tales of drinking, skiing, boxing, and bullfighting caused Hemingway to be called"amoral" about as often as gin was called "bathtub." This kind of label did not suit the bearded Papa, as he made increasingly clear in his late work: so clear that his readers came to wonder how they had missed it in his earlier work. The climactic lesson came in *The Old Man and the Sea,* which, if not a ritualistic religious parable, was at least a tale commenting on all the grand questions of man's relation to the stars, the sea, the fish, the town, the young, and the self.[27] The attitudes evoked by the Old Man's primitivistic reflections on these profoundly moral questions brought forth the classic Hemingway attitudes of respect, integrity, containment, and control. Looking backward at Hemingway, it became impossible to ignore the theme of man's selfless responsibility in *The Sun Also Rises* or to give less than total stress to the implications in the title of *For Whom the Bell Tolls.*[28] Thus, the Hemingway "pose" became a metaphor for self-respect in shifting times.

Another writer of that same generation who has been even more widely misjudged is James Gould Cozzens. Because he has dealt undisguisedly with bigotry, some misguided critics have made Cozzens wear the bigot's cloak himself. Such reactions have absurdly confused the collective judgment on a man whose major works—*The Last Adam, The Just and the Unjust, By Love Possessed*—all made the central point that man must conceptualize a set of moral absolutes towards which he can guide his imperfect steps and thoughts.[29] Without these absolutes to establish the polar stars, man is rudderless in a featureless, relativistic sea. In his novel of World War II, *Guard of Honor,* Cozzens developed most fully the theme which pervaded all the good novels of the war, the question of individual responsibility in a world where the questions are posed with seeming impersonality and the answers can be met only by collective action.[30] In such a world, represented by a minesweeper at sea or an infantry platoon on patrol, what standards can fairly be applied to the behavior of the individual? *The Caine Mutiny, The Naked and the Dead,* and *From Here to Eternity* were major novels because they saw beyond the camps, jungles, and atolls and into the heart of the modern dilemma where the threat to the individual was exaggerated by the military condition of arbitrary groupings and unbreakable hierarchies.[31] Surely there is no more pressing moral assignment than the restatement of individual ethics in a collective age.

Out of the World War II generation came the Beat writers, whose most eloquent voices—Allan Ginsberg and Lawrence Ferlinghetti—were joined in a complaint against a materialistic, unlovely America wherein individualism had surrendered to the centers where mass behavior is putatively controlled: Wall Street, Madison Avenue, Detroit, and the Pentagon. As Ferlinghetti has put it, we have become a nation of "conscientious nonobjectors" in a "kissproof world."[32] Although the rhetoric was different, the complaint did not differ much from similar ones issued by James Fenimore Cooper, Walt Whitman, Henry Adams, Henry James, George Santayana, and countless artists in all ages. Always more subtly and often more adroitly, this same complaint has been perpetuated by another generation of poets including Robert Lowell and Theodore Roethke. This complaint forms an important part of the public conscience: the conscience of those who wish this civilization judged by more than material standards.

Beyond the poets, Beat and clean-shaven, it is hard to detect a "school" of morally engaged writers. Sometimes, there is reason to suspect that the western might mature into an indigenous literary genre with philosophic as well as adventurous ingredients. Retelling the Cain-Abel, Jacob-Esau stories in small-town Texas, William Humphrey added a chapter to the use of western settings for a reexamination of some of our inherited cultural values in *Home from the Hill*.[33] A work like this allows one to speculate on the possibility of a kind of American morality play in a tradition tentatively defined by Stephen Crane's "The Blue Hotel," Owen Woster's *The Virginian,* Walter Van Tilberg Clark's *The Ox-Bow Incident,* and possibly Tom Lea's *The Wonderful Country* and A. B. Guthrie's trilogy.[34] Frederick Jackson Turner and Walt Whitman could readily serve as joint deities for a literary form which would implant the code of the frontier on the intellectual passage to India, extracting a uniquely American meaning. Someday we may have such a body of letters; today not even the skeleton is complete.

If there is no narrow theme to unite them, there is at least a group of contemporary writers who center their literary efforts around important moral questions. Saul Bellow is deservedly the best established of them. He is not only an important chronicler of the mid-century reaction to urbanism. Having followed Augie March along his complicated trails through the asphalt jungle, Bellow then placed Henderson the Rain King in a literal African jungle but with a more highly allegorical motivation.[35] Whether the protagonist is dangling at the loose end of unarrived military orders or writing unfinished letters to unheeding editors, he is constantly pacing the cage of the individual's mid-century limitations, testing the bars for expressionistic escape or the floor for existential assurance. Nor is any Bellow hero allowed to forget that his cage is not an irresponsible solitary confinement.

Though considerably younger, John Updike appears to be the closest companion to Bellow when it comes to composing accomplished fiction with a serious moral relevance. Updike has rejected, without regret, the accepted forms of collective action from team sports through protest marching. Instead, haunted by teachers and preachers, he has searched the mythological past and the Pennsylvania countryside, looking for an arrangement in time and place where a man can live in peace with his universal-yet-personal sense of being. The enigmatic J. D. Salinger has been making a similar search, causing the magic carpet from the Glass family's living room to hover dangerously close to Gautama's boh tree. Many Eastern readers of American literature take Salinger seriously; his American relevance seems to be evaporating. Among the newer names, that of Thomas Pynchon seems most likely to associate itself with writers who engage literature and morality constructively and skillfully. His wild first novel, V, had much that was no more than slapstick and no less than black comedy.[36] But there was also an insistent thread that united the novel: the quest for connections in history and tradition that give more than physical and sociological meaning to life. The hero, Benny Profane, discovered in himself an unselfishly sacred sense of responsibility which he could not abandon. His visceral probings, combined with Stencil's archival traceries, produced a network of associations more suggestive of humane meaning than of a senseless chain of circumstances.

What is new about American literature? Stylistically it can only be called experimental. The innovations—impressionism, symbolism, stream of consciousness—were made by older generations. These techniques are still subject to experimentation and sometimes to refinement. A new public morality has permitted a broader use of language and subject matter. Sometimes this license has resulted in obscene rejections of social patterns; more often it has permitted a more detailed, realistic literal-mindedness. Philosophically, recent literature has introduced a recognizable stream of nihilism and of crude, misunderstood existentialism, but the major point of departure is still the romanticism of Coleridge and Emerson or its dark cousin, the naturalism of Zola and Dreiser.

Basically, however, it seems clear from the answers to the questions on which this essay has been based that American literature will continue at mid-century to follow its historical patterns; it will illustrate the democratization of American culture; it will be inextricably bound up in the literal details of its environment; it will perform as an important aspect of the public conscience both as to superficial social questions and as to profound moral issues. Not to be ignored is a skillfully embittered minority; but so far, this minority remains outside the American character mold as represented by Hemingway and Faulkner, Bellow and Updike. To most American writers, the lotus lullabies of psychedelic drugs and social drop-out celebrations have proved less alluring than the humanistic clarion of Faulkner's Nobel acceptance speech. They may need to remind themselves now and again, but fundamentally they agree that the writer's privilege and duty is ''to help man endure by lifting his heart, by reminding him of the courage and honor and hope and pride and compassion and pity and sacrifice which have been the glory of his past'' and which can ''help him endure and prevail.'' [37]

Afterword

The editor has generously allowed an afterword to the foregoing pages viewed at a mean distance of a dozen years. To impose order on contemporary events is risky at best, and the perspective provided by a single decade gives no great assurance. Limited by space if not by prudence, the following paragraphs review in order the main features of the essay, at once revising and updating.

The first generalization concerned the democratization of American literature, a process that surely continues. Writers and readers in this country come from an increasingly broad spectrum, as witness for example the large creative outpouring from the inner city once avenues to publication were opened. Popular and serious literature grow ever more difficult to distinguish. The paperback revolution has become an established—if expensive—mode. Yet literature between book covers has given way even more noticeably during the past decade to other media as expression of popular interests and preoccupations. The most widely circulated poetry today is the lyric sung or accompanied by music. These verses carry the humor and melodrama of country-and-Western ballads; the folk wisdom of Johnny Cash and John Denver; the pop symbolism of a ''Miss American Pie''; as well as the more subtle observations of Simon and Garfunkel, Stevie Wonder, Joni Mitchell, and Carly Simon. Similarly, few novels have crystallized social attitudes as widely as ''Patton,'' ''A Thousand Clowns,'' ''Easy Rider,'' or ''Super Fly.'' Of course the printed word has never monopolized the public eye; yet today even more than yesterday it may be essential to include in discussions of popular literature the disc, the tape, and the film.

Literal-mindedness, identified in the foregoing essay as a primary and distinctive characteristic of American letters, has continued unabated. With the final disappearance of puritanical and Victorian repressions in the 1960s, this addiction to persuasive detail took on the look, in some fiction, of an anatomical handbook or the log of a sex clinic (see Philip Roth, *Portnoy's Complaint;* John Updike, *Couples, Rabbit Redux*[38]). The seemingly endless penchant of modern verse makers for sexual specifics caused one participant in a Library of Congress reading to exclaim that "The poet's privates are now public." Roy Basler, the poet and critic who reported this remark, went on to catalog an abundance of verse explicitly sexual as opposed to mystically romantic. This kind of literal-mindedness, speculated Basler, may herald a final triumph of Darwinism over humanism.[39]

Literal-mindedness still pertains to subjects outside the bedroom. In the aftermath of Watergate, many tales have owed their currency to a fictionalized realism directed at White House plots, espionage, counterespionage, and the acts of journalistic exposure. For a time it looked as though every single member of the committee to reelect President Nixon would force the American readership through a narrative justification of his own part in the drama of the world's most thoroughly documented oval office.

Literature and social issues are still closely interwoven, and attention is still shared by urban and international questions with some interesting variations in subcategories. The misadventure in Southeast Asia inspired many novels, none of paramount quality. The best recent war novel (*Winds of War*) is by a familiar writer (Herman Wouk) about a war already subject to nostalgia (World War II).[40] International intrigue and diplomacy have replaced Hollywood and Madison Avenue as focal points for the institutional novel. A new respect for nature, akin to Rachel Carson and the Sierra Club, shows itself particularly in verse. All genres reflect a more informed interest in urban issues, in the unexplored potential of women, and in the status of minority groups. A new tolerance covers extended literary treatment of alternatives to marriage, monogamy, and conventional heterosexual relationships. Perhaps the most important socioliterary fact, however, is the flowering of black literature, to some degree in verse and fiction, but particularly in the autobiographies of Maya Angelou, James Baldwin, Claude Brown, Horace Cayton, Eldridge Cleaver, LeRoi Jones, Malcolm X, and Alex Haley. Also growing is a corpus of imaginative literature dealing with the more diffused experiences of Americans of Spanish and Indian backgrounds.

In fact the concentration on issues that concern the dominant culture has been seriously diluted not only by attention to native subcultures but also by newfound international appetites. American literature—not so long ago—used to suffer from a kind of lingering colonial-mindedness which overvalued both the literary products and the literary criticism of France, Germany, and especially Britain. Now the view from the United States no longer exaggerates Western Europe but turns increasingly toward poets from Brazil and Czechoslovakia, novelists from Nigeria and Russia. Jean Luis Borges and Alexander Solzhenitsyn are but two notable examples in a chain of ''discoveries'' and translations. If the powerful impact of oriental verse and philosophy is waning a bit, it is surely being replaced by other exotic and subcultural themes and not by a return to the domestic mainstream.

The diffusion of interests, however, does not account for the continuing shift from constructive protest toward a mounting dismay with the consensus culture reflected as early as the middle 1950s. This tide of rejection has continued to swell in both number and proportion. It can be defined most clearly by what it rejects: the rational American present. A current rage for nostalgia beats a retreat for the American reader into the African villages of Alex Haley or the nearer nostalgia of E. L. Doctorow and Jack Finney. Owing its origins to John Barth's *Sot-Weed Factor* and Eudora Welty's *Losing Battles,* the current reader seems to thirst for settings that predate the impersonalism of modern cities while offering the reassurances of a more structured and static society to an age which has become exhausted by growth and mobility.[41]

Fantasy, mysticism, and insanity preoccupy legions of successful writers whose works collectively suggest a disenchantment with contemporary realities. Whereas the literary fantasies of Kurt Vonnegut continue to make a wild kind of social comment, the spirit of ''Star Trek'' and ''Star Wars'' more nearly summarizes the public interest in pure escape. Jack Finney (in *Time and Again*[42]), Walker Percy (in *Love in the Ruins*[43]), and Thomas Pynchon employ varieties of socially interesting fantasy; but the cult of Tolkien doubtless mirrors a public attitude more clearly.

Madness, one of literature's permanent fixations, seems uncommonly evident these days. Ken Kesey's 1962 novel, *One Flew over the Cuckoo's Nest,* never really reached the public mind until it was released as an award-winning film in 1975.[44] Walker Percy in his first novel (*The Moviegoer*) confronted madness head on.[45] Joyce Carol Oates has made a deservedly high reputation for her craft in depicting the individual's uneasy truces with what are called the facts of life. John C. Gardner, in works like *Sunlight Dialogues* and *Nickel Mountain,* probably comes closest to using ''divine madness'' as a way of transcending earthly dimensions.[46] Except for Kesey's Rabelaisian questionings as to whether true sanity lies inside or outside our mental institutions, these works have very little superficial social relevance.

Mysticism, ever a popular undercurrent, showed again its appeal to the populace in the extraordinary success of *The Exorcist* and related films and novels. Yet another eerie film may be scarcely worth noting; but when a writer such as Saul Bellow, so firmly identified with the earthly dimensions of New York and Chicago, begins to talk (in his Jefferson lecture) and write (in *Humboldt's Gift*) about the dimensions of light and the solace of disengaged contemplation, then the serious literary scene can be said to have suffered another major distraction from its engagement with contemporary reality.[47]

To explain this large and growing quantity of literature which either escaped from social engagement or subjected the culture to drastic abuse, I was only able (in the earlier part of this essay) to wonder whether the writer was being cumulatively oppressed by conformity and mass culture while failing to find an acceptable avenue of dissent. The problem, it has since become clear, goes deeper than even that. The writer has been constructing a kind of negative inventory, enumerating all the things that disturb him—from plastic and pollution to war and racial persecution. At the heart of these discontents lies a value system anchored in an emotional commitment to growth through urban industrialization. In rejecting this root value the writer has identified a generalized target in that insatiable and indiscriminate technology which gave birth to The Bomb while compromising the pristine air, water, and woodlands. In growing numbers of characters, plots, and stanzas, the writer now asks his fellow citizens to protect their sacred individualities against invasions of privacy, pressures of conformity, and lures of consumerism. Rather than responding to the traditional incentives, we are to be cool, open, and undemanding. Realizing that the nation is living through an era of basic value shifts (particularly as values relate to the growth ethic), the writer implicitly concludes his negative inventory with a new license for experimentation. We are to try the alternative modes that appeal to each of us, keeping open the potential access to new patterns and values. Meanwhile, writers as diverse as Tom Wolfe, Saul Bellow, and John Updike have been heard to complain that the mainstream American writer suffers from the lack of hardship, and persecution. Well paid, often idolized, free from censorship, he has lacked that profound and tragic background which has given meaning to many great achievements in the history of literature.

Stylistically literature is still best briefly categorized as experimental. The novel is receiving at least as thorough a redefinition as did poetry under the assault of free verse earlier in the century. Philosophically literature is still concerned with the general position of romanticism and naturalism albeit more critically than in earlier decades. Poetry and fiction, contrary to expectations, may have shifted their relative positions. Verse, frequently diagnosed as moribund, has by no means expired. Although few poets earn riches, their work springs forth from prairie and ghetto, from library and campaign trail. Meanwhile fiction, seemingly secure upon the literary throne, has seen some defections. Energies of prose writers have invested reporting with new dimensions, biography with increasing immediacy. The failure of many of the magazines that made a flourishing marketplace for short fiction may account in part for the relative prominence of various kinds of nonfiction at the expense of the short story and the novel.

Were I to begin this entire essay again, there is but one generalization I would seriously qualify: the one that found current literature, on balance, to be an affirmation of the human condition in the American setting. The balance has been affected by the fact that many kinds of popular literature are less abundant and sunny. Further, although great writers will still be defined by their ability to deal with great moral questions, few examples spring to mind. Of those cited previously, many have gone silent or turned negative or superficial. *Mr. Sammler's Planet* (Saul Bellow), *Gravity's Rainbow* (Thomas Pynchon), and possibly *Sunlight Dialogues* (John C. Gardner) must stand as the only recent works from this group of writers which harbor sustained consideration of the age's large moral issues.[48] Even these works are colored with resignation, shaded with doubts, and tinged with desperation. Yet Mr. Sammler still stands for continuing rediscovery, literally and metaphorically, and for the unquenchable sense of collective human responsibility; and Pynchon's protagonist, possessed and fragmented, is still an American Puritan with a sense of mission. And before the hero of *Humboldt's Gift* retreats into otherworldly contemplation, he remarks, "There's the most extraordinary, unheard-of poetry buried in America, but none of the conventional means known to culture can even begin to extract it" (p. 461). That there are not more examples of substantial minds wrestling imaginatively and positively with the ethics of contemporary life tells more about the age than about its literature. We are indeed undergoing a profound value shift, and literature is only one of many areas of expression which show us rejecting the old, enduring doubt and uncertainty as a necessary prelude to a new affirmation.

Notes

1. *Life* 23 (September 1, 1952): 35–54.

2. New York: Scribner's, 1964. This work was also excerpted in *Life* one month before book publication.

3. New York: Harcourt, Brace, 1957; Boston: Little, Brown, 1962.

4. Herman Melville, *Moby Dick* (New York: Harper, 1851).

5. Walt Whitman, *Leaves of Grass* (New York: n.p., 1855).

6. Boston: Houghton Mifflin, 1952.

7. New York: Doubleday, 1959.

8. New York: Doubleday, 1958.

9. Richard Henry Dana, *Two Years Before the Mast* (New York: Harper, 1840); Harriet Beecher Stowe, *Uncle Tom's Cabin* (Boston: Jewett, 1852), first serialized in *National Era,* Washington, D.C., 1851–52; Henry David Thoreau's famous essay first appeared as "Resistance to Civil Government," in Elizabeth P. Peabody, ed., *Aesthetic Papers* (New York: Putnam, 1849), pp. 189–213.

10. John Steinbeck, *The Grapes of Wrath* (New York: Viking Press, 1939).

11. In *Man with the Hoe and Other Poems* (New York: Doubleday & McClure, 1899).

12. For the many allusions to the fictitious Tilbury Town see *Collected Poems* (New York: Macmillan, 1937); Williams's work appeared in five volumes (New York: New Directions, 1946–58).

13. *Maggie: A Girl of the Streets* (New York: n.p., 1893).

14. Boston: Houghton Mifflin, 1959; New York: Simon and Schuster, 1957.

15. New York: Random House, 1951.

16. New York: Harper, 1940.

17. New York: Macmillan, 1965.

18. New York: Harper & Row, 1962; New York: McGraw-Hill, 1962.

19. London: Heinemann, 1955.

20. New York: Norton, 1958.

21. Upton Sinclair (New York: Doubleday, Page, 1906).

22. New York: Random House, 1939.

23. See note 3.

24. New York: Simon and Schuster, 1961.

25. *Course of American Democratic Thought*, 2nd ed. (New York: Ronald, 1956), Preface.

26. New York: Smith & Haas, 1932; New York: Random House, 1954.

27. New York: Scribner's, 1961.

28. New York: Scribner's, 1926; New York: Scribner's, 1940.

29. New York: Harcourt Brace, 1933; New York: Harcourt Brace, 1942; New York: Harcourt Brace, 1957.

30. New York: Harcourt, Brace, 1948.

31. Herman Wouk, *Caine Mutiny* (New York: Doubleday, 1951); Norman Mailer, *The Naked and the Dead* (New York: Rinehart, 1948); James Jones, *From Here to Eternity* (New York: Scribner's, 1951).

32. See the third stanza of the title poem in *A Coney Island of the Mind* (New York: New Directions, 1958).

33. New York: Knopf, 1958.

34. Crane's work appeared in *The Monster and Other Stories* (New York: Harper, 1899); *The Virginian* (New York: Macmillan, 1902); *Ox-Bow Incident* (New York: Random House, 1940); *Wonderful Country* (Boston: Little, Brown, 1952); the Guthrie trilogy as follows: *Big Sky* (New York: Sloan, 1947), *The Way West* (New York: Sloan, 1949), and *These Thousand Hills* (Boston: Houghton Mifflin, 1956).

35. *Adventures of Augie March* (New York: Viking, 1953); *Henderson the Rain King* (New York: Viking, 1959).

36. Philadelphia: Lippincott, 1963.

37. The speech was delivered November 11, 1950, printed in the *New York Times* (pp. 49–50) of that date and elsewhere.

38. New York: Random House, 1969; New York: Knopf, 1968; New York: Knopf, 1971.

39. "The Taste of It," in *Muse and the Librarian* (Westport, Conn.: Greenwood Press, 1974).

40. Boston: Little, Brown, 1971.

41. New York: Doubleday, 1960; New York: Random House, 1970.

42. New York: Simon and Schuster, 1970.

43. New York: Farrar, Straus & Giroux, 1971.

44. New York: Viking, 1962.

45. New York: Knopf, 1961.

46. New York: Knopf, 1972; New York: Knopf, 1973.

47. New York: Viking, 1975.

48. New York: Viking, 1970; New York: Viking, 1973; New York: Knopf, 1973.

ROBERT A. CORRIGAN

Literature and Politics: The Case of Ezra Pound Reconsidered

Robert A. Corrigan is Provost for Arts and Humanities at the University of Maryland – College Park where he is also Professor of English and American Studies. An American Studies graduate of Brown University and the University of Pennsylvania, he has contributed articles on American Studies and Afro-American Studies to a variety of journals including American Quarterly, American Studies, *and the* Journal of Popular Culture. *Before coming to College Park he was Dean of Arts and Sciences at the University of Missouri – Kansas City, a position he assumed after nine years of teaching in the American Civilization Program of the University of Iowa.*

The twenty-third of March marked the sixty-eighth anniversary of one of literary history's most remarkable but least celebrated events—the invasion of Europe by Ezra Pound.[1] That imaginative, excitable, and extremely talented young Turk who stormed the gates of literary London died in Italy in November 1972, a calm, withdrawn, old man, living out the butt end of his life in a self-imposed vow of public silence. But if the poet's voice was stilled at last, his public's was not; fittingly enough, Pound left the literary world as he had entered it, in a swirl of bitter controversy and angry debate precipitated by the decision of the prestigious American Academy of Arts and Sciences to deny him its coveted Emerson-Thoreau medal.[2] No one can say for sure that Pound desired the prize; so many times in the past such honors had mattered greatly, but often they had been more desperately sought for him by members of that protective coterie of friends and relatives who clustered about in his Italian retreat.[3] It is the relationship of Pound to these associates, the impact of his turbulent career upon his family and friends, and the effects of their well-meaning, if misdirected, efforts in his behalf, that need charting here; not another intricate route through that much surveyed ideomatic jungle he called his *Cantos*.

Those who remember the young Pound recall a slim, fair-haired, six-footer; an intensely handsome man whose good looks brought him great advantage with three generations of female admirers and whose physical size served him well in athletics: hiking through Germany with Ford Madox Ford, sparring with Ernest Hemingway in Paris, fencing with experts in London (and a duelling challenge to an antagonistic amateur literary critic), playing tennis throughout half of England and southern Europe, and demonstrating everywhere he traveled his mastery of the best-known of the indoor sports. Most certainly he was not the shy, weak, effeminate, graceless man of genius so often conjured up for us by the burly opponents of modern verse.

He is remembered as a big man in other ways as well, with so many owing so much to his generosity: the aging W. B. Yeats, whose poetic spirit, renewed by Pound, earned a Nobel prize; the desperate James Joyce, who might have died blind, unknown, and unread in a Trieste hovel were it not for Pound; the ambitious, unpublished, middle-aged, Robert Frost, thrust into literary prominence due to a fortuitous, perhaps calculated, meeting; and most of all, the shy possum, T. S. Eliot, who paid, and some say constantly repaid, that early debt of sustenance, criticism, and friendship for more than forty years. (Pound may have been contemptuous of usury, but no poet ever paid such exorbitant interest charges as did Eliot; perhaps because none was ever so indebted.) The list of his beneficiaries is long, an impressive cortege from the past of writers, painters, musicians, composers, architects and, even, avante-garde film makers. This unequaled record of patronage is well known, of course, partly because his debtors so readily acknowledged the loan, but more often because Pound was so quick to publish the mortgage notice.

Less well known than his magnanimity was a penchant for pettiness which exasperated even the closest of friends. There is, for instance, the case of the elderly philosopher George Santayana, interned throughout the war in Rome, who braved Communists and Fascists, Italians and Germans, Americans and assorted international bureaucrats to visit Pound at the Pisan detention center when not even the poet's family knew he was alive. Presumably Pound was grateful at the time for this courageous gesture of concern, but only acknowledged the visit some years later in conversation with a Washington friend, to whom he confided harshly that in his travels throughout northern Spain he had often run across the name of Santayana—always borne by a Jew.[4] Pound's unpublished letters also reveal a surprising degree of contempt for Archibald MacLeish, the poet whose unselfish fifteen-year campaign saved his life and freed him from St. Elizabeths.[5] As for Robert Frost, the reluctant MacLeish front man who is erroneously praised for engineering Pound's release through his powerful New Hampshire friend, and presidential assistant, Sherman Adams, the only accolade he ever received for his efforts was the laconic aside to reporters: "He ain't been in much of a hurry."[6]

Any attempt to study the history of Pound's endless legendary battles is complicated by the fact that the legends surrounding the battles are equally endless. No other major American writer, with the possible exception of Nathanael West, has ever so manipulated, or had manipulated for him, the basic facts of his life. For example, though actually born in Hailey, Idaho, Pound was only eighteen months old when the family left the raw frontier town in a raging blizzard aboard the train with that now famous rotary snow plow, feeding the infant Ezra kerosene to ward off the croup. What, then, we might ask, is the source of all those early British and European stories about the wild "youngster from the Wild West (who) made his first English appearance wearing a large cowboy hat, and flourishing in his hand a cowboy whip, which he would crack to emphasize his remarks."[7] The "frontier" of this "Dakota Dante" (as poet H. D. once described him)[8] was Philadelphia's Forty-third Street, his "Wild West" being the sedate West Philadelphia faculty neighborhood where the family first settled before moving on to a wealthy suburb. The educational pilgrimage from the exclusive Cheltenham Academy, to the University of Pennsylvania, to Hamilton College, and back to Pennsylvania for an M.A. degree and credit hours enough for a Ph.D. in Romance Languages[9] is hardly the route of an Idaho Christopher Newman; nor are two European tours and six months of college teaching the background expected of a serious rival to that other contemporary London favorite, Buffalo Bill.

Cowboy whip in hand or not, the young Philadelphian who arrived in London in 1908 with a shilling in his pocket and a sheaf of poems under his arm[10] had already established himself as an impetuous, lecherous, argumentative, bohemian willing to pay society's price for his treasured independence; a man quite capable of manufacturing the legends necessary to support a *persona* large enough to take on the Edwardian literary establishment.[11] Described by Richard Aldington as "a small but persistent volcano in the dim levels of London literary society," Pound quickly succeeded in associating himself almost immediately with the major malcontents planning even then the overthrow of the London establishment, and soon he became the revolution's self-appointed leader.[12] Despite an exhibition of all the worst mannerisms of a London music hall parody of the bumptious American,[13] Pound was soon on his way to becoming what Alfred Kazin has called the "Johnny Appleseed of the 'Little Renaissance.'"[14]

Having exhausted Kensington's supply of literary sparring partners, Pound moved on to Paris, and when it became overcrowded with other American expatriate authors, traveled to Italy and Spain, finally to settle in Rapallo, a pleasant little Mediterranean town where he lived and worked until arrested for treason on May 3, 1945. It was at Rapallo in the 1930s that Pound began to propagate his peculiar economic philosophy based on an offshoot Marxist assumption that because civilization depends upon economic influences, and since prosperity is the primary goal of all governments, it is necessary to guarantee this prosperity that governments must manage their own money and not be dependent upon moneylenders, banks, or usurers. For Pound, the backbone of a sound economic system was "social credit," which meant that in times of economic prosperity a nation should not only cease to collect taxes, but actually distribute surplus government funds to its citizens as a national dividend. Increasingly, Pound's belief in the correctness of his economic philosophy became dogmatic; drifting further and further from acceptable Marxist principles, he ceased writing altogether for Communist weeklies and by 1939 had actually become the chief critical target of a number of leftist journalists.[15]

At first Pound seemed to believe that President Franklin Delano Roosevelt could be educated to accept social credit, but as the New Deal wore on, he became convinced that FDR was idealogically the prisoner of those insidious enemies of economic democracy, the Jews, whose influence he doubted had ever been anything but a "stinking curse" to Europe.[16] He became openly hostile to Roosevelt and vicious in his denunciation of the Jews — or "the shitten kikes" as he called them. It has been argued that in his hatred of Jews, distrust of major banking interests, and contempt for federal authority, Pound was simply a populist following in the Western tradition of his birthplace. As early as 1922, he can be found objecting to the prevalence of Jews among the contributors to *Dial* and predicting that within a half-century Caucasians would have been replaced by Jews, blacks, and the Chinese[17] — thus discounting an unfortunate recent assertion that Pound stumbled into anti-Semitism in 1939.[18] The University of Pennsylvania, which he attended for four years, was rife with anti-Semitism, even among the faculty, and there is no reason to expect Wabash, Indiana, was any more tolerant of Jews than of bohemian instructors. Anti-Semitism among Edwardians, so prevalent as to go unquestioned, was a staple ingredient for London music hall comedy. Many of Pound's closest associates — T. S. Eliot and John Quinn, for example — had publicly expressed anti-Semitic sentiments, and the Christian church, he felt, was anti-Semitic by definition![19]

There is, regrettably, nothing intrinsically insane in hating Jews or of advocating social credit, cursing FDR, and even admiring Mussolini's Lion Cubs.[20] But Pound's unpublished correspondence, as well as the personal recollections of his closest friends, would suggest that somewhere in the late 1930s he began to lose touch with reality even as he became more and more convinced of his own power, wisdom, and influence. A strong-minded man, used to getting his own way, partly through sheer charisma, more often by the strength of his convictions and the power with which he presented them, Pound was quite aware of the important role he had played in shaping the careers of many talented people and through them the very structure of modern art. He was personally responsible, by anyone's account, for the success of a score of major literary and artistic figures and generally held to be the most important force in establishing the canon of the new poetry. A legend in his own time, so to speak, he turned to politics and economics, where he discovered his ideas acceptable and, as in literature, often the subject of intense debate on the part of highly intelligent people.

Puzzled as to why the American people did not accept his economic platform, Pound concluded, characteristically, that influential members of Congress and the press, out of stupidity or deceit, had kept the public ignorant of his ideas. To counteract this influence, he sailed to America in 1939, where he strode the halls of the Capitol buttonholing unwary congressmen, arguing his theories, granting interviews with any reporters who cared to listen, and even accepting his first honorary degree from Hamilton College to obtain more publicity for his economic philosophy. Except for the honorary degree, however, the trip was a total disaster: Congressmen wouldn't listen, Roosevelt refused to see him or even answer his letters, and the press generally ignored him. He returned to Italy convinced that the Jews and Roosevelt, having corrupted the American people and blasphemed their heritage, were about to plunge his country into an unconscionable war. He was insistent to the very end of his life that it was to prevent war between Italy and America that in February 1941 he began his famous broadcasts over Radio Rome, directed not at a European audience but at American listeners who had been shielded for too long from his theories by what he considered to be a hostile press, a Jewish conspiracy, and the malevolence of an insane president.[21]

As the months wore on, the content of the broadcasts became increasingly confused and convoluted, the charges more obscene and undocumented, the ideas less and less rational, and the tone more and more hysterical. Imprisoned by his own will in a foreign country officially at war with his native land, Pound began to lose contact with the outside world: The number of incoming letters trickled off, the English language newspapers ceased to arrive, and money was in short supply. What began in February 1941 as an idealist's argument against war became by February 1942 a paid act of propaganda on the part of a dogmatist completely isolated from any modulating influence or contradictory opinion. Radio brought out in him all of the latent egomania his good friends had learned to cope with over the years; with a potential international audience totaling millions, Pound lost all sense of proportion or responsibility.

Then came the shock of Mussolini's capitulation, Pound's desperate winter flight across Italy, and his secret spring return to the Mediterranean.[22] The Germans confiscated his apartment to build harbor fortifications, forcing the Pounds, as enemy aliens, to move into the hills above Rapallo to live with Olga Rudge in her rustic chalet.[23] It was there that he was arrested by the Italian partisans who turned him over to the Allied Army for questioning. By then, Pound was a desperate man filled with hate and fear, an egomaniac believing in the correctness of his own ideas and the malevolence of all government. Exposure in the infamous wire cage at the Pisan detention center certainly did not help his condition, and soon his mental and emotional decline was reinforced by a dramatic physical breakdown. Thus when he was deposited in the tank of the Washington, D.C., jail on November 18, 1945, Ezra Pound was a very sick man.

If Pound was mentally ill in 1945, and there is considerable evidence to suggest that he was, it docs not follow that his friends and family were equally incapacitated. To speak of the "tragedy" of Pound is not simply to describe an individual's solitary downfall, but rather to emphasize the influence of one man's career upon the lives of many; it is to describe the effect of his ideas, his personality, even his irrational fears on those who should have been better prepared to cope with them. By 1945 Pound's fate was fixed, but the political web which was to entangle the lives of so many for so long was just being woven. The tragedy is that the incarceration of Ezra Pound led friends with the otherwise highest of ethical and ideological principles to behave in a harried, secretive, conspiratorial, and often seemingly irrational manner; behavior which succeeded only in prolonging his punishment for an additional decade.

Despite all of his legendary quarrels, Pound still possessed in 1945 a number of very important close friends; always a generous man, both with his time and with his advice, he commanded the loyalty of even those who despised his anti-Semitism and deplored his political values. He had been cut off from a great many of these friends for most of the five years following his return from America and for a year and a half his actual whereabouts was known to only a handful of very close friends and relatives; indeed, a number of people gratuitously assumed he was dead. The circumstances of both his capture and subsequent imprisonment, particularly his being held incommunicado for months, contributed greatly to the anxiety of these friends and relatives.[24] In addition, the combination of American anti-Fascist sentiment, the newly discovered enormity of the horrors of the concentration camps, the fierceness of the Marxist journalistic assault on Pound,[25] and the British execution of two radio propagandists, John Amery and William Joyce, increased this tension almost to the point of hysteria. There were, as well, great psychological implications in Pound's transfer from Italy to Washington, a move which took him from the company of loyal friends and family and put him at the mercy of a tasteless assortment of political camp followers, publicity-seeking self-styled poets, racist civil servants, and literary psychopaths. Pound's London friends thought of them as half-baked literary parasites who were not really concerned with straightening out the legal tangle because they liked having him in Washington and knew that if freed he would return to Italy.[26]

This sense of isolation and separation, felt both by Pound and by family and friends, is crucial to an understanding of the Pound tragedy. Ezra Pound, it is to be remembered, had not resided in the United States for over thirty years and, except for that very brief trip in 1939, had been a stranger to the land of his birth until returned in handcuffs on November 18th. Dorothy Pound, who had exchanged British citizenship for American upon her marriage in 1914, had never seen her adopted land until she arrived in the summer of 1946 to comfort her institutionalized husband.[27] Both children, Mary and Omar, though American citizens, had never even visited their homeland. Left behind were all those solid European friendships developed over a twenty-year residence in Italy, including such British associates as T. S. Eliot, Ronald Duncan, Wyndham Lewis, John Drummond, and countless others the Pounds had come to trust during thirty years of marriage.

In America, to be sure, there were William Carlos Williams, E. E. Cummings, James Laughlin, Marianne Moore, H. L. Mencken, and Archibald MacLeish, but until his wife's arrival, Pound saw virtually no one but psychiatrists and legal counsel. Because Dorothy Pound's passport had expired in 1941 and all of her funds had been impounded by the British government under the alien property act, it took several months of negotiations to get to the United States. For months after her arrival she was often her husband's only visitor, and then for only fifteen minutes per day. Finally in 1947, after five hundred days in the very restrictive Howard Hall, Pound was moved to the less confining Chestnut Ward, where not only could Dorothy visit him daily for three hours at a time, but friends were welcome as well. Some, like H. L. Mencken,[28] came right away; others, like Archibald MacLeish, waited ten years;[29] a few, like Ernest Hemingway and Robert Frost, never made it at all. Most of his closest friends, however, were in Europe, and he had yet to acquire that entourage of "literary parasites" who became so visible in the 1950s.

The principal, if highly irrational, fear of Pound's friends in 1945 was that he would be tried for treason, found guilty, and executed; the Christmas Eve *New Masses* symposium recommending he be shot for treason did little to ease their minds. World War I precedent, later confirmed by the generous treatment accorded Axis Sally and Tokyo Rose, suggested that the most he would get was a jail sentence, but the fear remained. The diagnosis of insanity, concurred in by the four psychiatrists, at least brought some respite.

None of his friends seemed alert enough, at the time, to question the wisdom of the legal strategy of declaring Pound insane at the point of the trial rather than on the occasion of the alleged crime, probably because they believed it merely the first of several legal maneuvers which would eventually free Pound without a trial. Certainly Pound's lawyer, Julian Cornell, convinced those closest to the poet that the indictment would be dropped, the old man declared harmless, and released from custody.[30] Eventually, it was believed, the four psychiatrists would state more clearly that he was not in control of his senses at the time the broadcasts were made, thus clearing his character with the American public.[31] There was some fear that Pound might fight the insanity plea, but even he was convinced how hopeless would be the job of attempting to make "stupid" jurors understand what his life and work had been about.[32] The debilitating influences of eight months' incarceration had taken its toll, and Pound unquestioningly placed his future in the hands of those he was forced to trust; he could speak rationally about matters literary or economic but, according to friends, broke down completely when questioned about his own predicament.[33] The plan, then, was to wait until a decent interval had elapsed while Julian Cornell worked on the psychiatrists to produce an affidavit affirming that they considered his condition would not improve, at which point the lawyer could move to have the indictment dropped on the basis of the statute of limitations and the fact that the prosecution had shown no guilt.[34]

Perhaps a lawyer more experienced in such matters than Cornell could have foreseen in 1945 that this would lead to Pound's imprisonment in St. Elizabeths for almost thirteen years — longer than most of the German war criminals convicted at Nuremburg served in European prisons — but poets, publishers, and frantic family could hardly be expected to possess such legal omniscience. Had Pound been declared insane at the time of the crime, he would have been hospitalized in St. Elizabeths only until he was declared sane, at which time he would have been released and never required to stand trial on the treason charges. The unfortunate result of Cornell's plea was to keep the threat of a treason trial hanging over Pound's head for the entire thirteen years of his incarceration, which, in turn, led to all of the notorious indecision on the part of Julian Cornell, Dorothy Pound, and even Ezra Pound, and provoked much of the confusion, anxiety, and distrust on the part of their overseas friends. Even worse, it led to an embarrassing stalemate with the U.S. Attorney General's office, which did not wish to prosecute Pound in 1958 and ultimately to the final degradation which made Pound the legal ward of his wife to the very hour of his death.

Over the years, questions have been raised as to the accuracy of the psychiatric diagnosis of a "paranoid state in a psychopathic personality," and it is generally assumed that this was just a legal dodge on the part of government lawyers and defense counsel alike. But one of Pound's closest associates during this ordeal confided to T. S. Eliot his own fear that the judgment was all too accurate. Pound, he explained, could not understand why the Jews hated him, since he had had in mind a plan for resurrecting their old temple in Jerusalem. Moreover, he insisted that war never would have occurred if the world's leaders had read, understood, and acted upon his "translation" of the Confuscius. The latter belief, according to the psychiatrists, was a symptom of delusions of grandeur. Evidence of hypochondria was seen in continual complaints of being exhausted, despite physical tests which confirmed his sound health and strong condition for a man his age. His inability to pursue a subject for more than a few sentences was a sign of distractability, and confabulation was evidenced in his invention of things in the past which had never happened. All were considered classic symptoms of a paranoid state by the psychiatrists, and Pound's friend, despite himself, concurred in their judgment.[35]

The organized attempt to free Pound can be traced back to discussions held before he was even captured; at least as early as January 3, 1945, when T. S. Eliot disclosed to the Pound's family lawyer, A. V. Moore, that Omar Pound had borrowed a copy of *Jefferson and/or Mussolini* in order to determine if there was something in it which could be used to his father's advantage.[36] Although Pound had been indicted for treason by a federal jury in July 1943, Moore had not yet seen the indictment nor had he seen a transcript of the broadcasts from Italy; thus, he was not sure what action to take or even under whose jurisdiction Pound would be tried. Nevertheless he believed, as did Eliot, that Pound's friends should be prepared to come to his assistance. Beginning with this exchange of letters, T. S. Eliot became the invisible force behind the thirteen-year effort to bring about Pound's release. Working behind the scenes from London, "Ol Possum," as Pound called him, was never identified publicly with the campaign until the unexpected fierceness of the 1949 debate over the Bollingen Prize brought out his involvement.

Friends other than T. S. Eliot and A. V. Moore were also concerned about Pound prior to his capture; some Americans, fearful of his fate at the hands of the federal government, even wrote to U.S. Attorney General Biddle urging a pardon on the grounds of his international standing as a poet. One such letter, protesting the association of Pound ("whose deathless poetry was near to madness") with the names of completely rational traitors, came to the attention of Malcolm Cowley, who published it, not to embarrass Pound, but because he objected to what such statements implied about Pound in particular and poets in general. Pound was a man, not a child, argued Cowley, and poet or not, he should be held responsible for his actions just as any other man would be; to pardon him would be an affront to all other artists: "I want to see Pound and all other poets keep their human dignity. If they have to be punished in order to keep it, then let them be punished, but no more severely than their acts merit."[37] A somewhat different response came from poet Rolphe Humphries, who asked: "If we accept the premise that Pound, being a traitor and a good poet, should be pardoned the vice of being the former by the virtue of being the latter, what conclusion should we reach concerning those who are bad poets and aggressive patriots? Should they be shot or hanged? I have in mind certain individuals, nameless for the moment, who ought to be doing quite a little worrying until this matter is settled."[38] In general, those responsible critics and poets not emotionally attached to Pound shared Cowley's position that punishment was deserved but not execution or a very lengthy prison sentence. There were, of course, exceptions such as Louis Untermeyer's proposal of "life imprisonment in a cell surrounded by books— all of them copies of the works of Edgar A. Guest,"[39] or a callous classics professor's recommendation that Pound be executed, not for treason, but for the errors of his translations.[40] Despite such occasional insensitivity, the seriousness of Pound's predicament was generally recognized, even by those who privately condemned the insanity plea as a legal maneuver which, as poets and critics, they greatly resented.

Pleased as they were by the psychiatrists' verdict, Pound's strategists still feared that some of his close friends would find it a hard judgment to accept.[41] Such was Cornell's concern in writing to Dorothy Pound about the upcoming formal hearing to determine whether her husband's paranoid state would permit him to stand trial. Confident that the result was a foregone conclusion, Cornell predicted, ironically enough, that within a matter of months, the whole affair would be over and her husband set free. His strategy called for having Pound released quietly on bail and secretly transferred to a private sanitorium, eventually to be released and sent home to live with his family.[42] T. S. Eliot had even written Dorothy to suggest the conditions for which she might check in seeking a suitable private hospital for her husband.[43] But bail, to their surprise, was denied, and Pound once more was remanded to St. Elizabeths to be held until the hospital psychiatrists considered him well enough to stand trial.

Once the shock of this unexpected decision had worn off, Pound's friends consulted again by mail and agreed to refrain from further activity until the conclusion of the 1946 congressional election in order to prevent the controversial poet from becoming a campaign issue.[44] After the election, Cornell prepared a petition for Pound's release from St. Elizabeths on the grounds that he was harmless, even though paranoid, and further confinement in a federal institution would be injurious to his mental health. Hearing of this plan from a reporter, Assistant U.S. Attorney General Theron Caudle vowed that should the maneuver succeed, he would start immediate proceedings to have the poet brought to trial on the treason indictment.[45] The *PM* columnist who provided Caudle with his information was Albert Deutsch, the very same reporter whose widely reprinted reports of the 1946 insanity hearings had been "bitterly excoriated" by Julian Cornell, who believed that such unwelcome publicity prevented the government from quietly dropping the charges against his client.[46] Caudle did not have to make good his threat, however, since Judge Bolitha J. Laws rejected the bid for bail. At this point, Cornell wished to appeal — all the way to the Supreme Court if necessary — but on March 13, 1948, Dorothy Pound requested that he drop all such plans.[47] To all extents and purposes, this ended legal action for almost ten years. The family was determined to explore another route.[48]

Initial responsibility for planning the campaign to release Pound through the reestablishment of his literary reputation appears to have rested with T. S. Eliot in London and Pound's American publisher. Agreeing that the great publicity given to Pound's alleged treason needed to be offset by a campaign to revive his literary reputation, they speculated as to whether fascism's chief literary opponent, Ernest Hemingway, would state publicly what he had admitted in private, that he could not condemn the actions for which the poet was not mentally responsible.[49] But although Hemingway did put such an opinion into a letter to Charles Norman, he did not allow it to be printed, nor would he agree to being quoted on the subject of Pound's "crime" for several years. Another part of the noncourtroom strategy was to influence well-known literary critics, at home and abroad, to write favorably of Pound's verse and to persuade the better little magazines to commission articles praising his poetry and even to devote special issues to his work.

The major problem faced by the strategists was that critical interest in Ezra Pound's poetry had declined greatly during the 1930s, to such an extent in fact that the 1940 publication of his new *Cantos* provoked only a smattering of reviews; indeed his publisher even thought it necessary to include two articles on his poetry for inclusion with half of the copies of the book sold.[50] Major public attention from 1940 to 1947 was with his politics, not his verse; in the six and a half years from 1940 to September 1946, for example, there was only one major nonpolitical article published — and that was highly critical of his verse.[51] But beginning with T. S. Eliot's famous 1946 *Poetry* essay[52] and the 1947 Pound section of the *Yale Poetry Review* — one of the better little magazines referred to by Eliot and others[53] — and continuing through the special *Quarterly Review of Literature* issue,[54] a reawakening of interest in Pound on the part of both critics and editors is clearly evident. Naturally such attention was partially the result of the publicity accorded his wartime activities, but to a greater extent than might be expected it reflected the influence of the effort to improve the poet's image; a movement which gained in strength when the Pound family realized that, although the immediate threat of execution had passed, he still faced the dismal prospect of life imprisonment in St. Elizabeths unless something were done to interest influential people in his release.

There can be no question that Pound's work was richly deserving of critical reevaluation; nor can it be denied that he had had more than his share of unfavorable publicity. The charge that the government handled him with kid gloves because of his literary standing is balanced by the knowledge that his rough treatment in the press was also due to his status as a well-known poet. Little attention was given to the other seven "radio traitors" indicted with Pound in 1943;[55] whatever dishonor they suffered was largely private. But Pound was tried, as it were, in the public arena, and it was there that his defenders sought to clear his name.

If a good deal of the favorable criticism published was inspired by this need to refurbish the image of Pound as poet, much of it, nevertheless, was worthwhile; Eliot's 1946 essay is a superb piece of writing, a rich informative study. Nor are those earnest, if tentative, probings in the *Yale Poetry Review* to be dismissed; and if D. D. Paige's motives for putting together the special Pound issue of the *Quarterly Review of Literature* (with Pound's autobiography, and contributions by Paige, Wyndham Lewis, and Marianne Moore) are questionable, the quality of these essays must still be acknowledged. On the other hand, little of the material appearing in special journals devoted to Poundian theories started by the young converts who surrounded "grampaw" at St. Elizabeths is today worth the attention of the serious student of literature. Nor does the work of many of the young critics and scholars drawn to Washington by Dorothy and Omar Pound have much to recommend it; a monument to the absurdity of politically motivated biography, surely, is the Eustace Mullins study of Pound, a tissue of fabrication, innuendo, and outright bigotry.[56] There is also John Kasper, the misguided racist from New York who spent two years in a federal penitentiary for interfering with the integration of the Tennessee schools.[57] Not all of the members of the Pound circle, to be sure, were as objectionable as Mullins and Kasper. They were sincere in making a study of the poet's life work their chief enterprise and the teaching of his philosophy their major obligation. But few were able to separate their concern for the fate of the man from their assessment of the value of his work.

An interesting case in point is the young University of Pennsylvania graduate and Wellesley College English instructor, D. D. Paige, who first learned of Pound's predicament from Theodore Spencer at a reception following a lecture by T. S. Eliot. One of the first to make the requisite Washington pilgrimage to gain the confidence of the Pound circle, Paige volunteered to undertake the most ambitious project of all — an edition of Pound's letters which would indicate to the public at large the immensity of his contribution to literature and inspire a whole new generation of scholars. Paige's typescripts of Pound's letters not only confirm that he neglected to publish the complete texts of the originals, as he readily admits in his introduction, but prove that the material which was routinely deleted were statements of opinions most likely to alienate a public already sensitive to his unpopular political and social positions.[58] Thus, there are no anti-Jewish comments in the letter to Hemingway on banking, none of the typical anti-Semitic jibes in letters to Louis Zukofsky,[59] no antireligious statements in the exchange with the Reverend Henry Swabey,[60] nor the texts of such contempt-ible letters as the one to William Carlos Williams comparing the horrors of the Spanish Civil War to the necessary draining of a swamp.[61] Paige's edition of *The Letters of Ezra Pound* is, in retrospect, a very disappointing book; not only because of the deletions the editor thought politic to make, but because a generation of literary scholars has incorrectly assumed that the scholarship was sound and the book a sincere attempt to present a representative collection of Pound's letters. To be sure, the collection does illustrate Pound's literary mind at its best; as Mark Van Doren observed in his preface, it was worth publishing if only for the Eliot-Pound exchange on the manuscript of *The Wasteland*. But as an accurate reflection of Pound's social, political, and economic thought or as a historical-cultural document, the volume is very inadequate, reflecting as it does the fears of the St. Elizabeths circle that the public was not prepared to tolerate an uncensored Ezra Pound.

Fittingly enough, the early St. Elizabethan period ended with the celebrated fracas over Pound's winning of the 1949 Bollingen Prize in Poetry for *The Pisan Cantos,* written in 1945 while he was imprisoned in Italy and published in 1948 by New Directions while he was incarcerated in a mental institution.[62] Given under auspices of a Library of Congress Committee chosen to honor the best volume of verse published in America by an American, the award was roundly criticized for ignoring the anti-American and anti-Semitic content of some of the poetry. In retrospect, it seems obvious that the award was politically motivated, as many of its detractors had maintained, the culmination of the combined efforts of T. S. Eliot and Pound's publisher to win back his lost respectability and, ultimately, his freedom. The publisher of *The Pisan Cantos,* after all, had had the manuscript in its possession since 1945 but chose to delay publishing until

1948;[63] and Eliot was Pound's chief advocate on the Library of Congress jury, his public protestations to the contrary notwithstanding. Longtime supporters of Pound on the original jury or appointed during the controversy were Conrad Aiken, Allen Tate, W. H. Auden, Robert Lowell, Theodore Spencer, Archibald MacLeish, and William Carlos Williams. They seem to have completely underestimated possible public reaction, for instead of generating sympathy for Pound and contributing to the campaign to bring about his release, the award instigated the most intense and prolonged debate over Pound since his arrest in 1945, making him such a controversial figure and bringing such negative criticism of his poetry that another decade was to pass before his freedom could be obtained.

Whether or not Pound was guilty of treason, thirteen years in St. Elizabeths was a harsh punishment under the circumstances, and the question therefore remains as to who should be held responsible for this miscarriage of justice. Consider the conditions which helped to shape the poet's own attitude in that crucial period: after nearly two years of fleeing from Germans, Italian partisans, Allied Forces, and Communists, he was physically and mentally exhausted when finally captured. Pushed from one detention area to another, exposed to the humiliation of his animal-like confinement in a cage, surrounded by murderers, rapists, and the worst possible criminal element in the whole European theater, he was nearly out of his mind from exposure, loneliness, and fear. Handcuffed in a jeep for an all-night trip to Rome and a sleepless military flight to Washington, he arrived in America suffering from shock and exhaustion to be greeted by the angry voices or the cold avoidance of former friends and the public debate over whether he should be shot for treason. Attacked in the press as a traitor and the willing associate of history's foulest murderers, he was thrown into a jail bullpen, locked up with maniacs, deprived of the stable influence of family and friends, and sought out increasingly by those who were themselves as wild and as irrational as he had ever been.

Or take the situation of Dorothy Pound: a quiet, dependent woman who had lived for thirty years in the shadow of the tall, gaunt, domineering man who was her husband; forced to face alone and penniless the cold officialdom of both the American Consulate Service and the British Foreign Service for months on end as they debated whether she should be allowed to go to her husband's side. For five months, he had been a prisoner without her even knowing where he was, let alone if he were still alive.[64] From America she received conflicting reports as to his fate: Was he to be hanged, electrocuted, or committed to an insane asylum for life? Once in America, a stranger in her new country, there was the loneliness of a rented room broken only by the fifteen minutes spent each day with her imprisoned husband in the shadows of iron bars, within the sight of uniformed guards, and amid Howard Hall's frightening collection of lunatics and criminals.

It is not surprising, therefore, that both Dorothy and Ezra Pound should have hesitated to leave the newly acquired security of the Chestnut Ward for the strange hostility and experienced hatred of the savage world outside the brick walls of St. Elizabeths. They saw only anger expressed in the daily press, and, with fear their constant companion, they tried desperately to analyze the situation, fearful all the while that Pound would become the political pawn in someone's election campaign. Fear, confusion, and alienation prevented the once proud Pounds from seeking an intelligent, unemotional solution to their predicament, and thus the famed poet was obliged to spend that extra decade in captivity, almost forgotten by the hostile public for most of that time.

It is not accurate, either, to blame the Justice Department or the U.S. Army for Pound's fate. Despite horror stories circulated by his U.S. friends, Pound was, except for the first two weeks, extremely well treated in the Pisan camp; if no other evidence were available, the completion of eleven new cantos during this time would support this contention. His own letters are filled with praise for the agent who conducted the investigation, and Justice Department files suggest the thoroughness with which the case was prepared. It was not government action, or inaction, that caused the problem.

Although no single individual or group is wholly to blame, some attention should be given to assessing the attitudes of those closest to Pound during the early imprisonment. What they shared, it seems in retrospect, was his contempt for American government, the U.S. people, their legal system, and even, in some instances, tragically enough, his attitude to her Jewish citizens.[65] Instead of relying upon the courts for a just verdict, his advisers concluded that they should circumvent due process and arrange for his quiet release. The insanity plea, whether justified or not, was merely a subterfuge to gain time while they masterminded the behind-the-scenes activity. The charge that special attention was accorded Pound due to his reputation was only half true; it did not matter to the prosecution, but it was crucial to the defense. Deliberately, they set about to resurrect his almost dead reputation in an attempt to justify his release to the public. It is the supreme irony that the culmination of this effort, the Bollingen Prize, should have been the act which led to the final tragedy, that one man paid such a harsh penalty for a guilt shared by so many.

Notes

1. See Dorothy Pound, *Etruscan Gate* (Exeter, Private Publication, 1971), p. 2; notebook passage indicating that on March 23, 1909, EP took her and her mother to tea after a concert to celebrate the anniversary of his landing in Europe.

2. See Robert Reinhold, "Ezra Pound Is Focus of New Dispute," *New York Times*, July 5, 1972, Section 1, p. 29; "Pound's Prize," July 17, 1972, p. 10; L.V.D., "Veto of Academy's Award to Ezra Pound Stirs a Bitter Debate Among Scholars," *Chronicle of Higher Education*, October 2, 1972, p. 3; and Irving Howe, "The Return of the Case of Ezra Pound," *World*, October 24, 1972, pp. 20–24.

3. The latest critic to honor EP with a book, for example, had not only speculated openly about a campaign to get him the Nobel *Peace* Prize, but had even intimated to her secular friends that his Holiness the Pope might be prevailed upon to consider canonization.

4. From an unpublished memoir in the manuscript division of the Library of Congress.

5. See for example Dorothy Pound's letter to Ronald Duncan, October 5, 1947, quoting EP that "The MacLeish level of Kulchur is not high enough to fool the world."

6. See interview in the Washington *Daily News,* April 30, 1958, and quoted in Eustace Mullins, *This Difficult Individual, Ezra Pound* (New York: Fleet Publishing Corporation, 1961), p. 196.

7. Logan Persall Smith, *Milton and His Modern Critics* (Boston: Little, Brown and Company, 1941), p. 10, claims to have received this information from EP's first English publisher, Elkin Mathews.

8. Hilda Doolittle, *Bid Me To Live* (New York: Grove Press, 1960), p. 41.

9. Emily Mitchell Wallace, "Penn's Poet Friends," Pennsylvania *Gazette* (February 1973), p. 35. Ms. Wallace also discovered that EP had failed a graduate course—literary criticism!

10. Mary Dixon Thayer, "Ezra Pound's Father Tells How Son Went to London with a Shilling and Found Fame," Philadelphia *Bulletin,* February 20, 1928, p. 12.

11. A case in point is the legend (or legends) about Pound's mid-year dismissal from the faculty of Indiana's Wabash College. Pound provides two versions, both of which recount an evening walk in which he was accosted by a stranded dancer who needed a place to stay the night. (The two versions differ as to whether she was a ballet dancer or a burlesque queen.) Pound generously offered the destitute dancer his own bed, chivalrously spending the night asleep in a chair, but went off to teach his morning class leaving the girl in his bed where she was quickly discovered by his spinster landladies. The girl *may* have been a dancer and she was undoubtedly discovered in his bed, but the rest is fabrication; his guest was actually a resident of the same rooming house, and this particular incident had been the last in a series of nocturnal events which led to his discharge from both the respectable boarding house and ultraconservative college.

12. Reported in Richard Aldington, in "Des Imagistes," *Saturday Review of Literature,* March 16, 1940, pp. 3, 4; "A Farewell to Europe," *Atlantic,* October 1940, 518–29; and *Life for Life's Sake* (New York: Viking Press, 1941).

13. See, for example, the much quoted salute by C. L. Graves and E. U. Lucas, "Mr. Welkin Mark's New Poet," *Punch,* June 23, 1909, p. 449: "Mr. Wilkin Mark (exactly opposite Long Jane's) begs to announce that he has secured for the English market the palpitating works of the new Montana (U.S.A.) poet, Mr. Ezekial Ton, who is the most remarkable thing in poetry since Robert Browning. Mr. Ton who has left America to reside for a while in London and impress his personality on English editors, publishers and readers, is by far the newest poet going, whatever other advertisements may say. He has succeeded, where all others have failed, in evolving a blend of the imagery of the unfettered West, the vocabulary of Wardour Street and the sinister abandon of Borgiac Italy."

14. Alfred Kazin, *On Native Grounds* (New York: Harcourt, Brace & World, 1942), p. 403.

15. The *New Masses* started to attack EP as early as September 1931, with an open letter from Mike Gold. See also attacks on April 10, 1934, and March 17, 1936. On December 11, 1945, Isidor Schneider published his "Traitor or Holy Idiot?" in the same journal, and two weeks later it came out with its infamous symposium "Should Ezra Pound Be Shot?" See also Donald McKenzie, "T(h)inker Pound and Other Italian Legends," *The Left* 1 (Summer and Autumn 1931): 48–52.

16. Letter to Wydham Lewis, February 1949, in the Beineke Library, Yale University.

17. Letter to Mr. Jeanne Robert Foster, February 2, 1922, in the Houghton Library, Harvard University.

18. Hugh Kenner, "Incurious Biography," *The New Republic,* October 17, 1970, pp. 30–32.

19. See, for example, T. S. Eliot, *After Strange Gods:* " . . . reasons of race and religion combine to make any large number of free-thinking jews undesirable." See also John Quinn, letter to Mary Maguire Column, January 3, 1919, in the Humanities Research Center, University of Texas: "I used to hate Germany and the Germans beyond words. Now I despise them beyond words. I have nothing but loathing and contempt for their whining and for all the low instincts that make the lowest of the low Jews contemptible."

20. On several different occasions EP reported to friends that he had told Mussolini at their meeting that the only thing he envied about him was the cubs. See, for example, letter to Ronald Duncan, May 8, 1946, Beineke Library, Yale University. On the other hand, T. S. Eliot wrote to Virginia Woolf on April 17, 1936, that he writes "sarcastic letters about Mussolini to Ezra Pound"— presumably to provoke him. See letter in the Berg Collection, New York Public Library.

21. See my "Ezra Pound and the Italian Ministry for Popular Culture," *Journal of Popular Culture* (Spring 1972), pp. 767–81, for a detailed discussion.

22. See Harry M. Meacham, *The Caged Panther* (New York: Twayne, 1967), for Dorothy Pound's version of the events, and Mary de Rachewiltz, *Discretions* (Boston: New Directions, 1971), for his daughter's. There are also unpublished letters at the University of Texas that bear upon this subject.

23. For a year or more, all of them — husband, wife, and mistress — lived together, and had the poet's mother not been so old and feeble, she might have left her Rapallo flat to join them in literary history's most remarkable ménage. Dorothy did manage a weekly trip into town to visit her "ma-in-law" as she called Isabel Pound, and it was during one such absence that those rough partisans took EP prisoner and trundled him off to Genoa for questioning by the Allied command.

24. See letter from Dorothy Pound to E. E. Cummings, November 4, 1945, Beineke Library, Yale University: "I am now allowed to communicate with my good man and he to receive letters from outside. . . . He is thankful for *any* news after five months in communicado . . . . I have been allowed one visit, after five months of not knowing where he was."

25. "Should Ezra Pound Be Shot?" *New Masses,* December 25, 1945, pp. 4–6. For a discussion, see my article *"What's My Line:* Bennett Cerf, Ezra Pound and the *American* Poet," *American Quarterly* 34 (March 1972): 101–13.

26. Ronald Duncan, Letter to John Drummond, May 4, 1948, Humanities Research Center, University of Texas.

27. Arthur V. Moore, Letter to Ronald Duncan, February 20, 1946, Humanities Research Center, University of Texas, indicates she was to sail on February 25. But EP reports the ship's name in a letter to Eileen Lane Kenney dated July 3, 1946, in Beineke Library, Yale University: "D. is reported to have sailed. . . . " Noel Stock, *The Life of Ezra Pound* (New York: Pantheon Books, 1970), p. 420, indicates her passport was finally renewed in June 1946 and that by July 14 she had visited her husband twice. Julien Cornell, *The Trial of Ezra Pound* (New York: John Day, 1966), p. 50, says she sailed in June.

28. In a letter to D. D. Paige, May 20, 1947, Beineke Library, Yale University, Pound says "Mencken wrote year before last on my arriv.— came here with 5 lb. cand and a stack of books . . . . "

29. According to correspondence in the Humanities Research Center, University of Texas.

30. James Laughlin, Letter to T. S. Eliot, December 23, 1945, Humanities Research Center, University of Texas.

31. Ibid.

32. Ibid.

33. Arthur V. Moore, Letter to Ronald Duncan, December 19, 1945, Humanities Research Center, University of Texas.

34. James Laughlin, Letter to T. S. Eliot, February 15, 1946, Humanities Research Center, University of Texas.

35. Ibid.

36. T. S. Eliot, Letter to A. V. Moore, January 3, 1945, Humanities Research Center, University of Texas. Moore wrote back to Eliot on January 6.

37. Malcolm Cowley, "Books and People," *New Republic,* November 15, 1943, pp. 689–90.

38. Rolphe Humphries, "Poets, Traitors and Patriots," *New Republic,* November 29, 1943, p. 748.

39. Louis Untermeyer, Letter to Charles Norman, October 8, 1945, Van Pelt Library, University of Pennsylvania; published in Charles Norman, "Ezra Pound," *PM,* November 15, 1945, p. 17, but not reprinted in Charles Norman, *The Case of Ezra Pound* (New York: Bodley Press, 1948).

40. Clarence A. Forbes, "Ezra Pound and Sextus Propertuis," *Classical Journal,* 42 (December 1946): 177–79.

41. James Laughlin, "Letter to T. S. Eliot," December 23, 1945, Humanities Research Center, University of Texas.

42. See Julien Cornell, *The Trial of Ezra Pound*.

43. T. S. Eliot, Letter to Dorothy Pound, November 13, 1946, Humanities Research Center, University of Texas.

44. Ibid.

45. Albert Deutsch, "Ezra Pound, Turncoat Poet, Seeks Release From Federal Mental Hospital," *PM*, January 25, 1947, pp, 1. 24.

46. See Albert Deutsch, "Pound Gets 'Unsound Mind' Verdict, Escapes Trial," *PM*, February 14, 1946, p. 7.

47. Dorothy Pound, Letter to Julian Cornell, March 13, 1948, in *The Trial of Ezra Pound*, p. 67.

48. This does not mean, however, that Pound's English friends were to give up the legal procedures; they continued to press for court action.

49. James Laughlin, Letter to T. S. Eliot, December 23, 1945, Humanities Research Center, University of Texas. Hemingway made quite a splash, however, in December 1954 on the occasion of his winning of the Nobel Prize for literature when he mentioned it was "a good year to release poets." See "An American Storyteller," *Time*, December 13, 1954, p. 72.

50. Ezra Pound, *Cantos LII – LXXI*, Norfolk, 1940. Actually there were 1,000 copies printed but only the first 500 contained the pamphlet, *Notes on Ezra Pound's Cantos: Structure and Metric*, consisting of two essays "Notes on the Cantos" by HH (James Laughlin) and "Notes on the Versification of the Cantos," by SD (Delmore Schwartz). See Donald Gallup, *A Bibliography of Ezra Pound* (London: Hart-Davis, 1963), pp. 90 – 91.

51. Hyatt H. Waggoner, "The Legend of Ezra Pound," *University of Kansas City Review* (Summer 1944): 275–85. See also, Elizabeth Delehanty, "Day with Ezra Pound" (New York, April 13, 1940), pp. 76–77; "Weston," *New Yorker* 19 (August 14, 1943): 16–17; Douglass MacPherson, "Ezra Pound of Wyncote," *Arts in Philadelphia* (May 1940): 10–28, is a historical piece written by a friend of EP.

52. T. S. Eliot, "Ezra Pound," *Poetry* 68 (September 1946): 326–38. The same issue contained George Dillon, "A Note on the Obvious," and R. P. Blackmur, "An Adjunct of the Muses' Diadem: A Note on E.P.," pp. 338–46, and J. V. Healy, "Addendum," pp. 347–49.

53. Edited by Rolfe Fjelde, issue no. 6 contained EP's Canto LXXXIII, and two articles: H. H. Watts, "Pound's Cantos: Means to an End," pp. 9 – 20, and Laurence Richardson, "Ezra Pound's Homage to Propertius," pp. 21 – 29.

54. Edited with an editorial note by D. D. Paige, *Quarterly Review of Literature* 5 (November 2, 1949) contains three EP poems and his "Indiscretions," plus: Wydham Lewis, "Ezra: The Portrait of a Personality"; Harold H. Watts, "The Devices of Pound's Cantos"; Richard Eberhart, "Pound's New Cantos"; and Ray B. West, Jr., "Pound and Contemporary Criticism."

55. Edward Delaney, Constance Drexel, Jane Anderson, Max Kolschwitz, Robert Best, Douglas Chandler, and Frederick Kaltenbach.

56. Eustace Mullens, *This Difficult Individual Ezra Pound* (New York: Fleet Publishing Corporation, 1961).

57. See Arthur Gordon, "Intruder in the South," *Look*, February 19, 1957, pp. 27 – 31.

58. D. D. Paige, *The Letters of Ezra Pound 1907 – 41* (New York: New Directions, 1950). At least one reviewer, "Instruction from Mr. Pound," Times Literary Supplement, September 21, 1951, p. 595, considered this a mistake, since the "inclusion of such letters . . . would have helped Mr. Pound and his numerous supporters to uphold his innocence . . . . "

59. It was in response to one such letter in 1938 that Zukofsky wrote to Pound: "There hasn't been a feud in these parts and thousands of innocent Americans have not been killed because of the crimes of Messrs. Dupont, Rockefeller, Morgan, etc. On the other hand, if Coughlin seconded by yourself continue to mention the names of Kahn, Rothschild, etc. to the same innocent Americans, one foresees a program in N.Y.C. in 1 year or less, in which thousands of innocent Jews will be killed." Louis Zukofsky, Letter to Ezra Pound, December 14, 1938, Humanities Research Center, University of Texas.

60. See, for example, Ezra Pound's letter to Henry Swabey, February 28, 1940: "Prot/ism was

a new bilge — wave from the Jew scriptures, I think O.T. is probably an over-willing fountain of pus.''

61. Paige includes no letters from EP to Williams written after 1931, nor do the Paige typescripts at Yale contain any letters to Williams between 1940 and 1947.

62. Ezra Pound, *The Pisan Cantos* (New York: New Directions, 1948). It was published by New Directions on July 30, 1948, in a printing of 1,525. A second impression of 1,023 copies was issued in June 1949. Faber and Faber issued a British edition of 1,976 copies on July 22, 1949. See Donald Gallup, *A Bibliography of Ezra Pound* (London: Oxford University Press, 1963), pp. 103 – 4.

63. See, for example, Dorothy Pound's letter to Ronald Duncan, December 21, 1945, indicating that twenty pages of typescript were sent to Laughlin of New Directions and to T. S. Eliot at Faber and Faber on December 20.

64. See Dorothy Pound, Letter to E. E. Cummings, November 4, 1945, Houghton Library, Harvard University.

65. See, for example, Letter to T. S. Eliot, December 23, 1945, Humanities Research Center, University of Texas, in which a close associate of Pound's describes the chief government lawyer, one Israel Matlock, as a ''rat-faced little_____I won't say it,'' who was ''banking... on making his reputation out of the trial.''

BRUCE A. LOHOF

A Morphology of the Modern Fable*

Bruce A. Lohof is Associate Professor of History at the University of Miami in Coral Gables, Florida. He recently completed a two-year term as Director of the American Studies Research Center in Hyderabad, India. His publications and teaching have involved American history, popular culture, and community outreach.

Good Housekeeping, as each of its more than five million readers must know, is "the magazine America lives by." Born a subliterary organ in 1885, expanded in the 1930s to include both fiction and household hints, it has in recent years become nothing less than a trade journal for the American homemaker, a continuing compendium of advice and instruction, to quote the late Professor Mott, on "family life and children, medical matters, cookery and foods, fashions and decorating, appliances, budgeting, [and] diet."[1] Never were the subliterary origins of *Good Housekeeping* forsaken, however, for even now the editors continue the regular publication of novelettes, short stories, and a genre particularly appropriate to consumer journalism, short short stories.

The short short story is, first of all, brief. "A complete story on these two pages," the billing inevitably promises. But it is not marked by brevity alone. It is also entertaining, familiar, and didactic. The short short story is, as it were, a modern variant of the fable, a genre so prevalent in oral tradition. For, like the *Fables of Aesop* before them, the fables of *Good Housekeeping* are meant to convey some moral or useful lesson to their readers, that, having read them, those readers might in some transcendent sense become good housekeepers.

One ponders these fables—perhaps a thousand or more of them over the decades—perused in kitchens and dentists' offices across the land. And the obvious queries come to mind: *What systems of morality are proffered by these little fables?* And, equally compelling: *How would one determine what systems of morality are proffered?*

* This article appeared originally in the *Journal of Popular Culture* and is reproduced here with permission of that journal.

I

Significantly, the answer to the second of these questions comes from folklorists and anthropologists, from such seminal minds as Vladimir Propp and Claude Lévi-Strauss.[2] It was they, after all, who explained what housewives have presumably known by intuition: Whether by Aesop or *Good Housekeeping,* fables are constructed rather than written, and the structure of the fable is the key to the fable.

Between 1965 and 1970, fifty-two short short stories appeared in the pages of *Good Housekeeping.* These stories had been contributed by nineteen different authors—or pseudonyms—many of them professional writers whose works have been widely published. Hugh Cave, for instance (whose "To Trust in Andy" is republished here as a sample of the genre[3]), has contributed to more than sixty anthologies and schoolbooks, and at the 1978 World Fantasy Convention, his *Murgunstrumm and Others* won the award for "best collection."

One might place these fifty-two stories, in the manner of Lévi-Strauss, behind each other thusly:

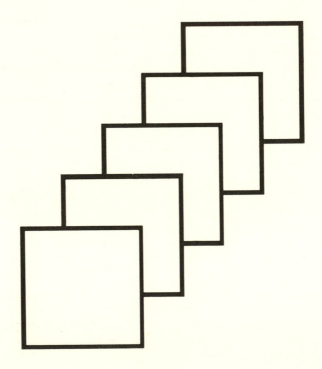

After Claude Lévi-Strauss, "The Structural Study of Myth," *Journal of American Folklore* 68 (1955): 435.

and read them not from upper-left to lower-right but, rather, from front to back, simultaneously perusing the progress of *all* the stories even as, reading casually, one would note the progress of a single story. In time it becomes clear that there *is* but a *single* story. And, written in morphological terms, the story is this:

Table 1   *Linear Structure*

	Structural Bundles	Functions
I.	Introduction Bundle	. . . in which the hero, villain, and tertiary characters are identified
I.A	Introduction of Hero	
I.B	Introduction of Villain	
I.C	Introduction of Tertiaries	
II.	Problem Bundle	
II.A	Confrontation Motif	. . . in which the struggle between hero and villain is revealed
II.B	Transformation Motif	. . . in which the villain is revealed to be heroic
III.	Resolution Bundle	
III.A	Solution Motif	. . . in which the solution to the confrontation motif is identified
III.B	Denouement Motif	. . . in which it is revealed that hero, villain, and tertiaries will live happily ever after

Hugh Cave's "To Trust in Andy" is a useful example:

Table 2   *Linear Structure in "To Trust in Andy"*

	Structural Bundles	Functions
I.	Introduction Bundle	
I.A	Introduction of Hero	Andy Graham is introduced
I.B	Introduction of Villain	Maria is introduced
I.C	Introduction of Tertiaries	Andy Graham's parents are introduced
II.	Problem Bundle	
II.A	Confrontation Motif	Andy's relationship with Maria threatens to jeopardize his plans for a college education
II.B	Transformation Motif	Maria is revealed to be eligible for college, and, thereby, becomes heroic
III.	Resolution Bundle	
III.A	Solution Motif	. . . in which the solution to the confrontation is identified
III.B	Denouement Motif	"With that they knew his future was safe. In his own strong hands."

To Trust in Andy

■ "I won't be late," their son Andy said. "Just going over to Maria's and then to Prof Newell's house." He disappeared into the back hall and they could hear him polishing his shoes, slapping the cloth rhythmically as he hummed the high school song.

Hands in pockets, he strolled back into the living room where they sat. "There's a good band on Channel 10 at nine o'clock," he offered, smiling fondly at them. "If you want to hear some smooth trombones, don't miss it. See you." The door closed behind him.

It took a moment, or seemed to, for the echo of his presence to fade from the room. Then Grace Graham bit her lip and said, "Arthur, I'm worried. I think you ought to talk to him."

Arthur Graham put aside the evening paper and studied his wife's face. Twenty-six years of marriage had taught him to read it well, and he saw concern in it now. "You think it's serious?"

"I don't know," she said.

"Have *you* talked to him?" he asked.

"Not in that way. He's eighteen, and if you remember what our other son was like at that age—"

"I remember." He felt himself smiling. "No explanations, no communication. But he seems to have survived it all, Grace. His grades are up and he's a big man on the campus."

"There wasn't any girl, dear," she reminded him. "No *one* girl who really mattered."

"And this girl of Andy's . . . what makes you think she matters?"

"He's rushing her," she said. "Tonight is the fifth straight night."

"What's she like?" he wanted to know.

"I've never laid eyes on her."

"I mean what does he *say* she's like?"

"He hasn't said anything."

"He did tell us about meeting her."

"Well, yes. But that was over a month ago."

Arthur frowned; it *had* been quite a while back. He had not paid much attention to Andy's tale that evening, he recalled. He'd been tired after a long and difficult board meeting. Andy had taken part in some music affair out of town, some competition for high school students—the sort of thing he always won. This time the boy had been beaten by a girl who—what were his words?—"didn't even own her own instrument, but had to play on an old, beat-up horn she borrowed."

The girl was a senior at Hillwood High and had gone to the competition by bus, all alone. Andy had told her that, though he went to Lincoln, he lived in Hillwood, too, and offered to drive her home. At first she'd refused. Then, discovering that she'd have to wait nearly two hours for a bus, she'd accepted.

She lived in a part of town that Andy did not know well: near the railroad tracks, on a street of run-down small houses that seemed to squeak when you looked at them. And did indeed squeak, he learned as he walked her to the door.

The girl at their son's side was lovely, her dark eyes shining with happiness.

DON DE MAURO

At the door she hesitated, then finally asked him in. Maria, he discovered, had four brothers and two sisters—all younger than she and all living with their mother in four crowded rooms. Her father had died the year before in a mill accident. Her mother worked in a café on the same street. The girl introduced him to her mother—a small, tired woman who had nothing to say—and thanked him for his kindness. That should have been the end of it.

But it wasn't. Less than a week later, Andy had gone back.

When he had gone over it in his mind, Arthur Graham looked at his wife and said quietly, "We ought to decide just what it is we're against. Are we worried because he is spending too much time with *one* girl, or because it happens to be *this* girl?"

"The girl herself doesn't enter into it," Grace said quickly. "Not at all."

"Good. Because if we're objecting on that basis, we haven't a leg to stand on. Andy is what we've brought him up to be, and I think we ought to be very proud of him."

"We've never had reason not to be," she said simply, "and we've no reason now. Just yesterday I ran into Mildred Cummings—you know her; she teaches at Hillwood High. She'd seen Andy with Maria and she said Maria was one of the nicest girls she'd ever taught. Smart, too." She tried to smile. "No, it isn't Maria I object to. It would be any girl, Arthur. Andy's just so terribly young to get . . . to get involved."

"No question about that." Arthur's fingertips drummed the end table beside his chair. "He's never gone steady before, has he? With all the girls he's brought around—all the many—there's never been anyone special like this."

"No. And that's another thing. He always *has* brought them around. But he hasn't brought Maria to meet us."

"Have you suggested he bring her?"

"No-o. If I seem to encourage it—"

"You're right, of course. If we put pressure on him, he's going to think we object to the girl herself, because of her home, her family. We both know how he'll react to that."

"He'll fight for her," Grace said. "He'll fight for the *idea* of her."

"We'd be disappointed in him if he didn't. All his life we've taught him to despise snobbery." He smiled assuringly at his wife. "Well, nothing much can happen, I suppose. Not really. He'll be going off to college in September."

"The Perkins boy was going off to college *last* September," Grace reminded him.

They were silent. Then Arthur stood up, thrusting his hands in his pockets. "I'll do what I can. When he comes in, I'll talk to him. Not about the girl, but about the importance of college and how fortunate he is that we can afford to send him." He crossed the big, comfortably furnished room and halted in front of the television set. "Let's look at that program he told us about."

The program was just ending when they heard their son's car in the driveway. The front door opened and closed. "Mom," Andy called. "Dad. Got company."

Tall, smiling, wholly at ease and self-assured, their son came into the room. The girl at his side was lovely, with dark hair and dark, luminous eyes —eyes so full of happiness that Arthur glanced quickly at his wife and saw, only because he knew her so well, her darting look of concern.

"This is Maria," Andy said. "Remember I told you about her."

Grace and Arthur greeted her warmly, and she accepted their welcome with those marvelously bright eyes and a gracious nod of her head.

"Got some news," Andy said excitedly, and Arthur could practically hear Grace's heart skip a beat as Andy's face lit up with pride. "I told you we were going over to Prof Newell's? The head of the music department at State?"

"Yes?" Arthur Graham said.

"Well, he says there are at least a dozen colleges that Maria can get into—on a full scholarship. And he's going to see to it that she does. Now, how about that?"

"College?" Grace Graham said faintly.

"With her talent and marks, she *has* to go to college. I've been telling her for weeks. And now she really can."

"I never thought I'd be able to," the girl whispered. "I just never even dared to dream that it was possible. I wouldn't even let myself think about it. Even now—well, it's just too much to believe."

"She's been laughing and crying all the way home," Andy said. "You never saw anyone so happy in your whole life."

"How wonderful for you," Grace said, reaching out to pat Maria's trembling hand.

"Look—Maria has to tell her mother," Andy explained. "Wait up for me, huh?"

Then they were gone, leaving Grace and Arthur staring at each other in silent astonishment.

Andy was gone longer this time. In fact, it was nearly midnight when they heard the car in the driveway again. But they were not alarmed. Even when he flung himself into his favorite chair and told them he had taken Maria out again after taking her home—out to a drive-in for hamburgers and shakes "to celebrate the big event"—they could smile in their feeling of security and laugh a little inside.

For as he sat there with them in the living room, in his usual slouch with his long legs outthrust and the backs of his hands propping up his chin, they were aware of the difference in him. The change was not yet complete, perhaps, but it was there.

When he said "Boy, what an evening," he was still the eighteen-year-old they had worried about. But with a kind of solemnity they had never heard before, he could also say—and did—"Can you imagine a girl with talent like that and no one *doing* anything about it? No one trying to help her?"

With that they knew his future was safe. In his own strong hands.   THE END

Like its fellow fables, ''To Trust in Andy'' is constructed in distinct modules—motifs and bundles—which are strung together in a linear pattern: *linear morphology*, it might be called, meaning simply that the modules are arranged sequentially.[4]

Variations exist, of course. An occasional story alters the initial bundle by introducing the villain before the hero, or by deleting the tertiary characters. More important, there are two major variations. One of these can be called the *schizoid variant,* in which heroism, villainy, and, therefore, confrontation all exist as opposing forces within a single individual. In a typical example the housewife (hero) nostalgically confronts her premarital status as a career girl (villain) until some tertiary character (e.g., a thoughtful husband, an injured child, or a lonely spinster) recalls to her attention the intrinsic merits of housewifery.[5] The second major variation might be called the *vanishing-villainy variant,* for here the villain is neither transformed (as in the basic structure) nor banished or destroyed (as is usually the case in oral tradition), but simply disappears from the story. A good example is the story ''Double Wedding,'' another Hugh Cave contribution to which we will return, wherein two stereotypical sisters, one a ''Plain Jane'' (hero), the other a ''Prima Donna'' (villain), marry their respective grooms in a double ceremony. During the reception which follows, ''Prima Donna'' simply disappears, leaving ''Plain Jane'' and her heroic values an unpretentious victory.[6]

But these variations, whether minor or major, do little to disturb the linearity of fables by *Good Housekeeping.* Introduction bundles are repetitiously succeeded by confrontation motifs and transformation (or vanishing-villainy) motifs, which are repetitiously succeeded by solution motifs and denouement clauses. There is, however, a second—though not contradictory—morphological pattern to these little fables, one which is suggested by those stereotypical sisters in ''Double Wedding.'' We might call it *binary morphology.*[7]

II

Now ''Plain Jane'' and ''Prima Donna'' are actually the Nickerson sisters, Mary and Beverly. Yet their personas are immediately recognizable. For instance:

Not that the girl [Mary] was an ugly duckling, mind you. She wasn't anything like that, and was such a sweet child that most people wouldn't have noticed anyway. It was just that her sister Beverly was such an outright beauty that she became the main attraction at *any* affair, and Mary was bound to be second fiddle.

Or:

Nobody paid much attention to her part of the wedding. Her sister Beverly was the prettiest bride you could ever hope to see, and marrying a mighty handsome fellow in the bargain, and, to be blunt about it, people were scarcely aware that Mary and her freckled Will Prentice were there in the church at all.[8]

Or, using "To Trust in Andy" as the example, one finds the hero disappearing "into the back hall and they could hear him polishing his shoes, slapping the cloth rhythmically as he hummed the high school song." Andy's older brother is a college student and "a big man on campus," while their father Arthur Graham is an important executive who, on the evening that we meet him, is ".'tired after a long and difficult board meeting." Maria, by contrast:

lived in a part of town that Andy did not know well: near the railroad tracks, on a street of run-down houses that seemed to squeak when you looked at them. . . . Maria . . . had four brothers and two sisters — all younger than she and all living with their mother in four crowded rooms. Her father had died the year before in a mill accident. Her mother worked in a café on the same street . . . a small tired woman who had nothing to say.

Fortunately for Maria — not to mention Andy and the linear development of the story — she is qualified to attend any one of "at least a dozen colleges . . . on full scholarship," a fact which satisfies the requirements of the transformation motif and opens the path to solution and denouement.[9]

In short, Andy is the conventional "fair-haired boy," a flat character but, nevertheless, a cultural symbol that speaks of clean-cut, all-American puberty. He is immediately recognized by the readers of *Good Housekeeping* because he shares and is heroized by their culture. Maria, for her part, is a "Cinderella," an equally flat and conventional figure who, though fraught with adversity, passes the ritual test and receives the endorsement of the culture.

These modern fables, then, are not simply linear arrangements of bundles and motifs; they are also sets of polar oppositions. Thus, a second morphological pattern of binary structure emerges:

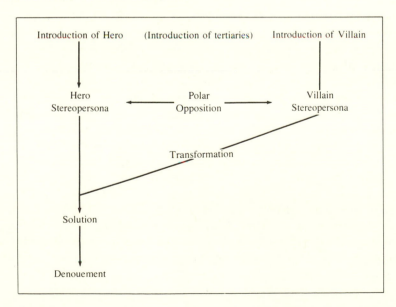

Now the focus is shifted. Now linear arrangements become secondary and the most important characteristic of the structure is its binary opposition. The critical elements of the story, whatever their order of appearance, are the rival value sets represented by heroes and villains. Indeed, so crucial is the binary nature of the fable that the competition always occurs between what can be called *stereopersonas,* each one a characterization so conventional in its attributes that it is a cultural cliché. Each fable swirls around these opposing stereopersonas: Andy, the white-Anglo-Saxon-Protestant *v.* the dark, probably-Roman-Catholic Maria from across the tracks; Mary ("Plain Jane") Nickerson *v.* her sister the "Prima Donna"; the all-American male *v.* the continental rakehell; the punctual husband *v.* the tardy wife; Mom&Dad&Bud&Sis *v.* the lonely spinster; the poor-little-rich-girl *v.* the fallen woman; and so on.

Conflict is the key. But the binary structure never lays waste to the linear. Conflict, therefore, is never severe enough to jeopardize solution and denouement, and most polarities are more apparent than real. Maria will go to college with the waspy, wealthy Andy. Career women, given half a chance, dissolve into happy homemakers. The tardy wife is punctual when the chips are down. The lonely spinster, abrasive and irascible at first, becomes the neighborly grandmother with the bottomless cookie jar once Bud&Sis work their adolescent wiles on her. Occasionally an authentic polarity is established, but even that can be quickly scuttled via the vanishing-villain variant. Always, as before, the "future [is] safe. In his own strong hands."[10] Or, to quote again from the larger tradition: "They lived happily ever after."

III

So the fable, whether ancient or modern, is to be understood in terms of its structure. It is to be known by its structure, however, not only architecturally, but morally. For when it is finally asked: *What systems of morality are proffered by these little fables?*—it is again the structure that holds the answer.

The world of the modern fable is a world of conflict, a world in which polar oppositions are literally built into every person's life. But between 1965 and 1970—years of critical conflict and dissension in the United States—polarities in *Good Housekeeping* were remarkably bland. Though war was raging in Vietnam, only once in fifty-two stories is there mention of the fact.[11] Though crime rates in the United States had reached new peaks, crime, like war, finds its way into only one of these stories. And, though poverty in America had become a concern of national proportions, on only three occasions did these fables by *Good Housekeeping* turn on issues of economics, and those, moreover, concentrate on the professional or economic problems of the middle class. Instead, most of the situations treated by these stories are personal in nature: courtship and marriage, family and friends. And here, too, no problem is too great for solution. (See table 3.)

Table 3   *Type of Problem by Percentage*

Type of Problem	Percentage
Personal Relations	
Courtship	14.3%
Marriage	34.7
Family	32.7
Friends	8.2
TOTAL	89.8
Economic & Professional	6.1
Crime	2.0
War	2.0

One compelling explanation for this easy solubility is the amazing homogeneity of the stories' characters. The hero, more often than not, is a woman, usually a young woman, and typically a housewife, career girl, or student. If male, the hero is usually executive: junior grade. And, whatever the gender, heroes are invariably white and typically middle class. Significantly, the demographics of villainy are similar to those of heroism. Villains, too, are usually young adults. They are more frequently women, never nonwhite — though, curiously, more frequently of Mediterranean stock — and involved in the same variety of middle-class occupations as their heroic counterparts. Tertiary characters, in turn, merely repeat the pattern.

In short, wherever one looks, the image is so many swatches from a single bolt of cloth. Homogeneity in this literally fabulous population far exceeds that of the "melting pot" or "salad bowl" society in which it is set. Indeed, it far exceeds the homogeneity to be found among the five million plus people who read *Good Housekeeping*. For, according to market research, nearly 10 percent of *Good Housekeeping's* readership is nonwhite, and nearly 60 percent of it belongs to the "working classes," as distinct from the white middle class that dominates the fables.[12]

The basic moral pattern of these stories, then, is not conflict in any usual sense, but *conflict within consensus*—gentle struggle among the like-minded, temporary debate within preordained unanimity. R. W. Alexander, one of the more successful of modern fablists, advises novice writers that the heart of the short short story is

some problem or situation that . . . has to be settled right away. . . . It is an important thing, this problem they [the characters] have to solve. It has a direct bearing on their happiness . . . . It is something big in their lives, though they may take only a few moments to get it straightened out . . . . It won't come up again, or certainly not in the same form. This is one hurdle they've got over safely, and they feel the better for it.

Table 4   *Demographic Analysis*

Demographic Variables	Hero	Villain	Tertiary
Age:			
Child	10.0%	6.3%	14.3%
Teenager	10.0	6.3	7.1
Young Adult	52.0	54.2	57.1
Middle Aged	28.0	31.3	21.4
Old Aged	0.0	2.1	0.0
Sex:			
Male	36.2	26.7	46.4
Female	40.4	51.1	42.9
2+*	23.4	22.2	10.7
"Race":			
Anglo-Saxon	97.6	91.4	82.1
Mediterranean	2.4	8.6	3.6
Occupation (Number of occurrences):	Executive (17)	Executive (9)	Executive (8)
	Housewife (9)	Housewife (7)	Housewife (5)
	Student (4)	Career Girl (5)	Student (4)
	Career Girl (3)	Student (2)	
	Businessman (2)	Worker (2)	
		Artist (1)	
		Pensioner (1)	

*2+ refers to heterosexual groups of persons—usually couples or families—who serve as heroes, villains, or tertiaries

Alexander, who understands the didactic nature of his genre, concludes the lesson by saying that "we can only hope the reader feels better for it, too. He should, if the story has been well done."[13]

This pattern of struggle and solution is, of course, the moral analogue of the genre's morphological patterns, both linear (which presumes not only problems but resolutions) and binary (in which polar oppositions are constructed, but quickly dissolved). Thus, the didactic content of the modern fable is as conventional, as much a cultural cliché, as the stereopersonas who give it life. The moral system implicit in these short short stories is consonant with that found some twenty-five years ago by the anthropologist Cora DuBois. "For the American middle class," she wrote in 1955, "it is postulated that: (1) the universe is mechanistically conceived, (2) man is its master, (3) men are equal, and (4) men are perfectible."[14] The world of *Good Housekeeping* is the demographic and moral equivalent of DuBois's middle America. The Newtonian mechanistics, the egalitarianism, buoyancy, and optimism—it is all here. To quote one of Alexander's own denouement clauses:

"Everything," she told him, feeling with all her being the truth of what she was saying.

"Everything's fine."[15]

The trouble, of course, is that everything *isn't* fine. Polarities in *Good Housekeeping* are easily dissolved only because the real polarities are fastidiously ignored. Where are the marriages that deserve to fail? Where are the people whose politics fall to the left of Kennedy or the right of Ike? Where are the kids who won't conform, or the women who have something other than housekeeping on their minds? Where are the ethnics, the Jews, the Slavs and the Greeks, the Asians, the Indians, the blacks? Is it not significant that, in analyzing these fables, one finds useful racial distinctions only by regressing to the now quaint notions of Anglo-Saxon superiority and Mediterranean inferiority?

But this, too, is part of the fable form. Fair-haired lads and dark-eyed Cinderellas are not real, of course—not as perfected by *Good Housekeeping's* short short stories. But, then, neither is Reynard the Fox or Brer Rabbit. They function didactically. They dramatize the great middle American mind set and bid us conform, that we might be accorded righteous.

Didactic journalism did not begin with modern women's magazines. If D. H. Lawrence is to be believed, it was an earlier journalist, Ben Franklin, who "set up the first dummy American . . . . Now wasn't that an American thing to do?"[16] *Good Housekeeping* merely maintains the tradition, constructing dummies in our image, that we may build our lives on theirs.

Notes

1. Frank Luther Mott, *A History of American Magazines* (Cambridge, Mass: Harvard University Press, 1938–68), 5: 143.

2. See Vladimir Propp, *Morphology of the Folktale,* 2nd ed. (Austin: University of Texas Press, 1968), and Lévi-Strauss, "The Structural Study of Myth," *Journal of American Folklore* 68 (1955): 428–44.

3. Cave, "To Trust in Andy," *Good Housekeeping,* April 1965, pp. 102–3.

4. On linear structure see Alan Dundes's "Introduction to the Second Edition," Propp, xi–xvii.

5. Examples abound in *Good Housekeeping* for 1969, when the schizoid variant became very popular.

6. Cave, "Double Wedding," *Good Housekeeping,* July 1965, pp. 88–89.

7. *Binary morphology* is Lévi-Strauss's term, although it carries a sophistication which goes beyond that of the short short story. See Dundes.

8. Cave, "Double Wedding."

9. Cave, "To Trust in Andy."

10. Ibid.

11. In "Good-bye Too Soon," by Leonhard Dowty (*Good Housekeeping*, October 1969, pp. 118–19), the hero is drafted and subsequently killed in Vietnam. This turn of events is so catastrophic that the basic structure of the genre is violated, making "Good-bye Too Soon," in the structural sense, something other than a modern fable.

12. W. R. Simmons, "Standard Magazine Audience Report, Selected Characteristics of Adult Female Readers," 1972.

13. Alexander, "The Short Short Story," *Writer* 80 (August 1967): 18.

14. Cora DuBois, "The Dominant Value Profile of American Culture," *American Anthropologist* 62 (1955): 1233.

15. Alexander, "My Young and Truly Love," *Good Housekeeping,* October 1966, pp. 102–3.

16. D. H. Lawrence, *Studies in Classic American Literature* (New York: T. Seltzer, 1923), p. 14.

NELSON MANFRED BLAKE

How to Learn History from Sinclair Lewis and Other Uncommon Sources

Nelson Manfred Blake is Professor of History Emeritus, Syracuse University. After receiving a Ph.D. from Clark University, he taught for thirty-eight years at Syracuse, where he held the rank of Maxwell Distinguished Professor of History from 1971 to 1974. He is the author of A History of American Life and Thought, Water for the Cities, Road to Reno, Novelists' America, *and other books and articles.*

The popularity of American Studies programs gives evidence of the desire of today's students to escape the strait jackets of the traditional disciplines. By combining the study of history, literature, and the arts young people are grasping the opportunity to share in the American experience in all its variety and color. To those of us trained as specialists in some traditional field of study such programs present a challenge to rethink our conclusions and to draw insights from other types of material than those we customarily use. In this spirit, let us consider what we may hope to learn of history from literature and the arts, first in a general way, and then with specific reference to Sinclair Lewis's angry novel *Elmer Gantry*.

I

Let me explain at the outset that it is not my purpose to give much attention to the type of literature known as the historical novel. Most fiction of this type is, in my judgment, neither good history nor good literature. Even more than most fiction, historical novels are likely to be written by formula. Take one part of warm-blooded heroine and one part of devil-may-care hero, add a generous portion of violence and drop after drop of tantalizing sex, and you may concoct a synthetic marvel that will be distributed by the Literary Guild and immortalized in Techni-color Vitavision.

No doubt, this indictment is too sweeping. Some historical fiction deserves the highest praise as providing a vivid and memorable reconstruction of the past.

Tolstoi's *War and Peace,* rated by some critics as the greatest of all novels, is, of course, a work of historical fiction. No American novel of comparable sweep and power has yet been written, but in the hands of men like Kenneth Roberts and Walter Edmonds our historical fiction has sometimes achieved a high level of competence. The most famous of American historical novels, Margaret Mitchell's *Gone with the Wind,* is a work of very uneven quality, but parts of it are very good indeed. Miss Mitchell's description of the burning of Atlanta is so vivid and memorable that academic historians may well read it with envy.

Even at its best, however, the historical novel is a secondary account of the past. It is true only insofar as the author has painstakingly accumulated his materials. The real historian is always impatient with learning history at second hand. He prefers to find out about the past from what he calls primary sources—that is, from the evidence left by the actual witnesses and participants of past events. It is from this point of view that literature and the arts open up the most exciting avenues for exploration.

II

Whether consciously or unconsciously, the author of a novel or a poem usually leaves a record of his own experience and observation. The nuggets to be mined out of this material are particularly valuable to the student of social history. He is interested not so much in the deeds of statesmen and generals as in what humbler people were doing and thinking. Consider these lines:

> Bearing the bandages, water and sponge,
> Straight and swift to my wounded I go,
> Where they lie on the ground after the battle brought in,
> Where their priceless blood reddens the grass the ground,
> Or to the rows of the hospital tent, or under the roof'd hospital:
> To the long rows of cots up and down each side I return,
> To each and all one after another I draw near—not one do I miss,
> An attendant follows, holding a tray, he carries a refuse pail,
> Soon to be fill'd with clotted rags and blood, emptied and fill'd again.[1]

These lines were written by Walt Whitman, who spent many hours comforting the wounded of the Civil War in army hospitals. Here is an authentic fragment from the past, a sensitive man writing out of his own deeply felt experience, conveying to us a century later some conception of the grim aftermath of battle.

To the student of history, Mark Twain gives particular delight when he writes about mid-nineteenth-century life along the Mississippi—a region he knew as an inquisitive boy and as a steamboat pilot. When Huckleberry Finn floats down the river on his raft, we get a succession of fascinating vignettes of the social history of the day. We read, for example, of Colonel Grangerford who "owned a lot of farms and over a hundred niggers." "Sometimes," says Huck, "a stack of people would come there, horseback, from ten or fifteen miles around, and stay five or six days, and have such junketings round about and on the river, and dances and picnics in the woods daytimes, and balls at the house nights. These people was mostly kinfolks of the family. The men brought their guns with them. It was a handsome lot of quality, I tell you.''[2] To me, the Grangerfords in *Huckleberry Finn* are convincing in a way that the O'Haras in *Gone with the Wind* are not—and precisely for the reason that Mark Twain had seen southern planters with his own eyes, while Miss Mitchell saw them only through the eyes of romantic imagination.

Huckleberry Finn with similar success transfers us back to the world of rural camp meetings, strolling actors, and steamboats pounding up the Mississippi at night, "big and scary, with a long row of wide-open furnace doors shining like red-hot teeth.''[3]

Oftentimes the sensitive description of the novelist or the short story writer can help us to understand a whole great historical episode. Speaking of the Populist movement of the early 1890s, William Dean Howells wrote: "If anyone is still at a loss to account for that uprising of the farmers in the West which is the translation of the Peasant's War into modern and republican terms, let him read *Main-Travelled Roads.*''[4] If the student of history follows this lead and dips into Hamlin Garland's famous collection of short stories, he finds such grim pictures of agricultural poverty as this:

> It was humble enough—a small white story-and-a-half structure, with a wing set in the midst of a few locust trees; a small drab-colored barn with a sagging ridge pole; a barnyard full of mud, in which a few cows were standing, fighting the flies and waiting to be milked. An old man was pumping water at the well; the pigs were squealing from a pen near by; a child was crying. . . . he could hear a woman's fretful voice and the impatient jerk and jar of kitchen things, indicative of ill-temper or worry. The longer he stood absorbing this farm-scene, with all its sordidness, dullness, triviality, and its endless drudgeries, the lower his heart sank. . . .[5]

Hamlin Garland's grim picture was painted in 1887. During the next decade there were remarkable changes, and Willa Cather's *O Pioneers!* depicts Nebraska of the late 1890s in quite different terms. The hardships and bitterness of frontier poverty are now mostly unpleasant memories. This is a period when hardworking Norwegian and Bohemian farmers are enjoying a modest prosperity. In Miss Cather's words:

> The Divide is now thickly populated. The rich soil yields heavy harvests; the dry, bracing climate and the smoothness of the land makes labor easy for men and beasts. There are few scenes more gratifying than a spring ploughing in that country, where the furrows of a single field often lie a mile in length, and the brown earth, with such a strong, clean smell, and such a power of growth and fertility in it, yields itself eagerly to the plough, rolls away from the shear, not even dimming the brightness of the metal, with a soft, deep sigh of happiness. The wheat-cutting sometimes goes on all night as well as

all day, and in good seasons there are scarcely men and horses enough to do the harvesting. The grain is so heavy that it bends toward the blade and cuts like velvet.[6]

Social change in the cities can be similarly traced. William Dean Howells has left meticulously authentic descriptions of Boston and New York during the 1870s and 1880s. Theodore Dreiser has done the same for New York, Chicago, and Philadelphia during the 1890s and early 1900s. And James Farrell carries us on to the Chicago slums of the 1920s and 1930s. A half-century of urban experience can thus be relived through the pages of these three novelists.

Obviously the realistic school of fiction is of particular interest to the social historian, but this does not mean that he can learn nothing from writers of a different tradition. If one wants to learn about Philadelphia during the yellow fever epidemic of 1793, let him read *Arthur Mervyn,* one of the Gothic novels of Charles Brockden Brown. The story itself is one of lurid melodrama, but there can be no doubt that the novelist knew from his own experience the city and the episode that served as setting for his improbable story. For a more recent period there is abundant information in the novels of William Faulkner. Faulkner is obviously no realist. Even the most biased northerner will refuse to believe that Mississippi is exclusively populated by murderers, sadists, prostitutes, perverts, lunatics, and idiots. Yet Faulkner's horror stories are played out in a setting of great interest to the social historian. In his famous county live many authentic southern people—small-town bankers, merchants, lawyers, laborers, and household servants. The tension between the Old South and the New so often symbolized in the key figures of the novels is reflected more literally in the less grotesque minor characters—gentle folks cherishing the old traditions, aggressive newcomers, and village idlers. It is obvious that even when a novelist is writing a highly romantic or richly symbolic work he leaves abundant clues regarding the material of his own experience.

III

Literature is not the only survival from the past. Every building, every painting, every piece of music created in an earlier age and still in existence has something to tell us about the period of its birth.

If you wish to understand the Virginia society in which George Washington and Thomas Jefferson lived, visit Mount Vernon and Monticello. Reflect on the sites so carefully chosen, the formal gardens and lawns so lovingly cultivated, the large drawing rooms and dining rooms so reflective of a generous hospitality, the libraries so indicative of the bookish interests of these Virginia gentlemen. Examine what is left of the slave quarters and be reminded that a southern plantation was in fact a village, complete with its blacksmith shop, carpenter shop, spinning room, and bakery.

It is fascinating to compare this simple, dignified architecture with the ostentatious palaces of Newport, Rhode Island, built for the Vanderbilts and other millionaires during the 1880s and 1890s. Here are iron gates so ornate that it took fifty workmen a year to build them, staircases as wide as those of a railroad station, and dining rooms large enough to seat two hundred guests. To visit these Newport mansions is to see with our own eyes what Thorstein Veblen meant by conspicuous consumption.

We learn history from architecture mostly by reflection and interpretation. But painting often gives its information with unmistakable directness. For material on the seamy side of London life in the eighteenth century, what better data can there be than the engravings of William Hogarth? America has its own rich tradition of *genre* painting. George Caleb Bingham, who lived in Missouri during the 1830s and 1840s, shows us just how the fur traders, the slouching drunkards, and the top-hatted politicians of a frontier society looked. Bingham's contemporary, William Sidney Mount, lived on Long Island and depicted with equal faithfulness the daily life of his rustic neighbors. Mount is particularly valuable for his record of popular amusements like barn dancing, fiddle playing, and eel spearing. In a later day when America had become urbanized the painters derisively known as the Ash Can School painted scenes of New York City life around 1910. The work of John Sloan, George Bellows, and their contemporaries is an invaluable record of the barrooms, the skating rinks, the ferry boats, and the crowded streets of the shabby metropolis of fifty years ago.

Music is also a survival from the past. Many concert programs reflect this. We often hear a first group of compositions by Bach, Mozart or other eighteenth-century composers. A second group may include works by Beethoven, Brahms, Chopin, or other nineteenth-century figures. The third group may include twentieth-century composers like Aaron Copland or Roy Harris. Such a program carries us through successive chapters not only of musical history but of intellectual history as well. Eighteenth-century music with its restraint, its clarity, its fine sense of balance and form belongs to the world of Newton, Voltaire, and Pope. Nineteenth-century music with its passion and warmth, its surging emotionalism, and its soaring climaxes belongs as clearly to the world of romanticism of Goethe and Keats and Whitman. Twentieth-century music with its dissonant chords, its restless nervousness, its looseness of form reflects the intellectual trends of our own times. This is the world where the old certainties have been dislodged by the discoveries of men like Einstein and Freud. In literature the new spirit finds its outlet in experimental writers like O'Neill and Faulkner.

Sometimes the social historian can take his data even more directly from music. Nothing is more social than dancing, and the popular dance music provides data that needs no explanation. The minuet, the waltz, the polka, the foxtrot, and the Bossa Nova in their tempos and forms all speak for themselves. Genuine folk music as distinct from the synthetic variety now monopolizing the juke boxes is full of the colorful life of the past.

IV

But one may ask, are there not great dangers in drawing the materials for social history from literature and the arts? Isn't it true that writers and painters deliberately distort their materials? Everyone knows that Mark Twain was a cheerful liar indulging in outrageous western exaggeration and that Walt Whitman had not always had the experiences that he said he had. Painters from Hogarth's day to our own have deliberately chosen their subjects to make the points that they wanted to make.

All this merely means that one must apply to these unorthodox materials of history the same standards of historical criticism that he would apply to other sources.

In the first place, one must learn as much as he can about the author or artist and why he created this particular work. This is much more important to the student of history than to the student of literature or art. To the latter the work is to a large extent an isolated object of criticism. The artist's intention is to be inferred from his creation. Its value is a matter of internal qualities of arrangement, language, symbolism, and the like. To concentrate on the artist and his background is to deal with things largely irrelevant to the making of judgments about the significance of his work.

But to the historian every author or artist is a man testifying about something that has happened in the past. We can judge the value of his testimony only if we have some kind of knowledge about the man himself. Theodore Dreiser, born of lower-class German-American parentage, poorly educated, living in the cities as a struggling journalist, will look at the successful American businessman from one perspective, and Edith Wharton, born to a wealthy, old established family, carefully educated, moving with perfect ease through New York society, will deal with the businessman from quite a different point of view. Even more relevant are the philosophical assumptions underlying the work of the authors. Dreiser, eagerly swallowing all the determinist assumptions of nineteenth-century science, will seize upon evidence of man's helplessness to deal with relentless social forces. Mrs. Wharton, holding a code of values in which conduct is either honorable or dishonorable, will as naturally select the evidence that supports her theory. The question always is, did a particular author or artist set out to prove anything by this particular work?

A second rule is that we must try to determine when an author or artist is working out of his own direct observation and experience and when he is using material gathered from other sources. And in the latter case we must ask how reliable these sources may have been.

Take, for example, the passage in John Dos Passos's novel *The Big Money* where he deals with events in Boston immediately preceding the execution of Sacco and Vanzetti. He describes how liberals and radicals from all over the country converged on the city, how they organized petitions and demonstrations, how they financed their activities, how the police handled them, how the Communists sought the ultimate in propaganda even if their doings might harm rather than help the effort to save the condemned men. From the standpoint of the literary critic the only question is how this episode fits into the work as a whole and whether in style and tone it contributes to the impact of the novel. But the historian must ask quite different questions. How did Dos Passos know about these events? Has he dealt with them with careful accuracy, or has he rearranged episodes to suit his literary purpose? The answers to these questions are reassuring. Dos Passos did not have to rely on old newspaper files. He himself was in Boston during these hectic days. He stood on the street near the prison at the very hour of execution. He wrote his account out of his own experience, and he told the story as it actually happened.

In using any document as historical evidence, there is still a third step to take. We must consider the probable truth or accuracy of particular statements. It is not enough to evaluate the document as a whole, as to its authorship and general characteristics. In the end, we must weigh the value of any particular item of evidence.

As a specific example, consider a paragraph from Upton Sinclair's *The Jungle,* in which the novelist is describing the processing of ham:

Jonas had told them how the meat that was taken out of pickle would often be found sour, and how they would rub it up with soda to take away the smell, and sell it to be eaten on free-lunch counters; also of all the miracles of chemistry which they performed, giving to any sort of meat, fresh or salted, whole or chopped, any color and any flavor and any odor they chose. In the pickling of hams they had an ingenious apparatus, by which they saved time and increased the capacity of the plant—a machine consisting of a hollow needle attached to a pump; by plunging this needle into the meat and working with his foot, a man could fill a ham with pickle in a few seconds. And yet, in spite of this, there would be hams found spoiled, some of them with an odor so bad that a man could hardly bear to be in the room with them. To pump into these the packers had a second and much stronger pickle which destroyed the odor—a process known to the workers as ''giving them thirty percent.''[7]

Disregarding any general evaluation of Sinclair's novel, how are we to regard these particular statements? Did Chicago packers around 1905 in sober truth doctor their hams in this way? We must recognize that Sinclair did not write out of pure imagination. He spent many weeks in Chicago gathering the material for his novel, and our knowledge of this tends to make us believe him. Yet if we are to be truly critical, we must ask a further question. Did Upton Sinclair have any bias that might affect his truthfulness at this point? And the answer to this question is disturbing. We must remember that Sinclair was not only a muckraker with all the muckraker's disposition to believe the worst about contemporary business and politics, but a dedicated socialist as well. Now I don't believe that socialists are any more untruthful than Republicans—or than college professors.

But I do believe that we all have areas of passionate conviction that are likely to color our statements when we deal with certain sensitive issues. In Upton Sinclair's case, he obviously hoped to make the point that the private profit system exploited the worker and ignored the health of the consumer. The matter of the doctored hams lies so close to the central bias of the author that I think we should regard these statements with extreme caution.

The result of critically weighing these statements in *The Jungle* has not been altogether satisfactory. From one point of view, we have tended to give them credence; from another point of view, we have found reason to doubt them. Yet this is exactly the situation in which the historian frequently finds himself. When he does, he seeks further evidence. If we want to make a final judgment as to whether the Chicago packers did market spoiled hams, we shall have to study the testimony of as many other witnesses as possible.

V

Having considered both the possibilities and the pitfalls of using literary and artistic productions as sources of history, let us try out our theories in some detail with a specific document. From the literary critic's point of view *Elmer Gantry* is a bad novel—awkwardly constructed, intemperate in tone, grotesque in characterization. But the novel's deficiencies as a work of art do not necessarily destroy its interest as a document of social history. By depicting the condition of American church life in the early twentieth century, Sinclair Lewis provides data that may be of some value in correcting the impressions to be gathered from more pious sources.

But if we are to use the novel thus, we must first have a close acquaintance with the author. What manner of man was Sinclair Lewis? He describes his own boyhood in Sauk Centre, Minnesota, as perfectly normal—"dull school routine, skating, sliding, skiing, swimming, duck hunting."[8] Yet we may ask whether this was the boyhood he really had or the one he liked to imagine for himself. As Mark Schorer in his fine biography tells the story, Lewis's boyhood was far from happy. Lewis was always peculiar in appearance. His flaming red hair was matched with a flaming red face; he was thin and awkward; and he was the frequent butt of schoolboy jokes. At the age of seventeen this badly adjusted youth was sent away to school. First he spent six months at Oberlin Academy in Oberlin, Ohio. Though brief, this experience was important for reasons to be discussed later. The next four years were spent at Yale, where most of his fellow students detested him and he made relatively few friends.

Between graduation from Yale in 1907 and sudden fame in 1920 lay thirteen years of obscurity. After a little vagabonding adventure he supported himself by literary hack work on newspapers and in publishers' offices while he attempted to write stories and novels. Between 1914 and 1919 he published four novels, but none of them was very successful. Then came *Main Street* and a decade of great acclaim, culminating in the receipt of the Nobel Prize in 1930. After that it was mostly downhill until his death in 1951.

These are the bare facts of Sinclair Lewis's life, but they don't really tell us much about the man himself. Lewis's own estimate is that "there was never in private life a less attractive or admirable fellow,"[9] and this harsh judgment has all too much truth. Throughout life he shocked people by his extraordinary homeliness. Even when he was sober he was rude and quarrelsome, and when he was drunk—as he far too often was—he was intolerable. He was a bad husband to two wives; he was a neglectful father to two sons; he had numerous cheap affairs with women. Yet, despite all these unlovely traits, Lewis could be a highly entertaining companion. He was a master of one thing, he said of himself, and that was talk. A gifted mimic, he would convulse his friends by imitating "an American Babbitt boasting about his motor car, a Swede or a Yankee speaking German, a college professor lecturing ponderously on nothing in particular." If the performance sometimes seemed childish, particularly when too frequently repeated, the reason in Lewis's explanation was that he was "only practicing, only making a sketch for the next character he was to paint."[10] Pretending that he was George Babbitt or Elmer Gantry, he would improvise the long harangues that later appeared in these novels.

Explaining himself still further, Lewis said: "Besides a certain amount of lasting affection for his friends and this pyrotechnical conversation, the man seems to me to have no virtues whatever save a real, fiery, almost reckless hatred of hypocrisy—of what the Americans call 'bunk' . . . and this may not be a virtue at all, but only an envy-inspired way of annoying people by ignoring their many excellent qualities and picking out the few vices into which they have been betrayed by custom and economic necessity."[11] This "hatred of hypocrisy" is probably our most useful key to understanding Lewis's testimony about the social history of his time.

On what sources did Lewis depend when he wrote his novels? First of all, he drew on his own personal experience. Again and again bits of material are worked in that reflect Lewis's boyhood in a prairie village or his later life in other places. Of the six months that he spent at Oberlin Academy Lewis says: They were very valuable; they "gave him a notion of such small, highly pious and denominational Midwestern colleges as appear in several of his novels; and a notion of the Eastern Middlewest, in which is situated Zenith."[12] And Zenith, we must remember, is the city where not only George Babbitt and Sam Dodsworth lived but where Elmer Gantry eventually preached.

But Lewis depended not alone on his own experience but on the experience of other people. Commenting on his extensive foreign travels, he said: "The fact is that my foreign traveling has been a quite uninspiring recreation, a flight from reality. My real traveling has been sitting in Pullman smoking cars, in a Minnesota village, on a Vermont farm, in a hotel in Kansas City or Savannah, listening to the normal daily drone of what are to me the most fascinating and exotic people in the world—the Average Citizens of the United States, with their friendliness to strangers and their rough teasing, their passion for material advancement, and their shy idealism and interest in all the world, and their boastful provincialism—the intricate complexities which an American novelist is privileged to portray.''[13]

So much for the witness, now let us listen to his testimony. Certainly the Reverend Elmer Gantry is one of the most unpleasant characters in all literature. What are we to think of a preacher who seduces the deacon's daughter in his first church, never gets to his second church because he gets drunk, becomes the bedmate of a woman evangelist, and finally, a hypocrite to the end, rises to fame in the Methodist Church? It would be bad enough if Lewis had written in these disrespectful terms about one preacher, but the novel depicts a score of other ministers and most of them are not much better than Elmer.

Why did Sinclair Lewis make such a savage attack upon the Protestant clergy? May it not be because we often assail with the greatest passion the things that we once have loved? It is significant that Lewis passed through a phase of intense interest in religion. As a high school boy, he attended the Congregational Church and Sunday School and was a good member of Christian Endeavor. During his six months at Oberlin he participated eagerly in the activities of the Y.M.C.A. So seriously did he take all this that he decided he was going to become a missionary. He took on a Sunday School class in a nearby village, to which he used to go by railroad hand car—exactly as Elmer Gantry goes out to his first church. After continuing these religious activities for a time at Yale, Lewis gradually lost his faith, but he still retained a high degree of curiosity about American church life.

When Lewis made the decision to write a novel about American ministers, he put himself through an unusual briefing. He struck up a friendship with the Reverend William L. Stidger, a well-known Methodist clergyman of the day, and, through Stidger, Lewis was able to organize an informal discussion group that met once a week in a Kansas City hotel room. In this extraordinary company that called itself "Sinclair Lewis's Sunday School class," there were fifteen clergymen ranging the full religious spectrum from Catholic priest and Jewish rabbi to Unitarian minister and free thinker. Lewis pumped these new friends for all kinds of information about their respective churches. Often he needled them with accusations of not really believing what they preached and of being unwilling to sacrifice for their faith. One participant remembers that every now and then Lewis would begin to preach with all sincerity, then he would bring himself up short and would say, "I have to stop this! I *could* have been a preacher."[14] When this group met for the last time, Lewis bade them an extraordinary farewell: "Boys, I'm going up to Minnesota and write a novel about you. I'm going to give you hell, but I love every one of you." And as each minister left the room, Lewis embraced him and said, "Good-by, old man; God bless you!"[15]

Does this help us to evaluate *Elmer Gantry?* Lewis certainly fulfilled his promise to give his minister friends hell, but where is the evidence that he loved them? The most obvious clue to the mystery is to be found in Lewis's hatred of hypocrisy. Lewis could excuse the hypocrisies of the Babbitts, but the hypocrisies of the clergy infuriated him. Speaking of himself, Lewis said: "Why, this man, still so near to being an out and out Methodist or Lutheran that he would far rather chant the hymns of his boyhood evangelicism than the best drinking song in the world, is so infuriated by ministers who tell silly little jokes in the pulpit and keep from ever admitting publicly their confusing doubts that he risks all the good friends he once had among the ministers by the denunciations of *Elmer Gantry*."[16]

The Reverend Elmer Gantry appears to be all the separate hypocrisies that Lewis had observed, rolled into one incredible bundle of hypocrisy. For this reason, the social historian need not take Elmer himself very seriously. He is so unrepresentative of the clergy as to hardly merit consideration. More plausible, however, are Lewis's vignettes of other clergymen, in which there is some mixture of good and bad. Many of these are probably drawn from life from Lewis's minister friends. For the most part, they are a pretty poor lot also, but there are at least two ministers in *Elmer Gantry* for whom Lewis shows respect and affection. One is the Reverend Andrew Pengilly, of whom he writes:

If you had cut Andrew Pengilly to the core, you would have found him white clear through. . . . To every congregation he had served these forty years, he had been a shepherd. They had loved him, listened to him, and underpaid him. . . . Little book-learning had Andrew Pengilly in his youth, and to this day he knew nothing of Biblical criticism, of the origin of religions, of the sociology which was beginning to absorb church-leaders, but his Bible he knew, and believed, word by word, and somehow he had drifted into the reading of ecstatic books of mysticism. . . . [17]

Pengilly, Lewis implies, could be free of hypocrisy, because he had never been confronted by the challenges to faith implicit in modern knowledge, but the position of another character in *Elmer Gantry* is much more difficult. The Reverend Frank Shallard has read widely in modern science; it has shaken his faith to the point where he is really an agnostic, but he stays in the ministry. So he is, from Lewis's point of view, a hypocrite. Yet Lewis is very gentle with Shallard's hypocrisy because he understands its reasons. Shallard wishes, in the first place, to avoid giving pain to his minister-father; he also wants to protect his wife and children, whom he loves very deeply. And finally Shallard sees some chance of doing good. Taunted as to why he doesn't get out of the ministry before he is kicked out, Shallard replies:

Because I'm not yet sure—Though I do think our present churches are as absurd as a belief in witchcraft, yet I believe there could be a church free of superstition, helpful to the needy, and giving people that mystic something stronger than reason, that sense of being uplifted in common worship of an unknowable power for good. Myself, I'd be lonely with nothing but bleak debating-societies. I think—at least I still think—that for many souls there is this need of worship, even of beautiful ceremonial—[18]

Although Shallard is in many ways a weak character, Lewis portrays him in one final act of supreme courage, going through with a speech certain to bring down on him the terrible vengeance of a fundamentalist mob. Shallard is thus at last set free from all hypocrisy. In writing this passage, Lewis is certainly projecting himself. He gives to Shallard the kind of courage that Lewis wishes he had himself but knows he does not.

To the social historian these various character studies are less useful than the general excursion that Lewis conducts through American Protestantism as of about 1926. He gives an excellent picture of the way in which Methodist ministers anxiously attended their annual conferences, where they awaited uneasily the Bishop's announcement of appointments. He touches upon the problems of the urban churches occasioned by shifts of population, upon the new emphasis on ritualism among certain churches, and upon the vogue of the social gospel. Most of this is excellent reporting. Lewis was in many ways an extraordinarily perceptive observer of the religious scene in the mid-1920s. If one can keep his temper and make proper allowances for Lewis's strong biases, he can learn as much about American Protestantism by reading *Elmer Gantry* as he can about middle-class conduct by reading *Babbitt*.

What general judgment can we make about Sinclair Lewis as a witness to American life in the 1920s? Obviously he is far from being a perfect observer. He is a man of many flaws in character. He is lacking in objectivity and judiciousness. He is strongly opinionated and oftentimes malicious in what he writes. But the judge and jury in a courtroom cannot wait for perfect witnesses. They must listen to whatever testimony is offered, shrewdly noting each witness's shortcomings and prejudices and giving to his statements such credence as they deserve. In like manner the historian must deal with Sinclair Lewis, drawing such information as he can from Lewis's rich gifts for fact gathering and mimicry, but being constantly on guard against his weakness for exaggeration and caricature.

VI

A final word on this whole matter needs to be said. Historians, I am sure, have no wish to invade the province of other disciplines. We are not suggesting standards by which we think literature or the arts should be taught or judged. To believe that the highest value to be sought in looking at the *Mona Lisa* is an understanding of how sixteenth-century Italian women wore their hair or that we ought to read *Moby Dick* chiefly for the purpose of gathering facts about the whaling industry is obviously absurd. Every great work of literature and art has both a timely quality and a timeless quality. The historian is particularly interested in the data that the work reveals about the age in which it was created. The critic, on the other hand, is properly concerned with the things in the work which are as true for us as they were for the author or the artist. *Moby Dick* and *The Scarlet*

Letter are great novels because they deal with problems and conflicts that beset men in every age, such problems as evil, sin, guilt, and remorse.

All that I am attempting to say is that literature and art have their secondary delights—and one of these is that they hold the mirror to the society that produced them. I am entirely certain that historians should read more novels and poems, look at more buildings and paintings, and listen to more music. I am almost as sure that students of literature and art should read more history.

Notes

1. Walt Whitman, "The Wound-Dresser," *Leaves of Grass*, Inclusive Edition, edited by Emory Holloway (Garden City, N.Y.: Doubleday & Company, 1954), p. 260.

2. Mark Twain, *The Adventures of Huckleberry Finn* (New York: Harper & Brothers, 1899), p. 148.

3. Twain, *Huckleberry Finn*, p. 133.

4. W. D. Howells, "Introduction," in Hamlin Garland, *Main-Travelled Roads* (New York: Harper & Brothers, 1899), p. 4

5. Garland, "Up the Cooly," *Main-Travelled Roads*, p. 78.

6. Willa Sibert Cather, *O Pioneers!* (Boston: Houghton Mifflin Co., 1913), p. 76.

7. Upton Sinclair, *The Jungle* (New York: Viking Press, 1950), p. 134.

8. Mark Schorer, *Sinclair Lewis: An American Life* (New York: McGraw-Hill Book Co., 1961), p. 3.

9. Sinclair Lewis, *The Man from Main Street: Selected Essays and Other Writings: 1904–1950*, edited by Harry E. Maule and Melville H. Cane (New York: Pocket Book, 1963), p. 47.

10. Ibid.

11. Lewis, *The Man from Main Street*, p. 48.

12. Schorer, *Sinclair Lewis*, p. 48.

13. Lewis, *The Man from Main Street*, p. 55.

14. Schorer, *Sinclair Lewis*, p. 449.

15. Ibid., p. 454.

16. Lewis, *The Man from Main Street*, p. 48.

17. Sinclair Lewis, *Elmer Gantry* (New York: Harcourt, Brace and Co., 1927), pp. 240–41.

18. Lewis, *Elmer Gantry*, p. 381.

PART THREE
History and the Changing Culture

DAVID W. MARCELL

Henry Adams's Historical Paradigm: A Reexamination of the Major Phase

David W. Marcell is a graduate of Stetson and Yale universities. He was chairman of the American Studies Department at Skidmore College from 1964 to 1977. Since 1977, he has been the Provost of Skidmore. He has recently published a volume in Greenwood Press's "Contributions in American Studies," entitled Progress and Pragmatism.

If the central task for the historian is to explain how and why change occurs, the central task for the intellectual historian is to explain change in the realm of ideas and understanding. Accounting for change in public sectors of experience is difficult enough; explanations in the more ephemeral zones of meaning and knowing are often downright baffling. Issues which seize one generation are often mysteriously ignored by the next. As John Dewey once noted, we don't so much "solve" our more complex intellectual problems as we "get over" them. Yet explanations for this process of "getting over" are rarely precise or satisfactory. Witness, for example, how the language of intellectual historians when they deal with periodization becomes either fuzzy or derivative: They speak of shifting "climates of opinion," evolving "world views," or an age of "enlightenment" or "anxiety."

It is partly because of such problems that Thomas Kuhn's *The Structure of Scientific Revolutions* has been greeted with special enthusiasm by intellectual historians over the past decade.[1] Kuhn's achievement has been to offer a detailed, meticulous model for deciphering changing scientific outlooks and for identifying the recurring stages through which such changes seem necessarily to pass. In addition, Kuhn provides a clear, logical language for the many aspects of the stages he identifies. While Kuhn's theories are derived from the dialectic of change within a fairly restrictive scientific community, his theories have been profitably applied to other intellectual groups and enterprises. Kuhn's model, indeed, can operate heuristically, as a general "methodological postulate" for "other fields outside the history of science."[2] I want to offer yet another kind of application.

My purpose is not so much to test Kuhn's postulates as to attempt to make use of his conceptualization in explicating what Ernest Samuels has called Henry Adams's "major phase." While many scholars have written penetratingly about the major phase, few have discerned the peculiar unity of vision underlying Adams's diversity of style and subject in his later years. Kuhn, I think, provides a good deal of help in this regard, and Adams's last works in turn provide a superb illustration of how Kuhn's model can be applied to yet another context: the lifework of an extraordinarily sensitive and erudite thinker who, alone, attempted to formulate a model for historical change that was at once cosmic and personal, "scientific" and autobiographical. While Kuhn's theories were designed expressly to clarify the functioning of particular communities, they can also illuminate the work of a single individual examining how traditional communities change.

All scientific communities, Kuhn maintains, are unified by their acceptance of "paradigms": certain shared assumptions, beliefs, values, and techniques which provide the discipline with a unifying tradition that allows it to pursue particular investigations without having each time to go back and, as it were, reinvent the wheel. The paradigms or models explain in consensual, fundamental ways the realities that can be taken for granted before proceeding with work on a particular problem at hand. Most scientific work—most of the "problems at hand"—involve exploring in detail how a given paradigm relates or applies in a highly specialized, as yet uninvestigated, instance. This kind of work, which Kuhn calls "normal science," extends and amplifies the paradigmatic base from which it proceeds and simply enlarges the scientific tradition of which it is part; normal science is essentially "paradigm articulation."[3]

But as normal science proceeds, certain "anomalies" arise: Experiments produce results which cannot be accounted for by a given paradigm—phlogiston, say, or the Ptolemaic system—and a growing sense of "malfunction" arises. Attention focuses on the problem, a "crisis" is perceived in experimentation, and soon the basic paradigm must either be "transformed" so as to account for the growing "anomalies" or a new paradigm must be offered which not only explains acceptably the results of past experiments but also accounts for the incongruous new results, for the anomalies. This "paradigm shift" will then allow "normal science" to take place from a new, more adequate traditional base, and this new base of paradigm will prevail until still newer anomalies arise and a subsequent new crisis is precipitated. Of such evolutionary stuff is scientific "revolution," and Kuhn illustrates his theory carefully by demonstrating how each step occurred during such specific occasions as the discoveries of Copernicus, or the development of Maxwell's electromagnetic theory.

The Kuhnian model offers a concrete way of reconciling tradition and innovation, of seeing how each is necessarily part of the other. Without a coherent tradition, innovation is merely random action; without innovation, tradition is but stasis and the antithesis of growth. Tradition is viable only so long as it can be reconciled with new knowledge, but that new knowledge must itself have a beginning in a given tradition. The goal of inquiry is the largest, most harmonious reconciliation of what is known generally and what is as yet specifically problematic. That goal of harmony is most threatened when the number of specific anomalies has multiplied and gathered so as to create the stresses, the crises, that ultimately generate a paradigm shift.

Scholars from various fields have applied the Kuhnian model profitably to an enormous range of problems—albeit sometimes promiscuously so. Kuhn has helped illuminate such disparate problems as the demise of avant-garde art, shifting patterns in English social thought, the Darwinian revolution, the rise of Freudian psychoanalysis, and the industrial revolution.[4] There is little doubt that Kuhn is extraordinarily helpful in ordering large cultural dislocations, particularly those periods of crisis antedating a paradigmatic shift when so much is confusing, little seems certain, authority is fundamentally challenged, and only the most imaginative uses of knowledge will provide the sought-for resolution and harmony.

These were, in the largest sense, precisely the conditions that Henry Adams perceived during the decade of the 1890s, and his attempts to reconcile the accepted paradigms of Newtonianism and Darwinism with the anomalies of the *fin-de-siècle* world produced an artful, eccentric, new kind of paradigm. Adams's paradigm strove to explain, in the languages of science and art, the true nature of historical and personal change, and the skill with which he worked created the unique consistency of vision that demarks the major phase. Only if the paradigmatic character of the major phase is perceived, I would argue, can the individual works that comprise it be fully understood.

Henry Adams was born, as he put it, "under the shadow of the Boston State House" in 1838 and grew up in one of the most remarkable families in America. Presidents, vice-presidents, secretaries of state, senators, congressmen, ministers to France, Russia, Germany, and England, latter-day Puritans all, were as common in the Adams household as coffee cups; young Henry was almost a teenager before he realized every boy did not have a president for a grandfather. After graduating from Harvard in 1858 with a mind, as he wrote in his autobiography, "left open, free from bias, ignorant of facts, but docile," he spent the turmoil of the Civil War years in London, serving as secretary to his father, Lincoln's minister to England, where he witnessed firsthand the extraordinary uses and misuses of political power.

After the war Henry returned to America and tried his hand at journalism. This meant, of course, moving to Washington, the center of power, where an Adams was anything but a stranger. But while his reform-oriented journalism did him little harm, his name did him little good; no appointments came his way. Shocked and disgusted by the corruption and ineptitude of national politics, in 1870 Adams was rescued from further exposure to the indecencies of the Grant regime by an unexpected invitation from President Eliot to teach medieval history to Harvard undergraduates. He knew nothing about medieval history, he protested, but President Eliot was firm; that Henry's father then happened to be chairman of Harvard's Board of Overseers may have stiffened the president's resolve. In any event, Adams began in 1870 a seven-year tenure as assistant professor of history and editor of the prestigious *North America Review*.

In 1877 Adams resigned from Harvard, and he and his wife, Marion Hooper, whom he married in 1872, moved back to Washington to establish one of the brightest and most exclusive salons in the country. Adams began work on his opus, the nine-volume *History of the United States During the Administrations of Jefferson and Madison,* and he and Marion settled into a genteel, scholarly domesticity. Late in 1885, shattered by the death of her father, Marion Adams committed suicide, an event that left a searing, unhealed scar upon her husband. For the rest of his life, each November brought Henry depression and restlessness; in succeeding years he spoke of his life after that fateful day as his "posthumous existence." Stoically, he went into isolation, and mechanically he finished the *History*. Travel and time and the fastness of friends like Clarence King and John Hay helped with what healing there was, but in some respects Adams never fully recovered. One measure of this may lie in the extremity of the term "posthumous." Yet ironically, it was during those posthumous years that Adams reached the maturity and perspective so clearly evident in the writings of the major phase.

By the early 1890s Adams had turned again to his historical studies, but now with a new sensitivity, curiosity, and awareness. Marion's death, a fifteen-month sojourn in the South Seas with the artist John LaFarge (who taught him how to see and use and feel color as a mode of expression), the near collapse of the American economy in 1893, a number of extensive, probing conversations about history and economics with his brother Brooks, and a myriad of startling new scientific discoveries all combined to create in Adams both a new sense of alienation from his times and his country and a new passion for solving the riddle of historical change. Signaled briefly in his presidential address to the American Historical Association in 1894, "The Tendency of History," these new stirrings flowered into the consistent posture of the major phase: the distinctive evocation of thirteenth-century France entitled *Mont-Saint-Michel and Chartres* (1904), the incomparable autobiography, *The Education of Henry Adams* (1907), and two final works, "The Rule of Phase Applied to History" (1909) and the *Letter to American Teachers of History* (1910).

In "The Tendency of History" Henry Adams called upon his colleagues to create a new science of history, to construct with a precision paralleling the physical sciences a history that would "fix with mathematical certainty the path which human society has got to follow."[5] This, to be sure, was not a new tune; historians had played it in various keys throughout the eighteenth and nineteenth centuries. But they had played the tune primarily in Newtonian or Darwinian modalities—that is, as an ascending progression filled with order and harmony and, more important, with a charming assurance of upward movement toward "a possible human perfection." Such a tune few individuals could criticize and all social agencies could applaud. The only problem—and this was the reason for Adams's plea for a new kind of scientific history—was that by the late nineteenth century science no longer seemed to convey the order and the harmonies upon which Newton and Darwin had built. Both science and society, in Adams's view, gave evidence of a discord and fragmentation that the old systematic scientific histories could not account for. If the historians could not fit the recent "disasters and cataclysms" into their theories, a new one would have to be created.

The primary problem with such a new theory, of course, was that it would inevitably bring forth the wrath of those people and institutions who found in its projections an uncongenial future. If science determined that a "socialistic triumph" was inevitable, would the property interests allow its articulation? Or, on the other hand, if a new historical science proclaimed that present social evils would continue in augmented form, few would listen. "In whatever direction we look we can see no possibility of converting history into a science without bringing it into hostility toward one or more of the most powerful organizations of the era." Having sketched this dilemma, Adams characteristically retreated: He had called for a new science of history in one breath, only to chronicle all the obstacles in its path with the next. On the question of what such a new theory would actually look like Adams also demurred, and he concluded his address to the association in a characteristically ambiguous fashion:

Beyond a doubt, silence is best. . . . In these remarks, which are only casual and offered in the paradoxical spirit of private conversation, I have not ventured to express any opinion of my own; or, if I have expressed it, pray consider it as withdrawn. The situation seems to call for no opinion, unless we have some scientific theory to offer; but to me it seems so interesting that, in taking leave of the Association, I feel inclined to invite them, as individuals, to consider the matter in a spirit that will enable us, should the crisis arise, to deal with it in a kindly temper, and a full understanding of its serious dangers and responsibilities.

In Adams's view, of course, the crisis had already arisen. The contemporary paradigms of historians were shopworn and outmoded, and they could not account for the thundering anomalies that were the daily fare of Adams's generation: the fractured economy, sudden shifts in geopolitical power, the twin specters of anarchism and communism, the shocking discoveries of radioactivity and X-rays, the implications of electromagnetism and the intimations of nuclear fission. These shocking developments notwithstanding, historians still clung to their antiquated Newtonian or Darwinian models of historical progress and blithely ignored evidence to the contrary. Such conduct flew in the face of all scientific procedure; clearly a new era was dawning and a new paradigm based on a more adequate scientific foundation was required. To its formulation Adams now turned his considerable energies; the task would occupy him until his death.

Shortly before the turn of the century Henry Adams became convinced that history's movement was from unity to multiplicity, from—here he echoed Spencer—an orderly homogeneity to a chaotic, uncontrollable heterogeneity But locating precisely the principle behind this trajectory as well as illustrating it convincingly were deeply problematic tasks which required enormous research, study, and imagination. By about 1901 or 1902 Adams's theory and strategy were well in hand and he had begun to work them out in detail. The first requirement for a theory of history was a base line, an "anchor," as he called it, from which to chart the course of historical movement. That base line he found in thirteenth-century France, a time and place in which both literal and symbolic order could be found.

In *Mont-Saint-Michel and Chartres,* which has something of the aspect of a fantasy, Adams assumed the role of a kindly old uncle squiring a flock of nieces through the landscape and mindscape of medieval France. Beginning with the dramatic Norman abbey of Mont-Saint-Michel, Adams and his nieces explored a world that existed for a fleeting hundred years, a world in which the church of Mont-Saint-Michel, the Song of Roland, the "full and perfect Gothic" of Chartres Cathedral, and the systematic theology of St. Thomas Aquinas were all expressions of a unique historical unity presided over by the Mother of God. That world was tenuous and fragile and lasted only during the century or so of the Gothic Transition, roughly 1150 to 1250. But during that century man had a transitory glimpse of cosmic harmony brought to earth.

Adams was attracted to the medieval world because it was an ordered, precommercial, prescientific, precapitalist world in which the most profound spiritual, aesthetic, and psychological energies of men and institutions were linked in an organic way. Symbolized archetypically by the Virgin of Chartres, in whose presence all narrow logic and partisan confusion found acceptance and resolution, no individual in that century could feel as lost and futile, as alienated, as Adams did in his own times. In the thirteenth century, as symbolized by church architecture and articulated in the most detailed, explicit fashion by the *Summa Theologica,* thought and emotion, reason and feeling, logic and passion found a perfect reconciliation; for a too brief moment, the collective energies of men and history and the cosmos moved in unison; the city of man and the city of God became one.

It was the Virgin of course, who signified the rapprochement between man and history. It was she whose femininity presided over the energies that built at Chartres; it was she who, at the unconscious level, lovingly animated the masculine consciousness that created the forms of Gothic unity. In her grace and serenity the warlike posture of the archangel Michel, who, with sword upraised, dominated the church militant on the mountaintop, was tamed and made whole. The Virgin concentrated in herself, as Adams put it, "the whole rebellion of man against fate"; in her person the finite and the infinite conjoined, and souls starved for that reconciliation found assurance of succor. It was the Virgin who gave to men their individual and collective identities; it was she, the Queen of Heaven, who reconciled the paradox of the Trinity by absorbing it into herself. Out of that identity had come a strength to build and feel and create no mere discriminating, masculine energy could have supplied. Her presence was everywhere and its effects "united whatever goodness is in created being." She was fundamental to the age. As Adams wrote: "The Virgin filled so enormous a space in the life and thought of the time that one stands now helpless before the mass of testimony to her direct action and constant presence in every movement and form of the illusion with which men thought they thought their existence."[6]

After 1300 or so it was all over, and the world began to grow "cheap," to use Adams's term. The concentration of energies that produced Chartres and the fine balance of faith and logic that was the *Summa Theologica* dissipated in the secularism of the fourteenth century: The unfinished tower at Beauvais stood as a monument to the declension. The church became blatantly corrupt, the state became merely political, and men became primarily commercial. The aesthetic power of Gothic art degenerated into the incipient humanism of the early Renaissance. The fragmentation that is modernity, the fragmentation Adams came to diagram in his final works, "The Rule of Phase" and *Letter to American Teachers of History,* had begun. To understand that process in its intermediate stage we must turn to the *Education,* for that, essentially, is its story.

The Education of Henry Adams dominates the major phase and provides the linkage among the emotional, thematic, and stylistic extremes of *Mont-Saint-Michel* and the "Rule" and the *Letter*; it is the fulcrum on which Adams's paradigm rests. It is no ordinary autobiography, no mere chronicle of externally related events held together by the fact of a common participant-observer. On the contrary, the *Education* is a subtle, complicated rendering by a highly sensitive consciousness of the development of that same consciousness against the background of its times. It has all the formal unity and aesthetic symmetry that Adams found so wanting in the life of twentieth-century society. The *Education* added to a human life the infinite dimensions of art, the realized quality of meaning distilled from the facts of being and then, in a reflexive way, artfully used to reconstruct those facts. Inevitably the facts become in the process much more than their historical reality: They become microcosms for all of human experience at a given historical moment. For this reason, in reading the *Education* one must constantly keep in mind the question why, at a certain stage, Adams felt compelled to create such a work. For the *Education* was not simply an act of piety; it was an attempt to achieve salvation through the ordered reconstruction of a personal identity in its historical context.

The world into which Henry Adams was born was, in his words, an eighteenth-century world, a world from which the accelerating processes of disintegration had to some extent still been held in abeyance. In that world politics was still applied morality, and morality still was a transcription of the laws of nature. The world was still premodern. Adams's generation witnessed, however, in the last four decades of the nineteenth century, that world's final destruction. By 1900 Newtonian certitude had given way to the doubts and uncertainties of the age of Einstein, and the *Education* is the record of Adams's attempt to establish or maintain some vestige of equilibrium in the process. He chose to call this the task of education, and put the problem thus: "From cradle to grave this problem of running order through chaos, direction through space, discipline through freedom, unity through multiplicity, has always been, and must always be, the task of education as it is the moral of religion, philosophy, science, art, politics, and economy...."[7]

Order and chaos, unity and multiplicity, discipline and freedom—here in brief is the tension, the dichotomy, so fundamental to Adams's life and work. The dichotomy could be expressed variously: the one and the many; religion and science; emotion and reason; the feminine and the masculine; the preconscious and the conscious. Like many sensitive observers at the turn of the century Adams had perceived a fundamental schism running through the modern Western mind, a schism explicated by such disparate thinkers as William James, Carl Jung, Henri Bergson, Sigmund Freud, Alfred North Whitehead, and George Santayana, to mention only a few. Yet Adams's depiction of the schism, refracted through the reconstruction of his own life, is uniquely compelling. The *Education* is the story of one man's recognition that modernity had broken all the primary ties—psychic, social, aesthetic, and intellectual—and that if one is to be made whole he must construct for himself a unified vision of the cosmos that will fit the fractured contours of his life and explain his most deeply felt emotional experience.

Such a reading helps to account for the structure of the autobiography and for the recurring pattern of dashed expectations that lies at the heart of what Adams called "education." Through a complex but consistent manipulation of allusion, paradox, metaphor, and symbol, Adams recounts a pilgrim's progress from the ordered world of his grandfathers to the chaotic world of the twentieth century. The *Education*'s underlying theme is the problem of maintaining a coherent, integrated sense of self in a universe whose basic elements are changing from matter to motion, in a universe changing from confidence in the moral law to a universe in which "the only absolute truth was the subconscious chaos below, which everyone could feel when he sought it."[8]

To convey both the objective and subjective dimensions of this change, Adams carefully raised up a labyrinth of dualities, a symbol-laden double helix that spiraled upward through his autobiography in its own deliberate, widening gyre. Beginning with a tension between summer and winter, rural Quincy and urban Boston, the discipline of school and the sensuousness of freedom ("balanced like lobes of the brain"), the *Education* moved steadily toward its crowning dichotomy of the Virgin and the dynamo, symbols that dramatically establish the archetypal dimensions of his historical vision.

The Virgin and the dynamo became the dominating symbols for the various dualities defining that vision. To them all lesser tensions became tributary. We have already seen how he used the Virgin to represent unity. The dynamo, which Adams had witnessed with awe at the Chicago World's Fair, represented a force of "ultimate energy" suggesting the infinite acceleration of modernity toward certain destruction. The sciences that were producing these staggering energies were, like the Virgin, supreme and mysterious in their day. Yet their effect, unlike hers, portended chaos and disintegration. The dynamo gave Adams the complementary symbol he needed to complete his dynamic theory of history; in fact it was only after Adams's attention had been drawn to these two symbols that he was able to articulate his paradigm.

It is, of course, easier to represent unity than multiplicity, order than chaos. Although Adams sketched in extended fashion the chaotic, disintegrative meaning of the dynamo in the *Education,* it is in the end a less successful depiction than its symbolic complement. Not until the "Rule" and the *Letter* did Adams outline fully the dynamo's historic implications. Yet those implications were very much in his mind as he composed his autobiography; that this is so emerges from the *Education* in two ways. The first is the glaring omission of the twenty years bracketing his marriage, an omission which Adams cryptically dismissed as a period not bearing on the problem of "education." Yet it is an omission that takes on great significance in the disintegration of Adams's own life. The *Education* is, in fact, like Adams's life, broken into pieces. Repeatedly fate deals Adams what seem to be pat hands; upon playing them, however, he repeatedly and unaccountably loses. His customary response is "life broke in half," a phrase signifying not merely discontinuity but a sense of betrayal. That the betrayal is often presented in a mocking, self-deprecating way does not alter its true nature.

Secondly, the *Education* itself becomes unified, paradoxically, by this recurring pattern of logical assumptions and expectations rudely shocked and broken by the caprice of events and the rush of experience. Darwinian evolution, for example, fails to evolve; social "progress" produces economic disaster. The cumulative effect of these shocks is inescapable: Logic is no match for history, and every lawful uniformity will produce its exception. That exception, far from proving the rule, renders the hope of unity, law, order mere chimera. Thus Adams is driven to conclude that "Chaos is the law of nature; order is the dream of man," his way of saying that he lived in a universe in which the laws of nature were all under a mysterious and capricious statute of limitations. In the modern world, any moment's truth, however minutely verified, is sooner or later certain to self-destruct. Both the structure and the content of *The Education of Henry Adams* conveyed the sense of Henri Bergson's famous observation. "Life does not proceed by the association and addition of elements but by disassociation and division."

Despite this knowledge, Adams's own passion was for certainty, for comprehension, for assurance that his assumptions were valid and his facts accurate and complete. This passion of course served him well as scholar and historian. But his need for certainty went beyond the ordinary caution of the academic. Adams was a son of the Puritans, and somehow his personal fate was deeply involved in the quest for certitude. To borrow William James's terms, Adams's temperament revealed both the skepticism and empiricism of the "tough-minded," and the longing for unity and repose of the "tender-minded." This helps to explain, finally, why he turned to the autobiographical form as a vital part of his quest for certitude: In a world in which all assurance, even down to the level of the structure of the atom, seemed to disintegrate on close scrutiny, the only unity left was consciousness. And even that, as Adams well knew, was a precarious unity indeed.

Adams had, in fact, been compelled to write his autobiography out of the need to explore the nature of consciousness and its relationship to history. The exploration was a crucial, necessary part of the paradigm he was creating on a larger-than-personal canvas. The precise steps which led him to write the *Education* cannot be retraced, but this much we do know. By the late 1890s Adams had become convinced that history's movement was from unity to multiplicity, and working out the precise meaning of those terms had begun to take up his full time. By about 1900 or 1901 he had begun to define the first of those terms and *Mont-Saint-Michel* was the result. In 1902 he read William James's *Principles of Psychology* and it was this work, I am convinced, which crystallized his autobiographical resolve by confronting him with yet another shattering anomaly. For in the *Principles* James stated bluntly the extent to which modernity meant multiplicity when he observed that the most absolute disjunction in nature was the unbroachable gulf between two consciousnesses. This episode, alluded to only obliquely in the *Education*, marked a turning point in Adams's life work, and the autobiography itself was one of the eventual results. Perhaps it is fitting that it is Albert Einstein who best sums up the kind of paradigmatic process Adams went through. Einstein put it this way:

Man tries to make for himself in the fashion that suits him best a simplified and intelligible picture of the world; he then tries to some extent to substitute this cosmos of his for the world of experience, and thus to overcome it. This is what the painter, the poet, the speculative philosopher, and the natural scientist do, each in his own fashion. Each makes this cosmos and its construction the pivot of his emotional life, in order to find in this way the peace and security which he cannot find in the narrow whirlpool of experience.[9]

The *Education of Henry Adams* ended by illustrating the problem of historical change rather than giving it a precise, scientific formulation. History moved, Adams suggested, from unity to multiplicity—from the wholeness and completeness of a religious, feminine-dominated world to the partiality and fractionalism of a scientific, masculine-oriented world—and somewhere on the horizon, he hinted, there lurked an apocalyptic smashup, a point beyond which human attempts to control the energies unleashed by mere rationality would fail in some unearthly, spectacular cataclysm. The *Education* thus supplies the keystone to the paradigmatic arch of the major phase; it is the carefully hewn element uniting the subjective, poetic evocation of order in *Mont-Saint-Michel and Chartres* with the objective, scientific description of impending chaos found in the "Rule" and the *Letter*. Viewed thus, the works of the major phase can be seen to recapitulate the progression from unity to multiplicity that was the essence of his paradigm.

It was not until 1909 and 1910 that Adams was able to state the last formulation of his model with the scientific precision and vocabulary it required. Yet looking back from the "Rule" and the *Letter* one can see that Adams's progression from "The Tendency of History" to *Mont-Saint-Michel* through the *Education* to these final works was sure-handed, knowing, and linear. It was also, in the most profound sense of the word, artful, for each of the statements was rendered in a style appropriate to its particular message and truth. The declension Adams was documenting in history was at least partly aesthetic, and consequently when one reaches his final writings, one is struck by their sparseness of imagery and the apposite, mechanical quality of their language.

In the "Rule" and the *Letter* two nineteenth-century hypotheses, Lord Kelvin's second law of thermodynamics, or entropy, and Willard Gibbs's rule of phase, provided Adams with the principles for his final statement. In the "Rule" Adams drew an analogy between Gibbs's formula for the stages of equilibrium through which chemical compounds pass—solid, fluid, vapor, electricity, ether—when subjected to variations in pressure, temperature, and volume, and the stages of the concentration and expenditure of energies in history. Just as changes in the temperature and pressure of water transformed it from a fluid to a gaseous state, so changes in human thought and social institutions, he argued, transformed history in a measurable, deterministic fashion.

Under the Rule of Phase . . . man's Thought, considered as a single substance passing through a series of historical phases, is assumed to follow the analogy of water, and to pass from one phase to another through a series of critical points which are determined by the three factors of Attraction, Acceleration, and Volume, for each change of equilibrium.[10]

Geometric increases in the volume of thought operating under the law of squares were propelling man to a point beyond which intellectual equilibrium would soon no longer be physically possible and, presumably, chaos would then reign. Adams even went so far as to plot the trajectory of how the accelerating phase-changes of history threatened to bring thought itself to the "limit of its possibilities in the year 1921."[11]

A basic assumption of "The Rule of Phase," one which Adams went to great lengths to support, was that thought, like electricity or gravity, was a form of energy. As such, he reasoned, it functioned according to invariable physical laws. This being true, the historian's task had become greatly simplified: All he needed now was to master certain physical principles and axioms and apply them to history. In one sense, the historian's job was finished. In place of the historian now stood the physicist: Art was to yield to science. "Sooner or later," he declared, "every apparent exception, whether man or radium, tends to fall within the domain of physics." In the *Letter to American Teachers* Adams went on to exchange his artist's palate for the physicist's slide rule.

The physical principle underlying the *Letter* was the second law of thermodynamics, or entropy, which had first been set forth in 1852, and which Adams discovered around the turn of the century. It was Lord Kelvin's principle which, more than any other, gave unity and some aspect of scientific credibility to Adams's paradigm. As Adams interpreted it, the law of entropy stated that the fixed amount of energy with which the universe began was, with every expenditure of physical or mental effort in the cosmos, being dissipated: "... granting that the universe was a closed box from which nothing could escape,—the higher powers of energy tended always to fall lower...."[12] As degradation inexorably proceeded, the universe moved from primal heat and motion toward coldness, stillness, and a final resting place somewhere near minus 273 degrees Centigrade. All of life, society, and history had to yield before this total, constant, accelerating dissipation. The sun would condense and wither, the stars would grow cold, eternal night would descend; given the law of entropy, the end of the universe was assured.

To support his point Adams cited a variety of contemporary authorities in physics, mathematics, natural philosophy, geology, and anthropology, all of whom concurred that the cosmic energies were irrecoverably dissipating themselves at what he suggested was an accelerating rate. Generally, however, this scientific consensus was being ignored by students of history, particularly in America. "If the entire universe, in every variety of active energy, organic and inorganic, human, divine, is to be treated as a clockwork that is running down, society can hardly go on ignoring the fact forever. . . . The universe has been terribly narrowed by thermodynamics."[13] Committed to an archaic progressivism based on an uncritical acceptance of Darwin or Compte or Spencer, or some vagrant German Idealism, however, professors of history shunned entropy in favor of evolutionary or dialectical sentiment. Adams's goal was to shake his fellow historians out of their vast complacency by forcing them to take entropy into account in their systems and theories.

The vision of history contained in the *Letter* systematically took the dominant assumptions of American historians at the turn of the century and stood them on their collective heads. Under the law of degradation the most recent and advanced developments in thought and society became, by inversion, the latest and most powerful contributions to that ultimate extinction toward which all tended. Civilization itself, far from representing the culmination of upward-moving historical tendencies, was but the most recent and pervasive form taken by energy as it dissipated. So too with man and his works, his will and his intellect. Appearing late in the sequence of creation did not mean that man was the ultimate product of some cosmic teleological process but simply that he was the most recent (and hence lowest) form of universal degradation. The more refined and powerful his achievements, the more degrading were their implications. All that current opinion pointed to with pride—industrialization, technology, science, art—became evidence of the charging, impending doom toward which all human energies were directed. Adams's theory of degradation inverted the mainstream of contemporary historical opinion and turned progress against itself: Silence and death were to be the ultimate rewards of human effort.

There was in all of this so strong an element of Adams's dyspeptic personality and declining circumstances in life that at least one critic has dismissed the "Rule" and the *Letter* as "irony and tomfoolery," as Adams's last wry, mocking joke on those who took science and scientism as the Alpha and Omega of modern knowledge. And there was, to be sure, a Puckish, gleeful aspect to Adams's demolition of the prevailing historical refraction of his day. Adams had taken a familiar, apocalyptic vision, once couched in terms of Christian eschatology, and translated it into the formalistic jargon of modern science. The result was a resplendent irony, the kind of suspension Adams delighted in:

From the beginning of philosophy and religion, the thinker was taught by the mere act of thinking, to take for granted that his mind was the highest energy of nature. . . . (But) as a force (Reason) must obey the laws of force; as an energy it must content itself with such freedom as the laws of energy allow; and in any case it must submit to the final and fundamental necessity of Degradation. The same law, by still stronger reasoning, applies to the Will itself.[14]

Even the discovery of the second law of thermodynamics and its application to history represented but the most recent and hence degraded of acts. Adams's own intellectual endeavors, as he best knew and appreciated, were nothing more than further dissipations of an already enfeebled energy!

It is a mistake, however, to dismiss Adams's theory simply as a joke. Even though, as William Jordy has shown, Adams twisted the scientific theories with which he worked to fit his paradigm, it is the paradigm and not its specific warrantableness with which we are here concerned. Adams devoutly believed that the very adhesives of culture—commonly held faiths, values, purposes, obligations, and restraints—were being dissolved by modernity, and his paradigm aimed at the most precise and comprehensive explanation he could offer for such a sweeping declension. If minor distortions of either science or history were required to illuminate this larger truth, they had simply to be treated as poetic license; the larger truth held firm. It is, for example, pointless to quibble over the historical accuracy of Adams's depiction of thirteenth-century France. Doubtless no culture or times were ever as holistic as the unified structure Adams described. The point is that in *Mont-Saint-Michel and Chartres* Adams was not so much writing history as evoking a cultural and psychological ideal: a time and state in which men's hearts and minds and lives were made coherent because, to them, the universe had been made whole by faith, and reason and imagination could, for once, reinforce each other. Such a vision of order was absolutely necessary if he was to find a way of charting the chaos that surrounded him in the twentieth century.

What we are left with as we contemplate the major phase at first seems puzzling. Adams aimed to produce a "scientific" paradigm for change that perhaps in his own eyes—certainly in ours—ended up neither truly scientific nor, in conventional terms, historical. His was an extraordinary achievement, but in the final analysis it must be understood in terms very different from those of either science or history. For Adams, like Yeats, saw that the center could not hold; he too glimpsed the rough beast of the apocalypse, and tried to plot its course and discover its meaning with what seemed to him the best tools the mind of man had forged: the blended languages of art and of science. As his friend John LaFarge observed, Adams's historic sense amounted to "poetry," and it is in this way only that we can appreciate the larger dimensions of that paradigm he called his "education."

Adams witnessed, during his lifetime, the death of romantic possibility: the death of that belief in a sublime organicism that allowed men to celebrate—or at least to hope for—a sense of oneness with the universe. He knew that in the disjointed world of the twentieth century such hopes were futile and such celebrations empty echoes of the past. Yet, as the major phase reveals, he too kept hoping and, if not celebrating, at least trying to understand. The result was an eccentric, highly personalized kind of unified field theory for time that even he probably didn't believe in wholeheartedly, but which represented his most profound attempt at bringing conceptual, paradigmatic order out of the experiential chaos of his life and times.

In the end it was this task of "education," of comprehension, of seeing things whole, that mattered so vitally, because with each passing decade the task became more elusive and arduous and, correspondingly, more necessary to the business of being human. Adams's characteristic pose was to proclaim himself a failure at the task, and he found scant consolation in the fact that no one of his generation seemed more a success at it than he. If in the end he failed to educate himself, he left for others a compelling record of the kinds of things that were required. And if the paradigm of the major phase failed fully to suffice for anyone's education to modernity, it nonetheless contained a magnificently provocative interpretation of medievalism and an autobiography that stands, as Charles Beard once put it, as at least one book that made Columbus's journey worthwhile.

Notes

1. See, for example, David A. Hollinger, "T. S. Kuhn's Theory of Science and Its Implications for History," *American Historical Review* 78 (April 1973): 370–93.
2. Ibid., p. 371.
3. Thomas S. Kuhn, *In Structure of Scientific Revolutions,* 2nd ed. (Chicago: University of Chicago Press, 1970).
4. See Hollinger, pp. 371–72, and Anthony F. C. Wallace, "Paradigmatic Processes in Cultural Change," *American Anthropologist* 74 (June 1972): 468–78.
5. The following citations are from "The Tendency of History," in Henry Adams, *The Degradation of the Democratic Dogma* (New York: Harper & Row, 1969), pp. 125–33.
6. Henry Adams, *Mont-Saint-Michel and Chartres* (Boston: Houghton Mifflin, 1953), pp. 249–50.
7. Henry Adams, *The Education of Henry Adams* (Boston: Houghton Mifflin, 1961), p. 12.
8. Ibid., p. 435.
9. Albert Einstein, *Ideas and Opinions* (New York: Crown Publishers, 1962), p. 225.
10. Adams, *Degradation,* p. 281.
11. Ibid., p. 308.
12. Ibid., p. 141.
13. Ibid., p. 261.
14. Ibid., pp. 207–8.

Bibliography

General

Boller, Paul F. *American Thought in Transition: The Impact of Evolutionary Naturalism, 1865 – 1900.* Chicago: Rand McNally and Co., 1969.
Jaher, Frederick C. *Doubters and Dissenters: Cataclysmic Thought in America, 1885 – 1918.* New York: The Free Press of Glencoe, 1964.
Marcell, David W. *Progress and Pragmatism: James, Dewey, Beard and the American Idea of Progress.* Westport, Conn.: Greenwood Press, 1974.
May, Henry F. *The End of American Innocence: A Study of the First Years of Our Time, 1912 – 1917.* Chicago: Quadrangle Books, 1959.
Persons, Stow. *The Decline of American Gentility.* New York: Columbia University Press, 1973.

Writings by Henry Adams

Adams, Henry. *Mont-Saint-Michel and Chartres.* Boston: Houghton Mifflin Co., 1913.
———. *The Education of Henry Adams.* Boston: Houghton Mifflin Co., 1918.
———. *The Degradation on the Democratic Dogma.* Brooks Adams, ed. New York: Macmillan Co., 1919.
Arvin, Newton, ed. *The Selected Letters of Henry Adams.* New York: Farrar, Straus, 1951.
Cater, Harold Dean, ed. *Henry Adams and His Friends: A Collection of His Unpublished Letters.* Boston: Houghton Mifflin Co., 1947.
Ford, Worthington Chauncey, ed. *The Letters of Henry Adams, 1892 – 1918,* vol . 2. Boston and New York: Houghton Mifflin Co., 1938.

Writings About Henry Adams

Donovan, Timothy Paul. *Henry Adams and Brooks Adams: The Education of Two American Historians*. Norman: University of Oklahoma Press, 1961.

Hume, Robert A. *Runaway Star: An Appreciation of Henry Adams*. Ithaca, N.Y.: Cornell University Press, 1951.

Jordy, William. *Henry Adams: Scientific Historian*. New Haven, Conn.: Yale University Press, 1952.

Levenson, J. C. *The Mind and Art of Henry Adams*. Boston: Houghton Mifflin, 1957.

Stevenson, Elizabeth. *Henry Adams, a Biography*. New York: Macmillan, 1955.

GERALD E. CRITOPH

The Contending Americas

What is America? This is a question that has intrigued the world since the last decade of the fifteenth century. To many people it has meant a fabulous source of wealth. Others have seen in it opportunities not possible in countries still burdened with centuries of traditions. It has been a haven for the religiously oppressed, a second chance for social and economic failures, or an arena for making one's reputation. Because of the variety of visions which it has generated, America has attracted a broad diversity of persons to its shores. These different groups have contended for the fruits of the land and for the means of control over the land ever since. These competitive efforts have had a share in shaping the structure and the spirit of the United States as we know it today.

While the religious vision is persistent in American traditions, economic opportunity provided a greater appeal for emigrating Europeans in the seventeenth, eighteenth, nineteenth, and early twentieth centuries. Land was the lure. To Europeans, the possession of land meant economic independence and more desirable social status. Coming from areas with limited amounts of land to a continent where it was relatively free gave the migrants hope for new life for themselves and their children.

Of course, it was not just a matter of crossing the ocean and taking up a piece of unused land. Rival forces were making claims for different distribution and use of the land. The monarchs of Europe had divided up the hemisphere and incorporated their respective portions into their empires. Imperial policy makers usually assumed that the colonies existed for the benefit of the empire, not necessarily for the colonists. This was especially true in the mercantilist era when the colonists were expected to supply the imperial masters with gold, raw materials, and markets for the developing imperial economies.

So from the beginning of its settlement, there has been contention over the meaning of America. Was it to be a conglomeration of individuals each going his own way, each following his own dream; or was it to be a well-ordered society of generally cooperative groups whose immediate goals fitted in with a universally desired national destiny? The tensions set up in the beginning have continued to influence the development of American society: the tensions between freedom and order, between independent and collective goals, between individualism and statism.

I

Part of the motivation for autonomy and eventually independence from the British Empire came out of the feeling of frustration over individual goals blocked by imperial demands for colonial responsibility. The frontiersman, the farmer, the merchant, the embryonic industrialist, and the ambitious politician objected to the restraints (light as they were) that were imposed in the name of the British imperial system. Some Americans felt strongly enough to carry the colonies into a revolution, which the British prosecuted with great reluctance and surprising forbearance. Even in fighting for their independence the Americans resisted the temptation to organize their efforts with much unity. Only a small minority agreed with Alexander Hamilton and George Washington that national loyalty should transcend local allegiance.

The advocates of extreme individualism and localism were in the ascendancy during and immediately after the Revolution. Once the imperialists were run out of the country, there seemed no need for a strong, unified structure. The farmers went back to their land, and, since they constituted about 90 percent of the population, there was no great impetus to establish more than the minimum of governments.

Like many another war, the Revolution was followed by an economic decline. This depression brought out a split in American attitudes. There were Americans who were beginning to play the role that British moneylenders had played before the Revolution. They were the creditors of those whose ambitions were slightly greater than their pocketbooks. On the other side ranged those who borrowed money primarily because it was a factor in producing goods and services, rather than something to manipulate. The split centered on disagreement as to the nature of property and the nature of man.

This division developed out of differences between two of the most influential men of the early republic, Thomas Jefferson and Alexander Hamilton. The rivalry between their visions has been so profound that it has persisted in one form or another until the present. Henry Bamford Parkes, in his *The American Experience,* identifies Jefferson's view of an ideal society in terms of agrarian democracy and Hamilton's in terms of aristocratic capitalism. According to Parkes, nineteenth-century America was able to combine the two by selecting the democracy of Jefferson and the capitalism of Hamilton, only because free land existed to absorb the inconsistencies of the conflict.[1] The struggle has not been so patly resolved in the twentieth century.

The agrarians took their cue from John Locke's assertion that each person had a right to property and that no one should have any more than he could work. The agrarians also agreed that the person who works the land should have a primary right to the land. This would include a prior right to the fruits of the land.

The Hamiltonian view emphasized the deed or grant of the land. The deed was a contract and whoever held the deed had primary right to the land and its fruits.

This meant that the mortgagee and the landlord had a claim on the goods produced by the mortgagor and the tenant. Because the contract was the key to the Hamiltonian position, one of the major provisions of the Constitution assured protection of contracts and a number of Marshall's decisions reinforced their sacred nature. According to the contractual point of view, it was irrelevant who worked the land or who actually made a product. Legal possession of the land, the raw materials, and the tools of production determined who was to decide on the division of the profits.

II

Another way to look at the contention between agarian democrats and aristocratic capitalists is in terms of the evaluation of goods and services. What were they? Were they the products of work and creative ingenuity as the agrarians claimed, or were they primarily the objects of the market to buy and sell in the process of making a profit as the capitalists claimed? The agrarians identified the goods and services with the workman; they were his, because his work had produced them. The capitalists maintained that the forces of supply and demand on the market determined the values of goods and services. This would imply that goods and services were interchangeable; therefore it was fruitless and irrevelant to identify any specific good or service with a workman. By further implication, the workman was interchangeable, so his price (or wage) was determined by forces of supply and demand on an impersonal market.

The agrarian way of life generally supported the view that each man's production was his. His goods and services drew value from his identity with them. The urban way of life tended to put market values on goods and services—what profit could be made from the transaction. As long as the farmers maintained a high degree of self-sufficiency, they could act with the independence and forthrightness that have been marked traits of the traditional American character. As the farmers increasingly produced for the urban market, they lost more and more control of their personal destinies.

III

Because the majority of Americans gained their livelihood from the soil during the first three hundred years of American history, agrarian principles formed the foundation of American traditions. By the beginning of the nineteenth century, these principles had been incorporated into the Declaration of Independence, a number of state constitutions, the Bill of Rights, and the writing of Thomas Jefferson and John Taylor. Their widespread acceptance was indicated by the capture and control of the government by the Jeffersonian Republicans and their successors, the Jacksonian Democrats.

The agrarian preoccupation with land was something migrating Europeans brought with them to America. Most of them aspired to the European aristocratic prerogatives that went with the ownership and control of land. They saw the possession of land as a major means to independence and self-sufficiency. Because land was so much easier to obtain in America than in Europe, it was possible for almost every family to have its own farm. This led to the family-oriented farm instead of the village or manor-oriented operation. In time, the family became a basic principle of the American way of life.

The ideal was a self-contained, self-sufficient farm identified with a man and his family. In the agrarian view of life, each man had to contend with the forces of nature for his success in life, not with his fellowmen. His relations with other men should be occasionally cooperative, but seldom competitive. He should be self-reliant and independent of others, not only of their help but of their hindrance.

Americans could practice in large numbers the ideal of the free individual, the man who made himself what he was. They did not have to live out predetermined lives as they would have had to do in Europe. They thought of themselves as new men and of America as a new world. As R. W. B. Lewis has pointed out, in his *The American Adam,* Americans in the nineteenth century developed the concept of the American Adam. Nineteenth-century American writers often referred to humanity's "second chance" in America and to Americans as born free of the sins of the "Old World."[2]

Because each person is born basically good and because working with the soil in God's clean air keeps a person good, the agrarians maintained that each man could govern himself, especially if he were a farmer. If this is so, then "the best Government is that which governs least" and which is concentrated at the local levels. As a matter of fact, some American agrarians talked as though they preferred a political society close to anarchy.

In the few circumstances when agrarians considered collective action necessary, they tended to turn to what they termed "natural aristocrats." These were men who had demonstrated the wise and fruitful use of their land. Ideally, they would be those who held only the land they could work profitably and who worked profitably all the land they held.

A major agrarian precept, therefore, was that government should be in the hands of those who owned and worked the soil. They were the good men, the wise men, and the responsible men of society. In order to keep society clear of corruption, all men should have the opportunity to own and work the land. Crowding into cities should be discouraged, because the agrarians looked upon the cities and those who dwelt therein with suspicion.

As a matter of fact, most agrarians maintained that the city was a major source of evil in society. Those who had traveled in Europe in the eighteenth century had, like Jefferson and Franklin, developed a fear that the growth of cities in the United States would produce bestial masses similar to those they saw in London and Paris. As cities grew in the United States, their fears seemed to be justified when large sections of the northern cities degenerated into slums.

However, slums were not the only indication of the city's evil for the agrarians. Whenever a countryman went to a city for business or pleasure, he seemed to see around him all the sins against which the Bible warns. Gambling, covetousness, stealing, murder, lying, and fornication were concentrated in such greater degrees than he saw them in the rural areas that he was convinced that the city was their origin.

As if it were not bad enough that the agrarian saw the urbanites wallowing in sin and corruption, he discovered that when he or his children went to the city they often were personally affected by the city's evil forces. Because of his innocence or naïveté, the countryman often was lured into circumstances in which his money was taken from him, or he was beaten or killed, or his pristine virtue was lost in one of the city's dens of iniquity. In the case of the country girl, American fiction and songs are full of the "fate worse than death" waiting in the city for the unsuspecting and trusting virgin.

The city slicker was a character in American agrarian mythology from the beginning of the country's history. His main goal in life was to take in the country "rube" in any way available. He cheated the countryman of his butter and egg money on market days, or he took away his farm in the form of a foreclosed mortgage and then rented the farm to the former owner at an outrageous price. The city slicker has been anything from a fly-by-night confidence man to the most powerful eastern banker or merchant. In more recent times, the industrial monopolist has taken his place among the city slickers in agrarian lore.

As a result of these images of the city, agrarians have tried to regulate commerce and banking, especially as they relate to the agricultural sector of American society. They also believed with Jefferson that industry should be restricted to a bare minimum. When this proved to be impossible in the early nineteenth century, they tried every way they could to keep industrial development within narrow bounds, because they saw industry as one of the most powerful forces encouraging city growth.

Industry was especially insidious to the agrarians, because they predicted, quite correctly, that industrial workers could never be completely independent of their employers. And when the industrialists began bringing shiploads of immigrants across the Atlantic and setting up company-controlled towns and cities, they were convinced that industrial workers, native or foreign, were the slaves of the employers, except in the technical sense. Therefore, the agrarians fought to keep political control of the local, state, and national governments as long as they could. The fight against reapportionment of legislative districts in the 1960s was a consequence of this belief.

Some of the major American democratic beliefs resulted from the experiences of the majority of Americans in agrarian settings during the formative years of the republic. For instance, the strong, abiding conviction that a free individual's identity should be held sacred and that his dignity and integrity should not be violated was a belief that came out of situations in which an individual had to confront the forces of nature just about on his own. Life and death, success and failure appeared to be determined by personal merit.

IV

Because the agrarians were in the majority in the republic's formative years, their beliefs and their view of man and society became the dominant ones in American traditions. However, there was a growing body of urban attitudes which evolved along with, and often competed with, the agrarian. In the twentieth century, some elements of these two traditions are in conflict and underlie the social, economic, and political problems of our times.

The towns and cities of seventeenth- and eighteenth-century America were basically commercial in origin, as were many of those established in the nineteenth century. They grew from settlements around good harbors on the coast, at the junctions of river branches, or where highway trails crossed rivers or other trails. In the nineteenth century, railroads accelerated the growth of commercial cities and brought about the rise of some new ones. As the Industrial Revolution reached the United States in the nineteenth century, city development took on different traits, but trade route locations still acted as a determining factor.

For the urbanite, therefore, trade has been the fundamental activity of life and the market the central mechanism of society. It would follow, then, that society's leaders were the merchants and bankers. If exchange was basic, the masters of exchange must be the fittest of all in the competitive struggle that permeated the urban scene.

Competition not only determined the social structure for the urbanites, it provided explanations for the nature of man and society. Its rules were impersonal and absolute. Their violation, for whatever reason, invited disaster. Attempts at regulating trade by any non-merchant agency has prompted strong resistance by those whose interests lie in trade.

According to the capitalist writers in nineteenth- and twentieth-century United States, competition in the market operates best when each participant knows his own best interests and acts with them as ultimate goals. The argument has been that the greatest advances for society come out of the struggle among the selfish interests of society's members. So, ideally, the market mechanism with its rivalry of selfish interests should govern society, but practice demonstrated that some government was necessary to act as referee, to provide protection for property from the disgruntled losers in the conflict, and to assure a relatively stable monetary system within which to operate.

It was recognized that any government would be subject to these same principles of competing selfish interests. Therefore, the best kind of government in a capitalist society would be one in which each selfish interest was balanced by other selfish interests. Any man or small group of men could not be expected to be altruistic enough to govern others, so a constitutional system incorporating checks and balances to limit the power of any one group seemed to be the logical solution. From the beginning of the republic, one of the major arenas of contention has been in the government. Each interest group competed to gain as much control of the political machinery as it could. In this way it has hoped to get preferential treatment from the referee. One of the results of this process has been the steady increase in size of government on all levels, despite the pious statements by almost all leaders that they were working for the reduction of governmental centralization and power.

Adherence to the unregulated, competitive, open market carries with it some contradictions. Success in the market usually leads to the increase in the size of operation. Because loyalty and cooperation within an enterprise contribute to its success, the larger an operation gets the more cooperation and collective action it demands and the less competitive impulse on an individual basis is encouraged. In addition, the organization asks that its personnel give up personal individuality to the organization. The organization men are expected to blend their identity with that of their company. The individualism touted as an essential part of the market mechanism is discouraged to ensure the success of the overall enterprise.

There are other collective tendencies connected with the demands of urban life. Industrial and commercial operations have brought together larger and larger numbers of persons to live in close proximity. Many of the necessary services for human life must be shared, instead of being obtained by personal effort. Such things as water, maintenance of health, and sewage, as well as fire and police protection seem to be handled best by some sort of collective action. In each of them, cooperation is essential to effective results.

Bringing together large numbers of persons in an area provides greater potential for educational and recreational activities. With more persons involved, a greater variety of alternatives can be offered. The more concentrated wealth of the urban communities holds possibilities for public and private educational facilities that the rural areas cannot hope to equal. Nor can the agrarians duplicate the accomplishments of the cities in the realms of music, theatre, or other entertainment which requires sums of money and reasonably large audiences to support them continuously.

The urban contradictions often result in a rhetoric that espouses the idea of the free individual in competition with other free individuals in an open market, while acting to eliminate competition and establish exclusive control over particular sectors of the community. Some of the rhetoric has been borrowed from the agrarian tradition, particularly from the works of Jefferson. This has created the appearance of a resolution of the contention between the two Americas, with the blessing of a man who has become one of America's patron saints.

V

My intention in describing the two major traditions in American life has not been to imply that they are clear-cut in definition or that the American people have been split neatly along agrarian-urban lines. As a matter of fact, because Americans are as practical and pragmatic as they are, they tend to adapt the principles and arguments that seem to provide their specific cases with plausible rationalizations. A brief summary of some highlights in the agrarian-urban conflict should illustrate some of the twists and turns it has taken.

In the early years of the republic the rival forces tended to align themselves behind Jefferson and Hamilton. The Jeffersonian Republicans contended that agriculture was man's most exalted pursuit and that land was the most legitimate form of wealth. They maintained that the leadership of society should be in the hands of the most efficient and successful tillers of the soil and that the right to select the leaders should be restricted to those whose initiative and abilities were sufficient to earn them some property. They argued that the economy and the government should favor those whose lives were related to the soil. They feared the development of commerce and industry beyond the point of providing minimum services to the agricultural sectors of society. Above all, they wished to restrict the growth of cities and towns to ensure an independent, responsible citizenry.

On the other hand, the Hamiltonian Federalists considered the general mass of Americans incapable of governing themselves. The rich and well-born were the Federalist choices for leaders and they would keep the voting franchise restricted to those owning a large amount of property. They disagreed with the Jeffersonian tenet that "the best Government is that which governs least." As a matter of fact, they advocated strong central government. This last carried the explicit assumption that the government should do all it could to encourage and advance commerce and industry.

In the first twelve years of the republic's history, Federalist control of the government established a reverence for contracts reinforced by over three decades of John Marshall's leadership in the Supreme Court. Respect for the Presidency and the central government's fiscal responsibility were other legacies from the Federalists. In somewhat ironic fashion, these erstwhile nationalists became states' rights advocates and secessionists during the War of 1812.

The Jeffersonian Republicans opposed the centralizing tendencies of the Federalist administrations, issuing the Kentucky and Virginia resolutions advocating states' rights. However, after 1801 they found it difficult to govern without contributing to the increase in the central government's powers. Louisiana was purchased to provide room for agrarian expansion, but it was accomplished with Hamiltonian methods. The Embargo and Non-intercourse acts were passed to maintain the nation's neutrality, but the reduction of overseas trade encouraged the industrial development that agrarians dreaded. The western agrarians were largely responsible for inciting the fervor that took the country into the War of 1812, but the capitalists gained from industrial growth and the country's leaders became convinced that a second Bank of the United States was needed for monetary self-sufficiency. They even went so far as to pass a protective tariff in 1816 that was designed to stimulate commerce and industry throughout the country.

By 1824, the agrarians in the Republican Party were beginning to feel the old suspicions toward the merchants and industrialists of the cities, especially the cities of the East. The Bank of the United States, located in Philadelphia, was gaining more power and influence to what seemed to be the detriment of the agrarians. Under the leadership of Andrew Jackson, agrarians gained control of the central government in 1829. Many had old scores to settle dating from the panics that had wiped out savings and taken away hard-earned, but mortgaged, farms.

Nicholas Biddle, president of the Bank, was confident that such a powerful institution could control the inroads of the Jackson administration. He moved against Jackson through his cohorts in Congress, Daniel Webster and Henry Clay, who were beginning to represent the moneyed and privileged interests. Jackson destroyed the Bank, but the conflict precipitated the Panic of 1837 which wiped out thousands of farmers and accelerated the Westward Movement. In the fight against the privileged groups, the agrarian defenders strengthened the central government as the agency most able to cope with great concentrations of wealth and power.

Another showdown between the agrarians and the capitalists helped to bring on the Civil War of 1861–65. By this time, however, the agrarians were split in goals and methods. The northern and western agrarians still adhered to the ideal of the family farm, run by an independent, self-reliant family unit. The southern agrarians had developed what might be called an industrialized agriculture based on slave labor organized in the plantation system. In addition to these fundamental differences in style of living, the western and southern agrarians were further separated by the development of east-west railroad lines that linked the growing industries of the Northeast with the food and raw material-producing areas of the West.

The war replaced the plantation system with the share-crop system, which might be described as the southern version of the family-farm model. The demands of the war accelerated the use of machinery on western farms and contributed to the increasing dependence of western agriculture on eastern markets. One of the major results of the war was to establish the financial, commercial, and industrial interests of the East and Old Northwest as the directors of American destinies for the rest of the nineteenth century.

One of the conflicts that demonstrated this ascendancy was the struggle between the agrarians, represented by the Granges, and the capitalists, represented by the railroads. The Granger laws, passed by a number of western states in the 1870s to regulate the railroads, were examples of the Jeffersonian concept of local and state action by voluntary organizations of independent citizens. These laws were declared invalid by the U.S. Supreme Court on the grounds that the states did not have jurisdiction in the area of interstate commerce, according to the U.S. Constitution. The use of this Hamiltonian legacy by the railroads forced the agrarians, in self-defense, to move into the national arena where they gained the passage of the Interstate Commerce Act of 1887. While this act did not accomplish all their desired goals, it taught the agrarians that they needed to have a strong hand in national affairs.

One of the decisive battles in the war between the agrarian democrats and the aristocratic capitalists was the presidential campaign of 1896 between William Jennings Bryan and William McKinley. In one of the most clear-cut campaigns of presidential history, the western and southern agrarians, financed by the silver-mine owners, attempted to capture the central government from the financial, commercial, and industrial leaders of the Northeast and Midwest. A number of factors seem to have contributed to McKinley's victory: Mark Hanna's systematized collection and spending of campaign funds, effective pamphleteering against "free silver," intimidation of employees by industrialists, casting of Bryan in the role of a "dangerous radical," and the increasing aspirations of Americans for middle class comfort and respectability.

After the 1896 campaign, agrarian power and influence experienced more setbacks than successes. The United States became increasingly urbanized and industrialized, so that today less than 4 percent of the population gains its livelihood from agriculture.[3] The farmers have been reduced to the position of just another of the interest and influence groups in our society.

Those who are successful are no longer really agrarian. While the family farm ideal continually crops up in legislation and farm literature, U.S. agriculture is becoming more and more industrialized and the farm family is acquiring more and more urban ways. In order to remain on the farm and to earn a living income, farmers have had to face the fact that their operations must be efficient, businesslike, and profitable. This has required larger outlays for machinery and more elaborate organizations. The contemporary farmer either learns to be a businessman, or he is forced to work for someone else.

As this brief sketch would indicate, the agrarians and the capitalists have not practiced either the Jeffersonian or the Hamiltonian ideals with much systematic consistency. The farmers have turned to the central government more and more to salvage what they could of their way of life in an increasingly industrial society. In addition, the small, self-sufficient unit is no longer typical in U.S. agriculture. On the other hand, while the capitalists have welcomed the subsidies Hamilton advocated (whenever they could get them), they have argued for freedom from government regulation in obviously Jeffersonian terms. At the same time, American corporate entities have become so large that they rival the government in many areas of life. It would seem that whatever explanations farmers or businessmen thought were rational they used as legitimate arguments for their cases, regardless of whether any particular principle fitted into a logical system.

VI

Nevertheless, one of the marked characteristics of U.S. history has been the struggle between the agrarian and the capitalist conceptions of life and society. Because of the forces of economic growth, the capitalist concept of life is dominant in practice. According to the 1960 census, about 70 percent of all Americans lived in urban or suburban areas.[4] Most work for large, complex organizations. Few own the means with which their goods and services are produced. Few can act as independent, or autonomous, self-reliant beings. What individualism is possible must be practiced within contexts somewhat narrowly defined by the organizations with which one is affiliated. For most practical purposes, the individual destinies of Americans are determined, or at least largely directed, by those whom Hamiltonians advocated as leaders—the rich and well-born.

Of course, American mythology does not readily admit this. The individual proprietorship in business and agriculture is still extolled as the ideal, even though this economic form comprises a smaller ratio of U.S. enterprise every year. Government regulation is resisted by giant corporations in the name of the small businessman. Union activity is opposed by companies in the name of the individual workman under the guise of "right-to-work" laws. Commonly accepted individual rights are denied the members of some minority groups under the fiction that insisting on them would violate the personal right of choice held by members of the dominant groups. The interpretations of individualism have become so ambiguous and varied that American society is working out a new definition of what an autonomous individual in the second half of the twentieth century can be.

While it is quite apparent that agrarianism is no longer a major force in American life, many of its principles are held to be desirable even in a highly industrialized, urbanized society. They may not be valid in the form that Jefferson expressed them, but their adaptations have wide appeal. Their validity for today's United States seems to depend on their flexibility within an increasingly corporate society and the success with which they can be used in grappling with everyday problems.

One notion that seems to maintain some of its strength is that the city is evil and corrupt. Political statements still ring with that implication. Advertisements seldom picture the joys of city life. Mass media news accounts play up the sensational and sensual aspects of it. Because more and more Americans are living in the urban areas, concerted efforts ought to be made by public and private institutions to improve urban living and to demonstrate that there are possibilities for a fruitful life in the city.

Another ideal that has clung to the American mind is the desire to own land and other forms of property. Homeowners are still considered to be the more stable members of a community. They usually have more voting rights on local matters. While the independence that went with the ownership of one's own farm was not the same as the freedom of action possible in one's own home, the feeling that there is at least one place in a person's life where he can be his own boss is an attractive one for millions of Americans. The wish to own productive property has been satisfied to some extent by the ownership of corporate stock. Even though this carries with it little or no voice in company decisions, the feeling of personal independence can be increased as the size of one's stock portfolio expands.

A third agrarian principle that has been translated into urban and industrial terms is the belief that the prior right to property should go to the person who has established a squatter's claim and has put time and effort into improving that claim. This can be seen today in the labor union insistence upon seniority rights in questions of raises, promotions, and layoffs. It has its political counterpart in legislative committee appointments and advancements.

One of the major tenets of agrarianism has lost its exclusiveness, although it maintains a great deal of appeal. That is the idea that land is *the* major source of wealth. Today, it is generally accepted that land is *one* of the major sources of wealth, sharing its place with a number of other economic factors of production.

Jefferson's vision of the United States as an agrarian republic did not come to pass. Many of the dire consequences that he foresaw for an industrial, urban United States did. They came about as byproducts of the embracing by Americans of Hamilton's vision of a well-balanced economy and a systematic cooperation between the governing and the economic forces.

As a result, the United States tends to combine an ideological rhetoric taken largely from Jefferson and his disciples with practices advocated by Hamilton and his followers. The ideology does not always square with the practice, but it provides the individual with a spirit and a set of long-range goals which carry distinctive American characteristics. These are commonly agreed to be: freedom of choice in most circumstances, equality of opportunity, and the recognition and maintenance of the rights of others.

By adhering to the Jeffersonian ideals which center on the integrity and dignity of the individual, Americans have had a tremendous opportunity to modify the crassness and materialism that lie at the base of Hamiltonian capitalism. These ideals modify the selfishness implicit in the principles of free enterprise with the tolerance and respect for others implicit in agrarian doctrines. As long as corporate, organizational life is qualified by the principles respecting the individual, Americans can claim the Jeffersonian heritage.

Generally, American historians agree that the greatness of the United States stems partly from the combination of Hamiltonian and Jeffersonian precepts. Without the cooperation and support of the government, the industrial and financial development of the country would have gone much slower and might not have gone far at all. Without the insistence upon the rights of all persons, some kind of autocratic society might have developed. Through the contending of the capitalist and agrarian impulses in U.S. society an outstanding civilization has developed with possibilities of attaining goals beyond present imagination. The problem of the present generation of Americans is to maintain the viability of their ideology in the midst of a dynamic, complex world.

Notes

1. Henry Bamford Parkes, *The American Experience* (New York: Vintage Books, 1959), pp. 110 – 14, 141 – 49.
2. R. W. B. Lewis, *The American Adam* (Chicago: University of Chicago Press, 1955), pp. 1–5.
3. Bureau of Census and Economic Research Service, "Farm Population," *Current Population Reports* (Washington, D.C.: U.S. Government Printing Office, 1977), Series P-27, no. 48, p. 1.
4. Bureau of Census, *Statistical Abstract of the United States, 1976* (Washington, D.C.: U.S. Government Printing Office, 1976), p. 18.

MORRELL HEALD

Technology in American Culture

Morrell Heald is Chairman of the American Studies Program at Case Western Reserve University and of the Division of Interdisciplinary Studies in Humanities and Arts. His teaching emphasizes comparative approaches to American culture, and he is now studying the role and experiences of American foreign correspondents in Europe. His most recent book, published by Greenwood Press, and coauthored by Lawrence Kaplan, is entitled Culture and Diplomacy: The American Experience.

What is the promise of technology for America today? And under what circumstances, likely or unlikely, is that promise capable of achievement? On the one hand, we hear that science and technology make possible levels of leisure and material well-being without precedent except in the most utopian of dreams. On the other, we see the distress and dislocation of societies now entering upon industrialization; we recognize discrepancies between the ideal and the real in our own experience; and we find to our dismay that the Russians—and presumably others as well—are able to build an industrial order upon foundations which challenge many of our most cherished values. As if this were not enough, the technology of mass destruction advances at a pace so swift as to outstrip not simply our control but even our comprehension. Is it conflict and destruction, then, which technology offers us rather than a new freedom? Can hopes prove so unfounded and reality so grim?

I

Despite the contemporary concern such questions represent, they are, after all, far from new. In almost every age men have mingled pride with fear at their own audacity in harnessing nature to serve their ends. In Greek mythology Prometheus—giver of the practical arts of healing and the utilization of the earth's mineral resources, as well as of fire, to mankind—suffered the relentless wrath of Zeus. Christianity, too, consistently has taught men to value material well-being below spiritual, however wide the gap between preachment and practice at any given time. Beyond the limits of Western culture, traditions and philosophies other than our own have supported an even more rigorous asceticism. While religious or ideological scruples seem never to have triumphed entirely or for long over countervailing incentives toward earthly comfort and security, strong impulses—rooted no doubt in basic psychological and sociological insights—seem periodically to warn men against the temptation to set too much store by material values, techniques, and achievements. The conflicts, real or presumed, between spiritual and material values which constitute so central a concern of twentieth-century thought are contemporary variations, then, on a perennial theme.

From these conflicts we Americans have ourselves by no means been immune. The form they have taken in our experience is, nevertheless, in some respects distinctive. The intellectual foundations of American culture were laid at a period in European history, the seventeenth and eighteenth centuries, when a reconciliation of matter and spirit seemed a reasonable hope in many quarters. Joseph Addison's acknowledgment of a divine "Original" manifest in the material firmament is a familiar expression of this belief. In America a Crèvecoeur, Franklin, or Jefferson—even a more skeptical John Adams—would surely have rejected the suggestion that scientific and technical progress were incompatible with human freedom and happiness. Nor have the hopes and expectations of successive generations of immigrants to the United States provided a useful text for sermons on the inevitable conflict between material and spiritual or intellectual concerns. More recently, the unprecedented abundance which Americans in overwhelming numbers enjoy has relieved some at least from the necessity of undue preoccupation with worldly needs. Taken together, then, it appears that a combination of forces in our history should have alleviated, if not entirely eliminated, the bitterness of traditional controversies.

Yet, to judge by popular interpretations of American culture, one might conclude that these factors have exercised little or no lasting influence on our attitudes and behavior. A few observers, to be sure, have discovered in the United States a remarkable freedom from gouging materialism, but their insights have largely been overwhelmed in torrents of social criticism insisting that America somehow uniquely reveals the consequences of a progressive subordination of humane values to technical and materialistic drives.[1] Whatever advantages in origins and circumstances the United States may have enjoyed, it is clear that in the view of many of our most influential and articulate critics we, too, have failed to achieve the hoped-for harmonies. As a symbol and instrument of man's age-old struggles with his material environment, technology seems to have won little more intellectual respectability in America than it has been accorded elsewhere.

While such misgivings have seldom been strong enough to interrupt scientific and technical progress, they have nevertheless greatly distorted appreciation of its social consequences. Despite a record of pragmatic adjustment and social innovation in the face of rapid technical change which can command a modest pride, Americans continue to speak in terms reflecting the preconceptions of an earlier age. At times we behave as if pressing human and social dislocations could be left to find automatic solutions and insist that preindustrial institutions can encompass the needs of a complex industrial order with little strain and less amendment; at others, faced with the necessity of changes we are unable to accept, we invoke the notion of conspiracy, foreign or domestic, social or intellectual, to justify continued resistance. In such erratic responses the meaning of our actual experience in combining technological change with human advancement eludes recognition. We have claimed too much or too little for the American experiment and, in so doing, have failed to probe the terms of some of our most significant successes and failures.

Events of recent decades indicate that, whatever our ability to pay the price of such confusion and misunderstanding in the past, we can do so no longer. From the depression of the thirties to current and anticipated problems of automation, the rolling impact of industrial technology has made it ever clearer that social stability and well-being under modern conditions must be effortfully won. Revelation of the enormous power of modern techniques of mass communication and of the destructive force of science and technology in a world of clashing nationalisms has aroused new fears and deepened old. On the surface, the record would seem to have confirmed many of the darkest fears of technology's critics. In reality, it demonstrates with undeniable force that rejection of science and technology and neglect of their social implications has become a fatal luxury. The reception accorded so simple a statement of this fact as C. P. Snow's essay, *The Two Cultures and the Scientific Revolution,* reveals widespread discontent with a world in which science and traditional values confront each other across a canyon of prejudice and confusion. Without more imaginative translation into social and humane values, technology bids fare to become the monster its critics have long feared. And without a more meaningful involvement in the material experience of men, the arts deteriorate into private and querulous laments.

II

Nineteenth-century American critics of technical progress drew upon a combination of traditional European and uniquely domestic sources for their arguments. The Industrial Revolution, which gave rise in some quarters to extravagant hopes of unlimited social improvement, was less enthusiastically received by those who sensed in it disturbing personal, social, or esthetic implications. Romantic writers fled from factory and town to the countryside, shunning the encroachment of industry and bourgeois values. From Blake's strictures upon England's "dark, satanic mills" to the New England transcendentalists' attitudes toward Boston and the rising industrial order it represented, their reaction was one of deep suspicion, if not outright hostility.[2] Nor was reaction against the impact of industrialization confined to literary circles: Its influence can be found in such diverse nineteenth-century American movements as the Gothic revival in architecture, early labor and utopian reform programs, nativism, and self-conscious southern feudalism—each in its way a protest against the rise of an urban, industrial culture.

In Europe, opponents of industrialism could draw support and authority from a landed artistocracy with a tradition of cultural leadership. No such backing was available in democratic America where critics had, therefore, to be more circumspect or more willing to stand alone in their attacks upon a business community increasingly aware of the profits inherent in technological innovation. As business gradually assumed virtual sole patronage over technology, the absence of a self-conscious urban proletariat in the United States meant that opponents of the alliance between technical progress and middle-class values lacked still another audience available in Europe. Thus, whether they turned to the upper or to the lower strata of American society, opponents of the advancing industrial technology found a cool reception. While resentment at the speed and direction of social and technical change could be found at both levels, American "aristocrats" and workers shared too many of the attitudes and ambitions of businessmen, inventors, and artisans to form an effective opposition.[3]

To compensate for the weakness of traditional sources of hostility to middle-class materialism and the technological revolution upon which it had seized, America did offer still another social class and, equally important, a social myth whose appeal, while never strong enough to block industrialization, has nevertheless effectively prevented appreciation of its meaning. Ironically, the man whose name and authority have been most effectively invoked by the enemies of industrial technology and its social consequences was Thomas Jefferson. Few more enthusiastic promoters of science and technology can be found in our early history. Yet Jefferson feared the doom of the agrarian society he loved and of democracy itself as a probable outcome of industrialization. His suspicions of the "mobs of large cities" were no less characteristic of the man than was his interest in and support of the work of Eli Whitney. Sufficiently the realist and man of affairs to recognize the irrepressible advance of industrialism, Jefferson late in his career was able to make his own uneasy peace with it; but his commitment to an ideal society of small farmers and independent artisans was fundamentally incompatible with the progress of science and invention to which he was also devoted. This faith in science and technology coupled with a reluctance to face their social consequences are representative of an enduring pattern in American thought. In a kind of double irony, Jefferson's emergence as a full-fledged national hero and symbol of democracy has coincided broadly with the triumph of industrial culture over agrarianism, thus reemphasizing the ambiguity of American attitudes he so well typifies.

Whatever its author's personal contradictions and hesitations, the tradition of Jeffersonian democracy has proved a strong bulwark against social adaptation to the conditions of industrial life. Jefferson's own resistance to the Federalist program of national economic consolidation; agrarian opposition to tariff subsidies for infant industries; Jacksonian suspicions of an intellectual and scientific elite; southern resentment of a dynamic, industrial North; Populist and Progressive fears of the implications of large-scale enterprise; conservative opposition to the new role of government in modern society: each has found in the Jeffersonian tradition strength for resistance to the causes or consequences of technological change. While literary culture has couched its critique of technology primarily in traditional, aristocratic, intellectual terms—themselves the product of a preindustrial order—Jeffersonian democracy has provided a seedbed for popular confusion as to the nature and needs of a dynamic, technological culture.

Closely allied with the tradition of agrarian democracy is the American faith in the common man, the untutored, unspecialized jack-of-all-trades whose practicality and "know-how" enable him to surpass the achievements of more conventionally privileged contestants in the race for favor and fortune. The practical talents and common sense of the amateur are essentially the hallmark of a relatively undifferentiated, rural way of life, although in a McCormick, Edison, or Ford they marked the transition to industrialization. The American legend of the "self-made" man exercises, thus, a double appeal stemming from roots in our agrarian past as well as relevance to an era of rapid industrialization; but its suitability for a society geared to the dynamisms of science and technology is dubious at best. The sense of anxiety and inadequacy which plagues even the intelligent citizen in this age of specialization and expertise was clearly reflected in President Eisenhower's Farewell Address:

Today, the solitary inventor, tinkering in his shop, has been overshadowed by task forces of scientists in laboratories and testing fields. In the same fashion, the free university, historically the fountainhead of free ideas and scientific discovery, has experienced a revolution in the conduct of research.

Partly because of the huge cost involved, a Government contract becomes virtually a substitute for intellectual curiosity. For every old blackboard there are now hundreds of new electronic computers.[4]

Outside the economic arena the transition has proved still more difficult for Americans to explain to themselves and accept. The confrontation of agrarian simplicity and virtue with the urban-industrial complexity and deviousness has been a perennially popular theme in our literature as well as in our politics. Organized religion in the United States, more than half a century after the rise of the Social Gospel movement, still finds itself desperately struggling to adjust to the facts of industrial life. The temptation for present-day devotees of the common man to resort to obscurantism and anti-intellectualism can be documented in popular attitudes toward education and the arts, as well as toward religion, politics, science and technology. For those less actively inclined there remains the ritual release of seeing the experts "stumped" on countless television quiz and panel shows.

Still other examples of the agrarian-industrial confrontation present themselves. While the contemporary cult of the Civil War has drawn its strength from many sources, it is scarcely accidental that this most popular of all episodes in American history is precisely that in which the forces of agrarianism and industrialism faced each other in outright combat. The appeal of the frontier as a refuge from advancing technological society and as a subject for literary and political myth-making rivals that of the Civil War. On the far frontier could be projected perhaps most effectively of all the rugged and simple verities of preindustrial life.[5]

Americans, thus, have found the agrarian ideal a constant source of inspiration for critiques of industrial society. Yet its attractions have exacted a price in frequent and repeated frustration. Not only have the critics found the industrialists whose ways they deplored appealing to the same symbols and declaring allegiance to identical values; too often the preconceptions and proposals of would-be reformers have also proved monuments to a passing rural order rather than guidelines to a new industrial democracy.[6] Again, no sharper irony can be found, I think, than the sensitivity of contemporary televison to the inexhaustible nostalgia of the public it serves. The spectacle of millions of Americans reliving ''frontier days'' with the aid of all the techniques of modern mass communication is worthy of a Dooley or Mencken. The humorless fury into which the popularity of the TV western drives many of its critics suggests that they resent such bald exposure of the irrelevance to an age of science and technology of the good old days for which they, too, yearn.

III

Indeed the status and mood of the arts in contemporary America present an arresting paradox. If ever there were a time in which one might anticipate a new flowering of the creative imagination and a restatement of the perennial themes of human experience in fresh and compelling terms, that time would seem to be the present. Ours is an era of discovery and exploration in which a new universe is being exposed to view, full of wonder and hope. Rapid social and economic change presents both strains and opportunities for individuals in many walks of life, as well as new patronage for the arts and the intellect. To this vivid social setting is added the dramatic dimensions of international ideological conflict. Meanwhile, the media through which critical and imaginative insights can reach a broadly literate public are at hand in unparalleled variety. Radio, records, television, magazines, paperbacks, the theatre, libraries, museums, and orchestras all are patronized as never before in history. The general level of public taste has probably never in history been so high. Americans, young, middle-aged, and elderly alike, have wealth and time at their command to an unprecedented degree. All of these resources, plainly the product of scientific knowledge coupled with technical and organizational ingenuity in its application, lie at our command. Yet the quality of the civilization to which these elements contribute has failed to satisfy either the sensitivity of the artist or the intelligence of the public.

Instead we Americans find ourselves accused of excessive preoccupation with material values. Mass production and the mass market are said to have created a mass taste. Critics may differ as to whether mass culture leads inevitably to the level of the lowest common denominator—"comic book culture"—or whether it merely produces a leveling of taste in which distinctions and gradations of sensitivity are sacrificed to a common standard of mediocrity. In either case they agree that the unique individual vision and its communication are drowned in the insatiable demands of the mass. As in the arts, so in economics, politics, morality, education. Wherever we turn, we are assured that individuality and creative endeavor are being stifled by standardization, commercialism, and apathy. If we are to believe those who fear the encroachments of an impersonal technology, our scientific and technical virtuosity have produced a society in which art is alienated, the individual diminished, intellect trivialized and distracted. No small indictment, indeed!

It is impossible to dismiss as wholly inaccurate or irrelevant either the substance of these charges or the concern they represent. At the same time one suspects that the bemoaners of our technological civilization have failed to comprehend the full range of its qualities and tendencies in their analyses. No simple formula or phrase can adequately describe the revolution in institutions and values through which America has been passing in the course of the past half-century. Its outlines have been sketched and its dimensions suggested but a full appreciation of its character requires the perspectives which only time and more perceptive scrutiny can supply.

Among the fruits of modern technology which, thus far, neither American society nor its critics have successfully savored or digested is the phenomenon of mass leisure. One hears frequent references to the fact that no other society known to history has made available to its people the resources of time and wealth now at our command, yet the full meaning of this astonishing fact continues to elude us. Statistics showing the reductions which have taken place in the hours and years of labor are sufficiently impressive in themselves, but beyond mere quantitative considerations we can discern the outlines of social revolution. The prospect of mass unemployment and dislocation through automation looms nearer, despite the bravest prophecies of inevitable progress and prosperity. Within the context of work itself a leisure morality has steadily encroached on traditional patterns, as David Riesman and others have noted.[7] Feather-bedding, the coffee break, office parties, and the pleasures of expense-account living raise serious questions not only for the business executive and the tax examiner but for the student of society as well. Together with the growing involvement of both unions and management in the social as well as the working lives of employees, they suggest that the sharpened distinctions between work and leisure which characterized earlier stages of the Industrial Revolution may once again be receding.

Before such fundamental shifts in human relationships, it is scarcely surprising if insight and imagination falter, traditions crumble, and anxiety abounds. To explain the unexpectedly high birth rate which Americans have sustained in recent years, Walt Rostow has suggested that, to avoid the trials and uncertainties of unwanted leisure, we may have chosen to reimpose upon ourselves the disciplines and scarcities that larger families bring.[8] And one is regularly tempted to conclude that we prefer to explore even the relatively certain consequences of mass violence and destruction rather than face the unparalleled possibilities of leisure and plenty now available to us. Forty years ago, it is well to remember, the notion of a ten-hour working day struck many employers as demoralizing and subversive.

The conservatism of vested economic interests in the face of social and political change is a familiar matter. Yet businessmen have managed, with the help of substantial profits, to be sure, to reconcile faith in a progressive technology with adherence to traditional economic values. Our social and intellectual conservatives have been more consistent, if less adaptable. Tracing the threat to established values directly to science and its applications, they have aimed their barbs accordingly. In so doing, they have minimized, when they have not denied, the function of science and technology as fundamental expressions of man's deeply felt need to know and control his environment. Unready for the new conditions of life which material abundance and leisure present, they have heaped scorn—when understanding and imagination were needed—upon society's fumbling efforts to incorporate these riches into new patterns and opportunities.

IV

Responsibility for the reaction against science and technology can be charged only in part to conservatism and bias on the part of vested cultural interests. Equal contributors have been the overenthusiastic spokesmen for science and material progress themselves. Sharing the widespread utopianism which science helped to sustain, these men—much like the abolitionists, pacifists, and other reformers of the nineteenth century—tended to believe that their new techniques alone held the key to the fulfillment of all human needs and the reconstruction of society. As the prestige of science and engineering soared with successive achievements, extravagant optimism and a casual dismissal of disturbing social implications were readily encouraged.[9] These heightened the sense of displacement and alienation among the devotees of the ancient culture, steeped as they were in a more sensitive evaluation of human ambiguities and a less obviously materialistic ideal of social harmony. Out of injured pride on the one hand and smug complacency on the other grew the resentments which divided the intellectual community into opposing camps.

Yet by the beginning of the twentieth century, science itself was moving in a direction which eventually made possible a reunification of divergent values and points of view. The history of science and technology in America, as elsewhere, shows a steady progression toward professionalism and specialization out of the amateur status they so often enjoyed in the early phases of the Industrial Revolution. The gentleman-scientist and the artisan-inventor, familiar figures well into the nineteenth century, are familiar no longer. The career of Thomas Edison illustrates the rapidity with which specialization overtook one of this country's legendary scientist-inventors. Matthew Josephson shows that, while Edison in the 1870s was able without benefit of formal training to carry on significant experimentation at the forefront of knowledge in the field of electricity, by 1900 he had been left far behind through the development of organized industrial research and professional scientific and technical education.[10] Paralleling the advance of specialization has been the liberation of science and technology from domination by "practical" and material interests alone and their emergence as preeminently intellectual disciplines. The rapid narrowing of the gap between application and theory in science has led to new appreciation of the role of ideas and imagination as its truly creative elements. James B. Conant has compared the theoretical structures of modern science with the Parthenon and the medieval cathedrals as monuments of the human spirit; no one today would seriously deny the claims of science to an honored place in the record of man's intellectual achievements.[11]

Similarly, the traditional contempt of the down-to-earth engineer for the theoretician, a standard theme of nineteenth-century discussions, is rapidly passing away. In an urban-industrial context, furthermore, advances in technology impinge upon social conditions with an often startling immediacy. As the engineer comes to recognize that the success of his efforts depends frequently as much upon human factors as upon technical, the practical basis for cooperation and understanding between humanist and technician is rapidly being extended. As the nineteenth century brought growing recognition of the mutual dependence of science and technology, so it now appears the twentieth promises a further reunification of these disciplines with the social sciences and the arts.

The very fruitfulness of modern conceptual science has produced a deeper sense of the limits, as well as the extraordinary power, of this system of thought. The scientist has come face to face with the fundamental fact of his inability, however sophisticated his techniques, to escape the confines of his own perceptual apparatus; and this, in turn, has led to a new caution and humility in advancing the claims of reason alone to comprehend the universe and disclose its universally applicable laws.[12] Science has increasingly recognized the extent to which it shares with other forms of thought in the tentative character of all human experience and achievement. Meanwhile, the raw destructiveness of uncontrolled science arouses men of all talents to explore more diligently the terms of their common humanity. In the search for a more humane world, science, technology, and the arts share a joint dependence and responsibility.

V

Recognizing in technology and related disciplines a dimension of man's experience no less valid than others can free us, at last, from past controversies to face the insistent issues of today. A realistic analysis can no longer dismiss the vulgarity, futility, and cruelty which characterize so much of contemporary culture merely by attributing them to an essentially brute technology. Much more study is needed of the conditions which foster or hamper the creative release of human and material resources. Even more than new facts, however, we need the stimulus which only new conceptions of the structure and ends of a dynamic, technological civilization can supply. Past experience indicates all too clearly the frustrations which result either from blind acceptance or blind rejection of technological change; and both acceptance and rejection will remain essentially blind until a new framework of social understanding enlarges our vision.

The issue is not merely of academic, but of practical and immediate, concern. Daily decisions as well as long-range programs inevitably hinge upon social and individual priorities arising from concepts, however vague, of an ideal social order. Whether we choose better schools or lower taxes, billboards or beauty on our highways, respectability or misery for our aged, definition of problems and choice of measures appropriate to them will reflect a system of valued means and ends. When this system is not subjected to critical reexamination, particularly at times of rapid social change, it inevitably distorts the policies through which we attempt to manage our lives. The problem which science and technology pose for contemporary society lies precisely here, that they make reevaluation of ends and means at once more necessary and more difficult.

Nor it is enough to label the resulting impasse as an example of "cultural lag" and let it go at that. While the concept may help us to define the problem, it has proved less useful than once was hoped in enabling us to surmount our difficulties.[13] Too often it has served to enable us to deplore society's plight while minimizing its capacity for remedial action. Science and technology have made possible, for Americans and for an as yet undetermined portion of the rest of mankind, a "new world." We Americans have taken pride in our contributions to technical progress, to the point at times of exaggerating them. It is equally true, I believe, that our social institutions have demonstrated a remarkable capacity to absorb and adapt to change. The modern business corporation, the community chest, the American system of education, and the Tennessee Valley Authority — to cite several familiar examples — testify to an impressive degree of social ingenuity. Such social inventiveness, however, has won less recognition than it deserves; and it is still fashionable to deplore helplessly an essentially mythical contrast between progressive technology and a supposedly changeless social order.

One reason for our failure to take full credit for a record of social adaptation which the experience of other nations has shown to be commendable lies, surely, in a realistic sense of imperfect achievement. A second source of our excessive modesty can be found, I believe, in the lingering appeal of preindustrial values and traditions. The advocates and architects of social change in the United States have usually felt constrained to justify their handiwork not in functional terms, primarily, but in the language of an earlier day. The conservatism of American social philosophy has thus obscured American daring in social experimentation. We continue to preach "individual enterprise" as we practice highly centralized private and public planning. In government we still defer to "states' rights" a century after the Civil War, while evolving an intricate, if not very efficient, system of national controls and initiative. In education we struggle manfully, although not always successfully, to balance general education for effective citizenship with the insistent demand for specialized knowledge. That we have managed in the face of entrenched resistance to achieve any social advances at all is a tribute both to the strength of the forces which impel us to search out new directions and to our ingenuity, or luck, in shooting the rapids of social change while pretending to lie at anchor.

It is in the light of this experience that the new mass leisure and the media which serve it can be more effectively studied. As fruits of a new technology offering choices and resources never before so widely accessible, their use can be guided and enlivened by traditional values, to be sure; but new insights and imaginative departures from established patterns will be equally necessary. That these new resources have contributed to a strong and active popular interest in the arts is already clear. Similarly, one has only to travel the country to confirm the fact that long-standing differences between rural and urban life are being drastically modified. Farming has become a major industry in the do-it-yourself suburbs; urban renewal promises parks and green belts in the metropolis; factories and their workers invade and obliterate the fields. At the same time, by land, sea, and air, Americans in unprecedented numbers sample the landscapes and experiences which a continent, a planet, and, indeed, a solar system offer. That the consequences of this social explosion are often offensive to the senses and the intellect is undeniable. To persist in judging them by preindustrial standards is both unilluminating and futile.

As contemporary American culture is approached, not with the hauteur of old habits but in a spirit which searches for new patterns and potentialities, both our understanding and our capacity for self-direction may be greatly enhanced. There is no reason to imagine, certainly at this early date, that a simple formula or standard will emerge to guide us in achieving a harmonious balance between freedom and control, spontaneity and discipline, chaos and overorganization in modern life. It may well be that differing times and circumstances warrant a sensitive and continuous adjustment of our social scales. New levels of knowledge and material wealth make possible, if they do not necessarily foster, more sophisticated social controls than we have relied on in the past. Nor need answers be sought always through the application of more sweeping political controls. The mess which private initiative has created in television may well call for experimentation with new forms of public competition and control in the interest of taste and variety. Yet, in another sector, it now seems probable that relaxation of public and private policies governing the ages of employment and retirement will prove desirable. The simple truth is that it is not technology but our own inertia and lack of imagination which have produced the cultural excesses we deplore.

To trace in detail the record of American responses to technological change or to offer specific prescriptions for the social ills accompanying the impact of modern science would be inappropriate here. Rather, I have tried to indicate what I believe to be a paradox at the core of American culture. Despite our technological virtuosity and our commitment as a people to a broad sharing of the benefits it makes possible, we have achieved no consensus as to the quality and character of the industrial civilization we want. Whatever our shortcomings in institutional adaptation to change, a more fundamental weakness can be found in our failure to envision in compelling terms the framework and ends of a democratic society in full mastery of the dynamic forces of science and technology. Institutions ultimately function no better than the human understanding which informs and shapes them. Without more adequate conceptions of what technology offers, and upon what terms, our adaptations are piecemeal and ramshackle at best.

Such conceptions can emerge only from a union of intellect and imagination in common concern for the quality of social and individual life; all the resources of the arts and sciences can now be joined in such an undertaking. Upon our ability to achieve a greater harmony among these discordant elements of American culture, indeed, depends the ultimate meaning of technology for our time.

In the years since this essay was written, recognition of the key role of technology in American, or, indeed, any, culture has grown significantly. Although it has not been possible to revise the essay in the light of recent scholarship, those interested in pursuing the subject in greater depth can find important substantive and conceptual resources particularly in the disciplines of history and anthropology. The following studies will provide an introduction to the range of topics, materials, and perspectives upon which contemporary students can draw.

Notes

1. Among the dissenters from, and critics of, the prevailing view have been: Jacques Maritain, *Reflections on America* (New York: Gordian, 1958), pp. 29–42; David Riesman, *The Lonely Crowd* (Garden City, N.Y.: Doubleday Anchor Books, 1953), pp. 263–64; also Mary McCarthy, "America the Beautiful," *Commentary* 4 (1947): 201–7, cited by Riesman. See also David M. Potter, *People of Plenty* (Chicago: University of Chicago Press, 1954).

2. Leo Marx, "Two Kingdoms of Force: Technology and the Literary Imagination," *The Massachusetts Review* 1 (October 1959): 62–95; Leo Marx, "The Machine in the Garden," *New England Quarterly* 29 (March 1956): 27–42.

3. American artists and writers could, and often did, turn to Europe for the social and intellectual support they missed at home. Expatriation was, after all, a form of social criticism exemplifying many of the attitudes referred to. The influence of American class structure on social and political thought is discussed with penetration by Louis Hartz, *The Liberal Tradition in America* (New York: Harcourt & Brace, 1955).

4. *New York Times,* 18 January 1961, p. 22.

5. Henry Nash Smith, *Virgin Land* (Cambridge, Mass.: Harvard University Press, 1950), pp. 189–92, 201–6.

6. Richard Hofstadter, *The Age of Reform* (New York: Knopf, 1955), pp. 9–10, 242–50, 255–69.

7. Riesman, *The Lonely Crowd,* pp. 305–8.

8. W. W. Rostow, *The Stage of Economic Growth: A Non-Communist Manifesto* (London: Cambridge University Press, 1960), pp. 11, 80–81.

9. Rene Dubos, *The Dreams of Reason* (New York: Columbia University Press, 1961), pp. 101, 149–52.

10. Matthew Josephson, *Edison, A Biography* (New York: McGraw-Hill, 1959), pp. 411–13, 466–67.

11. James B. Conant, *Modern Science and Modern Man* (New York: Doubleday Anchor Books, 1952), pp. 99, 187.

12. Ibid., pp. 55–101; Dubos, *The Dreams,* pp. 102–2.

13. William F. Ogburn, *Social Change* (New York: Viking Press, 1950), p. 200.

Bibliography

Boorstin, Daniel. *The Americans: The Democratic Experience.* New York: Vintage Books, 1974.

Hughes, Thomas Parkes. *Elmer Sperry: Inventor and Engineer.* Baltimore: Johns Hopkins University Press, 1971.

Jenkins, Reese V. *Images and Enterprise: Technology and the American Photographic Industry, 1839–1925.* Baltimore: Johns Hopkins University Press, 1975.

Kouwenhoven, John A. *Made in America: The Arts in Modern Civilization.* New York: Doubleday and Co., 1948; reprinted by Octagon Books, 1975.

Layton, Edwin T., Jr., ed. *Technology and Social Change in America.* New York: Harper & Row, 1973.

Rosenberg, Nathan. *Technology and American Economic Growth.* New York: Harper & Row, 1972.

Sinclair, Bruce. *Philadelphia's Philosopher Mechanics: A History of the Franklin Institute, 1824–1865.* Baltimore: Johns Hopkins University Press, 1974.

Smith, Merrit Roe. *Harpers Ferry Armory and the New Technology: The Challenge of Change.* Ithaca, N.Y., and London: Cornell University Press, 1977.

STOW PERSONS

Public Opinion—A Democratic Dilemma

Stow Persons is Professor of American History at the University of Iowa. A noted teacher and scholar, his most recent books are The Decline of American Gentility *and a revised edition of his distinguished American Intellectual History textbook,* American Minds: A History of Ideas.

Almost from the very beginning of colonial settlement in Anglo-America, more than three centuries ago, governments have taken the form that would be classified, broadly speaking, as the popular type. Even the Puritans formally affirmed the theory of popular sovereignty, though their practice seems to us to have been a caricature of that principle. The whole course of American political development might be characterized, not improperly, as a quest for more effective popular government.

I

While the implementation of the theory of popular government may be accomplished in a variety of ways, at least one constant factor will always be present. This is the responsiveness of public officials to the will of the people, expressed in the form to which we have attached the term public opinion. For us, public opinion is simply the articulation of that sovereign authority that embodies the ultimate will of the community. Every political thinker and every reflective politician from the days of John Winthrop to those of Franklin Roosevelt would have assented to these propositions.

One might appropriately assume, therefore, that American political theorists, working as they all have within the traditions of popular government, would have had a good deal to say about so fundamental an aspect of political life as the characteristics of public opinion. In fact, however, this is not at all the case. Conditioned as we have become in recent times to an intense — almost morbid — preoccupation with public opinion and its dictates, it is doubly surprising to discover that until very recent years American political theorists have had virtually nothing to say on this subject. The general histories of American political thought ignore the matter. With the sole exception of some fragmentary investigations by Professor Francis Wilson, I have been unable to find any indication that historians have concerned themselves with the subject.[1] The reason for this neglect is found, of course, in the fact that the sources the historian uses, namely, the writings of political theorists, do not deal explicitly with public opinion save for an occasional parenthetical remark. Not until the early years of the twentieth century did analysis of public opinion take its place among the fundamental problems of democratic political theory.

The temptation to speculate on the causes of so remarkable an oversight is almost overwhelming. Why was it that the political thinkers of the eighteenth and nineteenth centuries could have ignored so fundamental and obvious a branch of their subject? Walter Lippmann asked this same question forty years ago, and he suggested an ingenious explanation.[2] Every living political faith, said Mr. Lippmann, contains a central axiom or assumption upon which the whole system rests. The validity of the axiom itself is taken for granted, not simply for the logical reason that any system of thought must rest on some premises, but also for the practical reason that men are less likely to challenge assumptions of which they are unaware. In the democratic ideology the central unexamined axiom is the sovereignty of public opinion, and for many years this axiom remained hidden from view in the innermost sanctuary of the public piety.

However esthetically satisfying Mr. Lippmann's disposition of this problem may be, it does not absolve the historian from the prosaic task of conducting his own investigation. After all, Mr. Lippmann wrote as a political philosopher and not as a historian, and as every hardworking historian knows, no temptation is stronger than the temptation to substitute a theory for research. But the difference between the philosopher and the historian is scarcely indicated by the mere fact that the philosopher passes up the opportunity to play tricks on the dead. The philosopher quite properly looks at his problems from his own point of view. He stands at the center of his universe, and his own mind is the focal point on which all experience is centered. For this very reason, I think, a good philosopher is likely to be a bad historian, because the historian must purge himself of the natural and healthy human impulse to place himself or his times at the center of the human drama, and to interpret his own advent as its fitting and proper climax. So far as he is a good historian he will attempt to detach himself imaginatively from the conventions and assumptions of his own day and age in order to minimize that form of distortion which flows from the common tendency to explain the past in terms of the present.

Applied to our present problem, such reflections may serve as a caveat to look again at the question as it was first phrased. On further scrutiny it is obvious that to ask why something did not happen in history — or at least why it did not happen sooner — is a singularly inept question, the sooner abandoned the better. It should also be apparent that our first impulse to search for the reasons why the theory of public opinion had for so long been ignored reflected the implicit assumption that the modern preoccupation with public opinion is a proper and inevitable concern, and that it is therefore necessary to discover why our fore-bears had been so benighted as to overlook it. This temporal provincialism is, of course, precisely the kind of fallacy against which I have suggested that it is a prime function of the historical style of thinking to guard. By what right do we assume that wisdom and virtue are on our side, and that history may properly be summoned to the bar of this day and age? As a salutary corrective, let us experiment with turning the question around, and instead of inquiring why Americans succeeded in evading the theory of public opinion for so long, ask rather how it came about that in spite of the practical experience and accumulated wisdom of more than two centuries of popular government, Americans in our own times could yet be seduced by the blandishments of utopians or demagogues into subscribing to the preposterous notion that a stable foundation for political society could be found in the direct expressions of public opinion? Needless to say, I do not offer this question as an adequate working hypothesis. But I do suggest that it is no more arbitrary than the commonly received alternative.

In brief then, the object of this review will be to inquire into the train of events and ideas that led to the modern theory of public opinion. And we will try to maintain the pose that the modern state of affairs was not a foreordained outcome, not the inevitable product of a matured political intelligence, but that a succession of circumstances, each with its own contingencies, led to this particular outcome rather than to some other.

II

If we commence our survey more or less arbitrarily with the eighteenth-century era of independence and constitution making, we must strive to do justice to the peculiar American relationship between theory and practice. Americans had deeply rooted traditions of colonial self-government, and their political philosophy could and frequently did skim lightly over topics upon which the judgments of experience appeared to be firmly fixed. For our present purposes, one of these topics was the nature and functions of representation. And representative institutions are the key to the whole problem.

The theory and functions of representation were not extensively discussed in eighteenth-century writings, perhaps for the very reason that a distinctive pattern was well developed in all of the colonies before the Revolution.[3] Everywhere, the popularly elected legislative assemblies provided the circumstances within which this pattern was nourished. Save in two small colonies, Connecticut and Rhode Island, the colonial legislators were the most important and sometimes the only public officials to be chosen by the electors. The requirements or qualifications which surrounded their selection were of great significance. First, a residence requirement, both for suffrage and for candidacy for office, was usual, though not universal. Annual terms of office were also usual. Everywhere, the intimacy of association of office seeker with the electorate was a striking feature.

Electoral districts were numerically small, usually numbering their votes in the mere hundreds. The absence of political parties meant that campaigns for office had to be conducted by the candidates themselves, who had to be personally known to the voters to have much chance of success. The weight of these factors was so great that the theorist could take it for granted that in America the representative represented his constituents and no one else, regardless of what the contemporaneous British theory of virtual representation might hold. Furthermore, although the Massachusetts practice of instruction by the constituency was exceptional, the American representative tended to be something of a delegate, scrupulously regardful of the views of the majority of his constituents, especially if he wished to remain in office. These practices might be characterized as direct constituency representation, a form of representation which has always remained a principal feature of the American political system.

It is true that during the later eighteenth century an alternative theory of interest representation was popular with conservative theorists and constitution makers. According to this theory, advocated most notably by James Madison and John Adams, means should be devised to secure representation of the different interests in the community. In practice, this boiled down to finding ways in which to protect the rich from the poor. It is instructive to observe that even at that early date the rich were on the defensive, and were hence compelled to master the gentle arts of recouping in the marketplace the losses suffered at the polling place. Although historians have frequently referred to Madison's exposition of the theory of interest representation in *Federalist #10*, it seems to me that the significance of the theory has been rather overestimated. In spite of the common recourse to the bicameral legislature with differing property qualifications both for membership and electorate, interest representation found hard sledding in the states, where it survived for scarcely more than a generation.

The prevailing characteristics of direct constituency representation were confirmed and strengthened by the federal character of American government under the Constitution of 1787, and by the rise of political democracy in the early nineteenth century. Because the Constitution provided for a federal union of sovereign states, it was inevitable that senators as well as congressmen should represent their respective states, regardless of the expectations of Alexander Hamilton, who hoped that senators at least would emancipate themselves from parochial interests.

The impact of democracy upon representation was perhaps even more decisive. Short terms and rotation in office, the conversion of appointive to elective offices, proposals to abolish the Electoral College and to make U.S. senators and state governors popularly elective, all reflected the democratic impulse to make representative institutions responsive to the public will as expressed by the majority. The rise of democratic political parties also served to strengthen and implement constituency representation. From the beginning, these parties were federations of state parties rather than centralized national parties. Their electoral techniques were sensitively attuned to the impulses which were expressing themselves in direct representation. As constituencies became larger, and the electoral process necessarily more impersonal, it became the prime function of the party to reduce political ideas and problems to manageable proportions. This was accomplished by simplifying issues to alternative patterns between which voters could choose, and particularly by identifying issues with personalities, the candidates for office. My point here is that the rise of the political party is to be understood not as the intervention of a third force between the constituent and the office holder, but, at least in part, as the fashioning of a device suitable to modern conditions for mediating between voter and representative.[4]

This kind of direct constituency representation achieved its appropriate fulfillment in the reduction of the function of a representative to that of an agent. In the words of the journalist, Parke Godwin, "A representative is but the mouthpiece and organ of his constituents. What we want in legislation as in other trusts, are honest fiduciaries, men who will perform their duties according to our wishes."[5] It was appropriate, therefore, for Godwin and those who thought like him to sanction the practice of instructing representatives. Several state constitutions made such provision, apart from the informal practice of state legislatures in instructing U.S. senators whom they had chosen. The rationale behind the practice of instruction was stated categorically by the journalist Hezekiah Niles, in 1825: "The people are generally right, and, at any rate, their opinions are the only opinions that can be safely respected as reaching that degree of infallibility which is presumed to exist in every government. . . ."[6] The Virginia legislature had declared that laws reflected the general will, and that "the general will is only the result of individual wills fairly collected and compared."[7] Hence the appropriateness of furnishing explicit instructions.

I have stressed the theory and practice of constituency representation because out of it was precipitated the modern preoccupation with public opinion as a political problem. During much of the nineteenth century the concept of public opinion seems to have occupied the same kind of position with respect to popular sovereignty as did suffrage. Popular sovereignty was admittedly meaningless without an informed and responsible public opinion, and unless men could implement that opinion effectively through the use of the franchise. And yet the striking historical fact is that these associations were not frequently and explicitly made. Every thoughtful student of history knows how the logic of a situation runs ahead of practical behavior. In this case, the institutions of representation stood between government and the popular will. Any potential concern for the theory of public opinion was submerged within the preoccupation with direct representation.

A theory was nevertheless present, even though in embryo, and those who were disturbed by its implications were quicker to explore its meaning than were those who complacently took it for granted. James Madison stated the theory succinctly when he observed that public opinion was the opinion of the majority;

and he expressed his own reservations about it when he added that it would always reflect the interests of the majority.[8] Again, John C. Calhoun was at pains to show that the assumptions of the prevailing practice of direct constituency representation rested on a theory of public opinion which was inadequate because it provided no solution to the problem of protecting the rights of the minority.[9]

The assumptions of constituency representation had become so firmly rooted in the American political consciousness that when, by the end of the nineteenth century, representative institutions began to sag under the impact of industrial concentration, urbanization, and utilities monopolies, the obvious solution seemed to be to secure the same object, namely, implementation of the will of the majority, more effectively by resort to expressions of that will through forms of direct democracy. Alfred de Grazia has pointed out how the social and political problems of the nineties were understood by populists, reformers, debtors, and progressives in terms of their conditioning in the representative tradition.[10] They found good government being balked by malevolent individuals, such as monopolists and speculators, working through bosses and corrupt political machines. The solution they proposed was to circumvent institutions no longer truly representative by having recourse to such forms of direct democracy as the initiative, referendum, recall of officers and of judicial decisions, ballot reform, and women suffrage. All of these were devices calculated to implement effective majority rule. They admittedly presupposed a higher standard of citizenship, in terms of which ignorance and apathy were now to be branded major political sins. Political maturity and public spirit were now to be equated with active political participation. And in all of this there was considerable confusion of political techniques with programmatic objectives.

The utopian strain in the thinking of the direct democrats was clearly apparent in Frank Parsons, one of the most active and vocal of the proponents of direct legislation. Successively civil engineer, lawyer, law professor, and reformer, Parsons gave himself over wholly to the cause of progressive reform at the urban and state levels. Direct democracy, he believed, would purify political life by drawing better men into politics, by minimizing partisanship, purifying the press, and educating the public. Direct democracy would somehow restore a proper political balance between the rich and the poor. But at the same time, the intelligent and public-spirited citizens who would take the trouble to study issues and vote in referenda as the occasion offered would gain an advantage over the uninformed and uninterested citizens too preoccupied with their private affairs to exert themselves politically. Parsons evaded the unpalatable ideological implications of this distinction by persuading himself that in a democratic society in which civic responsibility was taught to be an obligation it could safely be assumed that the public spirited citizens would constitute a majority. Majority opinion, therefore, could safely be accepted as both morally and politically superior to minority opinion. Like many other Progressives, Parsons was concerned chiefly with the formulation of public policy, to which end he conceived the techniques of direct democracy to be appropriate means, and he gave little thought to the rights of the minority or to their protection.[11]

What was significant in this line of thinking was that it led directly to the unmasking of public opinion. The assumptions involved in the thinking of the direct democrats continued to be the assumptions of many of those concerned with public opinion as an aspect of the political process. Thus, for instance, George Gallup tells us that the function of the pollster is to ascertain public opinion more precisely than can the politican using traditional techniques of sounding his constituency.[12]

III

But when did public opinion emerge from the chrysalis of representation to pursue a career under its own colors? Without attempting to fix a precise date, I think we can risk the guess that it was somewhere around 1890. Professor Wilson says that Bryce, whose *American Commonwealth* was published in 1888, was one of the most important of the writers who made the modern world conscious of the problems of public opinion.[13] And yet, in spite of all that Bryce had to say about the influence of opinion in America, he still found its expression in the institutions of political representation.

Here is a paragraph from the St. Louis *Globe-Democrat*, in 1893, which will serve to signalize the arrival of public opinion in its own right, independent of all forms of implementation:

It is trite to say that public opinion is the supreme power in this country; but the fact is illustrated now and then in a way which gives it special interest and significance. Nobody can tell just how the force is generated, or just how it makes itself decisively felt in given emergencies. When we undertake to trace it to its origin and analyze its development, we are soon lost in a bewilderment of surmise and conjecture, from which nothing definite can be derived. There are times, we know, when a certain opinion or sentiment begins to make its way over the country, apparently from many different starting points, and it grows day by day until finally it becomes predominant, gaining recognition in legislation and substituting one policy for another in the regulation of our affairs. The people in various localities seem somehow to think the same thoughts upon a subject at the same time, without collusion or any chance of consultation, and the first thing we know the influence thus set in motion is directing the course of events in spite of all opposition. It is a great psychological mystery which our statesmen and philosophers have not yet been able to solve.[14]

It was indeed a great mystery, and we can begin to appreciate the good sense or good fortune of earlier students of public affairs who were content to assume that the techniques of direct constituency representation gave effective voice to public opinion, and to refrain either deliberately or instinctively from probing the mystery directly.

There is no doubt a universal impulse of human nature to bend the ear at times to a delphic utterance that is accepted as the voice of God, no matter what gibberish it may pronounce. But at least a few thoughtful Americans had a firm enough grasp upon the democratic ideal as a normative concept to insist that qualitative considerations should not be lost from sight. The *Baltimore Sun* declared in 1889 that public opinion was not a consensus of the opinions of everyone; if it were, it would be merely a compromise, inferior to the best opinion. The *Sun* was prepared to believe that in fact public opinion was usually the opinion of the wisest leaders, due to the fact that the strongest men furnished the unthinking masses with their opinions. But by the same token, public opinion should always be challenged by thoughtful citizens whenever they believed it to be misguided, for then it might be set right. The *Sun* was inclined to view public opinion as the outcome of a Social Darwinian struggle for the control of men's minds. "Public opinion follows the leaders who triumph in a battle of reason."[15] This ingenious effort to salvage quality from numbers, to get an *ought* from an *is*, must command our admiration, even if it leaves us unconvinced.

IV

No sooner had public opinion been isolated as an ingredient of public affairs, than it was subjected to searching criticism from two different quarters. On the one hand, the new social science of sociology insisted upon viewing the problem from a broader and more detached perspective. Professor William Graham Sumner of Yale made a characteristic distinction between the basic psychological matrix within which social life is embedded and public opinion defined as attitudes towards public affairs. The former was composed of the inherited patterns of behavior and belief, the mores and folkways, that governed men's conduct. This psychological matrix was subject to very gradual change in response to basic technological and economic changes. It might perhaps be regarded as public opinion of a kind; but in comparison with it, public opinion in the ordinary sense of the term—that is, attitudes towards public affairs—was of only trivial importance as an element in the social process.[16]

Lester F. Ward took a similar position when he distinguished between the *Zeitgeist*, "that part of human thought which lies below all doubt, question, schism, or discussion," and public opinion. The latter consisted of the questions under discussion, the issues that divided men. Questions closed to discussion, such as democracy, monogamy, or the separation of church and state, were part of the *Zeitgeist* of our society.[17]

The sociological distinction between the fundamental unifying forces in the community and the relatively superficial attributes of public opinion permitted the Michigan sociologist Charles Horton Cooley to state the problem in a different way. Approaching public opinion as an aspect of the social process, Cooley defined it as a "certain ripeness and stability of thought resulting from attention and discussion.'' It was not to be understood necessarily as agreement or disagreement upon some question of policy. Admittedly, a body of agreed opinion was the usual definition because of the common presumption that public opinion was the basis for decision and action. But Cooley insisted that while decision and action might result, they were not of the essence of the definition. After all, the resultant action might be a compromise, or there might be no action at all; yet the formation of a public opinion on the matter might be of great importance. Public opinion, then, was deliberation rather than agreement. The superficial conception of public opinion as agreement was considered by Cooley to be a remnant of the eighteenth-century idea that men are normally isolated and that social life consists of their coming together or agreeing in certain ways. Such a view failed to do justice to minorities, conceiving of them as stubborn refractory remnants.

Public opinion properly conceived was part of the social process, a complex growth forming and dissolving in time and perhaps partially unified on occasion for action. So far as people displayed sufficient interest in affairs to discuss them, there was public opinion, even though no common conclusions emerged. ''Communicated differences are the life of opinion, as cross-breeding is of a natural stock.'' From a dynamic point of view, Cooley believed that great importance attached to the role of the minority. All notable change began in the comprehension of a few only. Originality, faith, desire for improvement were always found in the minority, while every majority was composed of inert and dependent elements. Therefore, Cooley concluded, if one wished to consult public opinion as a means of prognosis, let him look to the minority, not because the minority must necessarily become a working majority, but because creative leadership was to be found there. ''There is nothing more democratic than intelligent and devoted non-conformity, because it means that the individual is giving his freedom and courage to the service of the whole. Subservience, to majorities as to any other authority, tends to make vigorous democracy impossible.''[18] These were noble sentiments to which we all breathe a fervent Amen, but where did they leave public opinion?

V

A second line of attack was taken by traditionalists who argued that representative institutions provided a more valid and defensible expression of public opinion than did the techniques of direct democracy. In 1907, the elder Senator Henry Cabot Lodge readily acknowledged the dependence of representation upon public opinion. It was precisely the public forum for responsible debate provided by the legislative chamber that, in Lodge's eyes, furnished the necessary link between public opinion and public policy. In contrast the devices of direct democracy made no provision for discussion. In the referendum, the voter would be presented with a ballot upon which he was to express a preference with or without benefit of discussion of the issues, as the circumstances of the individual voter might determine. Lodge thus attempted to turn the weapon of public opinion upon opponents who must have thought themselves in firm possession of it.[19]

Much of the most extended and discriminating discussion of the problems of public opinion within the context of traditional political assumptions was furnished by Abbot Lawrence Lowell of Harvard in his *Public Opinion and Popular Government* (1913). Lowell took up the question where the sociologists had left it. His problem was to mediate between the universally accepted mores or *Zeitgeist* and the controversial issues of opinion. His solution leaned markedly toward the former alternative. He was prepared to define an opinion as a public opinion when its implementation was acceptable to the minority in spite of its opposition. Thus the issue must clearly fall within the ends of policy and methods of government upon which the whole community was agreed. This was a profoundly conservative view. Lowell was at pains to emphasize the great restraints under which a government responsive to public opinion as truly conceived must operate. Public Opinion as he understood it functioned in much the same way as did Calhoun's notorious concurrent majority.

The events of the First World War introduced radically new elements and thus transformed the terms of the discussion. The war of 1917 was the first ideological war in American history. For the first time, a deliberate manipulation of mass opinion by governmental agencies was undertaken. The propaganda campaign rested on the assumption that the maximum war effort could be obtained only by persuading the American people that theirs was the cause of civilization and righteousness, and that the enemy represented tyranny, deceit, and inhumanity. Unquestionably, the campaign was oversold. The cynicism of the twenties was just one facet of the deeper sophistication which flowered from the painful realization of a gullible and innocent people that they had been used. Public opinion as a subject of study became indissolubly wed to propaganda, a union which is witnessed in virtually every textbook even today. The effect of these circumstances was clearly apparent in the writing of Walter Lippmann in the early twenties. Before the War, the central issues had been concerned with the nature and implementation of public opinion, with the ways in which public opinion was suitably translated into public policy. Now, however, in the second phase of the discussion, it was apparent to Mr. Lippmann that the assumption earlier taken for granted, namely, that the average citizen is both capable and willing to form adequate opinions about the world around him, must itself be subjected to careful scrutiny. What had been done deliberately in wartime appeared to be merely a special case of the distortion that always entered into the formation of opinions about the external world. Man's normal behavior was governed by symbolic pictures or stereotypes compounded of the individual's sense of values and his observations of life. These stereotypes varied enormously in adequacy, but were always simpler and more rigid than the flux of events.

Public opinion, Lippmann believed, was inevitably conditioned by the circumstances of group life. The stereotypes governing individual behavior were shaped largely by the community. In the formation of public opinions, individually centered emotions were transferred by means of conditioned responses to certain public symbols, to which were attached the desired policies. Lippmann clearly understood the emotional involvement which transformed a passive idea into a politically potent public opinion. The real opinion makers were the individual's associates, his parents, friends, teachers, employers, and colleagues. The forces at work in the process were those that in part assured the unity and solidarity of the community.

It was no longer possible, therefore, to accept the traditional assumption of democratic theory that political society was composed of self-sufficient individuals. The conversion of private opinions formed in the manner just indicated into public opinions required the subordination of the personal factors ordinarily involved in opinion formation to the objectivity and patience necessary to the fashioning of adequate opinions about the external world.

Lippmann concluded that only after a thorough education, after the attainment of adequate economic resources, with the possession of leisure, and with accurate information available could individuals hope to form opinions that would meet the qualitative criteria of public opinion. It was no longer possible to be as complacent on this matter as the prewar generation had been.

VI

The third and final phase of the discussion of public opinion is concerned with efforts to measure public opinion quantitatively. Heretofore, theorists had been preoccupied with the place of public opinion in political theory. So far as I am capable of judging, nothing more of significance has been said on that subject since the twenties. In other respects, however, popular interest in the matter had then scarcely commenced. George Gallup organized the American Institute of Public Opinion in 1935, and that date may be taken as the conventional starting point of the current practice of public opinion surveys.

But the pollster is interested in private opinions rather than in public opinion as traditionally conceived. He has devised elaborate techniques for the development of questionnaires free from distortion or ambiguity. He has mastered the statistical problems of sampling, and he has perfected the organization that makes national and even international surveys of opinion possible. With these aspects of opinion measurement I have no quarrel, nor indeed have I the competence to discuss them critically. The question which I raise is simply the question whether the individual opinions that the pollster records in answer to his inquiry constitute public opinion. The validity of the sample is not in question. But the political reality of the thing sampled is.

It seems to me that the pollster, by eliciting casual responses to his own arbitrarily chosen questions, is actually creating a partially artificial opinion which he labels ''public opinion.'' Furthermore, he appears to be largely oblivious of the profound consequences of this irresponsible act of creation. The pressures for conformity about which we hear so much nowadays are the result in part of a deliberately cultivated sensitivity to whatever is alleged to be public opinion.

It is no accident, I suspect, that public opinion polling and its rationale are products of the academic mind rather than of the practical political world. The opinion survey fails to make a distinction, crucial for political purposes, between what might be called active and passive opinions. Active opinions are those held with such conviction or felt to be of such practical importance to those who hold them as to impel these individuals to seek their actual implementation. As we say, they make their opinions felt as well as known. Passive opinions, on the other hand, are those which all of us hold on many subjects, and which we willingly indicate to the pollster when he questions us, but in which we are not sufficiently involved to work actively for their realization. As a practical matter, the politician will necessarily be concerned primarily with the active opinions of his constituents. Successful politicians working within representative institutions have always recognized this distinction. Democratic theory would probably prefer not to have to grapple with the distinction between active and passive opinions, but this is a dilemma which the unmasking of public opinion forces upon it.

But I cannot gainsay the fact that while polling may neglect some of the implicit assumptions of constituency representation, it does appear to be in accord with the theory of direct democracy. In this respect, polling is the authentic culmination of a clearly marked development. Just as John Adams felt no dishonor in receiving the instructions of his constituency, so today a U.S. senator may solemnly poll every second householder. But I am certain that Adams accounted it an important fact that when the town of Braintree instructed its representative, it did so by vote in open meeting, after the issues had been thoroughly hashed over. As for the modern politician's poll, the senator himself frames the questions out of his own intimate knowledge of the problems and interests of his constituents; nor does he feel obliged to tell us what the results are, or how he will use them. But for those engaged in the direct sampling of opinions verbally expressed the assumptions of direct democracy provide a convenient rationale. When Dr. George Gallup lectured at Princeton in 1939 on ''Public Opinion in a Democracy'' he found representative processes inefficient because they failed to reveal the popular will with certainty. On the other hand, the pollster had demonstrated by his preelection surveys that he could accurately measure public opinion, and could thus promptly give voice to the popular will. Aided by the opinion analyst at his elbow, the function of the statesman was simply that of discovering and implementing public opinion. It was apparent that the pollster had little patience with the problems which the theory of public opinion had posed for philosophers.

If the modern interest in public opinion is the direct outcome of the theory and practice of constituency representation, so is polling clearly in accord with the assumptions of direct democracy. But in political terms polling is also open to all of the criticisms to which the techniques of direct democracy were exposed, and I suspect, partly for this reason, that representative institutions will survive this as they did the earlier challenge.

Notes

1. Francis G. Wilson, "The Federalist on Public Opinion," *Public Opinion Quarterly* 4 (1940): 563–75; "James Bryce on Public Opinion: Fifty Years Later," *Public Opinion Quarterly* 3 (1939): 420–35.

2. Walter Lippmann, *Public Opinion* (New York: Macmillan, 1922), pp. 254–55

3. For a perceptive discussion of the development of the theory and practices of representation in America see Alfred de Grazia, *Public and Republic: Political Representation in America* (New York: Alfred Knopf, 1951).

4. A succinct acknowledgment of the proper responsiveness of a democratic political party to its constituency was contained in a manifesto of fourteen Pennsylvania congressmen issued in 1824. See *Niles Weekly Register* 25 (January 27, 1824): 306–7.

5. *Political Essays* (1856), quoted in de Grazia, p. 124.

6. *Niles Weekly Register* 28 (May 28, 1825): 193.

7. de Grazia, p. 126.

8. Madison, *Letters and Other Writings,* 4 vols. (Philadelphia: J.B. Lippincott & Co., 1867), 1: 326.

9. Calhoun, "Disquisition on Government," *Works,* Richard K. Cralle, ed. (New York: Appleton, 1854–55), 1:1–39.

10. de Grazia, p. 178.

11. Frank Parsons, *Direct Legislation: or, The Veto Power in the Hands of the People* (Philadelphia: C. F. Taylor, 1900), pp. 6–30.

12. Gallup, *Public Opinion in a Democracy* (Published under the University Extension Fund, Herbert L. Baker Foundation, Princeton University, 1939).

13. *Public Opinion Quarterly* 3 (1939): 420.

14. Quoted in *Public Opinion* 15 (September 23, 1893): 575.

15. Quoted in *Public Opinion* 8 (November 23, 1889): 168–69.

16. Sumner, *Folkways* (Boston and New York: Ginn & Co., 1906), pp. 2–4, 16–20, 30–59.

17. Lester Ward, *Applied Sociology* (Boston and New York: Ginn and Co., 1906), p. 44.

18. Cooley, *The Social Process* (1909. New York ed., 1927), pp. 378–81.

19. Henry C. Lodge, *The Democracy of the Constitution and Other Essays and Addresses* (New York: Freeport, 1915), pp. 1–31.

NELSON MANFRED BLAKE

Was Nat Turner Right? Violence in American History

I read about the slave preacher Nat Turner who put the fear of God into the white slavemaster. Nat Turner wasn't going around preaching pie-in-the-sky and "non-violent" freedom for the black man.[1]

The Autobiography of Malcolm X

Put to death on a Virginia gallows in 1831, Nat Turner became eligible for admission to the American Valhalla during the 1960s. Thousands of young blacks, disillusioned with the slowness and hardships of Martin Luther King's nonviolent protests, found their hero in the avenger, whose rebel band took fifty-seven white lives during three days of terror. White youths were as ready as black to admit Nat Turner to veneration along with such saints as Che Guevara and Mao Tse-tung.

The new heroes were men of action and violent deeds. The worship of violence, moreover, was not just a matter of rhetoric. On the contrary, history seemed to be unfolding in a succession of bloody chapters during these years. Assassins wiped out John F. Kennedy, Robert Kennedy, and Martin Luther King, Jr., and crippled George Wallace. Milling mobs burned and looted in Watts, Newark, and Detroit. Trigger-happy lawmen gunned down students at Kent State and Jackson State. Black Panthers shot it out with policemen. Inept Weathermen blew themselves up in the process of making bombs to use against other people. As though all the real violence were not enough, the moviemakers provided a gory feast of vicarious violence in films like *Bonnie and Clyde, The Godfather,* and *Clockwork Orange*.

Those who hated violence hoped that all this was merely a passing phenomenon. They noted with satisfaction that by 1972 former black militants were donning neckties and running for political office and that college students were returning to the puerile pranks of academic normalcy. But had the plague of violence really run its course; or was it merely in remission? Certainly in other countries violent men were doing ever more desperate things: Palestinian exiles hijacked planes, sent letter bombs through the mails, and murdered Olympic

athletes; French-Canadian nationalists kidnapped and killed; Catholic and Protestant zealots gunned each other down in the streets of Belfast. And in the
United States there were new explosions of violence. Unseen assailants fired
from overpasses at drivers ignoring the truck boycott during the fuel crisis of
1974; the "Symbionese Liberation Army" kidnapped Patty Hearst as an act of
war against corrupt "Amerika," while Patty turned bank robber to dramatize her
conversion to the cause of her captors. And in 1975 Lynette Fromme tried to
strike a blow for the conservation of natural resources by attempting to shoot the
president of the United States.

How should the historian interpret this plethora of violence? Does it represent
a radical break from the continuity of American history? Or is it merely a
recurrence of a basic pattern? In the words attributed to the black militant Rap
Brown, is violence "as American as cherry pie"?

Those who read American history in a spirit of piety will indignantly deny that
violence stains its mainstream. The real story, they will insist, is one of peaceful
development—the drafting of the Constitution, the widening of democracy
through the gradual enactment of laws, the ever more efficient production of
goods, the rising standard of living, the building of schools and colleges,
libraries and churches. Such a view of American history conforms to the ideals of
the eighteenth-century founders. It combines the rational and humane goals of
Thomas Jefferson with the rational and efficient goals of Alexander Hamilton.

But a realistic account of American history must find room for material of a
very different character. White men began to fight against the Indians in the early
days of settlement and continued to shoot it out with them until long after the
Civil War. In sober truth, our ancestors stole a whole nation from its native
owners by violence. In similar fashion they won their independence, not by the
soaring rhetoric of Sam Adams and Tom Paine, but by the bloody campaigns of
Saratoga and Yorktown. Another generation of Americans rounded out the
national borders by the violence of the Mexican War; they preserved the Union
and freed the slaves by the violence of the Civil War. Still later Americans seized
an overseas empire and then resorted to violence in two world wars and the wars
in Korea and Vietnam.

Of course, the historian stresses an important difference between the violence
of these wars and the violence on city streets and on college campuses. Soldiers
killed because the government ordered them to do so. No matter whether the
official policy was justified or not, the violence was "legal." But recent urban
and campus riots belonged to a different category of violence. This was violence
not sanctioned by the government, but violence perpetrated in defiance of law
and authority.

Is defiant violence something new in American history? Not really. During our
"Age of Reason" Sons of Liberty sacked houses and terrorized royal officials;
pseudo-Indians dumped tea into Boston Harbor; angry followers of Daniel Shays

forced the courts to close; and outraged frontiersmen defied President Washington in the sacred cause of untaxed whiskey. In later decades Catholics and Protestants broke each others' heads in the streets of eastern cities; northern mobs assaulted abolitionists; antislavery mobs roughed up slave catchers; irate Irishmen strung up blacks to protest the Civil War draft; striking workers destroyed property and shot at their oppressors.

The realistic historian obviously cannot close his eyes to the red thread of violence that runs through the American experience from the days of the Jamestown colony to the present decade. But he needs to interpret this aspect of our history. Did violence always, sometimes, or never achieve its goals? Applying the pragmatic test, did violence "work" in the American context?

If one analyzes various examples of defiant violence in American history, he finds at least three different kinds. The first is the apparently successful act of violence—the one in which a group of people defy authority, do violent things, achieve their goal, and escape punishment for their violation of the law. An early example of this would be the Stamp Act riots. In several towns mobs roamed the streets, destroyed the property of colonial officials, and terrorized the stamp agents into resigning. Violence in this case seems to have been highly successful: The rioters made it impossible to collect the tax; they ultimately got rid of the hated law; and they suffered no punishment for their illegal actions.[2]

Equally successful acts of violence occurred in defiance of the federal Fugitive Slave Act of 1850. In 1851, for example, a throng of respectable citizens broke into the office of the U.S. commissioner in Syracuse, New York, took out of his custody an alleged fugitive named Jerry, and helped this black man to escape to Canada. The good people of the community willfully defied the authority of the United States and nullified an act of Congress. Grand juries would take no action against the rioters; there were no indictments and no punishments.[3]

The sit-down strikes of 1937 provide still a third example of successful thwarting of the law. In Flint, Michigan, auto workers seized the plants of the General Motors Corporation and held them for six weeks in defiance of admonitions from the police and orders from the courts. Their protest was nominally nonviolent, but police who ventured too close to the seized plants had to dodge barrages of bottles and auto parts. No one was killed, but the danger of serious injury was real. Yet the sit-down strikers escaped punishment for their illegal conduct and won a union contract for the United Automobile Workers.[4]

Do acts of violence such as these have common characteristics that might explain their success? The first feature to impress us is that the acts were not indiscriminate in character. Each was sharply focused on a single issue; each had a kind of symbolic character. By their drastic action against representatives of British authority, the Stamp Act demonstrators dramatized the asserted injustice and unconstitutionality of a particular piece of legislation; by concentrating their wrath on one unfortunate officeholder charged with enforcement the Jerry rescuers acted out their contempt for a despicable law; by occupying the GM factories the sit-down strikers proclaimed their conviction that the right to join a labor union was a right superior to the right of property.

In the second place, these acts of violence had strong support in community opinion. Besides the riots, opposition to the Stamp Act took the form of resolutions by various representative bodies and a boycott of English imports. Millions of other northerners agreed with the Syracuse lawbreakers that the Fugitive Slave Act was an intolerable piece of legislation. And the sit-down strikers enjoyed a substantial immunity because many liberals including the man who happened to be governor of Michigan and the one who was president of the United States sympathized with their cause.

The whole Revolutionary War may be regarded as a successful resort to defiant violence. From the viewpoint of the weary British troops marching back to Boston after the skirmishes at Lexington and Concord, the Yankee farmers sniping at them from every barn and hedge were certainly criminals and assassins. The minutemen of 1775 have been canonized as patriots only because they eventually won. Their acts have been awarded a kind of retroactive legality. Yet even if the historian recognizes their acts for what they were—deliberate defiance of British law—he must remember certain other things. Although there was occasional mob action against the person and property of Loyalists, most of the violence of the Revolution was of an organized and disciplined kind. The colonists formed regiments and armies; they fought the king's soldiers under the rules of war as they understood them. Moreover, they sought from the very first to give their defiance some kind of plausible legal basis. They organized committees of correspondence, provincial congresses, and continental congresses to provide the country with government. When they could no longer pretend that their acts were legal under British law, they appealed to the higher law of Nature and Nature's God. American success, moreover, depended on much more than violence. By a skillful use of propaganda the colonists undermined the British will to persist in the war; by bold diplomacy they found European allies to help them.

The second category of violence is what we may call the sacrificial act. This is the act of violence that fails in its immediate objective and brings about the destruction of its perpetrators, but eventually serves their cause. The so-called Boston Massacre provides a good example. The episode grew out of the hostility of artisans and laborers to the British troops stationed in Boston in 1770. One winter night a crowd—egged on by a black militant named Crispus Attucks— began to rough up some British sentries. The immediate results were disastrous to the demonstrators. British troops opened fire and killed five of their tormenters, including Crispus Attucks himself. The demonstrators paid for their resort to violence with their lives, but Boston radicals made skillful use of the incident to inflame American opinion against the British. One night of rather unheroic disorderly conduct became the Boston Massacre of American patriotic legend.[5]

An even better example of the sacrificial act of violence is the John Brown raid. It was an act of fanaticism bordering on madness when old John Brown seized the federal arsenal at Harper's Ferry, Virginia, in an attempt to free the slaves. Brown failed completely. Virginia militia companies and U.S. troops attacked him. Ten of Brown's followers were killed in combat; Brown and six others were captured, tried, and hanged. Yet Brown's act of violence had far-reaching consequences. His attempt to incite the slaves against their masters alarmed the South and inflamed the secessionist spirit. His martyrdom on the gallows touched the hearts of Emerson and Thoreau and thousands of other northerners. In both sections the affair contributed to that polarization of passions that made the Civil War inevitable and eventually brought about the emancipation of the blacks.[6] No wonder federal troops sang as they marched:

John Brown's body lies a'moldering in the grave
But his soul goes marching on.

There is still a third type of violence in American history. This is the defiance of law that may either fail or succeed in its immediate effects, but in the long run seriously injures the cause for which the violence is employed.

The history of the American labor movement after the Civil War involves many such futile outbursts of violence. In 1877 the railroads cut the wages of their employees, and the embittered men not only refused to work but attempted to stop the trains. Since the strikers often had a good deal of sympathy from local opinion, they won temporary victories in many localities. But their resort to violence only resulted in the mobilization of more and more force against them. The governor of Maryland dispatched the state militia to the scene; President Hayes sent in federal troops; and the strike was crushed. Elsewhere the story was the same. In Pittsburgh there was one glorious night of rioting in which the citizens had the exhilarating experience of destroying the property of the hated Pennsylvania Railroad. The mob put the torch to the Union Station, the round house, the machine shops, and a grain elevator. They wrecked 2,000 freight cars and 25 locomotives. It was an altogether memorable night in the history of American violence, but the morning after was grim. State and federal troops took over the city, and the strikers had to go back to work on their employers' terms. The violence of 1877 left railroad management supreme in its labor relations for years to come.[7]

In the Homestead strike of 1892, there was another example of strikers winning a battle but losing the war. Determined to prevent the Carnegie company from running its steel mills with scab labor, the strikers and their sympathizers took control of the town and defeated an attempt at amphibious invasion by Pinkerton guards. After ten lives were lost in a pitched battle, the Pinkertons suffered the humiliation of surrendering, being manhandled by the crowd, and then expelled from the town. Violence triumphed, but the victory was short-lived. The governor of Pennsylvania sent in troops, scabs took over the jobs of the strikers, and the cause of organized labor in the steel industry was set back for almost a half-century. Not until 1937 did Carnegie's successor, the United States Steel Corporation, make a general contract with the steel workers' union.[8]

For still another illustration of violence injuring the cause of the protestors, consider the somber results that followed an outburst in Chicago's Haymarket Square in 1886. On this occasion there was a labor rally, the police attempted to break it up, and some unknown person threw a bomb. In the ensuing chaos seven policemen received mortal injuries and sixty more were wounded, as against only four deaths and an undetermined number of injuries among the demonstrators. This grim profit and loss statement might suggest that the police got the worst of the clash, but the aftermath was quite different. Unable to identify the actual bomb thrower, the authorities arrested and put on trial eight anarchists on a charge that their advocacy of force had made them accessories before the fact. All eight were convicted; four were hanged; one committed suicide; and the other three served prison terms. Harsh though this punishment was for men whose only crime was inflammatory language, the incident has its greatest significance in the setback that it gave to the Knights of Labor. During 1885 and early 1886 the Knights had enjoyed a dramatic rise in membership; they seemed to have a bright future ahead of them. There was no real connection between the Knights and the anarchists; yet conservative opinion lumped all agitators together. In the reaction that followed the Haymarket affair employers joined forces to combat the Knights; frightened workers left the unions; and during the next four years this labor organization lost 85 percent of its membership. There were other reasons than the Haymarket tragedy for the collapse of the Knights, but the recoil from this act of violence was a major cause.[9]

If we compare the acts of violence that failed with those that succeeded, we find that the violence of these strikes and labor disputes was more general in scope, less rational in purpose, less focused on a key issue. More important, these disorders took a form that outraged large sectors of public opinion, not only in the business community but in all the citadels of middle-class respectability. Solid citizens demanded that the government use whatever force was necessary to crush the fomenters of trouble. More than that, the spirit of fear and repression was extended to the cause associated with the violence. Again and again the whole organized labor movement was made to suffer for the hot-headed acts of a few militants. Oftentimes constitutional rights were ignored—particularly at the level of local government; tough sheriffs and deputies jailed union organizers on absurd charges or ran them out of town—all with the blessing of fearful middle-class opinion. In still other cases there was no pretense of legal formality. Vigilantes beat up and even lynched hated radicals. Such was the fate of IWW leaders during the overheated days of World War I.[10]

The great peril of violence is that it sets off counterviolence. The issue is decided not on its merits but on which side can exert the stronger force. Almost every victory for the violent acts of one party is a defeat for the violent acts of the other. To be sure, the North won the Civil War; violence brought victory to the cause of national unity and antislavery. But to the South violence brought defeat. To bombard Fort Sumter in 1861 was a heady act of violence, but it was a violence that ultimately brought destruction and ruin on the whole section. White men conquered the Indians; through violence they won control of the country. But the Indians lost. The Indians' resort to tomahawk and gun doomed them to destruction.

Except under the most unusual circumstances, it appears, violence is a dangerous weapon. The problem is not that violence is uncharacteristic of American history; on the contrary, it is all too common. Every American Babbitt has a tiger in his tank; beneath his placid exterior lurk primitive fear and anger. It is just because of this that acts that provoke fear and anger are so dangerous to American minority groups. Mayors who walk the streets with their poor constituents and value human life above property are a rare breed; mayors who order their police to shoot to kill reveal the spirit likely to gain more and more middle-class applause if protest groups return to violence.

Since violence is so dangerous both to the dissident himself and to his cause, why has he continued to employ it? Why did groups like the Black Panthers and the Weathermen indulge in the rhetoric of violence, whether or not they were guilty of the specific acts of which they were accused? The principal reason, of course, was the desperate anger of young radicals—whether white or black—at the terrible things they saw in American society during the sixties—the unjust war in Vietnam, the horrors of the urban ghettos, the pollution of the earth and the atmosphere.

But something else was involved in the recent epidemic of violence. With many young radicals, violence became not just an explosion of rage but a cult. White militants venerated heroes like Che Guevara, and black militants inevitably exalted the example of Nat Turner. During the sixties, history suddenly became important to intelligent young blacks. They looked to history to help them understand who they were and what their destiny was. These blacks disliked much of the history that white professors had written and taught. The older accounts devoted many pages to the institution of slavery, the antislavery movement, and the controversies of the Reconstruction period, but these were usually written as though the blacks had played an entirely passive role, as though all that counted was what white men were saying and doing about black men. Blacks now wanted to hear what blacks had done. Specifically they were eager to hear about the ancient glories of Africa, about the transfer of African culture to America, and, above all, about the black man's long, long struggle to be free. They did not want to hear how dearly old master and his slaves loved each other; they wanted to hear about how the restless slaves sabotaged production on the old plantation and shot old master whenever they could get the drop on him. Herbert Aptheker gave them what they wanted in his book *American*

Slave Revolts. The concluding sentence in that book reads: "The data herein presented makes necessary the revision of the generally accepted notion that the response was one of passivity and docility. The evidence, on the contrary, points to the conclusion that discontent and rebelliousness were not only exceedingly common, but, indeed, characteristic of American Negro slaves."[11]

It was in this context that Nat Turner became a major hero. Malcolm X was not his only fervid admirer. In 1965 the magazine *Negro Digest* reprinted the rare old document by T. R. Gray, containing the authentic confession of Nat Turner. In his introduction the editor said: "To T. R. Gray, Nat Turner was a murderous villain, but Mr. Gray was white. To the millions of American Negroes, then and now, Nat Turner, the insurrectionist, was a hero."[12]

Putting aside the question of whether Nat was a hero or a villain, how does his resort to violence fit into the analysis attempted in this essay? Was the Nat Turner uprising a successful act of violence, or was it a failure? For a few hours Nat and his followers were triumphant. But their act of violence aroused the whole countryside. The whites mobilized overwhelming force against them. They scattered Nat's little company of followers and methodically destroyed them. Some twenty blacks including Nat himself died on the gallows after trials in the county courthouse. But the grimmest aftermath was a white reign of terror. A Richmond newspaper deplored "the slaughter of many blacks without trial and under circumstances of great barbarity." A minister wrote: "Many negroes are killed every day. The exact number will never be known." According to one contemporary estimate, over one hundred blacks were destroyed in this orgy of counterviolence.[13]

Clearly, the Nat Turner insurrection failed miserably in its immediate consequences. But was it perhaps one of those sacrificial acts of violence that contributed to the eventual victory of a noble cause? It is difficult to contend that this is so. On the contrary, this night of terror seems to have strengthened rather than weakened the institution of slavery. Throughout the South frightened white men, whether slave owners or not, joined ranks to keep the blacks in subjection. Old laws repressing the slaves were vigorously enforced; new laws were passed making it more difficult for individual masters to free their slaves. White critics of slavery were assaulted and murdered, not only in the South but in the North as well.

Even as a martyr in the black cause, Nat Turner is a somewhat ambivalent figure. Why did he kill? In his confession he used language such as this: "... I heard a loud noise in the heavens, and the Spirit instantly appeared to me and said the Serpent was loosened, and Christ had laid down the yoke he had borne of the sins of men, and that I should take it on and fight the Serpent, for the time was fast approaching when the first should be last and the last should be first."[14] Is this the language of a black Spartacus, or that of a man crazed by religious obsession? Of course, one theory does not necessarily exclude the other. In the case of Malcolm X, it can be seen how black nationalism may assume a passionately religious form.

Nat Turner is truly a mysterious figure. Gray says of him that he had "an uncommon share of intelligence with a mind capable of attaining anything, but warped and perverted by the influence of early impressions."[15] What were these early impressions? William Styron has exercised his imagination on the problem in a fascinating novel. He has provided a biography for Nat, complete with sexual repressions and all the modern hang-ups. This makes readable fiction, but it does not really serve the purposes of sober history. We shall never know just what formed the personality of Nat Turner, but we do have evidence that he was an unusual man—not at all the Sambo type that Stanley Elkins describes as resulting from the slave experience.[16] Consider further testimony from T. R. Gray: "The calm, deliberate composure with which he spoke of his late deeds and intentions, the expression of his fiend-like face when excited by enthusiasm, still bearing the stains of the blood of helpless innocence about him; clothed with rags and covered with chains, yet daring to raise his manacled hands to heaven; with a spirit soaring above the attributes of man. I looked on him and my blood curdled in my veins."[17]

Clearly Nat Turner was a most impressive person, a proud and defiant man, a highly symbolic figure. Yet the realistic historian must regard his outburst of violence as a failure. No one ever sang:

Nat Turner's body lies a'moldering in the grave
But his soul goes marching on.

Poor Nat never even made the grave. On the last page of his novel Styron quotes without comment another early account of the insurrection. The author, William S. Drewry, wrote: "The bodies of those executed, with one exception, were buried in a decent and becoming manner. That of Nat Turner was delivered to the doctors, who skinned it and made grease of the flesh. Mr. R. S. Barham's father owned a money purse made of his hide. His skeleton was for many years in the possession of Dr. Massenberg, but has since been misplaced."[18] The symbolism is shattering. White violence took its last mean vengeance against the body of the man who had organized black violence.

Advocates of social change—both black and white—may draw profit from Nat's example. They will of course admire his defiant courage and preserve his memory. Yet—unless they are suicidal—they will not follow him as a model. If one resorts to violence against impossible odds, if one commits deeds so terrifying that they provoke an orgy of retaliation, if one strengthens the very institutions he seeks to overthrow, his sacrifice is in vain. He ends up, like Nat, a misplaced skeleton.

Effective radicalism in the American situation demands other strategies. The example of Frederick Douglass is in striking contrast to that of Nat Turner. Douglass was a rebellious slave also. He maintained a sturdy independence and was many times flogged for his impertinence. He tried to run away once and was captured. He ran away again and made it. In the North he encountered the familiar prejudices that kept most black men in poverty. He made a precarious living as a day laborer until the antislavery people made him one of their agents. The life of an abolitionist in those days was one of difficulty and danger, but Douglass became one of the movement's most effective men. He was an orator, a newspaper editor, and a politician. He used all the weapons available to him: He worked both within the system and against the system by helping other fugitive slaves to maintain their freedom. And he stayed alive. He lived to see the abolition of slavery. He lived to sit in the White House and tell Abraham Lincoln to his face how he should treat black soldiers if he wanted to get recruits. This, it seems clear, was a form of black power much more effective than Nat Turner ever achieved.[19]

What then is the place of violence in American history? It would be futile to deny that it has been a persistent pattern in the American experience. Not only do episodes of violence run through our nation's history; violence has a particularly strong grip on the American imagination as evidenced both in the popular culture and in serious literature. Note, on one hand, the popularity of western stories and movies, murder mysteries, gangster films, and lurid comic books. And note also that some of our best novelists—Melville, Hemingway, Faulkner, Mailer—have written about violent men and violent deeds.

Occasionally acts of violence have advanced some worthwhile cause in American history; more frequently they have injured one. In either case, violence begets violence, and issues get settled on the basis of which side can exert the greater force. Rather than accept the cult of violence, any oppressed group stands a better chance to help itself by basing its appeal on the ever-fresh philosophy of the Declaration of Independence—the philosophy that all men are entitled to basic human rights and that it is the obligation of government and society to secure these rights. Within the American tradition there are many useful weapons for protesting against injustice—political action, economic boycott, marches of protest, civil disobedience, black power, yellow power, red power, student power, woman power. But the weapon of violence seems to the sober historian too dangerous to wield except in clear cases of self-defense.

Notes

1. *The Autobiography of Malcolm X,* with the Assistance of Alex Haley, paperback ed. (New York: Grove Press, 1966), p. 178.

2. Lawrence H. Gipson, *The Coming of the Revolution, 1763–1775* (New York: Harper, 1954), pp. 89–94.

3. Allan Nevins, *Ordeal of the Union* (New York: Scribner's, 1947), 1: 391.

4. Irving Bernstein, *Turbulent Years: A History of the American Worker, 1933–1941* (Boston: Houghton & Mifflin, 1969), pp. 519–51.

5. Gipson, *Coming of the Revolution,* pp. 201–2.

6. Allan Nevins, *The Emergence of Lincoln* (New York: Scribner's, 1950) 1: 70–97.

7. Foster Rhea Dulles, *Labor in America: A History,* 3rd ed. (New York: Crowell, 1966), pp. 118–22.

8. Ibid., pp. 166–71.

9. Norman Ware, *The Labor Movement in the United States, 1860–1895* (New York: Appleton, 1929), pp. 313–19.

10. Joseph Rayback, *A History of American Labor* (New York: Macmillan, 1959), pp. 282, 289.

11. Herbert Aptheker, *American Negro Slave Revolts* (New York: International Publishers, 1943), p. 374.

12. T. R. Gray, "The Confessions, Trial and Execution of Nat Turner, the Negro Insurrectionist," *Negro Digest* 14 (July 1965): 28

13. Aptheker, *American Negro Slave Revolts,* p. 301.

14. Gray, *Negro Digest,* p. 37.

15. Ibid., p. 44.

16. Stanley M. Elkins, *Slavery: A Problem in American Institutional and Intellectual Life* (New York: Universal Library, 1963), 81–139.

17. Gray, *Negro Digest,* pp. 44–45.

18. William Styron, *The Confessions of Nat Turner* (New York: Random House, 1967), p. 429.

19. Rayford W. Logan, ed., *Life and Times of Frederick Douglass* (New York: Collier Books, 1962), pp. 115–44, 155–75, 197–214, 259–70, 347–49.

Bibliography

Aptheker, Herbert. *American Negro Slave Riots.* New York: International Publishers, 1943.

Bernstein, Irving. *The Turbulent Years: A History of the American Worker, 1933–1941.* Boston: Houghton Mifflin, 1969.

Boskin, Joseph. *Urban Racial Violence in the Twentieth Century.* 2nd ed. Beverly Hills, Calif.: Glencoe, 1976.

Brown, Richard Maxwell. *Strain of Violence: Historical Studies of American Violence and Vigilantism.* New York: Oxford University Press, 1975.

Brown, Richard Maxwell, ed. *American Violence.* Englewood Cliffs, N.J.: Prentice-Hall, 1970.

Dulles, Foster Rhea. *Labor in America: A History.* 3rd ed. New York: Crowell, 1966.

Elkins, Stanley. *Slavery: A Problem in American Institutional and Intellectual Life.* New York: Universal Library, 1963.

Gipson, Lawrence H. *The Coming of the Revolution, 1763–1775.* New York: Harper, 1954.

Graham, Hugh Davis, and Ted Robert Gurr. *Violence in America: Historical and Comparative Perspectives.* 2 vols. Washington, D.C.: U.S. Government Printing Office, 1969.

Gray, T. R. "The Confession, Trial and Execution of Nat Turner, the Insurrectionist." *Negro Digest* 14 (July 1965): 28–48.

Hofstadter, Richard, and Michael Wallace, eds. *American Violence: A Documentary History.* New York: Knopf, 1970.

Logan, Rayford, ed. *Life and Times of Frederick Douglass.* New York: Collier Books, 1962.

Malcolm X. *The Autobiography of Malcolm X,* with the Assistance of Alex Haley. Paperback ed. New York: Grove Press, 1966.

Nevins, Allan. *Ordeal of the Union.* 2 vols. New York: Scribner's, 1947.

———. *The Emergence of Lincoln.* 2 vols. New York: Scribner's, 1950.

Rayback, Joseph. *A History of American Labor.* New York: Macmillan, 1959.

Rose, Thomas. *Violence in America: A Historical and Contemporary Reader.* New York: Random House, 1969.

Styron, William. *The Confessions of Nat Turner.* New York: Random House, 1967.

Ware, Norman. *The Labor Movement in the United States, 1860–1895.* New York: Appleton, 1929.

MORRELL HEALD

Foreign Relations, American Style

America began, in the minds of the English and other Europeans who settled that portion of it that later became the United States, as a country distinctively different from others.[1] This sense of difference was originally grounded in those European conditions that between the sixteenth and the eighteenth centuries sent explorers, settlers, religious reformers, common laborers, prisoners, refugees, and others across the ocean to seek a new life. It soon drew support from other sources as well. Not only friends and families left behind but the migrants themselves and, inevitably, the native American peoples whose lands were invaded and lives disrupted by the newcomers had many occasions to ponder the significance of the new society quickly spreading from its coastal bases across the North American mountains and plains. Both the idea and the reality of America had meaning for many more than merely Americans themselves.

The combination of religious and economic motives that had led the early settlers to undertake the risks of transatlantic migration grafted a dynamism born of great expectations upon the resources of an undeveloped continent. Idealism and opportunity — the ambition to serve God or to build a society unfettered by traditional institutions and prescriptions — defined and energized a pervasive sense of American distinctiveness. By the time recognition of a distinctively American character, interest, and destiny had emerged to support a successful revolution against Old World political domination, Americans had evolved a widespread set of assumptions about their relationships to other nations and peoples. The commitment to mission[2] and opportunity, to a better and freer society both at home and abroad, reflected the experiences and outlook of an expansive, self-confident people.

The conviction of American uniqueness, even superiority, and the simultaneous claim to be a model and guide for others have shaped our foreign relations and foreign policy from the beginning. If America was fortunately different from other lands, its mission was not only to preserve and protect that difference but included also the responsibility to favor and foster the advancement elsewhere of the universal principles upon which it was assumed to rest. Such a view implied fellowship and identification with the aspirations of men everywhere, to be sure, but it nevertheless took for granted America's primacy and priority in the achievement of those virtues for which others still yearned or struggled. The conflicting perspectives within this double vision of America's relations with the rest of the world have emerged into clearer focus with changing times and circumstances. The tensions they have given rise to intensify, but limit, our isolationism while they simultaneously restrict, yet stimulate, our internationalism.

In the process of breaking through the bonds of empire, Americans acquired a third commitment which seemed initially to accord well with those of mission and opportunity. Resistance to British encroachments upon their freedoms popularized the concept of the limited state, as set forth in Lockean political theory, Adam Smith's economics, and the writings of the French *philosophes*. As children of the Enlightenment and its first self-conscious exemplars, the leaders of the American Revolution leaned toward a liberalism which in its exaltation of the individual aimed to reduce the role of the state to a minimum. Manifested in such movements as Jeffersonian and Jacksonian democracy, as well as later versions of "rugged individualism," this doctrine has heretofore been considered primarily in its domestic applications, where it offered the widest possible license to private individual and group initiatives. In so doing it reinforced the idea of American distinctiveness from Europe, whose monarchies, in contrast, were ponderous, corrupt and tyrannical. The new, limited American state thus also served as a unique model of democratic virtue.

Ideas exercise their influence not primarily as materials for intellectual speculation and analysis, but as lenses or filters through which men can focus or distill the meaning of their experience. If freedom multiplied opportunities for Americans, it correspondingly reduced their dependence upon government. And the new social and political order they were building in turn defined their mission to preserve, to further, and to extend it. This new society had come into being not only on a continent of untold dimension and wealth but on the fringes of the European metropolis mired, in the early nineteenth century, in a cycle of wars and revolutions from which Americans were eager to remain aloof. The ideal of American isolation from the alliances and conflicts of Europe, as enunciated by Washington, Jefferson, and John Quincy Adams, was an attempt to guarantee the security of the young nation and its ideals. Isolation assured the preservation of American opportunity and distinctiveness. It offered the firmest assurance for the fulfillment of America's mission in a troubled world. And isolationism, of course, was consistent with the liberal concept of the state. In foreign, as in domestic, relations it prescribed a limited role for government — circumscribed, inactive, and concerned primarily with the maintenance of basic interests and freedoms.

In describing the foreign policy of the United States in the nineteenth century as isolationist, however, we have usually overlooked the fact that the limitations implied were directed almost exclusively against the state, hardly at all against individuals. Indeed, with the exception of defense, the chief role Americans assigned their government in international affairs was that of underwriting private liberty of movement and enterprise by promoting freedom of the seas and winning most-favored-nation status for the benefit of its citizens. True, government itself might be restricted to a modest, nominally isolationist posture; but private citizens in pursuit of the distinctive (yet curiously universal) American doctrine of opportunity were free to extend their interests and activities wherever it beckoned. American isolation was never conceived of as confining the dynamism and expansiveness of the American people within their own national boundaries. Commitment to the multiplication and defense of private opportunity was the common assumption underlying both American foreign and domestic policies.

Only by recognizing this distinction between private and public roles can we reconcile the rhetoric of isolationism with the reality of widespread private international activity. American citizens as individuals and in groups — merchants, missionaries, soldiers of fortune, and others—ranged widely across the Caribbean, Latin America, the Pacific, and into Asia. The role of diplomacy was twofold: to support and extend their aims as far as limited governmental means made possible; and to uphold a framework of principled idealism within which Americans could reassure themselves and others that, in foreign as well as in domestic affairs, private advantage and the general welfare were complementary.

Two leading pronouncements of American diplomacy, whose development and application spanned nearly a century of private expansionism and governmental restraint—the Monroe Doctrine and the policy of the Open Door— clearly exemplify the balancing of opposites characteric of the American approach to foreign relations. The assertion of a moral imperative to promote the extension of freedom rationalized policies whose immediate effect was to enlarge the circle of overseas opportunities for private exploitation. The rhetoric of active commitment on the part of American government screened policies whose enforcement actually rested on the self-interests or rivalries of other powers. American foreign policy attempted to persuade other nations to forgo the exercise of powers the United States was unable, by virtue of its own ideological or material limitations, to wield. The success of American diplomacy in framing policies that reconciled its government's weaknesses with its citizens' wideranging interests by assuming moral postures in the international arena further encouraged those citizens to see their own activities in pursuit of profit or of religious and political converts in the same light. Since private initiative and freedom had proved themselves at home, all that remained was to demonstrate by example or, sometimes, merely by assertion that they were moral and beneficial overseas as well. As missionaries of freedom and morality, Americans could in principle justify intervention abroad, whether private or governmental, without seeming seriously to contradict their commitment to isolationism and limited government at home.

In the course of the nineteenth century technological change and industrialization greatly accelerated the rate and range of American expansion. Enthusiasm for international expansion in some quarters even outran the rapid extension of actual economic and political interests. By the 1890s it had become increasingly difficult for the American government to cling to a limited role in foreign relations. In the wake of the Spanish-American War President McKinley undertook the task of reconciling the nation to an increasingly active governmental role in foreign relations, a responsibility his successor assumed with greater gusto. The shift did not come easily or quickly; indeed, it hardly won general acceptance until World War II. Since then, America has of course experienced an intensive increase in international involvement, with government overtaking and matching private initiative. With this change has come a convulsive, reluctant, and evidently still incomplete relinquishment of the illusion of isolation.

Governmental activism both in domestic and in foreign relations may have been encouraged by deepening involvement with Asian and Latin American peoples whose social, political, and racial characteristics many Americans considered inferior, appropriate subjects for patronizing. Toward Europe and the Europeans, on the other hand, Americans had long displayed an ambivalence in which presumptions of superiority rooted in that sense of distinctiveness already referred to were counterbalanced to a considerable degree by deference and insecurity.

Over the years the stridency of American critiques of Europe, and sensitivity to overt or imagined slurs upon the New World by governments and citizens of the Old, had offered persuasive evidence of the persistence of feelings of inferiority beneath the surface. Uneasy though they might be in the face of European power and tradition, Americans still affirmed their country's present and future superiority. It was an awkward stance to maintain but one made necessary by the fact that they or their ancestors had staked their lives, fortunes, and convictions on the choice. Yet, by mid-twentieth century events seemed at least partially to have vindicated American claims. Sapped by two wars, Europe had been forced to acknowledge American leadership, if not superiority. And the United States had meanwhile moved with only temporary hesitancy to assume the role of heir and defender of Western freedom in a cold war against communism.

The doubts and hesitancies which complicated Americans' attitudes toward Europe faded quickly, however, when they faced in other directions. To the south, Latin America had struggled to create sister republics in the traditions of European liberalism and American democracy; but the Latins were hybrid democrats at best who strangely failed to appreciate or imitate the social and economic virtues undergirding the forms of North American republicanism. They were racial hybrids, too, mixing European blood with that of the Indians and Africans in ways deeply disturbing to a people that, even when they denied the fact, were attempting to maintain lines of distinction and separation between the races. Catholicism added still another suspicious element to the Latin compound in the view of straight-laced North American Protestants. The American doctrine of mission, after all, had descended via Puritanism directly from the Reformation attack upon Catholic idolatry, corruption, and repressiveness. It was little wonder, all things considered, that North Americans felt free to deal with their Latin brothers as distinctly second-class democrats.

When they confronted the peoples and religions of Asia and Africa, Americans encountered cultures so unfamiliar as to require new images and categories. Yet, even here, past experience offered clues and tendencies for further development. Their earliest contacts with non-Western peoples had been with the American Indians and with black Africans. The relationships arising from those encounters had matured in contempt, hostility, and violence. As heathens or pagans, these strangers could claim little respect on the part of those who had come to do their own or the Lord's work in a new land. Backward, by European standards, in the technologies of economic exploitation and accumulation, they could scarcely resist the onward drive of those who found ways to express their sense of mission in the opening of new regions for development as much or more than in the opening of new souls to the vision of God. For blacks torn by force from their African homeland and lacking continuous contact with it, only submission to the institution of slavery provided terms on which they could live in peace with white Americans. The Indians were hardly more fortunate; the cycle of struggle, retreat, negotiation, and settlement which bought time for survival left them finally even weaker and more helpless. Conversion to Christianity might offer a claim for more humane treatment, but it soon became clear that race outweighed religion on the scale of American values. Nonwhite Christians could at best hope for acceptance as second-class human beings within the broad circuit of American society.[3]

Racism, precipitated in the contest for continental domination, combined with religious conviction and confidence in Western technological virtuosity to unfetter the missionary and opportunistic urges with which Americans confronted Asia and Africa. It denied to peoples of non-European origin any values or virtues worthy of consideration. It replaced the lingering sense of inferiority that checked American dealings with Europe with smug superiority, justifying beforehand ignorance and lack of concern for the traditions and preferences of the benighted. There were, of course, exceptions: men and women whose human concern or cultural sensitivity led them to approach the non-Western world in the spirit of brotherhood or genuine respect. Unfortunately, they were too few in number and slight in influence.

In the face of evidently inferior and backward peoples, Americans could more easily rationalize an augmented role for the state in the regulation of human affairs. If the presumably universal values of freedom and equality were to be applied to these peoples, it could only be after a long period of tutelage under the benevolent eyes of the American government. Such paternalism toward the Caribbean and Pacific dependencies acquired in the course of the Spanish-American War justified the unexpected acquisitions in acceptably idealistic terms while diverting attention from less moral expectations of profit and power. The opportunity for the United States to set an example for European imperialists by establishing colonial regimes dedicated to the democratization and uplift of subject peoples offers a strong temptation. Through a policy of service to others America's fulfillment of her historic mission might be demonstrated to the world. Post-Civil War efforts to help Negroes prepare for full participation in American society had floundered, among other reasons, on the lack of support American liberalism offered for an ambitious social and economic welfare program. Forty years later American colonial policy instituted a program of education, health, political, and economic uplift on behalf of the Caribbean and Filipino peoples as an essential justification of its new acquisitions and role. The initiatives and experience gained in these remote regions in turn provided precedents for a more active governmental role at home when individual and institutional weaknesses there became apparent in the 1930s.

The twentieth century has seen a notable increase in the role of the state in both domestic and international affairs. Isolationism, in the traditional sense of negation of governmental activism in foreign relations, became increasingly untenable as did the attempt to insulate the government from active responsibility for domestic, social, and economic conditions. The decade of the 1930s was in many respects crucial. The years which saw the New Deal undertake sweeping domestic initiatives also demonstrated the futility of efforts to dissociate the United States from the international arena behind a screen of neutrality.

From the beginning Americans had considered it the responsibility of diplomacy to advance the interests, economic or otherwise, of private citizens. As those interests grew in scope, complexity, and scale of organization, foreign policy assumed an ever-larger role in public affairs. By the end of World War II the American government had emerged as a major participant if not the dominant partner in an economic system characterized by public and private collaboration at virtually every level. Viewpoints differed as to whether private interests, more affluent and powerful than ever, could effectively be constrained by the modern state or whether in fact they controlled and manipulated it to their own ends. Whatever the balance of this intricate relationship, there could be little disagreement concerning the central role played by government in what had come to be termed the military-industrial complex. At the very least, it served as a coordinator and clearinghouse for a combination of public and private agencies and interests: corporations, foundations, communications networks, and policies which constituted the American economic system. In the absence of effective international controls, a policy of limited government involvement in international affairs was clearly no longer viable, reluctant though traditionalists might be to acknowledge the fact.

Like racism, anti-communism in the twentieth century has helped to justify major departures from the American tradition of governmental non-involvement in foreign affairs. The Cold War, coming on the heels of the Great Depression and

World War II, sanctioned an enormous enlargement of the role and responsibilities of American statecraft—all in the name of protecting private freedoms. Not without qualms, the United States had recognized, and, under extreme pressure, even allied itself with the Soviet Union. But Russia's postwar emergence as a superpower with ideological and missionary pretensions equaling if not surpassing our own was too threatening to be ignored. The last vestiges of the old isolationism were abandoned as the United States moved in the 1940s and 1950s to mobilize a worldwide structure of multilateral alliances. Once again the concept of an American mission for freedom helped rationalize the assumption of unprecedented commitments both in Europe and in Asia while complicating rational analysis of respective claims of national interest and idealism in the making of foreign policy.

More recently, controversies generated by the American experience in Vietnam have revived fears of a renewed isolationism. The term itself has become a weapon of attack upon those who called for the withdrawal, or the severe limiting, of American intervention — political, economic, cultural — in the affairs of other nations. Conversely internationalism, with all the uncritical prestige that isolationism once enjoyed, is now widely used to justify virtually every form of American intervention overseas. Yet, a review of the interplay among the concepts of mission, opportunity, and isolation as they arose in the early stages of the nation's history can help us reconsider the significance of the terms internationalism and isolationism as they are used in contemporary polemics.[4]

The isolationist principle had from the beginning aimed to defend as a matter of national policy, and to spread through private initiatives, a concept of man and his relationship to society held to be both distinctively American and ultimately universal. It could justify withdrawal from the world, but it could also rationalize the obliteration of those groups or nations that stood in the way of its fulfillment. Such interventions to extend the sway of American institutions and value patterns were once undertaken on the western plains, in the southern plantations, and in the urban ghettos, as well as in the foreign missions and commercial compounds. Then, they were primarily the initiatives of private individuals and groups with government limited to a secondary, although far from insignificant, role. Today, when government and multinational corporate interests bestride the international arenas, such blindness to hostility toward foreign cultures and values constitute the essence of modern isolationism.

Internationalism, however, calls for the acknowledgment of the divergent rights and values of others. That Americans from the beginning have found it difficult to accept and respect such differences is a dimension of the national character and mission we have yet to take full account of. Despite these difficulties, international and cross-cultural influences could never be fully evaded by a people whose isolation proved, after all, so limited. The slow and painful awakening among Americans of many walks of life and under many kinds of circumstance, both foreign and domestic, of a sense of the reality and the vitality of human differences is the foundation of contemporary internationalism. It is such a perspective, and not an isolationist one after all, that would limit American intervention and pressure in the internal affairs of others.

The pluralism implicit in the ideal of equal opportunity, which the American Revolution attempted to secure and which isolation once attempted to preserve in a hostile world, can today be achieved only through cultural comity and an international concert of powers. The concept of an American mission, that once could reconcile simultaneous state isolation and private expansion, now points toward a conscious effort to share with others the responsibility for balancing public and private values in international relations. The long effort to separate public from private and foreign from domestic concerns can no longer be successfully sustained. Indeed, we can now see that that effort was never entirely realistic or successful. The ideals of mission and opportunity that helped to define America's understanding of itself and its role in the world were broadly, if not self-consciously, enough conceived to comprehend both public and private roles, foreign and domestic interests. In recognizing the essential unity of these elements, more obvious and compelling today than ever before, we may be able to relate an understanding of our past more effectively to reasonable hopes for our future.

Finally, it may be appropriate to note two additional dimensions of America's missionary approach to its foreign relations. Perhaps because of their conviction of the universal validity of the democratic ideals to which they subscribed, Americans have been inclined to pride themselves upon the generous, disinterested, constructive motives with which they have entered into their international engagements. This self-congratulatory view often led them to expect gratitude and welcome, and to experience bitter disillusionment when the results proved otherwise. It would be foolish, and patently unfair, to deny that benevolent motives have often manifested themselves in America's foreign undertakings — more often, perhaps, than has been the case with most other major powers. Yet, the record shows that such motives often also served to screen or rationalize other, more self-centered, concerns.

There is, however, still another sense in which Americans may be said to have encountered other nations and peoples as missionaries, or representatives, of a distinctive way of life. Louis Hartz has noted — as did the French aristocrat, Alexis de Toqueville, before him — the circumstances under which American society may be said to have been ''born free'' of the feudal, hierarchical institutions and traditions of the Old World. To the extent that this analysis is valid, Americans may be seen, from the perspectives both of the social democracies of Europe and of the preindustrial societies of the world, as advance agents first of an individualistic liberalism and, more recently, of modern mass consumption-oriented culture. In either guise they have indeed come as missionaries and revolutionaries of the established order of things, in a sense they themselves may not fully have understood. As, often unconscious, saboteurs of the established cultural orders, Americans might on occasion "win friends and influence people"; but they inevitably provoked resentment and hostility as well.

Expectations of gratitude or emulation on the part of other nations, then, appeared certain to face recurring frustration and disappointment irrespective either of American motives or performance. Such expectations were themselves more a measure of the lingering missionary world view than a realistic assessment of human probabilities. A reexamination of the cultural and historical sources of such misunderstandings will surely benefit us more than repeated denunciations and repetitions of them can ever do.

Notes

1. This essay, in modified form, appears in Morrell Heald and Lawrence S. Kaplan, *Culture and Diplomacy: The American Experience* (Westport, Conn: Greenwood Press, 1977).

2. The concept of mission as an element in American attitudes toward our relations with the rest of the world has been thoughtfully considered in Ralph H. Gabriel, *The Course of American Democratic Thought* (New York: Ronald Press, 1940); David M. Potter, *People of Plenty* (Chicago: University of Chicago Press, 1954); and Ernest Lee Tuveson, *Redeemer Nation: The Idea of America's Millenial Role* (Chicago: University of Chicago Press, 1968).

3. Recent scholarship has greatly enlarged our understanding of the cultural dimensions of contact and conflict among Europeans, Native Americans, and Africans in North America. See especially Gary B. Nash, *Red, White and Black: The Peoples of Early America* (Englewood Cliffs, N.J.: Prentice-Hall, Inc., 1974); Francis Jennings, *The Invasion of America: Indians, Colonialism and the Cant of Conquest* (Chapel Hill: University of North Carolina Press, 1975); Winthrop D. Jordan, *White over Black; American Attitudes Toward the Negro, 1550–1812* (Chapel Hill: University of North Carolina Press, 1968).

4. The interdependence of American isolationism and internationalism has also been noted in Louis Hartz, *The Founding of New Societies* (New York: Harcourt, Brace & World, 1964), pp. 116–18, especially.

PART FOUR
Special Groups—Visions and Problems

DAVID M. POTTER

American Women and the American Character

At the time of his death in 1971, David Potter was President of the American Historical Association and of the Organization of American Historians. He was also Coe Professor of American History at Stanford University. This article, first given as a lecture at Stetson University in 1959, was one of the first efforts by a major historian to reexamine the role and image of women in American culture.

There is an old riddle which children used to ask one another concerning two Indians. One was a big Indian, the other was a little Indian, and they were sitting on a fence. The little Indian, the riddle tells us, was the big Indian's son, but the big Indian was not the little Indian's father. How, asks the riddle, can this be?

Boys and girls for a long time have found that this riddle succeeds very well in mystifying many people. And the fact that it does presents another puzzle as to why the riddle is hard to answer. If we were to state the question in more general terms: There are two human beings, one adult and one child; the child is the son of the adult, but the adult is not the father of the child, probably no one would have much difficulty in recognizing that the adult is the mother. Why then do the Indians on a fence perplex us? If we examine the structure of the riddle, I think we will find that it contains two devices which inhibit our recognition that the big Indian is a female. First, the two Indians are described as being in a very specific situation—they are sitting on a fence. But women, at least in our culture, do not usually sit on fences; if the two Indians had been roasting some ears of corn, or mending their teepee, how much easier the riddle would have been. Second, we are perhaps especially prone to think of Indians as masculine. If the riddle had said two South Sea Islanders, or perhaps, two Circassians, the possibility of their being female might occur to us more easily.

But most of all, the riddle owes its baffling effect to the fact that our social generalization is mostly in masculine terms. If we said that the little Indian is the big Indian's daughter, but that the big Indian is not the little Indian's mother, the possibility that the big Indian is the father would come to mind readily enough.

For in our culture, men are still in a general category, while women are in a special category. When we speak of mankind, we mean men and women collectively, but when we speak of womenkind, we mean the ladies, God bless them. The word humanity is itself derived from *homo*, that is man, and the species is *Homo sapiens*. Neuter nouns or general nouns which are ambiguous as to sex—nouns like infant, baby, child, sibling, adolescent, adult, spouse, parent, citizen, person, individual, etc—all take masculine pronouns. In our culture, a woman, at marriage, takes her husband's name. Though born a Cabot, if she marries Joe Doaks, Mrs. Joe Doaks she becomes and Mrs. Doaks she remains, usually for the rest of her life.

This masculine orientation is to be expected, of course, in a society which is traditionally and culturally male dominated—in what we call a patriarchal rather than a matriarchal society. Even women themselves have connived at maintaining the notion of masculine ascendancy, and in the rather numerous concrete situations in which they actually dominate their men, they often dissimulate their control by pretending to be weak, dependent, or "flighty." In such a situation one must expect that men will be regarded as the normative figures in the society, and that, in popular thought at least, the qualities of the masculine component in the society will pass for the qualities of the society as a whole.

If this habit were confined to popular thought, it would hardly be worth examining. But it also sometimes creeps into academic and scholarly thought, which ought to have more rigor, and when it does so, it can sometimes distort our picture of society. Thus a writer may sometimes make observations on the traits or values of American men, and then may generalize these as the traits or values of the American people. If he did this deliberately, on the theory that since male values dominate the society, they must therefore be American values, we would have to concede that he is aware of what he is doing, even though we might question his results. But when he does so unconsciously, his method may easily lead him to assume first that since American men are dominant, the characteristics of American men are the characteristics of the American people, and that since women are people, the characteristics of the American people are the characteristics of American women, or in short, that the characteristics of American men are the characteristics of American women.

To avoid this trap, when one meets with a social generalization it is frequently worthwhile to ask concretely, does it apply to women, or only to the masculine component in the population? Does the statement that Prussians are domineering mean that Prussian women are domineering, or only Prussian men? Does the statement that Americans are individualistic mean American women as well as American men? The question seems worth asking, for it appears more than possible that many of our social generalizations which are stated sweepingly to cover the entire society are in fact based on the masculine population, and that if we took the feminine population into account, the generalization might have to be qualified, or might even run in an entirely different direction.

I

A notable example of this can perhaps be found in Frederick Jackson Turner's famous frontier hypothesis, stated so brilliantly at Chicago almost seventy years ago. The gist of Turner's argument was, of course, that the frontier had been a basic influence in shaping the character of the American people. Primarily, as he saw it, the frontier provided economic opportunity in the form of free land. When this free land was suddenly conferred upon a people who had previously been held in dependence by the land monopolies of the Old World, it made the American economically independent and this independence made him more individualistic and more egalitarian in his attitudes. Also, the necessity for subduing the wilderness by his own personal exertions, in a situation where he could not call upon doctors, dentists, policemen, lawyers, contractors, well-drillers, repairmen, soil analysts, and other specialists to aid him, made him more self-reliant.

Not even Turner's harshest critics deny that there was much truth in his observations, but many of them have pointed to his lack of precision, and it is fair to question to what extent Turner's generalizations applied to all frontier people, or to what extent they applied restrictively to frontier men. Sometimes it becomes clear that the life process which he identifies with the frontier was primarily though not wholly an experience shared by men rather than by women. There is one famous passage, for instance, which begins,"The wilderness masters the colonist." Now *colonist* is a neuter noun, and could apply to a female colonist. But the passage continues to say that the wilderness, finding the colonist "European in dress, industry, modes of travel, and thought, . . . takes him from the railroad car and puts him in a birch canoe [this sounds progressively less as if it could be a woman]. It strips off the garments of civilization and arrays him in the hunting shirt and the moccasin." Soon, this colonist hears the call of the wild almost as clearly as Jack London's dog, and when he does, "he shouts the war cry and takes the scalp in orthodox Indian fashion."[1] Here, at least, the pioneer in question is hardly a woman.

Certainly it is true that the frontier offered economic opportunity, and certainly, also, frontier women shared in some of the social consequences which flowed from the fact that this opportunity was available to their men. But is it not true, in cold fact, that the opportunities offered by the West were opportunities for men and not, in any direct sense, opportunities for women? The free acres of the West were valuable to those who could clear, and break, and plow and harvest them. But clearing and breaking, plowing and harvesting were men's work, in which women rarely participated. The nuggets of gold in the streambeds of California in 1849 represented opportunity to those who could prospect for them. But the life of the prospector and the sourdough was not a woman's life, and the opportunities were not women's opportunities. Similarly, the grass-covered plateau of the Great Plains represented economic opportunity for those who could use it as an open range for the holding and grazing of Longhorn cattle. But the individuals who could do this were men; the Cattle Kingdom was a man's world. Thus, when Turner says that "so long as free land exists, the opportunity for a competency exists," he means, in effect, an opportunity for males.

Again, it may bear repeating, there is no question here that the frontier influenced women as well as men. It had its Molly Pitcher and its Jemima Boone, as well as its Davy Crockett and its Kit Carson. It left its stamp upon the pioneer women as well as the pioneer men. But when Turner states that it furnished "a new field of opportunity, a gate of escape from the bondage of the past," one must ask, exactly what was the nature of women's participation in this opportunity? Before this question can be analyzed, it is perhaps necessary to recognize that women's place in our society is invariably complicated by the fact that they have, as men do not, a dual status. Almost every woman shares the status of the men in her family — her father or her husband — and if this is a privileged position, she is a recipient of some of the privilege. This is an affiliated status, but if her men gain, she gains with them. Thus, if her family became landowners on the frontier, she participated in their advancement, and no one can deny that free land was, in this indirect sense, opportunity for her also. But woman also has a personal status, which is a sex status, as a female. As a female, on the frontier, women were especially dependent upon having a man in the family, for there was no division of labor there, as there was in settled communities, and most of the tasks of the frontier — the hunting, the woodchopping, the plowing — could hardly be performed by women, though many of them, of course, rose to these tasks in time of emergency. In fact, the frontier was brutally harsh for females, and it furnished its own verdict on its differential impact upon the sexes. "This country," said the frontier aphorism, "is all right for men and dogs, but it's hell on women and horses."

If we accept Turner's own assumption that economic opportunity is what matters, and that the frontier was significant as the context within which economic opportunity occurred, then we must observe that for American women, as individuals, opportunity began pretty much where the frontier left off. For opportunity lay in access to independent employment, and the employments of the frontier were not primarily accessible to women. But in the growing cities, opportunities for female employment began to proliferate. Where the work of the frontier called for the strong back and powerful muscles of a primeval man, the work of the city—clerical work, secretarial work, the tending of machines—has called for the supple fingers and the ready adaptability of a young woman, and it was in this environment, for the first time in America, that women found on any scale worth mentioning access to independent earning power. Once women possessed access to such earning power, whether she used it or not, the historic basis for her traditional subordination had been swept away. The male monopoly upon jobs was broken, and the breaking of this monopoly was no less significant for American women than the breaking of the landlord's monopoly upon fertile soil had been for American pioneer men. As a symbol, the typewriter evokes fewer emotions than the plow, but like the plow, it played a vital part in the fulfillment of the American promise of opportunity and independence. The wilderness may have been the frontier for American men, and the cabin in the clearing the symbol of their independence, but the city was the frontier for American women and the business office was what gave them economic independence and the opportunity to follow a course of their own.

II

Another social generalization which is often stated as if it applied to all Americans, men and women alike, is that our society has experienced a vast transformation in the occupational activities of its people, and that we have passed from the independent, self-directed work, of the kind done by a landowning farmer, to the regimented, externally directed activity of the employee who labors for pay. In 1850, 63 percent of the gainfully employed workers in the United States were engaged in agriculture, and a high proportion of these were landowning farmers—perhaps as nearly independent as people can be. In the past the farmer, more than most of his fellows, was in a position to plan, decide, and act for himself—to maintain his own values without regard for the approval or disapproval of his fellowman, to work at his own pace, to set his own routine. But today, as the census figures show, the American who labors is no longer self-employed. In 1958, it was estimated that 50 million people gainfully employed in the United States received salaries or wages, while only 8 million were self-employed, which means that in general the American worker does not work for himself. He works under direction in an office or a factory. He does not decide what to do, when to do it, or for what purpose, but he waits for instructions which come to him through channels. Even the junior executive, despite his prestige, is no more a self-employed man than the factory worker, and if we may believe *The Organization Man* he is in fact considerably less independent after hours. With these ideas in mind, we speak in broad terms about the disappearance of the old forms of autonomous, self-directed activity.

Yet none of this applies in any sense to women, except for women who are employees, and although female employment has increased steadily to a point where nearly one-third of all women are employed it is still true that two out of three American women are not employees, but find their occupation chiefly in the maintaining of homes and the rearing of children. Millions of housewives continue to exercise personal choice and decision not only in arranging their own timetable and routine but also in deciding what food the family shall have and how it shall be prepared, what articles of purchase shall have the highest priority on the family budget, and, in short, how the home shall be operated. Despite strong tendencies toward conformity in American life, it is clear that American women exercise a very wide latitude of decision in these matters, and everyone knows that there are great variations between the regimes in various American homes. Indeed it seems fairly evident that the housewife of today, with the wide range of consumer goods available for purchase and the wide variety of mechanical devices to free her from drudgery, has a far broader set of alternatives for household procedure than the farm wife of two or three generations ago. [2] Moreover, there are now great numbers of women working independently in their own homes, who a generation ago would have been working very much under direction as domestic servants in the homes of other women. If we based our social generalizations upon the experience of women rather than that of men, we might drop the familiar observation about the decreasing independence of Americans in their occupational pursuits. Instead we might emphasize that in the largest single occupational group in the country — the group which cooks and rears children and keeps house — there is a far greater measure of independent and self-directed work than there was in the past.

III

Closely connected to this question of the disappearance of the independent worker is another commonplace generalization, namely that the American people have become the victims of extreme specialization. Everyone is familiar with the burden of this lament: American industry has forced the craftsman to abandon his craft, and with it the satisfaction of creative labor, and has reduced him to operating a machine or to performing a single operation on the assembly line as if he were a machine himself. Further, the complaint continues, modern conditions provide fewer and fewer opportunities for a worker to be an all-round person of varied skills and resources, as the American farmer used to be, and instead conditions make of him a diminished person, a narrow specialist hardly fit for anything save his narrow specialty.

Despite the exaggerated and somewhat hackneyed character of this outcry, it contains an important element of truth as regards the work of American male workers. But this generalization, too, is in fact applicable largely to the male component in the population rather than to the American people as a whole. For the American housewife is not a specialist, and in fact her modern role requires that she be far more versatile than her grandmother was, despite the greater skill of her grandmother in cooking, sewing, and other household crafts. A good housewife today must not only serve food to please the family palate, but must also know about calories, vitamins, and the principles of a balanced diet. She must also be an economist, both in her knowledge of the quality of the products offered to her and in her ability to do the impossible with a budget. She must not only maintain a comfortable home, but must also possess enough skill in interior decoration to assure that her own ménage will not seem dowdy or unappealing by comparison with the latest interiors shown in Hollywood films. She must not only rear children, but must also have mastered enough child psychology to be able to spare the rod and still not spoil the child. She must not only get the children ready for school, but must also, in many cases, act as a kind of transportation manager, participating in an elaborate car pool to convey them to and fro. In addition to all this, society now enjoins her not to rely upon the marriage vows to hold her husband, but to keep her personality and her appearance so attractive that he will have no incentive to stray. Whatever else she may be she is certainly not a specialist, and even if she fails to meet all these varied demands upon her, her mere effort to do so would remove her from the category of specialists. If we based our social generalizations upon women rather than upon men, we might quite justifiably affirm that the modern age is an age of diversified activity rather than an age of specialization.

IV

The profound difference between the patterns of men's work and women's work is seldom understood by most men, and perhaps even by most women. In terms of the timetables of life, however, the contrasts are almost startling. For instance, man usually begins work in the early twenties, labors at precisely timed intervals for eight hours a day and five days a week, until he is sixty-five, when his life as a worker may be cut off with brutal abruptness and he is left idle. Woman also usually begins work in the early twenties, perhaps in an office on the same timetable as a man, but after a very few years she becomes a wife, whose work is keeping house, and mother whose work is rearing children. As such she labors often for from fifty-one to fifty-six hours a week, and she does not have the alternation of work and leisure which help to lend variety and pace to the life of her husband. Her work load will continue to be heavier than her husband's until the children are older, after which it will gradually diminish, and she may ultimately reenter employment. But most women do not; they continue to keep house.[3] And as long as a woman does keep house, either as a wife or as a widow, she never experiences the traumatic, sudden transition from daily work as the focus of life to enforced idleness — the transition which we call retirement.

Another far-reaching consequence of the difference between man's work and woman's work is forcibly expressed in a recent public interest advertisement in *Harper's Magazine* by Frank R. Neu, entitled "We May Be Sitting Ourselves to Death." Neu presents some very impressive data about the poor physical fitness of a large percentage of American men, and about the deleterious effects of the sedentary life of Mr. Joe Citizen as an office worker whose principal exercise is to go around a golf course on an electric cart on the weekend. Then Mr. Neu says, "Let's consider Jill, Joe's wife, for a moment. Chances are, on the basis of current statistics, Jill will outlive Joe by anywhere from five to 25 years. Medical science is not sure yet whether this is because Jill has different hormones from Joe or whether it is a result of the different roles which Joe and Jill fulfill in our society.

"The average suburban Jill is likely to be a home-maker responsible for rearing two or more children. It is safe to assume that any woman with this responsibility is going to get a lot of daily exercise no matter how many gadgets she has to help her do her housework. A homemaker does a lot of walking each day merely to push the buttons and start the machines that wash the clothes, cook the meals, and remove the dust. And she also does a good deal of bending each day to pick up after Joe and the junior members of the family. All in all, Jill is likely to get much more exercise than Joe. This may have a significant relationship to Jill's outliving Joe, who no longer hikes the dusty trail to bring home the buffalo meat and hides to feed and clothe his family."[4]

In the light of differences so great that they may radically alter the duration of life, it is again evident that a serious fallacy results when generalizations derived from the experience of American men are applied indiscriminately to the American people in such a way as to exclude the experience of American women.

V

As a further illustration of the readiness with which one can fall into a fallacy in this way, let me suggest one more generalization about Americans which has been widely popular in recent years. This is the proposition, formulated by David Riesman in *The Lonely Crowd,* that the American has been transformed, in the past century, from an inner-directed individual to an other-directed individual. A century or so ago, the argument runs, the American learned certain values from his elders, in his youth. He internalized these values, as matters of principle, so that, in Riesman's phrase, they served as a kind of gyroscope to hold him on his course, and he stood by them throughout his life whether they were popular or unpopular. When these values were involved, he did not hesitate to go against the crowd. Thus he was inner directed. But today, says Riesman, in a universe of rapidly changing circumstances, where the good will of our associates is more important to our success than it ever was to the nineteenth-century farmer, the American no longer internalizes his values in the old way. Instead, he responds very perceptively, very sensitively, to the values of others, and adjusts his course to meet their expectations. Indeed their expectations are a kind of radar screen for his guidance. Thus he is other directed, or to use an older and less precise term, he is much more a conformist.

Riesman does not discuss whether his thesis about "the changing American character" is applicable to American women, as well as to American men.[5] But we are entitled to ask, does he really believe that American women were so inner directed as his analysis would suggest? Perhaps yes, if you believe that women have been more steadfast than men in defending the values on which the security of the home is based. But on the other hand, woman, historically, was a dependent person, and as a dependent person, she developed a most perceptive sensitivity to the expectations of others and a responsiveness in adapting herself to the moods and interests of others. She has always had a radar screen. If women are quicker to conform to the expectations of a group of other women than men are to a group of other men, and if we should say that this has been true in the past, what it would mean is that women have been other directed all along, and that when Riesman says Americans are becoming other directed, what he means is that American men are becoming other directed. As women gain more economic and social independence, it might be supposed, in terms of Riesman's own analysis, that more than half of the American people are becoming less other directed rather than more so. With the gradual disappearance of the so-called "clinging vine" type, who dared not call her soul her own, this is, in fact, apparently just what is happening.

VI

If many of the generalizations which apply to American men, and which purport to apply to Americans generally, do not actually apply to American women, anyone who attempts to study the American character is forced to ask: to what extent has the impact of American historical experience been the same for both sexes, and to what extent has it been dissimilar? Viewed in these terms, the answer would probably have to be a balanced one. Certainly the main values that have prevailed in American society — the belief in individualism, the belief in equality, the belief in progress, have shaped the thought of American women as well as of American men, and American women are no doubt more committed to individualism, and to equality, and to progress, than women in many other societies. But on the other hand, some of the major forces that have been at work in American history have impinged upon men and upon women in differential ways. For instance, as I have already suggested, the frontier placed a premium upon qualities of brute strength and of habituation to physical danger which women did not possess in the same degree as men, either for biological or for cultural reasons. The result has been a differential historical experience for American men and American women which must be analyzed if there is any basis to be found for asserting that there are differences in the character types of the two sexes.

What then, we might ask, have been the principal transformations that history has brought in the lives of American women? Surprisingly enough, this is largely an unexplored field, but there are certain answers which appear more or less self-evident.

One of these is that our society has, during the last century and a half, found ways to do most of its heavy work without the use of human brawn and muscle. Water power, steam power, electric power, jet power, and the power of internal combustion have largely eliminated the need for brute strength and great physical stamina in most forms of work. This transformation has emancipated men to a revolutionary degree, but it has even more strikingly emancipated women, for women are physiologically smaller than men, and they lack the muscular strength and physical endurance of men. As the factor of hard labor in human work is reduced and the factor of skill is enhanced, therefore, women have found that inequality in ability to meet the requirements of work is greatly diminished. This basic fact, by itself, has probably done more than anything else to promote the equality of women.

But if this is the most fundamental effect of the mechanization of work, mechanization has also had a number of other sweeping consequences. One of these is that it has destroyed the subsistence farm as a unit of American life, and the disappearance of the subsistence farm, in turn, has had the most far-reaching implications.

To appreciate this, we must remember what life was like on the subsistence farm. The only division of labor that existed in this unit was the primitive division between men and women. The men constructed the dwelling, planted and cultivated the crops, raised the cattle and hogs and poultry, sheared the sheep, and chopped wood for the stoves and the fireplaces. In short the man was the producer—the producer of food, of fuel, of the raw materials for clothing. The farm wife, in turn, not only cooked, kept house, and cared for the children, as modern wives still do, but she also performed certain other tasks. She used ashes to make her own soap, she put up vast quantities of preserved food, she spun fibers into cloth, and made cloth into garments. In economic terms, she and her daughters were processors. Together, they worked in a small, close-knit community, in which all lived very much together.

It hardly needed saying what happened to this typical unit of life in an earlier America. The use of machinery, the increased specialization of labor, and the development of an economy of exchange superseded it, and rendered it almost obsolete. Today a limited number of farmers with machines raise enough food for the entire population. Men go out to work instead of working on their own place, with their own sons, and their reward is not a harvest but a weekly wage or a monthly salary. Instead of "making a living" they make an income. All this is obvious, and oft-repeated. But what are the implications for the American woman?

Some embittered critics have retorted that modern woman, no longer a processor of goods, has lost her economic function, and she retains only a biological function as mate and mother and a social function in the family. This loss of function, they would say, accounts for the frustration and sense of futility which seems to plague modern woman even more than it does modern man. But if we take a hard look at this argument, clearly it will not stand up. What has happened is that women have acquired a new role, in a new division of labor. With her husband away from the home, held by the compulsions of the clock, it falls to her, first of all, to use the family's income to take care of the family's needs. In short, while her husband has changed from a producer to an earner, she has changed from a processor to a consumer in a society where consumption is an increasingly important economic function.

The responsibilities of the consumer are no mean task. To handle them successfully, a person must be something of a dietitian, a judge of the quality of many goods, a successful planner, a skillful decorator, and a budget manager. The business of converting a monthly sum of money into a physical basis for a pleasant life involves a real art, and it might be counted as a major activity even if there were not children to rear and meals to prepare. But the increased specialization of the work of men at offices and factories away — frequently far away — from the home has also shifted certain cultural duties and certain community tasks in ever-greater measure to women.

In the Old World, upper-class men, claiming leisure as the principal advantage of their status, have made themselves the custodians of culture and the leaders in the cultural life of their communities. In America, upper-class men, primarily businessmen, working more compulsively and for longer hours than any other class, have resigned their cultural responsibilities to women and then have gone on to disparage literature and the arts because these pursuits, in the hands of females, began to seem feminine. Women have shouldered the responsibility, have borne the condescension with which their cultural activities were often treated, have provided the entire teaching force for the elementary schools, and most of the force for the secondary schools, and have done far more than their share to keep community life alive. This is another of the results, impinging in a differential way upon women, of the great social transformation of the last two centuries.

VII

So far as we have examined them, all of these changes would seem to operate somewhat to the advantage of woman, to have an emancipating effect, and to diminish her traditional subordination. No longer handicapped by a labor system in which biceps are at a premium, she has moved into the realms of employment, and has even preempted the typewriter and the teacher's desk as her own. If she has exercised a choice, which she never had before, and has decided to remain in her home, she has encountered a new economic role as a consumer rather than as a processor, with a broad range of activities, and with a new social role in keeping up the vigor of the community activities. In either case, the orbit of her activities is far wider than what used to be regarded as women's sphere, and it has been wide enough in fact to lead some optimistic observers to speak of the equality of women as if it were something which had reached some kind of absolute fulfillment and completeness about the time of the ratification of the woman's suffrage amendment in 1920.

Yet before we conclude our story with the ending that they all lived happily ever after, it is necessary to face up to the fact that women have not found all these changes quite as emancipating as they were expected to be. Indeed, much of the serious literature about American women is pessimistic in tone, and makes the dissatisfactions and the sexual frustration of modern American women its principal theme. Great stress is laid upon the fundamental dilemma that sexual fulfillment seems to depend upon one set of psychological attitudes—attitudes of submissiveness and passivity—while the fulfillment of equality seems to depend upon an opposite set—attitudes of competitiveness and self-assertion. At its grimmest level, this literature stresses the contention of Sigmund Freud that women instinctively envy the maleness of a man and reject their own sex. There is no doubt that these psychoanalytic views are important and that attention to questions of the sex life of an individual is basic, but a very respectable argument can be and has been made that what women envy about men is not their maleness in purely sexual terms but their dominance in the society and their immunity from the dilemmas which the needs of sexual and biological fulfillment on one hand and of personal fulfillment on the other pose for women.[6] The inescapable fact that males can have offspring without either bearing them or rearing them means that the values of family life and of personal achievement can be complementary for men, where they are conflicting values for women.

This one immutable and timeless fact, more than anything else, seems to stand forever in the way of the complete and absolute equality of men and women. Political and legal emancipation and even the complete equality of women in social relations and in occupational opportunities could not remove this handicap. So long as it remains, therefore, no one who finds a measure of inequality still remaining will have to look for an explanation in social terms. But it is legitimate to ask whether this is the only remaining barrier to emancipation, or whether other factors also serve to maintain adverse differentials against women, even in modern America, where she seems to be more nearly equal than she has been in any other time or place, except perhaps in certain matriarchal tribes.

There are, perhaps, two aspects of woman's role as housekeeper and as consumer which also contribute, in a new way historically, to work against the prevailing tendencies toward a fuller equality. These aspects have, in a subtle way, caused society to devalue the modern activities of women as compared with those of men, and thus may even have contributed to bring about a new sort of subordination.

One of these is the advent of the money economy, in which income is the index of achievement, and the housewife is the only worker who does not get paid. On the farm home, in the days of the subsistence economy, neither she nor her husband got paid, at least not very much, and they were economic partners in the enterprise of making a living. But today, the lowliest and most trivial job which pays a wage counts as employment, while the most demanding and vital tasks which lack the sanction of pecuniary remuneration do not so count. A recent and in fact very able book entitled *Women Who Work* deals, just as you would expect, not with women who work, but with women who get paid for their work. Sociologists regard it as an axiom that the amount of income is as important as any other criterion in measuring social status today, and in one sense, a woman's status may reflect the income of her husband, but in another sense it should be a corollary of the axiom that if income is esteemed, lack of income is followed by lack of esteem, and even by lack of self-esteem. If it needed proving, Komarovsky has shown that the American housewife tends to disparage herself as well as her work, as both being unworthy because they do not receive recognition in terms of cash income. [7]

If woman does not command respect as an earner, she is also likely to incur a certain subtle lack of respect for herself in her role as a consumer. For there is a strong tendency in some phases of American advertising to regard the consumer as someone who may be flattered or may be bullied, but who need not be treated as a mature person. Insofar as the consumer is an object of condescension, someone to be managed rather than someone to be consulted, someone on whom the will of the advertiser is to be imposed by psychological manipulation, and insofar as consumers are primarily women, it means that women become the objects of more than their share of the low esteem in which the consumer is held, and more than their share of the stultifying efforts to play upon human yearnings for prestige and popularity or upon human psychological insecurities. Anyone who recalls the recent publications about the rate at which the blinking of women's eyes increases when they view the display of goods in a supermarket, and the extent to which this display causes them to spend impulsively, rather than according to need, will recognize that the role of the consumer has not enhanced the dignity of women. [8] This aspect was very clearly and wittily recognized by Sylvia Wright in an article in *Harper's* in 1955, in which she dealt ironically with the assertion, which we sometimes hear, that America has become a woman's world.

"Whatever it is," she wrote, "I'll thank you to stop saying it's mine. If it were a woman's world, people wouldn't yammer at me so much. They're always telling me to do, be, or make something. . . .

"The one thing they don't want me to be is me. 'A few drops of Abano Bath Oil' they say, 'and you're not you . . .you're Somebody New lolling in perfumed luxury.' But I'm not allowed to loll long. The next minute I have to spring out in order to be Fire and Ice, swathed in satin, not a thing to do but look stark, and wait for a man to pounce. Turn the page, I've got to make sure it's Johnson's cotton buds with which I swab the baby. A few pages later, the baby gets into the act yelling for fullweight diapers. . . .

"I'm supposed to use a lot of make-up to keep my husband's love, but I must avoid make-up clog. I'm supposed to be gay, spontaneous and outgoing, but I musn't get 'expression lines.' [Expression lines are to wrinkles as morticians are to undertakers.]

"In the old days, I only had to have a natural aptitude for cooking, cleaning, bringing up children, entertaining, teaching Sunday School and tatting. . . .

"Now I also have to reconstitute knocked-down furniture and build on porches."[9]

If woman's status is somewhat confused today, therefore, it is partly because, at the very time when efforts to exploit her as a female began to abate, the efforts to exploit her as a consumer began to increase. And at the time when the intrinsic value of her work was gaining in dignity as compared with that of the male, the superficial value as measured in terms of money income was diminishing. The essential strength of her position has increased, but the combined effect of the manipulation by the media and the emphasis upon monetary earning as a standard for the valuation of work has threatened her with a new kind of subordination, imposed by the system of values which she herself accepts, rather than by masculine values imposed upon her against her will.

If a woman as a consumer in a world of producers and as an unpaid worker in a world of salaried employees has lost some of the ground she had gained by emancipation as a female in a world of males, even the emancipation itself has created some new problems for her. For instance, it has confronted her with a dilemma she never faced in the days when she was confined to her own feminine sphere. This is the dilemma that she is now expected to attain a competence in the realm of men's affairs but that she must never succeed in this realm too much. It is well for her to be intelligent, but not intelligent enough to make a young man feel inferior; well for her to find employment and enjoy it, but not enjoy it enough to be unwilling to give it up for the cradle and the sink; well for her to be able to look after herself but never to be so visibly able that it will inhibit the impulse of the right man to want to look after her; well for her to be ambitious, but never ambitious enough actually to put her personal objectives first. When a man marries, no one expects him to cease being a commuter and to become a farmer because it would be good for the children — though in fact it might. But when a woman marries, her occupation becomes an auxiliary activity.

Here we come back to the presence of a fundamental dualism which has made the so-called "emancipation" of women different from the emancipation of any other group in society. Other emancipated groups have sought to substitute a new condition in place of an old one and to obliterate the old, but except for a few of the most militant women in a generation of crusading suffragettes, now almost extinct, women have never renounced the roles of wife and mother. The result has been that their objective was to reconcile a new condition with an old one, to hold in balance the principle of equality, which denies a difference, and the practice of wifehood and motherhood which recognizes a difference in the roles of men and women. The eternal presence of this dualism has not only caused a distressing amount of confusion and tension among women themselves; it has also caused confusion among their many volunteer critics. The result is that we encounter more wildly inconsistent generalizations about modern American women than about almost any other subject.

For example, modern woman, we are told, is gloriously free from the inferiority of the past, but she is miserable and insecure in her new freedom. She wields the purse strings of the nation and has become dominant over a world of increasingly less maculine men who no longer trust themselves to buy a suit of clothes without their wife's approval. But also she does the routine work at typewriter and sink while the men still run the universe. Similarly, we are assured that the modern woman is an idle, parasitic, bridge-playing victim of technological unemployment in her own mechanized home, and also that she is the busy manager of a family and household and budget whose demands make the domestic chores of the past look easy by comparison. She escapes from reality into the wretched, petty little world of soap opera and neighborhood gossip, but she excels in her knowledge of public affairs and she became an effective guardian of literary and artistic values when her money-grubbing husband defaulted on the responsibility. She is rearing the best crop of children ever produced on this planet, by the most improved methods ever devised, while her overprotectiveness has bred "momism" and her unwillingness to stay at home has bred delinquency.

VIII

Clearly, we are still a long way from having arrived at any monotonous unanimity of opinion about the character of American women. Yet if we will focus carefully upon what we really know with some degree of assurance, we can perhaps begin the process of striking a balance. We certainly know, for instance, that many of the trends of American history have been operative for both men and women in somewhat the same way. The emphasis upon the right of the individual has operated to remove legal disabilities upon women, to open many avenues to gainful employment, to confer the suffrage, and so on. Even our divorce rate is an ironic tribute to the fact that the interests of the individual, and perhaps in a majority of cases the individual woman, are placed ahead of the protection of a social institution — namely, the family. The rejection of authority in American life, which has made our child rearing permissive and has weakened the quality of leadership in our politics, has also meant that the relation of husband and wife is more of a partnership and less of an autocracy in this age and in this country than at any other time or place in Western civilization. The competitive strain in American life has impelled American women as well as American men to strive hard for their goals, and to assert themselves in the strife—indeed European critics complain that they assert themselves far more strenuously than European women and entirely too much for the tranquility of society.

On the other hand, we also know that the experience of women remains in many ways a distinctive experience. Biologically, there are still the age-old facts that women are not as big as men and not as strong; that the sex act involves consequences for them which it does not involve for the male; that the awareness of these consequences conditions the psychological attitudes of women very deeply; and that motherhood is a biological function while fatherhood is, in a sense, a cultural phenomenon. Historically, there is the formidable truth that the transformations of modern life have impinged upon men and women in different ways. The avenues of employment opened to men are not the same as the avenues of employment opened to women. The revolution in our economy has deepened the division between work in the home and work outside the home by according the sanction of monetary reward to the one and denying it to the other — thus devaluing in a new way work which is distinctively woman's. The economic revolution, while converting most men from producers to earners, has converted most women from processors to consumers, and the exploitation of the consumer has, again, added a new devaluation to woman's role. Society has given her the opportunity to fulfill her personal ambitions through the same career-activities as a man, but it cannot make her career aspirations and her family aspirations fit together as they do for a man. The result of all this is a certain tension between her old role and her new one. More of an individualist than women in traditional societies, she is by no means as wholeheartedly individualistic as the American male, and as a study at Berkeley recently showed, she still hesitates to claim individualism as a quality of her own.[10] If she enters the competitive race, she does so with an awareness that the top posts are still pretty much the monopoly of men, and with a certain limitation upon her competitive commitment. In short, she is constantly holding in balance her general opportunities as a person and her distinctive needs as a woman, and when we consider how badly these two go together in principle, can we not say that she is maintaining the operative equilibrium between them with a remarkable degree of skill and of success?

The answer to my childish riddle was that the big Indian is the little Indian's mother. To say that she is a squaw is not to deny that she is an Indian — but it is to say that she is an Indian for whom the expectations of the masculine world of Indians, or of Americans, do not apply. It is to say that her qualities and traits, whether she is an Indian, or an American, will reflect the influence of the same sweeping forces which influence the world of men, but that it will reflect them with a difference. In this sense, what we say about the character of the American people should be said not in terms of half of the American population — even if it is the male half — but in terms of the character of the totality of the people. In this sense, also, attention to the historic character of American women is important not only as a specialty for female scholars or for men who happen to take an interest in feminism, but as a coordinate major part of the overall, comprehensive study of the American character as a whole. For the character of any nation is the composite of the character of its men and of its women and though these may be deeply similar in many ways, they are almost never entirely the same.

Notes

1. Frederick Jackson Turner, *The Frontier in American History* (New York: Henry Holt and Co., 1920), p. 4.

2. Robert Lynd, "The People as Consumers," writes that there is "probably today a greater variation from house to house in the actual inventory list of family possessions . . . than at any previous era in man's history." *Recent Social Trends in the United States* (New York: McGraw-Hill, 1933), pp. 857–911.

3. In 1957, of the 21 million women in the work force, 11 million were wives. Female employment was highest (45 percent) in the age bracket 20 to 24, declined to 39 percent in bracket 25 to 44, rose to 40 percent in the bracket 45 to 64, and declined to 10 percent in the bracket 65 and over.

4. *Harper's Magazine* 223 (November 1961): 23.

5. David Riesman, *"The Lonely Crowd:* A Reconsideration in 1960," in Seymour Martin Lipset and Leo Lowenthal, eds., *Culture and Social Character: The Work of David Riesman Reviewed* (Glencoe, Ill.; The Free Press, 1961), p. 428, discusses an investigation by Michael S. Olmsted which showed that Smith College girls regarded themselves as more other directed than men and regarded other girls as more other directed than their group; but Riesman does not state what his own belief is in this matter.

6. Probably the best of the literature which emphasizes the sex frustration of the modern American woman is found in professional publications in the fields of psychology and psychoanalysis which do not reach a popular audience. In the literature for the layman, probably the best presentation of this point of view is Simone de Beauvoir's excellent *The Second Sex* (New York: A. A. Knopf, 1953), but other items have enjoyed a circulation which they hardly deserve. Two cases in point are Ferdinand Lundberg and Marynia F. Farnham, *Modern Woman: The Lost Sex* (New York: Harper, 1947), and Eric John Dingwall, *The American Woman: An Historical Study* (New York: Rinehart and Co., 1958). Denis W. Brogan's judicious and yet precise evaluation that Dingwall's book is "strictly for the birds" would be equally applicable to Lundberg and Farnham's. For an able argument that the condition of modern women must be understood partly in social terms, and that the concept of "genital trauma" has been overdone, see Mirra Komarovsky, *Women in the Modern World: Their Education and Their Dilemmas* (Boston: Little, Brown and Company, 1953), pp. 31–52.

7. Komarovsky, *Women in the Modern World*, pp. 127–53.

8. Experiments on the rate of eye blink, as conducted by James M. Vicary, a leading exponent of motivation research, were reported in Vance Packard, *The Hidden Persuaders* (New York: David McKay Co., 1957), pp. 106–8.

9. Sylvia Wright, "Whose World? and Welcome to It," in *Harper's Magazine* 210 (May 1955): 35–38.

10. John P. McKee and A. C. Sheriffs, "Men's and Women's Beliefs, Ideals, and Self-Concepts," in *American Journal of Sociology* 64 (1959): 356–63.

ALICE KESSLER-HARRIS

American Women and the American Character: A Feminist Perspective

Dr. Alice Kessler-Harris is a Professor of History at Hofstra University and Director of the Institute of Applied Social Science sponsored jointly by Hofstra University and the Distributive Workers of America. Previously, she has been Director of Women's Studies at Sarah Lawrence College.

I

David Potter argues, in his now well-known essay, that traditional definitions of American character undergo sweeping revision when viewed through the eyes of the female majority of the population. But he says nothing about how women's self-definitions have altered conceptions of national character in the direction of what we might call "feminization." In Potter's world, women are passive people who have not participated in the creation of normative prescriptions and values of our society. Their particular role enables them to escape some modes of behavior expected of men. In the real world, women are active proponents of their own sets of behavior patterns and meaning systems which interact with and alter commonly accepted norms. The contemporary women's movement offers striking illustrations of how women's own experiences can bend the direction of American character into new shapes. In the course of denying male supremacy, women are nurturing a cultural revolution that may alter the structure of power in America.

Women have, for the most part, lived within the core values and beliefs that constitute the boundaries of what we call national character. I take national character to mean a mode of behavior that reflects a composite of commonly accepted meanings, practices, ideas and expectations that are, as British sociologist Raymond Williams says, "reciprocally confirming." But a debate about national character needs to consider the ways a society distributes its rewards and the effects of the distribution system on patterns of behavior. Where an economic system rests, as ours does, on the production of profits, the critical components of behavior are those that enhance the power to control capital and to regulate access to its attainment. Emphasis on competition, efficiency, and individualism reflect the way our economic system confirms patterns of behavior that sustain it. Useful behavioral characteristics are soon integrated into laws, schools, families, and personality formation until they seem to be part of the natural order of things.

Because women have in the past normally participated in the structure of power through men—fathers, husbands, and employers—the behavioral consequences of the distribution of rewards have manifested themselves differently. Women have been discouraged from competing in the marketplace, from striving for their own success. They have instead been called upon to provide support and to nurture men who are engaged in the upward struggle. As David Potter so accurately notes, women have been encouraged to be generalists, to be autonomous within the framework of the household, and to guard humane and moral values. These are qualities normally excluded from definitions of U.S. national character; yet they are essential to sustaining behavior patterns that confirm beliefs in progress, individualism, and equality. From the mid-nineteenth century to the present, we have acknowledged, indeed insisted, that one of the particular tasks of women was to preserve these values in the bosom of the family.[1] There they have rested, salving the moral conscience of a society otherwise propelled towards a competitive lifestyle. These "feminine" qualities nourish the seeds out of which alternative conceptions of life-styles might grow and which now seem to be challenging the distribution of power itself. Women, in other words, harbor values, attitudes, and behavior patterns potentially subversive to capitalism.

These alternative conceptions are not merely requests for access to male bastions of power, though in the past, as in the present, women have frequently pressured to be included. Ann Hutchinson wanted to be acknowledged as a teacher in the Puritan church. Elizabeth Cady Stanton demanded the vote. Betty Friedan laid the groundwork for recent pressure for equal employment opportunities. Stern measures silenced their outbursts, and token compromises shaped their protests to fit thoroughly established patterns. Hutchinson was declared a heretic and banished. Women got the vote after they became too insistent to ignore, but the shape of the electorate remained the same. And so it has gone: Technology has reduced the time necessary to maintain a household, yet housework remains the major preoccupation of women, not of men; vast numbers of women are entering the labor market, while jobs remain largely segregated along sexual lines; the state has undertaken the formal education of children, removing them from their homes for a few hours each day, but child care is still primarily a mother's responsibility. And all the while women have simply been denied access to centers of power.

A much smaller group of women, encouraged by a persistent stream of utopian thought and experimentation, has suggested redistributing power in ways that could release all people from competitive modes of being. Charlotte Perkins Gilman and Emma Goldman are among the best-known examples of a strong opposition that has refused to ratify prevailing values and norms. These women reflect a search for humane values: for individual and collective activity that has as its first aim the perpetuation of freely chosen, unalienated, productive work. Whatever the differences in their political philosophies, radical women agreed that their sex needed to be free of male economic and sexual domination as a first step towards altering the structure of power in the society. The women's movement seems to have breathed new life into this tendency.

Dramatic changes in the life experiences of many women account for new challenges to the power of men—challenges that raise fundamental questions about the distribution of power as a whole. In the past few decades, growing numbers of women, particularly in the relatively affluent middle class, have rejected the need to function in confined spheres. The family has loosed its grip; new jobs offer a perhaps illusory economic independence. As women have begun to search for access to the realms of power and the roads that lead to individual success, they have encountered barriers of credentialism, layers of hierarchy, and stone walls of entrenched status. To combat these obstacles requires elucidation of their nature and origin. Many women are driven to understand for the first time the social development of laws, theories, and ideologies which they have long accepted as natural. With students, ethnic minorities, and some workers who have come to these questions from different directions, women have begun to explore alternatives to the competitive search for success.[2] Notions of collectivity and nurturance, humanitarian and egalitarian goals, enter the national vocabulary— perhaps to stay.

Will these values modify or replace the old? Do they offer to reshape American culture, to redirect American society? The profit-maximizing imperatives of capitalism weigh heavily against their adoption. Yet there are strong forces working to redefine American character: The mid-1970s witnessed an enormous surge of investment and energy by right-wing political groups on behalf of such anti-feminist and traditional actions as abortion restriction, opposition to the equal rights amendment, and resistance to affirmative action programs. Yet the organized women's movement is only a symptom of the strong forces working to redefine American character. Recurrent economic crises, growing competition for scarce resources, fears for world survival, rising crime rates, and increasing social disorder create a sense of urgency which, along with reaction, yield a willingness to question old patterns. The direction of the current women's movement is still unclear: It has encouraged and symbolized tendencies towards incorporating women into the power structure as well as for altering entirely the distribution of power. Yet events that are changing women's lives hint at bigger things to come.

II

Americans have never, of course, been defined by a single set of categories. Individualistic and competitive values and the search for perpetual progress that we all take for granted have been accompanied by their opposites: community, cooperation, and an attempt to achieve humane values in an egalitarian society. But despite the lip service we pay to the latter, status, wealth, and power have drifted inexorably to those who have excelled in the former. The turning point seemed to come in the 1820s and 1830s when Jacksonian laissez-faire ideas choked off the remnants of a mercantile society with a sense of itself as an interdependent and organic whole. Since then, the expansion and development of competitive capitalism has increasingly relied upon and encouraged competitive and individualistic modes of being among workers.

Cooperative modes of behavior threatened to eat into the profits of capital, and to challenge the leadership of its owners. So they were ruthlessly destroyed. Conspiracy laws denied workers the right to act collectively. Bloody military intervention not infrequently became the resort of industrial entrepreneurs desperate to preserve their position. Hierarchical divisions in the work force separated workers from each other. It took most of the nineteenth century to convince workers that they too had a stake in social mobility and the success ethic. And in the end, capitalists agreed to restrict some of their absolute power over individuals, and to accept wage, hour, and social welfare legislation. The compromise accepted some forms of collective organization in return for help in preserving capitalist power.

Because the household remained outside the capitalist sphere and women were excluded from the channels of success orientation, deviant traits could surive longer among them. Long after such behavior had been discouraged among most men, women continued to display a sense of community that was the essence of a shared and generally noncompetitive relationship. Strong bonds existed among women in all economic arenas. Women who were isolated from each other on America's evolving frontier longed for the days when they could share each other's company. For them, quilting bees, house raisings, pressing sugar cane, and slaughtering hogs were more than social events. They were times for solace and aid. In the mining camps of Colorado and the West, poverty bred close and supportive ties. The legendary activities of Mother Jones forged bonds of affection with miners' wives and their children. Agnes Smedley, who grew up in a mining camp and later became a journalist, recalls a mother who consistently defended her prostitute sister against a husband who would have driven her out. Marie Hall Ets's Rosa vividly describes the horrors of an isolated pregnancy and childbirth. In the company towns of Kentucky and Tennessee, women shared beans, warmth, and their mutual fears for their husbands' lives.[3]

Kinship and friendship networks extended to women of all social groups. For ninteenth-century "ladies" they provided supportive ties as well as help in periods of illness, childbirth, or trouble. Women relied on each other for medical advice when they were embarrassed about seeing doctors, and for help in child rearing. Friendships not infrequently lasted over a half-century, spanned thousands of miles, and were passed on to daughters as a precious inheritance.[4] Women with leisure joined in voluntary groups to dispense charity, educate their young, or study literature. In the late nineteenth century, some daughters of well-to-do parents seem to have deliberately rejected marriage to create communal forms of their own: The social settlement is only one example of their search for satisfying ways of working and living together.

In the growing urban centers, group solidarity among women reflected their protest against poverty and misery. Women who worked for wages banded together in "working girls clubs" which provided advice and entertainment in scarce leisure hours. Unlike trade unions, these were tolerated because they were often sponsored by wealthy women who could offer financial and emotional support and simultaneously provide role models of upward mobility through marriage. Later, women's trade unions in addition to fighting militantly for better working conditions became havens for education and recreation as well as sources of solidarity on the picket line. [5] Married women shared reliable child care and household help. As the nineteenth century turned into the twentieth, networks of immigrant women provided each other with critical economic support. Sometimes shared sorrows camouflaged the outrages of unbearable poverty. Immigrant women often united to protest economic injustice. On the Lower East Side, riots against kosher meat butchers in 1902 were sparked by high prices. The urge for pure milk, cheap coal, and lower rents sent angry groups of women demonstrators into the streets. Women served as babysitters, enabling mothers of small children to work for wages. Occasionally they helped each other to find boarders who produced extra income for families of struggling immigrants. Additional income became the foundation on which many families built their social mobility: They saved to buy homes or small businesses or to keep their children in school.

These pockets of resistance eroded as industrial capitalism spread into all of America's hidden corners. They were discouraged by a network of legal and institutional structures that influenced family patterns in the direction of individual achievement. Nineteenth-century schools and labor force needs reinforced each other, leading women to raise their children in success-oriented ways. The family became both the training ground and the measure for economic success, and close relations among women gave way under the weight of economics, law, and custom. Most women married, fulfilling the expected condition of womanhood. Throughout the century, the household remained the focal point of their existence. Though many women protested, and others made lives for themselves outside its confines, most exceptions had a rough time economically. Employers welcomed women as secondary workers, treating them as if their services were marginal and their pay merely supplemental. Laws regulating property, divorce, and birth control, standards of propriety in dress, manners, and speech, all confirmed accepted roles for women. They were to support their husbands emotionally, to organize their households so that men could more effectively commit themselves to work and to raise their children with a proper respect for work, thrift, and authority.

Patterns of family life-style varied with different ethnic and class groups, but for women the result was often the same. Middle-class men who aspired to success, efficiency, and power required compliant and socially active wives. Manual laborers, physically exhausted at the end of a lengthy workday, needed household maintenance, sustenance for themselves, and child control. In both cases, women had the major task of socializing children to accept their positions in life, to believe in the ideology of success, to become the competitive, striving people we call Americans.

Paradoxically, networks of women may have helped to undermine their supportive structure. In pushing forward the process of upward mobility, they encouraged the acquisitive materialism that was later to divide women from each other. For the family was not immune to the competition that was generated by capitalism, and it soon came to participate fully in competitive social relations. As the ethos of upward mobility seeped into the cracks of personality development, it corroded bonds of affection and mutual aid that managed to exist outside accepted frameworks. Women, noted Thorstein Veblen in 1899, had begun to participate increasingly in the competitive structure that kept their husbands and fathers upward bound. Kinship ties loosened as social relationships transcended the bounds of narrow familial interests. The unmarried competed with each other for wealthy husbands or the hands of European nobility. Women became increasingly dependent on their husbands for material possessions that validated rising status, and divided from each other by visible evidence of success. Clothing, furniture, even leisure, became the competitive barriers that women were called upon to mount. This process accelerated in the twentieth century, producing its own reaction: a response that provides the backdrop to some of the trends of the 1970s.

III

Women were sucked into the competitive maelstrom in their families and in the job market, but they were eligible for none of the power and privilege that validated the struggle for men. They continued to rationalize their activities in terms of familiar humane and nurturing values—which encouraged inappropriate behavior patterns for participation in a competitive world. It was an uneasy compromise. Yet it led women to enter the job market in ways that would contribute to the well-being of their families without encouraging ambition. And it obscured their exclusion from access to the haunts of power.

In the 1920s, family size declined significantly. The number of live births, which occurred at the rate of twenty-five per thousand women in 1915, began to fall, anticipating the decline of the depression years to come. By 1940, only seventeen of every thousand women of childbearing age gave birth. The divorce rate began its unremitting climb to its current high, reflecting the search for more satisfying affective relationships. Nearly half of all marriages now end in court.

And, most significantly, women began to look for jobs. The total proportion of women who worked for wages increased steadily in the 1920s, held its own in the 1930s, and burst into a flood in the war and postwar period. More important, the genteel daughters of the middle class were joining their less privileged sisters in the labor market. At first, only the unmarried looked for work, unless poverty dictated otherwise. But slowly, wives, then mothers, and in the sixties, even mothers with small children entered the labor force, until, in 1975, most school-age children had mothers who worked outside the home.[6]

New jobs beckoned them on every hand. Bursting offices in expanding corporations, then the growing education and social service networks and spreading medical facilities offered work that had none of the exhausting and unhealthy aroma that still surrounded women employed in factories. These rapidly expanding sectors of the labor force begged for women who were, it was said, grateful for decent jobs. They learned fast, commanded little pay, did not expect rapid promotion, and quit to marry and have children before they became eligible for expensive pensions and paid vacations. Moreover, after 1917, a growing number of publicly supported vocational training schools offered to teach new office skills like typing, stenography, bookkeeping and office machine operation.

At the same time smaller, less permanent, and more affluent families encouraged individualism on the part of women—permitted a demand for their share of the world's rewards. Yet most of the jobs open to women offered only limited social mobility. For women were hired precisely because employers needed a transient labor force. How, then, would women measure their rewards? The illusion of glamour with which employers draped women's jobs offered some satisfaction, but many women, drawing on years of socialization and a consciousness bred to serve, justified their work in other ways. They wanted jobs, not for power and money, but for personal satisfaction in the service of humanity. They would become the nation's housekeepers. At least, that was the rationale.

No better symbol of an age exists than the flapper provides for the 1920s. She represents not so much what women became in that decade, as what a business community would have liked its young women workers to be: glamorous, economically independent, sexually free, and of course, single. In the guise of the flapper, and for a price, women emerged from their homes and into the business world. In return for limited economic and sexual independence, they were expected to adopt a flighty, apolitical, and irresponsible stance. The image should have guaranteed only peripheral involvement in the task of earning a living: an extension of women's supportive roles to the male world without the threat of competition.

In practice, it contained the seeds of every woman's freedom. Many women escaped their fathers' houses to leap beyond temporary secretarial jobs into graduate and professional schools. Women doctors, lawyers, and college professors multiplied. For the first time, sizable numbers of women became executives in their own right. Loosening sexual inhibitions had equally unforeseen consequences. Companionate marriage, trial marriage, divorce, all augured a new search for satisfaction. For the first time significant numbers of women challenged male sexual dominance, and rejected their subservient positions. Like Mae West's aggressive ability to use her body for her own ends, sexual freedom was an assertion of the self: bursting the bonds of societal constraints and affirming an autonomy that transcended economic dependence. The newly achieved right to vote, won by the united efforts of women of all classes, opened a psychic, if not yet a physical, breach in the walls that barred women from the realms of power.

Depression and war briefly distorted an emerging vision. Then, with a pause to cope with the shifting structure of jobs and to absorb the barrage of propaganda urging them to stay at home, women rushed back into the work force in the 1950s. The married among them did so guiltily convinced that they were flying in the face of custom and tradition, unsure of the effect their work would have on their husbands' masculinity, and threatened with dire predictions of their children's juvenile delinquency. The press of inflation combined with the temptation of new items to consume after years of deprivation, to offer both a necessary incentive and a convenient rationalization. The wages of most women were, after all, essential to family subsistence. For a while, the rationalization restrained many women from full participation in the competitive labor force. If a job was acceptable, a career was clearly beyond the pale. The typical woman of the 1950s invested her energy and her dreams in her home and her family, even when she worked for wages.

But in the intertwining network of family, self, and jobs, new opportunities, new achievements, and new freedoms have exerted tremendous pressure to remove limits on women's access to competitive modes of behavior. Women have taken the lead in battering down the restraining walls, raising questions that would not wait for answers. If household roles were restrictive, why could they not be shared? If family interests limited women's vision of their roles, could families not be modified, communalized, and extended—male and female relationships altered to approach a new equality? If childbirth restricted access to jobs, then why not extend birth control and abortion to all? If jobs were structured so as to prevent women from participating in them fully, then how about introducing staggered hours, shorter days, and half-time jobs? Questioning the institutions into which people had so long been socialized exposed the system of ideas they were constructed to perpetuate. At last, the institutions could no longer contain the ideas they had so long regulated and a widely accepted and seemingly natural system of meanings, values, and practices fell under scrutiny.

In the 1960s, in a political and social climate born of affluence, civil rights protest, and an unpopular war, questions about the fundamental precepts that guided American character were the property of no single group. Civil rights activists had continuously asserted that equal opportunity and social mobility were no more than myths. A broad spectrum of public opinion in the 1960s questioned the value of material possessions, of individual success, of business-motivated competition, of work that provided no satisfaction, of media-manipulated leisure, of schools that credentialized without educating. Many disaffected people drifted off to communes and rural farms where they tried to create a simpler and more honest life in which human needs took precedence over the drive for profits. The issues had hardly been raised before they retreated in the depression mentality of the early seventies.

They did not, however, disappear. The contradictions between the rhetoric of egalitarianism and the reality of discrimination remained, even while protest against the competitive individualism diminished under the threat of economic crisis and some token compromise. Colleges admitted a few more black students and set up programs in Afro-American studies; the war and its accompanying draft wound down; and as jobs became scarce, protests about the meaninglessness of work diminished. But the protests of women have proved harder to contain. In part this is because for some women, issues of credentialism and hierarchy, of power and profits, grew out of a desire to gain access to the competitive structure and not to alter it. The strength of groups like the National Organization of Women (NOW) rests on their demands, not for radical change, but for such things as unrestricted work opportunities, equal pay, access to credit, and nondiscriminatory pension and insurance benefits. NOW has left to more radical women, involved in groups like Redstockings and the New York Radical Feminists, questions about family and sexual relationships, about job satisfaction and the need to do good in the world. These women see one solution to their dilemmas in altering the distribution of power in the family, and argue that the sexual division of labor reflects an unequal distribution of power in the society as a whole. For both radical women and those who want access to male power, the issues emerge from their inability to reconcile their functions as mothers and women, with an ideology of egalitarianism. For almost all, they strike responsive chords in a deeply bred subculture of humane values and of collective strength and action. Women's increasing role in the marketplace has opened a Pandora's box of problems that are proving difficult to reconcile with traditional expectations.[7]

New ways in which women are thinking, and for which they are struggling, threaten to burst the bonds of old institutions and to force a rethinking of national priorities. Yet they exist in tandem with incentives for individual women to emulate the male competitive world. In what direction will women move? In at least four areas, the women's movement seems to harbor significant signposts for change. Women are exploring modes of collective strength and action that threaten to reveal the economic priorities at the root of an individualistic ideology. They are beginning to see that personal problems are consequences of political issues and to recognize the relationship between socialization and economics. They are uncovering the limitations of an egalitarian ideology and exposing social mobility as little more than a myth. They are rejecting the constraints of assigned roles imposed by institutions like the family and schools and as a result undermining the very structures that have sustained national myths in the past.

An emerging understanding of the contradictions between real economic roles and the burdens imposed by an ideology whose purpose is to maintain social order could have unpredictable consequences. On the one hand, these pressures could lead to demands that women who make economic contributions, either in the home or in the wage labor force, receive all of the rewards that have long been given to men. On the other, they encourage skepticism about the rewards themselves and could easily lead to rejection of the ideas and values that maintain them.

IV

The combined experience of wage work and of household maintenance has played a key role in raising questions about the value of individualism in the minds of many women. Two sets of facts are crucial: Jobs open to women are often in the social service and low-level clerical sectors, where they extend traditionally female-nurturing roles, and women who choose to work carry to the workplace the humane and fulfilling values that accompany work done at home. Women, to quote one suburban wife, bring to their jobs "different priorities. They don't start with the defense budget. They tend to start with things that have to do with humane living — whether it's health care of the education system or cooperative work rather than competitive." [8]

But the attempt to translate nurturing and cooperative modes into jobs produces tensions both at work and at home. Ideas about individual responsibility and fiscal priorities that place military expenditures far above social services, obviate the possibility of eliminating poverty, of guaranteeing adequate housing and food to the poor, and of providing medical care to all. Social welfare aid is given grudgingly. National health insurance has fallen victim to the medical profession and insurance companies. Budgetary decisions eliminate remedial and appropriate education for youngsters caught in the vise of the ghetto. Decaying and violent inner cities testify to our neglect. Large portions of women holding jobs in social work, education, and health care, where they are trained to "do good," are the first to feel the impact of such outmoded notions as self sufficiency.

At the same time the growing numbers of women who are wage workers and also have primary responsibility for families need reliable and inexpensive child care and socialized household maintenance. Again, the price women pay for an individualistic society appears in stark perspective. Potential solutions are grounded in the kinship networks that so long supported women and encouraged cooperative activity even while the work situation was isolating men from each other. People like Charlotte Perkins Gilman argued seventy-five years ago that the form of the private household fostered isolation and competition, a cry now echoed by many advocates of women's liberation. In the early years of this century, Henrietta Rodman proposed apartment dwellings with communal kitchens and nurseries to supplement family care.[9] Child care has become one of the persistent concerns of people interested in equality for women from radical and liberal perspectives. Yet most day-care centers are notoriously understaffed and poorly tended, discouraging all but the most needy from using them.

Notions of collective responsibility in the home raise questions about the structure of jobs and the possibility of part-time work for all. Questions about the disciplinary function of work emerge. People begin to understand that individual attempts to share responsibility in housework and child rearing run afoul of rigid job structures and a competitive labor market. The desire to get ahead, which requires endless hours of work, contradicts attempts to share family responsibility, which rests on part-time jobs, and flexible hours. Moreover, communal forms threaten the economic function of individual households deeply embedded in the mass consumption that underlies our national well-being. Women's interests collide with the desire of the state to perpetuate the traditional nuclear family. When Richard Nixon vetoed the comprehensive Child Development Act in 1971, for example, he argued that he could not commit the "vast moral authority of the national government to the side of communal approaches to child rearing . . ."[10] But the possibilities of collective household modes persist and the questions that women raise are continuing to batter down the assumption that individual family units are the "American" way.

Out of the separate struggles to resolve problems related to transitions in roles for women have come one of the most meaningful slogans of the contemporary women's movement, as well as one of its most important techniques for stirring an awakening consciousness. "The personal is political," women told each other in consciousness-raising groups in the early 1970s. The slogan embodied a recognition that individual problems represented socially derived and created attitudes that were both the cause and condition of women's commonly shared oppression. A sexual taunt hurled to a passing woman on the street reflected the general perception of women as "sex objects" who were not to be taken seriously in the world of ideas or of work. A husband who demanded service from his wife echoed society's insistence on nurturing and passive roles for women. Each woman who protested these presumably personal acts raised her voice against deeply held convictions that were themselves responsible for restricting her ability to function as an independent human being.

More powerful was the dawning recognition that women had colluded in perpetuating their own secondary status. Economic and psychic dependence, the absence of self-esteem, and the failure to aspire to success were pieces of a much larger problem. They involved the nature of a child-rearing process designed to socialize people into appropriate work and social roles, and they recognized the realities of the division of the labor force into hierarchical and segmented layers. As women become aware of the ways in which school books, television, advertisements, and ordinary social relationships confirm limited self-images and restrict the free choice of adults, they have been able to see the close relationship between child-rearing patterns, self-esteem, and labor force needs. Their vision has been confirmed and extended by the demands of ethnic and social groups not simply for greater representation and job rights but for better role models. Control over black schools by black people, a resurgence of interest in women's colleges in the mid-1970s, and the rapid expansion of women's studies programs and courses in schools all over the country reflect a trend with enormous implications for altering the self-images on which oppression rests. Persistent and continuous exposure of the way roles are limited negates the kind of self-abnegation characteristic in the fifties, and encourages women to exert themselves to the point of rejecting male supremacy. Resulting pressures on the media and the job market could permanently alter the landscape of women in positions of some prestige and authority. They, in turn, will encourage others to try similar roles. Women may thus be challenging not simply the job structure but the entire fabric of psychic oppression that limits aspirations and stifles creative growth.

All this points to a third area. Women often take jobs far below the levels to which their education, skills, and social background entitle them. As long as family commitment and ideas of femininity rationalized their low place in the system of status and rewards, the inequity of their position remained hidden. But as women have begun to unmask these rationalizations, they have been able to see clearly the false nature of social mobility. Demands for equal treatment in the job market have led to confrontation with others competing for the same jobs. In a tight job market when unemployment is high and workers are played off against each other, women begin to understand how class position protects certain workers from economic ruin while it exposes others to the hazards of joblessness and the degradation of welfare. From 1970 to 1974, the heyday of women's demands for job and educational equality, no statistically significant change occurred in the sex structure of jobs and the earnings gap between male and female workers widened. In some academic jobs the proportion of employed women declined and in traditionally female sectors like telephone operators and secretaries, males made inroads into jobs that had always been held by women.[11]

As egalitarian pressures for more jobs for women have exposed the inability of the system to provide for all, they have concretized and rendered questionable among many the social stigma attached to welfare, unemployment, and other social programs like food stamps and medicaid. Living on welfare has become acceptable to people who would have shuddered at the thought not long ago, and students are now among the largest groups of people applying for, and getting, food stamps.[12] Extensions of social services have become so deeply institutionalized as to be seen as right. Failure to care adequately for the poor now induces protest — raising questions about the inability of the "system" to provide jobs for all. The growing number of people who can survive without jobs reduces the value attached to work as a means of self-support. Although women are of course not alone responsible for raising these questions, their entry into the job market in a time of steadily diminishing employment opportunity has aggravated them.

Women who enter jobs voluntarily often have contrary reactions. Since they come from relatively autonomous household situations and are often second wage earners in their families, they are sometimes unwilling to put up with role work and unsatisfying jobs. Yet some have argued that because women have major commitments to the home, they prefer jobs that carry little responsibility. In both cases, however, a new measure of success emerges, pinned to self-satisfaction and autonomy either on the job or off it. It raises questions about the primary commitment to efficiency in work and concerns about whether the production of profits should outweigh the search for humane work relationships.

Finally, questions being raised by women are undermining the institutions that socialize us all into accepting the values of this society: Families, households, and schools are challenged by the search for new roles and ways of relating. As relative affluence frees some women from spending much of their lives maintaining households and rearing children, it also forces them to look for alternatives. Many women develop a growing sense of the way families restrict their options. The household appears as an inefficient unit in which every woman repeats her neighbor's activity. Far from being the bastion of independence David Potter describes, it is experienced as confining, isolating women in trivial tasks and consumer roles and leaving many women bored and dissatisfied. As the standard of living rises among the middle-class, material possessions become less satisfying in themselves and women, who are the major consumers, begin to question the time and energy they spend acquiring goods. Many young people have already begun to reject possessions as a mark of status.

As long as schools could fulfill the promise of upward mobility that education carried, they remained protected from serious attack. But education no longer guards against unemployment and the humane and critical values taught by schools have no place in expanding bureaucratic structures. Women confront these problems as mothers and as workers. They have to deal with children for whom education seems irrelevant. And they often work in the social service bureaucracies (including the schools themselves) where their training to serve is contradicted by the need to keep order and shuffle papers. Schools themselves are increasingly becoming scenes of violence as they continue to teach values and offer possibilities that the job market cannot meet.[13] This is especially painful for women because it further restricts options that have always been limited. Women have traditionally been channeled into low-level dead-end jobs in which the social mobility promised by their high educational levels fails to materialize. Now that rationalizations about family roles can no longer explain this deprivation, women have begun to protest. The changing shape of the family throws questions about the value of education into stark relief. For women, education has always been a questionable means of "getting ahead," and now men are beginning to share their fate.

The institutions that are responsible for teaching us to rely on ourselves, to obey authority, to strive for power, and to be efficient are in travail, threatening to wash away elements that make up the commonly accepted definition of American character. Egalitarian households threaten to eliminate sex roles. New options for women create the possibility of autonomy for all individuals. Dissatisfaction with child rearing and materialistic pursuits yields pressure for more satisfying outlets. Perhaps all this augurs a new kind of family: one in which sexual equality presages an end to relationships of domination within the family as well as outside it.

V

The most important continuing consequence of ferment among women in the 1970s and perhaps the reason why it will not soon be ended is that it provides a clear vision of the way that things we take as natural really represent the unseen ideas of a hidden socialization process. Elucidating the rationale that regulates our roles and aspirations provides insight into the way that all manner of things are condoned in the name of unquestioned slogans. Phrases like "That's not women's work," and "Women belong at home" form a veil of obscurity over sex role, family, and job divisions that are no longer necessary.

But one veil is easily replaced by another, and women can be enticed into the competitive framework that restricts our vision of reality. A few women are already being offered plum jobs in traditional bastions of power and prestige. For many others, it is easy enough to provide the outward appearance of social mobility: new job titles and small salary increases. Women are expected to accept their rewards gratefully, adopting prevailing modes of what we might call masculine behavior (valuing efficiency and power) and thus assuring their continuation. At the same time they act as models for younger women to emulate. While such a process might eventually end distinctions between male and female jobs, it would do so by socializing women into prevailing definitions of work, without threatening "male supremacy" or questioning the values and belief systems that sustain an unequal distribution of power.

But the economic independence of all adults could encourage more egalitarian living arrangements. "Feminine" modes of behavior (nurturing and collective) would thus be expected from both men and women in the home. Already we begin to see what John Kenneth Galbraith has labeled an "emancipation of belief." Sexual behavior is less inhibited and not necessarily confined to the marriage relationship—even nominally. Sex-stereotyped jobs in families and in the job market are beginning to change hands. "Macho" ideals for men are no longer attractive to women among whom a new independence is prevalent. Men are beginning to question the assumption that they must support their families alone. Many women now accept economic responsibility as wage workers and define themselves by their own jobs instead of as their husbands' wives.

These tendencies to alter power relationships in families demand some compromises to accommodate new visions of self. Employers are making tentative gestures in the direction of job sharing, job satisfaction, worker control, day care, and increased emphasis on security. I suspect that these are only the beginning of the accommodation and adjustment required of institutions that have so far validated and perpetuated our sense of ourselves as a nation. And I suspect that they will be insufficient to satisfy a growing number of women who see access to real equality as part of a challenge to the way all decisions are made. No one knows what the end result will be. But the process will surely forbid future speculation about the making of an American character that neglects the active and distinctive input of women.

Notes

1. See Barbara Welter, "The Cult of True Womanhood: 1820–1860," *American Quarterly* 18 (Summer 1964), for a full description of the "lady." Aileen Kraditor's introduction to *Up From the Pedestal* (New York: Quadrangle, 1968), has an incisive analysis of the lady's role in an emerging business society.

2. This is analogous to the turn-of-the-century labor movement when the contradiction between the rhetoric of equal opportunity and the reality of exploitation led many workers towards socialism and anarchism. These movements were undermined by compromises (better working conditions, higher pay, shorter hours) that seemed to narrow the gap between the rhetoric and the reality.

3. Mary Parton, *The Autobiography of Mother Jones* (Chicago: Charles Kerr, 1972); Agnes Smedley, *Daughter of Earth* (Old Westbury, N.Y.: Feminist Press, 1973); Marie Hall Ets, *Rosa: The Life of an Italian Immigrant.* (Minneapolis: University of Minnesota Press, 1970). See also Anzia Yezierska, *Bread Givers* (New York: Braziller, 1975), and Kathy Kahn, *Hillbilly Women* (Garden City, N.Y.: Doubleday, 1972).

4. Carroll Smith-Rosenberg. "The Female World of Love and Ritual: Relations Between Women in Nineteenth Century America, an Ethno-historical Inquiry," *Signs 1* (September 1975): 1–30.

5. The women who first demanded such activities in the early 1900s were subject to ridicule by their male colleagues. Yet they proved to be an effective and important organizing device.

6. See Richard Flaste, "The Family: Pressured by Economics and Public Policy," *New York Times,* June 6, 1975, p. 39.

7. Alice Kessler-Harris, "Stratifying by Sex: Notes on the History of Working Women," in David Gordon et al., eds., *Labor Market Segmentation* (Lexington, Mass.: Lexington Books, 1975), offers an explanation of women's changing labor force roles.

8. Lisa Hammel, "Consciousness Was Raised, Lives Were Changed," *New York Times,* May 19, 1975, p. 34.

9. See June Sochen, *The New Women in Greenwich Village: 1910–1920* (New York: Quadrangle, 1972), for some of these alternatives.

10. Quoted in the *New York Times,* December 10, 1971, p. 20. For an analysis of day care see Katharine Ellis and Rosalind Pecheskey, "Children of the Corporate Dream: An Analysis of Day Care as a Political Issue Under Capitalism," *Socialist Revolution* (November 1972).

11. See the articles in *Monthly Labor Review* 97 (May 1974) for figures on women's labor market participation. And see articles in the *New York Times,* January 6, 1975, p. 16, and August 31, 1974, p. 24, for indications of how slowly change is occurring.

12 The *New York Times* has provided a number of illustrations of changing attitudes towards work. See especially Paul Wilkes, ''Jobless in the Suburbs,'' *New York Times Magazine,* June 8, 1975, p. 13.

13. Enid Nemy, ''Violence in the Schools Now Seen as Norm Across the Nation,'' *New York Times,* June 14, 1975, p. 1.

Bibliography

Ehrenreich, Barbara, and Deirdre English. ''The Manufacture of Housework.'' *Socialist Revolution* 5 (October–December 1975): 5–40.

Ets, Marie Hall. *Rosa: The Life of an Italian Immigrant.* Minneapolis: University of Minnesota Press, 1970.

Gordon, Linda. *Woman's Body, Woman's Right: A Social History of Birth Control in America.* New York: Grossman, 1976.

Kahn, Kathy. *Hillbilly Women.* Garden City, N.Y.: Doubleday, 1972.

Kraditor, Aileen, ed. *Up From the Pedestal: Selected Writings in the History of American Feminism.* Chicago: Quadrangle Books, 1968.

Lasch, Christopher. *Haven in a Heartless World.* New York: Basic Books, 1977.

Parton, Mary. *The Autobiography of Mother Jones.* Chicago: Charles Kerr, 1972.

Piercy, Marge. *Woman on the Edge of Time.* New York: Knopf, 1976.

Smedley, Agnes. *Daughter of the Earth.* Old Westbury, N.Y.: Feminist Press, 1973.

Smith-Rosenberg, Carroll. ''The Female World of Love and Ritual: Relations Between Women in Nineteenth Century America, an Ethno-historical Inquiry.'' *Signs* 1 (September 1975): 1–30.

Sochen, June. *The New Women in Greenwich Village: 1910–1920.* New York: Quadrangle Books, 1972.

Veblen, Thorstein. *The Theory of the Leisure Class.* New York: Macmillan, 1899.

Welter, Barbara. ''The Cult of True Womanhood: 1820–1860.'' *American Quarterly* 18 (Summer 1964): 151–74.

Yezierska, Anzia. *Bread Givers.* New York: Braziller, 1975.

BENJAMIN D. BERRY, JR.

Some Issues in the Proper Study of Black America

Benjamin D. Berry, Jr., is a sociologist who has taught at the University of South Florida and at Heidelberg College before becoming the Director of Black Studies at the College of Wooster. He is currently teaching in the American Studies Department of Skidmore College.

I am an invisible man. No, I am not a spook like those who haunted Edgar Allan Poe; nor am I one of your Hollywood-movie ectoplasms. I am a man of substance, of flesh and bone, fiber and liquids — and I might even be said to possess a mind. I am invisible, understand, simply because people refuse to see me.

Ralph Ellison, *The Invisible Man*

The first edition of this book contained no essay dealing with the role of black people in American culture. This fact does not imply that the book or its editor was significantly different from other works and writers of the time. In those days, which were not too far in the past, black people were not considered a part of the American scene by either politicians or scholars of the national character. There was a "racial problem" which demanded some attention, but that was not a subject for serious scholarly work.

American scholarship has been plagued with the same malaise as has the general society. Simplistically, this is racism. However, many liberal academics, especially those involved in the American Studies movement, would recoil in horror at such a suggestion. These are the men and women who have left the quiet of the hallowed halls of academe to walk the dusty roads of Alabama and Mississippi in the struggle for black equality. And beyond that, they have brought that struggle into the classroom, destroying the atmosphere of quiet contemplation with hard questions of race and equality.

Indeed, these men and women would not stand still for a charge as simple as racism. Therefore, let me state it another way. American scholars, including those involved in the American Studies movement, assume, along with the rest of American white society, that those social structures, values, behavior and speech patterns, and religious practices that have their foundations in Anglo-European society are REALITY. All else is either a pathological deviation, a temporary adaptation, or simply inferior. These assumptions accompanied my learned colleagues to Selma and to Birmingham.

These same assumptions have produced some fascinating scholarly results. We have, for example, the often-quoted and well-respected professors Morison and Commager, who wrote in *The Growth of the American Republic:*

As for Sambo . . . there is some reason to believe that he suffered less than any other class in the South from its "peculiar institution." The majority of slaves were adequately fed, well cared for, and apparently happy. . . . [1]

Or that paragon of sociological virtue, Gunnar Myrdal, who writes in *An American Dilemma:*

In practically all its divergences, American Negro culture is not something independent of general American culture. It is a distorted development, or a pathological condition, of the general American culture.[2]

These two examples demonstrate how the study of black America has reflected the biases of the general society. What follows in this essay are some suggestions which, if taken seriously, might help release the university from its current predicament. These are presented as propositions — a kind of Berry's Three Theses nailed to the classroom door.

Thesis

1: Black America comprises both a racial *and* an ethnic group in American society.

While this statement appears fairly obvious at first glance, a look at the literature on black America will reveal that much, if not all, of the work has ignored the implications of the statement. The racial identification, that is, the classification of humans on the basis of physical characteristics, is so obvious as seemingly to eliminate the necessity for consideration of that sociopsychological phenomenon called ethnicity. Scholars have assumed that this group is simply American, sometimes "exaggerated," or "under the skin" the same as white men, but in no significant way different or distinct from the general American population.

The problem for scholars, therefore, has not been to understand the black American, but rather to devise a rationale for his exclusion from full participation in the society, or a public policy that would overcome the pathology of black life. At each of these extremes, the concern is with race relations, not with the content of black life, or the dynamics of social interaction between black people within the confines of the social ghetto created for them.

Yet any person who has spent any time talking to, and, more importantly, listening to nonacademic blacks, is aware of the sense of PEOPLEHOOD that is present. In my early childhood I was aware of it, and the fact that the Supreme Court decision in *Brown* v. *Topeka Board of Education* placed factors in my life which threatened that sense of peoplehood prompted my father to send me south to a black college in order to preserve "some race pride." This was in the late 1950s when black people were fleeing the South in large numbers. This sense of peoplehood is, as Milton Gordon has defined it, both ancestral and future oriented.[3] The "people" are my ancestors; they are my people; they will be the people of my children and of their children. This is the other side of the dual identity of black Americans. Race is a category imposed by the racist social structure of the nation; ethnicity is the internalized awareness of peoplehood.

The implications of taking the ethnicity of black Americans seriously are significant. First, the "nationalist" strain in black history is brought into sharp focus and the names of Martin R. Delany, Henry McNiel Turner, and Marcus Garvey become more central to any analysis of the black past than has heretofore been realized. These men touched the core of that sense of peoplehood in ways that their integration-oriented peers could not and did not, even though these latter spokesmen are the recipients of a greater level of scholarly attention. The actor Ossie Davis said of Malcolm X that he was our manhood, our living black manhood. The same could have been said of the others who touched the nationalist strain in black America.

A second implication is more relevant for the study of contemporary black life. At a meeting called to plan a symposium on the conflict between traditional African values and those of Western culture, the statement was made that we find it almost impossible to force African thought patterns and values into the categories developed by Western scholarship. The same is true, albeit to a lesser degree, of the attempt to force black American values into white American categories. This is not the case simply because of the residue of African culture in black American life, but because of the isolation blacks have experienced and the necessity it brought about to develop patterns of life that would be protective both psychologically and physically. American scholars have displayed an almost total ignorance of this fact, and have instead termed the degree of deviance from white behavior, language, religion, and so on, sick. If the ethnicity of black America becomes a part of the intellectual baggage of American scholars, much of the mystery of the ghetto life-style will be removed. Let me offer an example.

In the ghetto culture, most preadolescent males (and a surprisingly large number of females) participate in a game of insults called "the dozens." The game involves exchanging insults about an individual and/or members of his family, usually his mother.

Your momma wear combat boots.
I'm not goin' to talk about your momma 'cause she's one of the boys.

In most instances "the dozens" involves talk about the sexual habits of the opponent's mother.[4] White scholars who have collected these sayings have had much difficulty explaining a game which involves such a great deviation from white standards of decorum. "The dozens" has been seen as a means of cutting the apron strings which have bound the growing male to the dominant mother. By degrading another's mother, he indirectly degrades his own, and demonstrates his toughness to his peers. This analysis assumes that preadolescent girls do not engage in the game, and that the mother in ghetto society is the dominant factor. Both of these assumptions have been called into serious question by recent literature.

All too frequently the role of language in the black community is either ignored or given only a passing notice. Ulf Hannerz suggests that good use of language is one of the symbols of status among black adult males, but he fails to notice that preadolescent playing of "the dozens" functions as a training ground in which appropriate linguistic skills are developed. "Good use of language" does not imply correct use of Standard American English, but rather the creative construction of images. Take, for example, the version of the Black Toast Stagolee found in *Black Folk Tales* by Julius Lester:

Stagolee was, undoubtedly and without question, the baddest nigger that ever lived. Stagolee was so bad that the flies wouldn't even fly around his head in the summertime, and snow wouldn't fall on his house in the winter. He was bad, jim.[5]

While "the dozens" is a part of what Hannerz terms "ghetto specific culture," those blacks who are closer to the American mainstream culture are able to identify with and appreciate the use of language involved, and do play "the dozens" on occasion. Most importantly, they are aware of the circumstances which require that a black male develop this specific type of language skill. All of us have had to talk our way out of situations involving whites and in which the use of physical, economic, or political power was not a viable option.[6]

While there are class distinctions within black America, the sense of peoplehood remains, for we have all shared the past of our people, we are all part of the present condition, and we all look toward a similar future.

Thesis

2: As an ethnic group, black Americans form a "subsociety" with a distinct set of cultural patterns.

This second proposition is a direct outgrowth of the first, and has suffered similar treatment (or nontreatment) from American scholars. Here, again, the work of Milton Gordon serves as a launching platform, for it is his concept of the subsociety that informs this discussion. He defines it as

...a network of organizations and informal social relationships which permits and encourages the members of the ethnic group to remain within the confines of the group for all of their primary relationships and some of their secondary relationships throughout all the stages of the life-cycle.[7]

The term "subculture" is reserved for the cultural patterns of the subsociety.

Simply interpreted, this means that those key events in the individual's life are carried on within the ethnic group, and that there are social institutions present to allow for this and to encourage it. This allows for the preservation of cultural traits within the group—the creation and preservation of a distinct subculture.

It is difficult to find an appreciation of this distinction in the works of students of the American culture. Myrdal set the tone when he wrote that the Negro spiritual is the only non-pathological element of black culture. Following that lead, a few elements of the black life-style have been granted a degree of legitimacy by scholars. Some are even willing to admit that some important aspects of American popular culture find their roots in black culture. But it remains the rule that the cultural forms of the black subsociety are seen as "sick" approximations of the general culture.

One contributing factor appears to be the debate over the existence of African-isms in black life. Scholars have argued that, since the African culture was destroyed by slavery, black Americans cannot possibly have a culture of their own. Others have argued that remnants of African culture are present in black life and constitute the foundation for the black culture.[8]

This debate clouds the academic view of the phenomenon of "cultural gene-sis" in the United States, and only a few have seen how both the destruction of African culture and the process of acculturation to the Anglo-American culture have been incomplete. The descendants of the first Africans have created something new on American soil which is neither African nor European, but is at the same time, both. It is black!

These are questions which anthropologists, sociologists, and historians should be considering. However, they have not done so in the past. Myrdal's massive book contains little or no information on how black people live. Even some black scholars have been guilty of ignoring their own people's life-styles.

It is time that the existence of a separate and distinct culture of blacks be recognized. The problem of American society, and, thus the American universi-ty, is not the Negro/black/Afro-American. It is racism, and the academic approach to that issue should be concerned with that segment of the society in which it is found: white America. The development of what Allan Spear has termed the "institutional ghetto"[9] is a part of the black response to white racism. The problem for the students of black American culture is to understand that response and how the desire of blacks to function as humans in a dehumanizing environment has spawned a distinctive black culture.

It is also time that American scholars recognize that the key to much of black history is the development of that black subsociety and subculture. Blacks have shown the desire to preserve a duality of identification which Du Bois captured at the turn of the century in *The Souls of Black Folk* when he argued that we are Americans, but black also, and that both are valuable.[10] Put another way, black history might be seen as the struggle to survive as full human beings in a society that was and is dedicated to our destruction. All too many students of black history have researched only the attempts at becoming a part of American culture and society, and have ignored the internal struggle to preserve a sense of group identity.

I would suggest that those who would study black America, especially whites, begin by freeing themselves of their integrationist orientation where integration implies the death of those cultural elements of the black community. If a degree of cultural relativism is necessary and desirable for effective study of so-called traditional societies, it is equally necessary for the study of the complex society of black Americans. The culture of a people is designed to facilitate the survival of the group within the environment in which the group finds itself. It allows the individual members of the group to relate to each other, to the past of the group, to the physical and social surroundings in such a manner that their actions and reactions will not be physically, psychologically, or socially destructive. Black Americans have lived for several centuries in a very hostile environment, and the elements of black culture have facilitated both individual and group survival in that environment. When a scholar sets himself or herself to the task of evaluating a specific culture, black culture included, the culture should be evaluated in terms of its ability to perform these functions.

It has been demonstrated that blacks who adopt the culture of white America while at the same time being denied admittance to full participation in the social structure of that society face the threat of psychological if not physical destruction. The fact that thousands of blacks were lynched in the late nineteenth and early twentieth centuries because they attempted to break out of the boundaries created for them by the dominant group is demonstrative of the physical dangers inherent in failure to adapt to the environment.

At the psychological level, Grier and Cobbs[11] and Frazier[12] have provided many examples of the problems caused by the conflict created by the attempt to live a life-style that cuts the black individual off from those protective mechanisms devised by his community over the years.

The point is that black culture and the black subsociety have functioned well at a time when they were most needed, and should be evaluated *on their own terms,* not on the basis of criteria imposed from the outside. Just as the attempt to deny one's blackness has been shown to be destructive of the individual, the effort to ignore blackness is destructive of good scholarship.

Thesis

3. Black people function in the United States as a domestic colony, and as such suffer much of the ills of the classic colonial situation.

The third and final proposition will receive the greatest attention in this essay for several reasons. First, it is central to the development of a body of honest research on black America. Second, it is the least likely candidate of the three for wide acceptance by the American academy. Third, if one of the goals of our research is to effect significant social change, it is crucial that we clarify the relationship of the black community to the larger society.

The chief advocates of the model of domestic or internal colonialism as a conceptual tool are Robert Blauner and Robert Allen[13] and most of this discussion is based on their work. The central theme of the model is that black-white relations in this nation are in essence those of the colonizer and the colonized. While many of the characteristics of the classic colonial situation are missing, the process remains the same. Blauner writes that "classical colonialism of the imperialist era and American racism both developed out of the same historical situation and reflected a common world economic and power stratification."[14]

The purpose of employing the model of internal colonialism in the study of black-white relationships is to bring conceptual clarity to race relations theory, and to overcome some of the misconceptions of the models employed in the past. These conceptualizations assume that sufficient similarities exist between the black experience and that of the European immigrants to allow for a theoretical shift from one to the other. Yet the entry of blacks into this society, the length of time we have been here, the role of color in the American psyche, all point to the non-applicability of the traditional models to the black experience.

Internal colonialism as a model encompasses the best of the other models and more accurately reflects the true status of blacks in the society. The fact that no ocean separates the colony from the colonizer is of no consequence. As J. H. O'Dell remarks in *Freedomways:*

A people may be colonized on the very territory in which they have lived for generations *or* they may be forcibly uprooted by the colonial power from their traditional territory and colonized in a new territorial environment so that the very environment itself is "alien" to them. *In defining the colonial problem it is the role of the institutional mechanisms of colonial domination which are decisive.* (Emphasis in original)[15]

According to Blauner, there are four variables that interact to create the colonial situation: (1) the point and manner of entry of the racial group into the dominant society; (2) the process of acculturation; (3) control of the colonized group by the colonizer; and (4) the manifestations of racism. Let us consider each in order to see if they apply to the black situation in the United States.

Most blacks in this nation are descendants of Africans brought to this country as slaves. These "immigrants" did not leave their homeland with any semblance of delight, but underwent what Stanley Lieberson has termed "forced migration."[16] Other national groups have come to America voluntarily. It may be true that pressures in the old country made migration necessary, but the choice was open to come here, or to go elsewhere. No such option was open to the Africans who survived the Middle Passage. The black person's life in this nation began with a desire not to be here, and with treatment as a chattel.

Once the Africans had arrived in the New World, and especially in North America, there was a concerted effort by the slaveholding group to destroy their culture and to replace it with Anglo-American culture. African religious rituals were prohibited and African languages barred. Persons from several tribal and ethnic groups were placed together on the same plantation, thus preventing effective communication except in some form of the English language. Those institutions and structures which facilitate the transmission of culture from one generation to the next were destroyed as part of the effort to destroy African culture.

However, the effort to Anglo-Americanize the Africans was not itself entirely successful. As we noted earlier, blacks were isolated to the extent that they were not permitted full participation in the American culture. The culture that grew up among the slaves was neither African nor American. It was a mixture of the two hammered into its peculiar shape on the anvil of slavery. The process of acculturation is a part of the black past to the extent that the culture of Africa was largely destroyed, but not to the extent that the culture of the slaveholder was totally adopted.

The slaves lived under almost total control of the slaveholding class. Laws of the slave states show that the master had control over every aspect of the slaves' lives, from the conditions of their housing, to the arrangement of marriages, to the fact of life or death itself. There were some provisions for punishment of those masters who unduly mistreated their slaves, and community pressure served as a deterrent to sadism in some places. But it remains a fact that the affairs of the slaves were controlled by the masters.

After emancipation, with the exception of those few years of congressional Reconstruction, this control continued to be as real as it had been under the system of slavery. The situation in which the black American experienced the sense of being managed and manipulated by outsiders continued even to the present. The lives of the majority of blacks are administered by representatives of the dominant group, even when some of these representatives are themselves black.

And finally, racism, as defined by Blauner, is "a principle of social domination by which a group seen as inferior or different in alleged biological characteristics is exploited, controlled, and oppressed socially and psychically by a superordinate group."[17]

Some would argue that black people are being granted the same political rights as those accorded whites. They will point to the new laws passed and the relatively recent court decisions as evidence of this. In response to this argument,

Robert Allen writes, "black America is now being transformed from a colonial nation into a neocolonial nation; a nation nonetheless subject to the will and domination of white America."[18]

Allen's analysis of the neocolonial situation is much too involved to repeat in its entirety here. He takes a close look at the involvement of the major corporations in the recent Black Power movement, and the role of the rising black middle class, arguing that these two groups work hand in hand to maintain the economic control of the masses of black Americans. Allen relies heavily on the work of Frantz Fanon.[19] Some American scholars have argued that Fanon's concepts, drawn from the Algerian situation, are not applicable to the American scene. However, if we recall the Nixonian attempt at developing "Black Capitalism," Hoover's almost psychotic war with the Black Panthers, and look carefully at the fate of the black radicals of the late 1960s, both Fanon and Allen appear frighteningly close to the truth.

None of the traditional conceptual tools mentioned earlier allow for these phenomena. The concept of black capitalism can serve as an example of this conceptual failure. It is interesting to note that blacks have been involved in capitalist enterprises at least since the end of the Civil War, but that it was only when mass violence erupted in the major cities that we saw the national government and the major corporations stepping in to help establish black companies. Under a caste model, this kind of concern is not possible. If blacks had been allowed to follow the course of ethnic assimilation, it is entirely possible that the earlier efforts would have proved successful and the problems of the late 1960s would not have materialized.

The ramifications of the concept of domestic colonialism are great, and to some extent, obvious. They involve an admission that the "integrationist approach" which lies at the root of much contemporary writing on black people is simply wrong. A discussion of the effects of discrimination does not begin to deal with the actual situation.

It also involves the admission that liberal efforts at erasing those evils are much akin to attempting to stem the progress of a forest fire with a bucket of water. The colonial situation is a complex of political, economic, philosophical, and social concepts that resist such efforts as half-hearted programs of affirmative action.

On several levels, then, Americans have begun their approach to the question of black-white relations with the wrong assumptions. The dynamics of these relationships are such that the failure to place them within the context of the colonial concept prohibits a clear understanding of both the relationships and the internal dynamics of the black community itself. While it is shameful that such a situation does exist within the borders of the United States, this shame cannot deter the scholar from the active pursuit of truth.

These three propositions have been presented in a spirit of open inquiry.

Although they may not be ultimate truths, I offer them to the American Studies community for discussion. I hope that such discussion will ensue, and that our research and teaching will be the better because of it.

Notes

1. Samuel E. Morison and Henry Steele Commager, *The Growth of the American Republic* (New York: Oxford University Press, 1937), p. 433.

2. Gunnar Myrdal, *An American Dilemma* (New York: Harper and Brothers, 1944), p. 928.

3. Milton Gordon, *Assimilation in American Life* (New York: Oxford University Press, 1964).

4. See Roger Abraham, "Playing the Dozens," *Journal of American Folklore* 75 (1962): 209–20.

5. Julius Lester, *Black Folktales,* as quoted in Geneva Smitherman, *Talkin' and Testifyin' in the Language of Black America* (Boston: Houghton-Mifflin, 1977), p. 128.

6. For a detailed discussion of "the dozens," see Smitherman, p. 128.

7. Gordon, *Assimilation,* p. 34.

8. This debate has raged for some time. See Milvile Herskovits, *The Myth of the Negro Past* (New York: Harper and Row, 1941), and E. Franklin Frazier, *The Negro in the United States,* rev. ed.(New York: Macmillan, 1957).

9. Allan Spear, *Black Chicago, The Making of a Negro Ghetto: 1890 – 1920* (Chicago: The University of Chicago Press, 1967), ch.5.

10. W. E. B. Du Bois, *The Souls of Black Folk* (Chicago: A.C. McClurg, 1915), pp. 2–12.

11. William H. Grier and Price M. Cobbs, *Black Rage* (New York: Basic Books, 1968).

12. E. Franklin Frazier, *Black Bourgeoisie* (New York: Collier, 1962).

13. Robert Blauner, *Racial Oppression in America* (New York: Harper and Row, 1972); Robert Allen, *Black Awakening in Capitalist America* (Garden City, N.Y.: Anchor Books, 1970).

14. Blauner, *Racial Oppression,* p. 83.

15. *Freedomways* 7, no. 1, as quoted by Allen, p. 8.

16. Stanley J. Lieverson, "A Societal Theory of Race and Ethnic Relations," *American Sociological Review* 28 (August 1963): 550– 65.

17. Blauner, *Racial Oppression,* p. 84.

18. Allen, *Black Awakening,* p. 14.

19. See Frantz Fanon, *The Wretched of the Earth* (New York: Grove Press, 1963).

PETER W. DOWELL and DELORES P. ALDRIDGE

Bridging the Gap: The Challenge of Interfacing American Studies and Afro-American Studies

Peter W. Dowell teaches American literature and American Studies at Emory University. He is a graduate of the American Civilization program at Princeton, and the American Studies program at the University of Minnesota. He has written articles on twentieth-century American poetry and American literary and intellectual history.

Delores P. Aldridge is coordinator and assistant professor of Black Studies at Emory University. A Merrill, National Institute of Mental Health, and National Science Foundation scholar, she earned her Ph.D. in sociology at Purdue. She has published articles in the areas of marriage and the family and Black Studies.

I

Both American Studies and Afro-American Studies today are growing concerns. American Studies departments and programs have for some time been familiar, even conventional parts of the academic scene. The newer ones in Afro-American Studies or Black Studies, whatever hackles they still raise or doubtful glances are still cast in their direction within the academic establishment, have made a definite place for themselves in many colleges and universities. In recent years, moreover, junior colleges and high schools have looked increasingly to both fields in developing new courses and curriculums. As each has expanded and flourished in its own right, the two fields have by and large gone their separate ways. Despite the efforts of individual teachers and scholars to work in both, there has been too little formal and ongoing interchange of ideas, perspectives, and people between the two. Yet they have several things in common — notably, their interdisciplinary nature, their similar experiences as innovators within the traditional framework of higher education, and their concern with American life and culture, past and present, from their respective vantage points. In our view, each now stands to gain by drawing upon the questions asked, the findings produced, and the problems confronted by the other's ways of seeing. It is time to work towards bringing about closer communication between them and more coordinated efforts on their part, especially in the area of classroom teaching.

We have chosen to call this endeavor *interfacing* American Studies and Afro-American Studies. The term indicates that they have common boundaries and further designates the act of mutually exploring these common grounds. We intend it also to convey some of the meanings of the root word, *face,* which, whether it denotes the human physiognomy or the action of human beings seeing one another face to face, calls attention to the individual lives, the flesh-and-blood reality that lies behind these academic enterprises. As opposed to *integration,* which suggests amalgamating or uniting as one entity, *interfacing* purports to describe coordinated cooperative activities between partners who retain their independent academic identities. This mode of interaction appears to us best suited to the present conditions in both fields and most likely to contribute to their future development. *Interfacing* likewise carries with it none of the divisive connotations of *integration* with respect to the debates over specific policies and viewpoints for dealing with the racial situation in this country. This does not mean that the actual examination of black and white materials in teaching and scholarly research cannot take different positions on these matters — only that the concept of interfacing itself is not tied to a particular social or political stance.

We also speak here of Afro-American Studies rather than Black Studies. Although they are sometimes used nearly synonymously, we would distinguish between them on the basis of content and scope. Afro-American Studies refers to the study of all aspects of the life and history of black people in the United States. Black Studies, on the other hand, pursues this study in the world context of black experience, particularly in relation to Africa and the other Americas. Afro-American Studies, then, is used in this article to specify that segment of Black Studies that most directly pertains to American Studies.

Very simply, our argument for interfacing proceeds from two corollary premises: First, there can be no really meaningful understanding of American culture which slights, however inadvertently, the lives of black Americans, and, second, a true appreciation of the Afro-American experience involves not only what that experience is in itself but how it resonates with the larger American experience. Both premises rest on a recognition of the special place which black Americans occupy within American life, a place distinguished from that of other groups not only because blacks constitute the largest single racial or ethnic minority within American society and have participated in American history from its beginnings, but also because the heritage of racism which this history has produced is so deeply and pervasively interwoven into the fabric of American culture. The true business of interfacing is the perpetual task of the educator—the constant reexamination of assumptions and approaches in the effort to expand the bases of perception and understanding. In any field of knowledge, there is an inevitable relationship between the vision it has of its subject and itself, the approaches and techniques it employs, and the results it comes up with. Particularly when we look at something as vast and complex and various as American experience, the perspectives employed tend to dictate the questions that are asked of that experience and to foreclose other possibilities. The benefits of interfacing will be to broaden and sharpen the perspectives that have evolved in American Studies and Afro-American Studies, and to discover new ones generated by their interaction. For, as the comedian Flip Wilson would say, "What you see is what you get."

II

Before we examine more specifically what is presently called for in the way of an interfacing approach, a brief look at the past is in order. From the beginning, American Studies as an organized academic enterprise implicitly included, or should have included, black America. Given its avowed break with academic formalism, its open and experimental urge, and its goal of making the whole of American civilization its proper purview, the American Studies movement might well have given the study of black experience a much more prominent place than had traditionally been accorded it in higher education. Yet, in practice, as the movement grew, the black side fared much the same as it did within the established disciplines. This situation, which by and large held true until the past ten years, was the natural if not inevitable result of several factors—most notably, the relationship between American Studies and the older fields from which it emerged, and the nature of the vision that dominated the movement in the early years.

Even as it succeeded in establishing its own interdisciplinary identity in these years, American Studies maintained close ties particularly with the older fields of history and literature. The impetus which launched the movement in the thirties and early forties came from these two areas. Pioneering programs at Yale, Harvard, George Washington, Pennsylvania, Amherst, Princeton, Minnesota, and elsewhere were based entirely or in large part on a history-literature bridge, and the main intellectual and organizational stimulus came from individual teachers and scholars in these fields like F. O. Matthiessen, Perry Miller, Ralph Gabriel, Robert Spiller, and Tremaine McDowell. By the early fifties, American Studies had clearly gained a firm foothold in the academic world. More than sixty programs were active concerns on campuses around the country,[1] *American Quarterly* began publication in 1949 as the official voice of the movement, and the founding of the American Studies Association in 1951 provided both a national organization and the stamp of professional status. During the next dozen years or so, American Studies was marked by consolidation and expansion, a greater acceptance within the academy, and the appearance of several important scholarly works associated with it. The network of disciplinary ties widened considerably, giving fuller play to art history, the history of architecture, music, and the social sciences. But history and literature still held center stage in courses and programs. Most of those who taught American Studies, moreover, had another academic "home," more often than not in a department of English or history.

At the same time that American Studies was developing as an academic field, there emerged a prevailing intellectual perspective by which it looked upon American culture, an outlook which has been referred to in recent critiques as "high cultural history" or "the intellectual history synthesis."[2] Though not exclusively the product of the American Studies movement, it became especially identified with the teaching of American Studies and with a distinctive body of scholarship produced in the field, the work of the "myth and symbol" critics.[3] Rooted in the longtime intellectual and popular preoccupation with the question of what is authentically, typically, or quintessentially American, this vision grew out of the search for meaningful answers to this question that were verifiable in scholarly terms. It emphasized a "holistic" conception of American culture, and made it the primary task of American Studies to elucidate the unifying elements or underlying continuities which produced this wholeness. Most often, the wholeness was posited through attempts to define concepts such as "the American character" or "the American mind" and a search for constructs of thought and feeling which gave concrete expression to them. Given the origins of American Studies, it is not surprising that the quest was pursued mainly in the direction of imaginative literature and intellectual history, and gravitated towards uncovering ideas, symbols, and myths which appeared to be at the heart of the culture and were thus regarded as the most valid expressions of what America was or meant. By the same token, certain major thinkers (Jonathan Edwards, Thomas Jefferson, John Dewey) and artists (Walt Whitman, Herman Melville) were seen as the foremost spokesmen for the culture. Even though popular materials were sometimes drawn upon as particular evidences of larger ideational, symbolic, or mythic patterns, the general view held that these patterns and their implications were most fully articulated at the level of high culture.

The circumstances surrounding the evolution of the movement and the intellectual outlook which sustained its early development both contributed to the fact that American Studies did not bring about a change in the customary treatment of black American experience within the academy. Its considerations of this aspect of America largely paralleled those in other fields. It did not initiate significant new considerations of black life and black history. The close kinship with older disciplines, together with the desire to achieve academic recognition and respectability, undoubtedly mitigated against new departures; the influence of established fields was felt not simply through their support or criticism, but in the fact that their courses usually comprised much of the training ground for students in the fledgling enterprise. The upshot was that the scant attention accorded black materials and issues in higher education generally persisted in American Studies as well.

This predisposition was reinforced by the prevailing intellectual persuasion in American Studies. The "holistic" approach did not lend itself to focusing upon or illuminating the nature of the Afro-American experience. It implicitly underwrote the accepted view of white America as normative for American culture. Further, in relying most heavily on recognized sources from literature and intellectual history, it looked to selected experience of a special sort as the most important index of the culture. Black contributors in these areas were comparatively inconspicuous, especially in the earlier periods of American history on which much of the scholarly attention focused, and the emphasis on shaping intellectual and imaginative visions paid little heed to those black sources that did exist. Insofar as the black experience had a place in American Studies in these years, then, it was either treated as a problem for white American institutions and values (for example, the "problem" of slavery), or as it could be assimilated into the general patterns or preoccupations by which scholars characterized American culture. (For example, Booker T. Washington's thought proved more amenable to deal with as an expression of American beliefs and ideals than did the more trenchantly critical thinking of W. E. B. Du Bois.) When black America surfaced, and it frequently did, it was usually in the context of those historical periods when it most directly impinged on white America (the pre-Civil War struggle over abolition, the Reconstruction period in the South), or with regard to areas where the importance of black contributions to American culture had been acknowledged (religion, music). But the form and fabric of Afro-American life, history, and culture *in and of themselves* remained largely submerged beneath the other concerns of American Studies.[4]

The past decade has brought considerable turmoil and change in the American Studies movement. These years have witnessed the growth of many new programs and an increase in the number of students and scholars in the field. But, under the impact of the upheaval in colleges and universities during the sixties and contemporary events in American society at large, a good deal of controversy has also arisen over what American Studies is or should be all about. The result has been a significant turnabout from its earlier direction. The unofficial hegemony of literature and intellectual history no longer has the preeminence it once had. The "holistic" view of American culture and the approaches associated with it have been seriously questioned and even rejected in some quarters as well as simply supplanted by the emergence of several new foci and methodologies for American cultural studies, especially through the spread of quantitative approaches and the widening use of other sources besides the verbal records of the high culture. Several new specializations have proliferated either within or alongside American Studies—not only Afro-American Studies, but Native American Studies, Women's Studies, Urban Studies, Popular Culture Studies, Film Studies, and more. Pluralism, diversity, and conflict as leading characteristics of American culture dominate much of the current thinking in American Studies.

These changes have generated a new awareness of black American experience paralleling the visibility it has gained throughout the academy in recent years; yet American Studies has been on the periphery of this upsurge in academic and scholarly activity. The current American Studies emphasis on diversity and pluralism has promoted an openness to black materials and concerns. Some of the newly developing specialties other than Afro-American Studies have begun to examine certain aspects of black life in other contexts; women's studies are giving a good deal of attention to the place and roles of black women, and urban studies are taking account of the major importance of the black urban condition. Despite this overdue recognition, however, Afro-American Studies is one of several divergent areas competing for attention within American Studies. More importantly, the rise of the Black Studies movement has raised barriers between the two fields. Like the academic community as a whole, those in American Studies have been divided in their reactions to the black-oriented educational goals and demands associated with the growth of Black Studies. On the other side, many proponents of Black Studies have seen American Studies simply as an arm of the academic establishment and have dismissed it as "for whites only."

Black Studies has in the meanwhile developed as an independent field of learning with its own history. The era of the Civil Rights Movement had a profound impact on the moods and styles of students in American universities. Out of the sixties emerged a new breed of black collegian. At first he was a participant in civil rights efforts in the South—the sit-ins, freedom rides, freedom marches, wade-ins, pray-ins—and was commonly committed to nonviolence as the method and integration as the goal. Increasingly, he became disillusioned over the slow pace of school desegregation, the denial of the black experience in America, and his own uneasy ambivalence as a black student on a campus which was serenely content with its white image.

During the second half of the sixties, the nation's predominantly white campuses found themselves suddenly placed under great pressure to give dramatic demonstration to the reality of their commitment to racial justice. These pressures came from a variety of sources, including the impact of court decisions and legislation. Many campuses throughout the North and West had for some time been pursuing, in a leisurely and good-natured fashion, the goal of "better race relations" based in equity. In the South quite a different story obtained. By the mid-sixties the flow of events began to dictate a quicker timetable and to demand affirmative effort far exceeding that which most predominantly white campuses had as yet exerted. As the decade came to a close, the tempo of history had accelerated. Student protests and campus unrest (something more than polite petitioning) occurred on 232 campuses in the spring semester of 1968–69. Although other issues such as the Vietnam War were often present, most of these campus incidents (59 percent) were sparked by the issue of "Black recognition" in one form or another.[5]

Black Studies was one answer to black recognition—a humanistic approach as part of a true liberal arts education. And from the outset of the demand there has been much concern about Black Studies. Colleges and universities throughout the country have encountered the Black Studies movement. Because of the encounter they will never be quite the same again. Black students demanded and in many instances were granted Black Studies programs or departments almost instantaneously. While not all the programs were ushered in by verbal confrontations and physical violence, such tactics were used effectively at a wide range of institutions, from Cornell to San Francisco State, not only to institute a Black Studies program upon a campus but also to decide questions concerning the development of curriculum, the selection of faculty and staff, the admission of students, and the conduct of research. In many instances the more-or-less standardized methods of innovation in the university were either directly challenged or effectively circumvented during a chaotic period such as occurred at Harvard, Cornell, Duke, Ohio State, Berkeley, Washington, and Wisconsin, to name but a few examples.[6]

Everybody, it seemed, favored Black Studies in the abstract. The problems began on many campuses when the militants and the establishment sat down together to iron out specific details regarding format, direction, and control and discovered that neither group had the foggiest notion what the other really meant by "Black Studies." Academic traditionalists, including most scholars and nearly all administrators, thought of Black Studies as the body of subject matter relating to the black experience in Africa and the New World. Within this frame of reference, a curriculum in Black Studies would consist of various courses from various disciplines. These courses would be taught by professors, white or black, with the proper academic credentials (which meant the Ph.D.) and would be open to all eligible students, black or white. Nontraditionalists, particularly militants, regarded the traditional academic practices as irrelevant. They envisioned Black Studies not as encumbered by curriculum committees and degree requirements, but as a collegiate training ground with a single overriding purpose—the advancement of the black revolution in every facet of American life. Embittered by the oppressions of the past and impatient to undertake the reconstruction of the future, these black militants held very little reverence for traditional academics.[7] If many militants were dismayed with traditional ideas on curriculum, they were repulsed by the "power structure" of the university. Students identified white administrators with the hated white establishment. The idea of sovereignty over Black Studies resting in the hands of administrators such as deans was met head on.

Out of these feelings grew demands for autonomous status with black student power over curriculum and the hiring and firing of faculty. Perhaps the most explosive of all issues relating to Black Studies was the question of participation by white professors and students.[8] Of course, this position is basic to the age-old integration-separation controversy and served to alienate most of the white community and many blacks as well. The range of critical reactions among black scholars was indicated by the responses of Martin Kilson of Harvard and Kenneth Clark of Columbia, author of *Dark Ghetto*. Kilson voiced a negative view of Black Studies particularly as it was conceptualized in its earlier stages; Clark believed that Black Studies had an important role to play in the college or university curriculum and in education generally, but that the exclusion of white teachers and/or white students was but another form of segregation.

Clearly, matters such as course content, objectives, and teaching strategies in Black Studies have been areas of concern. The limited training that some of the teachers have received, coupled with their insecurity about it and their desire to prove their blackness or possession of ''soul,'' has caused many of them to teach what was and/or is popular or currently ''relevant.'' Frequently this has meant a glorification of the black experience and an interpretation of that experience that would serve contemporary efforts of ''revolutionary'' blacks. Different ideologies among proponents of Black Studies accentuate many of the controversial aspects of the field. Yet, in spite of the differing views, many agree on several essential points: Black Studies is a legitimate and long overdue intellectual enterprise; it should and will produce change in the attitudes of blacks and whites; it will lead to improvements in the black community and train more sophisticated leaders for it, and it should stress scholarly solutions to pressing social problems.

Since 1968, when the first Black Studies program was established at a predominantly white institution of higher learning, the focus of black scholars has shifted from the question *''Whether* Black Studies?'' to *''Whither* Black Studies?''* From 1970 to 1973, Nick Aaron Ford, at Morgan State College, conducted an evaluative study of 200 Black Studies programs in American colleges and universities. In his book *Black Studies — Threat or Challenge?* he contended that ''the battle for the acceptance of the idea of the validity of Black Studies as an intellectual discipline was fought and won.''[9] Early concerned with the question of direction, John Blassingame, at Yale University, offered ''A Model Afro-American Studies Program'' in his book *New Perspectives on Black Studies*.[10] He urged attention to guidelines, an area which he felt had been neglected in the initial fight for the recognition and establishment of Black Studies.

The issue of separation appears to be low-keyed in the seventies. Traditionalists appear to have survived the sixties and currently dominate the Black Studies scene with respect to matters such as curriculum, administrative and budgetary control, faculty selection, and interracial student participation. Perhaps the current social, economic, and political milieu has taken the sting out of militants, be it in education or some other arena. Indications are that there is a rising tide of reaction towards the tumultuous sixties which is less prone to radical or militant behavior and less tolerant of it either in the university or on the larger American scene.

It is highly unlikely in any case that colleges and universities would allow militants to define curriculum in terms of the philosophy of black revolution. To grant any ideology such privileged status would be a severe blow to the traditional concept of the university as a laissez-faire marketplace for the free exchange of ideas. And given the dominant forces at work in American society and culture, it is certain that, if special treatment were to be accorded officially to a political philosophy, it would not be one that advocated Black Power. At the same time, Black Studies courses and programs at many institutions are no longer simply experimental innovations, but have demonstrated that they are viable and valuable educational assets to higher education. The future directions of—and directives for—Black Studies and the role of predominantly white academic institutions in that future are neither resolved nor clearly defined. But the predictable increase in Afro-Americans at these institutions and the growing number of white students concerned with understanding more about the black world increase the need and urgency for dispassionate scholarly attention to pedagogical and social issues inherent in teaching black experience.

III

The present challenge is to bring American Studies and Afro-American Studies closer together on a new footing. The fluid and changing situation that currently characterizes interdisciplinary studies should encourage those in both fields to put aside past differences and look for viable ways to interrelate that will build upon the perspectives, special competences, and teaching strategies and techniques that each field has developed.

What Afro-American Studies can bring to American Studies is, to borrow the metaphor Ralph Ellison took over from the blues, the view from inside the jug. Some years ago, in a debate with Irving Howe over the proper role and obligations of the black writer, Ellison challenged the highly reductive view of what it means to be black in America which he felt so often characterized the thinking of even the most sympathetic white interpreters. Arguing that Howe "seems to see segregation as an opaque steel jug with the Negroes inside," he suggested that if their situation could be likened to living in a jug, it was a transparent jug from which the blacks could observe a good deal more of the world than just their racial predicament.[11] The growth of Afro-American Studies in recent years has carried Ellison's challenge forward through the development and dissemination of perspectives on the conditions and dynamics of black life largely from a black American point of view. These perspectives have revealed the richly variegated black culture which exists within the larger American culture. They impart a much fuller awareness than American Studies has heretofore possessed of the traditions, values, behaviors, roles, artistic forms of expression, and so on, whose complex patternings and interconnections give a unique and self-sustaining stamp to the culture of black Americans and to their ways of thinking and feeling.

The outlook of Afro-American Studies brings with it the recognition that racism is a central constituent of America's social institutions and cultural life. Looking beyond the overt manifestations of prejudice and discrimination, it has illuminated the forms and effects of covert or institutionalized racism which permeate our national life in subtle, sometimes even unconscious ways. Important as this contribution is, however, the views and evaluations of American society as a whole which Afro-American Studies provides are not solely related to black-white conflict and the black American's struggle against racial injustice and oppression. Its special insights shed light on all facets of American life as they are perceived by black Americans: material abundance, the American dream, industrialization and technology, urbanization, immigration and ethnicity, religion, work and leisure, relations between the sexes, the family — the list could go on indefinitely. The view from the jug, as Ellison observed, is more than "a special perspective on the national ideals and the national conduct," involving the memories of slavery, the promise of emancipation and its betrayal, and the southern and northern myths by which that betrayal was justified and perpetuated. The view also "has to do with special emotions evoked by the details of cities and countrysides, with forms of labor and with forms of pleasure; with sex and with love, with food and with drink, with machines and with animals; with climates and with dwellings, with places of worship and places of entertainment; with garments and dreams and idioms of speech; with manners and customs, with religion and art, with life styles and hoping."[12]

What American Studies brings to Afro-American Studies is its broad concern with the whole mosaic of American culture. It augments the possibilities for seeing the black experience within that total design. It affords opportunities for looking at white experience alongside its black counterpart as they interact and reflect upon one another in diverse contexts. In his recent appraisal of Black Studies, Richard Long notes that as an academic area it faces "more or less the same problems which lie in wait for any interdisciplinary study in American institutions. Significantly, the American Studies experience is the true paradigm for [its] situation."[13] American Studies has fashioned no fixed methodology, no single theoretical or practical orientation for courses or programs to offer its younger companion in the interdisciplinary arena. But the ongoing discussion of what American Studies is or should be has produced a substantial body of discourse concerning the right forms and approaches for interdisciplinary cultural studies which can be useful to Afro-American Studies as it develops and articulates its own answers to similar questions.

A greater rapprochement with American Studies counteracts the prevalent tendency for Afro-American Studies to become academically set apart as a special case. The approach followed in many institutions, whether it takes the form of introducing a few Afro-American courses into a college curriculum or celebrating Black History Week in a public school, is insufficient. Too often, it has had the effect of saying "Here's where we do the Black thing," while the rest of the educational program conducts business as usual. Afro-American Studies and Black Studies represent important educational innovations in themselves, but they do not obviate the need for the black American experience and heritage to have a more integral place in the study of all areas of American life at all levels of schooling.

A great deal of consideration is needed to determine the kinds of perspectives that should inform the interfacing of American and Afro-American Studies, and the pedagogical questions and problems attendant to incorporating these perspectives into the classroom. As teachers it is imperative that we thoroughly accept the fact that teaching the Afro-American experience involves more than simply presenting certain content or subject matter; it necessarily brings in perceptions and judgments of the dominant norms, myths, and values of white America, and alternative ways of seeing American society and culture. Both the black experience and the white experience must be allowed to reflect upon and illuminate each other, without blurring or softening the critical dimension in either direction. The tendency to avoid or dilute tough and sensitive issues in the classroom in order to keep the situation "nice" needs to be guarded against if there is to be an honest treatment of the two experiences under consideration.

While this propensity must be counteracted, it is no less significant that teachers be aware of the attitudes and feelings in their students and in themselves which the heritage of racism in American society has created and which frank and honest interchange between black and white perspectives must inevitably come to grips with. Only through such give and take can a sense of confidence towards dealing with these attitudes and feelings develop. It goes without question that attention must be given to helping teachers discover approaches and strategies which not only acknowledge the very real presence of these attitudinal and emotional factors, but make them constructive components of the learning process rather than destructive agents of defensiveness or mutual recriminations. Many questions must be raised and confronted if there is to be an open milieu of meaningful teaching and learning. Some of these questions might well be: how can a black perspective be most effectively introduced into various situations? What are the most fruitful strategies for creating interplay between the black and white perspectives? What are the best ways of eliciting the full and honest expression of individual opinions and feelings in sensitive areas and dealing effectively with them in the classroom? How can one handle conflicts and tensions that can arise so as not to create a negative atmosphere by making the students antagonistic or unreceptive?

These questions must be dealt with if there is to be an interfacing approach. Several such questions of pedagogy have been proposed by Afro-American Studies scholars such as Nick Aaron Ford, but little of this kind of exercise has obtained for interfacing Afro-American and American Studies. Dr. Ford has predicted that the trend

will be to increase the number and variety of individual courses by more and more institutions until all accredited colleges and universities will be represented. . . . In the future one role of the white college will be to increase the number of its courses in Black Studies until there will be at least one such course in every significant area of black life and culture.[14]

In spite of the predictions of black scholars, there are few if any programs designed specifically to give teachers and prospective teachers direction in pedagogy and content to meet the inevitable demands in the delicate area of teaching the black experience in courses in Black Studies or in incorporating it in American Studies courses.

And yet authorities agree that the student confronts a special kind of learning situation in dealing with such sensitive subject matter as that of the black experience and more especially when it is juxtaposed with or placed in the context of traditional academic content. James Banks noted the importance of having multiethnic and multiracial teaching materials in an effective program in interracial settings, but also emphasized attitudes, perceptions, and predispositions of the classroom teacher as being much more important than the materials used. Larry Cuban commented: "Less attention should be paid to additional books, and courses . . . and more to the craftman who will use the tools. Preachers of Black History know that the person is far more important than the materials he uses." The California ethnic studies research group, directed by the eminent scholar St. Clair Drake, asserted that "students' sensitivities and needs, in selection of material and manner of presentation, must be consciously and deliberately taken into account in teaching the black experience in interracial classroom settings. . . . The setting in which no black students or too few black students are present gains in simplicity from what it loses in richness but also lays an unusually heavy responsibility upon the teacher to exhibit sensitivity and tact, and to explain, clarify, and interpret." Among the most critical issues involved in teaching black experiences is the problem of achieving sensitive and interpretive presentation of *undiluted* black expressions and black perspectives.[15]

Importantly, the pedagogical problems that interfacing American Studies and Afro-American Studies entails must receive more explicit scrutiny in local academic settings. The varied teaching experiences of individuals should be utilized to the fullest as a major resource with sharing of experiences among teachers from differing settings (black teachers in predominantly black schools, black teachers in predominantly white schools, white teachers in predominantly black schools, etc.). Very practical and immediate questions which pertain to actual teaching and learning situations should be raised. At what point should I begin teaching about black experience? What resources or materials are available for teaching black experience? How may they be obtained? What specific subject matter or materials have individuals found especially successful and rewarding to teach? What subject matter or materials have failed to go over in the classroom and for what reasons? What difficulties have they encountered in getting at certain kinds of subject matter or raising certain issues? How did they solve these difficulties? In what ways have the students' own backgrounds or experiences proved to be especially useful for teaching purposes? What strategies have white teachers employed most successfully in working with white students? with black students? What strategies have black teachers employed most successfully in these situations? Are there approaches a black teacher can use that a white teacher cannot? How can teachers best examine their own backgrounds and feelings as related to the subject matter, irrespective of the race of the students with whom they are dealing? These are only some of the questions that all of us engaged in this endeavor need to ponder if we are to expand our awareness and capabilities as classroom teachers.

The comparative potentials of interfacing are considerable and should be drawn upon. There is the opportunity for expanding students' horizons as they reflect their understandings of the black experience and the larger American experience. White students might well see black experiences not only as a means of understanding black people but as a source of illumination of their own lives — how it helps them to understand white experience in a different way. Black students might well view their own experiences not as pathological or void of meaning but as very much a product of life in America and thus a part of the total American experience, though different in many ways from that of the white population.

The possibilities for promoting this kind of understanding can be illustrated by one specific example — the study of the family. From a careful analysis of black families and white families, students might better glean what each can learn from the other. It is meaningful to assess and understand what conditions have contributed to the stability and resilience of white families which are noted for their nuclear, two-parent structures. That black family patterns and structures have differed in varying degrees from those of white families is no less significant for appraisal. In fact, given the tremendous obstacles faced by blacks, many of the alternative life-styles among black families may demonstrate extraordinary creative capacities and might well be seen as models rather than problems. And both black and white students can learn from models.

What to teach? How to teach? Who can teach? Today these are the pressing questions in interethnic studies. Moreover, these questions have different nuances when applied to Black Studies, when applied to Black Studies at white schools in the South, when applied to general education courses attempting to incorporate black experiences, and so forth. It is clear that the potential benefits of interfacing extend beyond the parameters of subject matter, theory, and method into actual teaching and learning situations. Equally apparent is the fact that sharp departure from what one is accustomed to inevitably entails some problems and uncertainty not only in knowing what and how to teach but in personally adjusting to unfamiliar circumstances. Thus, if interfacing is to work, a critical task is that of assisting individuals in acclimating to such new challenges so as to make them less difficult and more rewarding.

While we recognize that many questions have to be raised, we are nonetheless cognizant that few, if any, have airtight answers. We offer no panaceas but submit that questioning is and must be an ongoing task. For those who would seek to glorify the black experience rather than "tell the whole story" many questions should be resolved. Firstly, is this the only way to build pride or a revolutionary ethic in black students and respect for black people among white students? Will the spurious sense of self-worth the black student gains and the respect for black students which the white student acquires from such a course survive their acquisition of knowledge about the complex and baffling facts of history? It can be argued that students will learn more about the contemporary world (and how to change it) from studying uncle toms, pimps, and numbers runners than from studying black revolutionaries exclusively. After all, are not these groups part of the reality of the past and the present? We need to see blacks as models but this does not mean a failure to be critical of problematic areas.

Secondly, can any Black Studies course guarantee the formation of racial pride if there is no support of such a feeling engendered in all courses in the academic community? Or, will the effect of other courses in the academic community, in which the student is subject to forms of institutionalized racism, counter the positive gains? Lastly, can any emphasis guarantee or be guaranteed to produce one particular kind of response? It is certainly possible that any thorough study of the black experience will produce criticism, ambivalence, and revulsion as well as pride and respect for the survival of such a people. Will the sense of self-esteem or racial respect necessarily be decreased because of the other feelings? We think it unlikely. In the end, however, and regardless of what teachers do, the student must determine his or her own emotional relationship to the black experience.

IV

One effort to address some of these complex questions was made by the three-week Atlanta Summer Institute: Interfaces of American Studies and Afro-American Studies in July 1975.[16] The institute was conceived of as a forum for high school, junior and community college, and four-year college teachers to explore the interconnection between the two fields. The program had six specific guidelines for its activities: (1) to explore the common grounds of interdisciplinary teaching in American Studies and Afro-American Studies; (2) to introduce teachers in traditional academic fields to ways of undertaking interdisciplinary teaching and relating new perspectives and materials to their present backgrounds; (3) to expose teachers in American Studies or Afro-American Studies to what others are doing in these areas and the fruitful possibilities for interaction between them; (4) to examine practical models for courses and programs suited to particular institutional settings and needs; (5) to demonstrate the rich variety of resources available beyond the classroom, utilizing in particular the city of Atlanta and its many facilities as integral components of the program; and (6) to make available through the National American Studies Faculty ongoing consultations with specialists to assist participants in implementing courses or programs at their home institutions. The first three objectives define the overall purposes of the institute; the latter three address concrete and practical ways of implementing these purposes. These objectives were met with varying degrees of thoroughness and success, but nonetheless they can stand as a statement of the task of interfacing.

The program brought together thirty participants and a diverse faculty from different geographic regions, different kinds of schools, and different academic specializations. Their institutional affiliations ran almost the full gamut: inner-city and suburban public schools; parochial schools; a junior college in a mixed urban and rural area; private and state-supported colleges, some largely white and others predominantly black; and large private and state universities. A majority of the participants had had little or no academic grounding in American Studies or Afro-American Studies. Less than half were teachers or students in courses or programs with interdisciplinary dimensions of either sort, and only a few in full-fledged curriculums in these areas. Eight out of thirty had either an undergraduate or an advanced degree in one of the two fields.

Clearly, the institute appealed to many different academic walks of life. The attendance of some elementary school teachers expanded the spectrum of teaching levels represented beyond the original expectation. The interaction among participants and faculty encouraged an exchange of ideas and viewpoints so that individuals became more aware both of unfamiliar teaching situations and of mutual needs and problems. The broad cross section of professional experience had the special value of overcoming the insularity of the different academic levels.

The three weeks of the institute centered on three broad topic areas — the city, the family, and nationalism — which were selected for their intrinsic importance to both American Studies and Afro-American Studies and their exemplification of different ways in which the interdisciplinary study of American society and culture can proceed. The topic of the city emphasized looking at the development of a concrete phenomenon in space and time, moving from the physical city to the complex of forces that have historically shaped it and finally to what it has meant for the lives of individuals and the life of community in our society. The topic is especially appropriate for interfacing black and white experience because the migration to the cities constitutes perhaps the paramount factor in black American history in the twentieth century and, conversely, knowledge of the black urban experience is crucial to any kind of meaningful understanding of urbanization in America. The concentration on a particular city (Atlanta in the case of the institute) presents many opportunities to utilize tangible features of the urban scene (banks, churches, neighborhoods, amusement facilities, etc.) that lend themselves to juxtaposing black and white life on a very direct and observable level. Extending this approach further, the perceptions different social groups have of the city offer a fruitful means of exploring the outlooks and values of these groups.

The topic of the family provided a perspective focused primarily on the individual vis-à-vis the group, the relationships between highly personal modes of interaction and more impersonal modes, and the intersections of the private and public spheres of American life. The interfacing approach opens up the question of the changing place and meaning of family in American society, and it allows for a consideration of white families and black families in their own right as opposed to seeing the black family simply as a monolithic entity that deviates from a white American norm. The institute participants were particularly struck by the possibilities of family history and saw its personal immediacy for their students as an effective means of kindling an appreciation of the past and developing an awareness of different life-styles within American culture.

Nationalism was chosen as a topic that bears upon the formation of beliefs and ideologies within a culture. As a vehicle for interfacing, it takes in the importance for both white and black Americans of such amorphous yet widely and deeply felt concepts as "Americanism" and "the American way of life," and varying responses to them. It likewise includes the importance of black nationalist movements and thought and their meaning and influence in American life. Its major value for an institute for teachers proved to be its relation to the educational process and the educational system, which most saw as intimately bound up with the promulgation and reinforcement of national values. The topic sharply focused the need for relating the issue of nationalism as a particular subject for analysis to nationalism as a pervasive or "given" presence in the classroom, especially at the elementary and high school levels. How to deal with the perpetuation of "Americanism" in the schools through standard texts, approved course content, and required classroom activities poses a major problem for many individual teachers seeking to present both black and white perspectives fully and honestly.

A series of workshops built around each topic constituted the core of the institute program. These workshops, conducted by various specialists in the topic area, dealt with different specific facets of the general topic or different disciplinary vantage points on it. In the case of the topic of the city, for example, three urban historians treated diverse subtopics within the purview of urban studies (the automobile and the city, urban planning and urban living, the black urban

condition) and their implications for examining black and white urban experience. By contrast, for the topic of the family specialists from different disciplines
explored using the family history approach, literary representations and images,
and some social science viewpoints as ways of looking conjointly at black and
white families.

The workshops essentially moved in two directions. They pursued general
issues, themes, or problems, and they broached specific ideas and techniques for
classroom use, though more could have been done in the way of examining
models for course units, courses, and programs as they related to different
institutional situations. The attention paid to practical teaching resources was
supplemented by tours, site visits, and films. The program included these
components as demonstrations of teaching activities with some consideration of
the advantages and practical problems involved in utilizing them for classroom
purposes. As part of the session on the topic of the family, for example, the
group toured a community health center and met with some of its staff members
in a seminar concerning family health services. This combination of a firsthand
inspection of the working of the facility and an in-depth discussion of its rationale
and operations illustrated very well how resources in the outside community can
be used as educational tools. The activities of the institute could have struck a
better balance between the broad questions concerning content, theory, and
methods and the practical issues of course models, teaching techniques, and
classroom resources. They make clear, however, the two fronts on which the
discussion of the interfacing approach needs to take place.

The Atlanta Summer Institute was meant, first and foremost, to be a community of teachers learning from one another. It did not set out simply to have the
participants instructed by "experts," but to create a setting where a group of
professionals could share the problems and know-how gleaned from their respective experiences. The specific objectives of the institute were not always carried
out as fully or effectively as they might have been. In particular, the pedagogical
questions raised earlier in this article concerning the interfacing approach received insufficient attention. Yet, on the whole, the institute fostered the kind of
interchange it sought to achieve, and the participants were very receptive to the
program and its aims. If their response can, in one sense, be taken as a measure
of the institute's success, in a more important sense it is a measure of the very
real need felt by many teachers for more endeavors to chart ways of exploring the
interfaces of black and white America at all educational levels. Much still needs
to be done to meet this challenge.

Further efforts can take several specific and practical forms. Some things can
best be undertaken by individual schools. The possibility of introducing new
courses or programs based on the interfacing principle should be seriously
considered. It is equally if not more important, however, to strive for a fuller
incorporation of the principle in existing courses and programs, since additions to
the curriculum, and especially ones of an interdisciplinary nature, are often

difficult to achieve, because of financial, staffing, and other limitations. Informal seminars or discussion groups for faculty members might also be set up, where persons from different areas of study can exchange ideas and questions that pertain to bringing black American and white American materials to bear upon each other in the classroom. Such get-togethers on a more or less regular basis can serve as a valuable resource for individual teachers and can also provide a forum for planning curricular changes.

Various other efforts should be made to formalize interchange between Afro-American Studies and American Studies at a wider level. Professional organizations, such as the American Studies Association, the Association for the Study of Afro-American Life and History, and the African Studies Association, should plan to hold some professional meetings together and to sponsor joint conferences. Such ventures could be convened for local and regional areas as well as nationally.[17] Additional summer institutes for teachers need to be offered as well as in-service training programs for different educational levels. Journals, newsletters, and other professional publications should include and even actively promote articles concerned with a comparative consideration of aspects of American Studies and Afro-American Studies, and particularly with interfacing approaches to teaching. An informational center for the exchange of course outlines, materials, and resources that utilize or lend themselves to the interfacing approach needs to be built up and maintained, and this service should be widely publicized.[18] Finally, there is a crucial need at all educational levels for textbooks, bibliographies, and classroom materials designed with interfacing in mind, and teachers and school administrators must continually urge publishers to satisfy this demand.[19]

All of these steps can contribute to the creation of an ongoing community of scholarly and teaching activity that bridges American Studies and Afro-American Studies. The idea of interfacing reaches beyond programs and academicians in the two fields. It extends to any teacher who is concerned with discovering new ways of seeing the substance and meaning of American life and society. In a larger sense, it has implications for the institutionalized educational process itself. Deeply embedded in our educational system is the paradox that, on the one hand, it espouses the liberation of the individual mind by developing the ability to examine and evaluate its social and cultural milieu, but, on the other hand, the system is a central agent for the inculcation of national, regional, and local ideals and values. As a result, conflicts arise which at times become glaringly public, as in the recent textbook controversy in Kanawha County, West Virginia, but often are more subtly felt in what is said or left unsaid in the individual classroom. The juxtaposition of black and white perspectives provides one means of creating a keener consciousness of this paradox and of dealing constructively with the conflicts it generates. This function is but another example of the effort to bridge contradictions that exist not simply in education but within the society itself. Ultimately, the interfacing of American Studies and Afro-American Studies is more than a strictly academic enterprise. Behind it lies the question of how all of us as black or white Americans can better understand ourselves and each other and thereby enrich the quality of our lives.

Notes

1. Based on the number of programs whose date of origin is listed as 1950 or earlier in Robert H. Walker, *American Studies in the United States* (Baton Rouge: Louisiana State University Press, 1958).

2. "High cultural history" is Robert Sklar's phrase ("American Studies and the Realities of America," *American Quarterly* 22 (1970): 597–605). Sklar's essay is a brief but acute initial venture at assaying the intellectual history of American Studies. More recently, Gene Wise has developed a similar and somewhat fuller analysis of what he calls "the intellectual history synthesis." Wise defines a body of shared premises, explicit or implicit, that constituted a kind of intellectual "consensus" or "low-level paradigm" at work in American Studies during the earlier years (" 'Paradigm Dramas' in American Studies: A History of the Movement," an unpublished paper delivered at the Biennial National American Studies Association Meeting, San Antonio, November 1975).

3. Major exemplars include Henry Nash Smith, *Virgin Land* (Cambridge, Mass.: Harvard University Press, 1950); John William Ward, *Andrew Jackson: Symbol for an Age* (New York: Oxford University Press, 1955); R. W. B. Lewis, *The American Adam* (Chicago: University of Chicago Press, 1955); Charles Sanford, *The Quest for Paradise* (Urbana: University of Illinois Press, 1961); Leo Marx, *The Machine in the Garden* (New York: Oxford University Press, 1964), and Alan Trachtenberg, *Brooklyn Bridge: Fact and Symbol* (New York: Oxford University Press, 1965). For two recent assessments of the "myth and symbol" approach, see Bruce Kuklick, "Myth and Symbol in American Studies," *American Quarterly* 24 (1972):435–50, and Cecil F. Tate, *The Search for a Method in American Studies* (Minneapolis: University of Minnesota Press, 1973).

4. One indicator of this situation can be seen from the articles that appeared in *American Quarterly* between 1949 and 1965. Out of the 429 articles published, only 5 dealt primarily with black American life and culture—2 on jazz, 2 on black intellectuals and movements, and 1 on black writers. Two articles dealt with the institution of slavery and another 9 treated white thinking concerning blacks or white treatment of them. To date (1977), *American Quarterly* has not published any sort of bibliographical article or survey of the state of Afro-American Studies, although it has carried such pieces on other areas like Women's Studies, Native American Studies, Urban History, and Film Studies; however, a bibliographical issue on Afro-American Studies is scheduled to be published in 1978 as a special supplement to the annual biographical number.

There were, of course, exceptions to the prevailing picture. Louis Filler, for instance, was both an early advocate of American Studies and for the study of black life and history.

5. *Report of the President's Commission on Campus Unrest* (Washington, D.C.: U.S. Government Printing Office, 1970), p. 109.

6. Joseph A. Califano, Jr., *The Student Revolution* (New York: W. W. Norton, 1970), pp. 57–60. James Friedland and Harry Edwards, "Confrontation at Cornell," in *Campus Power Struggle*, ed. Howard S. Becker (Chicago: Aldine Publishing Co., 1970), pp. 79–100. James McEvoy and Abraham Miller, "The Crisis at San Francisco State," in Becker, *Campus Power Struggle*, pp. 57–58. Nathan Hare, "The Battle for Black Studies," *The Black Scholar* 3 (1972):39.

7. John W. Blassingame, ed., *New Perspectives on Black Studies* (Urbana: University of Illinois Press, 1971), p. 21.

8. This scenario over who would participate in Black Studies programs was played out to its fullest at Merritt College in Oakland, California, and at Antioch in Ohio, where white students were forbidden admittance to courses. The entry of white students into Black Studies courses at Antioch only came about in the face of loss of federal funds based on a decision by the U.S. Office of Education, which declared such a policy was in violation of Title VI of the Civil Rights Act.

9. Nick Aaron Ford, *Black Studies–Threat òr Challenge?* (New York: Kennikat Press, 1973), p. 54.

10. Blassingame, *New Perspectives,* pp. 229–39.

11. "The World and the Jug," in Ralph Ellison, *Shadow and Act* (New York: Random House, 1964), p. 116.

12. Ibid., p. 131.

13. Richard A. Long, "Black Studies Falls into Place," *The Nation*, July 6, 1974, p. 20.

14. Ford, *Black Studies*, p. 152.

15. James Banks, *Teaching the Black Experience* (Belmont, Calif.: Fearon Publishers, 1970), p. 7. Larry Cuban, "Black History, Negro History, and White Folk," *Saturday Review*, September 21, 1968, p. 65. St. Clair Drake, *Teaching Black* (Stanford: Multi-Ethnic Resources Center, 1971), p. 2.

16. The institute was held under the joint auspices of Emory University and the National American Studies Faculty and was partly funded by the Southern Education Foundation. A second institute was held in the summer of 1976, funded in part by the Lilly Foundation.

17. The meeting of Americanists and Afro-Americanists in the New York area, organized by Lillian Schlissel at Brooklyn College in October 1975, was a step in the right direction. So were the concurrent sessions of the biennial American Studies Association convention and the New World Conference in San Antonio in November 1975, even though they were geared more towards a hemispheric dialogue among the Americas than a dialogue specifically between Afro-American and American Studies.

18. The National American Studies Faculty has the beginnings of such a collection as part of its clearinghouse for course materials in American Studies.

19. Several of these recommendations originated as part of a formal statement drafted by the participants of the Atlanta Summer Institute.

Bibliography

Books

Allen, Robert L. *Black Awakening in Capitalist America.* Garden City, N.Y.: Doubleday, 1970.

Banks, James. *Teaching the Black Experience.* Belmont, Calif.: Fearon Publishers, 1970.

Bettelheim, Bruno. *The Informed Heart: Autonomy in a Mass Age.* Glencoe, Ill.: The Free Press, 1960.

Billingsley, Andrew. *Black Families in White America.* Englewood Cliffs, N.J.: Prentice-Hall, 1968.

Blackwell, James E. *The Black Community: Diversity and Unity.* New York: Harper & Row, 1975.

Blassingame, John W. *The Slave Community: Plantation Life in the Antebellum South.* New York: Oxford University Press, 1972.

————, ed. *New Perspectives on Black Studies.* Urbana: University of Illinois Press, 1971.

Blauner, Robert. *Racial Oppression in America.* New York: Harper & Row, 1972.

Bright, Alfred L., et al. *An Interdisciplinarian Introduction to Black Studies.* Dubuque, Iowa: Kendall/Hunt Publishing Co., 1977.

Cleage, Albert B. *Black Christian Nationalism.* New York: Morrow, 1972.

Cone, James H. *God of the Oppressed.* New York: Seabury, 1975.

Cox, Oliver C. *Caste, Class and Race: A Study in Social Dynamics.* New York: Doubleday and Co., 1947.

Cruse, Harold. *The Crisis of the Negro Intellectual.* New York: Morrow, 1967.

Degler, Carl N. *Neither Black nor White: Slavery and Race Relations in Brazil and the United States.* New York: Macmillan, 1971.

Dillard, J. L. *Black English: Its History and Usage in the United States*. New York: Random House, 1972.

Drake, St. Clair. *Teaching Black*. Stanford, Calif.: Multi-Ethnic Resources Center, 1971.

DuBois, W. E. B. *Souls of Black Folk*. New York: Fawcett Press, 1903.

————. *Dusk of Dawn*. New York: Schocken, 1968.

Elkins, Stanley M. *Slavery: A Problem in American Institutional and Intellectual Life*. Chicago: University of Chicago Press, 1959.

Ellison, Ralph. *Shadow and Act*. New York: Random House, 1964.

Essien-Udom, E. U. *Black Nationalism*. Chicago: University of Chicago Press, 1962.

Fanon, Franz. *The Wretched of the Earth*. New York: Grove Press, 1963.

Fogel, Robert W., and Stanley L. Engerman. *Time on the Cross: The Economics of American Negro Slavery*. Boston: Little, Brown, 1974.

Ford, Nick Aaron. *Black Studies — Threat or Challenge?* New York: Kennikat Press, 1973.

Frazier, E. Franklin. *Black Bourgeoisie*. New York: Free Press, 1957.

Genovese, Eugene D. *In Red and Black: Marxian Explorations in Southern and Afro-American History*. New York: Pantheon Books, 1971.

————. *Roll, Jordan Roll: The World the Slaves Made*. New York: Pantheon, 1975.

Goffman, Erving. *Asylums: Essays on the Social Situation of Mental Patients and Other Inmates*. New York: Doubleday, 1961.

Gordon, Milton. *Assimilation in American Life*. New York: Oxford University Press, 1964.

Grier, William H., and Price M. Cobbs. *Black Rage*. New York: Basic Books, 1968.

Gutman, Herbert G. *Slavery and the Numbers Game: A Critique of Time on the Cross*. Urbana: University of Illinois Press, 1975.

————. *The Black Family in Slavery and Freedom, 1870 - 1925*. New York: Pantheon Books, 1976.

Herskovits, Melville. *The Myth of the Negro Past*. New York: Harper & Brothers, 1941.

Huggins, Nathan. *Harlem Renaissance*. New York: Oxford University Press, 1971.

Jordan, Winthrop D. *White over Black: American Attitudes Toward the Negro, 1550–1812*. Chapel Hill: University of North Carolina, 1978.

King, Martin Luther, Jr. *Stride Toward Freedom*. New York: Harper & Row, 1958.

Klotman, Phyllis R., ed. *Humanities Through the Black Experience*. Dubuque, Iowa: Kendall/Hunt Publishing Co., 1977.

Lane, Ann J., ed. *The Debate over Slavery: Stanley Elkins and His Critics*. Urbana: University of Illinois Press, 1971.

Levine, Lawrence. *Black Culture and Black Consciousness*. New York: Oxford University Press, 1977.

Mullin, Gerald. *Flight and Resistance in 18th Century Virginia*. New York: Oxford University Press, 1972.

Myrdal, Gunnar. *An American Dilemma*. New York: Harper and Brothers, 1944.

Nichols, Charles H. *Many Thousands Gone: The Ex-slaves' Account of Their Bondage and Freedom*. Leiden, Netherlands: E. J. Brill, 1963.

Phillips, Ulrich B. *American Negro Slavery*. New York: D. Appleton & Co., 1918.

Rawick, George. *From Sundown to Sunup: The Making of the Black Community*. Westport, Conn.: Greenwood Publishing Co., 1972.

Rose, Willie Lee. *Rehearsal for Reconstruction: The Port Royal Experiment*. New York: Vintage, 1967.

Sanford, Charles. *The Quest for Paradise*. Urbana: University of Illinois Press, 1961.

Shade, William G., and Roy C. Herrenkohl, eds. *Seven on Black: Reflections on the Negro Experience in America*. New York: Lippincott, 1969.

Smitherman, Geneva. *Talkin and Testifyin: The Language of Black America*. Boston: Houghton Mifflin Co., 1977.

Spear, Allan. *Black Chicago: The Making of a Negro Ghetto: 1890 – 1920*. Chicago: The University of Chicago Press, 1967.

Stampp, Kenneth M. *The Peculiar Institution*. New York: Alfred A. Knopf, 1956.

Thorpe, Earl E. *The Mind of the Negro: An Intellectual History of Afro-Americans*. Baton Rouge: Ortlieb Press, 1961.

Toll, Robert C. *Blacking Up: The Minstrel Show in Nineteenth-Century America*. New York: Oxford University Press, 1974.

van den Berghe, Pierre. *Race and Racism: A Comparative Perspective*. New York: John Wiley and Sons, 1967.

Yellin, Jean Fagan. *The Intricate Knot: Black Figures in American Literature, 1776 – 1863*. New York: New York University Press, 1972.

Periodicals

Abrahams, Roger. "Playing the Dozens." *Journal of American Folklore* 75 (1962): 209 – 20.

Cole, Johnetta B. "Culture: Negro, Black and Nigger." *The Black Scholar* 1 (June 1970): 41.

Cuban, Larry. "Black History, Negro History, and White Folk." *Saturday Review*, September 21, 1968, pp. 64 – 65.

Hare, Nathan. "Myth and Symbol in American Studies." *American Quarterly* 24 (1972): 435 – 50.

Lieberson, Stanley J. "A Societal Theory of Race and Ethnic Relations." *American Sociological Review* 28, no. 4 (August 1963): 550 – 65.

ALBERT E. STONE

Visions and Versions of Childhood

Albert E. Stone was educated at Yale (B.A. and Ph.D. in American Studies) and Columbia (M.A. in English). He is chairman of the American Studies program at the University of Iowa. Previously, he taught in the American Studies program at Yale University and at Emory University. He also held a Fulbright lectureship at Charles University, Prague, 1968– 69. The author of The Innocent Eye: Childhood in Mark Twain's Imagination, *Stone is currently working on a book on American autobiography from which the section on Louis Sullivan is taken.*

In 1960, when I wrote the earliest draft of "Henry James and Childhood: *The Turn of the Screw*," many of the disciplines allied to American Studies were, of course, deeply committed to the broad examination of childhood as a cultural phenomenon. As decisive stages in individual development and social interaction, childhood and youth have long been subjects for all sorts of scientific research and theorizing — since at least the days of William James and G. Stanley Hall. But as one trained more carefully in the humanities or belletristic side of American culture studies, I was more aware of the fresh possibilities of childhood as a theme for the literary critic and historian than of my responsibilities to connect fictional images to possible explanatory paradigms used in social psychology and psychoanalysis. Consequently my early explorations, in this essay and in *The Innocent Eye: Childhood in Mark Twain's Imagination* (1961), were largely literary exercises with a historical overlay; they were imitations of New Critical models more than truly interdisciplinary applications of both humanistic and scientific analysis. If the second essay on Louis Sullivan's childhood represents any advance in imagination or methodology, this is due less to my shift in interest from fiction to nonfiction than to my halting, incomplete, but invigorating forays into post-Freudian thought. I suspect that this postdoctoral experience may be recapitulated in the careers of other Americanists, for our field, as taught in many graduate programs, still has not discovered wholly adequate theories and techniques for linking the unique and the typical, the qualitative and the quantitative, the free and the determined, in American cultural life.

Hence I now reread my comments on James's story with a sense of how different my present perspective is on its general subject, and also how much the study of James and childhood has been advanced by others since my attention has been directed elsewhere. Simply as literary-historical theme, the child has continued to challenge the critics. Biographical tools for pursuing James through the decade of the 1890s in his repeated explorations of children and adolescents are now amply available: In the past five years Leon Edel has completed his masterly work with *The Treacherous Years, 1894–1901* and *The Master, 1901–1916*. Muriel Shine's intelligent monograph *The Fictional Children of Henry James* appeared in 1969, and it cites at least fourteen recent essays on *The Turn of the Screw*. Parts of other new books, including Martha Banta's *Henry James and the Occult* (1972) and Charles Samuels's *The Ambiguity of Henry James* (1971), also contain fresh interpretations of the governess, Miles, Flora, and the ghosts.

But it is literature as history and as psychological expression and communication which has more recently engrossed my attention as teacher and scholar. These concerns, at once quite traditional and the subject of new theoretical work, have led in the direction of the frontiers between "fact" and "fiction." Autobiography is but one of several kinds of American writing which straddles this frontier. The historical dimensions of nonfictional forms like personal history, documentary, and high journalism have awakened or have accompanied a revived concern for what J. H. Hexter calls "the rhetoric of history," what David Levin explores in the "literary criticism of history," what has provoked Roy Harvey Pearce and Wesley Morris to their reexaminations of "historicism." History making in all its manifestations merges with psychology in the new field of psychohistory, as practiced most responsibly by Bruce Mazlish, Joel Kovel, and Cushing Strout, and as related to large social groups by Fred Weinstein and Gerald Platt. At the other end of the cultural spectrum, where individual works of imagination and particular psyches in single stories, poems, and plays become the subject of analysis, the enterprise of the psychoanalysis of literature has been an immense stimulus to my own reading, teaching, and writing. Norman N. Holland, Frederick C. Crews, Simon D. Lesser, José Barchilon, and Joel Kovel are among those who have signally extended and made more precise the pioneer work of earlier critics like Edmund Wilson, Lionel Trilling, and Leslie Fiedler.

In many of these developments of the past decade the influence of two seminal books continues to ramify: Erik Erikson's *Childhood and Society* (whose revised edition of 1963 has been restored to cultural relevance in a recent *Commentary* essay by David Gutmann) and Philippe Ariès's *Centuries of Childhood*. Advances in our methodological treatment of American childhood can scarcely claim validity, it seems to me, without the cross-cultural or comparative dimension which Erikson, Ariès, Kenneth Kenniston, Robert Jay Lifton, and others show to be necessary. This commitment is reflected in contributions to the recently established journal *History of Childhood Quarterly*. Such cross-cultural approaches must also recognize the deep cultural differences *within* American culture. Here the new developments in Black Studies, in Women's Studies, and perhaps in other ethnic explorations may prove of wide significance for American Studies.

But it is the genre of autobiography which now preoccupies me, as it does a growing number of other Americanists who seek to connect these new developments in literary, historical, and social science research. Henry James is one avenue by which I came to this subject. An important inspiration was Robert Sayre's excellent book *The Examined Self: Benjamin Franklin, Henry Adams, Henry James* (1964). More generally stimulating, only because broader in scope, have been three challenging essays: W. C. Spengemenn and L. R. Lundquist's "Autobiography and the American Myth" (*American Quarterly,* 1965); James M. Cox's "Autobiography and America" (*Virginia Quarterly Review,* 1971); and F. R. Hart's "Notes for an Anatomy of Modern Autobiography" (*New Literary History,* 1970). My deep indebtedness to these pioneering essays may be seen in my own contribution to a growing field, a bibliographical introduction, "Autobiography and American Culture" (*American Studies: An International Newsletter,* 1972).

The present essay on Sullivan's *The Autobiography of an Idea* is intended ultimately to make one-half of a chapter in a larger work in progress on autobiography in America. The other part examines one black American artist's childhood — in Richard Wright's *Black Boy.* It is my hope that a careful juxtaposition of these two personal histories may reveal some plausible generalizations about the way American geniuses grow up. But if this proves too grandiose and elusive a goal, perhaps the close scrutiny of a pair of masterly autobiographies, in the light of hypotheses derived from psychoanalysis and psychotherapy, as well as in more traditional literary and historical terms, will sharpen appreciation for particular American works of art and enlarge awareness of the "patterned character" of such re-created lives.

ALBERT E. STONE

Henry James and Childhood: *The Turn of the Screw*

"But ah, the exposure indeed, the helpless plasticity of
childhood that isn't dear or sacred to somebody! That was my
little tragedy!"

James to Dr. Louis Waldstein, 1898

The scene has stamped itself upon our imaginations. A young governess awakens
one night in a big English country-house to discover that her two beautiful little
charges, Miles and Flora, are not in their beds. Gliding silently and breathlessly
through the dim rooms of Bly she comes first upon Flora, face pressed to the
pane, peering out into the garden. At another window the governess herself looks
into the night. There on the moon-flooded terrace stands Miles. He is gazing
raptly up at the house. But the boy is not looking either at his sister's or the
governess's window, to see if his nocturnal prank is detected and appreciated; he
is looking above the governess's head, up at the old tower of Bly. There, the
governess feels sure, stands Peter Quint, the dead man-servant whose ghost has
returned to claim Miles and Flora as his own. The chain, then, originates with the
governess who watches Flora who watches Miles who watches the ghost on the
tower. It is a circuit connecting young and old, innocent and corrupt, living and
dead, perhaps even the sane and the insane. But who is who? The mystery of
The Turn of the Screw is caught and crystallized in the complex pattern of words of
which, like all fictional art, the literary image is composed.

I

Literature is a matter of effective images, and this particular one has tingled the
spines of a large number of Americans since its initial appearance in the pages of
Collier's Weekly in the spring of 1898. Unlike many of the elaborate embroi-
deries in prose which James published during the later years of his long career,
this tale has always been popular, with critics and with the common reader. One
reason for this, of course, is that ghost stories possess a perennial appeal.
Furthermore, the presence of a child gives in this case, as the narrator points out,

"another turn of the screw" to the atmosphere of horror; and this story contains not one child but several. For if Miles and Flora personify childish beauty and defenselessness, the young governess is innocence itself, and even Mrs. Grose, the simple, illiterate housekeeper, is essentially a childlike figure. Four children in all are left alone to confront the ghosts at Bly. James has brought off something which even our master Gothicist Edgar Allen Poe did not attempt — the mating of a mystery story with a classic study of childish innocence and its involvement with corruption.

This achievement not only won *The Turn of the Screw*'s author an unwonted popular reception, it reaffirmed his connection with a tradition in American fiction, already well established by the 1890s, of writing about childhood. Miles, Flora, and the governess take their places beside Pearl and Ilbrahim, Phoebe Pyncheon and the Snow Maiden, Tom Sawyer and Huckleberry Finn, Daisy Miller and Nanda Brookenham, Joan of Arc and Maggie Johnson and the others in the cast of juvenile characters which during the nineteenth century was so conspicuously an American contribution to world literature. James added his cosmopolitan voice to the more indigenous accents of his master Hawthorne and his contemporaries Mark Twain and Stephen Crane in a national invocation to innocence and immaturity.

Instead of expressing — like most European writers, thinkers, and artists — cultural values and preoccupations associated with mature, adult, social life, James now appeared to join those who celebrated quite opposite norms. Purity as inexperience, intelligence as simplicity and intuition, behavior as solitude or withdrawal, the moral directness of the innocent eye of youth — this was the constellation of values asserted, albeit often ambiguously or ironically, in such works of the American imagination as "The Gentle Boy," *The Scarlet Letter, Tom Sawyer, The Prince and the Pauper, Huckleberry Finn,* and *Maggie, A Girl of the Streets.* James himself contributed *Daisy Miller,* "The Pupil," *What Maisie Knew,* and *The Awkward Age* to the emerging image of American Adam as adolescent.

One of the clearest ways in which *The Turn of the Screw* shares this tradition is through its principal actors. During the sixty-odd years following Hawthorne's "The Gentle Boy" (which in 1832 became the first piece of serious childhood fiction in America), the cast of childish characters assumed a formal, almost stereotyped identity. There developed at least three recognizable juvenile roles — the precocious infant (Hawthorne's Pearl or Elsie), the Bad Boy (Aldrich's Tom Bailey, Tom Sawyer), and the virginal maiden (Phoebe Pyncheon or Crane's Maggie).

Flora, Miles, and their governess are cut from the same three bolts of cloth. "Young as she was," the governess tells us of Flora at their first meeting, "I was struck, throughout our little tour, with her confidence and courage, . . . her disposition to tell me so many more things than she asked." The little girl's later conduct fulfills this promise of preternatural knowledge and aplomb; in many respects she is a reincarnation of Hester Prynne's child. The governess, on the other hand, appears quite traditionally, as *less* mature and sophisticated than her twenty years. The "youngest of several daughters of a poor country parson," she is a "fluttered, anxious" beginner in the schoolroom, as "young, untried, nervous" as Phoebe Pyncheon on her first day at the House of the Seven Gables. Little Miles, for all his suavity and good manners, is not unlike a British cousin of Tom Sawyer. "When I'm bad I *am* bad!" he confesses gaily after the midnight escapade. Like any normal boy (which he may, after all, be), Miles chafes under petticoat government and wants "what a boy wants!"

The plot pattern, too, of these American stories of childhood became in some respects as formalized as the character roles. What traditionally *happens* to the precocious infant, the Bad Boy, or the virginal maiden is some sudden and violent introduction to the world of grown-ups, a world discovered to be either ambiguously or flagrantly evil. Modern anthropologists would term this initiation experience "the rites of passage." For Pearl in *The Scarlet Letter* the moments of illumination occur on the scaffold. In the case of Tom Sawyer, it is the harrowing brush with death in the cave. Huck Finn's initiation is more difficult to define; in a sense, the vagabond boy has always known the worst about human nature; but the various forays ashore from the raft appreciably widen and deepen Huck's awareness of the personal and social evil that threatens his and Jim's world.

To be sure, the adolescent's arrival at maturity which the word "passage" implies does not invariably take place. Pearl is transformed by her father's death, but neither Tom nor Huck nor Henry Fleming quite lives up to the moral opportunities forced upon them in the cave, or the river, or on the battlefield. Either they do not *see* the significance of events, or else having seen, they renounce, as Huck does in the Evasion at Uncle Silas's farm, the moral vision so hardly won.

In spite of lapses, however, it is the quality of a young person's moral insight that is the keynote of many nineteenth-century American novels. Again and again, a boy or girl points the accusing finger at the adult world's moral spots. "Thou wast not bold! — thou wast not true." Pearl cries to her weak-willed father in the forest. "Aunt Polly, it ain't fair," says Tom Sawyer to the assembled grown-ups at the funeral reunion. "Somebody's got to be glad to see Huck." And Huck Finn's declaration of moral independence is the most agonizingly honest one of all. "All right, then, I'll *go* to hell,"rings in our ears as a clearer, pithier condemnation of slavery than all the histrionics of *Uncle Tom's Cabin*.

Because of the foreign setting and an unusual and overpowering aura of suspense and horror which distinguished *The Turn of the Screw,* James's tale does not at first display the affinity which it actually possesses with *The Scarlet Letter* or the novels of Mark Twain. Not only is a representative cast assembled at Bly, but something like a traditional initiation is taking place there. Innocence demonstrates its perception of, and opposition to, the depravity incarnated in the ghosts of Peter Quint and Miss Jessel. At the end, the malignant spirits are presumably routed, but the simple governess's world has been turned upside down and little Miles is dead.

This ironic, even tragic dénouement contrasts sharply with the tidier outcomes of previous childish encounters with adult sinfulness in the writings of James's fellow Americans. Furthermore, this different conclusion is a piece with James's deliberately confusing presentation of character, motive, and value judgment that differentiates *The Turn of the Screw* from other stories of childhood. The easy thing to say, of course, is that such characteristics are generic to the ghost story. But there are, I think, more fundamental questions at issue than simply the techniques of mystification. James has written, we must grant, a story that contains the ingredients of a conventional American exploration of childhood. But the final imprint that remains in the sensitive reader's mind is so murky and indeterminate that it must be more than the fault of the ghosts. Perhaps Henry James, in 1898, took this oblique way of disagreeing with his contemporaries about the value of innocence, about the significance of a child's violent immersion in adult affairs, and about the nature and worth of moral insight based on ignorance and inexperience, no matter how pure and blameless. These are at least some relevant questions which might be directed at the little "pot-boiler" and "*jeu d'esprit*," as James once deprecatingly called *The Turn of the Screw*. However, as Douglas, the narrator, pointedly warns, we are not necessarily to expect clear answers to such queries. "The story *won't* tell," he remarks to the curious group around the fireside, "not in any literal, vulgar way."

II

Since the fabric *is* deceptive, one might best begin to unmask the meanings of *The Turn of the Screw* by establishing the kind of "reality" James presupposes for his tale. By this I mean, for one thing, the inescapably mysterious quality of the events narrated. Though in a famous letter to H. G. Wells, James wrote of his trying for "absolute lucidity and logic" in the governess's account,[1] it is obvious that the "singleness of effect" actually achieved is that of unsolved and unsolvable enigmas. No matter how carefully we read and reason we shall never settle all doubts about the events, about the children, about the governess's sanity. As for the "reality" of the ghosts themselves, we must, I feel, accept the governess's word. They exist for her so they must exist for the reader. As Mary McCarthy has recently written, "The narrator is, precisely, an eyewitness, testifying to the reader that these things really happened, even though the reader knows of course that they did not."[2] The supernatural is a necessary part of the world at Bly as it is at Elsinore.

We must not, to be sure, limit ourselves to the perspective of the young girl who relates her battle with the phantoms. A further aspect of the tale's reality —

and this is something that the governess does not realize — is the sense of evil pervading everything. Corruption is clearly in the ghosts and may have infected Flora and Miles, but there are other and more subtle forms of iniquity abroad. Evil has tainted the thoughts and actions of the children's companion and even of the good housekeeper. It also exists in the world beyond Bly. The master in Harley Street bears a share of the general evil which the young lady finds in the ghosts but which the reader sees not merely in Quint but as omnipresent. Just as, in willing suspension of disbelief, one accepts the spirits, so ought we to acknowledge the pervasive miasma of sin in this story. Like any work of art, *The Turn of the Screw* enacts its own rules of reality.

Furthermore, James's story, despite special supernatural qualities that appear to set it apart, does in fact bear a distinct relationship to the author's other novels and stories. This is a literary truism often overlooked in the spate of criticism which has all but inundated *The Turn of the Screw* during the past thirty years.[3] In particular, Miles and Flora's story has links with the novels and stories about children which James wrote in the nineties. During this period (marked in another area by his distastrously unsuccessful attempts at playwriting) James devoted a major part of his imaginative powers to this facet of experience. Before that time, American innocence — especially as plentifully endowed with money and confronted by European cupidity and baseness — had been Henry James's special theme, but except for *Daisy Miller* (1878) and a few smaller pieces like "The Author of Beltraffio" (1884), his innocents had not been children. But with "The Pupil" early in the decade and in *What Maisie Knew* and *The Awkward Age* James turned deliberately to the exploration of European society as seen from the children's quarters. The moral worth of the sophisticated members of English and continental aristocracy, as well as that of some expatriate Americans, was measured through the innocent eyes of their children.

The result is a wholesale arraignment. James's rich, self-indulgent parents, too preoccupied with pleasure, social status, money, or sexual intrigue to bother with their offspring, stand condemned for their abuse of innocence. As for the beautiful, perceptive, reticent girls and boys — Maisie Farrange, Nanda Brookenham, Morgan Moreen, and the others — their fate is to languish in isolation or to be tossed like shuttlecocks from one indifferent adult to another. Between parents and children stands usually one devoted person, a tutor (like Morgan's Pemberton), a nurse (like Maisie's Mrs. Wix), or a governess, who remains true to a trust that all too often goes unappreciated and unpaid. An essential part, too, of the pathetic situation is the uncovering of a tragic limitation, either of intelligence or willpower or of financial resources, on the part of the child's would-be protector which makes defeat for both of them inevitable. As a consequence, each of these works chronicles the victimization of childhood.

The Turn of the Screw is precisely a tale of this sort. The master in Harley Street stands *in loco parentis* to Flora and Miles, and his instructions to the governess — "she should never trouble him — but never, never: only meet all questions herself, receive all moneys from his solicitor, take the whole thing over and let him alone'' — betray his kinship to the Farranges, the Brookenhams, and the Moreens. As for the governess, she does not, like Pemberton of "The Pupil," suffer from too little love of her charge (she errs, perhaps, in the opposite direction), nor is she limited in mind and imagination as Mrs. Wix. But there is abundant evidence that her egotism and rigid middle-class morality are weak weapons with which to fight Peter Quint. In the final scene, at any rate, Miles lies dead, even though his little heart has been "dispossessed" as a result of the governess's valiant, unavailing fight.

There is no doubt that James himself regarded his ghostly tale as linked to these other works by the theme of innocence betrayed. In the summer of 1898, the author made this comment in a letter to Dr. Louis Waldstein: "But ah, the exposure indeed, the helpless plasticity of childhood that isn't dear or sacred to *somebody!* That *was* my little tragedy!'' This statement points to one of the major motifs running through *The Turn of the Screw*. The key words here are "dear" and "sacred." Both terms draw attention away from psychopathological and metaphysical questions (legitimate and important as these are) and toward the social, moral, and religious dimensions of the story.

These are, it seems to me, aspects of a literary artifact of the greatest interest to cultural historians. For it is the writer and his work in their relation to culture and to historical problems of value arising in that culture which chiefly concern the literary critic when he dons an American Studies cap. In this instance, James's use of "dear" and "sacred" suggests value judgments arising from stress felt between certain social institutions (like the family) and traditional Christian ideology. Something is seriously wrong with a social order, James is suggesting, that allows and encourages the betrayal of an innocence deemed sacrosanct by its own religion.

Insofar as *The Turn of the Screw* dramatizes the exposure and plasticity of childhood it ceases to be simply a mystery story and becomes a social document. I would go further and assert that *The Turn of the Screw* is "about" the problem of social class stratification and the religious psychology of a person occupying a peculiarly vulnerable but important position in that social system. This is, of course, a gross oversimplification. Like all formulas, it omits a great deal. But if, recognizing this, we proceed to such positive insights as the comment may contain, it may be possible to throw fresh light on what surely is the most shadowy and elusive short story of modern literature.

III

How can any revelation of evil as largely sociological compare with ghosts or an insane governess or diabolical children as an emotionally satisfactory image of horror? The answer is obvious; none can. To admit this is to establish at once the limits of intellectualizing a ghost story in the manner I suggest. But horror has its vogues and fashions like any other human response. What could raise the genteel hackles of James's readers in 1898 may no longer prove so effective. Indeed, there appear to be several reasons why the reader of 1960 finds it difficult to respond emotionally to the atmosphere of *The Turn of the Screw* in the same manner as the previous two generations. For one thing, our age is familiar with some new forms of the supernatural which render apparitions or hallucinations tamer devices than they once were. I refer not only to our familiarity with abnormal psychology, but also to such experiments as those of Dr. Rhine on extrasensory perception; others might include flying saucers or the alleged achievements of the ouija board, Madam Blavatsky, or the Society for Psychic Research. Furthermore, the twentieth century has grown rather blasé about matters of sexual perversion with which the story of Miles and Peter Quint is unmistakably infused. Most important of all, perhaps, is the fact that the present day reader is far less excited than he once was by intimations of human depravity and corruption. We know too much for sure on this score to respond as we once did to hints. There is no doubt that Hiroshima and Buchenwald have made it harder to read *The Turn of the Screw*.

I do not deny the power of James's prose to arouse and control feeling. But for us to regard the tale as anything more than simply a scary story we must be able to feel the evil in *The Turn of the Screw* as actual and necessary to the events — "actual" in the sense that a verifiable social and psychological situation is being adumbrated, "necessary" because the story could not be told apart from the conditions James presents. What makes Henry James superior as a mystery writer to, say, August Derleth or John Collier, is this huge substream of social fact underlying his images of terror.

The Turn of the Screw portrays a nineteenth-century society organized so as to make victimization almost inevitable for children in the situation of Miles and Flora. Bly itself is the symbol of the English social order. "Wasn't it just a storybook over which I had fallen a-doze and a-dream?" muses the ingenuous, perceptive governess at the close of her first day. "No; it was a big, ugly, antique, but convenient house embodying a few features of a building still older, half replaced and half utilised, in which I had the fancy of our being almost as lost as a handful of passengers in a great drifting ship." One does not need to be familiar with James's use elsewhere of house-and-garden imagery, as in *The Portrait of a Lady*, to see that Bly is not simply a gentleman's country-seat but represents also hierarchy itself, a "big, ugly, antique, but convenient" institution. The drifting ship metaphor, so far from vitiating this intimation, further reinforces the notion of the house as microcosm of a society lacking proper control and moral responsibility.

There are at Bly but two aristocrats, for the actual master resolutely remains in London, enforcing his hands-off policy. As the governess sees them, Miles and Flora are "a pair of little grandees" or "princes of the blood" abandoned to the care of a staff of servants. At the head of and distinctly above these lower orders, but demonstrably below her grandees, is the governess. She stands at the very fulcrum of the social tensions with which the story is filled. (A vicar's daughter, as Lloyd Warner or any sociologist would attest, is an ideal observer of social class.) Through her, we become acutely conscious not only of selfish irresponsibility at the top but of the reticent, conscious superiority of the two lovely children and of the mute humility of Mrs. Grose. We also sense the governess's own reserve and social timidity in her dealings with Miles and Flora. We gradually learn how Peter Quint, when he was alive, manipulated the class situation to his licentious ends. Comprehending all these various manifestations is the overwhelming fact of communication between classes at Bly as strained, formal, incomplete. Even the governess's love cannot make it otherwise.

One of Henry James's special marks as artist is his knack of suggesting obliquely, succinctly, but unmistakably a whole series of perceptions within a short scene or, indeed, paragraph. A notable instance of this symbolizing skill, illustrating James at his best as social commentator, occurs when, on their way to church one Sunday morning, the governess makes this observation to herself about young Miles at her side: ''Turned out for Sunday by his uncle's tailor, who had had a free hand and a notion of pretty waistcoats and of his grand little air, Miles's whole title to independence, the rights of his sex and situation, were so stamped upon him that if he had suddenly struck for freedom I should have had nothing to say.'' This brief comment, ostensibly about clothing, touches almost every manifestation of wrong already hinted at in the narrative. Clothes, of course, are to be taken no more casually in James's world than architecture or manners; each can be endowed with profound implications. Here the reference to waistcoats recalls at once Peter Quint, his peculiar pretensions, and his corrupting influence. In the first conversation between Mrs. Grose and the governess (after the ghost's initial appearance on the tower), Quint's history and character are revealed in a series of questions and answers having to do with social appearance. ''He has no hat.'' . . . ''He never wore his hat, but he did wear— well, there were waistcoats missed!'' . . . ''A gentleman?'' gasped Mrs. Grose, ''confounded, stupified: a gentleman *he*?'' Miles's debonair appearance, then, may derive not from innocent, embellished beauty but from a tailor's ''free hand'' (the master is always giving some servant a free hand with his dead brother's children) and from the example of another waistcoat-fancier. Thus a fond, innocuous remark assumes sinister overtones, just as the boy's ''grand little air'' may now be a similarly deceiving description of duplicity.

His demands for freedom, too, can no longer appear simply as boyish impatience; they hint at licentious revolt, conditioned by ''sex and situation,'' against the governess's moral restraint. But, again, is not Miles's ''title to independence'' a valid one? Might not the sexual aggressor (if there is one) be unconsciously the living companion and not the dead one? Each of these innuendoes is wrapped in the language, so to speak, of a society columnist reporting a scene. This reporter, however, is a young girl from the provinces, very much on the defensive before the waistcoat and what it represents.

Another essential ingredient of the mystery and horror of this tale consists of words and confidences that are *not* spoken. Conversations in *The Turn of the*

Screw are always skirting "forbidden ground." This helps immeasurably to thicken the dramatic atmosphere, throwing as it does so much weight on the frantic imaginings of the twenty-year-old girl. But secrets and silences, useful as they are for ghostly effect, often originate in the social relation of superior and subordinate, whereby confidences may go downward but not up. "There were things enough, taking one with another, to chatter about," she remarks at one point of the children, "if one went very fast and knew by instinct when to go around. They pulled with an art of their own the strings of my invention and my memory; and nothing else perhaps, when I thought of such occasions afterwards, gave me so the suspicion of being watched from under cover. It was in any case over *my* life, *my* past, and *my* friends alone that we could take anything like our ease. . . ." The conspicuous reticence of these charming small aristocrats effectively stifles the "monstrous utterance of words" that would bring the ghosts and their corruption out into the open. But as these gross questions "died away on my lips," the governess reports, "I said to myself that I should indeed help them to represent something infamous, if by pronouncing them, I should violate as rare a little case of instinctive delicacy as any schoolroom, probably, had ever known. When I said to myself: '*they* have the manners to be silent, and you, trusted as you are, the baseness to speak!' " The ironic freight which the words "delicacy" and "manners" is made to bear here is considerable, as James makes vividly clear later when little Flora loses her patrician secretiveness and goes to pieces in a flood of filthy invective. Miles alone keeps his aristocratic guard up until the very last minute.

I trust no one has received the impression from these summary quotations and comments on the sociological aspect of *The Turn of the Screw* that the story can be reduced to this dimension or that James, in some simple-minded American way, intended a wholesale condemnation of social class. His sense of the complexity of human experience and motive is, I trust, sufficiently obvious to destroy both simplifications. By the tale's end it is equally clear that the governess has been both the instrument and object of exploration; we see through her as we see the events unfolding through her eyes. The narrative exposes both her insights and insecurities, her perceptions of the situation and her involvement in it. If the ghosts are in one sense her personifications of past and present social iniquity at Bly they have also been magnified and distorted by her ignorance, given a sexual twist by her infatuation with the master and by her middle-class taboos. Her all-too-human vision of evil is then forced violently and prematurely upon little Miles in the final, fatal confrontation with the ghost of Quint. The boy's death, consequently, is both her fault and that of the system which permits the abuse of childhood. It may, of course, also be Miles's own fault.

IV

To return for a moment to Miles in his pretty waistcoat; it is not, I think, a coincidence that the party at Bly is on the way to church. The phrase "turned out for Sunday'' points to a religious — indeed, Christian — side to *The Turn of the Screw*, one apparent to every reader, and a dimension that Robert Heilman has examined brilliantly in *"The Turn of the Screw* as Poem.'' To approach this matter from the angle of clothing and social behavior, however, puts it into a somewhat different perspective from that most critics have employed. That viewpoint is heavily ironic, for the religious problem which James dramatizes is as much a personal as a universal parable; it is one of individual shortcomings, idiosyncracies, and eventual failure. Miles's death must be accepted as a defeat for the forces of righteousness; for the causes of catastrophe for the child lie so clearly in his governess's theory and practice of Christianity that any theological view of the tale as a modern morality play, a latter-day version of the Fall, must also consider the social psychology of the Christians involved.

For this purpose, as for the illumination of class tensions, James's choice of an immature vicar's daughter as actor-narrator was a brilliant one. There is, first of all, the religious vocabulary that falls so naturally from her lips. ''I had an absolute certainty that I could see again what I had already seen,'' she remarks early in the story, ''but something within me said that by offering myself bravely as the sole subject of such experience, by accepting, by inviting, by surmounting it all, I should serve as an expiatory victim and guard the tranquillity of my companions. The children, in especial, I should thus fence about and absolutely save.'' These brave words do not, as it turns out, do the trick. This is not to say that James mocks the girl's self-sacrifice, but he does employ the Biblical imagery with heavy ambiguity. The governess imagines herself ''an expiatory victim'' assuring salvation for her threatened innocents, the ''angels,'' the ''holy infants.'' The ghost of Quint, to her mind, is the Devil himself invading Bly-Eden with his ''poison.'' Her own role, as this Miltonic vocabulary suggests, is more than a ''sister of Charity'' or a saint; it is closer to the atonement of Christ.

For an inexperienced young girl to cast herself so confidently in the guise of savior inevitably raises questions both as to the adequacy of her formulations of the evil she fights and the quality of her own spiritual life. On each count the weakness of her mere unaided innocence is implied. Though Professor Heilman believes she has ''an inquiring lay mind with a religious sense but without precise theological tools,'' I see the governess rather as a child bravely but mistakenly grappling with a problem she does not comprehend. Hence much of the responsibility—and this tale is at heart a study of responsibility—for Miles's fatal ''dispossession'' must be laid to the governess's insistent oversimplification of evil. Here is a religious imagination that defines iniquity as an either-or condition. One is either pure or vile, never a human mixture. Thus the language of her naïve dualism converts Flora at one bound from ''angel'' to ''demon.'' As for the boy, ''If Miles is innocent, what, then, am *I?*'' is her instinctive query to Mrs. Grose when doubts begin to assail them.

This doctrinaire outlook stems, as Joseph Firebaugh has pointed out, from the governess's almost frantic fear lest her little charges learn too much about life.

To her black-and-white mind, Quint's influence on Miles has not been merely permissively lax; instead, "the imagination of all evil *had* been opened up to him." If the boy is allowed to go off to another school (the obvious symbol of knowledge) he will simply be "turned out again" with more "bravado" and "dishonor" on his little head. Far better, then, to remain innocently and, if need be, ignorantly within the park grounds. Such a cruelly narrow vision of childish development marks the final scene with special irony, for when the phantom appears for the last time at "the haunted pane" he is "a sentinel before a prison." May not Miles's desperate search for a way out of the prison of Bly mean that the governess and not the ghost is his warden? It is she who has sought to suppress the child's natural desire to see the world. Like Jo March in *Little Women*, she appears to long for flat-irons to put on the heads of her charges to keep them from growing up. Her whole philosophy of time slips out within a pair of parentheses when she observes "(for all futures are rough!)."

On herself, however, the governess imposes no such limits to the knowledge of corruption. Like Oedipus, "a dreadful boldness of mind" urges her to uncover every secret. "But I shall get it out of you yet!" is her cry to poor timid Mrs. Grose. To herself she confesses, "all the justice within me ached for the proof that it [Miles's imagination of all evil] could ever have flowered into an act." Like Oedipus, too, the young guardian at Bly exhibits at times *hubris* so boundless that even the diclosure of Flora's depraved vocabulary is welcomed because it "so justifies" her suspicions. But though the girl shares with the Greeks a belief in "absolute intelligence," she never, within the narrative at least, achieves that spiritual humility before the gods which would make her a genuinely religious person. She can perhaps unravel the Sphinx's riddle of original sin but she never arrives at Colonus.

In fact, the governess never gets inside a church. "Oh, I'm not fit for church!" she wails after glimpsing the ghost, and this remark, like almost everything in this remarkable tale, has its ironies. Though she yearns for "the almost spiritual help of the hassock" during the crucial interview with Miles in the churchyard, it is not to God she turns. Indeed, this girl never once prays. Any impartial appraisal of her spiritual life would find her neither contrite, nor merciful nor joyous nor trusting in divine power.

Her religion instead is an absolutist love of purity that issues in blind truth-seeking and insistence upon innocence at any price. In mistaken devotion to this rigid creed she sacrifices Flora almost gladly and even, reluctantly, Miles. Hers is a shallow and dangerous Christianity that by turns sentimentalizes and derogates the innocence of youth. Yet the melancholy fact is that this naïve girl is the only conscience, the sole moral imagination in the tale. For everyone else at Bly, religion consists simply of proper Sunday attire, walks through the park to Evensong, and the day off. As a consequence, there exists in the world of *The Turn of the Screw* no moral force adequately and maturely able to arm the governess's defense of childhood against the depravities and laxities of a secular order. This is the pathetic but unavoidable conclusion we are forced to when we accept Bly as the image of an actual nineteenth-century society with real people in it as well as ghosts.

V

The common reader who has read and reread, with growing perplexity, *The Turn of the Screw* and even followed some of the critics through the winding maze of words they have constructed about the tale, may well conclude by throwing up his hands. After all, he has an invitation to dismiss the work from Henry James; "it is a piece of ingenuity pure and simple," he wrote in the Preface to the collected works, "of cold artistic calculation, an *amusette* to catch those not easily caught (the 'fun' of the capture of the merely witless being ever but small), the jaded, the disillusioned, the fastidious." If the author himself admits to having composed nothing more serious than an *amusette* to "catch" blasé readers of *Collier's Weekly*, what possible use, then, can this ghost story serve for students of American culture? Can a piece of fiction so filled with calculated irony and ambiguity, artfully designed to pull the reader's leg, tell *anything* about James's world of 1898? These are legitimate queries which raise the larger issue of art's function in cultural history, of which *The Turn of the Screw* is but an exaggerated instance.

There is no doubt that humor, irony, hyperbole, and all the other modulations of tone and mode available to the novelist distort what the historian or sociologist would call the content of his work. But they do not destroy it, any more than the writer's individuality and the privacy of his utterance destroy the essential publicness of his book. All artists — even Emily Dickinson behind her father's hedge in Amherst or Ezra Pound behind the bars at St. Elizabeth's—play a triple role. They are of necessity the creatures, creators, and critics of their culture. Henry James is no exception, though certain allowances must be made for his Anglo-American outlook.

In the case of *The Turn of the Screw*, for instance, we may not take his parable of aristocratic family life (or absence thereof) as applying necessarily to the United States. But the author *is* American-born, writing for an American maga-zine audience, and with marked success. He chooses children as actors and childhood as theme, and thus, consciously or not, connects himself to an American literary tradition. The task of the historian of culture becomes that of distinguishing James's contribution to that running dialogue about innocence carried on by his fellow American writers during the greater part of the nine-teenth century.

Stated in the refreshing idiom of Leslie Fiedler, *The Turn of the Screw* signals an end to Wordsworth and Jean Jacques Rousseau. So far from continuing to celebrate the innocent eye of youth as moral norm, James dramatizes, through his precocious infant, his Bad Boy, and above all, through his virginal maiden, the inadequacies and dangers of inexperience and immaturity. After a century of sentimentality, this ghost story asserts with deadly seriousness the presence of original sin in the minds of the very young. Of course, James does not deny the beauty of innocence. It is of the very essence of this story that the tensions between the two never relax. As the governess observes of the ghosts' influence on Miles and Flora, "they've made them — their two friends, I mean — still cleverer even than nature did; for it was wondrous material to play on!" This, in a nutshell, is the tragic insight of *The Turn of the Screw*.

To be merely innocent is no longer a condition worth venerating by adults. But to be bereft of innocence in the sudden, violent fashion of Miles and his governess is equally tragic — and, in a morally aware society, unnecessary. The searing scene of Miles's dispossession is dramatically and emotionally needed, but part of its delayed impact is the reader's realization that socially and pyschologically such moral experiences are neither necessary nor desirable. They are, in fact, disastrous. Without directly mentioning it, James sets the reader to imagining counterversions of adult-child relations, like, for instance, Horace Bushnell's notions of Christian nurture, in which childhood is protected against its own innocence and sinfulness and gradually introduced to the meaning of moral maturity. For the reader of 1964, at any rate, these are legitimate implications to be drawn from James's fairy tale and ones that set *The Turn of the Screw* off from, and criticize, other American versions of initiation experience.

Does not James, too, redefine nineteenth-century platitudes about the moral imagination of childhood? Without losing admiration for the governess's pluck or sympathy for Miles's wavering allegiance to corruption, one is made to see how fatally much children and adolescents *cannot* see. Not that adults in *The Turn of the Screw* are more aware; Mrs. Grose and Peter Quint each, in opposite ways, are inferior moralists to Miles's and Flora's companion. There is on this score, James asserts, no qualitative or guaranteed difference between young and old. It is the author's tactic, however, to explode the contrary myth by pretending to honor it. In the process James revises what in earlier writers had all too frequently been sentimental or false values. More significantly, he prepares the way in the twentieth century for writers like Hemingway, Faulkner, Eudora Welty, and Salinger, carriers of the tradition of writing about childhood's "primal unwarped world" that for a century and a quarter has been one distinguishing mark of our national letters. In this history the little *amusette* Henry James wrote plays a more central role than its sly author may have foreseen. For *The Turn of the Screw*, despite all ambiguities, pays childhood the ultimate tribute of taking it with utter seriousness.

Notes

1. See Leon Edel, ed., *The Selected Letters of Henry James* (New York: Farrar, Straus, and Cudahy, 1955), p. 146.

2. Mary McCarthy, "The Fact in Fiction," *Partisan Review* 27, no. 3 (Summer 1960):451.

3. For a representative but by no means exhaustive collection of essays, see Gerald Willen, ed., *A Casebook on Henry James's The Turn of the Screw* (New York: Crowell, 1960). In addition to the text of the story and James's own Preface, this volume reprints the following articles: Edna Kenton, "Henry James to the Ruminant Reader: The Turn of the Screw"; Edmund Wilson, "The Ambiguity of Henry James"; Nathan Bryllion Fagin, "Another Reading of *The Turn of the Screw*"; A Radio Symposium: Katherine Anne Porter, Allen Tate, Mark Van Doren, "James: *The Turn of the Screw*"; A. J. A. Waldock, "Mr. Edmund Wilson and *The Turn of the Screw*"; Robert Heilman, "*The Turn of the Screw* as Poem"; Glenn A. Reed, "Another Turn on James' 'The Turn of the Screw'"; Oliver Evans, "James's Air of Evil: *The Turn of the Screw*": Charles Hoffmann, "Innocence and Evil in James's *The Turn of the Screw*"; Oscar Cargill, "Henry James as Freudian Pioneer"; John Silver, "A Note on the Freudian Reading of *The Turn of the Screw*"; Harold C. Goddard, "A Pre-Freudian Reading of *The Turn of the Screw*"; John Lydenburg, "The Governess Turns the Screws"; Joseph J. Firebaugh, "Inadequacy in Eden: Knowledge and *The Turn of the Screw*"; Alexander E. Jones, "Point of View in *The Turn of the Screw*." One additional essay of considerable insight might be added: Donald P. Costello, "The Structure of *The Turn of the Screw*," *Modern Language Notes* 75, no. 4 (April 1960): 312–21.

Bibliography

Banta, M. *Henry James and the Occult: The Great Extension*. Bloomington: Indiana University Press, 1972.

Coveney, P. *The Image of Childhood; The Individual and Society: A Study of the Theme in English Literature*. Baltimore: Penguin Books, 1967.

Cranfill, T. M., and R. L. Clark, Jr., eds. *An Anatomy of The Turn of the Screw*. Austin: University of Texas Press, 1965.

Edel, L. *The Selected Letters of Henry James*. New York: Farrar, Straus, and Cudahy, 1955.

———. *Henry James: The Treacherous Years, 1894–1901*. New York: Lippincott, 1969.

———. *Henry James: The Master, 1901–1916*. New York: Lippincott, 1972.

Kimbrough, R., ed. *The Turn of the Screw. An Authoritative Text, Backgrounds and Sources, Essays in Criticism*. New York: Norton Critical Edition, W. W. Norton, 1966.

Samuels, C. T. *The Ambiguity of Henry James*. Urbana: University of Illinois Press, 1971.

Shive, M. *The Fictional Children of Henry James*. Chapel Hill: University of North Carolina Press, 1969.

ALBERT E. STONE

Autobiography and the Childhood of the American Artist: The Example of Louis Sullivan

Autobiography, it is a truism to observe, is one of the richest resources we have for the history of American childhood. Quantitatively, the bibliographies of Lillard and Kaplan mention nearly 7,000 personal narratives published in the United States before 1961, and very many have been added since that date.[1] Qualitatively, too, the variety of memorable life stories which concentrate on remembered experiences and emotions of childhood and youth is likewise great. The notable works of this sort cover virtually the whole history of American autobiography, which, as James Cox has pointed out, is a history almost exactly coterminous with our national experience.[2] From Benjamin Franklin to Maya Angelou, some of the most imaginative chroniclers of the self have been principally preoccupied with the early years and stages of their lives and careers. *The Autobiography,* we recall, turns away from the achievements of the scientist, diplomat, and sage to memorialize chiefly the life of the young Franklin. *I Know Why the Caged Bird Sings* closes with the birth of the sixteen-year-old author's illegitimate child. Other autobiographers between 1771 and 1969 whose re-created lives virtually end with adulthood include Lucy Larcom, Helen Keller, and Mary Antin; Mark Twain, Henry James, and Louis Sullivan; Frederick Douglass, Richard Wright, and Claude Brown. Hence anyone exploring the patterns and particularities of American childhood in all its somatic, social, racial, and sexual variety will find the autobiography an important avenue into the heart of our diverse, individualistic culture. As Lillard observes, "autobiography is as near as mankind gets to a unified, lasting, prima facie version of what happens in an individual's lifetime."[3]

But if by "history" we mean both the scientific and literary analysis of the available records of the past—an aim persuasively argued by J. H. Hexter—then autobiography is also one of the most elusive and ambiguous sources of cultural data.[4] This double-barreled aspect has long been recognized by literary scholars and social scientists interested in autobiography. Classic definitions of the genre like those of Gusdorf, Pascal, and Hart emphasize a problem all recognize— autobiography (including journal, memoir, and reminiscence) traditionally bridges history and fiction, because it mixes memory and imagination.[5] It is, in

Jean Starobinski's terms, both "history" and "discourse": "history" because it *re*-creates a past assumed actually to have occurred; "discourse" because it re-*creates* through imagination as well as memory. Historicity and fictionality merge in autobiography's overarching aim, which is the identity of the self as both actor and author. F. R. Hart has precisely defined this autobiographical impulse and distinguished it from that of fiction; "... in understanding fiction one seeks an imaginative grasp of another's meaning," he writes; "... in understanding personal history one seeks an imaginative comprehension of another's historic identity. 'Meaning' and 'identity' are not the same kind of reality and do not make the same demands. One has no obligation to a fantasy."[6]

Many social scientists, however, feel no obligation to take autobiography seriously, despite its relevance to problems of identity and individual experience of cultural process—hence the debate among sociologists, anthropologists, and even psychologists over the proper use of autobiography as an idiographic tool. Herbert Blumer was one of the first to point out that although personal documents of this kind contain a wealth of pertinent information, these data come in a form which resists theoretical application. He observes that "while the experiences [in autobiography] have a tough independent character which enables them to be a test of a theoretical conception, at other times they seem, metaphorically speaking, to be helpless before the imposition of a theoretical view." Blumer concludes that at best personal histories enable the scientist "to make out *a case* for the theoretical interpretation."[7] Two other scientists who have sought to demonstrate the usefulness of autobiography despite the difficulties of interpretation are Gordon Allport and Erik Erikson. Both have been alert to the pitfalls Blumer mentions. In *The Use of Personal Documents in Psychological Science* Allport has written: "Acquaintance with the particular case, a sense of its patterned character and its individualized laws of action, stand at the gateway of generalized knowledge and at its terminus at the point of application."[8] Erikson's studies of Luther and Gandhi, like his analyses of youthful identity, white and black, in contemporary America, are in part based upon a sensitive use of autobiographical writings. Of these sources Erikson writes with the insight of both a scientist and a literary critic: "... each given medium (diary, conversation or autobiography) has its own formal laws and serves tradition and personal style. As to unconscious motivation," he continues, "we must always remember that the autobiographer has not agreed to a therapeutic contract by which he promises to put into words all his 'free associations,' so that we may help him to compare them with inner and outer 'reality.' "[9] *Gandhi's Truth* is evidence of Erikson's own finesse in "helping" the autobiographer articulate the realities of his own experiences.

If Allport, Erikson, and others meet some of the social scientists' objections to autobiography — objections as to their representativeness, reliability, and adequacy — nevertheless some serious and intriguing issues remain. The problem of relating the individual text to general theory is particularly difficult in the special case of autobiographies of artists, writers, and other individuals of extraordinary talent. Genius is mysterious whatever its era or culture, and is likely to elude all abstractions. But when an artistic genius writes an account of his or her own life, and especially of the childhood and youthful years, some of the mystery ought to be dispelled. Through the proper understanding of such unusual narratives one should find light thrown on some crucial areas of human experience. Looking inward to the self therein created, one might observe new but common dimensions of personal identity and the process of its discovery and expression; looking outward to the history and culture within which that self and career unfolded, one ought to see more clearly certain social concomitants of the creative process. For as Phyllis Greenacre has pointed out, one of the social functions of the genius is to explore and articulate the most important of normal human problems. In modern culture, one of these crucial problems is personal identity. "The study of identity," Erikson has written, "becomes as strategic in our time as the study of sexuality was in Freud's time."[10] In a real sense, certain persons specialize in this problem. As Greenacre observes, "only young children, philosophers, artists, and certain sick individuals concern themselves constantly with questions of their own identity."[11]

Preoccupation with this double phenomenon of identity and creativity, as dramatized with special form and force in autobiography, impelled Greenacre in 1957 to publish a challenging essay, "The Childhood of the Artist: Libidinal Phase Development and Giftedness."[12] She was inspired to confront this age-old issue by reading a number of British autobiographies published in the 1940s and 1950s. Of these sources she remarks, "In a naive way it might seem that the study of autobiography supplemented by biography would be the method *par excellence* of understanding the individual genius. What could be more firsthand and authentic than what a man writes about himself? It is, as it were, from the horse's mouth."

This is of course an illusion. Every analyst knows that the account which a patient insistently gives at the beginning of his treatment, "for the record" as it were, is not only imprecise but often filled with gross distortions and characterized by startling omissions. It is not only that the patient is not onto himself and aware of his deeper motivations, but that the individual memory is a great remaker of events, modeling and remodeling them throughout life with an extraordinary plasticity to make the cloak of remembrance do duty for one occasion after another, to meet both needs and fashions—with all of the skill and less noise than a good tailor. (*EG*, p. 480)

Then she proceeds to specify some of the circumstances of the autobiographical act which catch her psychoanalyst's eye. It is "always produced for an audience, and often for an occasion. The audience always consists of at least two sections: the self and 'the others'—whoever they may be. These three factors," she adds, "(occasion, self-estimate, and impression on others) combine to make pressures here, expansions there, possible explanations at one time which in further editions are treated as facts; and so it goes" (*EG*, p. 481). The central aspect stressed is the autobiographer's reliance upon memory rather than pure imagination. This raises special problems which the psychoanalyst may perceive more readily than the literary critic: "If all memory, as we ordinarily use the term, would seem to be but a cloak constantly in process of renovation, sometimes with gross additions of new material—in other words, if all memory has a screening function, how else can we understand the man within it? Certainly we must examine the cloak and know that it reveals much of the man within and is genuinely a part of him, but neither mistake it for the man within, nor discard it as of no value because it is not he" (*EG*, p. 482).

Nevertheless, Greenacre does not proceed to examine any cloaks. Instead of a psychoanalytic reading, say, of Stephen Spender's remarkable memoir, *World Within World,* she generalizes broadly about the creative person's childhood and youth. To be sure, her theories are drawn from autobiographies like Spender's — she also mentions Helen Keller and Norbert Wiener — as well as from case histories and from other psychoanalytic writers like Ernst Kris.[13] But memory's records are everywhere subordinated to the hypotheses they have helped to suggest. The cultural critic familiar with the insights and the warnings of Blumer, Allport, and Erikson is in a quandary — anxious to use Greenacre's ideas and experience but deterred by the dangers of proceeding without specific evidence and illustration. What seems more fruitful than a theoretical analysis is a close look at an autobiography of the childhood of a genius, one whose "patterned character" and "individualized laws of action" may be explored both by the psychoanalytic perspective of Greenacre and by wider, more cultural approaches. In this way hitherto unconscious motivations may be identified in a text seen also in terms of form, tradition, and personal style. Examining a personal narrative in these ways may help one perceive more clearly how autobiography is both a unique artifact and an important idiographic tool for the study of personality and culture.

Such a potentially clarifying, exemplary text is Louis Sullivan's *The Autobiography of an Idea* (1924).[14] One of the most famous narratives of an American childhood, it is also the personal history and testament of the father of the skyscraper and one of the acknowledged geniuses of modern architecture. Since Sullivan was an architect and not a poet or novelist, his autobiography may provide a clearer (but not simpler) case study of identity and creativity than, say, Henry James's *A Small Boy and Others* or Richard Wright's *Black Boy*. Words were their natural medium of creative expression, but Sullivan's was stone and concrete. It is true that Sullivan was also a writer, the author of *Kindergarten Chats* and other essays and prose poems. But his prime mode of creativity was the public building; the Wainwright and Guaranty skyscrapers, the Chicago Auditorium, the Transportation Building at the Columbian Exposition of 1893, the Getty Tomb, the Carson, Pirie, Scott department store are some of his most famous monuments. The fact that Sullivan discusses in detail only one or two of these historic buildings in his autobiography is part of the puzzle confronting the reader. What is the relationship, we wonder, between those buildings and the identity revealed in the *Autobiography?* Moreover, the author keeps insisting that his is first of all a *child's* story and only secondarily the memoir of an adult and world-famous architect. Hence few American life histories would appear to offer a better opportunity for tracing the intricate, hidden lines and links between the experiences and emotions of childhood and the actual artistic achievements of later life. As a "cloak of remembrance," *The Autobiography of an Idea* is neatly tailored to fit — and mask — the form of its artificer, and the attentive reader must play literary critic, historian, and social scientist in order to appreciate its special sartorial style and significance.

We begin by noting that Sullivan deliberately invites us to interpret his life and identity as both particular and representative. This is the intent of its deceptively awkward title. The "idea" of which Louis Sullivan is the particular manifesta- tion is the traditional Romantic vision of life unfolding as emotion, instinct, intuition, imagination, Personality, Genius, Egocosm. The "autobiography," on the other hand, is the story of a single "compacted personality" (p. 168) created in the natural and social circumstances of a New England childhood. This "story of a child's dream of power" (p. 272) devotes fully three-fourths of its length to the first eighteen years of Sullivan's experience, for it is his repeated assertion that beginnings are vital. Man's personality and powers as creator are established in infancy and cannot be essentially altered. This tenet and didactic principle is articulated in a memorable passage whose oratorical rhetoric is likewise typical. "Thus from the abyss of Memory's stillness," he writes of himself,

that child comes into being within Life's dream, within the dream of eternal time and space; and in him we behold what we were and still are. Environment may influence but it cannot alter. For it is the child in multiple and in multiple series that creates the flowing environment of thought and deed that shall continuously mature in its due time. . . . Thus in a memory-mirror may we re-discover ourselves. . . .

We see the tidal wave of children moving on and on, we partly under their dominion, they partly under ours. But theirs is the new; and, as ancients, we move on, unchanged from the children that we were— . . .

With this image in view the narrator has laid extended stress upon an authentic study of child life. (p. 93)

The "child life" is Sullivan's own but is universalized, first of all, by means of a third-person narrative, a strategy reminiscent of *The Education of Henry Adams* and one which masks the individual behind the type or archetype. This enlarged self is invoked in very un-Adamsian language. "The only one is Ego—," exclaims Sullivan, "the 'I am'—the unique—. Without Ego, which is Life, man vanishes. Ego signifies identity. . . . It is what we call the spiritual, a term now becoming interchangeable with the physical. It is the sign and symbol of man's immense Integrity—the 'I am that I am.' To it the Earth, the world of humanity, the multitudes, the universe—become an Egocosm'' (pp. 271–72). Sullivan's language, echoing the romantic rhetoric and belief of nineteenth-century thinkers from Coleridge, Froebel, and Whitman to Nietzsche and Spencer, here imparts a deliberately vatic tone to the *Autobiography*. As their capitalization and overtones suggest, ''Ego,'' ''Identity,'' and ''Integrity'' are Transcendental rather than Freudian terms. In fact, Freud's name is never mentioned by Sullivan himself or by his biographer, Willard Connely, or by his most acute critic, Sherman Paul.[15] Nevertheless, though the autobiographer was apparently ignorant of Freudian thought, his linkage of spiritual to physical existence and his assumption of projection as a basic process connecting inner and outer experience indicate Sullivan's awareness of the somatic and social as well as the spiritual sources of identity. Man is indeed Spirit but not disembodied Spirit. This offers a challenge to the post-Freudian reader: confronting Sullivan's sometimes vague, often clumsy, but always symbolic (that is, overdetermined) language, to elicit its multiple meanings through the insights and theories of Greenacre, Erikson, and others. What encourages this neo-Freudian decoding, while also obstructing it, is the style of *The Autobiography of an Idea*, which has long confused and exasperated readers who, like Connely, find its ''by-paths of philosophizing or sentimentalism'' ambiguous and annoying.[16] John Summerson, too, is correct in calling Sullivan ''a colossal sentimentalist'' with a style ''singularly unpalatable'' to the modern ear. Nevertheless, he accurately identifies the expressive power and genuine fascination of this grandiloquent confession, which he sees as gushing ''with the innocent self-love of the self-made America of the turn of the century, the rugged, generous, loose-limbed, eternally philosophizing America invented by Whitman and Emerson.''[17]

Viewed in these terms as a late memorial to Transcendentalism, Sullivan's story represents a self-conscious effort to turn back the cultural clock, to reinfuse twentieth-century thought and architectural practice with the nineteenth-century values of subjectivism and organic naturalism. Through metaphors of his own experience the aging designer seeks to express the tenets of Whitman, Greenough, and Thoreau in a world now dominated by the followers of Dewey and Daniel Burnham. His book is ''historical'' in other respects as well. The account, child-centered and spiritual at the core, deals at its edges with significant public events and movements. Cultural experience is recorded from the perspective of a generalized democratic American voice which is in reality that of a highly idiosyncratic son of Irish and Swiss immigrants. The *Autobiography* is, therefore, one of the earliest imaginative works, along with the plays of Eugene O'Neill, depicting American life from the viewpoint of an Irish-American. His idyllic childhood in South Reading, the Civil War, the westward and cityward movements typified by Chicago, the Columbian Exposition of 1893 — these and other social events and institutions are memorialized, but presented in passing, recalled less for their intrinsic interest than as aspects and occasions for the definition of Sullivan's youthful identity. That self is not primarily a historic identity, nor is his narrative essentially a memoir. Despite its presentation of the author as a representative American in the era from 1856 to 1895, Sullivan's story, as Connely's biography makes plain, has too many signal suppressions and omissions for his aim to be principally historical. Even as architectural history, the *Autobiography* neglects matters of prime concern; not only are major buildings left undiscussed and the history of Adler and Sullivan's famous firm sketchily treated, but important names like Frank Lloyd Wright's never appear. In the private realm, too, the gaps are striking. There is no mention of Sullivan's brother, wife, sister-in-law, or of many other intimates, male and female. Equally significant is his virtual silence about the last twenty-nine years of his career. One has only to compare this narrative with the life of another highly self-conscious architectural genius, Wright's *An Autobiography,* to realize the narrow range of Sullivan's historical imagination.

These silences and suppressions can in part be explained by the circumstances of composition and publication. In 1922, when at the instigation of friends Sullivan began writing his autobiography for the *Journal* of the American Institute of Architects, the old man had to look back on a career and personal life in shambles. Separated from wife, brother, and sister-in-law, Sullivan had long since also been separated from Dankmar Adler. Equally sad were the artistic waste and disappointments of his last three decades, during which he executed plans for only about twenty buildings. So impoverished had Sullivan become that in 1918 the designer of the Auditorium Building was forced to give up the offices he had long occupied in its proud Tower. Moreover his attempts through *Kindergarten Chats* to instruct the younger generation of architects had proved a failure. Living alone in wretched health in a run-down hotel, Sullivan had ample grounds for ignoring the bleak present and the bitter years since 1895. Small wonder, indeed, that this autobiography leaps over these decades to re-create the world of his childhood and youth. Philosophy, personal pain, and the prospect of lonely death conspired in this choice.

Some readers, recognizing these limitations on the book's historical aims and achievements, look elsewhere for an appropriate handle by means of which to grasp Sullivan's central purpose as autobiographer. One promising option is to accept the *Autobiography* neither as history nor confession but as a self-conscious work of art, the effusion of a lyric poet in prose. Style, language, narrative structure — all direct attention to an essentially aesthetic effect, which more closely resembles that of Emerson's *Essays, Walden,* or *Democratic Vistas* than the personal histories of Franklin or Henry Adams. Dramatizing himself as the Sayer, the Orator, the Literatus, Sullivan offers his book as an unparaphrasable prose poem. This intent is implied from the opening lines. Here, rather than placing himself in social and historical time, Sullivan establishes his original identity as a figure in a pastoral romance. ''Once upon a time there was a village in New England called South Reading,'' he begins.

Here lived a little boy of five years. That is to say he nested with his grandparents on a miniature farm of twenty-four acres, a mile or so removed from the center of gravity and activity which was called Main Street. It was a main street of the day and generation, and so was the farm proper to its time and place.

Eagerly the grandparents had for some time urged that the child come to them for a while; and after a light shower of mother tears — the father indifferent — consent was given and the child was taken on his way into the wilderness lying ten miles north of the city of Boston. (p. 9)

Only after the "once upon a time" rural setting has been set against Main Street does the autobiographer locate his beginnings in the usual terms anticipated by the "exigent and meticulous" reader. "Now lest it appear that this child had come suddenly out of nothing into being at the age of five," he explains, "we must needs authenticate him by sketching his prior tumultuous life. He was born of woman in the usual way at 22 South Bennett Street, Boston, Mass., U.S.A., on the third day of September, 1856" (pp. 9–10). As Sherman Paul has emphasized, this opening establishes Sullivan in the natural world of a pre-Civil War Yankee America — an actual child playing a mythic, rural role. The "tumultuous" Boston and Bennett Street world is not denied but is clearly subordinated to the pastoral image. Sullivan's imaginative intent is repeated in the larger patterns of the narrative which follows; not only are beginnings emphasized over subsequent events, but metaphoric rather than matter-of-fact meanings predominate and persist.

Everywhere in this literary transfiguration of reality the presence of Walt Whitman presides. In style, ideology, and subject matter, Sullivan's story reflects its author's thirty-six-year infatuation with *Leaves of Grass*, announced in 1887 with characteristic passion in the letter to the old poet at Camden.[18] "There Was a Child Went Forth" is the particular lyric which serves as *leit motif* to the *Autobiography*. Sullivan explicitly models himself on Whitman's child who "went forth every day,/And the first object he look'd upon, that object he became." The child's intimacy with nature and "all the changes of city and country" is the chief tie, but the identification runs deeper than this. The poetic child possesses parents who anticipate Andrienne and Patrick Sullivan in significant respects. The poet's "mother with mild words" exuding peace and protection as a "wholesome odor falling off her person" is an older, milder figure than the young Swiss beauty who shed the "shower of mother tears" at Louis's departure into the "wilderness," but in both cases the intimate connection of son to mother is emphasized. Fathers, too, are shown similarly. Whitman's child has a "father, strong, self-sufficient, manly, mean, anger'd, unjust/ The blow, the quick loud word, the tight bargain, the crafty lure." As for Patrick Sullivan "no need for discussion — he was Irish," explains his son, who proceeds to characterize the "indifferent" father as a physically powerful and graceful but "unlovely" dancing master, with "small repulsive eyes—the eyes of a pig" and a personality "self-centered — not even cold" (pp. 11, 14, 16). Though later experiences alter and enlarge this opening impression, the paternal presence remains one emotionally close to Whitman's. The self, whether as Egocosm or

Kosmos, is seen from the outset as a child grounded and growing in nature and a mother's fond love, but tied also in pride and hatred to a powerful father. Other parallels and debts to Whitman appear — in vocabulary, imagery, and a common fondness for imitating in prose the rhythms of opera and oratorio. None, however, is more central to Sullivan's self than the reiterated evocation of "There Was a Child Went Forth."

As literary artifact, however, *The Autobiography of an Idea* cannot duplicate Whitman's lyric — or any other poem — for it is a *prose* narrative with its own distinctive form as an unfolding story about the past. The narrative shape Sullivan has discovered in and imposed upon experience is the looping line, an intricate design of linear and circular movements in action, thought, and emotion. This pattern begins before his birth with his parents' separate arrival as immigrants in Boston, in which "the finger of fate was tracing a line in the air that was to lead on and on until it reached a finger tracing a line now and here" (p. 15). Henceforth Sullivan's story — both as journey and as creative achievement with pencil and pen — is seen as a single line (history, time, action) intersecting with or becoming a series of curves or loops (the imagination). The first such looping line is the "vacation" which the child takes from school in the countryside near his grandparents' farm. This is followed by the equally decisive trip by railroad to Newburyport and the ocean. Then he moves cityward and with his father surveys Boston and its environs. Later the loop grows longer as the boy travels with his grandfather to Lyons Falls, New York, in Chapters 8 and 9. Then his discoveries of Philadelphia and Chicago precede and enclose the largest loop of all, the eighteen-year-old Sullivan's journey to Paris, the Ecole des Beaux Arts, the Sistine Chapel, and back then to Chicago and a meteoric career. Each circular movement represents a stage in psychic development as well as the imaginative possession of a larger territory of actual experience. Moreover it is important to note that the young traveler and the old author both recognize this unfolding form of fate. Thus on the return trip from Lyons Falls the writer relates how the fourteen-year-old boy deliberately "took account of himself; he viewed the long, loop-like journey he had but recently completed, still fresh and free in memory's hold. . . . All these things, these acts, with their inspiring thoughts and emotions and reveries he had drawn into himself and shaped as one imposing drama, ushering in a new and greater life" (pp. 160–61). Unlike other American autobiographers like Franklin, Adams, or Malcolm X, Sullivan seldom contrasts former innocence or ignorance with present experience or awareness. It is an essential part of his mature vision of himself that the child perceived *then* what the man writes *now*.

One reason for this unity of vision is that for Sullivan memory and imagination are virtually interchangeable human faculties. Both are expressed in the tension of line and loop, of action and recollection, of historic actuality and creative dream. Memory's marriage with the imagination is consummated in the incantatory, Wordsworthian opening to Chapter 6. "As one in tranquillity gazes into the crystal depths called Memory," he writes, in search of sights and sounds and colors long since physically passed out from what is otherwise called memory; when one is intent, not upon re-calling but re-entering, he finds a double motion setting in[;] . . . there emerges to his view, as through a thinning haze, a broad vision assuming the color and movement of life once lived, of a world once seen and felt to be real, so likewise, the intensive soul moves eagerly forward descending through intervening atmospheric depths toward this oncoming reality of time and place, a reality growing clearer, more colorful, more vibrant, more alluring, more convincing—filling the eye, the ear with sound and color and movement, . . . So moving, the two great illusions, the two dreams of the single dreamer, accelerating, rush onward, and vanish both into a single life which is but a dream. (p. 91)

This is a crucial passage in the *Autobiography,* for it defines the book itself as "a single life which is but a dream." Memory's intersection with imagination is the "double motion" which has produced the lines and loops of this dreaming narrative of real life. The reader who is also familiar with Sullivan's masterful buildings with their facades and inner decorated spaces—for instance, the Carson, Pirie, Scott store — will recall the intricately looped, organic ornament set into their soaring or sweeping lines. (See Illustration 1.) Sullivan's artistic imagination, whether expressed in a skyscraper, store, bank, or autobiography, exhibits a characteristic impulse and visual pattern linking its varied forms. Moreover, this unity of design and decoration, seen at least as early as the Wainwright Building in 1890, remained in Sullivan's mind to the last; it can be seen superbly articulated in the plates Sullivan was working on as he wrote the *Autobiography* and published as *A System of Architectural Ornament According with a Philosophy of Man's Powers* (1924). (See Illustration 2.) Here is one concrete link between autobiography and a creative career.

If indeed life as experienced and art as created are both dreams with a common source in the creative memory-imagination, then Sullivan's autobiography may be read — in fact, I would argue, *must* be read — not simply as impressionistic history or Whitmanesque pastoral narrative but as a dream whose psychic meanings are, as in all dreams, masked and manifested in event, image, and metaphor. These metaphors which come to characterize or identify Sullivan the dreamer arise naturally from the remembered past and are conjoined in patterns created by the psychic pressures of the present experience of composition. They constitute, therefore, what James Olney calls "metaphors of self"—order-producing and emotion-satisfying images through which the individual succeeds in making the world take on his own shape. Such images, Olney asserts, though born of actual experience, tell more of the self who deploys them than of the world from which they come. "Metaphor," he writes, "says very little about what the world is, or is like, but a great deal about what I am, or am like, and about what I am becoming; and in the end connects me more nearly with the deep reaches of myself than with an objective universe."[19] This insight offers, I believe, an illuminating approach to *The Autobiography of an Idea.* Examining Sullivan's narrative through its major metaphorical patterns will record the

Carson, Pirie, Scott & Co., Chicago. Detail of cast iron over entrance. Plate 25
from Louis Sullivan, *The Autobiography of an Idea* (New York: Dover
Publications, 1956), p. 218.

Plate 16 from Louis Sullivan, *A System of Architectural Ornament According with a Philosophy of Man's Powers* (New York: Press of the American Institute of Architects, Inc., 1924).

author's historical experience (or at least his historicism), and will exhibit his literary skill and imagination. Even more clearly, however, these metaphors will lead inside Sullivan's created identity. For the nature and affect of such images point to hitherto unconscious dimensions of a present and past self. If, therefore, Olney is right, we shall perhaps find Greenacre, Erikson, and other psychological critics useful, perhaps even necessary, guides through this labyrinth of childhood.

The first such pattern of imagery and event in the *Autobiography* shows a small boy identifying himself—that is, seeing himself—in natural objects in the Massachusetts landscape as forms of beneficent beauty and power. At the same time, these objects—an elm tree, an ash, a meadow with rivulet and a dam, the iron bridge across the Merrimack River—represent relationships with the boy's mother and father to be achieved, maintained, or altered. Memory has summoned these symbols from a remote but still vivid past. The field, trees, and bridge in the early chapters of the *Autobiography* represent, therefore, the fusion of fact and fantasy.

The episode of the ash tree opens as a classic Rousseauistic reenactment of childish rebellion against school. Like Henry Adams, another Massachusetts boy, Sullivan recalls being led, kicking and screaming, along a New England road to the schoolhouse. Unlike Adams, however, the gentle grandmother is also along. It is she who has dressed her darling in white jacket, bow tie, and pantalettes. These effeminate, aristocratic garments, and not school itself, are the ostensible cause of the child's rage. Again unlike Adams, Sullivan recalls the elders relenting, turning home again, and allowing him to reappear next day victoriously reborn as "a tousle-headed, freckled, more or less toothless, unclean selfish urchin in jeans" (p. 27). The grandmother is saddened by this transformation; she perceives that Louis "would continue to grow bigger, stronger, rougher, and gradually grow away from her—ever more masculine, ever more selfish" (p. 27). The episode echoes other life stories and fictions, but also fits Sullivan and his later experiences and so expresses his typical blend of fictive and historic truth. It is the first of several successful revolts against social discipline and academic convention by this self-styled "compound of fury, curiosity, and tenderness" (p. 27). But the sequel to this childish revolt does not resemble Henry Adams's or Tom Sawyer's. Instead of a humorous denouement or a didactic demonstration of the inevitability of social conformity, Sullivan's act issues in a vision of nature. This occurs next day as the boy returns hand in hand with the defeated grandmother. As they "leisurely mounted a gentle grade," he remembers,

just behind the stone wall to the right of the road—marvel of marvels—stood a gigantic, solitary ash tree. On account of a certain chipmunk, various flowers, pebbles, and other things, the child had not noticed it during the approach. But of a sudden, there it stood, grand, overwhelming, with its immense trunk, its broad branches nearly sweeping the grass, its towering dome of dense dark green; . . . The child stood transfixed, appalled. A strange far-away storm, as of distant thundering, was arising within his wonder-self. He had seen many trees, yes; but this tree—*this tree!* . . . It became *his* tree—his Great Friend. (pp. 28–29)

Under this "wondrous tree," the child's earliest embodiment of beautiful power, Louis experiences his first mystical union with nature as he watches one morning "the militant splendor of sunrise—the breaking of night's dam—the torrent and foam of far-spreading day" (p. 61). This water imagery as well as other trees will be encountered again and again in Sullivan's story.

The second symbolic tree emerges from Sullivan's memory-imagination as the elm standing in the field where the six-year-old boy spends the month-long vacation from school celebrated in Chapter 4. Though this pastoral interlude recalls Tom Sawyer on his island, it also resembles in other respects the escapade of an earlier Boston boy—Franklin and his friends stealing the stone to build their wharf in the marsh. But Sullivan's escape to the field and trees and his building a dam differ essentially from both Twain's and Franklin's accounts. To this self-liberated boy, landscape is not simply a setting or the occasion for learning a social truth. Nature becomes a possession, a part of himself, his "promised land." Under the lovingly averted gaze of grandparents and school-mistress, the boy enacts on nature's stage his scenario of self-discovery.

The account opens with Louis slipping away from home, a supply of dough-nuts, rolls, and cookies in his blouse.

One bright particular spot was his goal. It lay in the narrow bottom of the ravine just where the gurgling water passed hurriedly among field stones under tall arching oaks. Here was the exact spot for a dam. He got immediately to work. He gathered the largest field stones he could handle, and small ones too. He had seen Scotchmen and Irishmen build farm walls and knew what to do. He was not strong enough to use a stone hammer if he had had one. So he got along without. He found a rusty remnant of a hoe, without a handle; with this he dug up some stiff earth. So with field stones, mud, twigs and grass he built his dam. It was a mighty work.

He was lost to all else. The impounded waters were rising fast behind the wall, and leaking through here and there. He must work faster. Besides, the wall must lengthen as it grew higher, and it leaked more at the bottom. He had to plug up holes. At last child power and water power became unequal. Now was at hand the grand climax — the meaning of all this toil. A miniature lake had formed, the moment had arrived. With all his strength he tore out the upper center of the work, stepped back quickly and screamed with delight, as the torrent started, and, with one great roar, tore through in huge flood, leaving his dam a wreck. What joy! He laughed and screamed. Was he proud? Had he not built the dam? Was he in high spirits? Had he not built this dam *all by himself*? Had he not planned in advance just what happened? Had he not worked as hard as he had seen big men work? . . .

Then he loafed and invited his soul as was written by a big man about the time this proud hydraulic engineer was born. But he did not observe "a spear of summer grass"; he dreamed. Vague day dreams they were,—an arising sense, an emotion, a conviction; that united him in spirit with his idols—with his big strong men who did wonderful things. (pp. 54–56)

With a habitat now aggressively appropriated, the boy ranges the fields, defining "the full spread of his domain" (p. 63). This exploration uncovers his second tree; "there, solitary in the meadow, stood the most beautiful tree of all."

He knew it at once for an elm; but such tall slender grace he had never seen. Its broad slim fronds spreading so high and descending in lovely curves entranced him. . . . Her beauty was incomparable.

Then he thought of his great ash tree. How different it was — so grand, so brooding, so watchful on the crest of the hill; and at times, he firmly believed so paternal so big-brotherly. But the lovely elm was his infatuation—he had adopted her at first sight, and still gazed at her with a sweetness of soul he had never known. He became infiltrated, suffused, inspired with the fateful sense of beauty. (p. 64).

Equipped now with two natural objects with which to identify, one masculine and paternal, the other feminine and motherly, the boy completes his solitary domain. "His breast swelled with pride. It was all his. No other boy should ever enter these lovely precincts. No other boy could understand" (p. 68). The idyll of self-objectivation concludes with the boy turning from creative fantasy about himself, his parents, and these trees to the social world beyond the meadow. "While his heart was fixed in one spot," he writes,

he made many tours of exploration; he called on many farmers and shoemakers . . . . He went frankly to a workman, watched him a while and told the man he liked to see him work. The moulder, much amused, said he would show him how it was all done. The child was amazed; a new world had opened to him — the world of handicraft, the vestibule of the great world of art that he one day was to enter and explore. (p. 68)

This whole episode marks the crucial childhood stage of Louis Sullivan's self-discovery. Childish actor and aged author are both identified and united in this imaginative reentering of the New England landscape which is so transparently also the self and the significant others. Behind the scene's lyrical language, pastoral setting, and transcendental message lie significant psychological truths. Seen in terms of Greenacre's paradigm of the creative artist's childhood, certain features stand out in bold relief. First of all, Sullivan shows that he possesses in abundance the basic qualities Greenacre ascribes to all geniuses — acute sensitivity, empathy, awareness of rhythm and relationship, the sensorimotor equipment for expression. More specifically, the child's early capacity for discovering objects to receive and represent his loving desires is striking proof of Greenacre's assertion of the genius's "communion with outer forms which reflect inner feelings" (*EG*, p. 494). Here begins one artist's "genuine collective love affair" (*EG*, p. 490) with the world. These natural forms constitute what Greenacre calls "collective alternates" — external objects or relationships which the gifted child selects to represent and replace primary objects (his own body, the mother's body, more generally the mother and the father) with whom he is deeply and oedipally involved.[20] Mobility of libidinal energy, or the capacity to transfer or deflect feeling from primary to secondary objects, is for Greenacre the first hallmark of the artist or creative genius. Here, these particular natural objects express Louis Sullivan's earliest, most persistent wish not only to identify with the mother but to rival and imitate the father. The ash, elm, sunrise, broken dam, and the marsh symbolize various things to the growing boy—beauty, power, the self, the parents, solitude, and socially useful activity. Here, too, is one explanation why Louis's brother Albert is never to be named in the narrative. Alone and free to act out impulses, Louis has explored and defined his natural self, first in visions of masculine power and feminine beauty, then in creative and destructive play. If total freedom is the prerequisite of the "beneficent power" (p. 255) he seeks, then the breaking of the dam dramatizes the destructive urges implicit in that freedom. The willful, even gleeful destruction of something created by the solitary self foretells obliquely Sullivan's subsequent career as architect and designer, as brother and husband, a fate with triumphs and failures here declared to be self-induced. These possible meanings are not articulated by the autobiographer himself, but in numerous passages Sullivan represents both his own creativity and destructivity as dammed-up water to be released suddenly. One instance is the ecstatic evocation of the sunrise as "the breaking of night's dam." Later, as a restless Boston schoolboy, he yearns for "a *teacher*" with "a spirit utterly human that would break down the dam made within him by sanctioned suppressions and routine" (p. 100). This releaser of creative, libidinal force soon appears as Moses Woolson, Sullivan's teacher at the English High School. Shortly after meeting this dynamo of disciplined energy, Sullivan reviews his recent past and again sees himself as water long dammed up and now to be released. He remembers his "child-domain"

holding within the encircling woods, his ravine, his rivulet, his dam, his lovely marsh, his great green field, his tall, beauteous, slender elm; land of his delight . . . . This sanctuary of his visions and his dreams, had seemed at first, and hopefully, to extend itself progressively into a larger world as far as Newburyport and Boston, there, however, to stop, to remain fixed and bound up for seven long years, held as by a sinister unseen dam, the larger, urgently growing Louis, held also back within it, impatient, oppressed, confined, dreaming of power, storing up ambition, searching for what lies behind the face of things, agitated and at times morose, malignant. When, of a sudden, the dam gives way, the child-domain so far enlarged, rushes forth, spreading over the earth, carrying with it the invisible living presence of Louis's ardent soul, pouring its power of giving and receiving far and wide over land and sea. . . . (p. 161)

Here the image of the broken dam defines not merely the succession of actual events in his life but also the psychic process of repression and release which already in childhood marks the life rhythm of this "compacted personality." The sexual and oedipal aspects of the image and the action are never far beneath the surface of Sullivan's prose.

If total freedom — the power to make and destroy — is the first condition of Sullivan's creativity, the second requisite is discipline. This necessary condition for the transition from childhood to boyhood emerges at the end of Chapter 4, when the boy's father takes him away to Newburyport, ending the era of total permissiveness. In place of the mother — she who "vacillated, oscillated, vibrated, richochetted, made figures of eight and spirals in her temperamental emotionalism and mother love" (p. 77) and encouraged the indulgent grandparents — the father now enters to impose order, respect, obedience. Through Patrick Sullivan, the child is initiated into the somatic and social ideal he is to imitate consciously throughout life. Line is about to be imposed on loop or curve. The paternal regimen is spartan: early out of bed, a cold drink of water and a run, then to the sea for swimming. Louis, the later athlete of the Lotus Club in Chicago, re-creates the scene in vivid detail:

At the end of two miles they came upon a narrow arm of the sea, which spread into a beautiful sequestered pool, at the point reached, with water deep, and clear green, and banks quite high. Strip! was the order. Strip it was. No sooner done than the high priest dextrously seized the neophyte, and, bracing himself, with a backward-forward swing cast the youngster far out, saw him splash and disappear; then he dived, came up beside a wildly splashing sputtering unit, trod water, put the child in order, and with hand spread under his son's breast began to teach him the simple beginnings of scientific swimming. "Must not stay too long in the water," he said. "Would Sonny like a ride astride Papa's shoulders to a landing?" Sonny would and did. He gloried as he felt beneath him the powerful heave and sink and heave of a fine swimmer, as he grasped his father's hair, and saw the bank approach. (pp.78 – 79)

Under such exhilarating circumstances he recalls first seeing and admiring his father's naked body.

On land he took note of his father's hairy chest, his satiny white skin and quick flexible muscles over which the sunshine danced with each movement. He had never seen a man completely stripped, and was pleased and vastly proud to have such a father, especially when the father, an object lesson in view, made exhibition dives and swam this way and that way in lithe mastery. And he asked his father to promise him that he would teach him how to do these things, that too might become a great swimmer. For he had a new ideal now, an ideal upsprung in a morning's hour — a vision of a company of naked mighty men, with power to do splendid things with their bodies. (p. 79)

Here, manifestly, is another distinguishing psychic event — "the experience of awe in childhood" — which Greenacre has observed in the early lives of certain creative artists and geniuses. As part of the gifted child's deep oedipal involvement (which Greenacre terms, somewhat imprecisely, "family romance") there sometimes occurs, between the second and fifth years, an actual experience which typically issues in the same idealization of father or father figure as Sullivan articulates above. This is an occasion of mysterious exhilaration and bodily excitement brought about by a child's first sight of his father's naked body.[21] The oedipal dimensions of this vision are, I believe, obvious here. The boy's previous hatred of Patrick Sullivan is now forgotten or suppressed; a phallic phase identification with the father, together with an anal phase acceptance of the order and discipline he represents, now succeed the child's oral identification with the mother. Continuity with that earlier phase is maintained, however, by the natural setting and by the persistance of water as the medium and metaphor of communication.

Another decisive event confirming this oedipal stage in the boy's development towards a creative career as architect is his account of a Sunday picnic on the banks of the Merrimack River which climaxes in Louis's sight of the iron bridge. As with other crises, this one opens with the writer-as-child "musing about South Reading, recalling his rivulet, his dam, his marsh. How small they seemed. And then there arose his tall, slender elm, his great ash tree to comfort him." Then he relates:

Meanwhile something large, something dark was approaching unperceived; something sinister that silently aroused him to a sense of its presence. He became aware; he peered through the foliage. . . . The dark thing came ever nearer, nearer in the stillness, became broader, looming, and then changed itself into full view—an enormous terrifying mass that overhung the broad river from bank to bank. (p. 82)

Here the autobiographer seems deliberately to be exaggerating the childish terror of the boy on the bank who cries, "Papa! Papa! Instanter Papa appeared — ah, the good fairy had waved her wand in the enchanted wood" (p. 83). Patrick Sullivan calms his son's fears by explaining what a bridge is.

On their way to rejoin Mamma, the child turned backward to gaze in awe and love upon the great suspension bridge. There, again, it hung in air — beautiful in power. The sweep of the chains so lovely, the roadway barely touching the banks. And to think it was made by men! How great must men be, how wonderful; how powerful, that they could make such a bridge; and again he worshipped the worker. (p. 85)

To the future designer of skyscrapers whose technical innovations are to be profoundly influenced by two midwestern bridges (the Eades bridge at St. Louis and Shaler Smith's cantilever bridge over the Kentucky), this dreamlike memory has very concrete repercussions. Equally significant, however, are its anterior sources in the swimming scene, in which the boy observed the "lithe mastery" of his father's body. That the two moments, apparently so different, are connected is suggested not only by the watery locale but by the "shameful fear" the boy first feels towards the bridge, an unusual response here but suppressed in the swimming scene, where it might have been expected. The iron bridge, I suggest, symbolizes this other, more terrifying — that is, more castrating — vision of paternal phallic power. As the father's reassuring presence and words transform the boy's fear into "awe and love," we witness not simply an instance of oedipal dynamics but also a concrete demonstration of the linkages between identity, infantile sexuality, and one person's later impulse to create massive objects like bridges and buildings. Thus memories of a casual Sunday's picnic become parts of the chain of events and emotional response connecting skyscrapers to a childish self.

Subsequent stages in the growth of this genius are as rich in evidence of libidinal dynamics as these rural and seaside scenes. One of the most dreamlike and significant of all episodes is the opening to Chapter 7, which records Louis's first encounter with city buildings and his decision to become an "archeetec." This crucial moment has, however, a curious prelude. Sullivan begins by recalling an old cobbler whom he regularly met on Washington Street in his natal city of Boston. This Uncle Sam figure with chin whiskers and faded clothes has a remarkable skill as a whistler which the boy tries in vain to emulate. The encounter leads into the longer dream/memory of himself walking into the street in which he had been born:

> . . . as the Yankee passed on southward the boy turned east into South Bennett Street following the south sidewalk. About midway to Harrison Avenue a paper bag struck the sidewalk in front of him, burst, and hard candies scattered over the pavement. The boy, startled, looked around and then up. In a second story window, straight across the way, appeared two fat bare arms, an immense bosom, a heavy, broad, red face, topped with straight black hair. A fat finger beckoned to him; a fat mouth said something to him; and at the doorway of the house was the number 22 — the house he had been born in; but the silver name-plate marked P. Sullivan in black script was no longer there. (p. 109)

No scene in the *Autobiography* re-creates more powerfully the impression of a child's actual dream. Louis's oedipal fears and desires about adult sexual experience, with a mother figure who is utterly and safely different in appearance from Andrienne Sullivan, are obliquely but unmistakably expressed. The oedipal context of the screen-memory emerges not only from the setting but in Sullivan's explanation for his visit: "He had been led to the spot," he writes, "which he had not seen for years, by a revived memory of a sweet child named Alice Look, who lived next door when the two of them were three together. He had wished to see once more the sacred dwelling wherein she had lived and the walled yard in which she had mothered him and called him Papa in their play" (pp. 109–10).

The mixed pregenital emotions resurrected so vividly by the sixty-five-year-old writer continue to spill out in other images from this past moment. As the boy, "much troubled," continues along Harrison avenue,

> he noticed that the stately trees were bare of leaves and sickly to the sight, while on the twigs and among the branches and even on the trunks were hundreds of caterpillar nests which made the trees look old, poor and forsaken. While he was counting the nests on a single tree, caterpillars now and then would come slowly downward from the heights. Some of them would remain for a time in mid-air, suspended invisibly before completing their descent, perchance upon a passerby. (p. 110)

The reader is here invited to recall earlier, healthier trees and to connect these bare, blighted trees of Sullivan's birthplace with his present — that is, with his nine-year-old self — stage of removal from the "sacred dwelling" where he had once been mothered by both Andrienne and sweet Alice. One is tempted, moreover, to see in the dangling caterpillars a representation of the boy's intermediate stage between childhood and adolescence. What seems never in doubt is the boy's—and the writer's—acute nostalgia for that lost pregenital world.

Throughout this chapter Sullivan emphasizes that he is relating episodes and emotions but dimly understood. This ambiguity is manifest in the succeeding sequence of events. He "was examining one of these caterpillars undulating upon his coat sleeve, when his quick ear detected the sound of snaredrums." It is a parade of veterans returning from the Civil War, for if Louis is nine the year must be 1865. History thus impinges upon—but does not trigger—the re-entered dream. The sequel is recounted in prose as emotionally evocative as Whitman's in *Specimen Days:*

Onward, into distinctness and solidity, came the mass of faded blue undulating to the pathos of the drums.The drum corps passed — and in the growing silence came on and passed ranks of wearied men in faded blue, arms at right shoulder, faces weather-beaten, a tired slow tread, measured as a time-beat on the pavement, the one-two of many souls. And to these men, as they marched, clung women shabbily clothed, with shawls drawn over their heads, moving on in a way tragically sad and glad, while to the skirts of many of these women clung dirty children. Thus moved in regular mass and in silence a regiment of veterans, their women, their children, passing onward between two tense rows of onlooking men, women, and children, triple deep, many of them in tears. So vivid was this spectacle, that the boy, leaning against a caterpillared tree, overflowed with compassion. (pp. 110–11)

Deeply perplexed at his confused feelings, the boy hurries to confide in Julia Head, the family's hoydenish, warmhearted Irish maid. "What did it all mean? Why was it so sad; why did he have to cry?" Julia gives the troubled boy three answers, all of which show how historical and psychic meanings are inextricably intertwined in this as in other autobiographical episodes. The scene first of all dramatizes a social truth about war: " . . . those men ye saw had just been mustered out of the army," she explains, "they were good fighting men, but all tired out. From the shawls the women wore and the dirty childer, I know the whole crowd was Irish and poor; and as everyone knows, the Irish won the war. Think of it! Holy virgin! — the Irish fighting for the naygers!" (p. 113). Then Julia drives home another of the scene's implications — Louis's emotional iden-tification with but distance from these poor Irish folk. "And yerself, Louis, wid yere big heart and small head couldn't see with yer own eyes and without any books at all that thim very childer was part of what as ye say lies behind it all? . . . Yere all sintiment, Louis, and no mercy" (p. 114). Then, to illustrate and palliate this rather harsh judgment of the boy's self-pitying sympathy, Julia tells a story. It is of a Union volunteer from County Kerry who was one day "out a-walking for his health, and faring to and fro" on the battlefield, when

he came upon a blanket lying on the ground, and at once picked it up and with great loud laughter he sed, sed he: Sure I've found me blanket with me name upon it: U fer Patrick and S for McCarthy; sure edication's a foine thing, as me faather before me wud say.

"Oh, Julia, I don't believe that's true. That's just another Irish yarn."

"Will, maybe it isn't true and maybe it's just a yarn; but I belave it's true and I want to till ye this; the man from Kerry had a rale education. Ye may think I'm a-jokin' now, but when ye get older and have more sinse ye'll be noticing that that's the way everywan rades; and the higher educated they are, the more they rade just as Pat McCarthy did, and add some fancy flourishes of their own. (p. 115)

Julia's tale is the key linking the apparently disconnected figures and scenes of this enigmatic chapter. It emphasizes, moreover, her role throughout the later childhood chapters as an intermediate figure between Louis's idolized mother, Irish father, and other women, including here the fat seductress-ogress in the window of 22 South Bennett Street. Julia's folk wisdom shows up Louis's emotion at the sight of the soldiers to be wholly characteristic of the boy and of the older man. Here, as perhaps in later Whitmanesque invocations to the people, Sullivan projects private, pregenital feelings (triggered by the bittersweet return to his birthplace) onto the passing parade. This is what Julia means when she accuses him of sentiment but no mercy. Louis Sullivan can enter the lives of others only through his own childish memories and desires, just as Patrick McCarthy can only read his name on the army blanket. Beyond the evident shame and pride at his Irishness — feelings heavily laden with oedipal energy and here introduced, I believe, in the counterfigure of the Yankee whistler— the episode says much about Sullivan's adult character. His democratic philosophy with its intense but generalized ardor for mankind, his self-styled role as the people's architect, his complete silence about any mature relationships with women — all suggest that Sullivan remained throughout his life a man whose capacities for strong universal emotion masked underlying ambiguities about personal ties. These Boston scenes exhibit some of the pregenital and genital sources of this outlook, which Greenacre describes in theory thus: "The reaction of the artist to the collective object(s) also involves utilization of the most primitive but acute empathic responses to an extent greater than is true in relation to the personal object" (EG, p. 501).

As Sullivan's own words reveal, Chapter 7 is one of the richest demonstrations in the Autobiography of a struggle (largely successful) to make explicit the pregenital experiences and emotions at the core of his creativity. At the close he remarks that "Julia had told the story mockingly. She seemed to leave in it somewhere a sting he could feel but not understand; . . . She had set him vibrating at the suggestion of an unseen power and he became rigid in his resolve to penetrate the mystery that seemed to lie back of the tale she told'' (p. 116). The psychic resonances of these two phrases, ''vibrating at the suggestion of an unseen power'' and ''rigid in his resolve to penetrate the mystery,'' are so pervasively characteristic of the boy and the man that they may almost be read as expressions of Louis Sullivan's ''personal myth.''[22] They express, that is, a self defined in terms of a lifelong involvement with a mother continually invoked in terms of trembling emotion and with a father all rigid power and thrusting will. Both the nine-year-old boy and the aged architect are bound and liberated, inhibited and impelled, by this unseen power and rigid resolve. Greenacre could find ample evidence here for perceiving this creative career as firmly anchored in ''family romance.'' Indeed, the transformation of libidinal energy into a life's work is explicitly announced later in Chapter 7 when Louis, now twelve, first sees the dignified well-dressed ''archeetec'' who has designed Boston's new Masonic Temple. To Sullivan that Temple is the incarnation of his romantic childish ideals. ''How beautiful were its arches,'' he recalls, ''how dainty its pinnacles! how graceful the tourelles on the corner! rising as if by itself, higher and higher, like a lily stem, to burst at last into a wondrous cluster of flowering pinnacles and a lovely, painted finial. . . . If Louis chose to liken this new idol of his heart unto a certain graceful elm tree, the pulchritudinous virgin of an earlier day, surely that was his affair, not ours'' (p. 118).

However in order to duplicate such creative combinations of line and curve, of emotion and energy, the boy must actually become the man and the builder. In somatic terms, this means passing through adolescence; socially, it means education and entry into the architectural profession. These twin experiences engross much of the autobiographer's attention throughout the remaining pages of his history. The crucial event of Sullivan's adolescence occurs when the boy, now nearly fourteen, travels with his grandfather to Lyons Falls, where he comes under the spell of his eighteen-year-old cousin Minnie Whittlesey. This excursion, the longest loop so far of expanding consciousness, also includes a hiking trip into the Adirondack wilderness, which in context is the boy's escape from the social and sexual dangers Minnie represents. On the train the grandfather predicts the sexual awakening which both does and does not occur at Lyons Falls. When they arrive, Louis's aunt greets them ''with the dry kiss of superculture'' (p. 141), displaying ''the reserve of a gentlewoman whom long practice had enabled to speak with delicate precision in a voice scarcely audible, and to inhale her smiles'' (p. 140). Minnie, however, is far less forbidding a representative of refined femininity than her mother. She reads him Byron and Tennyson, takes him to church and into the woods for lectures on social and literary deportment. As Sherman Paul remarks, she ''plays Mary Jane to his Huck Finn.''[23] But the sexual realities behind their play are closer to the surface than in Twain's novel. She teaches him to repeat ''*je t'aime*,'' at the same time warning him mysteriously ''Louis, Louis, you are in danger!'' (p. 145). The excited boy feels like ''a human package not merely stirred, but churned to butter and whey''

(p. 146) under her spell. Part of the disturbance is not merely erotic but social, for Minnie and the Whittleseys open horizons on social class previously unimagined by the boy. In later years, after Sullivan had become what he wryly calls "a draughtsman of the upper Crust," and had learned to dress like a dandy, he may have reexperienced some of these boyish fears and desires. If the inner conflicts of this adolescent situation cannot account for the trajectory of Sullivan's career and his ill-fated marriage to Margaret Hattabough, perhaps they do throw light on the autobiographer's complete silence about women in the remainder of his narrative.

Far safer than such temptations are the woods and male companionship. Louis's account of his camping trip to Brown's Tract, which follows immediately, is less initiation than retreat to the same masculine realm once entered when his father first threw him into the sea-pool at Newburyport. New vistas on that world of aggressive, muscular men open when the boy finds himself in Woolson's class at the English High School. The ideal of male power just reawakened by the trek is now definitely confirmed by the "mental athlete" whom more than anyone else Sullivan credits with making him into a "compacted personality, ready to act on his own initiative, in an intelligent purposeful way" (p. 168). As the most important father surrogate in the narrative, Woolson anticipates other tense, orderly, passionate men like Monsieur Clopet of Paris and Bill Curtis and John Edelmann of Chicago.[24] From each Sullivan relearns the lesson of Newburyport: freedom and power through a disciplined body and will. Like the inanimate models drawn from nature, these masculine figures point backward to a common oedipal source in childhood. Their historical counterpart and artistic summation is the man whose work Sullivan sees in the Sistine Chapel, and it is revealing that Michelangelo's Last Judgment captures the young student's imagination more than the ceiling. Herein he perceives that the creative force of the "first mighty Craftsman" is *momentum* — "the work of a man powerful even in old age" (p. 234) because still the outpouring of pure Dream or Imagination. The parallels with Sullivan's own career are obvious and ironic. *The Autobiography of an Idea*, too, is a monument to momentum.

Movement from an impulse, however, always interests Louis Sullivan less than recovering the original impulse itself. Hence the overriding concern in chronicling his education and entry into an architectural career is with beginnings, not climaxes or completions. This principle neatly coincides with reality at several points; history as well as desire records the fact that he spent only two years at high school before entering MIT, where he remained only one year before leaving for an apprenticeship in a firm. By this extraordinary telescoping of time and training Sullivan became a full-fledged designer by twenty-one and Adler's partner at twenty-five. This much is told in the *Autobiography*. What is not directly revealed, in his dramatic account of cramming for the entrance exams to the Ecole, is the fact that he then remained in Paris only one short term. He accuses the Ecole of departing from "the profound animus of a primal inspiration'' (p. 240), which expresses again his deep-seated disdain for academic art and traditional training. Other sources for this attitude, and for the unusual chronology of a truncated youth and early manhood flowing from it, have already been hinted at. Education and tangible success fulfill a father's rigid drive for abstraction and mastery; they also promise escape from the dubious social status of the Irish immigrant's son. At the same time, however, Sullivan's rebellion expresses the infantile ideal, first caught under his mother's piano as a little boy, of life as pure emotion, spontaneity, complete and solitary freedom. As with his earliest experiences of discipline, Sullivan accepts only enough educational order to release but not to restrict his creative energy. As autobiographer, therefore, he must compose a narrative which goes against the reader's traditional expectations. As soon as he becomes in actuality the big, powerful worker of his childish dreams, he abandons the account of successful achievement. Instead he turns preacher proclaiming his Whitmanesque doctrine: ''The chief business now is to pave the way for the child, that it may grow wholesome, proud and stalwart in its native powers. So doing we shall uncover to our view the amazing world of instinct in the child whence arises genius with its swift grasp of the real'' (p. 275). For some readers, as for the architects who first read these pages in their *Journal*, Sullivan's grasp of the ''real'' world of postwar building in Chicago is much too ''swift,'' his penchant for philosophizing all too unrestrained. Connely for one criticizes the *Autobiography* as a masterpiece worthy in some respects of comparison with Cellini but ''ill-proportioned, lop-sided, truncated'' because its final chapters fail to meet these traditional expectations.[25] Viewed, however, in the psychological perspective which Greenacre's hypotheses and insights provide, the writer's aims have been amply, even eloquently accomplished. Memory has recovered through narrative event and metaphor the intimate connections in this creative career among actual experience, philosophical belief, and psychic drive. Sullivan's lifelong urge to penetrate appearance and reach an underlying reality, to give shape in stone, cement, and words to still-powerful infantile desires and fears, can be traced in these pages. Moreover, what lies behind is also right on the surface of his memory. ''Louis, long since had begun to sense and discern what lay behind the veil of appearances,'' he observes halfway through his narrative.

Social strata had become visible and clear, as also that hypocrisy of caste and cant and ''eminence'' against which his mother, time and time again, had spoken so clearly, so vehemently in anger and contempt . . . These outbursts of his mother sank deep into the being of her son; and in looking back adown the years, he had reason justly to appraise in reverence and love a nature so transparent, so pure, so vehement, so sound, so filled with yearning for the joy of life, so innocent-ecstatic in contemplation of beauty anywhere, as was that of the one who bore him forth, truly in fidelity, to be and to remain life of her life. Thus the curtain of memory ever lifts and falls and lifts again, on one to whom this prayer is addressed. If Louis is not his mother's spirit in the flesh, then words fail, and memory is vain. (p. 183)

Clearly words have not failed. Memory has indeed lifted the curtain on the presiding presence of *The Autobiography of an Idea*. Andrienne Sullivan's portrait, though less sharply etched than those of several powerful men — Patrick Sullivan, Moses Woolson, John Edelmann — diffuses her presence into every corner of the narrative her son has composed in praise and continued identification.

Author, reader, and psychoanalytic critic can all agree that on one level this autobiography is indeed the love gift to Andrienne Sullivan written by the true son of Patrick Sullivan. It is, of course, more than this. Tracing through language, metaphor, and narrative style the author's elaborations as recovered memories of hitherto unconscious or preconscious impulses leads necessarily into remembered social and historical experience. This intersection of psychic, literary, and historical forces and norms reveals the "personal myth" informing and unifying this book. Such confluence defines the only identity of Louis Sullivan available to us as readers of autobiography.

Greenacre's theories from "The Childhood of the Artist" have served effectively, I would claim, to open up this text, to account for major emphases and ambiguities, and to support claims for its organic coherence — claims to be denied if the work is read simply as memoir, prose poem, or architectural history. Incomplete as the testing has been, it suggests that Sullivan shares with many other modern autobiographers a willingness "to reveal much of their early emotional life and problems," and that the capacity to do so is an essential part of his creativity. The artistic self celebrated in the *Autobiography* is one firmly rooted in — but flexibly in control of — infantile and childish drives and dreams. Many of these, though expressed more in the idiom of Froebel than of Freud, are brought to the surface of consciousness. Others remain more deeply masked.

Nevertheless, this narrative is not the case history of a psychoanalysis any more than it is the biography of a whole career. Hence many questions to which the clinician or historian might wish answers cannot be found in it. Other approaches would doubtless provide different, more socially meaningful answers. Thus Erikson's eight-stage schema of somatic-social development in child and man, as elaborated in Chapter 7 of *Childhood and Society*, might throw a somewhat different light upon Sullivan's recorded experiences. Certainly an approach like Harold G. McCurdy's in "The Childhood Pattern of Genius"[26] differs markedly. This is chiefly true because McCurdy, unlike Greenacre or Erikson, treats autobiography exactly like other sources of biographical information. He places as much weight on asserted facts from Mill's or Goethe's autobiographies, for instance, as on statements in biographies. His three basic hypotheses — that the genius typically enjoyed in childhood a high degree of parental or adult attention; that much time was spent in isolation from other children; and that geniuses had therefore very rich fantasy lives — are perhaps applicable to Louis Sullivan. In the language of Herbert Blumer, Sullivan's autobiography lends *plausibility* to such generalizations. However, McCurdy's misuse of the special truth of autobiography is a fatal error which Greenacre and Erikson do not commit. If the study of autobiography as a special genre proves anything to the cultural critic, it is to demonstrate the basic differences in form, language, intent, and truth between it and biography.

A simple but significant example of this fundamental distinction has already been cited: Sullivan's omission of his brother's name and presence from his narrative. The reader might surmise that this childhood, like those of other geniuses, was passed in isolation. What seems closer to the biographical truth, as found in Connely's *Louis Sullivan as He Lived,* is that Sullivan spent a more normally social childhood than his autobiography gives any sense of. The *autobiographical* truth is that he wishes us to believe with him that he enjoyed in solitude the more or less exclusive attention of parents or their surrogates. These two ''truths'' are no closer than are the narrative accounts of the same events in the two kinds of life history. Thus in Connely we read the following account of Louis's vacation from school in which I have found so much autobiographical significance:

When the winter was passed Louis, at least, experimented in freedom. Bored with his school, he went in for roaming. A great place in the vicinity that appealed more to his fancy was a great marsh; there he staked out a domain for himself, and among the reeds, cedars and cattails peopled it with imaginary retainers. For lunch he had his blouse filled with rolls and cakes. He built dams and formed ponds. And whenever he tired of his kingdom he rambled in the other direction to the village, where he spent the remainder of the day watching a moulder or cobbler.

As soon as Patrick Sullivan discovered this truancy he took Louis away from the genial Lists, also away from his more amenable brother Albert.[27]

In certain respects this version of the events related in Chapter 4 is doubtless more accurate as history than the *Autobiography*. In other ways it seems highly inaccurate. Apart from factual divergences and simplifications, however, Connely's account shows a very real dimunition in both personal and cultural significance: It reveals less about the little boy *and* the designer of big buildings. What makes it clear that these events mean more and different things than the biographer perceives is precisely the close, sympathetic reading of the *Autobiography* which theories like Greenacre's facilitate. We recall here Greenacre's own hypothesis: ''that the study of autobiography supplemented by biography would be the method *par excellence* of understanding the individual genius.'' Despite problems and qualifications, her approach properly recognizes the actual complexity—the overdetermination—of autobiographical statement, its difference from and superiority for expressive purposes over biographical statement. Nevertheless, autobiography's special relevance cannot be understood in artistic or cultural isolation.

We need finally to try to define the scope of this special relevance. Are we closer to generalizations about cultural process of the childhoods of American artists after having followed in some detail the play of Louis Sullivan's memory/imagination in *The Autobiography of an Idea*? Does the apparent fit between Greenacre's hypotheses and this text lead through the gateway to the generalized knowledge Allport, Erikson, and others seek through autobiography? Answers to these repeated queries seem at once easier to offer and harder to sustain in light of the foregoing discussion. On the one hand, Greenacre's traditional Freudian generalizations seem much more plausible now than in their original unillustrated statement. Pregenital patterns, mobility of libidinal energy, the persistent and powerful presence of collective alternates, the dynamics of "family romance," even the actual moment of mystery or awe, are psychic components of one genius's early experience which now resonate with social and historical process. Their influence may even be traced aesthetically in the soaring treelike lines and intricately looped ornamentation of Sullivan's buildings. As in this narrative, so perhaps in others. On the other hand, examining this pattern of psychic forces in the architect's childhood and youth has produced, for me at least, a more vivid sense of personal identity than of Sullivan's representative status as "the genius." This tension between general theory and particular text, between common humanity and unique identity, is inevitable in the study of autobiography. No matter which scientific theory is conjoined to autobiographical text, the results will, I suspect, prove *both* fruitful *and* frustrating — fruitful in suggesting common features in the somatic-social roots of unusual lives, frustrating (and exhilarating) in affirming the unique combination of such common elements into an identity. Only after psychoanalytic theories such as Greenacre's have been applied book by book—to Henry James, Richard Wright, Conrad Aiken, Ellen Glasgow, Maya Angelou, and Helen Keller, and so on through the whole corpus of American autobiographies of the artist as child—will their adequacy be definitively established. Each new encounter, moreover, introduces a new set of somatic, social, and historical circumstances as well as another pattern of narrative and metaphor created to turn experience into identity.

Three critics of American life who comment usefully upon this autobiographical standoff in relation to scientific theory are Robert Nisbet, Francis Russell Hart, and Norman Holland. As a historically minded sociologist, Nisbet has been long concerned to find "better ways than we now have of dealing with the *Genius,* the *Maniac,* the *Prophet,* and the *Random Event.*" He offers a trenchant critique of certain traditional generalizations historians have used to explain these enigmas. Most generalizations about such phenomena, he believes, misrepresent or grossly simplify. Nisbet advises a more radical approach—one which, though he does not say so explicitly, applies aptly to autobiographical criticism. "Merely [give] full attention to time, place, and circumstance," he writes, as well as to "art," "form," and "metaphoric" language.[28] Russell Hart would agree. As an acute anatomist of modern autobiography, he, too, has been arrested in the process of generalization by the nature of his genre. "Autobiographers share certain intentions in varying degrees and in numerous distinctive patterns of interaction," he concludes.

Rather than deducing fixed expectations from distinctions of intentional "kinds," we should try to see how — why — with what effect distinct intentions evolve and interplay in individual autobiographies. . . . When such recognitions of individual autobiographies have accumulated and undergone testing and sorting, then and only then will it be possible to make real and meaningful descriptive generalizations about the historical development of modern autobiography.[29]

Norman Holland, writing as a neo-Freudian psychoanalyst of literature, echoes the caveats of the sociologist and the literary critic:

Even within the arts, "creativity" does not seem a useful level at which to generalize, because the created product is so individual. Adding up traits and averaging away individuality will tell us those abilities helpful to all writers (a good memory, for example, or ability at typing); but averaging will be just the wrong way to learn why *this* writer writes or why he writes the way he does. . . . I think we can learn more about creativity in general by studying one creative person in depth, and the function creativity plays in his singular psyche, than by studying multitudes.[30]

Here Holland goes a step beyond Nisbet and Hart, a step short but decisive towards the generalizations social scientists seek. As I have sought to show here, "studying one creative person in depth" is the necessary ground on which all generalizations about autobiographies like Sullivan's must rest. But in discovering and describing "the function creativity plays in his singular psyche" I have, like Holland, found psychoanalytic theorists like Phyllis Greenacre useful and potentially applicable to other childhoods of American artists.

Notes

1. See Richard Lillard, *American Life in Autobiography* (Stanford: Stanford University Press, 1956), and Kaplan, *A Bibliography of American Autobiographies* (Madison: University of Wisconsin Press, 1961).

2. See James M. Cox, "Autobiography and America," in *Aspects of Narrative,* ed. J. Hillis Miller (New York: Columbia University Press, 1971), pp. 143–72.

3. Lillard, *American Life in Autobiography,* p. 1.

4. See J. H. Hexter, "The Rhetoric of History," in *Doing History* (Bloomington: Indiana University Press, 1971), pp. 15–76.

5. See Georges Gusdorf, "Conditions et limites de l'autobiographie," in *Formen der Selbstdarstellung,* eds. G. Reichenkron and E. Haase (Berlin, 1956), pp. 105–23; Roy Pascal, *Design and Truth in Autobiography* (Cambridge, 1960), chap. 1; F. R. Hart, "Notes for an Anatomy of Modern Autobiography," *New Literary History* 1 (Spring 1970): 485–511.

6. See Jean Starobinski, "The Style of Autobiography," in *Literary Style: A Symposium,* ed. S. Chatman (New York: Oxford University Press, 1971), pp. 185–96; Hart, "Notes for an Anatomy of Modern Autobiography," p. 488.

7. Herbert Blumer, *Critiques of Research in the Social Sciences: I, An Appraisal of Thomas and Znaniecki's "The Polish Peasant in Europe and America"* (New York: Social Science Research Council, Bulletin 44, 1939), pp. 47, 80.

8. G. Allport, *The Use of Personal Documents in Psychological Science* (New York: Social Science Research Council, Bulletin 49, 1942), p. 185.

9. E. Erikson, "Gandhi's *Autobiography:* The Leader as Child," *American Scholar* 35 (Autumn 1966): 635.

10. Erikson, *Childhood and Society* (New York: W. W. Norton & Co., 1963), p. 282.

11. Greenacre, "Early Physical Determinants in the Development of the Sense of Identity," *Journal of the American Psychoanalytic Association* 6 (1958): 612, reprinted in *Emotional Growth: Psychoanalytic Studies of the Gifted and a Great Variety of Other Individuals,* 2 vols. (New York: International University Press, 1971) 1: 114.

12. *The Psychoanalytic Study of the Child* 12 (1958): 47–72, reprinted in *Emotional Growth,* 479–504; subsequent references will be to this version, identified parenthetically as *EG.*

13. Autobiographies of artists and writers are cited, but discussed only thematically, in a number of essays reprinted in *EG,* including "The Family Romance of the Artist" (pp. 505–32); "Experiences of Awe in Childhood" (pp. 67–91); and "A Study on the Nature of Inspiration: Some Special Considerations Regarding the Phallic Phase" (pp. 225–48).

14. The edition cited hereinafter is the Dover Edition (New York, 1957), foreword by Claude Bragdon and introduction by Ralph Marlowe Line. Subsequent references, cited parenthetically, will be to this edition.

15. See W. Connely, *Louis Sullivan as He Lived: The Shaping of American Architecture* (New York: Horizon Press, 1960), hereafter cited as Connely; and S. Paul, *Louis Sullivan, An Architect in American Thought* (Englewood Cliffs, N.J.: Prentice-Hall, 1962), hereafter cited as Paul.

16. Connely, p. 294.

17. Quoted in Connely, p. 295.

18. Reprinted in Paul, pp. 1–3.

19. J. Olney, *Metaphors of Self: The Meaning of Autobiography* (Princeton, N.J.: Princeton University Press, 1972), p. 32.

20. See *EG,* pp. 489–90. Greenacre's informal, somewhat awkward style in "The Childhood of the Artist" makes precise formulations difficult. The best definition of "collective alternates" occurs in "The Relation of the Imposter to the Artist" (1958): ". . . further, with his greater perceptive response to both form and rhythm, the personal objects of his immediate human environment may be invested with a greater range of other outer (often inanimate) objects, perceptions, which are related to the animate personal objects by similarities in form or in active and passive movement and rhythm. This increased range and deepened sensitivity include heightened reactions to his own body sensations as well as to the outer world. I have referred to this increased range of outer objects as the field of the collective alternates—'alternates' because they may on occasion substitute for the warmer personal human objects. . . . This means that all object relationships may be felt and expressed with a vast increase in their symbolic representations and that the tendency to anthropomorphism in observation and thought is increased and usually lasts throughout life." *EG,* pp. 538–39.

21. "It is possible that in children of potential genius this inner state of awareness of tumescent feeling may be especially strongly pervasive. Combining with the sensitive perception of external objects, it may give rise to sensations of invigoration, inspiration and awe. These depend not so much on the actual sight of the penis as on communion with outer forms which reflect inner feelings in a way which I have tried to describe under such title *collective alternates.* It seems to me also that under such conditions the development of the family romance in especially strong form is inevitable." *EG,* p. 494.

22. The phrase is Norman N. Holland's. See *Poems in Persons: An Introduction to the Psychoanalysis of Literature* (New York: Norton & Co., 1973), pp. 45–59.

23. Paul, p. 12.

24. "Fortunate is such a child," writes Greenacre, "if his own father fulfills the need for the model with which then to identify. It is my suspicion, however, that in some instances where this is not true, the child carries the ideal with him as though it were the real father, and that subsequent identification may be made and the development of direction of talent determined in part at least by the chance encounter with some individual or even some experience which strikes a decisive harmonizing note with a part of the hidden image of the father, belonging to the original experience of infantile inspiration." *EG*, p. 494.

25. Connely, p. 295.

26. See *Annual Report of the Smithsonian Institution* (1958), pp. 527 – 42.

27. Connely, p. 32.

28. Robert Nisbet, "Genealogy, Growth, and Other Metaphors," *New Literary History* 1 (Spring 1971): 363, 351.

29. Hart, "Notes for an Anatomy of Modern Autobiography," p. 511.

30. Holland, *Poems in Persons*, p. 6.

Bibliography

Aries, P. *Centuries of Childhood: A Social History of Family Life.* New York: Alfred A. Knopf, 1962.

Cobb, E. *The Ecology of Imagination in Childhood.* New York: Columbia University Press, 1977.

Connely, W. *Louis Sullivan as He Lived: The Shaping of American Architecture.* New York: Horizon Press, 1960.

Cox, J. M. "Autobiography and America," in J. Hillis Miller, ed. *Aspects of Narrative.* New York: Columbia University Press, 1971.

Erikson, E. "Gandhi's *Autobiography:* The Leader as a Child." *American Scholar* 35 (Autumn 1966): 632 – 46.

————. *Childhood and Society.* Rev. ed. New York: W.W. Norton, 1973.

Greenacre, P. *Emotional Growth: Psychoanalytic Studies of the Gifted and a Great Variety of Other Individuals,* vol. 2. New York: International University Press, 1971.

Hart, F. R. "Notes for an Anatomy of Modern Autobiography," in R. Cohen, ed. *New Directions in Literary History.* Baltimore: Johns Hopkins University Press, 1974.

Holland, N. N. *Poems in Persons: An Introduction to the Psychoanalysis of Literature.* New York: W. W. Norton, 1973.

Olney, J. *Metaphors of Self: The Meaning of Autobiography.* Princeton, N.J.: Princeton University Press, 1972.

Paul, S. *Louis Sullivan: An Architect in American Thought.* Englewood Cliffs, N.J.: Prentice-Hall, 1962.

Stone, A. E. "Autobiography and American Culture," in Robert H. Walker, ed. *American Studies: Topics and Sources.* Westport, Conn.: Greenwood Press, 1976.

————. "Psychoanalysis and American Literary Culture." *American Quarterly* 28 (Bibliography Issue, 1976): 309 – 23.

PART FIVE
Personality and Culture

DAVID W. MARCELL

Poor Richard: Nixon and the Problem of Innocence

Announcing that "our long national nightmare [of Watergate] is over," on August 9, 1974, Gerald Ford succeeded Richard Nixon as president of the United States. A month later, on September 8, President Ford issued his controversial pardon for any crimes Nixon might have committed during his six years in the White House. Ironically, Ford's pardon negated his claim that the nightmare was over, for despite the evidence amassed against him, after the pardon no formal adjudication of Nixon's alleged crimes could ever take place. Thus the question of Nixon's culpability and its meaning lingers on, a matter now for scholarly speculation rather than legal resolution. Despite the accusations of his critics, one thing is clear: Richard Nixon is and always will be legally innocent of the crimes that constitute the nightmare of Watergate.

Yet Richard Nixon may be innocent on a scale much vaster than that which a court might determine: He may also be innocent in that more abstruse sense that many cultural critics have found Americans characteristically to be. For there are many modes of innocence, and legal innocence is simply the most constricted and negative variety. Legal innocence signifies the inability to prove beyond a reasonable doubt behavior which violates specific statutes. Cultural innocence, on the other hand, implies a typical, normative cluster of what appear to outsiders to be naïve expectations about time and fate and will, and it is in this more fundamental, inclusive sense that Richard Nixon may be most significantly innocent. Moreover, it may well be that Richard Nixon's cultural innocence has been one of the underlying causes of his transgressions; if this is so, he may emerge as much a victim of American cultural expectations as a transgressor against its statutory law.

During the past quarter century nearly every major interpreter of American culture remarked upon what is usually termed Americans' "innocence."[1] Varied in expression, at bottom this innocence affirms Americans' belief that actions and traditions in the past do not necessarily limit the present, that there is, both for individuals and for society as a whole, always the possibility of absolution and the remission of sins. As a result of this view, the myths, fables, and gestures through which cultures convey their most fundamental messages in America have assumed a particular cast: They suggest, inexhaustibly it would seem, the possibility of renewal and rebirth, of escape from the past and of venturing onward to new beginnings. Gestures of casting off old mistakes and moving afresh into an unblemished future so constantly present themselves as to seem "characteristically American." A vital part of America's own historical success story, these notions of innocence have become articles of faith for countless believers. As models for the culture's historical sense of itself, they have reflexively conditioned Americans' personal sense of destiny. Consequently, this innocence at once furnishes justification for strenuous personal effort and a familiar, culturally stylized rationale for any triumph over adversity. For believers in its canons, American innocence in its most familiar guise teaches that in the abyss of every failure lies the prospect of spectacular success. While such expectations encourage believers to view history as open and malleable, they also perpetuate illusions of omniscience and a special exemption from the judgments of time and memory.

Yet no culture, however unified, presents itself as a monolith; no culture speaks with but a single voice on matters of deepest significance. Rather, as R. W. B. Lewis pointed out in his classic study of nineteenth-century innocence, *The American Adam,* cultures manifest their distinctiveness through emerging "dialogues" over crucial issues, dialogues which reflect, often imaginatively, many voices and perspectives.[2] Over time these dialogues create patterns which, when elevated and dramatized by art, legend, or folklore, become cultural archetypes. It is through the essential stories embodied in these archetypes that a culture most clearly reveals its conflicts, its changing styles, and its sense of what living most deeply means. In turn, these stories help to teach members of the culture its sanctions, its normative range of approved choices, its totems and taboos. To identify those patterns of innocence which, both by example and by contrast, best illuminate the dark complexities of Richard Nixon and Watergate, it is instructive to glance briefly at three archetypical stories of American innocence, one each from the eighteenth, the nineteenth, and the twentieth centuries.

Perhaps the paradigm of American innocence during the earliest years is the legend of Benjamin Franklin. This is no accident, for as Franklin himself well knew, his contemporaries perceived him to be the embodiment of a new national type, and when he came to write his *Autobiography*, the persona which emerged was a cunningly contrived, two-dimensional character sketched not so much for verisimilitude as for teaching his countrymen the very lessons of innocence itself. It is through the images of this book that we best learn the quasi-mythic story of Franklin, a poor, obscure youth in a strange land, who, by diligence in his calling, rises to fame and respectability. The *Autobiography*'s central messages to posterity are that human "errata" can be corrected, that private ambition, rightly conceived, synchronizes smoothly with social advance, and that fate yields its rewards to persistence, virtue, and hard work. Underlying the various defeats and triumphs Franklin records is a comfortable, Newtonian certainty that history is a rational series of *quid pro quos*, and a firm conviction that those who would emulate his strategies can similarly expect to rise from poverty to public esteem. Franklin's catalog of virtues, when harnessed to will, purpose, and energy, provided countless Americans with a formula for successful living that had all the self-evident verity of $A = r^2$.

The *Autobiography*'s confident message that Franklin was the cause of his own effect begged many complexities; yet it afforded readers both inspiration and a standard by which to measure their own successes. What saved Franklin from mere avariciousness and self-seeking was his intense commitment to civic improvement and his genius for linking the emerging needs of a new society to his own powerful need for self-esteem. Franklin's very identity, in fact, was fundamentally shaped by the successes he caused others to experience; his innocence lay in his unquestioning faith that these kinds of transactions involved no tyranny.

The Franklin archetype drew its historical strength not only from the simplicity of the *Autobiography*'s formula but also from the fact that Franklin represented a phenomenon much broader and deeper than that of a provincial success story. For Ben Franklin, as Max Weber later recognized, was the personification of the Protestant ethic, the "ideal type" for the rising bourgeoisie throughout the Western world. Yet Franklin's distinctive Americanness was both pronounced and prescient. A society that made Franklin its patron saint for better or worse pointed the way to the future, as Alexis de Tocqueville remarked upon observing American society in the 1830s. Such a society could hardly be expected to be static, but even the sophisticated Frenchman was awed by the social flux Americans generated as they exercised the Franklinesque virtues. Underlying the frenzy of those "expectant capitalists" de Tocqueville so piercingly analyzed was a deep commitment to social equality, a commitment that reflected the philosophy of history implicit in Franklin's legend and raised it to the level of a cultural axiom. As de Tocqueville explained it, America's general equality of social conditions was generating a new philosophy of individualism, a philosophy which encouraged each person to regard his own experience as intrinsically valuable as that of any other person. Implicit in this celebration of the democratic self was a vigorous if shallow denial of authority. The logic of equality, de Tocqueville found, reinforced the American tendency to denigrate the received wisdom of the past in favor of one's own experience in the here and now.

The most dramatic illustration of de Tocqueville's analysis provides us with a second perspective on American innocence, this time from the nineteenth century: Henry Thoreau's two-year residence at Walden Pond, and the extraordinary record of that residence, *Walden*. Nowhere in American letters is there a more heroic gesture proclaiming the determination to achieve selfhood without encumbrances; *Walden* celebrates as does no other American story the sufficiency of the first person singular. But both in the living and writing of his book Thoreau is more radical than some of his readers have guessed, for *Walden* proclaims nothing less than the possibility of perceiving the universe without the corrective lenses of culture, of perceiving the universe directly, as it were, with only the structure of language itself to give form to the experience, and of raising up on that perception a fully whole, fully independent human personality. *Walden* is, then, a story of beginnings, of a return to that state of consciousness wherein raw experience becomes translated into concepts and thus into the moral structures necessary to genuine humanity, that is, to the realm of knowing and meaning. To become acculturated, Thoreau seems to say, is to become distorted; throughout the book Thoreau uses nature — especially the mirror of the pond — to get a true reflection of his own dimensions as a man. To do this he must slough off the scales of his cultural nurturing much as a snake sloughs off his skin (the figure is Thoreau's). Only by deliberately repealing traditional, historical standards of measurement and perception can he glimpse that transcendent ideal of selfhood which lurks behind — indeed, which comes before — the clutter of time and custom and civilization. Any task less basic is a diversion from Thoreau's quest ''to front the essential facts'' of human existence.

It is in his assumptions of what is and is not ''essential'' to living meaningfully that Thoreau's mode of innocence shows most clearly, for if social effect is absolutely critical to Franklin's sense of self, the very opposite is true for Thoreau. Thoreau's thrust was toward the uninterpreted, brute facts of nature (and hence of the spirit) and away from the stream of history, tradition, social structure, and expectation. For Thoreau the highest forms of humanity were always found in the singular and in the simple; aggregations and customs inevitably blurred the primary sensibilities essential to the discovery of true selfhood. Ties to others Thoreau not merely rejects, but views as positively inimical to the business of being human in the first place. Thoreau's innocence, finally, is that of what Quentin Anderson termed the characteristically American faith in ''the imperial self.''[3]

Hence on one level of meaning Thoreau and Franklin seem to be saying diametrically opposite things; their modes of ''innocence'' at first glance seem poles apart. For Thoreau the ''essential'' facts of living were neither social nor historical; his mode of innocence was to proclaim the adequacy of nature and the solitary seer-witness in the creation of the self. By contrast, Franklin's vision was shaped by social perceptions and achievements, achievements of the very kind Thoreau found it necessary to repudiate in order ''to live'' meaningfully. (Actually, Thoreau's meticulous rendering of accounts in building his cabin and selling his beans is a cheerful spoof of Franklin's ledger mentality, and the fact that Thoreau deliberately begins his experiment in cultural and psychological independence on the Fourth of July is hardly a coincidence.)

But while Thoreau's and Franklin's styles and values clash, while one commemorated a public, social, pragmatic self and the other a private, natural, transcendental self, fundamentally both affirmed that one's destiny and one's identity, however one chooses to define them, are essentially in one's own hands. Thoreau, after all, emphasized that he *chose* to live deliberately and that he *chose* to begin and to end his experiments both in consciousness and in the woods. Their meanings, and Thoreau's own notions of the self, were as willfully achieved and as democratically accessible as Franklin's formulas for social identity and success. At bottom, despite their differences, both stories unconditionally affirm human purpose and will as central to the shape of human identity and hence to history.

Other voices in America's dialogue over innocence, however, have found the essential facts of living much more complex than either Franklin or Thoreau envisioned, much more imbued with the limitations on human choice imposed by time and chance and death. Indeed, the most powerful twentieth-century exploration of innocence draws its force from the combination of traditional American imaginings and a starkly classical sense of tragedy. Yet *The Great Gatsby* could scarcely have achieved its extraordinary poignancy were it not for the familiar resonance of the materials with which Fitzgerald worked. Moreover, those materials and their particular resonance take one very close to an understanding of Richard Nixon and his own distinguishing mode of innocence.

Like any classical tragedy *The Great Gatsby* is a tale with universal implications, a tale of human usurpation of the power of the gods and of their wrathful, holocaustic vengeance. Jay Gatsby fatally attempts what is reserved for the deities — to re-create and then live in his own distorted version of the past — and thus he must pay the inevitable price of his own destruction. At the center of this familiar kind of story, however, is an explicitly American message, for Jay Gatsby does not spring, as Fitzgerald misleadingly suggests, from a "Platonic conception of himself." Although young Jimmy Gatz does indeed assume a fabricated, fictional identity called "Jay Gatsby," he does so with materials explicitly drawn from the cultural vestiges of the Franklin legend. If in both Jimmy Gatz's cultural milieu and his imagination those materials have been warped into a gaudy, adolescent fantasy, the outlines of the original model are plainly visible.

Where does Jay Gatsby come from? Fitzgerald gives us many clues. At the end of the novel old Mr. Gatz, come east for his son's funeral, proudly shows narrator Nick Carroway a trophy from Jimmy's boyhood: a ragged Hopalong Cassidy book with a crude schedule for daily discipline and a boyish list of "General Resolves" penned inside the back cover. Included on the list are "study electricity" and "needed inventions," "read one improving book or magazine per week," "save $5.00 (crossed out) $3.00 per week." As Mr. Gatz explains, "It just shows you, don't it? Jimmy was bound to get ahead." The ambitious boy who scrawled those clichéd resolves was indeed bound to get ahead, but the traditional means for doing so were far too slow for him, and Fitzgerald deftly sketches Jimmy Gatz's early deviation from the ancient formula in a few lines:

An instinct toward his future glory had led him, some months before, to the small Lutheran college of St. Olaf's in southern Minnesota. He stayed there two weeks, dismayed at its ferocious indifference to the drums of his own destiny, and despising the janitor's work with which he was to pay his way through.[4]

At the end of two weeks Jimmy drops out of college to return to the lakeside, and thus the twig is bent.

The ragged youth who some months later introduces himself to a degenerate yachtsman as Jay Gatsby has explicitly rejected the Protestant ethic of the Franklin myth in favor of a much more extravagant form of ambition, and the yachtsman, Dan Cody, speeds him on his quest. For Cody, the "pioneer debauchee," is historically the product of the Nevada and the Yukon gold fields, but metaphorically, as his name suggests, he represents the popular, theatrical version of the West of Buffalo Bill and Dangerous Dan Magrew. Dan Cody is veritably a nineteenth-century prototype for Gatsby, a model of romantic decadence and meaningless opulence washed up on the tide of a receding frontier. After five years under Cody's influence, as Fitzgerald tells us, "the vague contour of Jay Gatsby had filled out to the substantiality of a man."

When this "substantiality" meets Daisy Fay, the extravagant dimensions of its composite identity are revealed, for Daisy is the objective correlative for the "fantastic conceits" that have become Jay Gatsby. In the final analysis it is impossible to separate the vapid, translucent Daisy from Gatsby's lurid fantasy, for his dream is actually a narcissistic projection of himself and so, in his imaginings, is she. This is in some senses the main point of the story, for Daisy is essentially the screen on which Gatsby fatally projects his "incorruptible dream" of romantic self-love. Indeed, his courtship, seduction, and later wooing of her are actually but exercises in the extraordinary power of that self-love. Portentously, Gatsby's early courtship is expressly fraudulent, for it is based on his deceptive representation of himself: His officer's uniform masks his anonymity, and he hastens his seduction lest "the invisible cloak of his uniform . . . slip from his shoulders." When we meet Gatsby five years after he has won and lost Daisy, it comes as no surprise that he has evolved into a full-fledged criminal who is using his ill-gotten wealth to concoct a ludicrous, extravagant scenario for regaining her.

As this scenario unfolds, it becomes clear that Fitzgerald is exploring a tragic story that spins out inexorably from the contrivance of the Gatsby fabrication itself, from the cultural accretion that is the "unbroken series of successful gestures" Nick mentions in the novel's beginning. For the artifice of Gatsby is in reality a compounded series of counterfeit but nonetheless characteristically American fact-and-fable identities that dance merrily around each other in a gorgeous, improbable three-ring circus: Jimmy Gatz and Dan Cody, Meyer Wolfsheim and Shoeless Joe Jackson, Buffalo Bill and Horatio Alger, Hopalong Cassidy and old Ben Franklin — all under the baton, in case anyone missed the point, of David Belasco. Gatsby's "vast, vulgar, and meretricious dream" is simply the latest installment in a host of ornate American fantasies that stretch back over time, reaching beyond the city to the frontier and even beyond. They are the bourgeoisie's aristocratic pretensions, the dreams of nobility that produced the brewer's imitation chateau Gatsby lives in, Tom Buchanan's string of polo ponies, and the yacht Dan Cody pilots on meaningless trips to nowhere. They hark back to America's very beginnings, to the trees that once flowered for Dutch sailors' eyes, "a fresh green breast of the new world" which ordinary men and their extraordinary dreams would one day turn into a valley of ashes. These dreams were at once vague and compelling, and their symbol of Daisy and the green light at the end of the dock merely hinted at their enchantments: "Gatsby believed in the green light, the orgiastic future that year by year recedes before us. It eluded us then, but that's no matter — tomorrow we will run faster, stretch out our arms farther. . . . And one fine morning—.'' Jimmy Gatz may have paid a high price for "living too long with but a single dream," but he is not alone in having done so.

The scene shifts. It is Miami Beach, August 8, 1968, and the new nominee for president of the United States, Richard M. Nixon, is addressing the Republican National Convention; he too speaks of a dream:

I can see . . . [a] child tonight. He hears a train go by. At night he dreams of faraway places where he'd like to go. It seems like an impossible dream. . . . But he is helped on his journey through life. A father who had to go to work before he finished the sixth grade. . . . A gentle Quaker mother . . . [who] quietly wept when he went to war but understood why he had to go. A great teacher, a remarkable football coach, an inspirational minister encouraged him on his way. . . . And tonight he stands before you, nominated for President of the United States of America. You can see why I believe in the American dream.[5]

The scene shifts again. President Richard Nixon is delivering the annual State of the Union address before a joint session of the Congress. It is January 22, 1971. After congratulating the newly elected leaders of the Ninety-second Congress, the President says:

To those new members of this House who may have some doubts about the possibilities for advancement in the years ahead, I would remind you that the Speaker and I met just twenty-four years ago in this chamber as freshman members of the 80th Congress. As you can see, we both have come up in the world a bit since then.

Turning to other matters, the President goes on:

In these troubled years just past, America has been going through a long, dark night of the American spirit. But now that night is ending. Now we must let our spirits soar again. Now we are ready for the lift of a driving dream.[6]

The scene shifts once more. It is August 9, 1974, and Richard Nixon's presidency — his own "driving dream" — has come crashing down, and the shaken, tearful President is taking leave of his staff at the White House. It is a wrenching, emotional scene but even so the President's words strike many as unusually inchoate and allusive. Part of the mystery comes from Nixon's emotional, rambling account of his childhood, of his hardworking, unsuccessful father, and of his sainted mother. At that point the President unexpectedly reads a passage from Theodore Roosevelt's diary which deals with the death of Roosevelt's first wife: ''And when my heart's dearest died, the light went from my life forever.'' ''That was TR in his twenties,'' Nixon says. ''He thought the light had gone from his life—but he went on. . . . We think, as TR said, that the light had left his life forever. Not true. It is only a beginning always.''[7]

What do these scenes tell us? They suggest, I think, that in some profoundly basic way the presidency became for Richard Nixon what Daisy became for Jay Gatsby: the objective correlative of his own narcissistic imaginings. That in leaving the presidency Nixon should personify it and link it to a lost, dead ''heart's dearest'' makes explicit the connection between the office and the man's most basic emotional attachments. Like Daisy, Nixon's presidency was fatally shaped and contoured to reflect his strengths and weaknesses, his sense of self and his sense of destiny. In the end, on one level Richard Nixon seemed almost to know this. That he could not see it—or himself—more clearly suggests the nature of his innocence.

A president's character is the nation's fate, as William Shannon has observed, and in no instance has this been made clearer than in Watergate. Yet getting a refraction on Richard Nixon's character is extraordinarily difficult, for the private Nixon remains unknown, and the public Nixon slips in and out of focus, at his best eloquently inspiring and at his worst, as Anthony Lewis once put it, a ''mixture of treacle and venom, whining self-justification and insult, moralizing and lawlessness, sheepish deference and lofty condescension.''[8] Yet two episodes from Nixon's public life speak with particular clarity about the man and his sense of himself. These two episodes, one from the beginning of his career and one from the end, in striking ways reveal both Nixon's strengths and weaknesses.

By any measure, the Checkers speech is one of the milestones in American political history. Before Nixon's extraordinary performance no one fully realized the political power of television; afterward no one could doubt it. The facts seem fairly simple. In September 1952 reporters discovered a secret political fund that had been used to defray the expenses of Senator Richard Nixon, recently nominated as Republican running mate to General Dwight Eisenhower. Fearful that Nixon would prove a campaign liability, the general maneuvered him into taking his case before the American people over network television; Eisenhower's strategy was to force Nixon's resignation from the ticket. The strategy backfired, however, when Nixon went on the air and on the offensive. Point by point he refuted his accusers, and then in a remarkable display of desperate candor he told his life story, a traditional American tale of rags to respectability. The story included his complete financial history—including, of course, acknowledgment that he had accepted the gift of a cocker spaniel puppy named Checkers for his children; Checkers, he vowed, would not be returned. As the clincher, Nixon demanded that all candidates in the 1952 election make similar financial disclosures, and he then dramatically put in the television audience's hands the question of his own fate on the Republican ticket. The response to his performance was overwhelmingly positive, and Eisenhower, who had carefully let it be known that Nixon had to be "clean as a hound's tooth" to stay on the ticket, was forced to keep his young running mate. Nixon had successfully convinced his countrymen that he was not a crook.[9]

The Checkers speech established a pattern that was to recur again and again in Nixon's career: the desperate, largely self-created personal crisis, the heroic, lonely gesture against heavy odds, the reassertion of his own belief in basic American values, and the dramatic protestation of innocence of wrongdoing (usually with careful attention to media coverage). The pattern would, over the next twenty years, become a familiar staple in American political life; indeed, during the Watergate years it became virtually daily fare. Only in the Checkers speech most of what Nixon said, and the image he projected, was essentially accurate. Although not publicized the fund was not exactly secret; it was independently audited and, while perhaps technically illegal, it was in many ways unexceptional. Moreover, Nixon's public rendering of accounts, supported by a legal brief and an independent audit by Price Waterhouse, proved him to be what he claimed: a relatively poor, hardworking, even Franklinesque, public servant whose wife unblushingly wore a "Republican cloth coat." But as subsequent events would show, those circumstances would not always prevail, and not all of Nixon's self-generated crises would be escaped so easily.

In many ways Nixon's television speech of April 29, 1974, marked the beginning of the end of his presidency, and the parallels to the Checkers episode are striking. In the April speech Nixon was once again desperately fighting for his life, again making a bold televised move designed to confound his critics and seize the initiative on his own behalf. This was the speech in which Nixon, under pressure of subpoenas from both the Special Prosecutor and the House Judiciary Committee, made public the so-called presidential transcripts. Nixon had set the stage in the Oval Office carefully. The President's hair was freshly trimmed, and the American flag by his desk was echoed by the pin in his lapel. With the thermostat turned down to keep him from sweating, and against the backdrop of a table on which fifty stacked loose-leaf binders massively held the transcripts, the President made what Anthony Lukas has called "his best speech of the Watergate ordeal."[10]

In his speech the President assured the American people that he was allowing an unprecedented relaxation of executive privilege by making public "everything that is relevant" to the Watergate investigations. There were in the binders, he said, "more than twelve-hundred pages of transcripts of private conversations I participated in between September 15, 1972 and April 27 of 1973. . . . " Furthermore, he went on, "As far as what the President personally knew and did with regard to Watergate and the cover-up is concerned, these materials, together with those already made available, will tell all." But before telling all—that is, before releasing the transcripts the next day—the President artfully released to the press a fifty-page brief prepared by counsel James St. Clair which interpreted the transcripts in the best light possible. "In all the thousands of words spoken," St. Clair asserted, "even though they are unclear and ambiguous, not once does it appear that the President of the United States was engaged in a criminal plot to obstruct justice." Nixon's strategy here was to capture the next day's headlines with the claims of the brief rather than the substance of the transcripts.

The President and his advisers had miscalculated, however, for as the press soon pointed out, the released materials, far from telling all, raised still more questions. First, the presidential transcripts were only part of what the subpoenas had called for; on the day of their release presidential attorney Fred Buzhardt revealed for the first time that nine of the subpoenaed tapes were, as he put it, "nonrecorded." Second, the published transcripts, while a weighty volume in their own right, were a ludicrous contrast to the inflated image created by all those loose-leaf notebooks. As the press quickly revealed, each of those fifty binders had in fact held only about twenty-five pages of typescript, and one of the binders held only one page. Finally, there were the peculiarities of the edited transcripts themselves. According to one count nearly 1,800 portions were marked "inaudible" and some 35 sections were excised as "material unrelated to Presidential action." Inexplicably, the President's conversations contained more than twice as many "inaudibles" as all the other speakers combined.

But the real problem with the Presidential transcripts was their contents. No amount of self-serving editing could conceal the sordid nature of the conversations themselves, and their effect was to undermine Nixon seriously with his own staunchest believers. Longtime Nixton admirer Joseph Alsop called the tapes "sheer flesh-crawling repulsion. The back room of a second-rate advertising agency in a suburb of hell." Even Billy Graham, whom Nixon had ostentatiously courted while President, could "not but deplore the moral tone" of Nixon's conversations. And Senator Hugh Scott, who had often been maneuvered by the White House into excusing Nixon's worst transgressions, termed the transcripts "deplorable, disgusting, shabby, immoral."[11] Releasing the transcripts put the President's supporters in Congress still more on the defensive and led many Republicans to feel that their party's best interests would be served by a speedy removal of the tenaciously clinging President.

In the years between the Checkers speech and the release of the tapes Nixon had pursued his dream of the presidency with all the concentrated energy of a Gatsby pursuing his illusion. It is perhaps symbolic that his quest had begun with young Richard Nixon courting the California voters in 1946 deliberately wearing his officer's uniform. Over the years the image shifted somewhat according to the times: Nixon the veteran, Nixon the Communist hunter, Nixon the experienced world diplomat, the "new" Nixon, and finally the presidential Nixon who would, as he put it, "bring us together." At this point, with the dream finally in hand, his problems compounded and the dream and the self-image and the reality of the presidency became hopelessly, fatally ensnarled in the morass of Watergate. The criminal President fell back upon his old stock of familiar weapons: he made speeches and issued denials; he attacked his critics; he launched public relations campaigns such as "operation candor"; but it was now too late, "the foul dust that floated in the wake of his dream" covered even himself.

The tapes had caused Nixon's presidential mask to slip in a near fatal way. Nixon had always projected an image of prissy rectitude; he once chastized Harry Truman for saying "damn" in public. Now, as the deleted expletives were filled in by the Judiciary Committee and gradually became known, Americans could hear their president tell his former attorney general, "I don't give a shit what happens. I want you to stonewall it, let them plead the Fifth Amendment, cover-up or anything else, if it'll save it — save the plan." It was as if the cast of Fitzgerald's novel were somehow permitted to listen in on Gatsby's mysterious, offstage phone calls. Just as the fabrication of Jay Gatsby, finally exposed for the bootlegger he was, broke up "like glass against Tom's hard malice," so the carefully manufactured figurehead of President Richard Nixon shattered against the undisputable sordidness of his own recorded words. Yet to the end there is much to suggest that Nixon, like Gatsby waiting for the one phone call that never came, remained unknowing and unchanged. In the week before he resigned, with his presidency in shambles around him, David Eisenhower visited his father-in-law in the Lincoln Sitting Room. They went over all the options together. David thought it was hopeless, although he tried not to say so. Part of the President seemed to agree—but another part did not. Maybe what I should do, the President said slowly, is make "the best speech of my life."

But the tapes provided the kind of hard evidence of misconduct that could not be overcome by another heroic, video-gesture of denial and escape. Until this point in time Nixon throughout his career had enjoyed extraordinary success in constructing "scenarios" that avoided responsibility for past actions and that twisted, sometimes ever so slightly, historical truth to meet the requirements of the moment. And like the proud mother, who on being congratulated for her handsome baby exclaimed, "But you should see his picture!," Nixon sometimes seems to prefer the fiction to the fact, the scenario to the actuality. Indeed, one wonders if he could distinguish between the two.

In that wrenching farewell scene at the White House mentioned earlier, one small episode took place that illustrates the point. In recalling his youthful poverty and his family's chronic hard luck, Nixon mentioned that his father at one time owned a lemon ranch. "It was the poorest lemon ranch in California, I can assure you," he said. "He sold it before they found oil on it." In truth, Nixon's father had considered buying the property on which the oil was later found, although in fact he had never done so. But the image Nixon was trying to project of a hardworking, hard luck family seemed to require the distortion, and so it was done.

Yet meeting the requirements of some of Richard Nixon's distorted self-images was hardly so harmless or so inexpensive. No president in history used the powers of the office to serve his own conceits on such a scale or in such a style. From the Sigmund Romberg uniforms of the White House guards and the obligatory trumpet fanfares announcing the President's comings and goings, to the bloated executive staff and the multiple palatial residences, the Nixon administration distinguished itself as no other in furnishing a pomp for every circumstance of the imperial presidency. While the exact expense for all this cannot be determined, *Fortune* magazine estimates that running the Nixon presidency in its final year alone cost the taxpayers about $100 million. And the style with which this took place would have stretched the imagination of Jimmy Gatz himself, although he might have recognized the gaudy dream it sprang from.

For in the end Richard Nixon appears like nothing so much as Jimmy Gatz translated into politics, a veritable Jay Gatsby of the Oval Office. Like Gatsby, Nixon wooed and won and lost his heart's dearest by a succession of strategies involving fantastic counterfeits of familiar cultural coinage. Exhibiting at every turn and in every crisis Poor Richard's mannikin for public scrutiny, in reality and in private Nixon was radically other and different. Like Jimmy Gatz, he pursued the object of his dream of love with an ardor that seems nothing less than grotesque—until one realizes that the dream is nothing less than Nixon's own exalted reflection of himself. One can only speculate as to whether the extravagance of that exalted reflection was a measure of the emptiness within.

All of which bring us full circle. Every culture needs its dreamers, people whose vision is not limited by things as they are. And every culture supplies its dreamers with a traditional fund of images and metaphors and models which give proportion and inspiration to human striving. It is through such a fund of images and models that we learn to distinguish the mundane from the heroic, and the heroic from the grotesque. The distinctions are often subtle, and we need many kinds of teachers to learn them well. We need our Franklins to teach us pride in work and public esteem, and we need our Thoreaus to teach us to cultivate our inner lives. And we need our Gatsbys too, for they teach us, sometimes painfully, the limits of human possibility. But only at our peril do we elect our Gatsbys president. For when we do, their private, narcissistic dreams become our public nightmares.

Notes

1. Prominent among the most important interpreters of American civilization since 1950 who have employed various aspects of the concept of innocence in their analyses are David Noble, Leslie Fiedler, Henry May, R. W. B. Lewis, Charles Sanford, John William Ward, Louis Hartz, Daniel Boorstin, Leo Marx, Loren Baritz, Perry Miller, Richard Chase, A. N. Kaul, Ihab Hassan, Henry Bamford Parkes, Robert Skotheim, David Potter, George M. Pierson, Henry Nash Smith, Gene Wise, Richard Hofstadter, Marvin Meyers, Larzer Ziff, John Higham, Stanley Elkins, Rush Welter, Alan Trachtenberg, Max Lerner, Henry Steele Commager, John Cawelti, and Howard Mumford Jones.

2. Richard W. B. Lewis, *The American Adam: Innocence, Tragedy, and Tradition in the Nineteenth Century* (Chicago: University of Chicago Press, 1955), pp. 3–7.

3. Quentin Anderson, *The Imperial Self: An Essay in American Literary and Cultural History* (New York: Knopf, 1971).

4. F. Scott Fitzgerald, *The Great Gatsby* (New York: Charles Scribner's Sons, 1953), p. 100.

5. Richard M. Nixon, "Acceptance Speech," *Vital Speeches of the Day* 34 (September 1, 1968): 677.

6. Richard M. Nixon, "The State of the Union," *Weekly Compilation of Presidential Documents* (Washington, D.C.: U.S. Government Printing Office, January 25, 1971), p. 89.

7. Carl Bernstein and Robert Woodward, *The Final Days* (New York: Avon Books, 1976), pp. 507–8.

8. Anthony Lewis, "The Good Old Reliable Nixon," *New York Times*, March 15, 1976, p. 31.

9. For an account of the Checkers speech see Garry Wills, *Nixon Agonistes: The Crisis of the Self-made Man* (Boston: Houghton Mifflin Co., 1969), pp. 91–114.

10. J. Anthony Lukas, *Nightmare: The Underside of the Nixon Years* (New York: Viking Press, 1976), p. 487.

11. Ibid., pp. 488–91.

12. Bernstein and Woodward, *The Final Days*, p. 346.

13. Ibid., pp. 507–8. For an extended discussion of the difference between the public and private Nixon see David Abrahamsen, *Nixon vs. Nixon: An Emotional Tragedy* (New York: Farrar, Straus and Giroux, 1976), *passim*.

Bibliography

Archer, Jules. *Watergate: America in Crisis*. New York: Crowell, 1975.

Bernstein, Carl, and Bob Woodward. *All the President's Men*. New York: Simon and Schuster, 1974.

Breslin, Jimmy. *How the Good Guys Finally Won: Notes from an Impeachment Summer*. New York: Viking, 1975.

Dean, John. *Blind Ambition: The White House Years*. New York: Simon and Schuster, 1976.

Drew, Elizabeth. *Washington Journal: The Events of 1973–74*. New York: Random House, 1975.

Lukas, J. Anthony. *Nightmare: The Underside of the Nixon Years, 1969–1974*. New York: Viking, 1976.

Magruder, Jeb Stuart. *An American Life: One Man's Road to Watergate*. New York: Atheneum, 1974.

Mankiewicz, Frank. *U.S. v. Richard Nixon: The Final Crisis*. New York: Quadrangle, 1975.

Rather, Dan, and Gary Paul Gates. *The Palace Guard*. New York: Harper & Row, 1974.

Safire, William. *Before the Fall: An Insider's View of the Pre-Watergate White House*. New York: Doubleday, 1975.

Schell, Jonathan. *The Time of Illusion*. New York: Knopf, 1976.

Sussman, Barry. *The Great Cover-up: Nixon and the Scandal of Watergate*. New York: Signet, 1974.

White, Theodore H. *Breach of Faith: The Fall of Richard Nixon*. New York: Atheneum, 1975.

MARSHALL W. FISHWICK

The Hero in the Context of Social Change

Truth is one, the sages speak of it by many names.

The Vedas

Success is men's god.

Aeschylus

The heroes whom we see everyday through the TV screen may
be the gods of our age.

Hidetoshi Kato

God, I'm glad I'm not me!

Bob Dylan

Does not the pebble, entering the water, begin fresh journeys?

Kung Fu Meditations

Prologue

Oh, East is East, and West is West, And never the twain shall
meet . . .

Rudyard Kipling, The Ballad of East and West

Wrong, Mr. Kipling. In ways which the nineteenth century could hardly have
dreamed of, the twentieth century has broken barriers, boundaries, and barri-
cades. We have created new environments of invisible power, embedded in such
things as the Bomb, the Pill, the Tube. We have melded space and time into a
single concept — space-time — and sent it in orbit. Suddenly we live not only in
visual but also in accoustic space, creating electronic space by simultaneous
information. Nations, states, and culture regions of the world are transformed or
dissolved by such an environment.

The key is iconic; the pattern is multisensuous and multilevel. Hence I find
myself en route to New York, to research a paper for the East – West Communi-

cations Center in Honolulu. I am reading *The Decay of the Angel* by Yukio Mishima, ''the most Western of contemporary Japanese novelists,'' who delivered the manuscript to his publisher and committed suicide to stop the rush of history.

Nor is this remarkable interest in the martial arts the only visible evidence of Western fascination with the East. One need not go to New York to observe the influence of Transcendental Meditation, yoga, Zen Buddhism, and the vogue of various gurus (currently, Maharaj Ji). Nothing is more fashionable than the Mao jacket, and fan clubs for Japanese movies flourish.

What does all this mean in 1979? How is communication between East and West altering? Is a new kind of popular hero inevitable? Do we see in actors like the late Bruce Lee (whose movie *Enter the Dragon* will gross over $25 million) the basic formula emerging? What can we say of the hero in the context of social change?

The Hero

A new international style and outlook are surfacing in every part of the world. Far more pervasive than earlier national or regional styles (classic, gothic, baroque), it transcends political, class, language, and racial barriers. One senses this when he visits Paris, Prague, or Peking; New Delhi, New York, or New South Wales. The basis of the new style is electronic popular culture. What effect will it have on our old, and new, heroes?

So great is the rate of change, so abrupt the transitions, that one finds it difficult even to find a place or discipline from which there is enough perspective to attempt an answer. Perhaps the best place would be in skylab or satellite, looking down at the whirling green ball that has for so many millions of years been known as Earth: the home of man.

And the home of heroes. The very word itself (from the Greek *heros*) means ''superior man, embodiment of composite ideals.'' The *heros* has, and always will have, no matter what the style or culture, a reputation directly related to the social and religious structure of his society. A gift of heaven, the *heros* is a force sent by destiny.[1]

Civilizations which flourished long before the Greeks knew this. ''The entire Sumerian civilization,'' writes Hidetoshi Kato, ''can be seen as one great pantheon.'' Live heroes became deified in death; for the people of the Shang dynasty of China (1400 B.C.) the worship of heaven was synonymous with ancestor worship. In Japan, too, man's worship was tied to service to gods. Kunio Yanagita notes that the verb *matsuru* (to worship) is akin to the verb *matsurau* (to be at the service of).[2]

This kinship has persisted over the centuries. When Tokyo emerged as the Japanese capital in the mid-nineteenth century, it was necessary to establish not only a new sacred place but also new gods: The emperor himself had to be invented instantaneously.

The search and need for heroes is inherent in human history. Preliterate societies allow men, heroes, and gods to stand on a footing of tolerable equality. "Throughout the inhabited world, in all times and under every circumstance, the myths of man have flourished," writes Joseph Campbell. "It is necessary for men to understand, and be able to see, that through various symbols the same redemption is revealed."[3] The hero's story is a monomyth—and it has endless variations.

When one takes seriously the task of a *comparative* study of heroes, and to see if (as Campbell implies) one monomythic hero has a thousand faces, he quickly realizes the magnitude of his task. How can a Westerner come to understand the "Middle" or "Far" East? The terms themselves are significant — Occidental inventions implying distance from the West. That distance, Kenneth Scott Latourette points out, is not only geographical but cultural: "Until the latter part of the 19th century, fewer contacts and less interchange existed between Western European and Far Eastern people than between the Occident and any other of the civilized folk of Asia."[4]

Latourette goes on to point out that the term "Far East" has its counterpart in the Far East itself: Nippon, in its more familiar form, Japan, means the land where the sun rises.

If history has forced most Westerners to deal with the great and expansive cultures of Japan, China, and India in the twentieth century, it has still kept the historic and heroic patterns of many other Oriental cultures removed from wide understanding: Tibet, Sinkiang, Mongolia, Korea, Thailand, Burma, Laos, Cambodia, Ceylon, the Malay Peninsula, the East Indies, and the Phillippines, for example. How many Westerners can name "the four Buddhist lands of the White Elephant and the Sacred Sword—"[5] let alone name the nations' heroes? Or tell us why there are memorial parks to M. Ohmura and T. Saigo in Japan?

Yet a surprising number of young Westerners know the name of India's Ravi Shankar, who became a superstar in the global culture of the 1960s. He and other Eastern musicians brought about what is called the "sitar explosion." By 1968 Shankar could write: "I find myself adored like a movie star or singer. I love young people very much, and since they know I love them, they listen to me and are very receptive."[6] This appeal, Israel's Yehudi Menuhin comments, "is a tribute both to his great art and to the intuitive wisdom of the searching young."

This intuitive wisdom, and this search, takes on the guise not only of the culture but the epoch. In what Westerners call classic times, their heroes were god-men; in the Middle Ages, God's men; in the Renaissance, universal men; in the eighteenth century, gentlemen; in the nineteenth, self-made men. Our century has seen the common man and the outsider become heroic. In keeping with the times they have reacted to our social and scientific revolutions. Some of them now go where once only gods could dwell — in outer space. Heroes must act their ages. History is not meaningful without people, and people are ineffective without leaders. The search for paragons is inherent in human nature. In remote areas of the world men are still deified in their own lifetimes. The idea of aloofness in superhuman power comes late in history.

Just as there are many roles, so are there many meanings. Historians see heroes as shaping the flow of events, philosophers as altering thought patterns, social scientists as evoking attitudes of behavior, folklorists as evoking legends and ballads, politicians as winning elections. Messiah, emancipator, founding father, preserver, creative genius are related terms for one whose influence or personality captivates the people. Emerging at a moment when men's emotions are deeply stirred, the hero appeals to both imagination and reason. No one knows just when and why he comes. The gift of heaven, he is a force and a rallying point.

Like a stream, history moves in one direction for a time, then veers off in another. Gaining momentum it washes away old banks and gouges out new channels. Those who perceive and justify this, altering with the flow of events, are heroes.

Some men flash into prominence — one-issue politicians, matinee idols, sports champions — only to disappear like a flash flood. During their golden moments, however, the maxim is "Winner take all." We quote and misquote them with equal ease. At this juncture no one knows if they are true culture heroes or faddish meteors. (Marshall McLuhan, oracle of today's media revolution, is a contemporary example.) Every age has thousands of aspiring heroes. Some carry through to the second generation, which feels the hero's power in stories told by their fathers. By the third generation his exploits take on a certain remoteness. Always susceptible to legend, a hero becomes superhistorical in myth.

This magic of leadership the Greeks called charisma. They imagined that the peaks of Mount Olympus were reserved for the men-gods who showed charismatic leadership. Such a figure was Heracles, called Hercules by the Romans. Beginning as a petty ruler subject to the order of a more powerful king at Argos, Heracles benefited from known exploits plus mythical stories attributed to him. Finally, he emerged as the Greek Happy Warrior, meeting (as Socrates points out in the *Gorgias*) deep psychological needs of his people. The Athenians, craving a hero of their own, elevated the soldier-seducer Theseus, strong in battle "for rich-haired Helen's sake." Ionian in spirit, he was fond of dancing and music, though city fathers toned down his amorous stories. They deleted Hesiod's references to Theseus' passion for Aegle. Bolstered by his role in plays by Aeschylus, Sophocles, and Euripides, Theseus becomes more deliberate, lofty, and Olympian over the centuries. Cimon brought Theseus' bones to Athens from Scyros, buried them in the heart of the city, and established his cult.[7] History has blotted out this particular shrine; but one can visit Francis's bones in Assisi, Lenin's in Moscow, or Kennedy's in Washington and see the same phenomenon at work.

In contemplating Theseus (or Francis, or Lenin, or Kennedy), his admirers found courage and faith. On Hadrian's Arch was inscribed "Athens, formerly the City of Theseus.'' Athenians did not respect him because he was Theseus; he was Theseus because they respected him.

Still a third Greek hero was chosen by Homer to tower over his great epic poem—Odysseus. His ten-year wandering after the Trojan War not only provided the material for one of the world's greatest stories; it also gave us the notion of odyssey—the long wandering marked by many changes of fortune. Adventurer-warriors all—but how different are Heracles, with his prowess and brute strength; Theseus, with his balanced personality; and Odysseus, with his craftiness and political sagacity. In neither Greek nor American culture is the heroic style monolithic. Perhaps, as Emerson suggests, the one characteristic of a genuine heroism is its persistency.[8]

So impressive, in fact, is this persistency that lesser men are convinced that the hero is a chosen one. The deaths of Roland, Heracles, and Kennedy all drew forth that opinion. The Greeks were certain that their mighty men were part gods and part men. "Those Greeks were probably best advised," Kerenyi writes in *The Heroes of the Greeks*, "who, like the inhabitants of the Island of Kos, burned a sheep at evening as a hero's offering and next morning sacrificed a bull to him as a God."

In Roman times the old gods declined and new ones quickly emerged. Pagan Olympus was supplanted by Christian heaven, where heroes dwelled in everlasting glory. During Christ's lifetime messiahs could be found on every street corner; but by the second century, with the martyrdom of Saint Polycarp, the method of Christian veneration was generally accepted in a sizable portion of Europe.[9] Europeans would eventually export these saints to the far corners of the earth. Working in the same terms as primitive mythology, saints perform the same heroic offices as did classical gods. They render the services of intercession and prediction, providing the focus for relic worship and canonization. Style, but not substance, changed. Heroes got halos.

Then and now the operative aura for heroes was *golden*. They sat on golden thrones, had golden halos, dreamed of heaven with its streets of gold. Today they project their golden glow in film and polychrome advertisements, for which they are given bags of gold which enable them to follow the golden sun in all seasons.

Every hero mirrors the time and place in which he lives. He must reflect men's innermost hopes and beliefs in a public way. No easy task this. First he will benefit from excess adulation, then fall prey to the hysteria of depreciation. The rise and fall of heroes is closely tied in with a culture's ultimate purposes.

The hero is always a barometer to the national "climate of opinion." For years the Radical Republicans and abolitionists of the 1860s were condemned for their abuse and scurrility by American historians. But in the civil rights revolution of the 1950s they form the nucleus of a New Left hero class.[10] Soviet idols today are unlike those venerated by czarist Russia or in Stalinist war years. The "climate of opinion" reflected in 1967 celebrations of communism's fiftieth anniversary bore little resemblance to the outlook of Lenin's day.

Eventually great men are accepted as acts of faith. No Dead Sea scroll could alter Jesus' place in the Christian hierarchy. No historical document could stop Pocahontas from flinging herself on the block and saving Captain John Smith's head. No retelling of the events of the Long March could detract from the heroism of Mao Tse-tung. Monomyths do not bow to the tyranny of facts.

Each hero is emphatically himself, but there are recognizable heroic themes and counterthemes. Time and again one runs into variants of Cinderella and the antithetical Sly Fox. The Persevering Tortoise is the antithesis of the Futile Searcher; the Escapist, of the Returning Prodigal; the Golden Fly, of the Ugly Duckling; Patient Griselda, of the Inconstant Lover. Heroic fairy tales are universal and primary stirrings of the human soul, and all heroic reputations seem to swing between two poles — the saint (Buddha, Paul, Malcolm X) and the conqueror (Alexander, Napoleon, Eisenhower). The former stresses meekness and renunciation, the latter aggressiveness and affirmation. Both groups require missions, martyrs, and disciples.[11]

In fact, a full-fledged culture hero must develop his own mystique and empower a whole array of hero makers to propound it. Napoleon's empire has crumbled, his code is outmoded, but his legend flourishes. He did not hesitate to order the pope to Paris for his coronation as emperor, or to substitute his name for the divinity in the school catechism. His appearance on battlefields, which he methodically documented, was a masterpiece of image making. French poets, patriots, and dramatists helped him to create and spread the Napoleonic legend, as A. J. Guerard shows in his *Reflection on the Napoleonic Legend*. Nor can we blame this on the gullibility of nineteenth-century man. There has probably never been a more effective hero-making device in history than the propaganda machine perfected by Hitler and his associates during the days of the Third Reich. We are forced to update Emerson's contention that "Reputations of the nineteenth century will one day be quoted to prove its barbarism."

To master the macrocosm one must first overcome the microscosm. The source of true heroic power is internal. When he tackles the outer world, the hero faces the inertia of his fellowmen; upsetting the social equilibrium brings conflict. Either his triumph or defeat restores the social equilibrium. His importance stems from perceiving the enduring significance of daily flux. Creative leaders are a leaven in the lump of ordinary humanity. They run out threads of relation through everything, fluid and solid, material and elemental.

When this occurs, man becomes symbol. Caesar symbolized the power of Rome, Kubla Khan the cruelty of Asian hordes, Saint Thomas the wisdom of Christianity, Descartes the method of science. Realizing this, scholars have long sought patterns and typologies in the heroic story. That there are similarities in such matters as birth, youth, and death has long been recognized. Johann Georg von Hahn advanced his "Aryan Expulsion and Return Theory" in 1864, expanded later by Alfred Nutt and Otto Rank. Antti Aarne proposed a tale-type system in 1910, and Vladimir Propp published his *Morphology of the Folktale* in 1928. All this paved the way for Lord Raglan's monumental book, *The Hero: A Study in Tradition, Myth, and Drama* (1936).[12] Raglan named twenty-two elements in the heroic saga, covering origin, early struggles, marriage, reign, death, and burial, opening the door to comparative study of content and internal structure. The stories of Oedipus, Theseus, Moses, Christ, and King Arthur have marked similarities; all are rooted more in myth than in history. Raglan's formula can be applied with interesting results to the leading American hero of my generation, John F. Kennedy. His father was called to a royal court (as ambassador to the Court of Saint James), and the son was educated by (presumably) wise men (at Harvard). Then he went off to fight an evil dragon (the Japanese navy), and after a bloody fracas (PT-109) triumphed and returned to marry the beautiful princess (Jackie). Having inherited his father's kingdom (politics), he fought and defeated a second contender (Nixon) before taking over as ruler (president). For a time he reigned smoothly and prescribed laws. Then he suddenly lost favor (the Bay of Pigs crisis), tried to rally his people, and died a sudden and mysterious death (did Oswald really shoot Kennedy?). Amid great mourning (the first worldwide television funeral) he was buried on a sacred hillside (Arlington). Now he has many shrines (a cultural center, an airport, a library, a highway, and a space launching site).

The single factor that links all Raglan and non-Raglan paragons together is heroic style. Style—a characteristic mode, manner, or method of expression, skill or grace. Umph. Zing.[13]

Ancient Egypt had style. From simple cubic masses they constructed buildings and monuments which were uniquely their own. Strong and refined, the Egyptian style was canonized, and changed little for thirty generations. The Greeks had style, and imposed it on much of the eastern Mediterranean. In the Renaissance, single cities in Italy (Siena, Florence, Venice) developed such distinctive styles that centuries later they are still the platform upon which much of the history of Western painting is based.

People as different as Socrates, Nero, St. Francis of Assisi, Kubla Khan, Robin Hood, Julius Caesar, and William Shakespeare all had style. Very good men, and very bad men, too, never seem to lack it. Take Henry VIII, for example. Whether he was launching a ship, gnawing on a mutton bone, or ogling a bosom, he was superbly himself. The same could be said of his daughter Elizabeth; and it is to her reign that we shall turn when our analysis of America's heroes begins. In her name men explored and subdued a New World in which nature herself was a major adversary.

From the first, life-style has been the dye which colors the total fabric of culture and the lives of all heroes.

Style, like nature, despite all our study and probing, remains a mystery. Not only the folk style of the peasants, with its earthly eternal flavor, but also that of people in all contexts reflects an élan vital which no simple or complex formula can encompass. Most of this paper will deal with people, not formulas. First we must establish some criteria for choosing these people, ordering their stories, and linking them into a single chain. Even if this inner-civilization style, like Walt Whitman's poetry, eludes us, we must continue to search for its meaning.

One finds the term "style" attached to almost everything — cultures, nations, dynasties, regions, periods, crafts. The voluminous literature of art is rooted in the labyrinthine network of the notion of style. Style always means more when it describes one specific figure in space than when it deals with a type of existence in time. Style is bound up with sequence — but who can determine what the sequence should be?

Fumbling for an answer, we end up with models or metaphors. In our minds we form a mental image or pattern that represents for us the "style" of a painter, writer, or period. Then we realize that practically all metaphors for style place matter on the inside, style on the outside. Jean Cocteau notes that decorative style has never existed. "Style is the soul, and unfortunately with us the soul assumes the form of the body."[14]

Styles belong to a time and place, and so do heroes. Our great men are not only eventful; they are event-making. They determine issues or events whose consequences would have been profoundly different if they had not acted. The event-making man not only finds a fork in the historical road — he helps to create it.[15] Just as myth is a charter for society, the hero is the personification of the ethos.

How then does the new electronic global hero personify the ethos of the 1970s? Where can we find evidence and clues that will help answer this intriguing question? What does Professor Kato mean when he says that the heroes seen everyday through the TV screen may be the gods of our age?

To begin with, we all know that sights and sounds penetrate quicker than words. For today's heroes, the mind is not so much a debating society as a picture gallery. Our icons are no longer in church but on the tube: the NBC peacock, the CBS Big Eye, the TV commercial. These images are part of the new world currency—and provide the stage upon which new heroes and heroines will walk.

The new celebrities, like the art of our time, will be truly ahistorical and international. For them nothing is too old, too new, too obscure, too banal, too distant, too close for the everything-all-at-once style. All human history is part of the usable past; literally all the world's a stage and a resource center   Art is not so much a discipline as a scavenger hunt. Walls between disciplines, like national boundaries in a jet plane, become meaningless. Today's art schools teach not only painting and sculpting but also electronics, wiring, and glass blowing, in addition to (often trademark of) international pop. Pop gives the formerly submerged and segregated peoples instant visibility. It links together the two-thirds of the human race who are colored — for the first time. "Say it loud, say it proud, I'm black!" sings Jimi Brown — and the whole world hears him. Black Pop Culture is one of the great potential weapons for world understanding and peace. Whether it will be used to create or to destroy remains to be seen. That it is now, and will continue to be, a major ingredient in the New International Style is certain.

This style supersedes ideology. I have never seen a group of young people enjoy pop music more, or respond more vigorously to it than Poles attending summer conferences in Krakow and Poznan. The new generation is no longer willing to die for communism, capitalism, or any other ism. Instead they want to be tuned in.

We should remember that when Lenin sparked the 1917 Revolution, he shouted not only "Bolshevism!" but also "Electricity!" He turned on the light and shocked a backward peasantry into the Electric Age. By 1960 the whole world was wired for sound. Anyone who would lead must face the Big Light; must live or die by his "image." The nineteenth century took its toll on workers' bodies; the twentieth, on their minds. In place of the illusion of progress is the illusion of technique. The abrasive process of rubbing information against information accelerates. Instead of simple sequence there is radical juxtaposition. Political science has become instant alchemy. "Don't *tell* us about politics. *Be* political."

In short, seek meaning through movement. From the trips to the frontier to the "trips" of hippiedom, Americans have followed this formula. Daniel Boone, Buffalo Bill, Teddy Roosevelt, Timothy Leary, and Matt Dillon went thataway. They took with them weapons of violence and seeds of the new style. Characters in novels by Cooper, London, Hemingway, and Bellow did too. We are the Huck Finns, not the Siddharths. Instead of watching the river flow by, we cross it.

"Instant" intrigues us. Mom thaws out instant meals to supplement instant coffee, instant soup, and instant sex. "Nobody has time any more to start from scratch," Arlene Dahl claims in *Always Ask a Man*. "We can't wait for the coffee to perk, the soup to simmer, or physical attraction to grow into love. Who has time to waste on preliminaries these days? Besides, you can always switch to another brand."

Fed up with old-brand newspapers and magazines, people are finding avant-garde publications and heroes fresh breezes in a smoggy culture. On a more scholarly level, the *Journal of Popular Culture* is making review essays on "Mission Impossible" and "Diana Ross and the Supremes' Greatest Hits" subjects for graduate seminars instead of pulp magazines. The significance of such ventures is stressed by Edgar Friedenberg: "The new music, films and newspapers are not just hippie curiosities. They may be the only thing keeping American society from being taken in by its own cant and drowning as if in a cesspool."

They are part of the New International Style. So are the heroes, emerging simultaneously in many parts of the world. If we can help to identify and explain these new heroes, we will have taken a giant step forward towards our obvious goal: to promote better relations between the United States and the nations of Asia and the Pacific. And we will go far towards explaining the global village to those of us who are suddenly in it.

Notes

1. See "Clio's Favorites," Chapter 1 of Marshall W. Fishwick's *American Heroes: Myth and Reality* (Washington, D.C.: Public Affairs Press, 1953).

2. Hidestoshi Kato, "From Pantheon to Presley: Changes in Urban Symbolism," in *Communication and the City: The Changing Environment,* Paper #7 of the East-West Communication Institute, Honolulu, Hawaii, November 1973.

3. Joseph Campbell, *The Hero with a Thousand Faces* (New York: Pantheon, 1949).

4. Kenneth Scott Latourette, *A Short History of the Far East*, 4th ed. (New York: Macmillan, 1964), p. v.

5. See John F. Cady, *Thailand, Burma, Laos, and Cambodia* (Englewood Cliffs, N.J.: Prentice-Hall, 1966). Important for the intercultural understanding is Chapter 6, "The Impact of Colonial Rule." Nor are other non-Western areas given the attention and understanding they deserve. See, for example, James W. Buel, *Heroes of the Dark Continent* (London: Faber, 1890), and Martha B. Banks, *Heroes of the South Seas* (New York: Macmillan, 1896).

6. Ravi Shankar, *My Music, My Life* (New York: Simon and Schuster, 1968), p. 9. Another helpful study in this context is Harold Rosenberg, *The Tradition of the New* (New York: Horizon, 1959).

7. See Walter R. Agard, *Classical Myths in Sculpture* (Madison: University of Wisconsin Press, 1953).

8. See Emerson's piece on "Heroism," in *Essays and Poems* (1844), p. 205. The matter is also explored in Harold Lubin's "Introduction" to *Heroes and Anti-heroes* (San Francisco: Chandler Press, 1968), pp. 9ff.

9. See D. Ribble's *The Martyrs: A Study in Social Control* (Chicago: University of Chicago Press, 1931), and J. M. Mecklin's *The Passing of the Saint* (Chicago: University of Chicago Press, 1941).

10. Arnold A. Rogow, "The Revolt Against Social Equality," *Dissent* 4 (Autumn 1957).

11. For a full discussion of these matters see Otto Rank, *The Birth of the Hero, and Other Essays* (New York: Vintage Books, 1964); David Malcolmson, *Ten Heroes* (New York: Duell, 1939); and Joseph Campbell, *The Hero with a Thousand Faces* (New York: Pantheon, 1949) (paperback ed., Meridian, 1956).

12. Details on these books, and the general growth of comparative methods, are presented by Alan Dundes, ed., *The Study of Folklore* (Englewood Cliffs, N.J.: Prentice-Hall, Inc., 1965).

13. The literature of style is extensive, the work of Heinrich Wilfflin, Joseph Margolis, Carl Friedrich, and John Rupert Martin being important. Wylie Syper's *Four Stages of Renaissance Style* (New York: Peter Smith, 1955) suggests an approach which can be applied to other periods. See also Meyer Shapiro's essay on "Style," in A. L. Kroeber's *Anthropology Today* (Chicago: Phoenix, 1953), and George Kubler's *The Shape of Time* (New Haven, Conn.: Yale University Press, 1962).

14. Quoted by Susan Sontag, whose essay "On Style," in *Against Interpretation* (New York: Farrar, Straus and Giroux, 1966), casts new light on this difficult subject.

15. These words paraphrase Sidney Hook's in Chapter 9 ("The Eventful and the Event-Making Man") of his study of *The Hero in History* (New York: Humanities Press, Inc., 1943).

NORMAN R. YETMAN

Slavery and Personality: A Problem in the Study of Modal Personality in Historical Populations

Norman R. Yetman received his doctorate in American Studies from the University of Pennsylvania and is currently chairman of the American Studies department at the University of Kansas.

Of the voluminous amount of attention devoted to the institution of slavery during the past two decades, no single essay has had a greater impact than Stanley M. Elkins's provocative Sambo thesis.[1] Elkins hypothesized that the stereotype of a docile, submissive, infantile, childlike slave was not necessarily a rationalization or projection of American slaveholders but represented a relatively valid description of the predominant slave personality structure exacted by the American slave system. But Elkins provided no empirical support of his thesis. Instead he advanced an implicit model of the relation between the social system of American slavery and its psychological consequences for the enslaved. He argued that Sambo was an adaptive character type, a response to and a product of the unique nature of the American system of slavery. His thesis was supported by three separate but interrelated arguments: (1) a comparison of the institutional arrangements of American and Latin American slavery; (2) a theoretical discussion, synthesizing features of Freudian, Sullivanian, and role theory, of the relationship between character and social structure; and (3) an ingenious analogy to Nazi concentration camps in which observers noted widespread "infantilization" among adult inmates.

Slavery was a bold and imaginative work, and the question of slavery and personality it raised is one with which every student of the "peculiar institution" must come to grips. However, as might be anticipated, the work has been vigorously challenged on theoretical and methodological, as well as ideological, grounds. And the attention devoted to the thesis shows little sign of abating more than a decade after its original publication.[2]

One of Elkins's stated objectives in *Slavery* was to shift the context of the debate about the "peculiar institution," to raise different questions, to develop a new framework for its analysis. Ironically, the central question raised in *Slavery* — the provocative Sambo thesis — itself became characterized by a coerciveness comparable to that Elkins sought to dispel. Most who reacted to the idea of Sambo retained Elkins's conceptual framework, categories (e.g., the ideas of Sambo, identification, infantilization, internalization, etc.), and assumptions. Above all, most critics became locked into a debate over *whether* Sambo existed, not the more general — and to me more fruitful — question of *how* the slave system affected its participants.[3] Most criticism obscured the import of the questions Elkins raised concerning the relation between social structure and personality functioning. Moreover, many of those who reacted against Elkins's argument did not consider the implications of more general questions of modal personality among historical populations. In this paper I would like to consider several theoretical and conceptual problems Elkins's analysis posed and to suggest an approach by which the general relation of slavery and personality can be assessed.

Elkin's Model

One of the most intriguing and fruitful aspects of Elkin's work was the model of power and dependency he *implicitly* suggested. According to Elkins, Sambo was the "dominant" (what I interpret to mean statistically most frequent or "modal") personality type, but it was not universal. He did not argue that the effects of the American slave system would be uniformly felt, that all slaves would be Sambos, or that the Sambo personality would be randomly distributed among the slave population. Rather, he hypothesized that the effects of the system would be differentially felt among certain categories of slaves. Sambo would be most frequently found among those most vulnerable to the direct effects of the master's power and sanctions.

It is recognized in most theory that social behavior is regulated in some general way of adjustment to symbols of authority. . . . The more diverse those symbols of authority may be, the greater is the permissible variety of adjustments to them — and the wider the margin of individuality, consequently, in the development of the self.[4]

Elkins's failure to emphasize the probabilistic nature of his model — that the degree of Samboism will vary relative to the power wielded over an individual — has contributed to the idea that *all* slaves were traumatized by and therefore total victims of the American slave system. But I would argue that his model was not, as several critics have charged,[5] a deterministic or absolutistic one. Elkins himself in responding to criticism of his thesis rejected this implication, asserting that he "would be more than happy to settle for 'degrees.' (For instance, something less than absolute power produces something less than absolute dependency.)"[6]

In Elkins's model, therefore, Sambo, "the typical plantation slave,"[7] was primarily a product of the agricultural plantation. The field hand on a large plantation and the urban slave who arranged his own employment represented

polar ideal types among the slave population. Sambo traits were most characteristic of the former and were relatively less pronounced in those slaves whose
experiences, in terms of the diversity and complexity of alternative roles available to them, were shielded from the "full impact" of the "closed" system.

It was possible for significant numbers of slaves, in varying degrees, to escape the full
impact of the system and its coercions upon personality. The house servant, the urban
mechanic, the slave who arranged his own employment and paid his master a stipulated
sum each week, were all figuratively members of the "underground."[8]

What is most important in this conceptualization is the model of power and
dependency that Elkins suggested. In this model Sambo traits were distributed in
the slave population relative to the statuses an individual held within the structure
of the plantation slave system. Personality structure was treated as a dependent
variable, a function of an individual's status positions. The model itself, however, need not be restricted to slavery alone but is potentially applicable to other
"closed" institutional systems. Implicit in this approach, therefore, was a theory
of the psychological effects of life in a "closed system," one where "childlike"
behavior in adults represented the most extreme psychological consequence of
such an experience. The pervasiveness of these characteristics, moreover, should
be directly proportional to the number of available roles in which the individual
can effectively exert personal autonomy. It may well be that these broader
conceptual implications concerning the psychological functioning of individuals
in "closed systems" will ultimately prove to be Elkins's most profound and far-
reaching contribution.

Unfortunately, there has been little social scientific attention directed to the
question of the psychological effects of institutional regimentation. The most
notable exception is Erving Goffman's perceptive essay delineating what he
terms "total institutions," a concept markedly similar to Elkins's characterization
of a "closed system."[9] Goffman defined a "total institution" as "a place of
residence and work where a large number of like-situated individuals, cut off from
the wider society for an appreciable period of time, together lead an enclosed,
formally administered round of life."[10] He suggested that the term be employed to
describe a number of institutions (prisons, concentration camps, mental institutions, religious orders, military organizations) "whose encompassing or total
character is symbolized by the barrier to social intercourse with the outside and to
departure."[11]

Goffman's analysis was limited as a predictive model in several respects, for
he did not adequately distinguish between behavioral and psychological levels of
inmate adjustment, nor did he relate the adaptations he distinguished to social
structural or institutional variables. Nevertheless, his analysis is useful for the
purposes of this discussion in that it provides a context within which the
institution of slavery can be conceptually considered. I would argue that both
slavery and the concentration camp experience must be considered in terms of

their relevance to a more inclusive social psychological model.[12] Analyses of both experiences suggest a range of total institutions along a continuum of power, the most extreme form of which was the concentration camp, where terror, brutality, and cruelty — the absolute tyranny and repression by those in superordinate positions—were more extreme than in any other toal institution. Even among concentration camps, however, the degree of "totalness" varied, as shown by differences between those camps where incarceration and economic exploitation, rather than extermination, were primary goals. Elkins, it will be recalled, maintained that such gradations occurred among slave systems as well as among different statuses within the same slave system. And, according to his model, personality functioning is a consequence of the degree of "totalness"— the more absolute the dominant group's power, the more pronounced an effect it will have upon personality structures of those in subordinate positions.[13]

The value of this model, therefore, lies in its predictive nature. That is, an individual's role network within a closed social system can influence his psychological adaptation. While Elkins restricted his analysis to the specific historical situation of slavery in America, the model upon which it is based might well be extended to explain the dynamics of other total institutions and other dominant-subordinate relationships (e.g., debt bondage, clientage, serfdom, caste systems, etc.) as well as slavery.

Elkins's concentration camp analogy was therefore germane to the question of Sambo to the extent that it contributed to an understanding of the functioning and effects of total institutions and to the idea that personality structure is a variable influenced along a continuum of power. In essence both Elkins and Goffman similarly utilized descriptions of the concentration camp to develop a more general theory of the psychology of certain types of social institutions. The analogy was employed by Elkins in the absence of an adequate theory of the psychology of total institutions. The concentration camp situation provided clues to a possible explanation of comparable characteristics occurring in both situations. If Elkins's thesis is conceived within this broader theoretical context, its validity no longer hinges upon the efficacy of the analogy but upon the reliability of this model.

Elkins's comparison of the slavery systems in Latin America and the United States reinforces this model. In the United States, the master's power, supported by religious and political institutions, was potentially absolute, and the slave's autonomy was consequently severely circumscribed. In Latin America, according to Elkins, the slave could perform in a greater number of roles than in the United States — as slave, religious communicant, father, and so on — and authority within the Latin system was widely distributed. There the conflicting and competing authority of both church and state neutralized and impeded the imposition of absolute authority by the master, permitting a substantial degree of freedom and individuality for the slave. The absence of Sambo in Latin American lore, in contrast to its pervasiveness in the United States, allegedly reflected this diffusion of power.

Elkins therefore assumed that Sambo was idiosyncratic to American slavery and absent from other societies that permitted legal servitude.[14] Finding no evidence for the existence of Sambo in the Latin slave situation led him to discount slavery "in the abstract" as an explanation. This conclusion, however, is not only open to question on empirical grounds but is incompatible with the very model that Elkins developed to explain the existence of Sambo. That the Sambo image was not so pronounced nor so pervasive in Latin America as in the United States does not mean that such a personality type did not exist elsewhere. In Elkins's model the basic variables concern the effects of "absolute power" upon personality. Therefore, if the distinctive feature of slavery is the "totality of the slave's powerlessness,"[15] a comparable personality type should be found in other systems of slavery, even if in a somewhat attenuated form. From the inherent logic of Elkins's model, therefore, one would conclude that the psychological syndrome he described is an inevitable and inherent concomitant of slavery; the Sambo personality type was a function of the situation of slavery in general, not of the American variant alone.[16]

This is not the place to attempt to assess the validity of Elkins's comparison of slave systems in the Americas, since this aspect of his analysis has already been subjected to critical scrutiny. Several writers have persuasively argued that Sambo was a more prevalent stereotype in Latin America than Elkins admits and that his delineation of the differences between the slave systems in the Americas has been overdrawn.[17] These criticisms do not, however, diminish the value of Elkins's comparative analysis in constructing a model of the psychological impact of slavery. The delineation of Latin American slave situations, as against the American system of slavery, suggested that a society's institutional arrangements are important variables affecting the psychological functioning of its members and that by varying the concentration of institutional power, different modal personality types will result.

In summary, Elkins placed substantial reliance upon the comparison with Latin American slavery and the analogy with the concentration camp situation to support his contention that Sambo existed. But while both approaches are illuminating and provocative, neither case is indispensable to this thesis. They illustrate the model by specifying the importance of the relationship between social structure (e.g., occupation, size of slaveholding unit, geographical location) and psychological variables. One of the unfortunate consequences of the controversies that have raged over the question of Sambo is that the importance of the theoretical model has been obscured. Within the logic of this model the important question is not whether the Sambo personality type existed or did not exist. Instead it is whether occupying different roles in a total institution exacted differences in the incidence of certain character traits. In other words, rather than asking *whether* slaves were affected by the "peculiar institution," the question becomes *which* categories of slaves were affected and *how*.

Sambo: The Need for Clarification

The least adequate aspect of the Sambo hypothesis concerns the actual content or dynamics of the personality type. What was meant by the term "Sambo"? Elkins was not clear on this point, for he nowhere defined his central concept with sufficient precision. His study was designed to suggest that stereotyped characteristics of the American slave should not be dismissed as mere propaganda, and that the pervasiveness of these stereotypes in the antebellum South might be understood without resorting to racist explanations. Consequently he was not so much concerned with the conceptual clarity of the psychological *components* of Sambo. But the considerable ambiguity inherent in the term must be resolved before the question of the hypothesized institutional effects upon slave psychological functioning can be adequately evaluated.

The term "Sambo" itself forestalled conceptualization, for it possesses a dramatic, evocative, and emotional quality that diverted attention from the crucial question of the components or dimensions of slaves' personality structure. It is likely that much of the ideological controversy that Elkins's thesis stirred might have been avoided had the term "Sambo," with its assumption of the emasculation of the black male, not been employed.[18] To many critics the "childlikeness" of Sambo impugned the "manhood" of male slaves. The response has been to attempt to reassert their machismo, to demonstrate that the effects of the system were insufficient to undermine the slave's masculinity. Nowhere is this more explicit than in Blassingame's *The Slave Community,* the primary thrust of which is to attack the validity of the Sambo concept by demonstrating the slave's "manliness."

All things considered, the few Africans enslaved in seventeenth- and eighteenth-century America appear to have survived their traumatic experiences without becoming abjectly docile, infantile, or submissive. The Africans retained enough manhood to rebel. . . .[19]

In the quarters . . . where he saw his parents most often, his father acted like a man, castigating whites for their mistreatment of him, being a leader, protector, and provider.[20]

What is important for the present analysis is that terms such as "manhood," "acting like a man," and so on, are equally as imprecise as "Sambo" as explanatory concepts; they reveal little of the nature of the psychological predicates of such action. For this reason this aspect of the debate — with its strong ideological overtones — has been analytically futile and unproductive.

Another source of confusion surrounding the Sambo concept is the tendency to conceive of it as a unidimensional entity, rather than as a composite of analytically distinct components. Elkins's own delineation of Sambo was ambiguous in this regard. On the one hand, he enumerated several *traits* — perceived as *behavioral* manifestations of the underlying psychological adjustment exacted by the slave system — allegedly characteristic of Sambo. Among these were irresponsibility, silliness, laziness, impassivity, docility, humility, obedience, dependence, boastfulness, resignation, improvidence, and loyalty and deference to authority figures. On the other hand, these several traits were all subsumed under the more inclusive rubric of "childlikeness"; Elkins's basic assumption is that Sambo represented a distinct personality type.[21]

Most critics have concurred in this unidimensional conceptualization, assuming that the traits enumerated previously all have the same psychological referent— that is, that each is merely a different behavioral manifestation of the same underlying personality structure. As the term "Sambo" has become widely used, it has become reified. Critics—even if they denied the validity of Elkins's assertion that Sambo was "dominant"—have come to accept the concept as a real and unitary phenomenon. Thus George Rawick referred to "the slave personality produced by [the slave] community," and argued that "the slave personality was . . . not one that should be described in the metaphor of static psychology as 'infantile.'"[22] Thus, as noted earlier, even though the Sambo concept is rejected, its critics have become locked into a search for a *single* personality, albeit one different from Sambo.

A basic assumption of this paper, therefore, is that any attempt to assess the effects of slavery upon personality structure cannot only be more adequately understood, but more effectively operationalized, if it is conceptualized not as a single psychological attribute but as a personality structure of n dimensions. As noted previously, a careful examination of his discussion of slavery and the concentration camp literature reveals that Elkins himself posited several *distinct* variables hypothetically related to the Sambo personality. This conceptualization, moreover, is theoretically consistent with the position advanced by Inkeles and Levinson, who have warned against the assumption that the distribution of personality characteristics in a population is unimodal. A multimodal conception, they have argued, "would seem to be theoretically the most meaningful as well as empirically the most realistic."[23]

Behavior and Personality Structure

In Elkins's analysis the effects of the slave system were assumed to be so profound that the slave seldom deviated from role prescriptions defined by the master; rebellion and resistance were atypical and infrequent when compared with the incidence of these phenomena in Latin America. The leaders of the major slave revolts in America (Gabriel, Vesey, Turner) were described as individuals who personified the antithesis of Sambo and whose exceptional behavior can be explained by the fact that they were not subject to the same sanctions as the typical slave—their qualities of leadership "were developed well outside the full coercions of the plantation authority-system."[24] Elkins therefore appeared to equate Sambo with full behavioral conformity to the master's norms, and a non-Sambo personality type with the rebellious or recalcitrant slave.

The relationship between the slave's overt behavior and his underlying personality structure has been one of the major sources of dispute in the Sambo controversy. Most critics have agreed that conformity to slave role prescriptions exceeded organized rebellion among American slaves. However, few have concurred in Elkins's assumption that such conformity provided an accurate index of the *psychological* adjustment of the slave. Rather, it has been argued, behavioral conformity represented merely situational accommodations that did not influence the essential character structure of the slave. According to Nichols, the slave was characterized by a highly sophisticated "stage presence — that is the capacity to play his role convincingly before the master, even while he [the slave] sabotaged the effort in actuality."[25] Likewise, Herskovits, writing several years before Elkins's essay appeared, rejected the validity of the Sambo image.

It is difficult to understand how the Negro obtained any reputation for docility. This may, of course, be due in part to the outer aspect of accommodation whereby, following the patterned flexibility of African tradition, the slave told his master what he believed his master desired, and for the rest kept his counsel and bided his time until he could make good an effect protest, or escape.[26]

More recently, Blassingame has argued:

In the quarters . . . where he saw his parents most often, his father acted like a man, castigating whites for their mistreatment of him, being a leader, protector, and provider. On the few occasions when the child saw him at work the father was obedient and submissive to his master. Sometimes children internalized both the true personality traits and the contradictory behavioral patterns of their parents. Since, *however, their parents' submission was on a shallow level of convenience* directed toward avoiding pain, it was less important as a model of behavior than the personality traits they exhibited in the quarters.[27]

As these examples demonstrate, generalizations concerning the slave's underlying personality structure drawn from socially required behavior are viewed with skepticism. While resistance to the slave system is frequently cited as evidence that the slave was not Sambo-like, servility and docile compliance with role prescriptions are interpreted as accommodative mechanisms that did not mitigate the slave's inner defiance or in any manner reflect his "true" personality.[28] But if the argument that the slave was merely feigning submission to the master is accepted, then one cannot assess the slave personality structure from overt behavior. Elkins inadvertently contributed to the tendency to perceive the problem of slave personality structure in terms of *behavioral* characteristics by arguing that the behavior of the runaway slave was evidence that Sambo was not universal among the slave population. But to interpret conformity and rebellion as antithetical qualities precludes the possibility that rebelliousness and docility (or their psychological predicates) could mutually *and simultaneously* coexist in the same individual. Just as it has been argued that conformity to the system may mask a rebellious spirit, by the same logic, evidence of protest, recalcitrance, rebellion, and disloyalty do not necessarily indicate that the psyche of the enslaved had been unaffected by the system. Slave behavior alone is therefore an inadequate index of the slave personality structure.

It is, moreover, theoretically doubtful that reliance upon behavior is sufficient to establish the existence and nature of slave personality characteristics. As Inkeles and Levinson have pointed out, modal personality "cannot be *equated* with societal regularities of behavior but must progress beyond the cataloging of behavior items to the psychological analysis of behavior. Modal personality must be defined conceptually as a determinant of behavior rather than concretely as a *form* of behavior."[29] One of the basic theoretical assumptions of this paper, therefore, is that analysis of the question of slave personality should not deal with whether the prevailing slave adaptation was one of conformity to or deviation from role expectations alone. The more appropriate question concerns the psychological consequences of enslavement; the theoretical issue is how the "peculiar institution" affected slaves' psychological functioning, not only their behavior. It is therefore necessary to identify and isolate some of the psychological variables comprising the slave personality structure.

Dimensions of Slave Personality Structure

In his analysis Elkins employed three separate approaches to account for the existence of Sambo: an analogy with another "total" institution — the Nazi concentration camp, a comparative institutional analysis — with the Latin American slave situation, and an explanation in terms of social scientific theoretical models. In the latter discussion Elkins considered the relevance of Freudian, Sullivanian, and role theories, but he did not succeed in clarifying the problem of the psychological components of Sambo. Especially in his discussion of Freudian and Sullivanian theories Elkins appeared more intent upon explaining the psychodynamics of the concentration camp inmate than those of the slave. His discussion of the Freudian model was confined solely to the concentration camp experience and failed to provide any theoretical interpretation for the existence of "Sambo." If Freudian terminology was to provide a relevant interpretation of the slave experience, it was left to the reader.

Only in his discussion of role theory did Elkins directly consider the phenomenon of slavery. As previously noted, role theory was integral to his model that explains the relationship between the social system of slavery and personality characteristics of the slave. The most significant variable in this model, the mediating link between the social structure and the person, is the status position an individual occupies within the slave social system. According to this model, individuals occupying similar statuses will not only exhibit similar behavior but will possess similar personality types as well. While role theory provides a useful means of conceptualizing this model — that is, of specifying the relationship between the social structure and the distribution of psychological types within the social system — it does not provide adequate definitions of the traits themselves, for there has been little empirical research dealing with the effects of role experience upon personality variables.[30] It is therefore necessary to look elsewhere for clues concerning the components of the Sambo type.

In his concentration camp analogy Elkins implied that the psychological mechanisms of adjustment among slaves in the antebellum South were qualitatively comparable to those of SS captives. Since in his discussion of the concentration camp Elkins delineated some of the salient effects of total institutions, a review of accounts of the modal concentration camp adjustment might suggest some psychological dimensions of greater precision than the method of trait enumeration Elkins employed.

Three interrelated but distinct characteristics of the prisoners' adaptations emerge from the accounts of the concentration camp: a regression into childlike or infantile behavior, the imposition of new superego content, and a sense of dependence upon and identification with direct authority figures. By implication, therefore, similar processes should have occurred in the psychological development of the slave. Elkins perceived infantilization as the paramount dynamic in the slave's adaptation. The typical slave's "relationship with his master was one of utter dependence and childlike attachment: it was indeed this childlike quality that was the very key to his being."[31] He did not employ the term "regression" to describe the slave's adaptation, since the slave was born into the system. Yet he implied that the end product of the camp experience—infantalization—was also manifested by the slave.

Elkins maintained that neither "childlikeness" nor "infantilization" need be interpreted literally, since the terms are metaphorical conveniences useful because both were employed by concentration camp observers and by apologists of slavery. But he did not specify *how* literally they should be interpreted. Moreover, he did not discuss the psychodynamic content of "infantilization"; the assumption is that the phenomenon involves similar dynamic processes in both the camp and under slavery. Elkins therefore discussed three roles exhibiting similar behavioral characteristics — concentration camp inmate, slave, and child. To characterize the slave or the concentration camp inmate as "childlike" is to imply that all three of these roles are psychodynamically, as well as behaviorally, similar. But this does not really inform us of the dynamics of each role. As Caudill pointed out in his study of Japanese-American modal personality types, a similarity in external personality (or in descriptions of external behavior) may be derived from different psychological structures.[32] Therefore, because "infantilization" and "childlikeness"may have different dynamic explanations in the child and in the adult slave and because the term is descriptive of a category of *behavior* — not necessarily of psychological components — these terms cannot be considered appropriate variables of Sambo. It is therefore necessary to consider further the psychodynamic components of the slave adaptation and conceptually to isolate relevant components or dimensions of Sambo — that is, to define what "infantilization" means in the case of the slave specifically.

Elkins's explanation of the dynamics of the infantilization manifested by concentration camp inmates was strongly influenced by his reliance upon accounts written by individuals trained in psychoanalytic theory. His model of the effects of both the concentration camp and the slave situation in America was based in large measure on Bettelheim's wartime (1944) article,[33] which explained the inmate's psychological adjustment in terms of his prewar psychoanalytic framework. This model, however, antedated the emergence of ego psychology, and Bettelheim himself regards the interpretations he advanced at that time as theoretically inadequate, since "both the data and their interpretations transcended the theoretical framework I tried to force them into."[34] But Elkins did not consider the relevance of Bettelheim's own theoretical reinterpretation of the concentration camp experience, nor did he interpret slavery from the perspective of ego psychology, which emphasizes the independent functioning of the ego processes as integral to an understanding of human personality.[35] Instead Elkins described the concentration camp in terms of traditional psychoanalytic theory, a fact that led him to slight the effects of the experiences upon the ego structure, which, as Bettelheim has noted, is crucial for an understanding of the dynamic processes of personality transformation that occurred in the camps.

In his reassessment of what occurred in the concentration camp Bettelheim emphasized the profound effects of that experience upon the ego structure. Most significant was the atrophy of the individual's ego resources and the substitution of external for inner controls. The objective of the concentration camp was to destroy the psychological capacity for self-determination, to eliminate inner or internal sense of control of the environment within which the individual operated. The camp achieved this objective with remarkable efficiency and thoroughness: all personal control was abolished; all self-initiated action was eliminated and substituted with externally imposed action. The individual was deprived of any sense of independence of action, decision making, or privacy. In such a situation the individual's sense of personal control over his own actions was effectively undermined; his sense of dependence upon external authority was increased.

Bettleheim's reinterpretation is especially relevant to the problem of delineating the components of slave personality because he emphasized the impact of the concentration camp experience not only upon the superego, which Elkins stressed, but upon the structure of the ego as well. Perceived from this perspective, the slave's dependence, improvidence, impulsiveness, and lack of effective internal controls would seem to indicate that a crucial variable distinguishing the Sambo type is a weak ego structure.

The concept of ego strength has been widely employed in personality theory, and a number of measures of this phenomenon have been devised.[36] According to Barron, whose scale has been widely used as an index of ego strength, it refers to the capacity to deal realistically and effectively with the environment. Among the characteristics that Barron included in the category of ego strength are a strong sense of reality, and feelings of personal adequacy and vitality.[37] Jerome Bruner's concept of self-potency, which refers to the "sense of being able to act effectively in a situation, to overcome obstacles, to 'make out all right,' "[38] would appear to be synonymous. It would appear that both concepts of ego strength and self-potency are similar to the popular term "self-confidence," or what might be more appropriately characterized as "self-strength." While there is considerable imprecision in attempts to define the concept of ego strength, the concept remains theoretically an important one for this analysis.

What the concepts of ego strength and self-potency appear to be dealing with is the extent to which individuals have developed ego or internal control structures that enable them to control their environment and satisfy their needs effectively. A fruitful approach to measuring this characteristic has been derived from the research of Julian Rotter and his associates and their distinction between external and internal control of reinforcements.[39] The basic effort in Rotter's research has been to identify the source of control — whether internal or external to the self — to which an individual attributes what happens to him. People characterized by external control perceive events in which they are involved as resulting from forces outside their own control (e.g., luck, chance, fate, other people), whereas individuals high in a sense of internal control attribute events to their own behavior, skills, or personal characteristics. While the relationship of the external-internal dimension to that of ego strength has not been adequately explored empirically, both would appear to be dealing with similar phenomena, since implicit in the concept of external control is the idea that the actor lacks confidence in his ability to control what happens to him in particular situations. And they would appear to represent a relevant dimension of assessing slave personality structure. Mullin, in his superb treatment of eighteenth-century Virginia slavery, argued that slaves involved in organizing the Gabriel conspiracy "were more autonomous than the slaves they would lead. They had a life of their own — masters are conspicuously absent from their lengthy & detailed dispositions. . . ."[40]

Rotter has developed a scale with which to examine individual differences on the internal-external control dimension, and much research has been undertaken in an attempt to establish its correlates.[41] Several of these studies conducted in situations that approach total institutions are relevant here. Seeman employed the I-E scale to measure a psychological equivalent of alienation — the sense of powerlessness—in both a tuberculosis hospital and a reformatory. In both places he found that internally oriented individuals were better informed and more concerned about their situations. Those individuals characterized by a high perception of external control, on the other hand, were convinced of their own powerlessness and were indifferent to the characteristics of their situations.[42]

It would be consistent with the thesis being examined here to suggest that racial segregation and discrimination in American society would create a situation in which blacks have a higher sense of external control than whites. Utilizing the I-E scale in a study of reformatory inmates, Lefcourt and Ladwig found that, controlling for social class, blacks scored higher on measures of external control than whites.[43] Similarly, studies by Gore and Rotter,[44] and Strickland,[45] were concerned with the relation between the dimension of internal-external control and involvement or expressed willingness to become involved in civil rights protest activities. Those favorable to an activist stance as well as those who themselves had participated in such activities scored significantly higher on internal control than individuals indifferent or unwilling to become involved in such activities. In a study of the responses of black Detroit youth to the 1967 urban riots Forward and Williams[46] found that riot supporters held strong beliefs in their ability to control events in their own lives and shape their own futures coupled with a realistic assessment of the role of external factors, such as discrimination, that may block their aspirations. Unfortunately, these studies of the internal-external personality dimension considered only relations among attitudinal variables — for example, riot supporters were more likely to manifest a stronger sense of internal control than those blacks opposing the riots. The studies thus did not relate the expression on this personality dimension to structural variables, such as socioeconomic status, which is the concern of this model.

Nevertheless, the implications for the present analysis of the slave population seem clear. The "totalness" of the slave system should hypothetically have generated a strong sense of external control and low internal control, a situation congruent with the passivity, dependence, and resignation that allegedly characterized Sambo. It would therefore appear that the variable of internal-external control would provide a most useful dimension along which to measure the slave's adaptation.

The related personality variables just discussed — ego strength and internal-external control — have been inferred from Elkins's discussion of slavery and concentration camp situations. Although Elkins did not mention these phenomena as variables, they appear logically consistent with his discussion of the Sambo type. Elkins most closely approached suggesting a variable of the Sambo concept in his discussion of a personality type that should represent its antithesis. Arguing that such a personality type appeared primarily among urban slaves, house servants, craftsmen, and slave foremen, he cited the case of William Johnson, the free Natchez barber, who was described as a "complex and highly developed individual."[47]

Johnson's diary reveals a personality that one recognizes instantly as a type — but a type whose values came from a sector of society very different from that which formed Sambo. Johnson is the *young man on the make, the ambitious free-enterpriser of American legend.*[48]

William Johnson is not only the antithesis of Sambo. He is also the prototype of the hardworking, industrious, diligent, self-reliant, achievement-oriented entrepreneur — the "black Horatio Alger" — that emerges from the portrait of slavery advanced by Fogel and Engerman in their controversial *Time on the Cross.*[49] At first glance the Elkins and Fogel and Engerman models appear to be antithetical. However, both models converge in the special significance they attribute to skilled occupations within the slave social system. While Elkins felt that William Johnson was highly atypical, Fogel and Engerman argued that this personality type was most characteristic of the entire slave society. Yet Fogel and Engerman characterized the skilled sector of slave society (the size of which they substantially exaggerate) as an elite — the primary source of leadership for the slave community. Moreover, they argued that entry into skilled occupations represented a "prize that was to be claimed by the most deserving"—those who were most able and industrious and who manifested the "extra effort" in the "competition" for these privileged positions.[50] Thus the Elkins and Fogel and Engerman models are not really antithetical. They concur in the assumption that Sambo and William Johnson are polar types and that the most fully developed examples of the latter will be found among males in skilled occupational positions. They differ primarily in their estimates of the degree to which these characteristics were attenuated among unskilled laborers—the extent to which unskilled laborers had internalized the values of dependence and docility, on the one hand, or independence and industriousness, on the other.

The Horatio Alger entrepreneur personified in Johnson also closely corresponds to the personality type McClelland has described as high on the dimension of need for achievement (*n* Achievement).[51] Since Johnson was, according to Elkins, highly atypical, what he was in effect describing is the pervasiveness of low *n* Achievement among the slave population, a phenomenon that McClelland has argued should hypothetically be a condition inherent in the nature of slavery. Therefore, it would follow from the model advanced here that high *n* Achievement—independence and industriousness—was not internalized among the vast majority of slaves. Rather slave society socialized obedience, dependence, and compliance to the master's definitions[52]—traits that closely coincide with Elkins's description of Sambo.

Conclusions

The preceding analysis has not been exhaustive, for it is probable that other psychological dimensions can be identified. Moreover, the critical problem of operationalizing these dimensions in relevant data remains to be dealt with. What I hope to have suggested, however, is that personality structure is theoretically related to an individual's role in the social system of slavery and that greater conceptual clarity is a prerequisite to dealing adequately with the question of slavery and personality. The model I have delineated admits a range of personality types among the slave population but does not, as Blassingame maintains,[53] admit that they were necessarily distributed randomly.

The basic objective of research dealing with the issue of slavery and personality should be to determine not whether there was diversity of personality types among American slaves, but whether there was a systematic pattern in the distribution of these personality types and the relation of these patterns to location within the slave social system.

Notes

I would like to thank the University of Kansas General Research Fund and the Institute of Southern History, Johns Hopkins University, for their support of this research.

1. Stanley M. Elkins, *Slavery: A Problem in American Institutional and Intellectual Life* (Chicago: University of Chicago Press, 1961).

2. There is an extensive bibliography of criticism; many of the criticisms are contained in Ann J. Lane, ed., *The Debate over Slavery: Stanley Elkins and His Critics* (Urbana: University of Illinois Press, 1971). See also Elkins's sensitive essay, "The Slavery Debate," *Commentary* 60 (December 1975): 40–54, reprinted in the third edition of *Slavery* (Chicago, 1976), pp. 267–302.

3. For example, although each comes to conclusions different from Elkins's on the question of the existence of Sambo, George Rawick and John Blassingame have both accepted Elkins's categories. See George Rawick, *From Sundown to Sunup: The Making of the Black Community* (Westport, Conn.: Greenwood Press, 1972); John W. Blassingame, *The Slave Community: Plantation Life in the Ante-bellum South* (New York: Oxford University Press, 1972). Similarly, one of the central issues in Eugene D. Genovese's monumental *Roll, Jordon, Roll* is the nature of slave accommodation. It is revealing that an early tentative title of Genovese's work was *Sambo and Nat Turner: Docility and Rebelliousness in the Negro Slave.* See Eugene D. Genovese, *Roll, Jordon, Roll: The World the Slaves Made* (New York: Pantheon, 1975).

4. Elkins, *Slavery,* p. 87.

5. Eugene D. Genovese, "Rebelliousness and Docility in the Negro Slave: A Critique of the Elkins Theses," *Civil War History* 12 (1967): 311; Roy Simon Bryce-Laporte, "Slaves as Inmates, Slaves as Men: A Sociological Discussion of the Elkins Thesis," in Lane, ed., *The Debate over Slavery,* pp. 269–92; Rawick, *From Sundown to Sunup,* p. 3. The model is deterministic in the sense that slave behavior and personality are conceptualized as responses to the degree of power exerted over them. One of the most penetrating criticisms of the Elkins model is that it ignored the dynamic aspects of the master-slave relationship; masters not only influenced slaves but, as Eugene Genovese has argued, slaves influenced masters (Genovese, *Roll, Jordon, Roll*). Although disproportionate power lay with the master, slaves did not, as Genovese and Herbert Gutman have pointed out, behave solely in response to the dicates of the master but played an active role in determining their own behavior. Gutman's criticism of Fogel and Engerman's

controversial "Horatio Alger" model of slave personality functioning is applicable to Elkins's model: "[Its] essential flaw . . . is its failure to make a place in the historical process for slave behavior not directly determined by the policies and practices of their owners. Slaves behave in their model, but only in response to master-sponsored stimuli." Herbert G. Gutman, *Slavery and the Numbers Game: A Critique of Time on the Cross* (Urbana: University of Illinois Press, 1975), p. 32. See also Gutman's *The Black Family in Slavery and Freedom, 1750–1925* (New York: Pantheon Books, 1976), especially pp. 305–26.

6. Stanley M. Elkins, "Slavery and Ideology," in Lane, *The Debate over Slavery*, p. 350.

7. Elkins, *Slavery*, p. 82.

8. Ibid., p. 137.

9. Erving Goffman, *Asylums: Essays on the Social Situation of Mental Patients and Other Inmates* (Chicago: Aldine, 1961). Other writers have also argued for a consideration of Elkins's thesis in terms of Goffman's conceptualization: George M. Frederickson and Christopher Lasch, "Resistance to Slavery," *Civil War History* 13 (December 1967): 315–29; Roy Simon Bryce-Laporte, "The American Slave Plantation and Our Heritage of Communal Deprivation," *The American Behavioral Scientist* 12 (March-April 1969): 2–8; Blassingame, *The Slave Community*, pp. 217–26.

10. Goffman, *Asylums*, p. xiii.

11. Ibid., p. 4. The historical nature of Goffman's analysis is revealed by his omission of slavery from among those phenomena included within the rubric of "total" institutions. This omission is especially revealing, since some of the features of "total institutions" are described metaphorically in terms of slavery.

12. Although he has subsumed the study of the concentration camp under that of the institution of slavery, H. G. Alder has made the cogent suggestion that the study of both phenomena be considered under the general category of the "sociology of the unfree," or, perhaps more accurately in terms of this paper, the social psychology of the unfree. See "Ideas Toward a Sociology of the Concentration Camp," *American Journal of Sociology* 63 (1958): 513–22.

13. M. I. Finley has also argued that the study of slavery be conceptualized in this manner. See "Slavery," *International Encyclopedia of the Social Sciences* (New York, 1968), p. 308. Blassingame recognizes that there is a continuum of total institutions, although he argues that the concentration camp is far removed on this continuum from plantation slavery. But he refuses to extend the idea of a continuum (with its implicit notion of qualitative similarities) to the psychological effects of such systems. Instead he argues that the differences between concentration camp and slavery were of such proportions (i.e., *qualitatively* dissimilar) as to preclude any such possibility. "If some men could escape infantilism in a murderous institution like the concentration camp, it may have been possible for the slave to avoid becoming abjectly docile" (Blassingame, *The Slave Community*, p. 226).

14. Elkins, *Slavery*, pp. 84–85.

15. Finley, "Slavery," p. 307.

16. For a similar argument see Arnold A. Sio, "Society, Slavery and the Slave," *Social and Economic Studies* 16 (1967): 342–43, and Genovese, "Rebelliousness and Docility in the Negro Slave." M. I. Finley and David McClelland have also hypothesized the development of distinctive psychological characteristics as an inevitable consequence of the institution of slavery. See Finley, "Slavery," p. 311, and David C. McClelland, *The Achieving Society* (Princeton, N.J.: Princeton University Press, 1961), pp. 376–78.

17. Genovese, "Rebelliousness and Docility in the Negro Slave"; Pierre van den Berghe, *Race and Racism: A Comparative Perspective* (New York: John Wiley & Sons, 1967), pp. 66–67; Sidney W. Mintz, review of *Slavery* in *American Anthropologist* 63 (1961): 581; Arnold A. Sio, "Interpretations of Slavery: The Slave Status in the Americas," *Comparative Studies in Society and History* 7 (April 1965): 289–308; David Brion Davis, *The Problem of Slavery in Western Culture* (Ithaca, N.Y.: Cornell University Press, 1966), pp. 223–61; Carl N. Degler, *Neither Black nor White: Slavery and Race Relations in Brazil and the United States* (New York: Macmillan, 1971).

18. Genovese, who has been among the more sympathetic of Elkin's critics, has suggested the more neutral term "slavish personality." Although less ideological, it is important to note that it, as

"Sambo," does not delineate conceptually distinguishable components of personality structure. Genovese, "Rebelliousness and Docility in the Negro Slave."

19. Blassingame, *The Slave Community*, p. 39.

20. Ibid., p. 100.

21. Elkins, *Slavery*, p. 32. Willie Lee Rose implicitly attests to the imprecision conceptualizing Sambo unidimensionally in her analysis of the adaptation of freedmen in the Sea Islands. She concluded that the Sambo thesis is invalid when applied to these freedmen because there occurred a significant diminution of servility and docility among the freedmen. On the other hand, she notes that other traits—characteristics that Elkins has included in the Sambo syndrome—persisted: lying, stealing, absence of individual initiative, poor work habits, and so on. Rose, *Rehearsal for Reconstruction: The Port Royal Experiment* (Vintage edition, 1967), pp. 346–79.

22. Rawick, *From Sundown to Sunup*, pp. 100–1.

23. Inkeles and Daniel Levinson, "National Character: The Study of Modal Personality and Sociocultural Systems," in Gardner Lindzey, ed., *Handbook of Social Psychology* (Reading, Mass., 1954), 2: 982.

24. Elkins, *Slavery*, p. 138.

25. Charles H. Nichols, *Many Thousands Gone: The Ex-slaves' Account of Their Bondage and Freedom* (Leiden, Netherlands: E. J. Brill, 1963), p. 74.

26. Melville Herskovits, *The Myth of the Negro Past* (New York: Harper & Brothers, 1941), p. 90.

27. Blassingame, *The Slave Community*, p. 109. My emphasis.

28. It should be noted, in this regard, that Blassingame's assertions earlier that "submission was on a shallow level of convenience," that "it was less important as a model of behavior," and that "it did not penetrate the slave's true personality" are all undocumented assumptions.

29. Inkeles and Levinson, "National Character," p. 932.

30. Daniel Katz and Robert L. Kahn, *The Social Psychology of Organizations* (New York: John Wiley and Sons, 1966), pp 195–96.

31. Elkins, *Slavery*, p. 82.

32. William Caudill, "Japanese-American Personality and Acculturation," *Genetic Psychology Monographs* 14 (1952): 93.

33. Bruno Bettelheim, "Individual and Mass Behavior in Extreme Situations," *Journal of Abnormal Psychology* 38 (1944): 417–52.

34. Bruno Bettelheim, *The Informed Heart: Autonomy in a Mass Age* (Glencoe, Ill.: The Free Press, 1960), p. 19.

35. Heinz Hartmann, Ernst Kris, Rudolph M. Lowenstein, "Comments on the Formation of Psychic Structure," in Anna Freud, *The Psychoanalytic Study of the Child* (1945), 2: 1–38; David Rapoport, "The Autonomy of the Ego," *Bulletin of the Menninger Clinic* 15 (1951): 113–23.

36. William G. Herron, "The Assessment of Ego Strength," *Journal of Psychological Studies* 12 (1962): 173.

37. F. Barron, "An Ego-Strength Scale Which Predicts Responses to Psychotherapy," *Journal of Consulting Psychology* 18 (1953): 327–33.

38. Jerome Bruner, "Personality Dynamics and the Process of Perceiving," in Robert R. Blake and Glenn V. Ramsey, *Perception: An Approach to Personality* (New York: Ronald Press Co., 1951), p. 144.

39. Julian B. Rotter, Melvin Seeman, and Shephard Liverant, "Internal Versus External Control of Reinforcement: A Major Variable in Behavior Theory," in Norman F. Washburne, ed., *Decisions, Values and Groups* (New York: Macmillan, 1962), 2: 473–516; Julian B. Rotter, "Generalized Expectancies for Internal Versus External Control of Reinforcement," *Psychological Monographs* 80, no. 609 (1966).

40. Gerald Mullin, *Flight and Resistance in 18th Century Virginia* (New York: Oxford University Press, 1972), p. 166.

41. Rotter, "Generalized Expectancies for Internal Versus External Control of Reinforcement."

42. Ibid; Melvin Seeman and J. W. Evans, "Alienation and Learning in a Hospital Setting," *American Sociological Review* 27 (1962): 709 – 16; Melvin Seeman, "Alienation and Social Learning in a Reformatory," *American Journal of Sociology* 69 (1963): 270 – 84.

43. Herbert M. Lefcourt and Gordon W. Ladwig, "The American Negro: A Problem in Expectancies," *Journal of Personality and Social-Psychology* 1 (1965): pp. 377 – 80.

44. Pearl M. Gore and Julian B. Rotter, "A Personality Correlate of Social Action," *Journal of Personality* 31 (1963): 58 – 64.

45. Bonnie R. Strickland, "The Prediction of Social Action from a Dimension of Internal-External Control," *Journal of Social Psychology* 66 (1965): 353 – 58.

46. John F. Forward and Jay R. Williams, "Internal-External Control and Black Militancy," *Journal of Social Issues* 26, no. 1 (Winter 1970): 75 – 92.

47. Elkins, *Slavery,* p. 138.

48. Ibid. Italics mine.

49. Robert W. Fogel and Stanley L. Engerman, *Time on the Cross: The Economics of American Negro Slavery* (Boston: Little, Brown, 1974).

50. Ibid., p. 150.

51. McClelland, *The Achieving Society.*

52. Ibid, pp. 376 – 77.

53. "There was great variety in slave behavior. Some slaves were always docile; others were docile most of the time and rebellious at other times. Likewise, some resisted bondage throughout their lives in various ways, while others, generally docile, might be rebellious only once. *In other words, the slave was no different in most ways from most men. The same range of personality types existed in the quarters as in the mansion.*" See Blassingame, *The Slave Community,* pp. 213 – 14. Italics mine.

MURRAY MURPHEY

Culture, Character, and Personality

Murray Murphey received his Ph.D. in American Studies at Yale University in 1954. He is currently Professor and Chairman of the American Civilization program at the University of Pennsylvania. He is the author of several books and a former editor of American Quarterly.

Since Fromm published *Escape From Freedom*[1] in 1941, the study of national character, and more generally of group personality, has become exceedingly popular. Psychologists and psychoanalysts, political scientists, and even historians have contributed to the ever-growing literature on the subject. As is usually the case with new fields, the rapid growth of both data and theory has been accompanied by some vagueness respecting the basic terms employed and their relations, and this has been particularly true respecting the relations between culture and personality. Some investigators have been accused of psychologizing the culture: others of culturizing the personality; some have held that personality and culture must be defined so as not to overlap; some hold that the concepts necessarily overlap.[2] There is, in short, considerable confusion in the field as to what personality is and how it is related to culture.

Definitions of personality are a dime a dozen, and few of them agree. This does not mean that most of them are wrong, although they may be; rather, it means that "personality is defined by the particular empirical concepts which are part of the theory of personality employed by the observer."[3] Definitions of personality therefore are theory specific. Accordingly, to discuss the relation of personality and culture in any reasonable way, one must start from a theoretical basis which affords such a definition. Moreover, this theoretical basis must be sufficiently articulated with the concepts used to describe the culture so that relations between personality and culture can be discussed. For purposes of this paper I shall adopt the stimulus-response theory (hereafter the SR theory) as such a basis. Whether the same results would be obtained on the basis of Freudian theory or field theory or McClelland's theory or the many other possible choices is a question which must be left to the proponents of those approaches.

I

In their brilliant book on child training and personality, Whiting and Child[4] also took SR theory as a basis. In order to relate the concepts of SR theory to those of culture, Whiting and Child sought to define the necessary cultural concepts in terms of the concepts of SR theory.[5] The basic definition they use for this purpose is the definition of "custom"—namely, "A custom is a characteristic habit of a typical member of a cultural category of persons."[6] Here the term "custom," which is a cultural concept, is defined in terms of "habit," which is a term of SR theory characterizing individual behavior. The definition does indeed relate these two terms, but it also involves other terms which are not terms of SR theory—for example, the term "characteristic" as here used is distinctively a cultural concept. So far as Whiting and Child are concerned, this fact creates no problem: They do not claim that custom is definable solely in SR terms and the definition as they give it does all that they require. But it is a question worth exploring whether or not custom can be defined solely by concepts of SR theory together with those of logic and mathematics. In fact, it is my contention that this can be done. Before endeavoring to justify this contention, however, we must clarify the meaning of Whiting and Child's definition.

There are three terms in the definition whose meanings are not obvious. When they speak of a "cultural category of persons," Whiting and Child mean any set of persons in a society who are distinguished by the members of that society as a distinct group.[7] By "typical" they "mean a central tendency such as the mode or the median but arrived at by the ethnologist's judgment."[8] The use of subjective rather than objective methods of determining the central tendency was due to the nature of the data: The authors would certainly have preferred objective methods had they been applicable. Finally, by "characteristic habit" they mean that "the habit must in some way be relevant to a person's membership in the cultural category."[9] The relevance here spoken of however is very complex. A simple association between membership in a category and performance of a given habit would not satisfy this definition: nor would a habit performance of which is a condition for becoming a member of the category. What Whiting and Child mean to describe is such a relation between the category and performance of the habit that the habit is performed because the person is a member of that category.

The basic concept of SR theory which is relevant to the concept of custom is habit. As Whiting and Child define it, "a habit is a relationship between a set of stimuli and a response (or series of responses) such that there is a probability that when the stimulus is perceived by a given organism the response will be evoked."[10] Several points about this definition require emphasis. First, habits are general. The stimuli in the stimulus set are not identical although they are similar—the degree of similarity being measurable in j.n.d.'s[11] and the same holds of the response set. The habit therefore is a connection among members of one class and members of another, not between one stimulus and one response. Second, we extend the habit concept to situations in which a given stimulus evokes a series of responses $r_1 \ldots r_n$ if reinforcement follows r_n but no preceding member of the series, and all responses from r_1 to r_n are conditioned to the stimulus. Third, the probability of the response being evoked by the stimulus is a measure of the "habit potential" of the habit in question (Hull's effective reaction potential).[12]

There are several types of habits of which we shall have need, and we may conveniently adapt the definitions used by Whiting and Child for most of these. A "belief" may be defined as a habit whose response symbolizes some relationship between events.[13] A "practice" may be defined as a habit "whose response directly affects a change in the environment, the performer, or the relationship between the two."[14] A "positive sanction" may be defined as a habit whose stimulus is the performance of a habit (or the failure to perform a habit) in given stimulus conditions, and whose response is a reward to the individual performer (or nonperformer). A "negative sanction" may be defined as a habit whose stimulus is a performance of a habit (or the failure to perform a habit) in given stimulus conditions, and whose response is a punishment to the performer (or nonperformer).[15] A "value" may be defined as a habit whose response attributes goodness or badness to some event.[16] A "motive" may be defined as a habit which is responsible for acquired drive in its performer, and a "satisfaction" as a habit which is responsible for acquired reward in its performer.[17] These definitions follow Whiting and Child precisely except that these terms are here defined in terms of habit rather than custom. The reason for this is that individuals can have beliefs, values, motives, satisfactions, and practices and exercise sanctions, so that these terms should first be defined for individuals and then extended to groups. It should also be remarked that the terms "reward" and "punishment" are well defined concepts of SR theory: A reward is that which reduces a drive; a punishment is that which creates pain.[18]

To these definitions we now add a further one. For any phenomenon y and any individual x, x recognizes y if and only if there exists a verbal expression V which is used by x to designate y uniquely — that is, to designate y and y alone. This definition coordinates recognition with the possession of a unique linguistic designation and implies that what cannot be named cannot be recognized. This thesis concerning the relation between language and consciousness is by no means new — it was asserted by Freud and has been incorporated into SR theory by Miller and Dollard.[19] By its use we obtain a definition of recognition which, like those of belief, practice, and sanction can be stated wholly in SR terms.

For habits to be customs, they must stand in peculiarly complex relations to social groupings. Any society may be regarded as a set of n people: By a well-known theorem there are then 2^n-1 non-empty subsets of this society. Any such subset might have associated with it certain characteristic behaviors, but as a rule only a few of these subsets actually do have a significant relation to behavior. Thus in our society women, priests, and lawyers do have peculiar behavioral patterns, but thirty-fifth cousins, brunettes, and men born on the third of March do not. Which subsets a given social system utilizes in its division of tasks is an empirical question of considerable interest: some subsets have distinctive behavior in all societies while others are behaviorally significant only in a few, or in none.

A subset may be recognized, or it may not. If it is, then there exists some set of people who recognize it — that is, who use a distinctive linguistic expression to designate that subset. Thus "women" designates uniquely adult females, and "men who wear spats" designates uniquely a certain class of men. It should be stressed that it is the use of the expression as a name which constitutes recognition: The fact that everyone in the society uses the words "men," "wear," "who," and "spats" does not mean that they apply the expression "men-who-wear-spats" as a set name. It is also important to see that recognition of a subset does not imply that its members have distinctive behaviors: We all recognize brunettes, but there is no distinctively brunette behavior. Finally, recognition is a relation between a set recognized and a set of recognizers. In any complex society there are many subsets having characteristic behaviors which are recognized by only a small fraction of the total society. This is obviously true in our own society, where there are thousands of job classifications known only to a minute fraction of the total population.

Habits may be related to sets of people in many different ways. The simplest such relation is ordinary association — a statistically significant relation between performance of a habit and membership in a given set. Such associations are obviously of great importance and much of the research done in social science is concerned with relationships of this sort. Nevertheless, this is not the sort of association between habit and set that constitutes custom. In fact, the relationship which makes a habit a custom involves at least three sets of people and four kinds of habits. In the first place, there are the performers of habit — the members of what Whiting and Child call the cultural category. Let us call the set of these people X and the members the x's. Secondly, there are those who recognize X and have beliefs about the behavior of the x's. It is not necessary that all who recognize X should have such beliefs, but it is necessary that all who have such beliefs should recognize X. Let us call the set of believers Y and its members the y's. Thirdly, there are those who perform sanctions upon the x's. Let us call this set Z and its members the z's. What relations must obtain among these sets? Clearly, all x's are y's, for performance must be guided by beliefs about the performance. It is also clear that all z's must be y's, for sanctions are applied as behavior does or does not conform to expectations, and such expectations are beliefs. But the x's need not be z's, although they may be. The x's can perform perfectly well without exercising sanctions upon themselves, although they cannot perform without beliefs about their performance.

To say that a habit h_1 is "characteristic" of X, in the sense in which Whiting and Child use this term, comes I think to saying that the y's believe that the x's perform h_1 and that the z's sanction the x's for such performance or the failure to

·perform. This is not indeed an explication of the meaning of ''characteristic'' but rather an assertion respecting the necessary and sufficient conditions for a habit's being ''characteristic'' in that sense, but I think it will be generally agreed that these conditions are necessary and sufficient. It is because certain people expect that habit of the x's and because some people reward and/or punish the x's as they do or do not perform the habit that being an x is relevant to the performance of that behavior.

Whiting and Child defined a custom as a habit characteristic of a ''typical member'' of a cultural category of persons rather than as a habit performed by all members of the set. They explained their preference for the ''typical member'' approach by raising two objections to a definition in terms of shared habits. First, there are customs which characterize single member sets, as, for example, the president of the United States. If ''shared'' is taken to mean ''common to more than one,'' then clearly no shared habits characterize a single member set, while if ''shared'' is construed reflexively, then every habit of the single member is a custom.[20] A possible answer to this objection is that although there is only one president at a time, still there have been thirty-six presidents over a period of time, and the customs of the presidency are the habits characterizing all thirty-six presidents. But this answer seems to me clearly fallacious. Had the office of president been abolished in 1796, it would still be true that there were customs characterizing the presidency which were not mere idiosyncracies of Washington. A better answer is provided by the definition given above, for according to this definition being shared is not a necessary condition for a habit to be a custom. It is only habits which are expected and sanctioned which are customs, and there can be expectations about and sanctions upon one person as well as many. Accordingly, Whiting and Child's objection does not touch the definition here offered.

But the objection does bring out the very significant difference between customs and habits which are merely shared by a group of people, and this is a difference which raises some important problems in itself. In the definition of custom given above, we made use of several types of shared habits — the beliefs of the y's and the sanctions of the z's. Are these shared habits customs or not? The answer must obviously be no, so far as the above definition is concerned: Otherwise we should be defining custom by custom. Yet it is also obvious that those beliefs and sanctions can be customary: There might be a set W of people who recognize Z and expect z's to sanction x's and there might be a set U of people who sanctions the z's for their performance of (or failure to perform) sanctions upon the x's. The important point is that we can determine whether or not a given habit is a custom without knowing whether the beliefs and sanctions which make it a custom are customary themselves. The definition of custom is therefore not circular: It refers to shared habits but not to other customs.

A further point about this objection should also be remarked. Suppose that $X = Y = Z = [x]$: That is, suppose X, Y, and Z have all only one member, x. Then is the habit in question a custom or not? It seems to me to make little difference which way we decide this question. Common usage does permit a man to refer to an idiosyncratic habit as his "custom," but such a usage violates somewhat the spirit of the concept as used by Whiting and Child. Accordingly, we should probably require that if X is a unit set, then X does not equal Y and Z does not equal X.

But Whiting and Child raise a second objection to the shared habit definition of custom which also applies to the definition given above. Within any reasonably large set of people there will be considerable variation in the performance of the custom. It is therefore inaccurate to speak of one habit being shared by all: We should rather speak of a limited range within which these variations fall.[21] There are two answers to this objection. First, it should be noted that habits themselves are general. A habit is a relation between a class of similar stimuli and a class of similar responses, so some variation is permitted within the concept of habit itself. Nevertheless, it is easy to find cases in which this answer will not suffice. For example, it may be customary in a society to greet strangers, and there may exist several forms of greeting which are equally acceptable but which are not similar. In this case all members of the society do greet strangers, yet there is no shared habit of greeting.

There are two cases here which must be clearly distinguished. If the form of greeting depends upon characteristics of the stranger, or of his behavior, then there is no problem: We have simply several distinct habits with different stimulus sets, but each habit is shared by the whole society. Thus, if all Irishmen salute all Germans and shake hands with all Frenchmen, there are simply two distinct customs each of which characterizes all Irishmen. The case which makes trouble is the case in which the stimuli are the same but there are different responses occurring with comparable frequency among the Irish, as, for example, if half shake hands and half bow, irrespective of the characteristics of the stranger or of his behavior. In this case, the shared habit definition of custom clearly collapses altogether.

But the objection also points the way to its own solution, for as Whiting and Child note, "culture does not mean precise uniformity but merely restriction of the range of variation in behavior."[22] What we have here is a set of habits which fall within the accepted limits of variation. We may define this class of equally acceptable alternatives in the following way: It is a class of habits $h_1 \ldots h_n$ such that each member of the class has an identical stimulus set, and at least one of the two following conditions is met; either, if any x performs any one of the habits $h_1 \ldots h_n$ but not the others then the z's positively sanction x, or, if any x performs any one of $h_1 \ldots h_n$ then no z negatively sanctions x, and if some x does not perform one of $h_1 \ldots h_n$ then the z's negatively sanction that x. This amounts to a definition of a class of habits which the z's—that is, the sanctioners—regard as equally acceptable. We may then define the custom of the x's as this set of habits equally acceptable to the z's. These habits need have no more in common than their stimulus sets, which makes them genuine alternatives to each other, and their acceptability, which makes them equally acceptable alternatives. Habits need not be shared to be customs, but they must be equally acceptable responses to given stimuli. If the responses which the x's habitually make to a given stimulus set are equivalent, then that equivalence class of habits is a custom, and in the limiting case where all x's make the same response, the custom is a shared habit.

There is a further reason for preferring this definition to that given by Whiting and Child — namely, the lack of clarity of the concept of a "typical member." Whiting and Child define "typical" as "a central tendency such as the mode or the median but arrived at by the ethnologist's judgment."[23] A central tendency is a characteristic of a distribution, and a distribution is a distribution of a variable. But in the phrase, "typical member of a cultural category of persons," it is not at all clear what variable is referred to. Consider for example the cultural category of women. What is the "modal woman"? If we consider the variable "height of a woman," then a modal value, and even a mean value, can be defined, since this variable has a distribution. But unless such a variable is specified, the phrase "modal woman" is meaningless. Nor is it obvious how to make the specification. For purposes of defining a habit as a custom, it would appear that the "typical member" must be typical with respect to his performance of the habit concerned. But in that case the "typical member" is defined in terms of the "typical habit," and the phrase "characteristic habit of a typical member, etc." becomes "characteristic habit of a member having the typical habit," which is far from clear. It is true that in describing the habit characteristic of a set of people it will very often be necessary on any definition to use measures of central tendency, but these measures must be applied to characteristics of the habit, not the performer. There are many variables on which habits may vary (habit potential, latency, amplitude of response, etc.) and a typical habit will be one which represents the central tendencies of these diverse variables. But it is the habit, not the member, which is typical.

II

If the argument given above is correct, then it appears that we can give a definition of custom which contains nothing but terms of SR theory, mathematics, logic, and set theory. What are the implications of this conclusion for culture theory as a whole? It must already be apparent that there is a strong analogy between the concept of custom presented above and the concept of role. Indeed, a role will appear in this theory as a complex of customs, or more precisely, as a set of equivalent habit complexes characterizing a set of people in the same way that a custom does. The specification of the exact nature of the complex which constitutes a role is too broad a subject to be treated here: What does need urging is that the relation of role and status is the same as that between custom and the set of performers, and that roles differ from individual customs only in being equivalence classes of complexes of habits rather than equivalence classes of single habits. And if role and status are definable in these terms, then so is the social structure as a whole, for the social structure is just the system of roles and statuses characterizing the society. It seems a fair inference, therefore, that the whole of the nonmaterial culture is reducible to these components. A proof of this thesis would require a book, but I think sufficient grounds have already been given to make it plausible, and I will therefore entertain this hypothesis for the remainder of this paper.

From the standpoint of SR theory, the personality is the structure of drives and habits characterizing the individual. This structure includes other people and their behavior as stimuli to which the individual responds, but the drives and habits and their organization lie within the individual. Culture, on the other hand, is the system of drives and habits which characterizes the group. It includes of course what is common to all members of the group, but it is particularly concerned with interrelations among the individuals and subsets of the group. Both personality and culture, therefore, are structures or organizations of drives and habits.

This assertion respecting the nature of culture and personality contradicts a number of well known views. Some writers, seeking to avoid an overlap between culture and personality, relegate behavior to culture, and restrict the personality to the organization of nonbehavioral psychological states and processes which are inferred from behavior and which are conceived as causes or conditions of the behavior.[24] But such an emasculation of the concept of personality seems hardly defensible. As the term "personality" is used in ordinary language it refers to an individual's characteristic ways of responding to stimuli, and such responses may obviously be behavioral. Most theorists employ the concept of personality as an integrating concept referring to the organization of the psychologically signifi-cant components of the person. To exclude behavior from the personality is therefore to deny that it is psychologically significant — a procedure which seems dubious at best. Habits involving behavioral responses are constituents of both culture and personality and little is accomplished by denying so obvious a fact.

On the other hand, there are definitions of culture which differ radically from that given above. Some writers use the term "culture" to refer to behavior patterns which are norms for the group, while other patterns are relegated to what is called the "social system."[25] But this usage need not be debated, since it only means that what I have called culture above, these writers call culture plus the social system. Other writers restrict culture solely to behavior and exclude all reference to drives and motives which they regard as belonging to an extracultur-al domain of personality. Yet such writers do regard sanctions as legitimate components of culture, and a sanction cannot be defined without reference to drives in the individual. Thus one cannot define a particular role in a given society without reference to the sanctions used to enforce conformity to the role prescriptions, and to say that a given act of z on x is a positive sanction for x is to say that it is drive reducing for x. Accordingly, these writers do include references to drives in their expositions of culture, albeit implicitly.

What is the relation of culture and personality? Both are constructed from the same elements — drives and habits. Each represents a particular organization of those elements. Personality is the organization of these elements in the individual: Culture is their organization in the set of people. If we find a given habit which characterizes all members of a set, that habit is a component of the culture; but it is also a component of the personality of each person who holds it. It is true that there may be habits in some personalities which are neither shared with others nor related to the beliefs and sanctions of others, and these habits we exclude from the culture as idiosyncratic, but every habit in the culture is first in some personality.

Nevertheless, many writers insist that culture and personality are radically distinct, and even that "culturally determined" behavior is not only not personality but also not indicative of personality. At its extreme, this position leads to the absurdity of saying that deviant behavior is more expressive of personality than conformist behavior, because, forsooth, deviant behavior is not determined by the culture so it must be the result of personality![26] What seems to underlie such arguments is the fact that some habits are intrinsic to the person while others are not. Indeed, if personality is simply an organization of drives and habits, then some habits must be intrinsic — in fact, constitutive — of personality, in such a sense that their alteration would create a new or different personality. But other habits appear to be extrinsic in such a sense that dropping those habits would not create a new or different personality. If one then says that the extrinsic habits are performed because they are enforced "by the culture" while the intrinsic habits "spring from the personality," one is in effect saying that intrinsic habits are those enforced by sanctions which the performer applies to himself while extrinsic habits are those in which the performer does not sanction himself but others do. Hence, since deviant behavior is (allegedly) not sanctioned by others, it is not extrinsic — therefore it is intrinsic.

The argument has its merits. Habits clearly do differ in some such way as that indicated by the intrinsic-extrinsic division, but this difference is a matter of degree. The organization of drives and habits constituting the personality is complex, and clearly some habits will have a more central role in that organization than others. One may expect that habits which carry strong self-sanctions are probably more central to the structure than those which carry little self-sanction, and it is reasonable to assume that the more central to the structure a habit is, the more far-reaching will be the consequences of its alternation. On the other hand, it seems doubtful that there are many behaviors performed by a person which are wholly devoid of self-sanctions of some kind. People are rarely indifferent toward behavior which they perform frequently. Moreover, even if a particular performer does not sanction himself for performing a given habit, still performance of that habit may be a means of obtaining a self-administered reward if it is followed by positive sanctions from another, and such positive sanctions are a stimulus to self-congratulation in the performer. Thus the interrelations among the component drives and habits of the personality can be very complex and devious, and there are probably very few habits performance of which is not in some respect self-sanctioned.

It follows from these remarks that conformist behavior very likely involves self-sanctions: Indeed, there is no reason why those habits most central to the personality may not be fully in accord with the expectations and sanctions of others. For most people, most of the time, customary behavior affords the most thoroughly satisfying method of drive reduction. Nor is there any reason to believe that deviant behavior is somehow a better expression of personality than conformist behavior. Deviance need not be self-sanctioned: It can arise from a host of factors, such as role contradictions, conflicting demands of different sanctioning groups, means-ends situations where an approved means to the goal is not available, and so on, which have as little, and as much, to do with personality as those which operate to induce conformity.

If personality is an organization of drives and habits characteristic of the individual, then a group personality is an organization of drives and habits characterizing the members of a particular set of people. The problem of how such an organization becomes associated with this set may then be approached in the same way that we approach the problem of how any complex of habits and drives becomes associated with a particular set. The simplest case of this sort is that of custom, in which a single habit, or a set of equivalent single habits, is induced in the members of a set of people. A more complicated case is that of role, in which a complex of habits, or a set of equivalent habit complexes, is induced in the members of a set of people. Viewed from this perspective, group personality is simply a case in which a still more elaborate complex of habits is induced in the members of the set, and what makes a personality customary will be essentially the same factors which make all habit complexes customary.

We are accustomed to viewing role as a complex of habits induced and maintained in the members of a set of people by the expectations of others and the due application of sanctions to the members of the set according as they do or do not perform the expected behavior. We are accustomed to viewing personality as a complex of habits and drives instilled in the individual by a process of child rearing and thereafter enduring with only slight modification until death. Both views require revision. If we consider the training to which a candidate for a role is subjected, it is clear that a large part of this training consists in the induction of appropriate motives, values, and satisfactions and in internalizing in the candidate a set of rules the violation of or conformity to which by the candidate will result in self-sanctioning responses. Role training thus involves both the organization of drives already present and the acquisition of new ones as well as the learning of practices and beliefs — a fact which is dramatically evident in the case of the training for such roles as the priesthood. Similarly, if we consider the induction of personality in an individual, it is clear that what we call child rearing is a process in which the child is led to comform in thought, action, and feeling to the expectations of others, and the means by which this conformity is obtained is the due application of sanctions by some set of sanctioners — usually the parents — according as he does or does not conform. Moreover, it is obvious that the formation of personality does not terminate at six, or twenty-one, or even forty: Personality is continuously modified, whether by life or psychotherapy, until death. The behavioral complex which is the role is thus a subsystem of the personality, and the personality, if it characterizes a set, is in a generalized sense a role. Being a doctor is the same kind of phenomenon as being an Englishman.

Personality and culture are not identical. There will be in every individual personality some elements which are purely idiosyncratic. But where an organization of drives and habits sufficiently extensive to qualify as a personality characterizes the members of a set of people, we are dealing with a cultural phenomenon. We do not hesitate to classify less extensive organizations of drive and habit such as roles as cultural phenomena: Why should we hesitate to do so with personality? Of course the culture is much more than just an aggregate of personalities, since it involves various kinds of relations among them and among their constituents, but group personality is as much a part of culture as custom or role.

From this perspective, it should be clear that the problem for culture and personality studies is not the interaction of personality and culture. To ask how personality and culture interact makes about as much sense as to ask how the planets interact with the solar system. The significant problem is how drives, habits, and social groupings are related. To determine the modes of personality characteristics — for example, aggressiveness — in a given society is usually fruitless unless we also determine how those characteristics are related to specific groupings and to the drives and habits of people in other sets. This has in fact been the focus in child-rearing studies, which have for this reason been the most interesting of the group personality studies, and in those few splendid studies such as Hallowell's work on the Ojibwa[27] which have made the field worth while. But such studies are not numerous and a raft of major problems remains virtually untouched. The attempt to divide culture from personality has created a pseudo-problem—the interaction of culture and personality—which has led us away from the problems which ought to engage our interest — the interrelations of drives and habits in individuals and sets of individuals.

Notes

1. Eric Fromm, *Escape from Freedom* (New York: Rhinehart and Co., 1941).

2. See the critical reviews of the literature in Alex Inkeles and Daniel Levinson, "National Character: The Study of Modal Personality and Sociocultural Systems," in *Handbook of Social Psychology,*

Linzey, ed. (Reading, Mass.: Addison-Wesley Co., 1954), pp. 977–1020, and H. C. J. Duijker and N. N. Frijda, *National Character and National Stereotypes* (Amsterdam: North-Holland Publishing Co., 1960).

3. Calvin Hall and Gardner Lindzey, *Theories of Personality* (New York: John Wiley & Sons, 1957), p. 9.

4. John W. M. Whiting and Irvin L. Child, *Child Training and Personality* (New Haven, Conn.: Yale University Press, 1958).

5. Ibid., p. 16.

6. Ibid., p. 22.

7. Ibid., pp. 22–23.

8. Ibid., p. 23.

9. Ibid., p. 24.

10. Ibid., p. 18.

11. Just noticeable differences. Cf. Clark Hull, *Principles of Behavior* (New York: Appleton-Century-Crofts, 1943).

12. Whiting and Child, *Child Training,* p. 18, n. 1. Hull, *Principles,* pp. 283–84.

13. Whiting and Child, *Child Training,* p. 28.

14. Ibid., p. 27.

15. Ibid., pp. 29–30.

16. Ibid., p. 28.

17. Ibid., p. 30.

18. Hull, *Principles,* p. 131. Neal Miller and John Dollard, *Social Learning and Imitation* (New Haven, Conn.: Yale University Press, 1941), pp. 41–42.

19. John Dollard and Neal Miller, *Personality and Psychotherapy* (New York: McGraw-Hill, 1950), p. 158.

20. Whiting and Child, *Child Training,* pp. 23–24.

21. Ibid., p. 24.

22. Ibid.

23. Ibid., p. 23.

24. Duijker and Frijda, *National Character,* p. 38. Ralph Linton, *The Cultural Background of Personality* (New York: Appleton-Century-Crofts, 1945), p. 84.

25. Duijker and Frijda, *National Character,* pp. 40–41. Cf. Talcott Parsons and Edward Shils, eds., *Toward a General Theory of Action* (Cambridge, Mass.: Harvard University Press, 1960), pt. 1.

26. Duijker and Frijda, *National Character,* p. 42.

27. A. Irving Hallowell, *Culture and Experience* (Philadelphia: University of Pennsylvania Press, 1955).

Bibliography

Books

Aaron, Daniel. *Men of Good Hope*. New York: Oxford University Press, 1951.

Adorno, T. W. *The Authoritarian Personality*. New York: W. W. Norton & Co., 1969.

Agard, Walter R. *Classical Myths in Sculpture*. Madison: University of Wisconsin Press, 1953.

Almond, Gabriel. *The American People and Foreign Policy*. New York: Harcourt, Brace & Co., 1950.

Andrews, Wayne. *Architecture Ambition and Americans*. New York: Free Press, 1964.

Atherton, Lewis. *Main Street on the Middle Border*. Chicago: Quadrangle Books, 1966.

Banks, Martha B. *Heroes of the South Seas*. New York: Macmillan, 1896.

Beard, Charles. *The American Spirit*. New York: Macmillan, 1942.

Bell, Daniel. *The End of Ideology*. New York: Free Press, 1965.

Bercovitch, Sacvan. *The Puritan Origins of the American Self*. New Haven, Conn.: Yale University Press, 1975.

Berger, Arthur Asa. *Li'l Abner: A Study in American Satire*. New York: Twayne, 1970.

Billington, Ray Allen. *America's Frontier Heritage*. New York: Holt, Rinehart & Winston, 1966.

Boorstin, Daniel. *The Genius of American Politics*. Chicago: University of Chicago Press, 1953.

———. *The Americans: The Colonial Experience*. New York: Random House, 1958.

———. *The Americans: The National Experience*. New York: Random House, 1965.

Boulding, Kenneth E. *The Meaning of the Twentieth Century*. New York: Harper & Row, 1964.

Brogan, Denis. *The American Character*. New York: Alfred A. Knopf, 1944.

Brooks, Van Wyck. *America's Coming of Age*. Garden City, N.Y.: Doubleday Anchor Books, 1958.

Brown, William R. *Imagemaker: Will Rogers and the American Dream*. Columbia, Mo.: University of Missouri Press, 1970.

Buel, James W. *Heroes of the Dark Continent*. London: Faber, 1890.

Burchard, John E., and Albert Bush-Brown. *The Architecture of America: A Social and Cultural History*. Boston: Little, Brown & Co., 1966.

Burns, Edward M. *The American Idea of Mission*. New Brunswick, N.J.: Rutgers University Press, 1957.

Campbell, Joseph. *The Hero with a Thousand Faces*. New York: Pantheon, 1949.

Cash, W. J. *The Mind of the South*. New York: Alfred A. Knopf, 1941.

Cawelti, John. *Apostles of the Self-made Man*. Chicago: University of Chicago Press, 1965.

———. *The Six Gun Mystique*. Bowling Green, Ohio: Bowling Green University Press, 1970.

———. *Adventure, Mystery, and Romance: Formula Stories as Art and Popular Culture*. Chicago: University of Chicago Press, 1976.

Chomsky, Noam. *American Power and the New Mandarins*. New York: Pantheon Books, 1969.

Cleaver, Eldridge. *Soul on Ice*. New York: McGraw-Hill Book Co., 1968.

Cochran, Thomas. *Railroad Leaders, 1845 – 1890: The Business Mind in Action*. Cambridge, Mass.: Harvard University Press, 1953.

———. *Business in American Life, a History*. New York: McGraw-Hill, 1972.

Cohen, Hennig. *The American Culture: Approaches to the Study of the United States*. Boston: Houghton Mifflin, 1968.

————. *The American Experience: Approaches to the Study of the United States*. Boston: Houghton Mifflin, 1968.

Commager, Henry Steele. *The American Mind: An Interpretation of American Thought and Character Since the 1880's*. New Haven, Conn.: Yale University Press, 1950.

Condit, Carl. *American Building Art: The Nineteenth Century*. New York: Oxford University Press, 1960.

Cox, Harvey. *The Feast of Fools*. New York: Harper & Row, 1971; 2nd ed., Cambridge, Mass.: Harvard University Press, 1972.

Degler, Carl. *Out of Our Past: The Forces That Shaped Modern America*. New York: Harper & Row, 1970.

Denney, Reuel. *The Astonished Muse: Popular Culture in America*. Rev. ed. Chicago: University of Chicago Press, 1975.

Dollard, John. *Criteria for the Life History*. New York: Peter Smith, Reprint of 1935 ed.

————. *Caste and Class in a Southern Town*. New York: Peter Smith, 1949.

————, and Neal Miller. *Personality and Psychotherapy*. New York: McGraw-Hill, 1950.

Duijker, H. C. J., and N. H. Frijda. *National Character and National Stereotypes*. Amsterdam: North-Holland Publishing Co., 1960.

Dundes, Alan, ed. *The Study of Folklore*. Englewood Cliffs, N.J.: Prentice-Hall, Inc., 1965.

Ekirch, Arthur A., Jr. *Man and Nature in America*. New York: Columbia University Press, 1963.

Fishwick, Marshall W. *American Heroes: Myth and Reality*. Washington, D.C.: Public Affairs Press, 1953.

Franklin, John Hope. *From Slavery to Freedom: A History of Negro Americans*. New York: Alfred A. Knopf, 1974.

Friedan, Betty. *The Feminine Mystique*. New York: W. W. Norton & Co., 1963.

Fromm, Erich. *Escape from Freedom*. New York: Rhinehart and Co., 1941.

Gabriel, Ralph H. *American Values: Continuity and Change*. Westport, Conn.: Greenwood Press, 1974.

Galbraith, John K. *The New Industrial State, 1967*. Boston: Houghton Mifflin Co., 1967; 2nd rev. ed., Houghton Mifflin Co., 1971.

Ginzberg, Eli. *The Optimistic Tradition and American Youth*. New York: Columbia University Press, 1962.

Glazer, Nathan, and Daniel P. Moynihan. *Beyond the Melting Pot*. Cambridge, Mass.: MIT Press, 1970.

Goodman, Paul.*Growing Up Absurd*. New York: Random House, 1960.

Gorer, Geoffrey. *The American People: A Study in National Character*. New York: W. W. Norton & Co., 1948.

Hackett, Alice Payne. *70 Years of Best Sellers, 1895 – 1965*. New York: R. R. Bowker, 1967.

Halberstam, David. *The Best and the Brightest*. New York: Random House, 1972.

Hall, Calvin, and Gardner Lindzey. *Theories of Personality*. New York: John Wiley and Sons, 1957.

Hallowell, A. Irving. *Culture and Experience*. Philadelphia: University of Pennsylvania Press, 1955.

Hamlin, Talbot. *The American Spirit in Architecture*. New Haven, Conn.: Yale University Press, 1926.

Hansen, Marcus. *The Immigrant in American History*. Cambridge, Mass.: Harvard University Press, 1940.

Harrington, Michael. *The Other American, Poverty in the U.S.* New York: Macmillan, 1962, 1969.

————. *The Accidental Century*. New York: Macmillan, 1965.

Hartz, Louis. *The Liberal Tradition in America*. New York: Harcourt Brace, 1955.

Heilbroner, Robert L. *An Inquiry into the Human Prospect*. New York: Norton, 1974.

Herberg, Will. *Protestant-Catholic-Jew*. Garden City, N.Y.: Doubleday, 1955.

Hoffer, Eric. *First Things, Last Things*. New York: Harper & Row, 1967, 1968, 1970, 1971.

Hofstadter, Richard. *Anti-Intellectualism in American Life*. New York: Alfred A. Knopf, 1963.

Horney, Karen. *The Neurotic Personality of Our Time*. New York: W. W. Norton & Co., 1937.

Hsu, Francis. *Psychological Anthropology: Approaches to Culture and Personality*. Homewood, Ill.: Dorsey Press, 1961.

Huber, Richard M. *The American Idea of Success*. New York: McGraw-Hill, 1971.

Hull, Clark. *Principles of Behavior*. New York: Appleton-Century-Crofts, 1943.

Iriye, Akira. *Across the Pacific: An Inner History of American–East Asian Relations*. New York: Harcourt Brace, 1967.

Johnson, Walter. *American Studies Abroad, Progress and Difficulties in Selected Countries*. Washington, D.C.: U.S. Government Printing Office, 1963.

Jones, Howard Mumford. *Education and World Tragedy*. Cambridge, Mass.: Harvard University Press, 1947.

———. *A Strange New World*. New York: Viking Press, 1964.

Kazin, Alfred. *On Native Grounds*. New York: Harcourt, Brace & World, 1942.

Keniston, Kenneth. *The Uncommitted: Alienated Youth in American Society*. New York: Harcourt, Brace & World, 1965.

———. *Young Radicals: Notes on Committed Youth*. New York: Harcourt, Brace & World, 1968.

Kirkland, Edward. *Dream and Thought in the Business Community*. Ithaca, N.Y.: Cornell University Press, 1956.

Klapp, Orrin. *Heroes, Villains and Fools: The Changing American Character*. Englewood Cliffs, N.J.: Prentice-Hall, 1962.

Kluckhohn, Clyde. *Mirror for Man*. New York: Whittlesey House, 1949.

Koedt, Anne, ed. *Radical Feminism*. New York: Quadrangle Books, Inc., 1973.

Kouwenhoven, John. *The Arts in Modern American Civilization*. New York: Norton Library, 1967.

Kubler, George. *The Shape of Time*. New Haven, Conn.: Yale University Press, 1962.

Kwiat, Joseph, and Mary Turpie. *Studies in American Culture*. Minneapolis: University of Minnesota, 1960.

Lane, Michael, ed. *Introduction to Structuralism*. New York: Basic Books, 1970.

Latourette, Kenneth Scott. *A Short History of the Far East*. 4th ed. New York: Macmillan, 1964.

Lerner, Max. *America as a Civilization: Life and Thought in the United States Today*. New York: Simon and Schuster, 1957.

Lévi-Strauss, Claude. *Structural Anthropology*. New York: Basic Books, 1963.

Lewis, R. W. B. *The American Adam: Innocence, Tragedy & Tradition in the Nineteenth Century*. Chicago: University of Chicago Press, 1955.

Linton, Ralph. *The Cultural Background of Personality*. New York: Appleton-Century-Crofts, 1945.

Lipset, Seymour Martin. *Culture and Social Character: The Work of David Riesman Reviewed*. New York: Free Press of Glencoe, 1962.

———. *The First New Nation: The United States in Historical and Comparative Perspective*. New York: Basic Books, 1963.

Lynd, Robert and Helen, *Middletown*. New York: Harcourt Brace and Co., 1929.

———. *Middletown in Transition*. New York: Harbrace J., 1963; 1st ed., Harcourt, Brace, 1937.

Lynes, Russell. *The Tastemakers*. New York: Harper, 1954.

Lynn, Kenneth. *The Dream of Success*. Westport, Conn.: Greenwood Press, 1972; reprint of 1955.

McDonald, Dwight. *Against the American Grain*. New York: Random House, 1962.

McDowell, Tremaine. *American Studies*. Minneapolis: University of Minnesota Press, 1948.

McGiffert, Michael, ed. *The Character of Americans*. Rev. ed. Homewood, Ill.: Dorsey & Co., 1970.

Malcolmson, David. *Ten Heroes*. New York: Duell, 1939.

Marcel, Gabriel. *The Existential Background of Human Dignity*. Cambridge, Mass.: Harvard University Press, 1963.

Marnell, William H. *Man-Made Morals, Four Philosophies That Shaped America*. Garden City, N.Y.: Doubleday, 1966.

Marx, Leo. *The Machine in the Garden*. New York: Oxford University Press, 1964.

Mead, Margaret. *And Keep Your Powder Dry: An Anthropologist Looks at America*. New York: William Morrow, 1942.

Mecklin, J. M. *The Passing of the Saint*. Chicago: University of Chicago Press, 1941.

Merideth, Robert, ed. *American Studies: Essays in Theory & Method*. Columbus, Ohio: Charles E. Merrill, 1968.

Mills, C. Wright. *White Collar*. New York: Oxford University Press, 1951.

————. *The Power Elite*. New York: Oxford University Press, 1956.

Moore, Arthur, ed. *The Frontier Mind*. New York: McGraw, 1957.

Morison, Elting. *The American Style*. New York: Harper, 1958.

Mott, Frank Luther. *A History of American Magazines*. 5 vols. Cambridge, Mass.: Belknap Press of Harvard University Press, 1930– 68.

Mumford, Lewis. *The Culture of Cities*. New York: Harcourt, Brace and Company, 1938.

Myrdal, Gunnar. *American Dilemma*. New York: Harper & Row, 1962.

Nash, Roderick. *Wilderness and the American Mind*. New Haven, Conn: Yale University Press, 1967.

Niebuhr, Reinhold. *The Irony of American History*. New York: Scribner's, 1952.

Noble, David. *The Eternal Adam and the New World Garden*. New York: Grosset & Dunlap, 1971.

Novak, Michael. *The Rise of the Unmeltable Ethnics*. New York: Macmillan, 1972.

Nye, Russel B. *This Almost Chosen People*. East Lansing: Michigan State University Press, 1966.

————. *The Unembarrassed Muse: The Popular Arts in America*. New York: Dial Press, 1970.

Osgood, Robert E. *Ideals and Self-interest in America's Foreign Relations*. Chicago: University of Chicago Press, 1953.

Packard, Vance. *The Hidden Persuaders*. New York: David McKay Co., 1957.

Parrington, Vernon Louis. *Main Currents in American Thought*. 3 vols. New York: Harcourt, Brace, 1927– 30.

Parsons, Talcott, and Edward Shils, eds. *Toward a General Theory of Action*. Cambridge, Mass.: Harvard University Press, 1960.

Paterson, Thomas G., et al. *American Foreign Policy: A History*. Boston, Mass.: D. C. Heath, 1977.

Perry, Ralph Barton. *Puritanism and Democracy*. New York: Vanguard, 1944.

Peterson, Merrill. *The Jefferson Image in the American Mind*. New York: Oxford University Press, 1960.

Potter, David M. *People of Plenty*. Chicago: University of Chicago Press, 1954.

Propp, Vladimir. *Morphology of the Folktale*. 2d ed. Austin: University of Texas Press, 1968.

Rank, Otto. *The Birth of the Hero, and Other Essays*. New York: Vintage Books, 1964.

Rapson, Richard L., ed. *Individualism & Conformity in the American Character*. Boston: D. C. Heath, 1967.

Ravage, Marcus E. *An American in the Making: The Life Story of an Immigrant* (with a new preface by Louise Ravage Tresfort). New York: Dover Publications, 1971.

Reich, Charles A. *The Greening of America*. New York: Random House, 1970.

Ribble, D. *The Martyrs: A Study in Social Control*. Chicago: University of Chicago Press, 1931.

Riesman, David. *The Lonely Crowd*. Garden City, N.Y.: Doubleday Anchor Books, 1953.

Rosenberg, Bernard, and David Manning White, ed. *Mass Culture: The Popular Arts in America*. Glencoe, Ill.: The Free Press, 1957.

————, eds. *Mass Culture Revisited*. New York: Van Nostrand Reinhold Co., 1971.

Rosenberg, Harold. *The Tradition of the New*. New York: Horizon, 1959.

Rossiter, Clinton. *Conservatism in America, the Thankless Persuasion*. New York: Alfred A. Knopf, 1955; 2d ed. rev. New York: Vintage Books, 1962.

Roszak, Theodore. *The Making of a Counter Culture*. Garden City, N.Y.: Doubleday, 1969.

Rourke, Constance. *American Humor: A Study of the National Character*. New York: Harcourt, Brace & Co., 1931.

————. *The Roots of American Culture, and Other Essays,* edited by Van Wyck Brooks. New York: Harcourt, Brace & Co., 1942

Schickel, Richard. *The Disney Version*. New York: Simon and Schuster, 1968.

Schrag, Peter. *The Decline of the WASP*. New York: Simon and Schuster, 1971.

Sennett, Richard. *The Uses of Disorder: Personal Identity and City Life*. New York: Alfred A. Knopf, 1970.

Slater, Philip. *Pursuit of Loneliness*. Boston, Mass.: Beacon Press, 1976.

Slotkin, Richard. *Regeneration Through Violence: The Mythology of the American Frontier*. Middletown, Conn.: Wesleyan University Press, 1973.

Smith, Bradford. *Why We Behave Like Americans*. Philadelphia: J. B. Lippincott, 1957.

Smith, Henry Nash. *The Virgin Land: The American West as Symbol and Myth*. Cambridge, Mass.: Harvard University Press, 1950.

Smith, Page. *As a City upon a Hill: The Town in American History*. New York: Alfred A. Knopf, 1971.

Stein, Maurice R. *The Eclipse of Community*. Princeton, N.J.: Princeton University Press, 1971.

Strout, Cushing. *The American Image of the Old World*. Chicago: Rand McNally, 1963.

Syper, Wylie. *Four Stages of Renaissance Style*. New York: Peter Smith, 1955.

Tate, Cecil F. *The Search for a Method in American Studies*. Minneapolis: University of Minnesota Press, 1973.

Taylor, William R. *Cavalier & Yankee: The Old South and American National Character*. New York: George Braziller, 1961.

Terkel, S. *Working: People Talk About What They Do All Day and How They Feel About What They Do*. New York: Random House, 1974.

Tillich, Paul. *Theology of Culture*. New York: Oxford University Press, 1959.

de Tocqueville, Alexis. *Democracy in America*. New York: Vintage Books, 1945.

Trachtenberg, Alan. *Brooklyn Bridge, Fact and Symbol*. New York: Oxford University Press, 1965.

Turner, Frederick Jackson. *The Frontier in American History*. New York: Henry Holt & Co., 1920.

Twelve Southerners. *I'll Take My Stand: The South & the Agrarian Tradition*. New York: P. Smith, 1951; published originally by Harper & Brothers, New York, 1930.

Vidich, Arthur J., and Joseph Bensman. *Small Town in Mass Society*. Princeton, N.J.: Princeton University Press, 1958.

Wade, Richard. *The Urban Frontier*. Chicago: University of Chicago Press, 1964.

Ward, John William. *Andrew Jackson – Symbol for an Age*. New York: Oxford University Press, 1955.

Ware, Caroline, ed. *The Cultural Approach to History*. New York: Columbia University Press, 1940.

Warner, W. Lloyd. *American Life: Dream and Reality*. Chicago: University of Chicago Press, 1962.

Webb, Walter. *The Great Plains*. New York: Gossett & Dunlap, 1957.

Weber, Ronald, ed. *America in Change, Reflections on the 60's and the 70's*. Notre Dame, Ind.: University of Notre Dame Press, 1972.

Wecter, Dixon. *The Hero in America: A Chronicle of Hero Worship*. New York: Charles Scribner's Sons, 1941.

West, James. *Plainville, U.S.A.* New York: Columbia University Press, 1945.

White, Morton. *Social Thought in America, 1957*. New York: Oxford University Press, 1976.

Whiting, John W. M., and Irvin L. Child. *Child Training and Personality*. New Haven, Conn.: Yale University Press, 1958.

Whyte, William H., Jr. *The Organization Man*. New York: Simon and Schuster, 1956.

Wiebe, Robert H. *The Segmented Society*. New York: Oxford University Press, 1975.

Williams, Robin. *American Society: A Sociological Interpretation*. New York: Alfred A. Knopf, 1951; 2d ed., rev., New York: Alfred A. Knopf, 1967.

Wood, James Playsted. *Magazines in the United States*. New York: Ronald Press, 1956.

Wood, Robert C. *Suburbia, Its People and Their Politics*. Boston: Houghton Mifflin, 1958.

Woodward, C. Vann. *The Burden of Southern History*. Baton Rouge: Louisiana State University Press, 1968.

Wyllie, Irvin. *The Self-made Man in America: The Myth of Rags to Riches*. New Brunswick, N.J.: Rutgers University Press, 1954.

Articles

In addition to the articles that follow, students will find valuable collections of articles in the volumes edited by Hennig Cohen and by Joseph Kwiat and Mary Turpie, Michael McGiffert, Robert Merideth, Richard L. Rapson, and Caroline Ware. All of these works have been cited previously in this bibliography.

DuBois, Cora. "The Dominant Value Profile of American Culture." *American Anthropologist* 62 (1955):1232–39.

Gurian, Jay. "American Studies and the Creative Present." *Midcontinent American Studies Journal* 10 (Spring 1969):76.

Hook, Sidney. "The Eventful and the Event-Making Man." *The Hero in History* (New York: Humanities Press, Inc., 1943).

Inkeles, Alex, and Daniel Levinson. "National Character: The Study of Modal Personality and Sociocultural Systems." In *Handbook of Social Psychology*, Linzey, ed. (Cambridge, Mass.: Addison-Wesley Co., 1954), 2:977–1020.

Kato, Hidestoshi. "From Pantheon to Presley: Changes in Urban Symbolism." In *Communication and the City: The Changing Environment*, Paper #7 of the East–West Communication Institute, Honolulu, Hawaii, November 1973.

Keniston, Kenneth. "You Have to Grow Up in Scarsdale to Know How Bad Things Really Are." *New York Times Magazine*, April 27, 1969, pp. 27–29.

Kuklick, Bruce. "History as a Way of Learning." *American Quarterly* 22 (Fall 1970):609–28.

———. "Myth and Symbol in American Studies." *American Quarterly* 24 (October 1972):435.

Lévi-Strauss, Claude. "The Structural Study of Myth." *Journal of American Folkore* 68 (1955):428–44.

Lifton, Robert Jay. "Protean Man." *Partisan Review* 35, no. 1 (Winter 1968):13–34.

Lubin, Harold. "Introduction" to *Heroes and Anti-heroes*. (San Francisco: Chandler Press, 1968), pp. 9ff.

Lynd, Robert. "The People as Consumers." *Recent Social Trends in the United States*. (New York: McGraw-Hill, 1933), pp. 857–911.

Maritain, Jacques. *Reflection on America*. (New York: Gordian, 1958), pp. 29–42.

Marx, Leo. "American Studies — A Defense of an Unscientific Method." *New Literary History* 1 (October 1969):75.

Riesman, David. "The Lonely Crowd: A Reconsideration in 1960." In Seymour Martin Lipset and Leo Lowenthal, eds., *Culture and Social Character: The Work of David Riesman Reviewed* (Glencoe, Ill.: The Free Press, 1961), p. 428.

———. "Some Questions About the Study of American Character in the Twentieth Century." *Annals of American Academy of Political & Social Science* 370 (March 1967):36.

Rogow, Arnold A. "The Revolt Against Social Equality." *Dissent* 4 (Autumn 1957).

Schapiro, Meyer. "Style." In A. L. Kroeber's *Anthropology Today* (Chicago: Phoenix, 1953).

Smith, Henry Nash. "Can 'American Studies' Develop a Method?" In Joseph J. Kwiat and Mary C. Turpie, eds., *Studies in American Culture: Dominant Ideas and Images* (Minneapolis: University of Minnesota Press, 1960), p. 14.

Stannard, David E. "American Historians & the Idea of National Character: Some Problems & Prospects." *American Quarterly* 23 (May 1971):202.

Symposium: Individualism in Twentieth-Century America moderated by Mody C. Boatright, *The Texas Quarterly* (Summer 1963), Austin, University of Texas Press.

Gordon Mills: Introduction

Louis Hartz: Individualism in Modern America

Leslie A. White: Individuality and Individualism

Paul A. Samuelson: Modern Economic Realities and Individualism

David M. Potter: American Individualism in the Twentieth Century

Frederick J. Hoffman: Dogmatic Innocence: Self-assertion in Modern American Literature

Index

Aarne, Antti, 344
Adams, Henry, xii, 73, 128-140, 299-300, 305
Adams, John, 158, 174, 182
Adams, John Quincy, 198
Adams, Samuel, 186
Adams, Sherman, 82
Adler, Dankmar, 299, 315
Advise and Consent, 68
Aeschylus, 339, 342
Aesop's Fables, 99-100
Aiken, Conrad, 93, 319
Albee, Edward, 17, 18
Adlington, Richard, 83
Aldridge, Delores P., xiii, 253
Alexander, R. W., 107-108
Alger, Horatio, 330, 362
Algren, Nelson, 68
Allen, Frederick Lewis, 6
Allen, Robert, 249, 251
Allport, Gordon, 294, 296
All the King's Men, 13
Alsop, Joseph, 334
Always Ask a Man, 347
Ambiguity of Henry James, The, 292
America and the World Revolution, 25
American, The, 7, 13
American Adam: Innocence, Tragedy and Tradition in the Nineteenth Century, The, 24, 146, 326
American Commonwealth, 177
American Dilemma, An, 244
American Dream, The, 17
American Experience, The, 144
Americans: A New History of the People of the United States, The, 20

Americans: The Colonial Experience, The, 24
American Slave Revolts, 192
American Studies Abroad, 23
Amery, John, 86
Anderson, Sherwood, 15
Angelou, Maya, 76, 293, 319
Antin, Mary, 293
Aptheker, Herbert, 191-192
Aquinas, St. Thomas, 132, 344
Ariès, Phillipe, 276
Arthur Mervyn, 112-113
Attucks, Crispus, 188
Auchincloss, Louis, 66
Auden, W. H., 19, 93
"Author of Beltraffio, The," 283
Autobiography, An, 299
Autobiography, The, 293, 326-327
Autobiography of an Idea, The, 277, 296-322
Awkward Age, The, 280, 283

Babbitt, 122
Bach, Johann Sebastian, 114
Bailey, Charles W., 69
Baldwin, James, 68, 76
Banta, Martha, 276
Barchilon, José, 276
Barth, John, 66, 77
Basler, Roy, 76
Beard, Charles A., 24
Becker, Carl, 6
Beckett, Samuel, 17
Beethoven, Ludvig Van, 114
Bellow, Saul, 74, 77-79, 347
Bellows, George, 114
Bergson, Henri, 134
Berry, Benjamin D., Jr., xiii, 243

Bettelheim, Bruno, 359-360
Biddle, Nicholas, 151
Bierce, Ambrose, 70
Big Money, The, 116
Billy Budd, 7
Bingham, George Caleb, 113-114
Bissell, Richard, 71
Black Boy, 277, 296
Black Folk Tales, 246
Black Panthers, 191, 251
Black Studies—Threat or Challenge?, 260
Blake, Nelson Manfred, xii, xiii, 111, 185
Blake, William, 159
Blassingame, John, 260, 354, 356
Blavatsky, Madam, 285
Blavner, Robert, 249-250
Blue Hotel, The, 73
Blumer, Herbert, 294, 296, 317-318
Bonaparte, Napoleon, 344
Bonnie and Clyde, 185
Boone, Daniel, 347
Boorstin, Daniel J., 24-25
Borges, Jean Luis, 77
Bowles, Paul, 70
Brahms, Johannes, 114
Brown, Charles Brockden, 112-113
Brown, Claude, 69, 76, 293
Brown, H. Rap, 186
Brown, John, 189
Brown v. Topeka Board of Education, 245
Bryan, William Jennings, 152
Bryce, James, 177
Buchanan, Scott, 12
Buntlin, Ned, 66
Burden, Jack, 13
Burdick, Eugene, 69
Burnham, Daniel, 298
Burroughs, William, 70
Bushnell, Horace, 291
Buzhardt, Fred, 334
By Love Possessed, 66, 73
Byron, (Lord) George Gordon, 314

Cady, Steve, 37, 44
Caesar, Julius, 345
Caine Mutiny, The, 73
Calhoun, John C., 176
Campbell, Joseph, 341
Camus, Albert, 19
Cantos, 81, 90
Carnegie Council on Children, 57-58

Carson, Kit, 212
Carson, Rachel, 76
Cash, Johnny, 75
Cassidy, Hopalong, 330
Catch-22, 70
Cather, Willa, 115
Caudill, William, 358-359
Cave, Hugh, 100-105
Cayton, Horace, 76
Center for the Study of Democratic Institutions, The, 12
Centuries of Childhood, 276
Chandler, Raymond, 66
Cheever, John, 66, 70
Child, Irvin L., 368-373
Childhood and Society, 276, 317
"Childhood of the Artist: Libidinal Phase Development and Giftedness, The," 295, 317
"Childhood Pattern of Genius, The," 317
Clark, Kenneth, 260
Clark, Walter Van Tilberg, 73
Clay, Henry, 151
Cleaver, Eldridge, 76
Clemens, Samuel, 11, 71, 114-116, 275, 280, 293, 306
Clockwork Orange, A, 185
Cobbs, Price M., 248
Cochran, Thomas C., 24-25
Cocteau, Jean, 346
Cody, Dan, 330
Cody, William (Buffalo Bill), 83, 330, 347
Coleridge, Samuel Taylor, 298
Collier, John, 285
Commager, Henry Steele, 244
Compte, Auguste, 138
Conant, James B., 165
Connely, Willard, 298-299
Cooley, Charles Horton, 178-179
Cooper, James Fenimore, 73, 347
Copland, Aaron, 114
Cornell, Julian, 87-88
Corrigan, Robert A., xii, 81
Couples, 76
Cowley, Malcolm, 89
Cox, James, 293
Cozzens, James Gould, 3, 72-73
Crane, Stephen, 68, 71
Crews, Frederick C., 276
Critoph, Gerald, xii, 27, 54, 143, 280
Crockett, Davy, 212
Cuban, Larry, 264

Cummings, E. E., 87

Dahl, Arlene, 347
Dahl, Robert A., 20
Daisy Miller, 280, 283
Dana, Richard Henry, 68
Dark Ghetto, 260
Darwin, Charles, 10, 130-138, 178
Davis, Ossie, 245
Day of the Locusts, 70
Decay of the Angel, The, 340
deCrèvecoeur, Michel G. J., 158
Degler, Carl, 5
de Grazia, Alfred, 176
Delany, Martin R., 245
Democratic Vistas, 299
Denver, John, 75
Derleth, August, 285
Descartes, Renée, 18
de Tocqueville, Alexis, 8, 10, 204, 327
Dewey, John, 8, 127, 256, 298
Dickey, James, 71
Dickinson, Emily, 66, 290
Doctorow, E. L., 77
Dollard, John, 369
Dooley, Mr., 162
Dos Passos, John, 116-117
Double Wedding, 104
Dougherty, Philip H., 40-41
Douglass, Frederick, 193, 293
Dowell, Peter W., xiii, 253
Drake, St. Clair, 264
Dreiser, Theodore, 67, 71, 75, 116
Drewry, William S., 193
Drummond, John, 86
Drury, Allen, 67-68
DuBois, Cora, 6, 108
Du Bois, W. E. B., 247-248, 257
Duncan, Ronald, 86
Durso, Joseph, 44
Dylan, Bob, 339

Eberhart, Richard, 71
Edel, Leon, 276
Edison, Thomas Alva, 161, 165
Edmonds, Walter, 112
Education of Henry Adams, The, 130, 133-136
    297
Edwards, Jonathan, 256
Einstein, Albert, 10, 114, 134

Eisenhower, David, 335
Eisenhower, Dwight D., 161, 332-333, 344
Eliot, T. S., 72, 82, 86, 88-92
Elkins, Stanley, xiii, 193, 349
Ellison, Ralph, 69, 243, 261-262
Elmer Gantry, 111, 118-122
Emerson, Ralph Waldo, 4, 7, 11, 25-26, 71,
    343-344
Engerman, Stanley L., 362
Erikson, Erik, 52-53, 276, 294
Escape From Freedom, 367
Essays, 299
Ets, Marie Hall, 230
Euripedes, 342
*Examined Self: Benjamin Franklin, Henry
    Adams, Henry James, The*, 277
Executive Suite, 67
Existentialism, 17-19, 70
Exorcist, The, 77

Fable, The, 72
Fail Safe, 69
Fanon, Frantz, 251
Faulkner, William, 12, 66, 72, 75, 113-114,
    194, 291
Federalist party, 150, 160
Feminism, 227-241
Ferguson, Harry, 37
Ferlinghetti, Lawrence, 73
Fictional Children of Henry James, The, 276
Fiedler, Leslie, 276, 290
Field, Eugene, 68
Finney, Jack, 77
Fishwick, Marshall W., xi, 17, 339
Fogel, Robert W., 362
Ford, Gerald R., 325
Ford, Henry, 8, 161
Ford, Nick Aaron, 260, 264
Forward, John F., 361
For Whom the Bell Tolls, 72
Franklin, Ben, 109, 146, 293, 299-300, 306,
    326-330, 336
Frazier, E. Franklin, 248
Freedomways, 249
Freud, Sigmund, 10, 114, 134, 298
Friedan, Betty, 228
Friedenberg, Edgar, 347
From Here to Eternity, 73
Fromm, Erich, 367
Fromme, Lynette, 186
Frontier evangelism, 4

Frost, Robert, 82, 87
Fugitive Slave Act of 1850, 187-188

Gabriel, Ralph, 22, 71-72, 255
Galbraith, John Kenneth, 240
Gallup, George, 177, 181-182
Gandhi, Mahatma, 294
Gandhi's Truth, 294
Gardner, John C., 77, 79
Garfunkel, Art, 75
Garland, Hamlin, 115
Garvey, Marcus, 245
Gatz, Jimmy, 330
General Motors Corporation, 30-31
''Gentle Boy, The,'' 280
George, Henry, 7
Gibbs, Willard, 137
G. I. Bill, 29
Gilman, Charlotte Perkins, 228, 237
Ginsberg, Allan, 73
Glasgow, Ellen, 319
Godfather, The, 185
Godwin, Parke, 175
Goethe, Johann Wolfgang von, 114
Goffman, Erving, 351
Goldman, Emma, 228
Goldman, Eric, 53
Goldwater, Barry, 11, 70
Gone with the Wind, 112
Goodbye Columbus, 68
Good Housekeeping magazine, 99, 105-109
Gordon, Milton, 245-246
Gore, Pearl M., 361
Gorgias, 342
Graham, Billy, 334
Grapes of Wrath, The, 68
Gravity's Rainbow, 79
Gray, T. R., 192-193
Great Gatsby, The, 329-331, 334–336
Great Society, 54
Green, Gerald, 68, 71
Greenacre, Phyllis, 295-296, 298, 307-309, 313-314, 317-320
Greene, Graham, 69
Grier, William H., 248
Growth of the American Republic, The, 244
Guard of Honor, 73
Guerard, A. J., 344
Guest, Edgar, 89
Guevara, Che, 185, 191, 194

Gusdorf, Georges, 293
Guthrie, A. B., 73

Hadrian, 342-343
Hague, John A., xiv, 3, 51
Haley, Alex, 76-77
Hall, G. Stanley, 275
Hallowell, A. Irving, 377
Hamilton, Alexander, 144, 150, 152, 186
Handlin, Oscar, 20, 25
Hanna, Mark, 152
Hannerz, Ulf, 246
Harris, Roy, 114
Hart, Francis Russell, 293, 319-320
Hartz, Louis, 204
Hattabough, Margaret, 315
Havemann, Ernest, 34
Hawley, Cameron, 67
Hawthorne, Nathaniel, 71, 280
Hay, John, 130
Hayes, Rutherford B., 189
Heald, Morrell, xii, 157, 197
Hearn, Lafcadio, 70
Hearst, Patricia, 186
Hegel, Georg W. F., 18
Heilman, Robert, 288
Heller, Joseph, 70
Hemingway, Ernest, 66, 72, 75, 82, 87, 91, 194, 291, 347
Henry James and the Occult, 276
Hero: A Study in Tradition, Myth, and Drama, The, 344
Heroes of the Greeks, The, 343
Hesiod, 342
Hexter, J. H., 20, 276, 293
History of the United States During the Administrations of Jefferson and Madison, 130
Hitler, Adolph, 344
Holland, Norman N., 276, 319-320
Holmes, Oliver Wendell, 3
Home from the Hill, 73
Hooper, Bayard, 39
Hoover, Herbert, 28
Hoover, J. Edgar, 251
Howe, Irving, 261
Howells, William Dean, 71, 112, 115
Huckleberry Finn, 280
Hull, Clark, 369
Humbolt's Gift, 77, 79
Humphrey, William, 73

Humphries, Rolphe, 89
Hutchinson, Ann, 228

I Know Why the Caged Bird Sings, 293
Image: What Happened to the American Dream?, The, 24
Inflation, 38-39
Inkeles, Alex, 361
Invisible Man, The, 69, 243

Jackson, Andrew, 151
Jackson, Shoeless Joe, 330
James, Henry, 7-8, 13, 66, 73, 279-293, 319
James, William, 60, 71, 134, 136, 275-277
Jefferson, Thomas, 27-28, 113, 144-147, 149-150, 152-154, 158, 160-161, 186, 198, 256
Jefferson and/or Mussolini, 88
Johnson, Walter, 23
Johnson, William, 362
Jones, Howard Mumford, 21
Jones, LeRoi, 76
Jordy, William, 139
Josephson, Matthew, 165
Journal of Popular Culture, 347
Joyce, James, 82
Joyce, William, 86
Jung, Carl G., 134
Jungle, The, 68-69, 117-118
Just and the Unjust, The, 73

Kasper, John, 91
Kato, Hidetoshi, 339-340
Kazin, Alfred, 83
Keller, Helen, 293
Kelvin, Lord, 137-138
Keniston, Kenneth, 51-52, 54, 57, 59, 276
Kennan, George, 20
Kennedy, John F., 185, 345
Kennedy, Robert, 185
Kerenyi, Karoly, 343
Kesey, Ken, 77
Kessler-Harris, Alice, xiii, 227
Khan, Kubla, 344-345
Khrushchev, Nikita, 15
Kierkegaard, Soren, 18
Kilson, Martin, 260
Kindergarten Chats, 296, 299
King, Clarence, 131
King, Martin Luther, 68, 185
King, Wayne, 41

Kipling, Rudyard, 339
Knebel, Fletcher, 69
Knights of Labor, 190
Kovel, Joel, 276
Kris, Ernst, 296
Kuhn, Thomas, 127-129

Ladwig, Gordon W., 361
LaFarge, John, 130, 140
Larcom, Lucy, 293
Last Adam, The, 73
Last Puritan, The, 13
Laughlin, James, 87
Lawrence, D. H., 109
Lea, Tom, 73
Leary, Timothy, 347
Leaves of Grass, 67, 300
Lederer, Charles, 69
Lee, Bruce, 340
Lefcourt, Herbert M., 361
Lenin, V. I., 347
Leonief, Wassily, 42
Lesser, Simon D., 276
Lester, Julius, 246
Letters of Ezra Pound, The, 92
Letter to American Teachers of History, 130, 133, 135, 137-139
Levin, David, 276
Levinson, Daniel, 355, 357
Lewis, Anthony, 332
Lewis, R. W. B., 24-25, 146, 326
Lewis, Sinclair, 6, 111, 118-122
Lewis, Wyndham, 86, 91
Lieberson, Stanley, 249
Life magazine, 29, 31, 34-36, 38-39, 43
Lifton, Robert J., 52-53, 276
Light in August, 72
Lillard, Richard, 293
Lincoln, Abraham, 12, 194
Lippmann, Walter, 9, 20, 172, 180-181
Locke, John, 144, 198
Lodge, Henry Cabot (Sr.), 179-180
Lohof, Bruce A., xii, 99
London, Jack, 71, 347
Lonely Crowd, The, 216
Long, Richard, 262
Longfellow, Henry Wadsworth, 71
Losing Battles, 77
Louis Sullivan as He Lived, 318
Love in the Ruins, 77

Lowell, Abbot Lawrence, 180
Lowell, Robert, 73, 93
Lundquist, L. R., 277
Luther, Martin, 294

McCarthy, Mary, 21, 282
McCormick, Cyrus Hall, 161
McCurdy, Harold G., 317-318
McDowell, Tremaine, 22, 23, 255
McKinley, William, 152, 200
MacLeish, Archibald, 82, 87, 93
McLuhan, Marshall, 342
McPartland, John, 68
McWhirter, William A., 35
Madison, James, 174-175
Maggie: A Girl of the Streets, 68, 280
Maharaj Ji, 340
Mailer, Norman, 73, 194
Main Street, 118-119
Main-Travelled Roads, 115
Malamud, Bernard, 70
Malcolm X; 76, 185, 192, 245, 301, 344
Manchild in the Promised Land, 69
"Man with the Hoe, The," 68
Marcell, David W., xii, xiii, 127, 325
Markham, Edwin, 68
Marquand, John P., 66
Marsh, George P., 22
Marshall, John, 145, 150
Marshall Plan, 11
Marx, Karl, 7, 72
Master, 1901–1916, The, 276
Matthiessen, F.O., 255
Maxwell, James C., 128
Mazlish, Bruce, 276
Melville, Herman, 7, 18, 25, 67, 71, 122, 194, 256
Mencken, H. L., 87, 162
Menuhin, Yehudi, 341
Meredith, William, 71
Miller, Neal, 369
Miller, Perry, 255
Mills, C. Wright, 213
Mishima, Yukio, 340
Mitchell, Joni, 75
Mitchell, Margaret, 112
Moby Dick, 67, 122
Monroe Doctrine, 199
Montaigne, Michel D. E., 18
Mont-Saint-Michel and Chartres, 130, 132-133, 136-137, 140

Moody, William Vaughn, 68
Moore, Marianne, 87, 91
More, Paul Elmer, 19-20
Morgenthau, Hans, 20
Morison, Samuel E., 244
Morphology of the Folktale, 344
Morris, Wesley, 276
Mount, William Sidney, 114
Moveable Feast, A, 66
Moviegoer, The, 77
Mozart, Wolfgang Amadeus, 114
Mr. Sammler's Planet, 79
Mullins, Eustace, 91
Murphey, Murray, xiii, 367
Murrow, Edward R., 23
Mussolini, Benito, 84-85
Myrdal, Gunnar, 244, 247

Naked and the Dead, The, 73
National Organization of Women (NOW), 235
Native Son, 69
"Naturalism" (literature), 71-72
Neibhur, Rheinhold, 10, 20
Nero, 345
Neu, Frank R., 215-216
New Deal, 202
New Freedom, 7
New History of the People of the United States, A, 25
New Nationalism, 7
New Perspectives on Black Studies, 260
Newton, Sir Isaac, 114, 130-131, 134
Nickel Mountain, 77
Nietzsche, Friedrich, 298
Niles, Hezekiah, 175
Nisbet, Robert, 319-320
Nixon, Richard, xiii, 76, 325-337
No Down Payment, 68
Norman, Charles, 90
Norris, Benjamin Franklin, 71
North Atlantic Alliance, 11
Nutt, Alfred, 344

Oates, Joyce Carol, 77
O'Connor, Edwin, 68
O'Dell, J. H., 249
Oepidus Rex, 12, 289, 345
O'Hara, John, 66
Old Man and the Sea, The, 66, 72
Olney, James, 302
One Flew over the Cuckoo's Nest, 77

O'Neill, Eugene, 114, 298
Open Door policy, 199
O Pioneers!, 115
Oppenheimer, J. Robert, 18
Organization Man, The, 213
Ox-Bow Incident, The, 73

Paige, D. D., 91-92
Paine, Thomas, 186
Parkes, Henry Bamford, 144
Parrington, Vernon Louis, 24
Pascal, Blaise, 293
Paterson, 68
Paul, Sherman, 298, 300, 314
Peale, Norman Vincent, 11
Pearce, Roy Harvey, 276
Pengilly, Andrew, 121
People of Plenty, 25, 33
Percy, Walker, 77
Perry, Ralph Barton, 3
Persons, Stow, xii, 171
Phillips, David Graham, 68
Pisan Cantos, The, 92
Pitcher, Molly, 212
Platt, Gerald, 276
Pocahontas, 344
Point Four Program, 11
Polycarp, Saint, 343
Pope, Alexander, 114
Porter, Katherine Anne, 66, 70
Portnoy's Complaint, 76
Portrait of a Lady, The, 285
Potter, David, xiii, 9, 21, 25, 33, 209, 227-228, 239
Pound, Ezra, xii, 81-98
Prince and the Pauper, The, 280
Principles of Psychology, 136
Prometheus (myth of), 157
Propp, Vladimir, 344
Psychohistory, 276
Public Opinion and Popular Government, 180
"Public Opinion in a Democracy" (lecture), 182-183
"The Pupil," 280, 283
Purdy, James, 70
Puritanism, 3, 15
Pynchon, Thomas, 74, 77, 79

The Quiet American, 69

Rabbit Redux, 76
Rabelais, François, 18

Raglan, Lord, 344-345
Railroad Leaders, 1845–1890: The Business Mind in Action, 24
Rank, Otto, 344
Rawick, George, 355
"Realism" (political), 20
Red Eye of Love, The, 17
Reflection on the Napoleonic Legend, 344
Republican party (Jeffersonian), 150
Reuther, Walter, 55
Riesman, David, 5, 6, 10, 21, 53, 163, 216-217
Roberts, Kenneth, 112
Robinson, Edward Arlington, 68, 71
Roethke, Theodore, 73
Romanticism, 3-16, 53
Roosevelt, Franklin D., 28, 84, 171
Roosevelt, Theodore, 7, 332, 347
Roth, Philip, 68, 76
Rotter, Julian, 360-361
Rousseau, Jean Jacques, 290

St. Clair, James, 334
St. Francis of Assisi, 345
Salinger, J. D., 74, 291
Samuels, Charles, 276
Samuels, Ernest, 128
Santayana, George, 13, 73, 82, 134
Sartre, Jean Paul, 18-19
Sayre, Robert, 277
Scarlet Letter, The, 122-123, 280-281
Science and the Common Understanding, 18
Scott, Hugh, 334
Sennett, Richard, 56
Seven Days in May, 69
Sewall, Samuel, 67
Shakespeare, William, 345
Shallard, Frank, 121
Shanker, Ravi, 341
Shannon, William, 332
Shays, Daniel, 186-187
Shine, Muriel, 276
Ship of Fools, 66, 70
Simon, Carly, 75
Simon, Paul, 75
Sinclair, Upton, 68, 117-118
Slave Community, The, 354
Slavery, 349-363
Sloan, John, 114
Small Boy and Others, A, 296
Smedley, Agnes, 230

Smith, Adam, 198
Smith, Captain John, 344
Smith, Henry Nash, 22-23
Smith, Shaler, 310
Smith, William D., 44
Snow, C. P., 159
Snyder, Richard, 31, 37
Socrates, 342, 345
Solzenitzin, Alexander, 77
Sophocles, 13, 342
Sot-Weed Factor, 77
Souls of Black Folk, The, 248
Spear, Allan, 247
Specimen Days, 312
Spencer, Herbert, 298
Spencer, Theodore, 92-39
Spengemenn, W. C., 277
Spiller, Robert, 22-23, 255
Sporting Goods Market at the Threshold of the Seventies, The, 37
Sputnik, 12
Stamp Act, 187
Stanton, Elizabeth Cady, 228
Starobinski, Jean, 294
"Star Trek," 77
"Star Wars," 77
Steinbeck, John, 68
Stone, Albert, E., xi, xiii, 275, 279, 293
Stowe, Harriet Beecher, 68-69
Strickland, Bonnie R., 361
Strout, Cushing, 276
Structure of Scientific Revolutions, The, 127-129
Studies in American Culture; Dominant Ideas and Images, 23
Styron, William, 193
Sullivan, Andrienne, 311
Sullivan, Louis, 275, 277, 293-322
Sullivan, Patrick, 300, 309-310, 317
Summa Theologica, 132-133
Sumner, William Graham, 178
Sun Also Rises, The, 72
Sunlight Dialogues, 77, 79
"Symbionese Liberation Army," 186
System of Architectural Ornament According with a Philosophy of Man's Powers, A, 302

Tate, Allen, 93
Taylor, John, 145
Taylor, Robert Lewis, 68
"Tendency of History, The," (address), 130, 137

Tennyson, Alfred Lord, 314
Theseus (myths of), 342-343
Thompson, Kenneth, 20
Thoreau, Henry David, 4, 7, 11, 71, 298, 327-329, 336
Tilbury Town, 68
Tillich, Paul, 15
Time and Again, 77
Titanic, 7
Tolstoi, Leo, 112
Tom Sawyer, 280
To Trust in Andy, 100, 102-105
Toynbee, Arnold, 25
Transcendentalism, 4, 22
Travels of Jamie McPheeters, 68
Treacherous Years, 1894-1901, The, 276
Trends in the Sporting Goods Market, 31
Trilling, Lionel, 276
Truman, Harry, 335
Tse-tung, Mao, 185, 344
Turner, Frederick Jackson, 9, 24, 73, 211-212, 355
Turner, Henry McNiel, 245
Turner, Nat, 185, 191-193
Turn of the Screw, The, 276, 279-292
"Turn of the Screw, as Poem, The," 288
Twain, Mark, 11, 71, 114-116, 275, 280, 293, 306
Two Cultures and the Scientific Revolution, The, 159
Two Years Before the Mast, 68

Ugly American, The, 69
Uncle Tom's Cabin, 68-69, 281
Untermeyer, Louis, 89
Updike, John, 66, 74-77
Use of Personal Documents in Psychological Science, The, 294
U.S. News & World Report, 45-46

V, 74
Valenti, Jack, 45
Van Doren, Mark, 92
Veblen, Thorstein, 232
Vedas, The, 339
Veterans Administration, 29
Vidal, Gore, 67
Villon, François, 18
Virginian, The, 73
Voltaire, François-Marie Arovet, 114
von Hahn, Johann Georg, 344
Vonnegut, Kurt, 77

Walden, 299
Waldstein, Louis, 279, 284
Walker, Robert, xi, xii, 22, 65
Wallace, George, 185
War and Peace, 112
Ward, John William, 21
Ward, Lester F., 178
Warner, Lloyd, 286
Washington, Booker T., 257
Washington, George, 113, 144, 187, 198
Wasteland, The, 92
Watergate, 325-337
Weathermen, 191
Weber, Max, 327
Webster, Daniel, 151
Weinstein, Arnold, 17
Weinstein, Fred, 276
Wells, H. G., 282
Welty, Eudora, 77, 291
West, Nathanael, 70, 83
Wharton, Edith, 116
What Maisie Knew, 280, 283
Wheeler, Harvey, 69
Whitehead, Alfred North, 134
Whiting, John W. M., 368-373
Whitman, Walt, 19, 67, 71, 73, 114, 116, 256, 298, 300, 312, 316
Whitney, Eli, 160
Wiener, Norbert, 296
Williams, Jay R., 361
Williams, Raymond, 227

William, Stanley, 22
Williams, William Carlos, 68, 87, 92-93
Wilson, Edmund, 276
Wilson, Francis, 172, 177
Wilson, Woodrow, 7
Winds of War, 76
Winthrop, John, 171
Wolfe, Thomas, 13, 78
Wolfsheim, Meyer, 330
Women Who Work, 220
Wonder, Stevie, 75
Wonderful Country, The, 73
Woodward, C. Vann, 22
Woolson, Moses, 317
Wordsworth, William, 290
World War I, 8
World Within World, 296
Woster, Owen, 73
Wouk, Herman, 73, 76
Wright, Frank Lloyd, 299
Wright, Richard, 69, 277, 293, 296, 319
Wright, Sylvia, 221

Yeats, W. B., 82, 140
Yetman, Norman R., xiii, 349
You Can't Go Home Again, 13
Young, Francis A., 23

Zola, Émile, 75
Zoo Story, The, 18

About the Editor

JOHN A. HAGUE is Professor and Chairman of American Studies at Stetson University in DeLand, Florida. He has contributed to *American Studies in Transition* by Marshall Fishwick and *Essays in Modern American Literature* edited by Richard Langford. He is currently at work on a book entitled *Cultural Traditions in American History*.